COCHABAMBA, 1550–1900

D0967489

Cochabamba, 1550–1900

Colonialism and Agrarian Transformation in Bolivia

BROOKE LARSON

Expanded edition

With a new foreword by William Roseberry

DUKE UNIVERSITY PRESS

DURHAM AND LONDON 1998

© 1998 Duke University Press
The text of this book originally
was published without chapter 10
by Princeton University Press in 1988.
All rights reserved
Printed in the United States of America
on acid-free paper ∞
Typeset in Trump Mediaeval
Library of Congress Cataloging-in-
Publication Data appear on the last
printed page of this book.

FOR CARTER, JOSH, AND DEVON

CONTENTS

LIST OF ILLUSTRATIONS

LIST OF TABLES

FOREWORD

Brooke Larson's book is the product of an earlier historiographical moment, and it is an enduring contribution to scholarship. Thinking about the relation between these two dimensions of the book helps us appreciate its special importance.

Let us deal, first, with the book as a contribution to scholarship. *Cochabamba, 1550–1900* is an examination of the formation of colonial society in the Cochabamba Valleys—the installation of Spanish colonial institutions, relations, and forms; the reconfiguration of indigenous social relations and identities; the emergence of indigenous communities as colonial forms and productions; the emergence of Cochabamba as a provisioner of grain within the economic orbit of the mines at Potosí and the consequent rise of haciendas; and the formation of a mestizo peasantry within and alongside haciendas. After two chapters that deal with sixteenth-century transformations, based on a magnificent reconstruction of precolonial Andean social and political organization, most of the book deals with eighteenth-century colonial society. While the institutional and structural dimensions of these transformations are examined in detail, a distinctive feature of the book is the care with which it explores the dynamics and unequal social relations within indigenous societies in the context of colonial rule, as well as the activities and social relations of the "rival peasant economy."

The documentary basis for the study is rich, including archives in Seville, Madrid, Buenos Aires, Lima, Sucre, and Cochabamba. The interpretive work Larson does with her archival sources is especially impressive. Let us take two examples. In chapter 4, she examines the internal relations, inequalities, and rivalries of Andean village society. For an interpretation of a mid-eighteenth-century rivalry between two cacique families, she begins with the record of the dispute, or *juicio,* in the Bolivian National Archives in Sucre but sup-

plements that information with material from censuses, wills, and
property transactions from the Archivo General de Indias (Seville),
the Archivo General de la Nación (Buenos Aires), and the municipal
archives of Cochabamba. This detailed and critical reading of a text
(the juicio), supplemented with other materials, can be contrasted
with a second use of documentary sources—a statistical analysis of
alcabalas, an ad valorem tax, to measure tithe revenues over a thirty-
five-year period as part of an analysis of the incomes and resources
of hacienda owners in relation to peasant agriculturalists (chapter 6).
In each case, the use of sources is innovative, and appropriate to the
particular story, or part of a story, she is telling.

This is, then, the work of a master historian, finding, analyzing,
and interpreting archival sources with both discipline and insight. As
a contribution to the historical and ethnohistorical analysis of indigenous societies under Spanish colonialism, it fits quite well within
traditions of work pioneered by scholars such as Charles Gibson and
John Murra. We can also consider Larson's book as part of a smaller
tradition that took to the study of indigenous societies under Spanish
colonialism a concern for processes of class formation, especially the
formation of agrarian institutions and structures—the emergence of
large landed properties and of peasantries, landlord-peasant relations
and conflicts, and the roles these institutions might have played both
in subsequent conflicts and in the creation of fundamental social,
economic, and political structures in postcolonial Latin American
societies. Here this relatively small group of scholars of colonial
societies connects with a rather large group of scholars working in
Latin America and elsewhere in the then-called "Third World" from
roughly the late 1960s to the mid 1980s.

(Of course, to even mention such dates indicates one of the problems with considering Larson's book a "product of an earlier time":
it remains a *recent* publication, first released in 1988, after the publication of much of the political-economic work and during the emergence of a kind of paradigmatic shift in Latin American studies. I
link her book with that earlier work because it is based on her dissertation, completed a decade before, and because its central themes
are linked to that earlier work. But I would also suggest that the
book goes beyond much of the political-economic work and that the
text bridges the paradigmatic gulf in important ways. I will consider
these below.)

The theoretical perspectives that informed these works were,
broadly speaking, political economic. That is, they placed local re-

gions and particular peoples within wider networks and forces of political and economic power and relationship, especially the forces associated with colonial rule and capitalist development; they examined the emergence and development of structured inequality, especially along class lines; and they understood these wider forces and structured inequalities as having a profound shaping power in the lives and livelihoods of ordinary people. Almost all of the historians, anthropologists, or social scientists who did this kind of work saw themselves contributing to "radical" scholarship; some, but by no means all, entered into an engagement with the writings of Marx.

This body of work—by no means uniform in perspective, politics, or quality—is now subject to two kinds of retrospective critique. One is the much publicized neoconservative attack on a whole generation of intellectuals and on the academy in which some of them (always only some) have been able to work—the "tenured radicals" for whom politics reigned supreme and who undermined both established standards of quality and scholarly discipline and the minds of subsequent generations of unsuspecting students. To this, the only appropriate response is one that considers actual texts. The neoconservative critique conflates political position and perspective with commitment to "quality" and "standards": conservative positions are implicitly (often explicitly) connected with a commitment to standards and "radical" work undermines standards. But many neoconservatives have shown themselves to be just as ready to let politics determine scholarly pursuits and conclusions as some radicals were.

The effective response was written in the late 1970s by E. P. Thompson, whose work served as inspiration and guide to several generations of radical historians. In a criticism of Louis Althusser and the current of Marxism that subsumed historical inquiry to the demands and conclusions of grand theory (and, it must be said, politics), Thompson wrote of the historical method itself as a form of inquiry bound by the determinate forms of evidence. Each generation might pose different questions or bring different preoccupations to historical inquiry and, in pursuing those questions, seek out new, previously unexamined, kinds of evidence. But the persuasiveness of the historical account rests upon the skill and insight with which the historian examines, "interrogates," and interprets the evidence. Discussion of evidence used (its type, range, representativeness, and reliability) and the quality of one's reading and interpretation of it represents, for Thompson, a kind of "court" where historians can "find one another out," despite a range of different political or generational positions, perspectives, and questions. This, and not the level of politics, is the arena where the question of "standards" would apply.[1]

There are, of course, important problems with Thompson's argument. He made it in defense of what he called "real history," a history that does not change with each generation, or each set of new questions or interpretive frameworks. But this grants to both the history and the evidence a fixity that cannot bear close scrutiny. If the questions are really new and good, and the interpretation of evidence penetrating, the "history" itself must change: the relationship between interpretation and interrogation of evidence is dynamic. Nonetheless, Thompson's argument is important in that it insists upon a discipline of inquiry that requires a sustained engagement with and a convincing interpretation of archival evidence. It is on that basis, not on the basis of criticisms prompted by intergenerational politics, that judgments of quality should be made.

In that arena, as I have already suggested, Larson applies and meets the highest standards of historical scholarship; her book, along with others written in the period, serves as effective refutation of the more careless, alarmist, and (it must be said) paranoid claims of the neoconservatives. But there are two other dimensions of Larson's book that refute such claims: her use of language and her attitude toward and understanding of historical process. One problem with much of the work inspired by Marxist perspectives in the 1970s had to do with its use of language, and of concepts. Especially in the application of the language and concept of "modes of production," the concept could stand for a whole range of social relationships and historical processes, making detailed description of them—or interrogation of evidence concerning them—unnecessary. Similarly, much of the analysis of the period was concerned with the development of capitalism and examined particular regions and peoples at particular moments in terms of their participation in or relationship to processes of capitalist development. In both senses, Larson is refreshingly skeptical. In her introduction, she offers a caveat: "This study of agrarian transformations neither seeks nor finds the origins of capitalist transition in eighteenth- or early nineteenth-century Cochabamba" (chapter 10). She then proceeds to distance her account from a variety of received wisdoms and teleologies. This is not the only received wisdom to be unsettled by Larson's account. While hers is a study of the formation of power-laden agrarian institutions, it is

1 E. P. Thompson, "The Poverty of Theory: or an Orrery of Errors," in *The Poverty of Theory and Other Essays* (London: Merlin, 1978).

not a story of "passive peons and tenant farmers bent in permanent subservience before the all-powerful *patrón*" (chapter 10). Instead, she pays close attention to the economic, social, and cultural forms and resources that peasants were able to use as they pursued their livelihoods, forms and resources that constituted, over time and in relation to the structures and relations of Spanish domination, alternative sources of power. Furthermore, the book itself is free of the jargon of much of the literature of the 1970s and 1980s and is therefore much more attentive to the particularities and specificities of the region, peoples, and processes that here draw our attention.

A second line of criticism of work done during this period comes from the standpoint of present-day social theory, for which various political-economic and structural questions concerning capitalist development and class formation have been displaced by concerns with discourse, the construction of social and cultural identities, and the constitution of modes of structured inequality that cannot be conflated with class (gender, race, ethnicity, and so on). To a certain extent this represents a generational shift, as new generations of graduate students and scholars embrace different theoretical orientations and central texts, and selectively read, ignore, and represent the work of an earlier period. But this theoretical shift is also confronted by authors who made important contributions to the political-economic and structural literature of the earlier period and continue to work in the present. This confrontation can be seen in prefaces to re-editions of books and in retrospective review essays and commentaries.[2]

To the extent that this shift is represented as a change of academic fashion—and it must be said that too much of the retrospective commentary takes the form of a presentist " 'we' did that then, and now 'we' do this, and it's better"—it is not especially interesting and can give rise to silly celebrations and reactions. It is more important to recognize that all inquiries are bound by the questions and assumptions they bring to a range of evidence, that inquiries illuminate certain relationships and processes but are necessarily silent or inattentive on others. Thus truths are partial, not because of the different subject positions of authors (a dangerous claim) but because specific questions and assumptions focus inquiry and results in certain ways

2 See, in addition to Larson's new preface and chapter to this edition, Frederick Cooper et al., *Confronting Historical Paradigms: Peasants, Labor, and the Capitalist World System in Africa and Latin America* (Madison: University of Wisconsin Press, 1993) and Ann Stoler, "[P]Refacing *Capitalism and Confrontation* in 1995," preface to *Capitalism and Confrontation in Sumatra's Plantation Belt, 1870–1979*, 2d ed. (Ann Arbor: University of Michigan Press, 1995).

and not in others. Questions and assumptions must change even as we continue to apply a common set of standards and disciplines of inquiry.

Thus all work is marked by the period in which it is written, by a set of questions, assumptions, and arguments, and much very good work is limited by its period. The best work, while marked, is not so limited, however, and transcends the assumptions and arguments of its period. I conclude by suggesting that Larson's is one such book, partly for reasons already advanced in this foreword. I make a partial case for this claim by asking readers to consider the two previously mentioned dimensions of her archival scholarship: her critical reading of the documents surrounding a cacique rivalry in eighteenth-century Cochabamba and her examination of tithe returns and tax records as part of a reconstruction of the hacienda economy. Both of these exercises are part of an argument that disrupts any simple or straightforward account of Spanish colonialism in Cochabamba or the Andes. The second is part of her examination of peasant activity and livelihoods within the hacienda structure, underscoring crucial gaps and weaknesses in the structure of power and emphasizing important sources and resources for peasant life and action. The first is part of an examination of the formation of indigenous communities under colonial rule, one that emphasizes precolonial and colonial diversity, differentiation, and inequality among indigenous subjects, and demonstrates how complex any consideration of the formation of indigenous subjects and identities must be.

In both ways, Larson's book contributes, directly, to the concerns of the present. That Duke University Press's republication of the book guarantees its availability to new generations of scholars is good news indeed.

William Roseberry
The New School for Social Research

PREFACE TO THE DUKE EDITION

When Duke University Press's editor, Valerie Millholland, called me in Vermont one sparkling August morning to offer me a contract for the republication of *Colonialism and Agrarian Transformation in Bolivia: Cochabamba, 1550–1900* (Princeton: Princeton University Press, 1988), I was deeply immersed in another project and had not thought about late colonial Cochabamba for several years. I had no intention of doing more research on the region, and initially I decided that I would simply make a case in the preface for the book's pertinence to ongoing historiographical discussions about the formation of particular agrarian societies under colonial rule. I had certainly sampled enough prefaces of recently republished books to appreciate the various ways that authors gracefully extolled the relevance of their own studies to a new generation of readers.

But as I began to reread the book, I soon grew skeptical about pitching the preface in such a way. The book's narrative and explanatory structure, and its muted theoretical preoccupations seemed incomplete. The recent epistemological lurch toward things postmodern, cultural, and literary, the collapse of class as an interpretive category, and the wholesale retreat from political-economic and structural analysis in much of the new historiography of the 1990s seemed to belie the ten short years that separated the two editions of this book.

But as I began to focus more deeply on the content of the book's interpretive arguments and evidence, Cochabamba—the case study and its broader significance—once more caught me in its clutches. Among other connected narratives, the book chronicles the formation of a distinctive mestizo, mercantile peasantry in nested fields of power—from local village society, to the regional political economy, and finally to the shifting imperial stage. The book's themes and approaches lend themselves quite naturally to political and cultural issues, and I began to bring new questions and assumptions to bear on them. In spite of myself, I began rethinking, almost re-interpreting, whole chapters. Where I had written a book about the formation of colonial power and agrarian classes in one Andean region tightly integrated into the Potosí mining economy, I now began to see in this regional case new possibilities for understanding the mutually interactive influences of class and ethnic identity-making and their implications for local peasant politics and consciousness. I was also eager to extend the study's time frame in order to make conceptual linkages between the region's colonial legacies (discussed in chapter 9) and Cochabamba's emergent peasant movement in the second and third decades of the twentieth century—just about the time when the original book ends! (To some degree, this implicit re-casting of the book reflects my current research interests in early twentieth-century nation-making in Bolivia.) Clearly, however, I was not going to rewrite the book.

What I have done, instead, is to preserve the integrity of the original study, as a reflection of the state-of-the-field of Andean social/regional history produced in the late 1970s and 1980s. The introduction and chapters 1 through 9 remain unchanged, but there is a new chapter for this edition. Much more than an afterword and yet not really part of the body of the text, chapter 10 is a hybrid chapter—part retrospective, part interpretive—written very much in the present historiographic moment.

On the one hand, chapter 10 reflects upon the history of this book as an unfolding research project that was shaped, and reshaped, by the ideas and experiences of doing research and writing about Bolivia over the 1970s and early 1980s. Like many other young social historians of that time, I found myself straddling the conceptual divide between political economy and social history. I was trying to nego-tiate the prevailing paradigms of the day and my own intellectual commitment to detailed local knowledge of class relations and struc-ture, understood in dynamic historical terms through specific pro-cesses of human agency, conflict, and force. These tensions were not abstract; they were all too tangible in the kinds of conceptual shifts and doubts that went into the multiple drafts of this book. But, in one way or another, they also shaped a historiographic agenda for a whole generation of social historians. As always is the case, living and working in Bolivia brought an urgency and immediacy to the intrinsic tensions between history and theory as no Talmudic Marx-ian text ever could. I first arrived in Cochabamba in April 1974, only three months after a brutal massacre of peasants had stained the roads leading into the city. The repressive Banzer dictatorship was a constant throughout most of the 1970s, followed by the brutality of García Meza, and later a tenuous return to civilian rule. In spite of them, Bolivian intellectual life flourished in the late 1970s and early 1980s. So too did insurgent ethnic politics and scholarship—much of it quite critical of Marxist paradigms. All these kinetic pressures left their imprints on this book, or so it seems to me in retrospect. Chapter 10 begins therefore as a critical self-reflection on the theories, politics, and research experiences that went into writing this history.

On the other hand, the new chapter also selectively reengages this regional study of peasantization (that is, the historical formation of particular peasant economies and societies within a long-term historical/regional context) from an explicitly cultural-political perspective. For, as William Roseberry recently noted, historical studies of peasant (or class) formation in the 1980s positioned historians and anthropologists to pose questions about rural politics, political culture, and peasant consciousness in the 1990s.[1] Indeed, there is a new crop of studies redefining regionalism around distinctive peasant political cultures, discourses, and identities in the Andes and elsewhere. Harnessing that new historiographic literature, taking stock of recent research on Cochabamba and the Andes, and rethinking the implications of my own earlier work here, chapter 10 remaps the contours of regional political culture onto the template of agrarian class formation. In pursuit of new conceptual tensions—this time those obtaining between political economy and popular culture—I use the final chapter to integrate perspectives on the formation of peasant political culture, power, community, and identity into this long-term regional study of agrarian colonial-class dialectics.

In addition to those many people who contributed to the production of the original book (acknowledged in the pages that follow), I wish to thank Valerie Millholland for her support and forbearance. Like all superb editors, she is part terror, part shrink, part friend. Maybe mostly friend, now that I have written my last word on Cochabamba. (I hope.) I am also grateful to Laura Gotkowitz and Sinclair Thomson for their critical reading of chapter 10. I also extend my heartfelt thanks to Carter for always being the calm at the center of

1 William Roseberry, "Beyond the Agrarian Question in Latin America," in *Confronting Historical Paradigms: Peasants, Labor, and the Capitalist World System in Africa and Latin America*, ed. Frederick Cooper et al. (Madison: University of Wisconsin Press, 1993), 359.

my interior storms; to Jodie for her abiding support and solidarity; to Josh, who often wishes me "happy writing" even though he hates to see me disappear upstairs into my attic study; and to Devon, who usually gets me to come down again to deal with snacks, pet snakes, and life's other important things.

ACKNOWLEDGMENTS

Authors of first books should be allowed to celebrate the rites of passage—not by passing through the process of tenure review, but in song, dance, and festivity. If this were a venerable academic ritual, my fiesta would take place on the alpine slopes of El Tunari, overlooking the fertile Valle Bajo, where I would toast the scores of friends, colleagues, and archivists who contributed to this project during its various phases.

In lieu of that happier alternative, I am forced to express but a few sober words of gratitude to all the people and institutions that helped me to carry out and complete this study. Perhaps my first intellectual debt is owed to my undergraduate professors in Latin American history, Ralph della Cava and Magnus Mörner, who opened up the field of Latin American history to me, encouraged me to pursue it, and gave me the courage to follow my star in spite of the bleak prospects of academic employment. I also want to warmly acknowledge the intellectual support and continuing encouragement of Herbert Klein and Karen Spalding, with whom I worked in graduate school. In spite of the fact that I did not take his advice to "publish the dissertation quickly," Herbert Klein never entirely lost faith in me—especially after I overcame my instinctual distaste for statistics, mastered SPSS, and processed a thousand punch cards on *alcabalas*! Karen Spalding, on the other hand, wasn't so interested in alcabalas, but she did stretch my horizons in Andean ethnohistory and anthropology, and she has been an unending source of inspiration and support over the years. In addition to my intellectual patrons, I wish to express my gratitude to my graduate-school *compañeros*—particularly Antonio Mitre, Adrian deWind, Carmen Ramos, Steven Volk, Elinor Burkett, and Elizabeth Dore—for their contributions to the early phases of this study and with a certain degree of nostalgia for more exciting political times. Numerous colleagues and friends have given me the benefit of their thoughts and criticism on various drafts of this book; in particular, Steve Stern, Antonio Mitre, Tristan Platt, Enrique Tandeter, John Murra, and Nicolás Sánchez-Albornoz were generous with their time and interest. I also appreciate the support I have received during the past three years from Barbara Weinstein and others of my colleagues at the State University of New York at Stony Brook.

During the course of my field research, I incurred many intellectual debts and received wonderful hospitality in Bolivia, Argentina, and Spain. I owe thanks to all the unsung employees of archives who carried dusty files to me day after day. I also am indebted to Gunnar Mendoza for his support and guidance during my work in the Archivo nacional de Bolivia. A host of people from Cochabamba offered me generous assistance, moral support, and warm hospitality. The municipal authorities responsible for opening the Cochabamba archive to me in 1974 (and, later, for the first time, to the public at large) should receive special mention. I will always be grateful to the Mitre family of Cochabamba for their loyal friendship, generosity, and hospitality. I also have had the good fortune of learning about various aspects of contemporary Bolivian society from several colleagues and friends over the years. I am especially grateful to Tito Jiménez, Jorge Dandler, Rosario León, Xavier Albó, Nancy Velarde, and Cassandra Torrico.

Of course, the project could never have been completed without the generous financial support I received from several institutions. An initial Foreign Area Field Program Fellowship from the American Council of Learned Societies and the Social Science Research Council allowed me to spend eighteen months in archival research. A Williams College faculty summer grant, an award for recent recipients of the Ph.D. from the American Council of Learned Societies, and a grant from the Inter-American Foundation allowed me to return to Bolivia for parts of several summers to expand the scope of my dissertation. I am also grateful to the Centro para el estudio de la realidad económica y social (CERES) for support enabling me to participate during the summer of 1981 in a collaborative project on the peasant economy of Cochabamba.

I wish to thank all those people who contributed to the laborious tasks of typing and editing drafts of this book. María Onestini, Carmen Díaz, Julie Franks, and Marie Murray deserve special mention for their work, as does my illustrator, Lisa Tingey Davis. I was most fortunate to have Robert A. Feldmesser as the book's copyeditor. His exacting criticism and valuable suggestions contributed in important ways to the final outcome. I am also indebted to the editor in chief of Princeton University Press, Sanford G. Thatcher, for his encouragement and support over the past several years.

Another part of the social infrastructure lies closer to home. As any woman (or man) involved in a high-pressured, two-career family can testify, the magnitude of the tasks of research and writing becomes clear only when parenting suddenly has to be balanced against all the rest. It has been possible for me to find joy in both work and family because Carter Bancroft has shared so fully and happily in the responsibilities of child raising, and because two wonderful grandmothers have always been there when needed. To them, and to Josh and Devon, who put it all in proper perspective, I owe more than I can ever say.

ABBREVIATIONS

AGI   Archivo General de Indias (Seville)

AGN   Archivo General de la Nación (Buenos Aires)

AHMC Archivo Histórico Municipal de Cochabamba (Cochabamba)

ANB   Archivo Nacional de Bolivia (Sucre)

BN   Biblioteca Nacional del Perú (Lima)

EC   Expedientes y Correspondencia (pertaining to the manuscript collections catalogued as Tierras e Indios and as La Audiencia de Charcas in the ANB)

EP   Escrituras públicas

f., ff.   *folio, folios* (front side of page of archival document)

ML   Mata Linares manuscript collection of the Real Academia de Historia

RAH   Real Academia de Historia (Madrid)

COCHABAMBA, 1550–1900

Introduction

This book traces the evolution of agrarian society in the region of Cochabamba, Bolivia, between the sixteenth and nineteenth centuries. It explores the long-term impact of colonial rule upon the formation and development of agrarian class relationships that were defined by European principles of property ownership and reinforced by Spanish imperial rule. The central aim of the study is to show how the pressures and contradictions of colonialism and class gradually gave rise to a distinctive Indian and mestizo peasantry that eventually became a powerful protagonist in regional society. The study also explores the consequences of the emergence of this peasant sector for the nature and balance of local class relations, for peasant-state relations, and for the regional economy as a whole in the late colonial and the postcolonial periods.

The region with which the study is concerned is the former colonial province of Cochabamba, which was incorporated into the vast intendancy of Santa Cruz de la Sierra in the late eighteenth century. Located to the east of the *altiplano* (high plains) at about the seventeenth degree of south latitude, this geopolitical space had no physiographic uniformity. It represented a cross-section of the vertical Andean landscape that swept down from the snow-capped peaks of the Cordillera Oriental, bordering the eastern edge of the altiplano, past the ancient lake basins and plains lying at middle-range altitudes of some 8,500 feet above sea level, to the eastern lowland fringes of the tropical frontier. In spite of the region's ecological diversity, it was known for its fertile, temperate valleys that caught the waters tumbling down from glacial lakes in the mountain chains to the north and west. A cluster of three contiguous valleys composed the unifying feature of the region (see figure 1). Their extraordinary fertility attracted Andean cultivators from the western *puna* who sought warm, moist soil to cultivate maize and other crops that

3

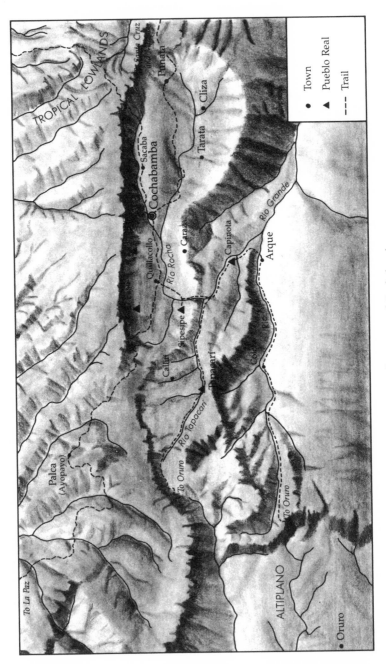

Figure 1 The Region of Cochabamba

did not thrive in the harsher alpine environments. Later, Europeans discovered the broad expanse of irrigated bottomlands and rich pastures in these central valleys. Although the region was always strongly oriented to the western altiplano, before and after the European arrival, it gained a territorial integrity and geohistorical identity of its own over the course of the colonial centuries.

The agrarian history of Cochabamba is no more representative of broader socioeconomic trends than any other Andean region. It is not my intention to project regional patterns onto the larger canvas of colonial Peru or Alto Perú. Rather, this study is focused on three specific aims. The first is to examine the region's strategic importance in the larger context of Tawantinsuyu and later of Alto Perú. The region's unique ecological endowments in the southern Andean landscape made it a vital area of surplus grain production for the Incas and the Spanish colonizers. In the late sixteenth century, Cochabamba was famous for the maize and wheat it shipped to the silver mines of Potosí. In some ways, the region became a classic agrarian hinterland of a dominant export sector.[1] Even as its functional role of granary in Alto Perú diminished over time, the region did not lose its importance as grain supplier to the cities and mines across the altiplano. In the late eighteenth and nineteenth centuries, Cochabamba's grains still supplemented the tuber diet of highland Andean peasants and provisioned some of the cities of the altiplano, particularly in times of drought and dearth. Moreover, Cochabamba became an important area of Spanish, mestizo, and Andean settlement in its own right. Intensive agriculture on the bottomlands sustained a relatively dense concentration of people who lived and worked in a network of towns, haciendas, and villages that crisscrossed the central valleys and hugged the banks of the western river valleys. But for a variety of reasons, which will emerge in the course of this study, the region gradually came to supply the dominant mining sector with another commodity: the labor power of impoverished peasants seeking wage work in the mineral lodes around the beginning of the twentieth century. One purpose of this history of Cochabamba, then, is to show the changing nature of the region's integra-

---

1 The seminal work on the formation of the internal colonial market revolving around Potosí is Carlos Sempat Assadourian, *El sistema de la economía colonial: Mercado interno, regiones, y espacio económico* (Lima: Instituto de Estudios Peruanos, 1982). See also the important article by Luís Miguel Glave, "Trajines: Un capítulo en la formación del mercado interno colonial," *Revista andina* 1 (1983): 9-76.

tion into the larger political economy and its link to the dominant mining economy and, through it, to the world market.

The second aim of this study is to illuminate the processes of structural change over a long period of time in an area of the Andes that was thoroughly integrated into the Spanish colonial empire. Through an examination of the long-term patterns of regional change in the context of mines, markets, and state formation in Alto Perú, it reveals the powerful extraregional forces of change that seemed to suck the region into the vortex of the expanding European economy during the first century of colonial rule. But it also seeks to show how Andean people conditioned the impact of those world-historical forces and sometimes set in motion counterforces that contained or limited the erosive effects of mercantile colonial pressures at the local level; and it identifies an important source of historical change in the internecine conflicts among factions of the colonial elite, as they tried to adjust to increasing competition for Indian labor during a protracted period of economic stagnation and a weak, decentralizing state in the seventeenth and early eighteenth centuries. Thus, considerable attention is given to the processes of market and state formation during the Toledan and post-Toledan periods in Alto Perú in order to explore how Andeans and Europeans in the Cochabamba valleys responded to (and to a certain degree impinged upon) the development of mercantile colonialism in this part of the Andes.

Cochabamba is a case study of radical transformation of preconquest patterns of life and work during the first century of Spanish rule. The market economy penetrated deeply, giving rise to new forms of exploitation and compelling Andean peoples to accommodate or to find new strategies of resistance. By the beginning of the seventeenth century, enterprising Spanish landowners (*chacareros*) had extended their reach across much of the valley land and created a servile class of peasants dependent upon them for the means of subsistence.

But the analysis of agrarian change in this region does not end with the transformation of native peoples into inferior "Indian" peasants. The broad temporal scope of this study allows for an exploration of the dynamics of ethnic and class relationships long after the dramatic confrontation between Andeans and Europeans had ended. The formation of European-style agrarian classes during the first century of colonialism did not establish a local hegemonic order that was either static or immutable to social pressures from below. Contrary to popular images of passive peons and tenant farmers bent in permanent subservience before the all-powerful *patrón*, most peasants who lived on haciendas were neither immobilized by debt nor limited in their livelihood activities to the boundaries of the "great estate." The study will show how a sector of the peasantry developed strategies of subsistence that combined Andean forms of communal labor and reciprocal exchange with small-scale commodity production and marketing, and in particular how the adaptive vitality of this peasantry eroded the economic power, prosperity, and hegemony of the landed elite in Cochabamba during the late colonial and the postcolonial periods.

At the same time, the study examines the dialectical nature of agrarian social relations. For if the emergent peasant economy began to challenge the landowning class (already suffering from the deleterious effects of estate fragmentation and market contraction), the landowners deployed their own schemes and strategies of accumulation and exploitation to shore up their eroding position in rural society. One consequence was a sharpening of class tensions in the region during the Bourbon period of increased state intervention and fiscal pressures. While the Bourbon state tried to smooth the raw edges of agrarian class relations in the region, the cumulative effect of its reforms was to deepen class antagonisms, as the burdens of colonialism grew heavier. The later chapters of the book therefore focus on the intersection of class and colonial relationships in rural Cochabamba in the late colonial period.

This analysis of regional change tries to demonstrate the historically contingent and sometimes precarious nature of agrarian classes in a colonial context. It assumes that the balance of class forces was subject to the internal social tensions, ecological disturbances (such as shifts in land-to-man ratios), and cyclical crises of subsistence that plagued all preindustrial societies. It also takes into account the initiatives of local groups and their responses to the continuing impact of larger historical forces, long after the watershed events of conquest and colonization.

However, one caveat is necessary. This study of agrarian transformations neither seeks nor finds the origins of capitalist transition in eighteenth- or early nineteenth-century Cochabamba. The study describes a regional economy that was in the process of diversifying into crafts, but that never saw peasant craft activity transformed into primitive manufacturing for the domestic market of a proletarianizing labor force. The study probes into agrarian estates, but finds little evidence of landlords bent upon rationalizing their enterprises to increase productivity or simply to enlarge their estates. Nor are there clear signs of enterprising capitalist farmers, an incipient kulak class, who harnessed their small-scale enterprises to expanding markets. The patterns of social realignments in the countryside were far more subtle. Under the intensifying fiscal pressures of the Bourbon state, each group struggled to maintain or improve its bargaining position in local society as the region was gradually drained of its meager capital resources in the late eighteenth century. Processes of social differentiation within the Cochabamba peasantry would have to advance much further before social pressures and uncertainties would turn a sector of the peasantry into a migrant work force in the distant industrial mines, or before a few prospering peasants would begin to acquire titles to pieces of crumbling haciendas around the beginning of the present century. Traditional haciendas continued to coexist uneasily with small-scale commodity production. Thus, while the balance and dynamics of class relations under colonialism and neocolonialism were characterized by historical motion and contradiction, the agrarian class structure in the Cochabamba region proved remarkably resilient throughout the late eighteenth, the nineteenth, and the early twentieth centuries.[2]

2 My interest in the development of agrarian class relations reflects, in an indirect way, some of the controversy among historians of early modern Europe over the relative autonomy of class and class conflict as forces of change. At issue, essentially, is where to locate the "motor force" of change in the gradual, uneven, and nonlinear process of transition toward capitalist relations of production: in the Malthusian dynamics of demographics; in the growth of trade and commercial capitalism; or in the internal class conflicts and contradictions embedded in the organization of production. Among Marxists, the issues of the debate were crystallized succinctly in the 1950s in a series of essays later gathered in Rodney Hilton, ed., *The Transition from Feudalism to Capitalism* (London: New Left Books, 1976). The debate was rekindled and broadened in the late 1970s with the publication of Robert Brenner, "Agrarian Class Structure and Economic Development in Pre-Industrial Europe," *Past and Present* 70 (1976): 30-75, and the subsequent commentaries under the same title by M. M. Postan and John Hatcher, *Past and Present* 78 (1978): 24-37, and Rodney Hilton, *Past and Present* 80 (1978): 3-19. Two additional Marxist essays on this "transition debate," which argued for the analytical primacy of class and class relations in the study of Eastern Europe and of Third World areas that were subordinate to, or penetrated by, European commercial capital, redirected the debate toward the world-systems approach to historical change; see Robert Brenner, "The Origins of Capitalist Development: A Critique of Neo-Smithian Marxism," *New Left Review*, no. 104 (1977): 25-92, and Aidan Foster-Carter, "The Modes of Production Controversy," ibid., no. 107 (1978): 47-78. A major object of their critique was, of course, Immanuel Wallerstein, *The Modern World-System: Capitalist Agriculture and the Origins of the European World Economy in the Sixteenth Century* (New York: Academic Press, 1974).

The third major aim of this study is to analyze patterns of agrarian change over the long term in comparative regional terms. The extraordinary cultural and social diversity of Andean rural societies, even after several centuries of colonial domination, dictates against insular approaches to regional history. Social historians and ethnohistorians have shown, in recent research, the persistent variation in social and economic organizations in Andean regions which, over five centuries, were subjected to common successive forms of political and economic domination.[3] From another angle, the ethnohistorical emphasis on the variety and adaptability of Andean forms of life and work reminds us that, in spite of the legendary wealth and world importance of Potosí, the market economy had an extremely variegated and uneven impact on southern Andean communities. Many Andean peoples managed to shield themselves against the most divisive effects of mercantile colonialism, sometimes through strategic engagement with the market or colonial state for purposes of preserving some semblance of economic autonomy and subsistence security.[4] The incursion of market forces (and of the colonial

3 David Lehmann, "Introduction: Andean Societies and the Theory of Peasant Economy," in David Lehmann, ed., *Ecology and Exchange in the Andes* (Cambridge: Cambridge University Press, 1982), 1-2. The ethnological literature on Andean diversity is too abundant to inventory here. For a succinct overview of recent research, see Frank Salomon, "Andean Ethnology in the 1970s: A Retrospective," *Latin American Research Review* 17 (1982): 75-128.

4 For contemporary ethnographic studies of Andean societies and of the interpenetration of reciprocal and market relations, see, for example, Billie Jean Isbell, *To Defend Ourselves: Ecology and Ritual in an Andean Village* (Austin: University of Texas Press, 1978); Barbara Bradby, " 'Resistance to Capitalism' in the Peruvian Andes," in Lehmann, ed., *Ecology and Exchange*, 97-122; Olivia Harris, "Labor and Produce in an Ethnic Economy: Northern Potosí, Bolivia," in ibid., 70-97; and Tristan Platt, "The Role of the Andean Ayllu in the Reproduction of the Petty Commodity Regime in Northern Potosí (Bolivia)," in ibid., 27-69. Ethnohistorical studies on the patterns and consequences of Andean market participation under colonial rule include John Murra, "Aymara Lords and Their European Agents at Potosí," *Nova Americana*, no. 1 (1978): 231-244; Thierry Saignes, "De la filiation à la résidence: Les ethnies dans les vallées de Larecaja," *Annales E.S.C.* 33 (1978): 1160-1181; Jorge Hidalgo Lehuedé, "Ecological Complementarity and Tribute in Atacama, 1683-1792," in Shozo Masuda, Izumi Shimada, and Craig Morris, eds., *Andean Ecology and Civilization: An Interdisciplinary Perspective on Andean Ecological Complementarity* (Tokyo: Tokyo University Press, 1985), 161-184; Karen Spalding, "Kurakas and Commerce: A Chapter in the Evolution of Andean Society," *Hispanic American Historical Review* 53 (1973): 581-599; Steve Stern, "The Struggle for Solidarity: Class, Culture, and Community in Highland Indian America," *Radical History Review*, no. 27 (1983): 21-48; and several of the essays in Olivia Harris, Brooke Larson,

state) was necessary, but certainly not sufficient, for the disintegration or erosion of Andean ethnic economies. The region of Chayanta, contiguous to Cochabamba, was but one area where Indian ethnic groups held on to their traditional lands and reproduced their social organization, with significant modifications, to withstand the pressures of colonialism.[5] The contrast in the colonial experience of the two regions, Cochabamba and Chayanta, stands as a vivid reminder of the differential impact of mercantile colonialism on Andean rural societies even in the economic heartland of Alto Perú. Furthermore, we need only recall that, at the birth of the Bolivian republic, some 70 percent of its Indian population still lived in autonomous communities to put the Cochabamba region into proper perspective, at least in the context of the southern Andes.

More than most regions of Alto Perú, Cochabamba experienced the economic and cultural shocks of European colonization. In contrast to Chayanta and many other highland areas, Andean peoples of the valleys were unable to contain the divisive forces of class within their communities or to slow the advance of Spanish land ownership. The challenge, therefore, is to determine the reasons why Andean peoples in Cochabamba succumbed so early to the European forms of domination, even as the Toledan state mounted its apparatus of indirect rule. Toward this end, it is necessary to explore the patterns and consequences of the unfolding struggles, conflicts, and alliances among and between Andeans and Europeans in the critical years between 1550 and 1600. The ethnic rivalry and disunity that weakened Andean resistance to European encroachment on valley land were similar to those that have been described for several other Andean regions in the same period.[6] But equally important was the peculiar legacy of late Incaic rule in the Valle Bajo of Cochabamba. Once the local Incan agrarian regime was shattered by the Spanish Conquest, Europeans could sift through some of the shards and piece together their own agrarian enterprises geared to the emerging market of Potosí. In this way, the deep imprint of particular precolonial state and social structures in Cochabamba created opportunities for

and Enrique Tandeter, eds., *La participación indígena en los mercados surandinos: Estrategias y reproducción social, siglos XVI-XX* (La Paz: CERES, 1987).

5 See Tristan Platt, *Estado boliviano y ayllu andino: Tierra y tributo en el Norte de Potosí* (Lima: Instituto de Estudios Peruanos, 1982), chaps. 1 and 2.

6 See, for example, Steve Stern, *Peru's Indian Peoples and the Challenge of the Spanish Conquest: Huamanga to 1640* (Madison: University of Wisconsin Press, 1982) and Thierry Saignes, *Los Andes orientales: Historia de un olvido* (Cochabamba: CERES, 1985).

European colonizers to engage in more extensive restructuring of patterns of production and exchange than was possible in many other Andean regions.

The study of regional change is approached here from several conceptual angles. Because the origins and evolution of this rural colonial society cannot be understood simply in terms of historical processes at the regional level, Cochabamba must be studied in the context of mercantile colonialism in Alto Perú. The early chapters of this book therefore approach regional history "from the outside." Necessarily, they chart broad patterns of change rather than the fine-grained detail of rural life. Chapters 1 and 2 locate the region in the larger colonial formation during the early period and consider the processes by which Europeans subordinated Andean traditions to their own economic, political, and ideological imperatives (which were not always congruent). Chapter 3 provides an overarching interpretive framework within which to trace secular trends over the course of the seventeenth and early eighteenth centuries and to explore the interaction between these trends and patterns of regional change. They seek to show how rural society in Cochabamba both adapted to and, in some measure, shaped the larger patterns of Andean population decline and dispersion, mineral decline and slow recovery, and political fragmentation in the period before the Bourbon reforms.

The later chapters narrow the temporal scope to the late colonial period in order to take a closer look at regional change. Chapters 4 through 8 explore various aspects of regional society and economy from the perspective of ethnic, class, and colonial relationships. Most of the data pertain to regional society during the second half of the eighteenth century, for which period there exists a wealth of quantitative and qualitative material on Cochabamba. But, as indicated earlier, the decision to focus on the internal dynamics of class and ethnicity in this period was motivated by more than simply pragmatic considerations. The eighteenth century seemed to be a period when regional patterns of landholding, agricultural production, and marketing began to configure and crystallize in forms that would endure well beyond the colonial period. Furthermore, the pressures of political reform in the late eighteenth century magnified the tensions intrinsic to peasant-landlord relations and threw into bold relief the social contours of class in this region.

Chapter 4 focuses on demographic characteristics and social relations in the Andean villages that were subject both to continuing encroachment from outside and to internal pressures and divisions.

In particular, this chapter studies the ways in which class differentiation in the village of Tapacarí created a crisis of authority for the caciques. Chapter 5 broadens the analysis to include the majority of the region's peasant families: those who lived outside the village on parcels of hacienda land, on small plots of their own, and on the outskirts of Spanish towns. It explores the nature and implications of peasant subsistence strategies, partly based upon small-scale commodity production and exchange. The next two chapters, 6 and 7, shift the analysis to the landed elite, who developed defensive strategies against the incursion of peasant smallholders, but who in turn contributed to their own declining position in rural society. These chapters explore the limits of reformist initiatives and the structural constraints that forced landlords to find rentier forms of income. Chapter 8 again enlarges the picture to examine the impact of the administrative reforms introduced by the Bourbons on the deterioration of the regional economy at the end of the colonial period.

Chapter 9 draws together the various strands of analysis to show the principal currents of change in the region over the course of the colonial period. Beyond this synoptic overview, the chapter explores the legacies of colonialism and class in Cochabamba in the nineteenth century and indicates the ways in which the acceleration of social differentiation in the valleys toward the end of the century both strengthened the peasant family economy in the region and simultaneously created the basis for peasant migration and proletarianization. The agrarian crisis and change in Cochabamba around the turn of the twentieth century had roots that lay deep in the subsoil of the colonial past.

Chapter 10 stands apart from the other chapters. Written expressly for the new edition, it selectively reexamines the conceptual premises and substantive findings of the original study, with an eye on the historical formation of local political cultures and discourses of peasantization and mestizaje in Cochabamba's central valleys and towns during the late colonial and postcolonial eras.

Along the
Inca Frontier

The traveler in the sixteenth century who set off southward from the shores of Lake Titicaca on a journey through Alto Perú (today Bolivia) left behind him one of the world's most arresting lacustrine landscapes. Pausing a moment in the hot morning sun to contemplate the landscape, a European traveler must have been struck by the lake's vast expanse and deep blue waters set off by the golden reeds that rose from the shallow waters near the shore. He saw great herds of alpaca and llama grazing on yellow-green pastures, and peasants planting quinoa and potatoes on hillsides sloping gently down to the lake. Across the inland sea to the northeast rose glaciered peaks that formed part of the endless eastern cordillera flanking the lake and the *altiplano*. Those mountains formed a topographic barrier between the dense human settlements around the lake and the vast, tropical frontier stretching eastward across the upper Amazonic basin. In the afternoons, the peaks vanished in white clouds that welled up from the tropical jungle beyond the cordillera, as if beckoning people of the high, arid plains to venture across the mountains into the steamy lowlands. From the altiplano, at 12,000 feet above sea level, the foreigner could feel the effects of the dry, "thin" air that seemed to lend an extraordinary luminosity to the landscape. The sun's warmth was deceptive, for the temperature would plummet to near freezing on most clear nights. The Aymara peoples who inhabited the high plains harnessed the extreme diurnal temperature contrast to make "freeze-dried" potatoes (*chuño*), a major source of their stored energy, and to preserve other staples. But for the European, the altiplano was bleak and inhospitable country.

Continuing southward, the sojourner encountered the bitter wind that scoured the high plains during the winter months, portent of a harsher climate. The southern reaches of the altiplano, near the towns of Oruro, Poopó, and Potosí, were considerably more arid and

13

cold than the lake region or points north.[1] Farther south, in the desolate territory of the Lipez, it was said that during the winter months the cold split stones and shrank the facial muscles of the dead, leaving ghostly smiles on their frozen, withered faces.[2] It was strange landscape, where shallow lakes were really salt marshes and where it was impossible to judge distance across the high plains to the next *tambo* or town. The luminous air seemed to play dangerous games with European perceptions of space.

The Southern Landscapes

Continental mountain chains border the altiplano on its western and eastern sides, so that in reality it is a series of high intermontane basins that formed a corridor of highland movement and settlement along a north-south axis between Cuzco and southern Alto Perú (see figure 2). To the west, the Cordillera Occidental juts sharply upward from the altiplano, its peaks reaching heights of 15,500 feet. A few rivers originate in this volcanic belt and flow westward toward the sea; the vertiginous western slopes drop off into the Atacama desert region bordering the sea. Mountain passages are few and treacherous, but the descent into the desert is the only outlet to the sea and the world beyond.

Crossing the eastern mountain chain, the Cordillera Oriental, the sixteenth-century traveler encountered a rugged, corrugated landscape that seemed more vertical than horizontal. Three or four days on muleback would bring the traveler through mountain passes near the snow line (at 15,000 feet) and across slopes and high pastures, where llamas grazed on *ichu* grasses, to cultivated fields where peasants planted tubers, barley, and perhaps some European wheat, at altitudes ranging from about 11,400 to 13,800 feet.[3] The puna lands

1 David Browman, "El manejo de la tierra árida del altiplano del Perú y Bolivia," *American indígena* 40 (1980): 145; Wendell C. Bennett, "The Andean Highlands: An Introduction," in J. Steward, ed., *The Handbook of South American Indians*, (Washington, D.C.: Smithsonian Institution, 1946), 2: 17.

2 Tristan Platt, "The Ayllus of Lipez in the Nineteenth Century" (paper presented at the Congress of Americanists, Manchester, England, September 5-10, 1982), citing Bernabé Cobo, *Historia del nuevo mundo* (1653) (Madrid: Atlas, 1956).

3 See Platt, "Role of the Andean ayllu," 30-31. For a discussion of agricultural tiers in the region, see Stephen B. Brush, "Man's Use of an Andean Ecosystem," *Human Ecology* 4 (1976): 147-166; and Olivier Dollfus, *El reto del espacio andino* (Lima: Instituto de Estudios Andinos, 1981).

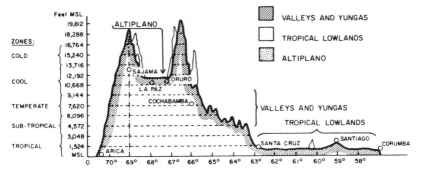

Figure 2 Ecological Zones of Bolivia
Source: E. Boyd Wennergren and Morris D. Whitaker, *The Status of Bolivian Agriculture*, p. 20. © 1975 Praeger Publishers. Reprinted by permission of Praeger Publishers.

were cold, but every so often the sojourner would come across a warm, sheltered valley that had a microclimate allowing peasants to cultivate less hardy crops than the tubers. This mountain range was wider than the western cordillera, and its tortured landscape sometimes seemed impenetrable, but actually these mountains were less hostile. Volcanic lakes fed streams that plunged into the cordillera and carved out rugged gorges and crevices. In the dry winter months, mountain streambeds became passageways into the warmer lowlands. There, the weary traveler at last began to feel at home: the *kichwa* region, ranging from 6,500 to 11,000 feet, was a temperate zone where European crops flourished alongside native ones. European colonists compared the valleys favorably to their own homelands in Spain.

In this longitudinal slice of the eastern cordillera, three broad intermontane basins created important agricultural regions in the kichwa ecological tier. Of the three valleys—Cochabamba, Chuquisaca, and Tarija—the northernmost, Cochabamba, was the largest and probably the most fertile. It consisted in turn of three contiguous, connected valleys, each with its own ecological characteristics (see figure 1).[4] The central valley, called the Valle Bajo or Lower Valley, was blessed with moist, alluvial soil deposited by a mountain river (known today as the Rocha River) that ran the length of the valley and spilled into the next, smaller valley, called Sacaba. In the richest lands, especially in the western reaches of the Valle Bajo, where the basin began to twist southward through the cordillera, peasants planted maize continuously on irrigated lands. There was no need to let the lands lie fallow where the alluvial soil was so deep and water readily available. A passage through a small mountain chain at the eastern end of the Valle Bajo led to the larger, higher, and more arid valley of Cliza. During winter months, its dry, dusty fields had none of the charms of the moister lands in the Valle Bajo or the Sacaba Valley, but its fields provided good pastures for European stock and pockets of moist soil that might be planted with maize and potatoes.

Though they opened on to each other, these central valleys of Cochabamba (as we shall refer to them) were fairly contained geographically. The cordillera rose sharply on all sides of the three valleys, isolating them from the altiplano and from other large settlements or valley regions. To the north and east, the rugged land jutted upward toward the sky, barricading the valleys from the tropical frontier on the other side of the eastern escarpment. South of the Cliza Valley, the landscape erupted in dry, jagged mountains that cut off the valley region from the southern intermontane basins and the large settlements of Chuquisaca and Tarija. The central valleys of Cochabamba were not cul-de-sacs; it was possible to travel eastward across the valleys and then, turning south, to follow winding mountain trails to the southern towns. But like most settlements in the warm kichwa tier along the eastern escarpment, the towns and villages of Cochabamba were off the beaten track—situated far from

---

4 See chap. 5 for a detailed description of the different zones in the late colonial period.

the altiplano and perched on the eastern edges of the colonial frontier, where the land dropped off precipitously into the untamed tropical expanse. The most heavily traveled routes followed the Arque and Tapacarí rivers in the western territory of the Cochabamba region through the cordillera to the altiplano.

The bleak puna and sharp, broken landscape of the cordillera that vexed and tortured Europeans provided an extraordinary variety of ecological niches which Andean peoples harnessed in precolonial times. The Aymara tribes, which inhabited the southern Andes long before the arrival of even the Incas, adopted pastoral and agricultural strategies that took advantage of the variations in climate and flora in the distinct ecological zones, often widely dispersed in space.[5]

The Aymara people implanted their core settlements in the bleak lands of the altiplano and puna. Highland settlements could take advantage of the tough grasses to graze their cameloid animals, chiefly llamas and alpacas. With careful planning and frequent rotation, tuber crops and quinoa also thrived in higher altitudes, where rainfall provided the only water. And the cold, dry climate proved ideal for preserving for ten or twelve months the vital foods that could supplement the consumption of chuño, which highlanders sometimes stored for years on end.[6] However harsh and forbidding the puna might seem to Europeans, it was the heartland of the domesticated cameloids and tubers that provided the staples of life for most Andean peoples. Furthermore, the puna tier was a strategic location for Andean communities. It usually formed a "middle ground" between the upper alpine pastures, too cold for even the hardiest crops to be sown, and the lower valleys and slopes in the kichwa zone. More important, puna settlements could be fortified more easily than villages nestled in remote valleys at lower altitudes.[7] But the

5 Carl Troll, "The Cordilleras of the Tropical Americas: Aspects of Climatic, Phytogeographical, and Agrarian Ecology," in Carl Troll, ed., *Geo-Ecology of the Mountainous Regions of the Tropical Americas*. (Bonn: University of Bonn Geographical Institute, 1968); John V. Murra, "El 'control vertical' de un máximo de pisos ecológicos en la economía de las sociedades andinas," in Iñigo Ortíz de Zúñiga, ed., *Visita de la provincia de León de Huánuco en 1562* (Huánuco: Universidad Nacional Hermilio Valdizán, 1972) 2: 429-476, as reprinted in John V. Murra, *Formaciones económicas y políticas del mundo andino* (Lima: Instituto de Estudios Andinos, 1975), 59-116 (citations refer to the reprinted edition).

6 John V. Murra, "Rite and Crop in the Inca State," in Stanley Diamond, ed., *Culture in History* (New York: Columbia University Press, 1960), 393-407, as translated and reprinted in Murra, *Formaciones económicas*, pp. 46-47.

7 Harry Tschopik, Jr., "The Aymaras," in J. Steward, ed., *Handbook of South*

puna not only nourished its inhabitants; it also formed the battle-grounds where rival Aymara kingdoms or clans engaged in ceremonial and real warfare. Small wonder that the Aymara word for highlands, *urco*, also connoted "virility associated with violence." In contrast, the warm, fertile lowlands were associated with feminine qualities, and valley settlements were considered to be subordinate to the core ethnic group of the puna.[8]

Life and agriculture at altitudes of 12,000 feet above sea level were fraught with uncertainty. Communities on the shores of Titicaca had the benefit of that large, deep body of water, which tempered the cold, dry climate of the altiplano. But most Aymaras lived with the expectation that frost, drought, or hailstorms would cut deeply into the harvest about three out of every five years.[9] It was not enough that abundant rain fell near harvest time if mild drought struck in the crucial months of September, October, and November, when highland peasants planted precious potato seed in the thin topsoil of the puna. And no season was free of the threat of frost; it could strike at any moment, sometimes claiming an entire harvest as winter approached.[10] Even under optimal climatic conditions, cultivators had to manage puna resources carefully, allowing their fields to rest—sometimes as long as twenty years—between crops. Highland peasants rotated potato, another tuber called *oca*, and the barley-like quinoa among multiple, dispersed plots of ground where the angle of the slope, patterns of light and shade, altitude, and soil condition combined in different ways to produce varied ecological conditions within the puna zone. In that way, cultivators didn't upset the delicate ecological balance, and they hedged their bets against natural calamity in any one locality.

Strict ecological constraints and the risks involved in puna agriculture impelled the highland communities to reach out to distant lands in the east. The moist lands in the kichwa zone meant that highland people could complement their everyday diet of potatoes,

American Indians, 7 vols. (New York: Cooper Square, 1963), 2: 547; Brush, "Man's Use of an Andean Ecosystem," 160.

8 Thérèse Bouysse-Cassagne, "L'espace aymara: Urco et uma," *Annales E.S.C.* 33 (1978): 1061 and 1063.

9 Juan Polo de Ondegardo, "Informe . . . al Lic. Briviesca de Muñatones sobre la perpetuidad de las encomiendas en el Perú" (1561), *Revista histórica* 13 (1940): 168.

10 R. Brooke Thomas and Bruce P. Winterhalder, "Physical and Biotic Environment of Southern Highland Peru," in P. Baker and M. Little, eds., *Man in the Andes* (Stroudsburg, Pa.: Doudon, Hutchinson, and Ross, 1976), 21-59.

chuño, and oca with such exotic products as maize, chili peppers (*ají*), and squashes. Without large-scale public works to terrace hill-sides and build irrigation systems, valley agriculture remained small-scale, dispersed, and secondary to highland subsistence agri-culture.[11] But scattered parcels of irrigated land in the river valleys of Cochabamba might yield maize crops large enough to allow some to be stored in communal silos against future emergencies—when, for example, drought in the *temporal* lands of the puna diminished the community's potato harvest. More than simply insurance, maize had symbolic value as a ceremonial crop, to be consumed (often in the form of *chicha*, or beer) at holiday festivities, work parties, or life-cycle rituals. It was a food of the gods as well as of the peasant fam-ily. Thus, rich maize fields in the eastern valleys provided precious resources to highland communities with which to appease the local deities and to guard against the frequent harvest failures.

Like most of the Andean peoples that inhabited the highlands south of the Cajamarca region, Aymara communities assured them-selves of a stable source of subsistence through their control of mul-tiple ecological tiers. At the local level of the *ayllu*, an extended kin group, this "vertical control of the ecology" might simply take the form of crop diversification across different microclimates located at great distance from one another. Even today in many parts of Bolivia, Aymara kin groups collectively control high pastures where came-loids and sheep are reared as well as crop land scattered throughout the puna and in the tucks and folds of the warm valleys, several days' journey away.[12] Murra's pathbreaking ethnohistorical study of the Chupaychu and Lupaqa kingdoms in the sixteenth century revealed extensive networks of "vertical control" that interlaced multiple settlements along the eastern and western cordilleras and nuclear political and kin groups in the highlands.[13] These ethnic kingdoms

11 Murra, *Formaciones económicas*, 47-48.

12 See Tristan Platt, "Espejos y maíz: El concepto de yanatín entre los Macha de Bolivia," in E. Mayer and R. Bolton, eds., *Parentesco y matrimonio en los Andes* (Lima: Universidad Católica, 1980), 139-182; Platt, "Role of the Andean ayllu"; O. Harris, "Labor and Produce"; Olivia Harris, "Ecological Duality and the Role of the Center: Northern Potosí," in Masuda, Shimada, and Morris, *Andean Ecol-ogy and Civilization*, 311-336; Joseph W. Bastien, *Mountain of the Condor* (St. Paul, Minn.: West Publishing, 1978); and Josep M. Barnadas, *Los Aymaras den-tro de la sociedad boliviana* (La Paz: Centro de Investigación y Promoción del Campesinado, 1976).

13 Murra, " 'Control vertical.' " See also his articles " 'El archipiélago vertical' Revisited" and "The Limits and Limitations of the 'Vertical Archipelago' in the

created "peripheral islands" of kinsmen in fertile pockets in the eastern kichwa regions, on oases along the Pacific coast, and on the edges of the tropical frontier. The inhabitants of these satellite communities, who were called *mitimaes*, cultivated coca, maize, ají, and cotton; they gathered guano along the seacoast to be used as fertilizer in the highlands; and they sent tropical fruit up from the *yungas*, the eastern mountains of the tropical zone. The same settlement pattern obtained for the Aymara kingdoms located far to the south of Lake Titicaca, though their vertical orientation was perhaps more eastward toward the kichwa lowlands.[14] This "archipelago" pattern of territoriality, so different from European nucleated settlements and contiguous territorial control, required kinsmen to trek many days through diverse landscape and "foreign" territory to their outlying colonies. Once they left behind their fortified core settlement in the highlands, they moved from ethnic island to island, navigating their way through neutral or enemy territory. A bird's-eye view of the eastern cordillera and intermontane basins would reveal a mosaic of multiple (often competing) hamlets, sealed off from their neighbors but bound tightly through kin ties and ideology to their distant ethnic "headquarters" in the highlands. Thus were Andean polities able to harness the ecological diversity of the vertical landscape and ensure their social reproduction, even in the face of high-risk puna agriculture, without embarking upon the indigenous development of a market system for the exchange of specialized or surplus products.

Yet, as Murra conceptualized it, "vertical control of the ecology" cannot be reduced simply to a model of ecological adaptation. "Verticality" was also an "ideal" that shaped the social relations of production and exchange within Andean society and formed an integral part of an ideology and world view.[15] In principle and in practice,

Andes," in Masuda, Shimada, and Morris, *Andean Ecology and Civilization*, pp. 3-14 and 15-20, respectively.

14 On the Aymara nations of the southern Collasuyu, see the testimony of Charcas Indians in Waldemar Espinoza Soriano, ed., "El memorial de Charcas: Crónica inédita de 1582," *Cantuta: Revista de la Universidad Nacional de Educación* (Chosica, Peru, 1969): 1-35.

15 For a discussion of the verticality model as an Andean ideal, see Olivia Harris, "Kinship and the Vertical Economy of the Laymi Ayllu, Norte de Potosí," *Actes du XLIIe Congrès International des Americanistes* (Paris: Société des Americanistes, 1976), 4: 165-177. For an exploratory essay on the concept of complementarity as applied to Andean societies, see Frank Salomon, "The Dynamic Potential of the Complementarity Concept," in Masuda, Shimada, and Morris, *Andean Ecology and Civilization*, 511-532. See also the important essays by Murra, " 'Archipiélago vertical' Revisited" and "Limits and Limita-

vertical control implied the existence of a communal tradition and ideology that bound people together in a web of mutual rights and responsibilities. Through reciprocity and communal labor, people coordinated their efforts to minimize and pool subsistence risks and ensure the social reproduction of their community or kindred. In its purest form, the principle of reciprocity involved the exchange of equivalencies, mediated by kinship and ritual kinship relations. As anthropologists have long argued, however, reciprocal relations may take a variety of forms, some symmetrical and some not, so that the term refers only vaguely to a relationship defined by a process of advances and restitutions over time.[16]

What was crucial in the precolonial Andean context, however, was that kinship provided a language and an ideology defining and legitimating patterns of give and take, at both the ayllu and the state level, which gave a certain cohesion and unity to kin groups scattered widely across space. In Andean societies, kin groups were bounded units composed of an extended network of households. Households were joined together to form larger, nested groups such as the ayllu, the lineage, and the community, tribe, or ethnic lordship (*señorío*). The ayllu, the cell of Andean society, was theoretically an endogamous lineage that traced its origins to a common ancestor. Ayllus were nested in extended lineages which, in turn, claimed descent from a mythical ancestor-god. These "confederated lineages" formed a half-dozen or so polities embracing thousands of households and extensive "vertical archipelagos." Before and after Incaic penetration, the Colla and Lupaqa kingdoms of the lake district, the Pacajes peoples south of the lake, and, to the far south, the Charcas, Caracaras, Chuyes, and Chichas all identified themselves

tions." A more critical view of "verticality" may be found in Rodrigo Sánchez, "The Model of Verticality in the Andean Economy: A Critical Reconsideration," *Actes du XLIIe Congrès International des Américanistes* (Paris: Société des Américanistes), 4: 213-226.

16 On the concept of reciprocity as a process of "advances and restitutions," see Claude Meillassoux, *Femmes, greniers, et capitaux* (Paris: Maspero, 1975). For critical discussions of the concept as applied in the Andean context, see Nathan Wachtel, "La reciprocidad y el estado inca: De Karl Polanyi a John V. Murra," in his *Sociedad e ideología* (Lima: Instituto de Estudios Peruanos, 1973), 59-78; O. Harris, "Kinship and the Vertical Economy," 172; Bradby " 'Resistance to Capitalism,' " esp. 114-115; and Benjamin Orlove, "Inequality among Peasants: The Forms and Uses of Reciprocal Exchange in Andean Peru," in Rhoda Halperin and James Dow, eds., *Peasant Livelihood: Studies in Economic Anthropology and Cultural Ecology* (New York: St. Martin's, 1977), 201-214.

as cultural groups distinguished by their Aymara dialects, styles of dress, music, weaving, and local rituals and deities (see figure 3).[17]

To realize the ideals of self-sufficiency and community, extended kin groups vested authority in an elaborate hierarchy of chieftains, including *mallkus*, or superior lords, and *hilacatas*, or secondary chiefs who governed at the level of the ayllu or moiety. These lords and chiefs symbolized the unity, common interests and identity of the ethnic group at the highest levels of social organization.[18] Vertical control of the environment thus implied a centralized political system which reproduced its own political, ideological, and religious power through the mobilization of peasant labor.[19] Theoretically, the contradiction engendered by the ideals of verticality and community, on the one hand, and the appropriation of surplus by ethnic elites, on the other, found its resolution in the services and gifts the mallkus (or *kurakas*, as they were called in the Quechua language) offered to the community at large or to individual kin. At all levels of the ethnic hierarchy, the principles of reciprocity and redistribution governed the social relations between direct producers and their lords. Andean chiefs gained authority and legitimacy by serving the

---

17 An important survey of Aymara peoples is the classic study by Luís G. Lumbreras, *The Peoples and Cultures of Ancient Peru* (Washington, D.C.: Smithsonian Institution Press, 1974), esp. 200-213. See also John Hyslop, "An Archeological Investigation of the Lupaqa Kingdom and Its Origins" (Ph.D. diss., Columbia University, 1976). On Aymara kinship organization, see Freda Y. Wolf, "Parentesco aymara en el siglo XVI," in E. Mayer and R. Bolton, eds., *Parentesco y matrimonio en los Andes* (Lima: Universidad Católica, 1980), 115-136, and Xavier Albó and Mauricio Mamani, "Esposos, suegros, y padrinos entre los Aymaras," in ibid., 283-326. Two recent regional approaches to Andean social relations and ideology, both of them focused on the central highlands of Peru, are Karen Spalding, *Huarochirí: An Andean Society under Inca and Spanish Rule* (Stanford, Calif.: Stanford University Press, 1984), esp. chap. 1-3; and Stern, *Peru's Indian Peoples*, chap. 1.

18 In his study of the Lupaqa on the western shores of Lake Titicaca, Murra identified two kings who reigned simultaneously around the time of the Spanish Conquest. This dualistic political organization, which split Lupaqa settlements into moieties, was a common Andean pattern which survived, at the local level, the transition to colonial rule. But it seemed to be particularly marked among some Aymara polities, which were also segmented in their political and social spatial organization. See John V. Murra, "An Aymara Kingdom in 1567," *Ethnohistory* 15 (1968): 115-151, as reprinted in Murra, *Formaciones económicas*, 207-209; Bouysse-Cassagne, "Espace aymara," 1058-1059; O. Harris, "Ecological Duality"; and Platt, "Espejos y maíz."

19 See Bradby, " 'Resistance to Capitalism,' " for a discussion of vertical control as a social relation.

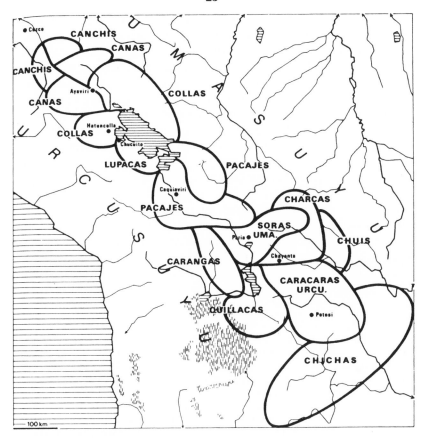

Figure 3   The Aymara Kingdoms
Source: Thérèse Bouysse-Cassagne, "L'espace aymara: Urco et Uma, *Annales
E.S.C.* 5-6 (1978): 1059. Reproduced by permission.

collective interests. They protected and maintained the community's property and norms; generously feasted laborers working on
communal projects; coordinated the production, storage, and redistribution of products among ayllus and across the vertical archipelago; mediated disputes and rivalries so as to preserve the group's solidarity; interpreted and appeased the gods and the sacred ancestors;
and defended community interests against outside threats. Above
all, they guaranteed to all kin who shared communal responsibility
a minimum of subsistence security and a cushion against natural
disaster.

Ethnohistorians who have reconstructed the social organization of

Andean societies prior to the European intrusion have found under-currents of conflict and contradiction that animated these societies and often pulled them in opposite directions. While they have not agreed on the course these societies might have taken had the European invasion not arrested their development, most Andean ethnohistorians take pains to demystify *lo andino*—the "Andean way"—as an egalitarian utopia or ideal.[20] Whether we are dealing with the powerful Aymara kingdoms of the southern steppes or the Andean tribes of the central sierra, power and access to resources were distributed unequally. Furthermore, the internal dynamics of communal organization that supported a powerful, often bellicose ethnic elite sharpened the contradictions within local Andean society and probably widened the gap between Andean ideals and social reality. Communal forms of work and life contained the germs of class differentiation; the ideology of reciprocity often masked relations of political domination and surplus extraction; and the ideal of vertical control intensified ethnic rivalry among polities struggling to extend their reach into the maize valleys.[21]

The crucial point, nevertheless, is that the ideals of verticality, community, and reciprocity established the ideological boundaries within which people defined and articulated social norms, created standards of justice and social legitimacy, and interpreted their world and cosmos. These principles formed the basis of "moral economy" that to a greater or lesser degree governed social relationships, bound together kinship and social hierarchy, and strengthened communal solidarity.[22] They endowed everyday subsistence activities

20 See esp. Murra, " 'Control vertical' "; Spalding, *Huarochirí*, chap. 2 and 3; Stern, *Peru's Indian Peoples*, chap. 1; and Nathan Wachtel, *The Vision of the Vanquished: The Spanish Conquest of Peru through Indian Eyes, 1530-1570* (New York: Harper and Row, 1977).

21 Stern, *Peru's Indian Peoples*, chapter 1; Bradby, " 'Resistance to Capitalism' "; Murra, " 'Control vertical.' "

22 Historians and anthropologists who study change in traditional societies within the framework of "moral economy" are not concerned simply with the apparent "objective" conditions of life and work within precapitalist agrarian orders. Rather, they emphasize the pattern of moral rights and expectations that both governed social behavior within a kin group or ethnically bounded community and provided the normative order or standards by which people judged their own behavior and that of outsiders. In many traditional agrarian societies, that moral order revolved around the shared expectation of distributing risks and scarce resources among members of the community in a way that guaranteed some form of subsistence to all members engaged in communal activities. Traditional ideals of reciprocity also governed relations between peasants and their

and labor prestations with symbolic, even religious, meaning. They gave peasants the right to call on their mallkus or hilacatas for assistance or generosity in times of need. On a broader level, the ideals of verticality, community, and reciprocity gave social cohesion to the Charcas or Caracaras who were scattered in isolated hamlets across a tortured landscape, because those ideals legitimated and preserved their moral claim to "subsistence rights" no matter what ecological niche they inhabited in their polity. Thus, while Andean societies may have been marred by social differentiation and accumulative processes, the normative order mandated a degree of social control that placed structural limits on the exploitation of the poorer peasants. The dominant ideology thus blunted the cutting edge of class formation based on property relations.

Yet the communal tradition and ideology had a double edge. It provided an overarching unity, but it could be manipulated in a way that had a disintegrating effect on the whole. Thus, for example, while Aymara lords could ensure the group's self-sufficiency and material well-being, and while they had to uphold minimum standards of justice and equity, they could also invoke the communal tradition to militarize their societies. Aymara lords of the Collao were famous for turning their peasants and herders into professional warriors. When the Incas expanded their empire into the southern Andes during the fifteenth century, the Quechua-speaking invaders began to appreciate the power and authority that Aymara lords wielded in their ethnic kingdoms and to turn it to their own imperialist ends.

Incaic Inroads

Under the emperor Pachacuti (1438-1471), Inca warriors from the north pushed their way into the rich, populous kingdoms of the Collao, the region around Lake Titicaca. The invaders from Cuzco encountered bitter resistance, but they finally managed to impose imperial control over the Aymara dynasties of the lake district. During two successive administrations, the Incas consolidated their rule over the Aymara nations, absorbing them into the Collasuyu "quarter" of the Incaic empire of Tawantinsuyu. The emperor Yu-

overlords and other members of the ruling group. On the politics of "moral economy," see Edward P. Thompson, "The Moral Economy of the English Crowd," *Past and Present*, no. 50 (1971): 76-136. On the moral tissue of peasant societies and the logic of reciprocal relationships, see James Scott, *The Moral Economy of the Peasant* (New Haven: Yale University Press, 1976), and Barrington Moore, Jr., *Social Origins of Dictatorship and Democracy: Lord and Peasant in the Making of the Modern World* (Boston: Beacon, 1966), esp. 453-483.

panqui (1471-1493) settled ethnically alien populations among the recently subdued natives, constructed a network of roads and tambos, and began to recruit Aymara warriors for his own imperial armies. As the Incas advanced the northern frontiers of their empire, they drew more heavily on the loyal Aymara, Pukinas, and Uru nations of the southern highlands for their soldiers. Military recruitment intensified under Huayna Cápac (1493-1527), as he elevated the status of certain Aymara groups to serve as his professional warriors. Many years later (in 1582), in litigation aimed at recovering some of their former privileges and status, the Charcas, Caracaras, Chuyes, and Chichas proudly described themselves as "soldiers of the [Incan] emperor," who had "fought and conquered the Chachapoyas, Cayambis, Canares, Quitos, and Quillaycincas, who are the [tribes] of Guayaquil and Popoyán." The Aymara warriors furnished the shock troops on the northern edges of the empire, and the Incas also stationed soldiers from the "four nations" along the southeastern escarpment to fortify their territory against the unconquerable Chiriguanos, who inhabited the tropical lowlands beyond the imperial frontier.[23]

The Incas' ability to mobilize Aymara troops to fight their own expansionist wars a thousand mountainous miles from the soldiers' homeland provides a striking example of indirect rule. The Incas grafted extractive institutions onto local ones and worked through the existing ethnic hierarchy, allowing the ayllu and the ethnic polity to retain considerable autonomy under their rule. Peasants had to contribute their labor to cultivate state and religious lands, but they did so in much the same way as they participated in ayllu tasks and in obligations to their ethnic lords and community. Tribute obligations to the state therefore overlapped and blended with communal obligations, without eroding the subsistence base of the local group. The Incan state skillfully manipulated the norms of vertical complementarity, reciprocity, and community to "absorb the surplus production of a self-sufficient population."[24]

In the case of the Aymara warriors, of course, the stakes were

23 Espinoza Soriano, ed., "Memorial de Charcas," esp. 24-25.

24 John V. Murra, "On Inca Political Structure," in Ronald Cohen and J. Middleton, eds., *Comparative Political Systems* (New York: Natural History, 1967), 357. See also John V. Murra, *La organización del estado inca* (México City: Siglo XXI, 1978); Franklin Pease, "The Formation of Tawantinsuyu: Mechanisms of Colonization and Relationship with Ethnic Groups," in George Collier, Renato Rosaldo, and John Wirth, eds., *The Inca and Aztec States, 1400-1800* (New York: Academic Press, 1982), 173-198.

higher: tribute was paid in blood. Precisely for this reason, the Incan emperors cultivated the allegiance of the Aymara chiefs, who mobilized the troops and ensured their effectiveness and loyalty. Invoking the principle of reciprocity, the emperors showered status, privilege, and wealth on the Aymara groups who contributed their young men. The "generosity" of the Inca was expressed not merely in the usual way of feasting those in the service of the state, though the emperor's soldiers did receive special rations of maize beer, quinoa flour, meat, and other valuable items. The Charcas, Caracaras, Soras, Quillacas, and Carangas were also rewarded with grants of precious maize land in the eastern part of the Valle Bajo; moreover, as the Aymaras pointed out in a petition to the Spanish king in 1582, the emperors had exempted them from all other tributes and "personal services such as guarding the [royal] herds ... serving in the *mit'a* [a system of rotative forced labor] in the ... court of Cuzco ... weaving *cumbi* and *abasca* cloth, and ... serving as ... field hands [on state lands.]."[25] Perhaps they exaggerated Inca beneficence, since they were seeking to recover some of the status and privileges they had enjoyed under the Spaniards. But their sense of indignation and abuse under the newly arrived overlords, and their collective testimony to Incaic generosity, bespoke the special relationship the Incas established with certain Aymara chiefs. The Incas depended upon them as crucial allies who could marshal the most valiant soldiers in Tawantinsuyu, and Cuzco demonstrated its trust, esteem, and alliance by enhancing the power, status, and probably even personal wealth of Aymara lords.

It may well be that this relationship of "reciprocity" between the Inca state and the ethnic elites of the far south created problems *within* Aymara societies. The Incas depended upon the loyal leaders of the Charcas and their neighbors to defend the Collasuyu against the European invaders.[26] But the shadowy underside of the alliance with Aymara lords was that—although it took young men away from their kinsmen and fields only periodically, in turns—it nonetheless sapped the community of its youth and vitality, leaving the old people to tend the herds and crops of their absent relatives.[27] The

25 Espinoza Soriano, ed., "Memorial de Charcas," 21 and 24.

26 For contrasting cases in the central highlands of Peru, where the Inca policy of assimilation was less successful in forging interelite alliances, see Stern, *Peru's Indian Peoples*, 22-23, and Spalding, *Huarochirí*, chap. 3.

27 John V. Murra, "La guerre et les rébellions dans l'expansion de l'état inka," *Annales E.S.C.* 33 (1978): 931.

Incas were wise not to burden those ayllus with any more obligations.

The Incas' conquest of the southern Andes gave them access to stratified societies rich in herds, lands, mines, and laborers. The Collao must have seemed like a treasure trove to the invaders from Cuzco. But the Incas also displayed imagination and initiative as they began to explore the sparsely settled kichwa frontier. There, on the edges of their empire, near the eastern precipice and the tropical lowlands, the Incas discovered the fertile, temperate valleys of Cochabamba. Within two generations, they mounted a state agricultural project of unprecedented scope. Wachtel's recent study of sixteenth-century litigation over *mitmaq* lands (i.e., the lands of the mitimaes) in the Cochabamba valleys and the publication of a portion of the trial records bring into focus an extraordinary example of direct colonization by the Incas and the collectivization of agriculture under state auspices.[28]

The appearance of the Incas in the fertile valleys of Cochabamba foreshadowed momentous change. Túpac (Emperor) Yupanqui swept through the valleys in the late fifteenth century, uprooting the indigenous Sipesipes, Cotas, and Chuyes. The first of these groups was allowed to remain in the Valle Bajo, as subjects of the Incan emperor. But Yupanqui transplanted the Cotas and Chuyes to Incaic fortresses along the eastern frontier in Mizque and Pocona, where they served as guards against the "barbarians" of the tropical lowlands. Yupanqui's "clean sweep" of the Valle Bajo left him free to claim its lands. However, the Incas' earliest annexation of the valley apparently was limited to the eastern zone, called (to this day) Calacala. Túpac Yupanqui knew little of "farming matters," preferring instead to carve out a small patrimony in a fertile corner of the valley.[29]

The human landscape began to change rapidly when Huayna Cápac appropriated extensive lands in the central valleys for state purposes. He assembled a mosaic of ethnic islands, adopting the model of the vertical archipelago and recasting it for purposes of political control.[30] He created maize-cultivating colonies of Charcas, Cara-

28 Nathan Wachtel, "The *mitimas* of the Cochabamba Valley: The Colonization Policy of Huayna Capac," in Collier, Rosaldo, and Wirth, *Inca and Aztec States*, 199-235; and *Repartimiento de tierras por el Inca Huayna Cápac* (1556) (Cochabamba: Universidad de San Simon, 1977). The subsequent discussion draws heavily on both these sources.

29 *Repartimiento de tierras*, 25, and Wachtel, "*Mitimas*," 201.

30 Murra distinguishes between the ancient model of vertical complementarity,

caras, Soras, Quillacas, Carangas, Urus, and other ethnic groups of the puna. In addition, he imported Plateros, who originated on the desert coast near Ica, and mitimaes from other distant lands. The central valleys were checkered by distinct ethnic mitmaq colonies, some cultivating state lands, others tending the fields of their own nuclear groups rooted in the puna.

Huayna Cápac did more than cluster mitmaq colonies in the maize valleys. Under his administration, the Incas assembled the pieces of an elaborate state enterprise which "rationalized" the large-scale production and distribution of maize and turned the Cochabamba region into a major exporter of that crop. The state annexed the western half of the Valle Bajo and stamped the valley floor with an intricate landholding grid. Westward across the valley from Quillacollo were five adjacent grain farms, or *chácaras* (as Indians later described them to Spanish magistrates), each of which was quartered and distributed to an ethnic group. The Soras, Collas, Quillacas, and Carangas each received land in one of the quarters of the chácara. Within each quarter, land was subdivided into long strips, which were distributed to different subtribes of the group. Wachtel's analysis of land tenure reveals that the Soras cultivated the largest number of strips, followed by the Quillacas and Carangas, and then by the Collas.[31] Except for one of the five chácaras, the fruits of the land were earmarked for the state. Harvests from the smallest chácara went to feed the field hands and state workers who inhabited the valleys. In this way, the Incas "reciprocated" by providing for the subsistence needs of their laboring tributaries.

The cultivation of maize on irrigated land, which sometimes yielded several crops a year, required intensive labor. People were needed to fertilize the soil, maintain the elaborate system of irrigation, plant and harvest the crop, and transport it to the royal warehouses both in the valley and in the highlands near Paria and points north. The Incas called upon two types of laborers. The Sipesipes tended the royal llama herds which grazed in the rich uplands at the southwestern end of the Valle Bajo (the *cabecera del valle*). The mitimaes who resided in the valleys were assigned strategic or skilled tasks, and others were entrusted with guarding the royal granaries. Though they worked on the "state project," under the authority of Incan governors, the mitimaes still owed their primary allegiance to

an ideal and a form of ecological control, and the Incas' use of mitmaq colonies—in a kind of political archipelago pattern radiating from Cuzco—to extend control over their vast empire; see Murra, " 'Control vertical,' " 109-112.

31 Wachtel, *"Mitimas,"* 210-211.

their own mallku or kuraka and their ethnic "family." The field
hands, however, were corvée laborers brought into the valley for
three months of intensive physical labor. In assigned groups, these
Soras, Carangas, Quillacas, and Collas migrated from their puna settlements across the altiplano and down through the mountains to
the Incas' chácaras. There, under the supervision of their own leaders
and Inca overseers, they produced the empire's maize crop. After the
harvest, these seasonal agricultural laborers (*mittayoc*) returned en
masse to their highland ayllus. Thus, the Incan m'ita set in motion
one of the largest seasonal migratory flows in Tawantinsuyu. The
trial records give some indication of its magnitude: they mention a
laboring population of 14,000, though not all were seasonal migrants.[32] But the seasonal influx of migrant workers, fresh from their
highland ayllus, kept alive separate ethnic identities and reinforced
the kinship ties that still bound the sedentary mitimaes in the valley
to their distant highland communities. Collectivization of agriculture under the Incas did not homogenize the cultures of the valley
peoples. On the contrary, it relied heavily upon Aymara kin groups
and elites to coordinate the flow of labor prestations to the state's
maize lands. While there existed signs of incipient class divisions
within the collective enterprise, patterns of social differentiation
were expressed primarily in ethnic terms.

Huayna Cápac's agrarian reform turned the Valle Bajo into Tawantinsuyu's principal cereal region. In volume of maize production, the
valley was rivaled perhaps only by the richest, irrigated valleys along
the seacoast.[33] Recent archeological research on the Inca's system of
grain storage in the valley provides clues to the scale of production.
Perched safely upon the plateau of Cotapati, overlooking the Valle
Bajo, stood row after row of round stone silos, in which it is estimated that at least 9,600 tons of maize could be stored.[34] The Incas
built more grain depositories on this site in the Valle Bajo than in
the entire valley of Jauja, which was once thought to have been the
granary of Tawantinsuyu. This stored grain was in addition to the
quantity of maize exported to warehouses in Paria and other highland sites. In fact, most maize was expropriated by the state for redistribution in far-flung corners of the empire. Carangas Indians who

32 *Repartimiento de tierras*, 28; Wachtel, "*Mitimas*," 214 and 219.

33 John Murra, "Rite and Crop," 55.

34 Geraldine Byrne de Caballero, "La arquitectura de almacenamiento en la lo-
gística incáica," *Diario*, Nov. 30, 1975, 2.

recalled earlier times when they worked in the Incan maize fields mentioned the destinations of Cochabamba's superior quality crop: "In the chácaras of Potopoto, Yllaurco, Colchacollo, Anocaraire, and Viloma, they harvested the crop and carried it by llama caravan to the tambo of Paria and from there to Cuzco."[35] But if Cuzco's nobility consumed the finest quality maize, the bulk of it went to feed the emperor's soldiers. Maize nourished "all the nations of Indians who marched in the Inca's army, alongside Huayna Cápac."[36]

This analysis of the policies that were designed to assimilate the peoples of the southern Collasuyu into the rapidly expanding empire of the Incas has shown that they operated in two ways. Through methods of indirect rule and strategic alliance with powerful Aymara lords in the highlands, the Incas drained off young men to stock their imperial armies with tribesmen known for their skill and valor in warfare. In return, the emperor granted the ethnic lords lands, personal retainers (*yanaconas*), and special privileges, in the process probably buttressing the lords' power and prestige within their own societies. In contrast, the kichwa valleys afforded entirely different opportunities, which the Incas exploited with remarkable success. They focused their collective efforts on the fertile valleys of Cochabamba, where they vastly expanded the empire's maize production. Unlike the case in the puna, where the Incas ruled in subtle, almost invisible ways through ethnic intermediaries, the Incaic presence in the valleys loomed large. The state intervened in the productive process, shaping economic life in the valleys partly in accord with traditional principles of reciprocity and ethnic communalism but turning it toward new, imperialist ends. The imperatives of the state's agricultural project also required massive coordination and control over migrant laborers. It was this very enterprise that provided the surplus with which to mount the military machine on the shoulders of the highland peoples. Whether as soldiers of the emperor, or as migrant field hands who harvested the crop that fed those soldiers, the peoples of the altiplano bore a heavy burden of empire under the Incas.

Transition to Colonial Rule

The peoples of the Collao who had sacrificed their youth to the imperial armies of the Incas had every reason to ally themselves with

35 *Repartimiento de tierras*, 24.

36 Translated from the Spanish quotation in Wachtel, "*Mitimas*," 214.

the earliest European invaders who ventured into the southern high-lands. Like the Lucanas peoples in the central highlands of Peru, the Aymara lords might have seized the moment of political crisis that gripped the Inca state in the 1530s and joined in military alliance with the small band of Europeans to challenge Incaic rule.[37] Yet when the moment arrived, the warrior-subjects stood fast against the plundering Europeans and their native allies. Proclaiming their loyalty to the emperor Manco Cápac and his brother Paullo, the Lupaqas and Pacajes of the lake district and then the confederation of Charcas, Caracaras, Chuyes, and Chichas waged a bitter defensive war against the white invaders.

The valleys of Cochabamba were the battleground for the final confrontation between the Europeans (and their allies) and the confederation of Charcas. Native warriors mobilized their troops in the fortified region of Pocona and ambushed the Europeans in the maize valleys. After weeks of fierce warfare, the Europeans finally defeated the Incas' loyal warriors in 1539 and established tenuous control over the "nations" of the Collasuyu.[38] It was a crucial victory, for despite the harsh and alien landscape of the altiplano, the Europeans soon realized that the dense native communities and rich mineral deposits in this southern zone offered extraordinary opportunities for commercial exploitation. Of immediate strategic importance was that the Europeans had succeeded in isolating the peoples of Charcas (as the territory became known) from the rebel forces of Cuzco and the Vilcabamba River valley, who continued to resist European rule. But the final battle deeply scarred the human landscape and temporarily turned the cropland of Tawantinsuyu into a wasteland. Native and European soldiers alike pillaged the royal granaries and destroyed the herds, crops, and irrigation works, flooding the fallow lowlands that had once yielded the Incas' richest maize harvest. The mittayoc and many resident mitimaes were gone, having abandoned the royal maize valley to return home to their highland ayllus all across the altiplano.[39] Amidst the turmoil, small mitmaq communities still clung to the tucks and folds of the sierra and valleys and continued performing the daily tasks of subsistence. But life would never be the same. As we shall see shortly, the collapse of Incan state

37 See Stern, *Peru's Indian Peoples*, 30ff.

38 Espinoza Soriano, ed., "Memorial de Charcas," 25-26; John Hemming, *The Conquest of the Incas* (London: Sphere, 1972), 245-247.

39 *Repartimiento de tierras*, 21; Wachtel, "Mitimas," 220.

power in the Cochabamba valleys—indeed, the very legacy of Incan colonization of Cochabamba—created a social vacuum in the post-conquest period which would soon be filled by a new set of historical actors locked in a power struggle over the valley's resources.

The Europeans in Alto Perú focused their initial settlement efforts on the southern territory of their new subjects, the Charcas. Hernando Pizarro established the first official Spanish town, Chuquisaca (or La Plata, now Sucre), in 1538-1539, in the large kichwa valley nearest the densely populated communities of the Charcas and the scattered mineral deposits in the highlands. Soon to become the administrative center of Alto Perú, or the *audiencia* (royal court) of Charcas, the town of Chuquisaca was laid out in classic grid pattern to provide a "civilized," urban setting in a temperate climate tolerable (if not pleasing) to Europeans. But in 1540s, it was the sole colonial town in a landscape that seemed desolate and untamed to European eyes. Europeans also established footholds at two mining camps: the old, pre-hispanic mines of Porco and, after 1545, the newly discovered mines of Potosí. At an altitude that dizzied most Europeans, the bleak mining site at Potosí nevertheless began to attract large numbers of Europeans as well as natives. No gleaming white, garden town like Chuquisaca, Potosí from the beginning was a gritty mining town nestled at the base of the Cerro Rico, where puna Indians, but not Europeans, felt at home in the harsh climate. Yet even as the Chuquisaca-Potosí axis of settlement grew in the 1540s, the first Europeans in Alto Perú felt vulnerable, isolated in the mountainous interior of the southern Andean zone, far from Lima, Cuzco, Arequipa, and other centers of colonial power and cut off from the sea links to Europe (see figure 4). Travel northward across the altiplano to the transit town of La Paz (and from there down to the seaport of Arica) seemed treacherous to most Europeans, because they would have to pass through Charcas, Caracaras, Carangas, and Pacajes territory before reaching the next "safe" city.[40]

The Europeans soon began, however, to alter the world they had conquered. Their first step was to parcel out the spoils of conquest: The king of Spain bestowed *encomiendas*—grants of native communities together with their inhabitants, who were obliged to pay the grantees tribute—on the privileged few deemed worthy of such rewards. (Hernando Pizarro was the first of these *encomenderos*.) The earliest of the encomiendas, or *repartimientos*, as they were also

40 Josep M. Barnadas, *Charcas, 1535-1565: Orígenes de una sociedad colonial* (La Paz: Centro de Investigación y Promoción del Campesinado, 1973), 34-39.

Figure 4   Cities and Towns of Alto Peru
Source: Peter Bakewell, *Miners of the Red Mountain* (Albuquerque: University of New Mexico Press, 1984), 27.

known, grouped the Indians in units (ayllus, moieties, and confederated lineages) that corresponded loosely to pre-Hispanic ethnic and kin patterns, and the caciques (as the Spaniards called the kurakas), and the mitimaes subject to them, remained with their units.[41] But soon after, expediency and European ignorance wreaked havoc on Andean social patterns and notions of territoriality (with a few notable exceptions). The Europeans began to fragment, disintegrate, and rearrange the ethnic kingdoms of the south. As they stamped large, contiguous administrative districts onto the Andean landscape, they arbitrarily severed ethnic confederations, split apart

41 Thierry Saignes, "Políticas étnicas en Bolivia colonial, siglos XVI-XIX," *Historia boliviana* 3 (1983): 5-6.

moieties, and truncated the ethnic "archipelagos." Even the territorial-administrative division between Peru proper and Alto Perú sliced the Aymara-speaking world into two parts. Where Aymara peoples saw in the deep, blue waters of Lake Titicaca a sacred, unifying force, the natural center of the cosmos, the Europeans saw a natural boundary dividing, along an east-west axis, the heartland of the old Inca empire from the southern district of Charcas. Ethnic lords saw their señoríos shrink and their coastal or kichwa islands of mitimaes placed under the jurisdiction of different kurakas and their encomenderos. Thus, for example, the Lupaqa lords of the lake district lost their mitmaq colonies in the valleys near Arequipa to the local encomendero and caciques until Juan Polo de Ondegardo—a prominent jurist, an encomendero, and a student of Andean cultures, who understood the importance of the pattern of verticality—arranged for their return to their ethnic homeland.[42] As we shall see, the Charcas and other highland peoples were dispossessed of their mitmaq lands and colonists in the Cochabamba valleys. Though colonial policy did not at first institutionalize the rupture of kinship ties binding mitimaes to their distant highland homelands, the imposition of European models of territoriality set into motion a protracted process of fragmenting ethnic señoríos into localized units more easily administered by colonial authorities.[43]

As already mentioned, the Spaniards initiated their colonial exploits in Alto Perú in the highland regions, where repartimientos were rich in tributaries. At first, private encomenderos enjoyed unlimited authority over their tributaries, but in October 1550, the audiencia of Lima made the first attempt to assert royal control over encomenderos by legitimating and regulating the amount and kind of tribute they could demand. Whereas the Europeans had laid the foundations of early colonial rule on the basis of precolonial extractive institutions, the new tribute requirements, and the very circumstances under which tributaries had to meet their new obligations, forced the native peoples to alter their lifeways. The new overlords asked caciques to commandeer peasant laborers for their own small

42 Polo de Ondegardo, "Informe . . . al Lic. Briviesca de Muñatones," 177.

43 In a report prepared for a research planning meeting on Andean ethnohistoriography, held at the Social Science Research Council, New York, in October 1981, Murra proposed this issue of the transformation of ethnic señoríos into "Indian communities," with a gradual loss of rights, as an important line of future investigation. See Spalding, *Huarochirí*, and Saignes, *Andes orientales*, for recent studies of precisely this process.

enterprises, but—unlike the Incan emperor, who expected to be paid only in labor power—the encomendero demanded tribute in labor, kind, and increasingly in money. It was no longer enough for the Carangas or Soras to send off a small band of their kinsmen to work for a season in the distant maize fields of the Incas, knowing they would be amply fed while they were gone. Furthermore, the Incas would reciprocate in material and spiritual ways for the labor rendered. Now, tributaries required to deliver a certain quantity of maize to their encomendero had to reallocate their valley lands and cut into their own subsistence in order to meet their new obligations. More ominous, new tribute requirements in fixed amounts of products threw the burden of agricultural risk onto the backs of the producers themselves. Where the Incan emperor used to absorb the loss of crops from a severe drought or sudden frost, ethnic communities now confronted an unbending encomendero who required payment in crops no matter how wide the fluctuation of agricultural yields in the puna. Tributaries also had to deliver wheat, sheep's wool, and other products introduced into the Andes by Europeans and added to the tribute lists by encomenderos. Small wonder that most Andean peoples began to complain of tribute dues and of the social changes they wrought in their communities.[44]

The seven ethnic nations of the south suffered a particularly sharp rupture with the Incaic past. The proud Charcas and their ethnic neighbors saw their status diminished and their identity as privileged warriors lost under the strictures of early colonial rule. Subordinated to encomenderos, they no longer sent warriors or claimed exemption from ordinary tribute dues. Like other "vassals" of the Spanish crown and encomienda "Indians," they had to deliver specified amounts of eggs, maize, honey, woolen garments, and workers to their appointed "lords." Moreover, tribute requisitions were increasingly skewed by commercial considerations. A case in point is Pedro de Hinojosa's repartimiento of Macha and Chaqui, in what would become the province of Chayanta. Platt's study of this encomienda in the pre-Toledan decades reveals the extent to which encomienda tribute was becoming commodified in the early 1550s.

Hinojosa, whose encomienda was one of the richest in Alto Perú, required tributaries to provide labor services, but the vast bulk of

---

44 For three regional studies of early colonial relations and, in particular, the transformation of tribute institutions under colonial rule, see Spalding, *Huarochirí*, chap. 4 and 5; Stern, *Peru's Indian Peoples*, chap. 2 and 3; and Wachtel, *Vision of the Vanquished*, 98-139.

encomienda tribute was paid in products that could be marketed in Potosí, Chuquisaca, and Porco. His tributaries were required to deliver annually 1,200 *fanegas* of maize (probably harvested from non-ayllu lands) and another 20 fanegas of maize and wheat planted on communal lands to the three towns. (A fanega is equivalent to 1.6 bushels.) Hinojosa also claimed the right to collect tribute in mineral ore. Caracaras of Macha and Chaqui mined ore deposits throughout their territory and probably in Potosí, and then exchanged the metal in the *qhatu* (open-air metal market) of Potosí for pesos *ensayados y marcados* (assayed and stamped under royal authority). They paid their encomendero the enormous sum of 27,300 pesos in 1559. Tribute exactions in crude ore reflected the fact that the Caracaras inhabited a region rich in mineral deposits, just as the Lupaqas' wealth was concentrated in herds. But in 1550, royal authorities sanctioned the commercialization of specie by requiring Indians to pay their dues in imported pesos.[45] The Caracaras were not alone. All across Alto Perú's highlands, the new tribute arrangements accelerated the commodification of indigenous staples and drew ayllu Indians into the developing commercial orbit of Potosí.

Yet it would be a mistake to assume that encomenderos, even the likes of Hinojosa, unilaterally extracted surplus from Indian subjects. After all, encomenderos still could not call upon the state to enforce extraction or the commercialization of indigenous products. Although the presence of royal authority was manifest by 1550 in the first ordinances regulating tribute, the colonial state was still inchoate and weak. Furthermore, encomenderos who received repartimientos in the highlands had to harness the labor power of peasants who belonged to strong, unified ethnic polities which still managed to preserve group self-sufficiency. Even many years after military conquest, the encomenderos were confronted with Aymara lords who still controlled the basic processes of production and distribution within Andean societies. The Spaniards depended upon the persisting ability of those lords to command the labor and loyalty of ayllu peasants and to channel the flow of tribute to the "outsiders." If the system of decentralized, indirect rule was to function smoothly, Europeans had to take care not to push ethnic lords too far, lest they violate the social norms and traditions that governed relationships in Andean society and transgress the acceptable bounds of their authority. For while in the short term a despotic

45 Tristan Platt, "Acerca del sistema tributario pre-Toledano en el Alto Perú," *Avances*, no. 1 (1978), esp. 34-39.

chief might squeeze his people enough to satisfy tribute requirements, such behavior would eventually sacrifice their social trust,
jeopardize his own ability to govern, and risk open rebellion. As
Stern has shown in vivid detail for the Huamanga area in the 1550s
and 1560s, encomenderos had to establish alliances, however uneasy, with native lords. In the process, they manipulated and negotiated with "their caciques," but they also devised strategies to enforce their compliance and obedience. This mixture of force,
negotiation, and alliance that characterized the early relations in the
highlands reflected the Europeans' heavy reliance on the traditional
power and prestige of native chiefs.[46]

In sharp contrast to the situation in the highlands, Andean tradition had little bearing on the relations and balance of power that obtained between encomenderos and caciques in the valleys of Cochabamba. When the crown created four or five repartimientos of native
inhabitants scattered throughout the region, it dispersed the broken
pieces of the Incas' state agricultural project. The collapse of the precolonial state, the mass exodus of agricultural laborers, and the sack-
ing of granaries and waterworks left the region relatively impoverished, at least for a time. Encomenderos of valley repartimientos
inherited only vestigial mitmaq communities, which now fell under
the jurisdiction of local caciques. There was no dominant ethnic
group in the region, no powerful ethnic lords who, in their role as
stewards of community norms and resources, could mediate labor
relationships. The Europeans who were granted repartimientos in
the valleys had to appoint caciques in the expectation and hope that
they would channel the flow of tribute and labor to their overlords,
even in the absence of Incaic state rule and the legitimacy of their
own power.

In the early 1550s, encomiendas were granted to Rodrigo de Orellana and Juan Polo de Ondegardo.[47] Together, these encomiendas included former Inca lands (the chácaras of Potopoto, Yllaurco, Colchacollo, Anocaraire, and Viloma) and all the mitimaes placed in the
valleys by the Incas to cultivate Incaic maize fields. Orellana's holdings included parcels of land toward the eastern end of the Valle Bajo,
some of which the Incas had appropriated for themselves. His encomienda, known later by the name Tiquipaya, incorporated miti-

---

46 See Stern, *Peru's Indian Peoples*, 28-35, and Carlos Sempat Assadourian,
"Dominio colonial y señores étnicos en el espacio andino," *HISLA*, no. 1 (1983):
7-20.

47 See Wachtel, *"Mitimas*," 202 and app. 2; also *Repartimiento de tierras*, 26.

maes of the Quillacas, Carangas, Chilques, Chiles, and Collas of Azángaro (see table 1). Polo's encomienda, El Paso, included Carangas, Urus, Soras, Caracaras, Charcas, and Yamparaes.[48]

In establishing these encomiendas, the crown placed them under the authority of the caciques Gerónimo Cuyo and Diego Tanquiri in El Paso and Hernando Cuyo in Tiquipaya. They were charged with assigning the mitimaes to cultivate the lands that had once belonged to the Incan emperor. These caciques did not readily command the respect and labor of their charges, since they did not belong to the same ethnic family. It is true that Tanquiri was the son of a former Inca governor in the valley, but his ability to capitalize on that kin relationship was doubtful now that he was collaborating with the enemy and was seen as a traitor to the neo-Inca state struggling to survive in the Vilcabamba backlands. This dilemma was shared by all native elites whose newly found status and position in colonial society derived primarily from their collaboration with the imperial power. Their legitimacy was defined in colonial terms and their authority rested precariously on the support and patronage of their

Table 1. The Encomiendas of Cochabamba

	Precolonial Land Use	Predominant Ethnic Groups	Caciques	Encomenderos
Tapacarí	Mitmaq colonies; pasture, maize	Moyos, Soras, Carangas, Aullagas, Quillacas	—	Alonso Pérez de Castillejo; Gómez de Solis; Hernando Zárate; Marqués de San Germán; Juan de Mendoza
Sipesipe	Cabecera del valle; royal pastures and maize lands	Soras, Yungas, Cotas, Chichas, Caris, Urus, Chuyes,	—	Hernando de Silva
El Paso	Royal maize fields	Chichas, Urus, Soras, Charcas, Caracaras, Yamparaes	Gerónimo Cuyo; Diego Tanquiri	Juan Polo de Ondegardo; Gerónimo de Ondegardo
Tiquipaya	Personal lands of Yupanqui and Huayna Cápac	Carangas, Quillacas, Charcas, Chiles, Chilques, Collas	Hernando Cuyo	Rodrigo de Orellana; Francisco de Orellana
Capinota	Mitmaq colonies; rich maize lands	Carangas, Soras	—	—

Sources: *Repartimiento de tierras*; "Tasa de la visita general del virrey Francisco de Toledo," AGI, Contaduría, Leg. 1786; Nicolás Sánchez-Albornoz, *Indios y tributos en el Alto Perú* (Lima: Instituto de Estudios Peruanos, 1978).

48 Wachtel, *"Mitimas,"* 202 and 230.

overlords. Unlike their Aymara counterparts, who bargained from a position of relative strength, the valley caciques leaned heavily on their European patrons to enforce their own authority over the disparate colonies of mitimaes. This became all the clearer during the 1550s and 1560s, when Aymara lords began to challenge the rights of valley caciques and encomenderos to rule their former mitmaq colonies that remained in the valleys.

For twenty years, the Caranga, Quillaca, and Sora Indians of the highlands waged a judicial struggle against Orellana and Polo and their caciques over land rights in Cochabamba. In 1556, one Hernando Asacalla, principal cacique of the highland repartimiento of Paria, petitioned the audiencia of La Plata for the return of "certain lands" in the Valle Bajo that had been granted to his people by Huayna Cápac and his governors. The Carangas, Quillacas, and Soras claimed as their own those parcels of land (suyos) in the chácaras of Yllaurco, Colchacollo, Anocaraire, and Viloma which they had received from the Incas at the time of the great land reform under Huayna Cápac. They rested their court case on the weight of pre-Hispanic tradition, elaborating in fine detail the distribution of valley land and tributary labor under the Incas. Their rich oral testimony, together with other records, provides the evidence from which Wachtel was able to reconstruct with such precision the extraordinary colonization project in the valley.[49]

The king's inspector (*visitador general*), Francisco de Saavedra Ulloa, corroborated their testimony with further details about the Incas' agrarian regime in Cochabamba, and he concluded that the parcels of land granted to the caciques and Indians of the Carangas, Quillacas, and Asanaques should be returned by royal edict to the highland peoples. But his argument did not rely simply on tradition and customary right. Saavedra appealed to the crown on pragmatic and humanitarian grounds as well. Valley lands ought to be granted to the highland Indians, he seemed to reason, because the lands were abundant and the highland peoples were in need of them. Through his European eyes, the lands of his native clients appeared "very sterile, producing little food," while the temperate valleys were lands of

49 The litigation records are located in the AHMC. Wachtel's pioneering article, "*Mitimas,*" is based on these records; an appendix to his article contains excerpts from a document of 1560 in which Polo defended his encomienda against the highlanders. Fragments of other trial records and reports have been published in *Repartimiento de tierras*. Unfortunately, the latter is poorly assembled and allows only a glimpse of the arguments and counterarguments of the litigants.

abundant harvests. Further, the puna Indians had sustained themselves with maize, which they were now forced to purchase in the valleys. "At the time of harvest, for two or three months each year, more than 600 . . . Carangas, Quillacas, and Asanaques [descend into the valleys] looking for food."[50] Saavedra suggested that they might populate a town in the valley, so that they could cultivate maize and supply their highland communities. Besides, he added, they could receive religious instruction in the valleys. Thus, he argued his case along both European and Andean lines. But while he hoped the crown would return mitmaq lands in the maize valleys and partially reconstitute the "vertical archipelago," and while he justified native demands on the basis of Incaic tradition in the valley, Saavedra focused on the periodic subsistence crises facing puna Indians who had lost their peripheral islands in the valleys and had therefore resorted to seasonal migrations. After all, how could elusive wanderers be properly converted to Christian ways or, for that matter, be taxed by encomenderos?

Faced with such powerful testimony, the valley caciques and encomenderos closed ranks and united in opposition to the threat. In a report submitted on behalf of this coalition, the visitador Diego Núñez rejected the claims to the *suyos* based on grants from the Incas. These grants did not constitute property rights, he argued, but only usufruct rights in return for tributary labor on state land in the valleys. Lands were not granted as personal possessions, but only to enable tributaries to sustain themselves while they cultivated the state lands. "The Indians had to sustain themselves," he reasoned, "since they were not permitted to take food from the [state] lands they cultivated and since they did not bring, nor could they bring, food [with them]."[51] He wondered where they would have found their sustenance had they not been granted lands by the Incan emperor, and he argued that once the Indians ceased to farm the Incas' lands they forfeited their rights to the suyos that had provided for their subsistence during their tributary season in the valleys. It was an astute argument, which evoked the principle of reciprocity that supposedly governed relations between the Incaic state and its mitimaes and

50 *Repartimiento de tierras*, 29. Other contemporary observations of migration of puna Indians are Polo de Ondegardo, "Informe . . . al Lic. Briviesca de Muñatones," 177, and Diego Cabeza de Vaca et al., "Descripción y relación de la ciudad de La Paz," in Marcos Jiménez de la Espada, ed., *Relaciones geográficas de Indios: El Perú* (Madrid: Atlas, 1965), 350.

51 *Repartimiento de tierras*, 30.

mittayoc. But more than that, Núñez declared that the highland caciques had no legitimate rights to valley lands, because most mitimaes had fled the valleys at the time of the Spanish Conquest and had not returned to settle in the lowlands for some forty years since their exodus. The Carangas appeared from time to time, but only for purposes of barter.[52]

Who, then, did have legitimate claims to valley resources? Núñez admitted that the Sipesipes did, for they were autochthonous peoples predating the Incas. So did those mitimaes who had remained behind in the valleys after the Spanish Conquest. Yet even many of those people, Núñez argued, had not received land grants from the Incas. They had held more privileged positions under the Incas, as loyal guardians of the maize granaries. But since they had chosen to settle in the valleys and thereby had ruptured their ties to their "natural kin groups" in the distant highlands, they surely had acquired subsistence rights in their adopted region. And besides, Núñez added, they had acute economic needs, precisely because they had lost their links to highland communities and resources.[53]

The conflict over land rights in Cochabamba unfolded slowly over the 1550s, 1560s, and early 1570s; native litigants discovered how tedious and labyrinthian the colonial juridical process could be. This particular dispute was finally resolved by Viceroy Toledo in the mid-1570s in favor of the Carangas and their allies, who received parcels of land in the valleys. In a small irony of history, the viceregal decision was issued at just the time when Toledo was preparing to implement his massive resettlement plan, which would irrevocably alter the social landscape in accordance with European spatial patterns (and which will be discussed later).

This judicial conflict threw into bold relief the shaky, vulnerable ethnic hierarchy that existed in the valleys. Caught on the defensive, the valley caciques had to enter into an alliance with their encomenderos to stave off their highland rivals and strengthen their control over mitimaes in the valleys. They were in an extremely ambiguous situation, since precolonial land tenure in the Cochabamba valleys was unique, and even traditional ethnic mitmaq colonies had been displaced and re-created by the Incas. The very meaning of Inca land

---

52 Polo de Ondegardo testified in 1560, many years before the Nuñez report (which was probably issued in the mid-1570s) that Urus had started to filter into the valleys to cultivate fields during the previous three or four years. Wachtel, *"Mitimas,"* app. 2, 234.

53 *Repartimiento de tierras*, 29-31.

grants to ethnic groups was now subject to interpretation and rein-
terpretation in the colonial context.

And yet, while Cochabamba was a special case, the emergence of
interethnic rivalry over former mitimaes and valley resources in the
eastern cordillera was not specific to that region. To the south, Lupaqa, Pacajes, and other Aymara lords hoped to recover the warm
lands and the colonists they had lost to the valley caciques and encomenderos. Saignes has studied the unraveling of the ethnic affiliations that had tied colonists in the eastern valleys of Larecaja to the
distant highland polities on the shores of Lake Titicaca and the ethnic conflict that accompanied that process.[54] Though still relatively
unexplored by historians, the enduring rivalry between highland ethnic lords and valley caciques over mitmaq colonies and land rights
in the kichwa region created a deep fault line in Andean society,
which judicial maneuvers could not conceal. Colonial policies that
territorialized ethnic groups along European contours only sharpened the endemic rivalry and competition among puna communities, which extended into distant kichwa pockets where other groups
also claimed resources. But this rivalry was carried into the colonial
courts in the 1550s and 1560s not merely as a way of recovering
communal rights to mitmaq lands. It reflected one strategy of communal defense and survival, among several, that Andean people of
both puna and valley seized upon as the economic pressures of colonialism began to bear down harder and as the opportunities for bargaining within the colonial judicial system began to open up.[55]

Mining and Commercial Capitalism in Early Potosí

As early as 1551, the eyes of colonial entrepreneurs were on Potosí—
"the key to all Peru," as an enthusiastic friar described the mining
town to the members of the Council of the Indies.[56] Traders, merchants, miners, and royal administrators all saw a bountiful future
in the rich silver veins that etched the interior of the Cerro Rico. In
the 1560s, the distinguished jurist Juan de Matienzo compiled the

54 Saignes, "De la filiation à la résidence," 1174-1175. See also Espinoza Soriano, ed., "Memorial de Charcas," for the petition of the Confederation of Charcas for land grants in Cochabamba.

55 See Stern, *Peru's Indian Peoples*, chap. 5, for a fascinating analysis of "judicial politics" and relations between Europeans and ethnic groups and among
ethnic groups in the Huamanga region.

56 Quoted in Barnadas, *Charcas*, 514.

first comprehensive report on Potosí. An *oidor* (judge or magistrate) of the audiencia of La Plata, Matienzo frequently traveled upland to the cold mining town to make his observations and gather his statistics.[57] As he looked closely at the mining enterprises, he was rather disturbed to find that Andean people actually controlled production. It was true that many Europeans held titles of ownership to slices of silver vein which they could exploit with minimal capital investment. But their enterprises were thwarted by heavy royal taxes and high labor costs.[58] Furthermore, Andeans controlled the refining of the mineral. Employing traditional metallurgy techniques, the skilled miners cut crude ore from the rich surface lodes, ground it in their simple stone mills, and smelted it in small clay furnaces (*huayras*), which caught the cold wind of the puna that fanned the fires built from dried ichu grasses and llama dung. It was this group of Indian miners, not the European titleholders to mines, who controlled the distribution of the finished product.

Under the circumstances, Europeans found themselves in a peculiarly weak bargaining position. To get the Indian smelters to take their crude ore, Europeans sometimes had to sell it to them, at prices representing only a fraction of the value of the ore's metallic content.[59] Furthermore, the yanaconas who dominated the refining also could organize the extractive activities, thus extending their control over the entire productive process. The Europeans, on the other hand, had difficulty mounting mining enterprises of any scale. Mine ownership was of little benefit at a time when mineowners were unable to hire workers simply because capitalist labor relations—the separation of workers from the means of production and development of a proletarianized work force—were still virtually nonexistent. Furthermore, the enforcement of seasonal migration of peasants to the mines and the distribution of corvée workers among selected mines were impossible as long as the colonial state sanctioned private encomiendas and failed to centralize and coordinate

57 Juan Matienzo, *Gobierno del Perú* (1567) (Buenos Aires: Cía. Sud-americana de Billetes de Banco, 1910).

58 David Brading and Harry Cross, "Colonial Silver Mining: Mexico and Peru," *Hispanic American Historical Review* 52 (1972): 552-554, and Carlos Sempat Assadourian, "La producción de la mercancía dinero en la formación del mercado interno colonial: El caso del espacio peruano, siglo XVI," in Enrigue Florescano, ed., *Ensayos sobre el desarrollo económico de México y América latina* (Mexico City: Fondo de Cultura Económica, 1979), 223-292.

59 Barnadas, *Charcas*, p. 366.

tribute to the advantage of the mineowners. Of course, mineowners could capture labor from the Lupaqa or Macha Indians who traveled to Potosí to deliver their dues or to find temporary work in order to pay off their monetary debts. But the chronic labor shortage and the inability of Europeans to enforce labor prestations sharply limited the scale of mining enterprise and relegated mineowners to a marginal, dependent position. For the time being, economic autonomy rested with a sector of the yanaconas of Potosí.

Matienzo's alarm at the strong position of Andean miners also suggested the internal dynamics of commercial accumulation at Potosí during the first "silver cycle" (1545-1570). He realized that as long as production was in the hands of Indians, Europeans had to rely upon commercial distribution and exchange for their profits. The old maxim urged buying cheap and selling dear, and this would be easier if Europeans could monopolize the supply of, say, woolen garments, or speculate in advance purchases of grain, and it would be still better if they could dispense altogether with "buying cheap" by commodifying tribute in kind. Potosí, after all, offered extraordinary commercial opportunities even in the early years. Demand seemed always to outstrip supply (at least until the economic slump of the late 1560s and early 1570s), and inflation was spiraling upward. In 1561, Polo de Ondegardo commented on the inflationary tendency in the audiencia of Charcas, such that "a llama once worth but a peso now sells for 12 or 15."[60] Like Polo, Matienzo realized the potential for commerce in indigenous articles of consumption. At Potosí, trade in native goods was essential to the accumulation of metallic money. Spaniards exchanged coca, maize, chuño, and cloth for silver; and the more commercial opportunities increased, the more power Europeans had to obtain refined silver from the Andean producers. "The more Indians at Potosí and Porco," Matienzo wrote, "the more silver they will mine; as their numbers increase they will consume more coca and bread and wear more garments, and thus they will have to mine more silver from the hills."[61]

60 Polo de Ondegardo, "Informe . . . al Lic. Briviesca de Muñatones," pp. 144-145. Polo de Ondegardo's statement neglects the fact that the prices of some goods had previously declined. For example, a random sample of forty-six sales of coca leaves at Potosí during the decade of the 1550s reveals that the average price per cesto (a basket containing about twenty pounds) declined from eighteen pesos in 1549 to six pesos in 1559. In subsequent years, the price stabilized at about four or five pesos. ANB, EP, Juan Luís Soto, 1549; Gáspar de Rojas, 1550, 1553, and 1555; Lázaro de Aguila, 1557, 1558, and 1559.

61 Matienzo, *Gobierno del Perú*, 73.

Matienzo's logic reveals the extent to which Potosí engendered commercial capitalism in the emerging political economy of Alto Perú even before the advent of Toledo's reforms. Assadourian's analysis of the early economy of the mining town also reveals the intense and wide circulation of indigenous commodities at Potosí, where almost 90 percent of imports were native products.[62] Even trade among Europeans themselves frequently involved transactions in indigenous articles. In 1549, one merchant of Potosí paid a debt of 10,000 pesos to another Spanish trader by delivering maize, coca, chuño, and native textiles.[63] During the first decade of mining at Potosí, it was commonplace for Europeans to form trading companies and partnerships with itinerant traders who set off into the countryside for months, sometimes for several years on end, and to establish commercial contacts with willing caciques, encomenderos, or other Europeans. The webs of trade they spun across the land created the commercial channels through which commodities could circulate and gravitate toward Potosí.[64]

Thus, Polo and Matienzo, who recorded their astute observations in the 1560s, only two decades after Andeans had stumbled upon the rich lodes of Potosí, witnessed the formation of a commercial economy in a remote part of the world where markets and commodity exchange were virtually unknown before the European intrusion. Almost instantaneously, the discovery and commodification of silver ore set into motion the commodification of native subsistence goods, from cumbi cloth and coca to chuño and oca. Telescoped into two decades was the transformation of basic subsistence goods, traditionally exchanged outside the domain of the market, into commodities that fetched inflationary monetary prices in the strange, bustling qhatu of Potosí. In that brief span, Andeans saw special, ceremonial crops like maize and coca become items of mass consumption in the mining town; they found themselves planting European wheat and hauling it by llama caravan across the mountains to the mines; and they experienced new pressures and hardships in producing the quantities and types of goods that now were demanded of them, simply because the products had acquired exchange value at the mining town.

62 Assadourian, "Producción de la mercancía dinero," 231ff.

63 ANB, EP, Soto, July 3, 1549.

64 The notarial records of Potosí provide detailed information about early commercial companies, long-distance trade, and wholesale transactions; see ANB, EP, esp. Rojas, 1550; Aguila, 1559.

Some natives adapted their ways in order to exploit the new commercial opportunities at Potosí. Several recent studies have documented the commercial engagement of Aymara chiefs in the lake district.[65] Some of these lords were able to channel their capital in ways that benefited the entire community. In other instances, commercial success led Indians to break their social commitments to the ayllu in their pursuit of profits. But by and large, the intensity of commercial exchange at Potosí and the great effective demand for food crops and special items like coca prompted many Indians to redirect the flow of goods and labor outward, toward the mining town. The shift in the balance between agrarian production for subsistence and for commercial exchange frequently had drastic consequences for the well-being of the social whole.

The disintegrating effects of agricultural commercialization were felt most acutely in those regions where coca could be produced by migrant encomienda Indians.[66] Coca was highly marketable in the early years of Potosí; the soldier and chronicler Pedro de Cieza de León speculated in 1553 that "there has never been in the whole world a plant or root . . . aside from spices . . . that is so highly valued [as coca]."[67] Matienzo reported that coca had even become a medium of exchange at Potosí.[68] But even the highland peoples on their "sterile lands" could not escape the incursion of commercial capitalism, as long as encomenderos could capitalize on the Potosí market and as long as colonial policies eroded the basis of "social insurance" that traditionally had buffered Andean communities from subsistence crises.

As early as 1550, the royal authorities formulated policies designed to mediate the relationship between private encomenderos and their repartimiento Indians. Pedro de la Gasca, president of the audiencia of Alto Perú (1547-1550), ordered inspectors to survey the

65 See Murra, "Aymara Lords"; Silvia Rivera, "El mallku y la sociedad colonial en el siglo XVII: El caso de Jesús de Machaca," *Avances*, no. 1 (1978): 7-27; and Roberto Choque, "Pedro Chipana: Cacique comerciante de Calamarca," ibid., 28-32.

66 See the published report of 1557 on the repartimiento of Pocona for descriptions of the "mass production" of coca for export to Potosí and its impact on native communities: "Visita a Pocona," *Historia y cultura* (Lima), no. 4 (1970): 269-308.

67 Pedro de Cieza de León, *The Incas*, ed. Victor W. von Hagen and trans. Harriet de Onis (Norman: University of Oklahoma Press, 1976), 260.

68 Matienzo, *Gobierno del Perú*, 90.

human landscape to ascertain the distribution of resources.[69] Anticipating the great royal *visitas* (inspections) under Toledo and his successors, La Gasca introduced reforms that would "rationalize" tribute collection even in private encomiendas. To some extent, the early efforts of royal authorities to develop institutions for the appropriation of surplus product aimed at protecting encomienda Indians from "excessive" rent. A 1551 ordinance of the audiencia of Lima was explicit on this point.[70] But La Gasca's reforms of 1549-1550 also rigidified the tribute schedule for encomienda Indians, compelling them to pay fixed rent in specified products, both native and European, and they had a negative impact on income collected over the following decade or so. Reporting in 1561, Polo de Ondegardo pointed to the decline of encomienda tribute since the reforms; and he declared that the tribute collected in his day was far less than that which Andeans had once rendered to the Incas. "The Indians are poorer in these times than they have ever been in the past."[71] But pauperization was only part of the story, in Polo's view. Increasingly, the Andean people tried to lighten the tribute burden by deceiving the royal inspectors. Ethnic lords found ways to reduce the official rent levied on their communities. Since tribute was adjusted in accordance with population counts, the Europeans were outwitted by hiding potential tributaries, keeping royal inspectors away from remote hamlets, and denying tributary status (and kinship ties) to recent migrants (*llactas runas*) who had come from distant homelands. Polo de Ondegardo advised royal inspectors to get around these subterfuges by surveying a community's cultivated fields, herds, and other resources not easily hidden from view.[72]

Political problems ran deeper, however. In the 1550s, sharp internal divisions within the colonial elite weakened the incipient state and allowed astute natives to exploit the factionalism for their own ends. As elsewhere in the Spanish colonies, encomenderos had to deal with prelates who were indignant about the treatment of natives. Conflict and rivalry over tutelage of the Indians in the southern Andes were aggravated by the coca issue. Following the First Council of Lima (1552), the church raised its voice against the commercialization and consumption of coca. Coca use was considered

69 Polo de Ondegardo, "Informe . . . al Lic. Briviesca de Muñatones," 160.

70 See Assadourian, "Dominio colonial," 11.

71 Polo de Ondegardo, "Informe . . . al Lic. Briviesca de Muñatones," 163.

72 Ibid., 161.

an evil in itself and an encouragement to paganism. Worse still, encomenderos often forced their subjects to plant coca, which they then sold to seemingly insatiable consumers at Potosí. But there was the rub. For Matienzo and other administrators soon realized that coca fetched high prices, allowing Spanish merchants and traders to accumulate enormous profits—on which the crown could levy taxes. "By means of the coca [trade], the Indians mine the greatest part of the silver which is exported and taxed each year."[73] The oidores of the audiencia of La Plata came down on the side of economics, counterbalancing the church's efforts at moral suasion.

Thus, in the two decades before the arrival of Viceroy Toledo, basic ideological issues concerning encomienda rent, the morality of coca commerce, and the legitimacy of Andean rights over former mitmaq colonies factionalized the colonial ruling elite and weakened its control over Andean peoples. The cleavages within the colonial elite afforded some leeway for Andean influence in shaping early colonial relationships. With the colonial state still in formation, the Andean peoples of Alto Perú increasingly turned to judicial procedures to test the limits of Spanish authority and to advance their collective interests. Later, when the state consolidated and began to draw the lines of colonial authority, power, and legitimacy more sharply, the Andean peoples resorted more often to clandestine, dangerous, and extralegal strategies of defense.

In the late 1560s, the alliances between some encomenderos and ethnic lords and among factions of the colonial elite were very precarious. In Madrid, far from the puna and valleys of Alto Perú and the chambers of Spanish justice in La Plata, the highest royal officials convened to consider the crisis in Peru. A millenarian movement, Taqui Ongo, which was sweeping through the mountains and villages of Huamanga, clearly posed the most immediate threat. But more ominous, perhaps, was the deterioration of silver mining at Potosí. Potosí's first cycle of silver was coming to a close: the rich surface lodes seemed to have evaporated almost overnight, and the Andean miners were vanishing. Royal expectations of unlimited supplies of specie suddenly confronted a harsh reality. From the imperial viewpoint, it was a singularly unfortunate moment for Potosí's silver enterprises to shut down. Only a few years earlier, King Philip II had been forced to default on his foreign loans, and his financial needs were growing each year. How could the king safeguard

73 Letter to the Spanish king from the audiencia of Charcas, Nov. 2, 1566, quoted in Barnadas, *Charcas*, p. 383.

Spain's power in Europe, fight the French, repel the Turks, and prepare for war with England, if a primary source of American treasure dried up? Taxing Castile's peasantry could yield only so much. It was essential to revamp the tribute system in the Andes, dislodge the private encomenderos from their position of power and privilege, and rejuvenate Potosí's mines. In short, the crown needed to constitute a colonial state that could serve as an agent of metropolitan interests and a claimant on the resources of native subjects. Across the ocean, ensconced in the Andean region, the colonial state was never to become simply a reflexive agent of the crown. But the royal impetus for a strong colonial state beginning in the late 1560s gave to the viceregal authority the power to intervene directly in and shape the emerging political economy of colonialism. Viceroy Toledo would go far toward fulfilling this mandate.

Yet on the eve of Toledo's administration, most Andeans and Europeans were too preoccupied with local struggles over lands, mitimaes, and tribute to worry about a new balance of imperial forces. Still engaged in negotiation, bargaining, and passive resistance, the ethnic elites of Alto Perú had no way of anticipating the power of a strong state. In the maize valleys of Cochabamba, the caciques and their patron encomenderos believed that it was the Carangas lords of the highlands who posed a threat to their autonomy. But by the middle years of the 1570s, the valley caciques would witness the collapse of their alliances with encomenderos and watch the state wrest lands away and award them to their highland rivals, and they would discover that Spanish settlers, not Aymara lords, were the most serious threat to their lifeways.

The Emergence of a Market Economy

As he stepped onto the desert coast of Peru in 1569, the new viceroy of Peru, Francisco de Toledo, walked into a political and economic quagmire of impressive dimensions. Beyond the peaceful, civilized city of Lima loomed the ominous Andes, where the early colonial order had broken down and social chaos and economic decline menaced the entire European colonial project in the Andean kingdom. Insurrection was brewing in the Huamanga highlands and threatened to spread to other areas. The Taqui Ongo rebellion of the 1560s in Huamanga was dangerous enough; but worse, it exposed the fragile political underpinnings of early colonial relationships, which rested ultimately on encomendero-cacique alliances and on the ability of the traditional Andean authorities to mobilize the surplus labor of native peasants. At any moment, subversion and revolt could turn another region into a Huamanga.

But Toledo also inherited a political crisis that ran deeper than native insurrection, for it divided the colonial elite against itself and thus heightened its vulnerability. At issue was the distribution of power and the "spoils of conquest," now that a first generation of European colonists harbored expectations of prospering by means of their political or entrepreneurial pursuits in the Andes. In towns all across the Andes, merchants, mining entrepreneurs, lawyers and notaries, adventurers, friars and priests, and Spanish nobles who sought political patronage or coveted fertile lands and a servile labor force opposed the "archaic" system of extraction which gave private encomenderos a virtual monopoly over the goods and services of the Andean peoples. Not only did a small group of encomenderos exercise enormous control over the commodity market in native products, but many encomenderos actually seemed to be wreaking havoc on the very communities they were entrusted to protect. How else to explain the dwindling of tribute, the proliferation of restless and

51

rootless inhabitants, and the increasingly aggressive protests and challenges by ethnic lords? And, as if the very cosmos were warning encomenderos of the consequences of unbridled greed, successive epidemics swept over the human landscape, claiming millions of victims among the tributaries.[1] Thus, Toledo's challenge during his twelve-year administration (1569-1581) was not simply to resolve internecine conflicts but to save the Andean kingdom itself from social chaos and decline.[2]

The crisis led to the imposition of a "political economy of colonialism." Paradoxically, the Toledan reforms, which drew heavily on the policy proposals of Juan de Matienzo, were designed both to centralize state power over the Andean population and the colonial elite and to open up the potential for mercantile accumulation to a broad spectrum of that elite.[3] The first requirement was to dislodge the encomenderos from their position of privilege, even if that could not be done in a day or even necessarily in a generation. But under Toledo, the state irrevocably altered the balance of power among colo-

---

1 There were epidemics of measles, smallpox, and influenza in the Andes in 1524, 1531, 1546, 1558, and 1589-1591, claiming millions of victims among the indigenous peoples. See Noble David Cook, ed., *Tasa de la visita general de Francisco de Toledo* (Lima: Universidad Nacional Mayor de San Marcos, 1975), xiii-xxiv, and Noble David Cook, *Demographic Collapse: Indian Peru, 1520-1620* (Cambridge: Cambridge University Press, 1981), esp. chaps. 8-10. See also Henry Dobyns, "An Outline of Andean Epidemic History to 1720," *Bulletin of the History of Medicine* 37 (1963): 493-515.

2 Spalding (*Huarochirí*, 136ff.) analyzes the crisis of the "economy of plunder" in the 1560s, which, she argues, was "at root a crisis of production, directly linked to a demographic disaster." Stern (*Peru's Indian Peoples*, 47-71) also studies this crisis decade in detail. However, he focuses attention on the growing disillusionment of Andean peoples who had previously collaborated with the Spanish overlords, only to see those alliances deteriorate as commercial pressures and state exactions grew heavier. Stern interprets the millenarian movement of Huamanga's peoples as the culmination of this disillusionment. A third approach is that of Wachtel (*Vision of the Vanquished*, 85-139), who argues that Andean society decomposed and fragmented under early colonial pressures, so that many kurakas had forsaken their traditional roles, principles, and norms for more opportunistic and despotic patterns of behavior.

On Toledo's career and works, see Roberto Levillier, *Don Francisco de Toledo, supremo organizador del Perú: Su vida, su obra (1515-1582)*, 3 vols. (Madrid: Espasa-Calpe, 1935-1942). Toledo's writings are collected in Roberto Levillier, ed., *Gobernantes del Perú: Cartas y papeles, siglo XVI*, 14 vols. (Madrid: Sucesores de Rivadeneyra, 1921-1926).

3 See chap. 1. For a discussion of Matienzo's influence on Toledan policies, see Stern, *Peru's Indian Peoples*, 72-75.

nial factions, by denying encomenderos the right of feudal jurisdiction and by asserting its own authority over the terms and limits of exploitation of the crown's native subjects. Encomenderos could no longer expect to bequeath their legacies to their immediate heirs and beyond, and, more important, they now had to deal with officials sent by the viceroy to determine the amount and kind of tribute they could legitimately extract. The encomenderos who were granted a "reprieve" were living on borrowed time, before the pivotal moment when the state (or its representatives) expropriated tribute directly for the royal coffers. Thus would the Toledan state become a direct, autonomous claimant on the resources of Andean communities and assume responsibility for maintaining the outflow of surplus and securing control over Andean peasants and chieftains.

Under the new extractive system, private individuals theoretically had no greater access to the wealth produced by Andean communities than they had when encomenderos reigned supreme. The colonial authorities now were supposed to shield Andean communities from enterprising Europeans. But there was an important difference between the destiny of tribute extracted by the state and that of tribute collected by private encomenderos. The state allocated a share of its tributary income to subsidize members of the colonial elite. Toledo was to create an "age of opportunity" and of upward social mobility for the bureaucrat who enjoyed a royal pension and other perquisites of office, the merchant who increased his control over the commodity market in Andean goods, and the big mercury or silver mineowner who received allotments of "Indians" drafted by the state for temporary mine work. As long as the state could commandeer Andean peasants to subsidize the colonial bureaucracy and strategic enterprises, it could rely upon its power of patronage to co-opt and control members of the colonial elite. Patronage enabled the state to mediate among conflicting colonial interest groups and channel conflicts in ways that did not threaten imperial ends.[4]

4 The discussion above draws on Spalding's analysis of colonial state formation in the Andes (*Huarochirí*, 156-158). The author argues that the state's extraction of the surplus generated within Andean peasant economies and its redistribution to members of the colonial elite "preserved the power of patronage upon which the state rested." The patrimony of the Toledan state undergirded a colonial system of European absolutism that protected and subsidized aristocratic wealth and privilege under circumstances of rapid commercialization in a peasant society, where most producers were still bound up in subsistence economies. But state patrimony, under a centralizing bureaucracy, also preempted the emergence of feudal jurisdiction on the part of encomenderos. For a discussion of absolutism in sixteenth- and seventeenth-century Europe, see Perry Ander-

Toledo achieved neither instant nor lasting success. As we shall see in chapter 3, the Toledan colonial project set in motion social processes that ultimately undermined the project itself. By the mid-seventeenth century, the state no longer had the capacity to set the limits of exploitation and extraction. Rather, it was the Andean peoples themselves who, by their collective and individual action, determined the limits of state autonomy. But long after the Toledan program of political economy had ceased to function effectively, it remained the definitive model of colonialism in the Andes. Later viceroys could not avoid dealing with the Toledan myth and legacy, regardless of their own philosophical or pragmatic orientations. Even in the late eighteenth century, administrators in Alto Perú looked back to the era of Toledo for reformist ideals and inspiration. The imprint of Toledan reforms was especially deep in Alto Perú, where the viceroy rescued the mining industry from the doldrums and turned Potosí, for a short while, into the world's premier silver producer.

Potosí's Second Silver Cycle

Toledo's primary task was to modernize the mining industry at Potosí. Over the previous half-decade, the rich oxidized ores had dried up. Gone were most of the *huayadores* who had smelted the metal in their furnaces. The times of "easy metal" were over; a great deal of capital and technology would be needed to extract the lower-content ore from deeper within the rust-colored hill of silver. Reflecting back upon those days, Luís Capoche, owner of one of the silver-amalgamation mills, painted a bleak picture of a mining town where "the power of silver was diminished . . . the hill's rich ore exhausted . . . and ruin and harm were felt more each day."[5]

The problems of the decline in ore quality and of technological obsolescence in refining were compounded by an acute shortage of labor. Although we have no reliable population statistics for the pre-Toledan period, contemporary observers did remark on the scarcity

son, *Lineages of the Absolutist State* (London: New Left Books, 1974), esp. 33-42 and 397-431. A controversial treatment of the colonial formation as feudal is Marcello Carmagnani, *Formación y crisis de un sistema feudal* (Mexico City: Siglo XXI, 1976).

5 Luís Capoche, *Relación general de la villa imperial de Potosí* (1585) (Madrid: Atlas, 1959), 115-116; Bartolomé Arzáns de Orsúa y Vela, *Historia de la villa imperial de Potosí*, 3 vols., ed. Lewis Hanke and Gunnar Mendoza (Providence: Brown University Press, 1965), 1: 127.

of mineworkers. In 1567, Matienzo expressed concern about the inadequate and erratic supply of Indians at Potosí and said that Potosí's economic woes would continue unless ways could be found to attract more Indians to the mining town.[6] But Capoche, writing later with the benefit of hindsight, realized the labor problem was even more serious than Matienzo's remarks seemed to suggest. Capoche reported that "each day more Indians disappeared," so that by 1572 Potosí "was almost abandoned, the buildings in disrepair, and the residents empty-pocketed."[7] Capoche perhaps exaggerated this picture of a ghost town to bolster his argument that the logical and just solution to Potosí's crisis of production was a system of compulsory, rotating labor known as the *mita* (modeled, of course, on the Incaic institution). Nevertheless, he was pointing to a critical problem that plagued mining enterprises in many precapitalist economies: the extreme elasticity of the labor supply.[8] After twenty-five years of silver mining, local Europeans still had not managed to anchor a proletarianized labor force to the base of the Cerro Rico. As the problem of diminishing returns worsened in the 1560s, Potosí lost its ability to obtain or hold sufficient numbers of Indian wageworkers. Further, most miners at Potosí were peasants by origin and orientation. Even though the colonial state began to tighten administrative control over Andean communities and obstruct migratory movement, most Andean miners still found ways to escape from the mining economy as conditions deteriorated. Capoche perceived the transient, almost elusive nature of the miners: "As smelting metals dried up and it became difficult to mine ore profitably, Indians returned home to their villages; others (in still greater numbers) set off for the valleys of Chuquisaca and other temperate lands."[9] The wage incentive did not function in such a shallow labor market, where most miners retained their peasant roots and ethnic identity.[10]

6 Matienzo, *Gobierno del Perú*, 71-72.

7 Capoche, *Relación general*, 116 and 135.

8 Bakewell stresses this point, in his discussion of the labor supply in colonial Zacatecas: Peter J. Bakewell, *Silver Mining and Society in Colonial Mexico; Zacatecas, 1546-1700* (Cambridge: Cambridge University Press, 1971), 124-125.

9 Capoche, *Relación general*, 135.

10 Early literature and legends about the mita have shaped historians' assumptions about the predominant role of forced labor in Potosí's mining industry. Institutional approaches to colonial Andean history, such as the classic article by John H. Rowe, "The Incas under Spanish Colonial Institutions," *Hispanic American Historical Review* 35 (1957): 155-199, have placed heavy emphasis on the

Potosí's crisis was not confined to production. The mining slump depressed trade and the commodity market that had flourished since the late 1540s. Tributaries who once trekked for days across the altiplano to exchange their products for specie no longer bothered. They resorted to payment in kind, as cash became restricted to the highest echelons of society.[11] The economy seemed to retrogress to a "natural" one. Scarcity of silver, sluggish commodity circulation, and depressed prices all plunged the southern Andes into a recession. "The value of tribute has fallen off sharply in this kingdom," Capoche wrote. "Indians now pay tribute in llamas, maize, and crude cloth—the products of their own pastures, harvests, and looms."[12] The earlier trend toward commodification in the wider economic space was being reversed. Potosí had come to occupy a strategic site in the Andean economy, and the exhaustion of silver ore spelled ruin for the encomenderos, merchants, traders, and colonial artisans who had to acquire the currency with which to purchase European goods and invest in their future. Capoche stressed this point: "All the repartimientos . . . and cities . . . of this kingdom acquire [specie] in . . . Potosí. Potosí's market bestows monetary value on all goods, even in the remote villages whence they come. . . . Without silver or a market outlet, [native] goods fetch no price, nor bring any return." The qhatu still existed, but Andean traders who remained at Potosí

---

mita as the bulwark of silver mining at Potosí. See also the recent study by Jeffrey A. Cole, *The Potosí Mita, 1573-1700: Compulsory Indian Labor in the Andes* (Stanford, Calif.: Stanford University Press, 1985). Traditionally, Potosí provided a sharp contrast to Mexican mining, where forced rotational labor remained small in scale. However, recent work on southern Andean history has challenged the earlier assumptions about the mita. The recent study by Peter J. Bakewell, *Miners of the Red Mountain: Indian Labor at Potosí, 1545-1650* (Albuquerque: University of New Mexico Press, 1984), illuminates the complexities of labor arrangements at Potosí, where less than half the work force in about 1600 was classified as draft, or compulsory, laborers. The mingas, or free wageworkers, were not only numerically dominant; they also enjoyed a limited degree of leverage in their relationship with mineowners. But Bakewell also shows that it was the mita workers (mitayos), not the mineowners, who paid the material cost of the mingas' slim economic advantages, in the form of below-subsistence wages and harsh, regimented work conditions. As we shall see in chap. 3, Tandeter advances this argument even further in his study of eighteenth-century Potosí.

11 Capoche, *Relación general*, 135.

12 Ibid., 115. See also Juan Polo de Ondegardo, "Relación de los fundamentos acerca del notable daño que resulta de no guardar a los indios sus fueros" (1571), in *Colección de documentos inéditos relativos al descubrimiento, conquista, y organización de las antiguas posesiones españolas de América y Oceanía . . . ,* 42 vols. (Madrid: Imprenta del Hospicio, 1872), 17: 116-117.

resorted to "ancient forms" of barter and exchange, "customs they practiced before the Europeans arrived."[13]

In an effort to revitalize the mining industry, the new viceroy, in a series of ordinances, mandated the introduction of sweeping technological reforms. Toledo imported amalgamation techniques that employed mercury and salt to separate out silver from its by-products. Although it was almost two decades before the technique was perfected at Potosí, refiners eventually used this "patio process" of refining more efficiently than their Mexican competitors. More important, the new method finally allowed mineowners to exploit the bulk of the Cerro Rico's primary ores: the hard, dark ores called *negrillos*, buried deep in the mountain. Mineowners began to sink shafts and tunnels deep into the middle zones of the Cerro. Eventually, some shafts were so deep that the workers who hauled ore and earth often spent half of their eight-hour shifts climbing rope or cowhide ladders.[14]

The technological changes produced almost immediate results. In 1576, an oidor of the audiencia of Lima issued an enthusiastic report about the early experiments with mercury amalgamation at Potosí, and he urged the crown to increase the supply of quicksilver.[15] That same year, Toledo decreed that Potosí was to be the destination of all mercury produced in Huancavelica. He already envisaged the Potosí-Huancavelica nexus as Peru's primary strategic export sector. He apparently had good reason for doing so; royal taxes on silver production had jumped from 105,926 pesos to 336,144 pesos during the first three years in which the amalgamation techniques were used (1573-1576). By the time Capoche wrote in 1585, royal *quintos*—the tax on silver production—had more than doubled again.[16] Improvements in the extractive as well as the refining processes set in mo-

---

13 Capoche, *Relación general*, 115.

14 Peter Bakewell, "Technological Change in Potosí; The Silver Boom of the 1570s," *Jahrbuch für Geschichte von Staat, Wirtschaft, und Gesellschaft Lateinamerikas* 14 (1977): 55-77; Brading and Cross, "Colonial Silver Mining," 547 and 554.

15 Lic. Ramírez de Cartagena to the crown, May 6, 1576, in Levillier, ed., *Gobernantes del Perú*, 7: 282ff., also cited and summarized in Silvio Zavala, *El servicio personal de los indios en el Perú*, 3 vols. (México City: Colegio de México, 1978), 1:100.

16 Capoche, *Relación general*, 177. Toledo to Juan de Ovando, Mar. 12, 1576, in Levillier, ed., *Gobernantes del Perú*, 5: 472-480; John J. TePaske, "The Fiscal Structure of Upper Peru and the Financing of Empire," in Karen Spalding, ed., *Essays in the Political, Economic, and Social History of Colonial Latin America* (Newark: University of Delaware, 1982), 86.

tion industrial changes that would allow Potosí's mineowners to accelerate production and to penetrate into the middle ore zones almost a century earlier than happened in the silver mines of Mexico. On the world market, the quantity of silver exported from Potosí would virtually eliminate the German silver mines from the European market by the end of the sixteenth-century.[17]

The imperatives of mining as "big business" shifted economic power away from the direct producers and concentrated it in the hands of the relatively few owners of mines and mills. Although in 1585 there were five hundred registered mineowners, the real power rested with some seventy-five "mercury men" (*azogueros*) who owned the great silver refineries. Behind them stood a smaller group of silver merchants who advanced cash and credit to the mineowners and the azogueros to tide them over during the frequent lulls in production and to allow them to import mercury. The silver merchants also lubricated the productive mechanism by channeling silver bar to the mint at Potosí, the final step in the production of the commodity money.[18]

This new interlocking elite that exercised control over the factors and processes of mineral production depended upon a new breed of laborer, one that was directly subordinate and beholden to the owners of mines and mills for its means of subsistence and survival. Capoche reported that, at Potosí in 1585, "in general, mine work is salaried labor; under the *jornal* [wage system], the *mitayos* [mita workers] receive 3 1/2 reales [a day] and the *mingas* [free wage earners] receive 4 reales."[19] To his way of thinking, the ideological and real distinctions between forced labor and free (wage) labor were less striking than the historical transformation of semi-independent An-

---

17 Pierre Vilar, *A History of Gold and Money, 1450-1920* (London: New Left Books, 1976), 125. On mineral production trends, see Alvaro Jara, "Dans le Pérou du XVIe siècle: La courbe de production de metaux monnayables," *Annales E.S.C.* 22 (1967): 590-608, and Peter J. Bakewell, "Registered Silver Production in the Potosí District, 1550-1735," *Jahrbuch für Geschichte von Staat, Wirtschaft, und Gesellschaft Lateinamerikas* 12 (1975): 67-103. On the more general impact of American silver on Europen price trends, see Fernand Braudel and F. Spooner, "Prices in Europe from 1450 to 1750," in E. E. Rich and C. H. Wilson, ed., *The Cambridge Economic History of Europe*, 7 vols. (Cambridge: Cambridge University Press, 1967), 4: 378-486.

18 Brading and Cross, "Colonial Silver Mining," 567. On the economic and social aspects of Potosí, see Arzáns de Orsúa y Vela, *Historia de la villa imperial*, and Lewis Hanke, *The Imperial City of Potosí* (The Hague: Nijhoff, 1956).

19 Capoche, *Relación general*, 144-145.

dean miners (who had once owned their own tools, enjoyed free access to perhaps one-quarter of the mines, and controlled smelting) into dependent wage laborers "deprived of their livelihood, unable to feed themselves or pay tribute except by means of wage work."[20] Though hardly disinterested, Capoche seemed to lament the passing of an age when Andean miners enjoyed a relatively strong bargaining position vis-à-vis European mineowners and a certain amount of economic integrity.

But the transition to wage labor at Potosí was neither easy nor complete during the second silver boom. The mingas who had intimate knowledge of the labyrinthian interiors of the mines, or who had established trading relationships in the city's qhatu, or who could mobilize the labor of kinsmen recently arrived from their villages—all had resources to draw upon in their struggle for a livelihood. They employed tactics that allowed them to recover some of their economic autonomy and enhance their bargaining power. As long as colonial authorities did not effectively suppress the flourishing trade in pieces of crude ore in the city's metal market, Andean miners could commodify the ore they managed to extract on their own, bypassing the wage circuit and supplementing their wages with the income derived from that ore. The miners would not work unless they were given the rights to *la corpa*, or "bonus" chunks of ore. As Capoche wrote, "to keep [the mingas] content and grateful so they will return to work each day, the mineowners allow them to take a chunk of metal, and altogether the mingas amass a great quantity of ore they sell at the qhatu." He estimated that la corpa constituted one-quarter of all the silver mined.[21] As long as miners continued to have the right to la corpa and were able to exchange it for other commodities in the city, they had ample incentive to smuggle ore out of the Cerro and evidently did smuggle large quantities of it. In effect, the institution of la corpa created a hybrid labor system that resembled sharecropping almost as much as it did wage work.

Toledo sought to resolve the conflict over the legitimacy of la corpa in favor of the mineworkers. At first sight, it seems curious that the viceroy allied himself with the refractory and lawless mingas. After all, if the state had eliminated the illicit trade in ore, it presumably would have significantly reduced production costs (the value of the crude ore the workers were allowed to take and of that

20 Ibid., 162.

21 Ibid., 154.

they smuggled out).[22] But Toledo must have accepted the custom of la corpa as a necessary evil that had to be tolerated if the mingas were to work for wages at all. Capoche suggests, in fact, that Toledo fixed the daily wage rate of four reales in full realization that mingas could not sustain themselves on such a wage. His strategy was not to outlaw the custom of issuing rights to metal, but to incorporate la corpa into the new wage system. Thus, Toledo's "wage regime" did not absolutely subordinate mingas to the owners of productive means. It left "space" wherein Andean miners could reassert control over a limited part of the production and distribution of crude ore. If Toledo's policies cut into the short-term profits of mineowners, they also provided an economic incentive for mine work on the part of workers who could still exercise other livelihood options. For the labor market was probably still rather shallow in the 1580s. Men who were wageworkers one month might vanish the next, to return to their villages at harvest time or simply to escape the harsh life of a miner. A fully proletarianized labor force, dependent upon wage work for subsistence and reproduction, was still small in scale. Under the circumstances, the state and the mineowners had to make certain economic concessions to the mingas for the sake of meeting the needs of the industry. Toledo was under no illusion, however, that these concessions would make it possible to attract and hold the much larger labor force that the new mills and mine shafts required. Labor would continue to be a major bottleneck if the big mineowners depended exclusively upon nonconscripted wageworkers. A plan was needed to harness the vast resources of Andean communities to the silver enterprises.

Toledo was not the first colonial authority to draft peasants by turns for temporary mine work at Potosí, but he was the first to use the power of the state on a large scale to enforce mass migrations of peasants to the mines. His model for the mining mita of Potosí was probably the Incaic labor drafts for maize agriculture in the Cochabamba valleys (see chapter 1). The viceroy called upon the labor power of peasants inhabiting some 139 designated villages in sixteen provinces, from Canas y Canches and Tinta in the north near Cuzco to Tarija in the south. This mita was to tap about one-seventh of the

---

22 Assadourian has calculated that, relative to the average value of quintos in 1580-1584, la corpa represented a cost of about 10 percent of the total value of silver output, while for the average minga, it represented an increase of 80 percent in monetary income: Assadourian, "La producción de la mercancía dinero," 269.

adult male population of those villages.[23] In all, the state drafted some 12,600 mitayos each year. Only a few southern provinces were declared "free territories": Larecaja, Tomina, Pilaya, Mizque, and Yamparaes, valley regions on the margins of the densely populated Indian highlands. Among the lowland dwellers, only Cochabamba's native inhabitants were not exempted from the mita and were forced to trek upland through the mountains to the cold puna of Potosí to serve their mita duty.

The infusion of mitayos into the silver veins and mills of Potosí increased the Indian labor force in the late sixteenth century by one-third to one-half.[24] The mitayos were assigned to the owners of the large mines and mills, except during their "rest weeks." Theoretically, only one-third of the mitayo population was subjected to the terms of the mita in any given week. Most mita recruits were permitted to hire their labor out as "free" workers during their rest periods. At close range, then, the proportion of forced workers was surprisingly small, and the boundaries between forced and free labor seemed blurred. But the institution's importance cannot be reduced simply to the fraction of the labor force that was actually under mita assignment, for it served three vital functions.

First, the mita ensured a stable, disciplined labor force that undercut the economic influence of the mingas. Fresh from the countryside, gangs of mitayos worked under the immediate authority of one of their own villagers in the assigned mines and mills. The mita system allowed mineowners to allocate labor "rationally" to the most dangerous and exhausting tasks. Furthermore, the mitayos who hauled ore up the long rope ladders or who tended the liquified metal in huge vats were less susceptible to the "corrupt western influences" that, in the opinion of local clerics and mineowners, bred violence and indolence among the mingas.

Second, the mita expanded the pool of people available for wage work in the mines. During their rest weeks, mitayos hired themselves out as wageworkers in order to support themselves during their year or more in residence at Potosí. In addition, the women and

---

23 On the mita, see Bakewell, *Miners of the Red Mountain*, and Alberto Crespo Rodas, "La mita de Potosí," *Revista histórica* 22 (1955-1956), 158-162. Zavala's monumental work, *Servicio personal*, touches on many aspects of the mita over three centuries of Spanish rule.

24 Assadourian, "Producción de la mercancía dinero," 242 and 255-257; Cook, *Demographic Collapse*, 242ff.; and Bakewell, *Miners of the Red Mountain*, esp. the conclusion.

children who accompanied the mitayos engaged in many types of economic activities in mining and petty commerce. The forced migrations therefore channeled peasant labor into both mining and subsidiary work at Potosí.

Third, and perhaps most important, the mita represented an enormous subsidy to the recipient mining enterprises.[25] An anonymous report (*memorial*) written in about 1610 presented a crude calculation of the labor costs saved by those mineowners who employed mita labor.[26] Mitayos were then apparently receiving a daily wage of four reales, half the wage of free workers. Moreover, mitayos did not enjoy any rights to bonus ore, representing a further saving estimated to average about five reales a day. Thus, a mitayo cost only about one-third as much as a minga. In addition, many mineowners received direct subsidies in the form of commutation payments from Indians purchasing their way out of forced labor. Combining the estimated value of commutation payments with the value of "lost wages" (as a result of the undervaluation of mita labor), the memorialist estimated that the mita system saved the mining industry more than 3,800,000 pesos ensayados each year. It was no trivial sum, even in those heady days.

The architects of the mining mita thus designed a labor system that drew heavily upon the resources of the ayllus and communities. It was widely recognized that the mitayo's weekly wage alone was below the minimum remuneration necessary for a peasant family to survive in the city. Even when supplemented by income earned during the rest weeks, it was still insufficient. Mitayos depended upon their kinsmen and communities to provide them with subsistence goods and with extra workers who accompanied them to the mines. The mita affected not only those who were forced to migrate to Po-

25 Assadourian's conceptualization of "Peruvian economic space" and of the formation of a mining economy dependent upon the coerced participation of Andean peasant labor in the internal market and the resultant subsidy to the mining industry broke new ground in the study of the complex and changing articulation of peasant subsistence-oriented economies and the mining export economy. His conceptual framework of the emergent colonial socioeconomic formation situates the peasant economy at its center, even though Potosí was the "growth pole" around which Peruvian economic space configured. See Assadourian, "Producción de la mercancía dinero;" see also his "La organización económica espacial del sistema colonial," in his *Sistema de la economía colonial*, 277-321.

26 "Discurso breve en razón de lo que pierden los indios que van a las minas de Potosí . . .," cited and summarized in Zavala, *Servicio personal*, 2: 44-45. See also Assadourian, "La produccion de la mercancía dinero," 255ff.

tosí, but also those left behind in the villages. To furnish mitayo teams with the means of survival, ayllus and villages invested several months in preparation: grinding corn into flour, reallocating community stocks, rounding up and equipping llama caravans for the long journey. Mitayo families took with them their herds, crops, and clothes.[27] Europeans who encountered mitayo "companies" en route to Potosí reported that they looked like villages in microcosm moving across the altiplano. In 1603, Alfonso Messía Venegas described 7,000 people moving south from the lakeshore villages around Titicaca. Men, women, and children accompanied an endless train of llamas carrying chuño, maize, charqui, dried fish, and quinoa flour. The mitayos themselves were only a fraction of the group.[28] If a European had stationed himself at the gates of the city and inventoried the goods that mitayos carried into Potosí, he might have been more impressed. A census of Potosí in 1603 estimated that mitayo households brought some 60,000 llamas and 40,000 fanegas of food into the city, with an estimated worth of 440,000 pesos ensayados.[29] It is unlikely that these food crops or herds were sold, except perhaps for a small proportion of the produce to raise hard currency for the mitayos' kurakas and communities. Most of the food was consumed, and eventually even the beasts of burden were eaten.

These images offer perhaps the most graphic evidence of the compulsory incorporation of the Andean peasant economy into the mining export sector. Toledo expanded and reinforced state power to coerce a surplus out of self-sufficient peasantries and to funnel massive amounts of cheap labor to the mines. Legendary fortunes made from mining enterprises were not simply the rewards of entrepreneurial success and advantageous market fluctuations; they were partially the result of the ability of the colonial state to supply the needed workers and hold wages at levels below subsistence requirements. The mita, as conceived by Toledo, was a form of subsidy to the owners of the silver mines and mills. Toledo's use of the coercive powers of the state to provide these subsidies was a response to the

27 "Discurso breve," and "Memorial que se dió a S.M. sobre el trabajo de los indios en las minas de Potosí" (1610), cited and discussed in Zavala, *Servicio personal*, 2: 44-45.

28 Alfonso Messía Venegas, "Memorial al virrey Luís de Velasco" (1603), in Rubén Vargas Ugarte, ed., *Pareceres jurídicos en asuntos de Indias (1601-1718)* (Lima, 1951), 94-115.

29 "Descripción de la villa y minas de Potosí, año de 1603," in Jiménez de la Espada, *Relaciones geográficas de Indias*, 380-382.

imperatives of Spanish imperialism and of world demand for the commodity money. The royal quintos not only filled the crown's coffers in Madrid and financed much of the cost of the swelling colonial bureaucracy, which both enforced and fed from the surplus product and labor of the native peoples; the taxes and profits from mining also lubricated the internal and overseas commodity trade. Potosí's spectacular second silver cycle was made possible by the colonial apparatus that reinforced extractive relationships and redistributed the surplus generated within the domain of Andean communities to the mining elites of Potosí.

The deployment of state power to enforce peasant participation in the colonial economy was not limited to the mining enterprises. State institutions, policies, laws, and social practices generated a complex, overlapping network of legal and extralegal levies that stimulated both the demand for and the supply of goods and labor in the colonial economy which, left to spontaneous market forces, would have remained embryonic in character and small in scale. Thus, as Spalding has argued, "the dynamism of the economy was generated not within the system of production itself but from the outside. It came through the coercive mechanisms applied by the colonial state."[30] Beyond the great silver mines, a host of private enterprises were springing up which produced commodities for Potosí and other growing towns and cities. Directly or indirectly, young commercial endeavors in the colony were tied into the network of surplus extraction. As long as the state continued to impose extractive institutions like tribute and the mita, it could offer subsidies to factions of the colonial elite. As we shall see shortly, the colonial state could also target its subsidies to strategic economic sectors and thereby exercise some degree of control over competing colonial interest groups. The state acted as an autonomous claimant on peasant resources, and its power of extraction furnished the political weaponry which enabled it to arbitrate among groups within the colonial elite.

Andean Villages and the Patron-State

If the state defined and enforced the "contributions" of Andean peoples to the colonial project, it also attempted to legitimate and protect their claims to a certain minimum of subsistence insurance.

30 Karen Spalding, "Exploitation As an Economic System: The State and the Extraction of Surplus in Colonial Peru," in Collier, Rosaldo, and Wirth, *Inca and Aztec States*, 325.

The new, intrusive economic demands of the state could be met by peasant households only if they could provide for their own sustenance and physical reproduction within the matrix of the ayllu or village economy. Toledo fully realized that the state had a vested interest in protecting the internal capacity of Andean communities to provide a basic level of social welfare for its members and to absorb the state's fiscal and labor demands. If the state was to ensure a stable source of revenue from the rural sector, to continue to drain ayllus of people for the silver mines, and to ensure some degree of compliance from its tributaries, then it would have to offer its rural subjects a bedrock of subsistence guarantees. Thus, the issue of the social reproduction of local Andean economies was inextricably linked with the enforcement of economic subsidies to strategic colonial enterprises and ultimately with the power and wealth of the state. The colonial regime not only imposed fiscal demands and set the boundaries of legitimate exploitation; it also began to reach into the very heart of Andean communities to dictate the terms of intraethnic social relations.

Among the first priorities in expanding the state's scope of extraction was to balance its levies against a population's resources and competing social obligations. In principle, the Toledan regime wanted to adjust its claims to the ability of its tributaries to pay. In preparation for the official tax assessments, colonial authorities fanned out to all corners of the kingdom to do their field research— cadastral surveys, head counts, interviews—following the example of Toledo himself, who traveled across the mountainous backlands for nearly five years. The agents were required to obtain detailed pictures of Andean villages, ayllus, and lineages. No fragment of data was lost to view. Royal inspectors were to record the expanse, quality, and variety of the dispersed crop lands and pasturage; the availability of water, salt pans, fisheries, and fertilizer; the villages' herds, silos of grain, and storehouses of cloth; and, not least, the number of Indian households. The past was considered, too; royal inspectors were to assess the amount of tribute (in labor presentations and in kind) that an Indian population had formerly paid to the Incas and to their encomendero.[31] In effect, an early form of anthropology was being put to the service of Spanish imperialism.

There was a contradiction in the Toledan policy of tax assessment.

31 Carlos A. Romero, ed., "Libro de la visita general del virrey Francisco de Toledo, 1570-1575," *Revista histórica* 7 (1924): 115-216; see esp. "Instrucción nueva para visitadores," 177-186. This document is also summarized in Zavala, *Servicio personal*, 2: 96-97.

The state wanted to exercise some degree of prudence in its fiscal claims so as not to erode the very tax base upon which the mercantile colonial system rested. It therefore had to intrude into local life and to map the rural Andean economies in order to determine (in accord with European preconceptions) the reproductive capacity of those economies. Yet in the process, the growing central authority of the state provided the administrative armature for tapping the resources of those communities more systematically and for reducing any slippage that may once have afforded peasants room in which to elude or resist outside claimants. State penetration into local communities, for the purpose of centralizing and rationalizing tax collection, therefore posed a threat to the well-being of those communities, for it led to a more rigid and regressive tax system. In good times and bad, an ayllu or village had to pay up; even if a peasant household eked out a living on the community's most marginal lands, it still owed a fixed head tax, unadjusted to take account of changing circumstances—and almost all tribute was now levied in silver coin. Viewed from below, the assessments threatened to impose new hardships and sharpened native perceptions of an omnipotent and intrusive state.[32]

The implications of preserving the agrarian subsistence base of the Andean communities went far beyond tax-adjustment policies. The state needed to define, legitimate, and rationalize (again, in accordance with European norms) land tenure among its native subjects. Now that private colonists were launching productive enterprises all across the Andes to capitalize on lucrative markets, they competed with each other and with Andean cultivators for access to fertile lands, good pasturage, irrigation streams, and hired field hands. How could the state protect its tributaries against the growing threats of encroachment unless it threw up legal barriers against these intruders? Furthermore, even in remote puna regions, where Europeans rarely ventured, the effort to institute centralized administration and systematic extraction mandated sweeping reforms that would regroup Indians into a network of rural communities. The dispersed and fragmented landholding patterns of the ayllus left too many spaces in which tributaries could hide from colonial authorities or slip between territorial jurisdictions. As we have seen, the pastoral-

32 The most extensive and detailed study through Andean eyes of the colonial system in the seventeenth century is the chronicle of Felipe Guaman Poma de Ayala, *El primer neuva corónica y buen gobierno*, 3 vols., ed. John V. Murra and Rolena Adorno (Mexico City: Siglo XXI, 1980).

ists and cultivators of the puna sought to minimize the risk of crop failure by cultivating patches of land dispersed among several different environments. Their own subsistence needs required some access to resources at lower altitudes. (To this day, many ayllus in Norte Potosí and other parts of Bolivia have access to multiple ecological zones.)[33] Thus, Andean kin groups needed to retain vertical landholding patterns. Toledo himself settled some disputes in favor of highland Indians seeking to reclaim their rights to distant valley settlements. But for purposes of tightened administration and authority over rural Andean society, the state was bent upon sharply restricting the dispersed settlement patterns. With varying degrees of success, Toledo advanced the process, begun by his predecessors, of fragmenting dispersed kin groups and destroying the vestiges of political archipelagos.[34]

Toledo's program of forced resettlement was an assault on Andean kin networks of unprecedented scope. The principle behind the plan was to designate towns and their rural surroundings as official "Indian communities" and to assign certain Indian populations to inhabit them. This meant that the viceroy's agents had to uproot many Andean peoples and sweep them into nucleated settlements. The multiple hamlets that speckled the mountain slopes and hid in deep river valleys would be "reduced" to orderly, administered towns, their sites chosen for purposes of administrative expedience and "good climate."[35]

The spatial layout of the new Indian towns revealed the degree of the state's intrusion into the everyday life of Andean people. "Orderly planning" required that the *reducciones* be fashioned after grid-patterned Spanish colonial towns, wherein a prison, schoolhouse, and parish church would flank the central plaza. There, colonial au-

33 Lehmann, ed., *Ecology and Exchange;* Dollfus, *Reto del espacio andino;* and Jürgen Golte, *La racionalidad de la organización andina* (Lima: Instituto de Estudios Peruanos, 1980).

34 John V. Murra, "Investigaciones en etnohistoria andina," in his *Formaciones económicas,* 286.

35 Levillier, ed., *Gobernantes del Perú,* 8: 330-331. See also Magnus Mörner, *La corona española y los foraneos en los pueblos de indios de América* (Stockholm: Almqvist and Wiksell, 1970) and his more recent study, *The Andean Past: Land, Societies, and Conflict* (New York: Columbia University Press, 1985), esp. 59-63; Alejandro Málaga Medina, "Las reducciones en el Perú (1532-1600)," *Historia y cultura* (Lima) 8 (1974): 155-167; and Daniel W. Gade and Mario Escobar, "Village Settlement and the Colonial Legacy in Southern Peru," *Geographical Review* 72 (1982): 430-449.

thorities could collect taxes, administer the sacraments, and instruct Indians in the lifeways of "honest and obedient Christians." Contact with the outside world could be readily monitored in such insular towns, since authorities could restrict the coming and going of Indians and outsiders. And the towns, beacons of Christian civilization, would draw solitary herders and cultivators into their orbit, removing them from their ancient and remote lands, where natural formations were imbued with strange, idolatrous spirituality and meaning. The influences of urbanization were to absorb even a community's shepherds, who would no longer remain isolated in the high pastures for more than six months at a time, so that they would not return to their rural, primitive ways. Against the strong centrifugal forces endemic to Andean society, the state designed a network of social control pivoting on the stable habitation of the Indians in their official towns.[36]

The naked force by which the state reduced Andean settlements into reconstituted Indian communities was buttressed by the viceroy's guarantees of subsistence rights for residents of the reducciones. A redistribution of land accompanied the creation of the Indian villages, such that the state legitimated usufruct rights for all Andean households whose menfolk were inscribed as tributaries and mitayos. In many instances, that meant taking land away from the host Indian community, the site of the new reducción, and parceling it out among the ayllus, *parcialidades* (moieties), or repartimiento Indians who were transplanted to the community. As Toledo noted in one of his ordinances, this policy provoked numerous land disputes and court suits. The more that royal officials infringed on Andean rights to dispersed fields, forests, and pastures and tried to create a uniform land tenure pattern, the more they had to intercede in the disputes. In principle, all resettled Indians were to be compensated with appropriate land grants, even if that meant that the crown had to expropriate lands from other (non-reducción) Indians or from Spaniards.[37]

Nor was that all. The state also moved inside the jurisdiction of the Indian towns to sanction and dictate the terms of redistribution of surplus crops. Toledo ordered communities to designate parcels of potato and maize lands as *chacras de comunidad*, whose yields were

36 Francisco de Toledo, "Ordenanzas para los indios de . . . Charcas, destinados a evitar los daños y agravios que recibían de sus encomenderos . . . ," in Levillier, ed., *Gobernantes del Perú*, 8: 304-382.

37 Ibid., 330-331 and 353-354.

to feed the poorest inhabitants. In good years, a village was to sell part of the crop and put the proceeds in its *caja da comunidad*, or community treasury. In times of dearth, the community's crop would be distributed directly to the poor and the savings in the caja would provide for food purchases to tide the people over until the next harvest. Through cultivation of communal lands and participation in the product market, the Indian community was to guarantee minimal subsistence even to the poorest peasant families. These risk-sharing mechanisms would establish some kind of social equilibrium within the village economy and presumably prevent the poorer peasants from fleeing their communities and their social obligations to the state in times of scarcity.

Thus, the Toledan state took advantage of traditional Andean norms of reciprocity and redistribution and turned them to its own ends. Even as royal authorities uprooted ayllus and drove people from their ancient lands, joining them with alien ayllus or lineages, stripping them of their traditional land rights, and subordinating them to the parish priest and the magistrate (*corregidor*) who were, for all practical purposes, in charge of the Indian town, Toledo sanctioned a normative order that absorbed elements of the moral economy that had governed social relations in Andean society. But, as Wachtel has noted, the underlying contradiction of the extractive system of exploitation was its preservation and legitimation of certain cultural traditions, customs, and norms wrenched loose from the total Andean socioeconomic formation.[38] Form without content, customs without context: the Andean cultural and ideological systems that gave meaning to kinship relationships were under assault by the very colonial policies that were theoretically meant to protect certain customs and traditions. Rituals and ceremonies that regenerated social bonds, communal commitments, and ethnic identity were eroded, though never stamped out successfully, by the religious and civil bureaucracy.[39] Often, Andean myths, rituals, and beliefs had to go underground to allow the people to seek material wellbeing and harmony from their local dieties (*huacas*) and ancestorgods.[40] And while people still expressed their norms of reciprocity in

38 Wachtel, *Vision of the Vanquished*, 85-139 and 164-165.

39 Spalding, *Huarochirí*, chap. 8; Pierre Duviols, "La represión del paganismo andino y la expulsión de los moriscos," *Anuario de estudios americanos* 28 (1971): 201-207.

40 Two recent ethnohistorical studies explore the transformation and preservation of rituals and symbolic systems among specific ethnic groups in the south-

the ideology of kinship, it was now the state which theoretically defined the outer boundaries of "community" and determined the local ethnic map. Even at the most mundane level, the state altered Andean lifeways even as it sought to preserve them. For example, while Indians were supposed to continue to observe their communitarian practices of sharing scarce resources (under state supervision), they were at the same time ordered to till their fields with oxen and plows rather than with the traditional digging sticks.[41] With the new protection and patronage of the state came a paternalism that reinforced its political and ideological authority over its Indian subjects. As we shall see in chapter 3, during the seventeenth and eighteenth centuries Andean peoples increasingly challenged certain colonial authorities and found ways to loosen state control over their lives. But in the immediate aftermath of the Toledan reforms, the colonial bureaucracy seemed to expand its scope of power and make its presence felt in all parts of the southern Andes. The colonial leviathan appeared more omnipotent than eventually it proved to be.

In order to execute and enforce the reorganization of rural Andean society, Toledo created an intricate, interlocking network of Andean and European power brokers. On the European side, a hierarchy of colonial functionaries—from corregidor and parish priest to royal protector of Indians, jailer, and judicial officer—served as links in the chain of command that began at the highest echelons of government. As agents of a centralized state, they oversaw the extractive institutions, maintained the colonial order through mediation and threat, and diffused the norms and ideology of the dominant colonial elites among the native peoples. But if these white administrators had relied mainly on the power vested in them by the state, they would have had little success. Instead, colonial authorities had to work through the ethnic hierarchy in order to carry out the massive relocations, enforce the extraction of tribute and labor, and ensure the health of the village economy that subsidized the colonial enterprises, although this native hierarchy had to be carefully groomed by the colonial state if it were to serve its new purposes. Thus, Toledo sought to assimilate native authorities into the new power structure. The terms under which they would be subordinated to, and co-opted

ern Andes during (and beyond) colonial rule: Thomas Abercrombie, "The Politics of Sacrifice: An Aymara Cosmology in Action" (Ph.D. diss., University of Chicago, 1986); and Roger Rasnake, "The *Kurahkuna* of Yura: Indigenous Authorities of Colonial Charcas and Contemporary Bolivia" (Ph.D. diss., Cornell University, 1982).

41 Levillier, ed., *Gobernantes del Perú*, 8: 333.

by, the colonial regime were the subject of much debate. Spalding writes that Toledo sought to convert the hereditary position of kuraka into an appointed office.[42] Though he did not prevail, he did manage to institutionalize state control over the succession of the kurakas. Indians could nominate a successor from among members of the noble lineage, but the nominee then had to be approved by the audiencia. This rule later provided a crucial mechanism for state intervention in the internal affairs of Indian communities in Alto Perú (see chapter 8).

Toledo also had other ways of whittling down the power and prestige of kurakas and converting them into agents of the state. One strategy was to restructure the normative order of Indian society. It was the state that now formalized and legitimated the relations between native elites and members of their own ayllu or moiety. The kurakas (or caciques), *principales* (heads of the ayllu segments within the parcialidades), and a host of secondary chiefs had formed a governing hierarchy that corresponded to the native grouping. In a series of ordinances, Toledo sought to define the status, function, and privileges of the members of this hierarchy.[43] They were to oversee the outflow of tribute twice a year and the dispatch of the mitayos. They were to track down fugitive Indians; mobilize work parties to build churches, bridges, and roads; and coordinate the traditional communal activities, such as terracing fields, cleaning irrigation works, and cultivating communal lands. And, as was customary, they were to reciprocate for labor services by offering drink, food, and seeds to their workers. They were also to distribute rights to land and pasturage, arbitrate local disputes, and mediate between the moiety or village and the colonial authorities. In return for exercising his power with prudence and in accordance with the law, the principal kuraka could call upon the community to provide him with laborers to cultivate four fanegadas each of corn and potatoes and two of wheat. A few other privileges accrued to the native notables, all spelled out in the new regulations.[44]

Thus, two principles governed the reforms that revamped the ethnic power structure. First, the state assumed the role of defining the

42 Spalding, *Huarochirí*, 220-221.

43 "De los caciques principales y lo que deben guardar por razón de sus cargos," ordenanzas 1-28, in Levillier, ed., *Gobernantes del Perú*, 8: 340-353.

44 Ibid.; Spalding, *Huarochirí*, 220-221; Waldemar Espinoza Soriano, "El alcalde mayor indígena en el virreinato del Perú," *Anuario de estudios americanos* 17 (1960): 183-300.

positions, powers, and privileges in the kuraka or cacique system (*kurakazgo* or *cacicazgo*). Second, the state sought to limit and control excesses and abuses in the system. Toledo apparently tried to walk a thin line between giving privileges to the native power brokers, on the one hand, and blocking the development of a native oligarchy which could abuse its power and prestige at the expense of the community, on the other. It was to prove impossible (see chapter 3).

The extractive system that Toledo designed sat heavily upon Indian communities throughout the highlands. The Aymara and, to a lesser extent, Quechua peoples who inhabited the puna between Cuzco and Tarija had to bear the brunt of the reforms. In the regions closer to the silver mines of Potosí, the four ethnic nations that formed the loose confederation of Charcas were the most deeply affected. These four nations—the Charcas, Caracaras, Chuyes, and Chichas (see figure 3)—were major sources of tribute and mitayos (they had had ten thousand soldiers and tributaries in the service of the Incas). The once powerful Aymara lords of the lakeshore region remained bountiful providers under the new order. Toledo's vision was focused on the potential wealth of the puna, traditionally the site of the most populous and powerful ethnic groups.

In the eyes of Aymara lords, Toledo must have seemed ruthless and unyielding: a man who took pleasure in stripping once powerful lords of their traditional sources of status, prestige, and wealth. In the span of a generation or two, the lords of the Charcas, Caracaras, Chuyes, and Chichas saw their former privileges and power wiped out by colonial law, and their ayllus forcefully dislocated and burdened with excessive tribute dues. Gone were the times of glory and pride, when the four nations enjoyed the respect and patronage of the Incas in return for their contributions to the imperial war machine. It is no surprise, then, that Toledo's reforms met with resistance. In 1582, the caciques of the Charcas confederation presented a petition to the king of Spain, listing a host of grievances against Toledo's policies, ranging from violations of the traditional prerogatives and privileges of the ethnic lords to the new economic hardships. "If, during the past seven years, repartimiento Indians have paid their tribute . . . it has been out of fear of Viceroy Toledo, because his ordinances all say that caciques who fail to deliver their full tribute quota shall be suspended from the cacicazgo and replaced by others." Impoverished, indebted, and bound to their creditors, their people were suffering under the new tribute schedule (*retasa*). The caciques, who had once enjoyed a status akin to that of Spanish dukes and counts and had ruled over as many as eight or ten thousand people, had now been stripped of the "yanaconas and services" that were appropriate to their positions.[45]

Furthermore, the lords complained, Toledan policies had led to sharp increases in the tribute rate, from four pesos ensayados to seven. The new assessments had not taken into proper account the absentee tributaries, who could no longer be counted on to contribute their share. Because of the reducciones, Indians had been herded into towns, many of them with insufficient pasturage and inadequate access to fertile land. The petition also touched on a new menace that threatened the Indian communities: Spanish colonists were beginning to occupy lands in the kichwa valleys to the east.

By the early 1580s, highland lords saw Spanish colonists as dangerous rivals in an emerging struggle over migrant Indians. If the communities were to pay their tribute in full, they needed to mobilize all their resources and distribute the tax burdens among all able-bodied inhabitants. Every absent tributary meant extra labor for others in the community. Fiscal adjustments were rarely made, so tax burdens also bore down harder on the remaining inhabitants. The leaders of the Charcas confederation therefore asked the crown to grant them jurisdiction over the cimarron tributaries who were in the "power of Spaniards: so that we may round them up and take them away from [their patron], no matter how wealthy."[46]

Another problem raised in the petition was royal toleration and legitimation of colonial land-tenure patterns. The caciques protested the right of the *cabildos* (town councils) and of the audiencia of Charcas to issue land grants (*mercedes*) to Spaniards covering traditional mitmaq lands in the eastern valleys. In particular, the lords formally requested that parcels of land in the Valle Bajo of Cochabamba be returned to their jurisdiction.[47] Presumably, they had been given hope by the earlier viceregal decision to return mitmaq lands in Cochabamba to the Soras and Carangas lords (see chapter 1).

The efforts of the Charcas peoples to recover lost valley lands was but one tactic in their struggle against a social and political system that seemed to grow harsher and more hostile every year. If they were to bear the burdens of tribute and the mita, they had to prevent economic "seepage" from their ayllus and villages. But as long as

45 Espinoza Soriano, ed., *"Memorial de Charcas,"* 14.

46 Ibid., 15.

47 Ibid., 15 and 21.

Spanish colonists could accept migrants on their private domains and shelter them from most levies and from forced labor in the mines, the highland lords had little control over disaffected or defiant Indians. In the 1580s, a decade after Toledo initiated his reforms, the Charcas had identified a fatal flaw in them. The growing Spanish agrarian enterprises in the eastern valleys offered a loophole through which highland migrants might slip if they chose to escape the fiscal net that was tightening around their communities. The Aymara lords not only protested the loss of their mitmaq colonies; they also challenged the existence of the Spanish *chácaras* that were offering havens to their people.

Land and Labor in the Valleys

It was in the kichwa valleys where the advance of Spanish colonization most threatened the self-sufficiency and economic autonomy of village life. The highland lords might challenge the right of individual chacareros in distant valleys to shelter Andean migrants, but the valley caciques were plunged into a confrontation over maize lands, water, herds, and native laborers. Caught at the cutting edge of the Spanish agricultural frontier, the valley Indians braced themselves against the threat of European penetration into the heart of their rural society. The Spanish agrarian advance gained momentum during the 1570s, but to prescient observers, the threat already loomed large in the 1560s. Early in that decade, the oidores of La Plata were concerned about (though not opposed to) the growing number of Europeans who had ranches and small farms in Charcas. They believed that about a thousand Spaniards were earning a livelihood from commercial agriculture there.[48] In Chuquisaca, Tarija, Mizque, Cochabamba, Tomina, Paspaya, Pilaya, and other temperate valleys, European settlers found ideal ecological and topographical conditions for European seed, livestock, and agricultural implements. They also found that the commodity market in Potosí could bring them a handsome profit. Beyond the fertile, moist bottomlands of the Valle Bajo, where maize often yielded two harvests a year and wheat flourished in the drier parts of the valley, Europeans discovered the rich, extensive pastures of Cliza and the sheltered and fertile valley of Sacaba (to the east of the Valle Bajo). These valleys and their surround-

48 Barnadas, *Charcas*, 378.

ing mountains inevitably impressed European travelers, who compared the region favorably to Spanish climes and landscapes.[49]

In 1562, the audiencia of Charcas reported some one hundred European inhabitants of the Cochabamba valleys.[50] It was probably a conservative estimate, for only a few years later, about forty or fifty Spanish families controlled resources in the valleys.[51] One of these families was the Orellanas. Garcí Ruíz de Orellana entered the valleys in 1540, establishing a foothold in the Valle Bajo before leaving to fight against Gonzalo Pizarro in the battles of Warina and Sacsahuamán. Later, Ruíz de Orellana returned to Cochabamba, where he eventually purchased lands from the caciques of Sipesipe, in encomienda to Hernando Silva, of Chuquisaca. The fertile lands of Canata, an undulating plain south of the Sacaba River, where Inca herds had grazed and royal maize had flourished, thus passed into Spanish hands. Over the next generation, the Orellanas consolidated their holdings in the eastern end of the Valle Bajo. Rodrigo and Francisco de Orellana controlled the encomienda of Tiquipaya, once the personal possessions of Yupanqui and Huayna Cápac. Francisco also extended control over rich pasturelands in the Valle Bajo.[52]

The herds of cattle, goats, sheep, horses, mules, oxen, and other European livestock, small and large, must have increased greatly during the 1560s, with the influx of Spanish settlers from the south. Attacks by the Chiriguanos on Spanish settlers in Tarija forced many of them to drive their herds to safer valleys in the interior, away from the tropical frontier and the "savage" tribes.[53] Even before the Toledan reforms, Spanish colonizers negotiated, cajoled, and coerced Andean ethnic groups into surrendering control over their lands. Often hidden from the public eye and from royal scrutiny, a host of land transactions took place in the 1560s, amounting to a piecemeal, de

49 Antonio Vázquez de Espinosa, *Compendio y descripción de las Indias occidentales* (1630) (Madrid: Atlas, 1969), 410. See below, chap. 5, for a detailed description of the region in the eighteenth century.

50 Roberto Levillier, ed., *La audiencia de Charcas; Correspondencia de presidentes y oidores,* 3 vols. (Madrid: J. Pueyro, 1918-1922), 1: 72.

51 Augusto Guzmán, *Cochabamba* (Cochabamba: Amigos del Libro, 1972), 84-85.

52 Ibid., 81-83. Excerpts and fragments of early notarial records, including land transactions, tithes, grain sales, and wills, can be found in José Macedonio Urquidi, *El origen de la noble villa de Oropesa,* 2nd ed. (Cochabamba: Municipalidad de Cochabamba, 1971).

53 Barnadas, *Charcas,* 379-380.

facto, and often ostensibly peaceful territorial advance. Notarized land transactions from this period commonly offer Spanish explanations for native willingness to sell land. One such transaction, dated 1563, registered the purchase of maize land in the Cliza valley. Several Europeans paid 560 pesos to the Indians of Pojo (?) for land parcels, claiming that the Indians needed cash with which to buy cows, sheep, and even llamas. According to the Spaniards, the investment in llamas was part of the Indians' plan to transport coca from the yungas (probably to Potosí).[54] Thus, the alienation of native lands in Cliza was seen as a means by which Indians would invest in pack driving and take advantage of the rising price of coca. To European eyes, it was all part of the mercantilization of native-European relations.

As European land acquisitions increased, the Spanish presence began to pose a threat to social equilibrium in the valleys. The Spanish settlers sought royal sanction and an official disposition of physical space in the valleys. They were not content with extending their reach, haphazardly and somewhat tentatively, across the valleys. Prominent landholders wanted royal permission to establish a municipality that would give territorial jurisdiction to a cabildo and a corregidor. In August 1571, Toledo granted to Captain Gerónimo Osorio the right to found the town (*villa*) of Oropesa in the Valle Bajo. For the next three years, the town existed in name only: a territorial unit of municipal government was designated, but no new town was actually built. The small native village of Canata, near Sipesipe, became the site of local administration. It was not until 1574 that Oropesa appeared, at the eastern end of the Valle Bajo, where the central plaza of the city of Cochabamba is located today.[55] Oropesa, which soon came to be called Cochabamba, was laid out in the classic grid pattern, with its requisite Augustinian and Franciscan chapels, jail, hospital, and town hall flanking the central square. The Spanish presence in the valley now had official physical and political visibility.

The establishment of Oropesa symbolized the shifting balance of power in favor of the white colonizers. For the formal foundation of the town, the Spanish corregidor called together the caciques of El

54 "Compra de tierras por D. Luís Abasire," AHMC, Leg. 1195.

55 Guzmán, *Cochabamba*, 86-90. Confusion due to the lapse of time between the Toledan authorization for the founding of Oropesa and its actual establishment created a minor controversy over the date of its founding (1571 or 1574) when preparations were being made to celebrate its four hundredth anniversary.

Paso (under encomienda of Gerónimo Ondegardo) and Tiquipaya (in encomienda to Francisco de Orellana), as well as the caciques of Sipesipe, Tapacarí, Paria, Sacaba, and Pocona at the site. By their presence, the caciques were to acknowledge Spanish settlement and municipal authority, and they were to dispatch two hundred Indians to lay out and build the town. The Europeans, in turn, were to choose their house sites and eventually move off the land into the town. The chacareros were to be "reduced" from their scattered dwellings across the valley to the urban nucleus of Christian civilization. But the town's establishment represented more than a physical concentration of European culture and power, amidst the few material amenities in the village of adobe huts and chapels. The founding fathers of Oropesa sought royal sanction for the chácaras that every Spanish inhabitant (*vecino*) "has and possesses" in the valleys. Further, the town charter denied the right of Indians to challenge the vecinos' title to their lands, even when a deed could not be produced. The status of original vecino was to confer, ipso facto, landholding rights.[56] The act of foundation thus gave local authorities a device for rejecting Andean protests against Spanish land occupation.

Meanwhile, the establishment of the Indian communities placed the caciques of the Cochabamba valleys in a paradoxical position. On the one hand, the centralizing colonial state superseded the authority of local encomenderos and legitimated a set of rights and obligations (albeit quite asymmetrical) governing relations between the state and the village Indians. In the kichwa valleys of Cochabamba, state designation of Indian communties, accompanied by the forced resettlement of Andeans, theoretically worked in favor of the local caciques. The reducciónes hardened territorial boundaries and jurisdictions that undercut or weakened traditional links between valley mitmaq colonies and their distant highland ayllus. Royal recognition of Indian villages also bestowed protection against encroachment by outsiders.

On the other hand, the colonial authorities were not always scrupulous about protecting the Andean communities. In the same years that the caciques of Tapacarí, Sipesipe, El Paso, and Tiquipaya saw the scattered rural hamlets of their people reduced into one or two Indian towns and placed under religious and civil authorities (even while they remained in encomienda), they also witnessed what they

56 The "Acta de la fundación de la villa de Oropesa" appears as an appendix in Francisco de Viedma, *Descripción geográfica y estadística de la provincia de Santa Cruz de la Sierra* (Cochabamba: Amigos del Libro, 1969), 285-286.

believed to be a betrayal of their communal autonomy, when Toledo resolved the long, bitter dispute between the Sipesipes and the Carangas, Quillacas, and Soras over local mitmaq lands in favor of the highland Indians (see chapter 1). The state's intervention in this old rivalry was a concern to the valley caciques, for they feared that it would encourage other highland ayllus to press similar claims. Further, it weakened the ability of encomenderos to protect their Indian subjects from the aggression of outside claimants.

Nor did the state act forcefully against the rapid advance of Spanish land ownership in the Valle Bajo. Toledo's concessions to the founding vecinos in 1574 legitimated all previous despoliation of Indian land and blocked Andean challenges through court proceedings. Valley Indians could challenge *future* encroachments on their communal resources, but that was no defense against the aggressive chacareros who had already staked out pastures and fields throughout the three central valleys. Ironically, then, the Toledan policies aimed at preserving the Andean communities ended by tipping the balance of political forces against them.

The valley communities suffered the same "internal shocks" as their highland counterparts did during the years of royal inspection, reduction, and administrative reorganization. The resettlement created five Indian districts in the *corregimiento* (magistracy) of Cochabamba. Three of them—Sipesipe, El Paso, and Tiquipaya—were carved out of the Valle Bajo, on former Incaic lands where a variety of ethnic groups was clustered. Tapacarí, the largest district, stretched along the valley of the Tapacarí River and into the surrounding highlands in the western reaches of the province. The fifth district, Capinota, was situated in the warm valley of the Arque River and its nearby highlands.[57] Tapacarí, El Paso, and Tiquipaya were still tied to encomenderos (of the second or third generation). Only Sipesipe was clearly designated as a crown possession. Nonetheless, all the communities were the objects of forced resettlement. Tapacarí's forty-two scattered hamlets and ranches were reduced to two central villages; Sipesipe's fifty-odd settlements were concentrated into one main village.[58] That is not to say that the state severed all vertical kinship ties that cut across the ecological tiers. As

57 Capinota does not appear in the census taken in 1573. A report made in 1618, however, gives population figures for that year and for earlier years. For a detailed discussion of the five districts in the eighteenth century, see chap. 4.

58 Nicolás Sánchez-Albornoz, *The Population of Latin America* (Berkeley and Los Angeles: University of California Press, 1974), 46.

we have seen, Toledo himself contradicted his own policies by granting landholding rights in Sipesipe and Tiquipaya to highland ayllus. Furthermore, the ayllus of Tapacarí clung to their mitmaq colonists, situated in tropical valleys in Ayopaya, well into the seventeenth century.[59] Kinship relations between Indians in Capinota and highland villages in Paria survived until the late eighteenth century (see chapter 4). But these links were but vestiges of another age. The thrust of Toledo's reforms in the valleys was to bind together the disparate, fragmented cultural groups into "royal villages" (pueblos reales) beholden to colonial bureaucrats (and their native intermediaries) for subsistence rights.

A census in 1573 revealed the size and "carrying capacity" of the Indian communities (see table 2). Tribute was set at seven pesos ensayados per tributary. Tapacarí's population was greater than that of the other pueblos reales, and its total tribute was correspondingly higher. But all the villages (with perhaps the exception of Capinota) confronted a tax schedule that commuted (i.e., converted from a tax in kind to a tax in money) the overwhelming proportion of their tribute. The maize each community was required to deliver had dwindled to a symbolic reminder of the past. Another relic was the labor prestations that tributaries owed in two of the villages. In El Paso,

Table 2. Population and Tribute of Indian Reducción Communities, 1573

Community	Total Population	Number of Tributaries[a]	Tribute[b]	Percentage Commuted
Tapacarí	6,014	1,173	7,733 p. e. 600 f. maize	94
Sipesipe	3,691	819	5,255 p. e. 600 f. maize	92
El Paso	3,298	684	4,460 p. e. 400 f. maize[c]	94
Tiquipaya	2,573	504	3,250 p. e. 350 f. maize[c]	84
Capinota[d]	—	419	2,926 p. e.	—

Sources: "Tasa de la visita general de Francisco de Toledo," AGI, Contaduría, Leg. 1786, ff. 26, 35, 37, and 39; for Capinota, AGN, Sala 13, 18.1.3, Leg. 43 (1612 revisita de Capinota). (A published version of the census of 1573 is in Cook, ed., Tasa de la visita general, 23-32.) [a] Married males between the ages of 18 and 50. [b] p. e. = pesos ensayados (1 p. e. = 12 reales). f. = fanegas. A fanega of maize was assigned a value of six tomines. [c] Plus labor prestations. [d] Data are for 1612.

59 AGN, Sala 13, Padrones, 18.1.3, Leg. 43, June 1, 1618. The census of the Indian population of Tapacarí listed ninety-two colonists living in Ayopaya in 1618.

peasants were still required to cultivate six fanegas of maize and two fanegas of wheat for the encomendero. Tiquipaya Indians also owed personal service on a maize chácara belonging to their encomendero, Francisco de Orellana.

Times were changing, however. The remaining encomiendas were destined for transition from private to royal jurisdiction. Sipesipe, the second largest village in the region, had already passed into the royal domain and almost all its tribute was owed to the state, which channeled a small portion back to the community, to serve as a cushion against calamity. Even in those communities still in private encomienda, the colonial state claimed almost one-third of their tribute as royal income, earmarked to cover the expenses of administration, including a parish priest in each of the villages, the priests at Potosí who ministered to the mitayos and other migrants to the silver mines, and such civil officials as the "protector of Indians" and the village caciques.

The royal visitadores who moved through the valleys drastically altered the conditions of life for most Andeans. Eventually, the peasants would find ways of adjusting to, mitigating, or resisting the harsher terms imposed by the state. But the region's great loss of native population during the decades following the Toledan reforms is testimony to the deep disruption they caused.[60] Yet it was the mita that had perhaps the most wrenching effect on the valley peoples. As mentioned earlier, Toledo was inclined to exempt most of the valley Indians from the mita, apparently because he feared the devastating physiological effects of the high altitude and the frigid climate on the native inhabitants of the lowlands.[61] But Cochabamba was not so exempted, perhaps because it was the site of the original Incaic mit'a, after which Toledo had fashioned the mining mita. In any event, Toledo mandated that the five Indian villages in Cochabamba fulfill a quota of 409 mitayos each year. The burden was to be distributed among the villages in accordance with the size of their tributary populations.[62] In absolute terms, Tapacarí bore the heaviest burden of the villages. However, it is quite unlikely that the Cocha-

60 See chap. 3. Migration and population loss and dispersion had probably had a substantial effect on the size and ethnic composition of the region's Indian population already during the pre-Toledan decades.

61 The effects of the climate at Potosí on Andean inhabitants of temperate valleys was still a controversial issue in the late eighteenth century. See Viedma, *Descripción geográfica*, 180.

62 Ibid., app. 4.

bamba quota was met, after the first several dispatches of mitayos. In 1617, for example, only 218 mitayos were sent to the mines.[63] In the most extreme case, almost all the men subject to the mita had abandoned the village of Tiquipaya, leaving mostly widows and spinsters in the pueblo. Nearby there beckoned the growing town of Oropesa and Spanish fields and orchards—free territory lying outside the confines of the "obligated" village. Even the corregidor of Cochabamba grumbled about the impossible task of finding mitayos to fulfill the quota.[64]

Passage out of the Indian villages into the "free" Spanish territory made possible a number of alternative labor arrangements. In the Cochabamba region, the Toledan reforms indirectly left most valley territory open for Spanish colonization. The early vecinos, unable to rely upon agricultural repartimientos,[65] had to secure their field hands, herders, muleteers, domestic servants, and weavers from among itinerant and seasonal laborers or Indian retainers. It was not uncommon for local ayllu Indians to spend a season or more on a Spanish estate and then return to village life. Day laborers (*jornaleros*) and seasonal migrants, temporarily away from their ayllus, might fulfill the intensive labor requirements of harvest during July and August. But most enterprising chacareros and hacienda owners (*hacendados*) depended upon a core group of permanent laborers, dependent upon their landlords and masters for access to the means of subsistence. By force of circumstance or bitter choice, Andeans who had lost their means of subsistence, severed themselves from their kin groups, or sought security from labor drafts often succumbed to long-term, exploitative relationships of personal dependence and servitude. The forms and content of incipient class relationships in the early agricultural enterprises in Cochabamba probably varied considerably. Cultural and class lines had not yet hardened, and there was a fluid movement of Andeans through the region and between village and chácara, chácara and town. Spanish landlords, unable to depend on the state to provide a reliable flow of laborers and faced with keen competition for the services of the Andeans, developed strategies to bind workers to their enterprises. They combined guarantees of minimum subsistence and gestures of patronage with coercive

63 *Digesto de ordenanzas*, 3: 4-7.

64 Ibid.

65 Juan López y Velasco, *Geografía y descripción universal de las Indias* (1574) (Madrid: Atlas, 1971), 255.

practices to extract the maximum of labor from their Indian retainers. If the chacareros were to profit from the emerging long-distance grain trade to Potosí, they needed to anchor a labor force amidst the turmoil and change provoked by Toledo's reforms.[66]

In the Toledan and pre-Toledan decades, there was a significant group of Andean laborers whose primary official status derived from their informal bondage to Spanish landlords. They were considered to be, in some ways, "rural yanaconas"—agrarian counterparts to the permanent, independent workers in the mines of Potosí who apparently had ruptured their links to their native villages or ayllus (see chapter 1) and who were called by the term yanaconas, which had been inherited from Incan times and had become a generic term for a "detached" indian who lived near and worked for a Spaniard.[67] Matienzo's categories of yanaconas gave some functional content to the term, so that Spanish colonists began to discriminate among yanacona artisans, town dwellers, independent miners, and agricultural laborers.[68] But long before the colonial nomenclature captured some of the nuances of the multiple niches that Andeans had carved out for themselves at the bottom of Spanish colonial society, authorities used the term yanaconas to refer to those Indians who had separated from their native lands and kin groups, escaping from encomienda and mita obligations and assimilating themselves (in varying de-

66 Stern (*Peru's Indian Peoples*, 138-157 and 189-193) discusses the emerging "political economy of dependence" in the colony, as many Andean peoples lost the independent means of subsistence they had had by virtue of communal membership and participation and were reduced to servitude and dependence on individual colonists. My own thinking about the rise of private modes of exploitation in early colonial Alto Perú, based upon incipient class and property relations, owes much to Stern's conceptual framework of distinct, and contradictory, forms of extraction in the colonial social formation. For another important conceptual approach to private modes of exploitation, within agrarian enterprise, see Pablo Macera, "Feudalismo colonial americano: El caso de las haciendas peruanas," in his *Trabajos de historia*, 4 vols., (Lima: Instituto Nacional de Cultura, 1977), 3: 139-227. Important historical studies on early haciendas in the Andes are Robert G. Keith, *Conquest and Agrarian Change: The Emergence of the Hacienda System on the Peruvian Coast* (Cambridge: Harvard University Press, 1976); Keith Davies, *Landowners in Colonial Peru* (Austin: University of Texas Press, 1984); and Rolando Mellafe, "Frontera agraria: El caso del virreinato peruano en el siglo XVI," in Alvaro Jara, ed., *Tierras nuevas: Expansión territorial y ocupación del suelo en América (siglos xvi-xix)* (Mexico City: Colegio de Mexico, 1969), 11-42.

67 Murra, *Formaciones económicas*, 225-242.

68 Matienzo, *Gobierno del Perú*, book 1, chap. 8.

grees) into Spanish society. It was estimated in 1571 that the Peruvian kingdom had some fifty thousand yanaconas integrated into Spanish urban and rural society.[69] In 1574, Toledo said that there were about 5,500 *yanaconas de servicio* living on 364 chácaras of Spaniards and mestizos in Charcas. He noted that some had come from various repartimientos, while others had fled their villages or the mines of Potosí.[70] The regional distribution of that population was not ascertained. But where chácaras flourished, yanaconas clustered, and the valleys of Cochabamba were a prime area of *yanaconaje* in the late sixteenth and early seventeenth centuries. No detailed census of yanaconas had been taken at the time, but over the ten-year period from 1656 to 1665, the yanacona miners of Potosí contributed more tribute revenue than yanaconas in any other part of Charcas. Among the rural districts, the yanaconas of Cochabamba generated the most royal income (see table 3). Although they were a small portion of the region's tributary population, there were probably more yanaconas in Cochabamba than in other areas of Alto Perú where chacareros had settled.

Like the other yanaconas of the southern highlands, the Andean immigrants to Cochabamba had diverse origins. Some had followed the conquistadores into the valleys of Cochabamba, shortly after the decisive battle against the Charcas conferderation. Other had been

Table 3.   Tribute Paid by the Yanacona Population of Alto Perú, 1656-1665

Province or Town	Total Tribute[a]	Percentage
Villa de Potosí	58,656	31.3
Porco	21,078	11.2
Cochabamba	30,408	16.2
Chayanta	2,392	1.3
Yamparaes	24,737	13.2
Chichas	19,909	10.6
Mizque	8,260	4.4
Tomina	13,338	7.1
Pilaya	8,715	4.6
Total	187,493	99.9

Source: AGI, Contaduría, Leg. 1818, Jan. 31, 1666.
Note: Discrepancy in total of percentages due to rounding.
[a] In pesos corrientes (8 reales each), converted from pesos ensayados (12 reales each).

69 Barnadas, *Charcas*, 296, n. 302.

70 Toledo to the crown, March 20, 1574, cited in Zavala, *Servicio personal*, 1: 92.

engaged as personal retainers of the early encomenderos.[71] Still others had moved into the region after 1550, as chácaras began to flourish and Andeans fled the harsh conditions of Potosí for rural work. Many contemporaries believed that the conditions of life and work were more tolerable on private rural estates than they were in the mines or even in the Indian communities.[72] But we still know little about labor relations or living conditions for yanaconas working in private commercial agriculture in the easter valleys. One scholar, Josep Barnadas, accepts Matienzo's judgment that the material conditions, physical environment, and work rhythms there were less alienating than the burdens that weighed on the yanacona miners. He believes that most yanaconas had adapted to Hispanicized ways by the late sixteenth century.[73] Thierry Saignes, on the other hand, questions contemporary assessments of yanacona alienation from their cultural roots or kin groups. Rural yanaconas, in particular, may have maintained ties to their ayllus over the course of a lifetime, or even across generations. Neither the ascribed, official status of yanacona, nor spatial separation, necessarily led to the complete severance of kin or cultural ties. Further, yanacona families may have woven new webs of reciprocal rights and obligations with each other, allowing them to spread risk and retain some of their traditional rituals, customs, and norms, even within the confines of the hacienda.[74] Until further research is done, we can only speculate about the labor arrangements and cultural lifeways among yanaconas on sixteenth-century chácaras. Projecting ahead, though,

71 "Juicio en grado de apelación ante la real audiencia de la Plata . . . entre d. Juan Durán y los caciques de Sipesipe . . ." (1584), ANB, EC no. 72; Franklin Pease, ed., "Una visita al obispado de Charcas" (1590), *Humanidades*, no. 3 (1969): 89-125, esp. 102-103.

72 Zavala, *Servicio personal*, vols. 1 and 2, passim, and Mario Góngora, *Studies in the Colonial History of Spanish America* (Cambridge: Cambridge University Press, 1975), 149-158.

73 Barnadas, *Charcas*, 293.

74 Thierry Saignes, "Ayllus, mercado, y coacción colonial: El reto de las migraciones internas en Charcas, siglo XVII," in Harris, Larson, and Tandeter, *Participación indígena*, 111-158; and Saignes, "Políticas étnicas," 13. Zulawski's work on the region of Pilaya y Paspaya in the early eighteenth century challenges the notion of yanaconas as relatively immobile, servile workers. She has found considerable labor mobility among a group of Indians registered as yanaconas in the censuses. Ann Zulawski, "Agricultural Labor and Social Change: Pilaya and Paspaya in the Eighteenth Century" (paper presented at the International Congress of Americanists, the Universidad de los Andes, Bogotá, July 1-7, 1985).

it is perhaps revealing that, among Indians and mestizos in the Cochabamba valleys in the eighteenth century, the yanaconas were stigmatized as the lowest-ranked laborers, who occupied inferior positions of servitude and subordination to a landlord and who passed their position on to their children (see chapter 5).

As long as the yanaconas were among the flotsam and jetsam of the conquest—the uprooted vagabonds of a land torn by strife and violence—they could be dismissed as "misfits" who had slipped between the cracks of encomienda and repartimiento. But as their ranks swelled and as the colonial state began to tighten control over the movement and labor of native Andeans, they could no longer be ignored. When Toledo traveled to Chuquisaca in late 1572, he was apprised of the magnitude of yanaconaje in Charcas, and he was confronted with an agressive group of chacareros who wanted royal sanction to tie the yanaconas down. Toledo felt that two concerns were at issue. First, the yanaconas were an untapped resource, as far as the state was concerned, and Toledo wanted them to be taxed. Second, since yanaconas dwelled outside state jurisdiction, on isolated rural estates, and were often witness to the corrupt behavior of their masters, they were in need of the sacraments and moral teachings of the church. Hence, the viceroy enacted, in 1574, a series of ordinances that was to govern relations between landlord and yanacona on the chácaras throughout Alto Perú.[75]

Among other provisions, the ordinances called for a priest on every rural estate, the religious instruction of Indian boys, a prohibition against intoxicating beverages among yanaconas, and the protection of Indian women from abusive behavior by unmarried landlords. The ordinances also established a set of mutual obligations between landlords and peasants. Landlords had to allocate land to each yanacona family for its subsistence needs, and they were to provide a plow and draft animals during planting season and grant the peasants time in which to cultivate their family plots. They were obligated to supply a piece of rough woolen cloth to their yanaconas each year, to care for the sick and infirm, and to grant one day of rest each week (except during planting and harvest). In return, the yanaconas were to work daily between dawn and sunset for the benefit of the landlord and at his behest.

Legally, the yanaconas were free, but in the context of colonial-

75 "Ordenanzas acerca de los indios yanaconas de la provincia de Charcas, como han de ser doctrinados y el tributo que han de pagar," in Levillier, ed., *Gobernantes del Perú,* 8: 241-256.

ism, their "freedoms" merely camouflaged the bonds that impeded their movement and crushed their will. Thus, yanaconas could not be legally sold along with rural estates, but at the same time they were declared to be perpetual tenants and were forbidden to own land. Yanaconas had rights to subsistence lands on the estate, but they could not abandon the property of their lord, nor could they sell their labor to others, except for ten days each year—enough time to earn their tribute dues. They were permitted to transport their master's grains to Potosí and to sell small surpluses of their own crops in the marketplace there, but they could not otherwise engage in commerce. Essentially, yanaconas were to be kept on the rural estates, sealed off from the market (and from corrupt European influences) and isolated from other rural laborers on nearby chácaras.[76] The intrusion of the state into the private, rural domain circumscribed landlord-peasant interaction and dictated the interaction of yanaconas with the wider world as well.

Toledo's attention to the rights and obligations of yanaconas arose out of more than his presumed moral responsibilities. In an encounter with Potosí mineowners and authorities in 1572, Toledo discovered an incipient but growing competition between the mining industry and the agrarian estates for Andean labor. As will be discussed in chapter 3, this conflict became the leitmotif of seventeenth-century politics in Alto Perú. But already under Toledo, the Potosí mineowners considered the chacareros of Chuquisaca and Cochabamba to be their economic rivals. They wanted the yanaconas returned to their ayllus and villages, where the Indians would again be subject to the mita.[77] The Spanish landholders, on the other hand, believed that such a measure would doom many chácaras to extinction. Thus, Toledo had to mediate between these rival factions and strike a balance between the dominant extractive mode of exploitation (upon which the mita rested) and the emerging, still subordinate private mode of exploitation. In geopolitical terms, the conflict pitted the western, highland mining interests against the eastern, lowland agrarian interests.

Toledo's bias was toward the mining interests. It was he who was assembling the machinery with which to force Andean communities in the highlands to subsidize the Potosí mines. But he was too wise an administrator to take a one-sided stand. Returning the yanaconas to their original communities (or transplanting them to new royal villages) would enlarge the pool of draft labor, but only at great

76 Levillier, ed., *Gobernantes del Perú*, esp. ordinance 11, 8: 251-252.

77 Barnadas, *Charcas*, 296ff.

cost to the colony. The chácaras had to survive simply because they produced much of the food sustaining the mining towns. Thus, he based his policies on the complementarity between mining and agriculture in Alto Perú. In spite of their opposition, the mineowners needed the chacareros. On the other hand, Toledo agreed that the private agrarian sector had to be kept subordinate to the export interests at Potosí. Above all, the leakage of Indians from their official communities to Spanish estates had to be halted. In the 1574 ordinances, Toledo granted legal status to all yanaconas who had lived on Spanish estates for four years or longer. They could not be evicted, nor could they abandon their landlords. More recent migrants were given the choice of staying or returning to their homelands. But the ordinances also forbade landlords to recruit new yanaconas to their farms and ranches. Thus, the size of the native labor force in commercial agriculture in Alto Perú was fixed (except for changes that might take place through natural growth). Chacareros would have to rely on sources of rural labor that were not subject to the mita—African slaves and contract or day workers.[78]

In the valleys and serranías of Cochabamba, the ordinances limiting yanaconaje probably had little impact on the quest for permanent, servile labor on Spanish lands. The chacareros there continued to press Indian migrants into peonage by whatever means available. In these efforts, they were opposed not by the mining aristocracy but by the caciques of Cochabamba's five pueblos reales. The chacareros' aggressive pursuit of Andean laborers threatened the caciques' already precarious hold over their peasantries. For beyond the maize fields lay Spanish territory and the seeming "freedom" from state and community obligations. Neither distance, nor mountain, nor climate was there to separate the villages from the chácaras, where an alternative way of life awaited. Thus, a bitter struggle erupted between chacareros and caciques over the legitimacy of yanaconas on private lands.

In 1598, the caciques of the five pueblos reales petitioned the audiencia of La Plata for an inspection of the province.[79] Their aim was to ferret out the chacareros who had "usurped" Indians from their

---

78 Levillier, ed., *Gobernantes del Perú*, 8: 247-249 and 253-254. In 1600, the audiencia of La Plata sought to legalize the status of yanacona only for those Andeans who had lived on Spanish estates for a minimum of ten years as opposed to the previously stipulated four-year period. Had this become policy, many fewer rural yanaconas would have enjoyed legal protection. Levillier, ed., *Audiencia de Charcas*, 3: 411-447, esp. 418-427.

79 "Los indios de Cochabamba sobre el pago de jornales," ANB, EC no. 15 (1598).

villages. The caciques said that, in times past, many Indians would spend a season on Spanish lands, often tending the herds of Spanish landlords. Presumably, such labor was one means by which communities earned money to pay their tribute. But many such Indians did not return to their villages, and their Spanish employers meanwhile refused to remit the accumulated wages to cover their tribute dues. To the caciques, the usurped shepherds were "lost" tributaries, whose dues then had to be covered by the rest of the village, and they demanded that a head count of them be taken. A census was commissioned by the oidores, and it was revealing. Sipesipe had lost 30 tributaries from Anansaya and 51 from Urinsaya to nearby Spanish estates. There were 22 tributaries missing from El Paso and about 29 from Tiquipaya. Many of these Indians had been absent for fifteen or more years. The caciques calculated that the missing tributaries had accumulated debts amounting to the worth of a "standard" ten-mule train loaded with maize and silver coin (*peara de mulas*). Such debts were an obstacle to those Indians who wished to reintegrate themselves into village life. Some of the usurped peasants may originally have sought protection from tribute burdens. Against state prohibitions and the objections of their own caciques, they had lived on Spanish lands until their status of jornalero or *indio usurpado* had been forgotten and they were indistinguishable from yanaconas. Their new status was apparently even becoming hereditary. The landowner Diego Pérez de Orellana had usurped an Indian herder, identified as Rodrigo in the special census. Rodrigo, a member of the Guaillanco ayllu of Sipesipe, had died on the chácara, leaving his children to become shepherds in his place and to serve the master in his house. Without the caciques' intervention, the children would have inherited, de facto, the servile status of yanacona.[80]

The audiencia's position was sympathetic to the caciques' pleas. It ordered the royal inspector to calculate the sum of Spanish debts owed to the five villages and to reduce all the usurped Indians they could identify to those communities. How effectively these orders were implemented is a matter of speculation. But as we shall see in chapter 3, such meliorating gestures did not stem the tide in any case. Ironically, Toledo's reforms, which were supposed to stabilize

---

80 Ibid. (Sipesipe census). The loss of several dozen tributaries to haciendas was not numerically significant, in terms of the percentage of the pueblos' tributary populations registered in the Toledan census of 1573 (see table 2). Rather, the point is that this struggle over usurped Indians from El Paso, Tiquipaya, and Sipesipe presaged a deepening conflict between village and hacienda over land and labor in the Valle Bajo.

the distribution of the Andean population between the royal villages and the private sector, threw open the floodgates of Andean migration in the seventeenth century.

In the struggle over land and labor in the eastern valleys, the chacareros had seized the advantage over the caciques by the end of the sixteenth century. Thereafter, the caciques were ever more on the defensive, engaged in a struggle for survival against the forces of attrition that gnawed away at the edges of communal life. Even under the encomienda, the caciques of the maize valleys had found themselves under siege by powerful and aggressive Aymara lords seeking to recover mitmaq lands. In that interethnic struggle, many of the valley chiefs fell back on their precarious alliances with local encomenderos to defend their territorial jurisdiction over lowland resources. They did not command the power, respect, or solidarity of the ethnically fragmented groups under their wing that they needed to confront the highland hereditary chiefs. Nor, on the other hand, could they count upon the centralizing colonial state to buttress their authority and protect their communities from outside incursions. Toledo was ambivalent toward the Indian communities of Cochabamba, and the caciques were increasingly vulnerable to a new threat—the private agrarian enterprise. While they were mounting their defenses against the chacareros, the Toledan state was erecting the apparatus of extraction. The valley dwellers would not be exempt from forced mine work at Potosí, after all.

Potosí cast yet broader shadows across the valley landscape. In the 1580s and 1590s, the mercantile power of the mining town stimulated commercial agriculture in the valleys and turned small-scale chacareros into wholesale cereal exporters. The short-term success of Toledo's mining reforms and the ensuing "silver rush" turned Potosí into a legendary boom town of some 100,000 people around the turn of the century. The dizzying pace of production fanned the fires of inflation, with rapid price increases even for the staples of life.[81] The city suffered from a chronic shortage of maize and wheat, and prices fluctuated wildly from year to year.[82] These conditions created

81 Levillier, ed., *Audiencia de Charcas*, 2:332, and Assadourian, "Producción de la mercancía dinero," 282ff.

82 The cabildo of Potosí was concerned about stabilizing commodity prices of imports, particularly food crops, and its records during the 1580s and 1590s are full of references to price fluctuations and the need for stricter regulation: ANB, Biblioteca Nacional de Bolivia, "Libros de acuerdos del cabildo de Potosí," vols. 5-8. See esp. the discussions about food shortages and price increases during the drought years of 1590 and 1591, when the price of maize rose by more than 50

a climate for mercantile and speculative investment in overland trade. Even such bulky products as wheat and maize could be transported profitably. Potosí drew cereal in abundant quantities and from distant regions across the broken landscape. In 1603, pack trains brought in sacks of wheat flour whose estimated worth surpassed one million pesos. Another one million pesos worth of maize flour entered the city that year (destined, no doubt, for fermentation into chicha).[83] Potosí's greatest commercial power rested not with exotic luxury goods from Europe, but with its capacity to attract the staples of life, hauled on the backs of men and beasts, from vertical niches scattered across a vast mountainous interior.[84] Under other circumstances, European and Andean grains could not have burst out of the circuits of a regional market network.

In this situation, the early commercial enterprises in Potosí rapidly turned into trading partnerships and speculative ventures and led to annual treks to the mines, where huge quantities of wheat and maize fetched prices that were often four times higher than local ones.[85] Cochabamba was emerging as one of the principal sources of grain for the mining town. In 1605, Bishop Reginaldo de Lizárraga reported that the valleys produced enough grain to feed Potosí and several minor mining towns besides. Some thirty years later, Váz-

percent, and that of wheat by more than 33 percent, over "normal" price ranges: ibid., vol. 6 (1591-1593), f. 70v. On the mercantilist role of the cabildo, see John Preston Moore, *The Cabildo in Peru under the Hapsburgs: A Study in the Origins and Powers of the Town Council in the Viceroyalty of Peru, 1530-1700* (Durham, N.C.: Duke University Press, 1954), 160-175, and Frederick B. Pike, "Aspects of Cabildo Economic Regulation in Spanish America under the Hapsburgs," *Inter-American Economic Affairs* 13 (1960): 67-86.

83 "Descripción de la villa y minas," 380.

84 Assadourian, "Producción de la mercancía dinero," and his "Integración y desintegración regional en el espacio colonial: Un enfoque histórico," in Assadourian, *Sistema de la economía colonial*, 109-134 (see also related articles in that book); Gwendoline Ballantine Cobb, "Supply and Transportation for the Potosí Mines, 1545-1640," *Hispanic American Historical Review* 29 (1949): 25-45; and Brooke Larson, "Merchants and Economic Activity in Sixteenth-Century Potosí" (Master's thesis, Columbia University, 1972).

85 ANB, Biblioteca Nacional de Bolivia, "Libros de acuerdos del cabildo de Potosí," vol. 5 (1585-1590), f. 309v. In the late sixteenth and early seventeenth centuries, various schemes were advanced in the cabildo to undermine the power of middlemen and grain speculators, whose activities even further inflated the prices of foodstuffs at Potosí: BNB, AP, Tomo 5 (1585-1590), f. 313; Tomo 6 (1591-1593), f. 44; Tomo 8 (1596-1599), ff. 5-12.

quez de Espinosa was equally impressed.[86] Perhaps they exaggerated, but it is worth noting that the archbishopric of La Plata counted on the Cochabamba province for its greatest source of tithe revenue around the beginning of the seventeenth century (see table A-1). It had become a major cereal bowl of Alto Perú.

During the process, the chacareros established their hegemony in the regional economy. By 1630, a landed aristocracy was in place. But it was neither autarkic nor immune to changes in the wider political economy of colonialism. Having triumphed over the contentious caciques in the region, Cochabamba's landlords would once more confront the mining elite, which resented their seeming control of Andean rural laborers.

86 Reginaldo de Lizárraga, *Descripción breve de toda la tierra del Perú, Tucumán, Río de la Plata, y Chile* (1609) (Madrid: Atlas, 1968), 74-75, and Vázquez de Espinosa, *Compendio y descripción*, 410.

Declining State Power and the Struggle over Labor

On Monday mornings, the mitayos gathered at the base of Huayna Potosí (the hill for which the town was named) to receive work assignments for the week; and on one of those Mondays early in 1617, the recently arrived corregidor of Potosí inspected the assemblage. Armed with official lists of the sixteen newly formed "companies" of mitayos (each usually consisting of the members of a single ethnic or community group), the corregidor checked over the contingents to see whether the required one-third of the companies had reported for mine work. The corregidor's inventory confirmed the alarming report that had been issued five years earlier by Viceroy Juan de Mendoza y Luna: the mita was shrinking. From a corpus of 13,500 mitayos in Toledo's day, the registries now showed only 10,460. Still worse, the corregidor discovered that only about half the men who were subject to the mita had come to Potosí at all. The remaining mitayos now appeared only on paper, as *indios de plata*—i.e., those who had commuted their service by monetary payments (*rezagos*).[1] These payments were made to the owners of mills and mines who were entitled to allotments of mitayos, and they were supposed to cover the expenses of hiring free wageworkers. But there was much contemporary dispute over this practice.[2] The concern continued as the magnitude of commutation grew in

1 "De la mita de Potosí y reducciones del reino," cited and discussed in Thierry Saignes, "Notes on the Regional Contribution to the Mita in Potosí in the Early Seventeenth Century," *Bulletin of Latin American Research* 4 (1985): 65-76. The document is also discussed in Zavala, *Servicio personal*, 2: 67-70. Its author was probably Rafael Ortiz de Sotomayor, the corregidor of Potosí in the second decade of the seventeenth century.

2 Jeffrey A. Cole, "An Abolitionism Born of Frustration: The Conde de Lemos and the Potosí Mita, 1667-1673," *Hispanic American Historical Review* 63 (1983): 313-314; and Zavala, *Servicio personal*, 2: 118-119, 143-147, 150, and 175.

later years, reaching annual levels of as much as 600,000 pesos in the 1660s.[3]

Reports issued during the second decade of the seventeenth century revealed how extensively Andean peoples engaged in mercantile activities of all kinds in order to purchase exemption from the dreaded mita. Particularly in the southern half of the "obligated provinces," numerous indios de plata commercialized charcoal, lumber, ceramics, and food crops to accumulate the necessary cash. Others bought their way out by working temporarily for wages in mining enterprises at Potosí and elsewhere, where they had somewhat more control over the conditions and terms of exchange.[4]

However, commercial activities were not the only method used by Andean peoples to avoid the mita. Many of them simply abandoned their official villages and dispersed among smaller hamlets in the region.[5] In 1610, for example, a company of Jesuits called attention to a group of Carangas communities on the shores of Lake Poopó that had become mere shells of the towns they once were.[6] The depopulation of these villages, as of many others, was the result both of the spread of European diseases and the flight of the villages' inhabitants. This turn of events signaled the deterioration of the institution of forced mine labor itself and the declining ability of the state and its ethnic collaborators to mobilize mitayos. The Toledan scheme to rationalize extraction, even while preserving communal access to resources, had set migratory streams in motion all across the Peruvian landscape.

Effects of Andean Flight

Flight and migration were more radical strategies of resistance than market participation. Although the latter entailed European means,

3 Manuel A. Fuentes, ed., *Memorias de los virreyes que han gobernado el Perú durante el tiempo del colonaje español*, 4 vols. (Lima: Felipe Bailly, 1859), 3: 175; Cole, "Abolitionism," 310-311; and Nicolás Sánchez-Albornoz, *Indios y tributos en el Alto Perú* (Lima: Instituto de Estudios Peruanos, 1978), 71.

4 Saignes, "Ayllus." Sánchez-Albornoz (*Indios y tributos*, 108) notes the irony of the fact that so many Indians migrated to Potosí to work in the mines as mingas, in order to earn enough money to buy their exemption from the mita.

5 Nicolás Sánchez-Albornoz, "Mita, migración, y pueblos: Variaciones en el espacio y en el tiempo—Alto Perú, 1573-1692," *Historia boliviana* no. 3 (1983): 40.

6 "Sobre la mita de Potosí y reducción del reino: Los padres de la Compañía del Colegio de Potosí," March 31, 1610, in Vargas Ugarte, ed., *Pareceres jurídicos*, 116-131; also cited and summarized in Zavala, *Servicio personal*, 2: 45-48.

the end result was not necessarily adverse to indigenous norms. After all, the peasant family that engaged in long-distance trade and paid its commutation fees was essentially buying back its right to continue to participate in the labor and ceremonial life of its kin group and community. It represented one less family that the silver mines would claim. But the residents who fled were not only abandoning their ancient lands and huacas, relinquishing their kinship ties, and forsaking their complex of rights and responsibilities to the group; they were also throwing the burden of their mita turn onto the rest of the community. It was the entire community, and ultimately the cacique, which carried responsibility for the mita. Cash payments might make up for shortfalls for a season or two, but an increase in the rezagos also meant greater pressures on caciques and kin groups to find the money, or else to recover their human resources. Thus, in the wake of the Andean "economic refugees" there followed a dogged group of caciques, hilacatas, collectors (*cobradores*), and sometimes Spanish judges. They pursued the migrants across provincial boundaries, into distant lands, cities, and mining camps, in hopes of redeeming the debts owed to the community and the state. Even in the late seventeenth century, caciques were still tracking down errant kinsmen to demand their outstanding dues.[7] But they often ran up against the resistance of host Indian communities, local corregidores, or hacendados willing to shield their workers from the claims arising out of previous affiliations.

The flight of Andeans, however, did not always lead to alienation from their ayllus. The recent work of Saignes cautions us against oversimplified views of the migrants who appeared on tribute registries as "foreigners" (*forasteros*), "tenants" (*agregados*), or yanaconas.[8] Many forasteros—migrants to Indian communities or Spanish estates, mining towns, or cities who had neither rights to land nor obligations to the colonial state—maintained the kinship links and the rights and responsibilities they had had in the villages from which they had come. They could reaffirm their relationship and loyalty to their distant kin group by paying tribute dues or in symbolic ways that were not recorded and so are not easily traced today. Indeed, the very question of ethnic identity was an elusive one that defied the colonial schemes of categorization. Astute colonial au-

---

7 Ibid., 37, and Sánchez-Albornoz, *Indios y tributos*, 92ff.

8 Saignes, "Ayllus" "Políticas étnicas," and "De la filiation à la résidence." See also the recent work of Ann Zulawski, "Labor and Migration in Seventeenth-Century Alto Perú" (Ph.D. diss., Columbia University, 1985).

thorities like Polo de Ondegardo had distinguished between llactas runas—temporary migrants, who retained strong links to their original ayllu (see chapter 1)—on the one hand, and forasteros or *yana-conas del rey*—"rootless Indians," who had ruptured all ties to their ethnic group—on the other.[9] But by the middle of the seventeenth century, such nuances were a fiscal nuisance. Authorities wanted to be able to classify every Andean in a clear-cut category for purposes of more orderly taxation.[10] The migrants themselves by then had less ability to maintain ethnic associations over politically divided distances. Nevertheless, some forasteros still hoped to return home and reintegrate themselves into their kin groups. Illustrative is the case of Diego Paredes, a forastero in the village of Tiquipaya, whose grandfather had come from the town of Arapa, in the province of Azangaro, in the late sixteenth century. In the 1650s, Paredes found himself designated a forastero and working on a chácara "as if he were a yanacona." Through the royal protector of Indians, Paredes petitioned for the right to return to his original village "to pay tax and serve the mita," and his petition was granted in January 1658.[11] Forastero in the fiscal records, yanacona in his host community, Paredes managed, in effect, to establish a "subjective status" as a llacta runa.

The very fact that Diego Paredes had to petition for permission to leave his adopted community suggests that migratory and settlement patterns were less fluid than before. For if once it was difficult for migrants to break social and ideological ties to their original community, it was now increasingly hard to remain socially isolated in the new one. A host of new obligations and subsistence needs bound the migrants to their host communities. Departure remained an option for forasteros and yanaconas, but there were obstacles, especially as the native population continued to decline and competition for labor sharpened in the seventeenth century. Furthermore, the fiscal system hardened, making forasteros increasingly liable for tribute, at least in theory. If they were to escape paying double taxes, the migrants had to sever ties to their original ayllus and forsake their rights to communal resources. The Toledan system of colonial ex-

9 Polo de Ondegardo, "Relación de los fundamentos," 158, cited and discussed in Nicolás Sánchez-Albornoz, "Migracion rural en los Andes: Sipesipe (Cochabamba), 1645," *Revista de historia económica* 1 (1983): 31.

10 Sánchez-Albornoz, "Mita," and Sánchez-Albornoz, *Indios y tributos*, chap. 2.

11 "Petición del Diego Paredes, indio de Tiquipaya, 1594-1659," AHMC, Leg. 1046 (uncatalogued and erroneously dated 1804).

ploitation militated against the flight of Andean peasants, but once Indians had broken out of the cultural orbit of their ayllus, it was in the interest of the state to reroot them in their host communities or on haciendas, in order to register them as forasteros (and potential tributaries).

A detailed study of one pueblo real in Cochabamba affords a glimpse of the impact of Andean migrants. Sánchez-Albornoz has analyzed a census taken in 1645 of Sipesipe, which was situated at the western edge of the Valle Bajo, where the Incas' royal herds once grazed.[12] In the preceding fifty or sixty years, Sipesipe's population of tributaries—i.e., the total number of adult males—had shrunk from 815 to 160. The magnitude of its population loss was even greater if the numbers of mitayos and *ausentes* (those who had fled the community temporarily or permanently) are considered. Most of the mitayos came from two ayllus of Anansaya, and thus their loss was borne unevenly within the community. So, too, most of the 33 ausentes came from a small sector of the community: the plateros (originally from Ica on the Pacific coast), the ayllu Guaillanco of Anansaya, and the moiety Urinsaya.[13] On the other hand, like many other Andean villages in the fertile maize valleys of the kichwa zone, Sipesipe had absorbed a substantial migrant population, which mitigated the effects of its population loss. Sipesipe had 145 forasteros, a number not much smaller than that of its *originarios* (native tributaries). The total population of Sipesipe, including women and children, was 648 originarios and 551 forasteros. Birthrates were so low, however, that neither group physically reproduced itself. The stabilization of Sipesipe's population thus depended upon a steady in-migration of Andeans who chose to stay and assimilate themselves. The 1645 census showed that the forasteros had come from villages scattered across the Collao, to the west and north of Lake Titicaca; from the provinces of Sicasica, Pacajes, Omasuyos, and others near La Paz; and from southern Charcas. Most of them, however, had come from the nearby town of Toledo, in the province of Paria, which still had mitmaq clusters in certain localities in Cochabamba (including Capinota).[14]

Some of the migrants to Sipesipe may have maintained their ties of kinship to their native villages, but most seemed to be in the proc-

12 Sánchez-Albornoz, "Migración rural."

13 Ibid., 21.

14 Ibid., 19, 23, 25-27.

ess of assimilation. One indication is the extent to which they inter-married. At least 41 percent of the forastero population whose original communities were identified had married exogenously. Many of the men from the lake region had married women from villages in the Collao and apparently had migrated to the Cochabamba valley thereafter. But many other marriages coupled people from different regions; in almost one-third of the cases, they united forasteros with originarios of Sipesipe.[15] These marriage patterns intensified the ethnic amalgamation that had been going on since the creation of encomiendas from the vestiges of mitmaq and Incaic settlements. The continuing inflow of first-generation forasteros may have regenerated ethnic strains within the village, but the frequency of ethnic intermarriage suggests that most migrants adjusted to the new circumstances and attached themselves to their adopted village. Nevertheless, the permanent forastero population composed a stratum of peasants subordinate to the originarios. The migrants, composing almost half of Sipesipe's population in 1645, not only diluted the community's original ethnic mix but also created a cleavage in village society which deepened in the eighteenth century (see chapter 4).

Sipesipe was not unusual in the proportion of forasteros in its population. In the middle of the seventeenth century, contemporary authorities were beginning to suspect that migration was destroying the system that Toledo had established almost a century earlier. Indeed, a group of azogueros at Potosí issued a dire prediction that the silver industry would collapse if the mita were not revitalized.[16] To do so would mean that the colonial authorities would have to curb migration and population dispersion. In the early 1680s, the Duque de la Palata, the then viceroy of Peru, was ordered to undertake the first comprehensive census of Andean communities since the Toledan inspections, in preparation for a new labor repartimiento.[17] Furthermore, the ambitious viceroy launched a project to enumerate the Indian population in all eighty-three Peruvian corregimientos, not

15 Ibid., 28ff.

16 Jeffrey Cole, "Viceregal Persistence versus Indian Mobility: The Impact of the Duque de la Palata's Reform Program on Alto Perú, 1681-1692," *Latin American Research Review* 19 (1984): 40.

17 On Palata, see Fuentes, *Memorias de los virreyes*, 2: 244-264; Rubén Vargas Ugarte, *Historia del Perú*, 5 vols. (Lima: Librería Stadium–Imprenta López, 1956), 2: 389-394; Sánchez-Albornoz, *Indios y tributos*, chap. 3; Margaret Crahan, "The Administration of Don Melchor de Rocafull, Duque de la Palata, Viceroy of Peru, 1681-1689," *Américas* 27 (1971): 389-412.

simply in the southern *provincias obligadas*, and at the same time to have the corregidores (in collaboration with local priests and caciques) register the forasteros living outside their native domain. Palata's intentions were, among other things, to redistribute the burden of tribute and mita among the originario and forastero population, close the loopholes in the system, and extend the mita to formerly exempt corregimientos.[18]

The census project ran into formidable obstacles, and it took five years to complete. Ironically, it precipitated a new wave of migration among Andeans fearful of being subjected to tribute and the mita. The viceroy himself died before any of his reforms could be implemented. But the census did reveal the magnitude of population decline and dispersion that had taken place. It found, for example, that the Indian population had declined by almost 50 percent since 1573.[19] Ten corregimientos in central and southern Alto Perú had lost 57 percent of their originario population between 1573 and 1683; in Cochabamba, the originario population had declined by more than 75 percent. The overall number of tributaries had fallen from 34,621 to 14,858 during that period.[20] However, as in Sipesipe, the decline of originarios in Alto Perú was offset by the rise in the number of Andeans who had resettled in "foreign" places. The census counted 12,138 of these forasteros: adult male Indians and their families living apart from their kin units in the central and southern provinces of Alto Perú—45 percent of all tributaries.

The magnitude of *forasteraje* in the southern Andes was confirmed by another census in 1754. By then, forasteros composed more than half the tributary population in both the northern bishopric of La Paz and the southern bishopric of Chuquisaca (see table 4).[21] Within each area, the distribution of forasteros was extremely

18 Cole, "Viceregal Persistence," 41-42 and 44; Sánchez-Albornoz, "Mita." Palata initiated a number of other reforms, including a reduction in the ratio of work weeks to rest weeks for mitayos from 1:3 to 1:1 and a standardization of wages.

19 Cole, "Viceregal Persistence," 43, and Sánchez-Albornoz, *Indios y tributos*, 30.

20 Sánchez-Albornoz, *Indios y tributos*, 29-30.

21 This census was partially compiled from earlier estimates and is somewhat unreliable. See Sánchez-Albornoz, *Indios y tributos*, 52; Karen Spalding, "The Colonial Indian," *Latin American Research Review* 7 (1972): 71, n. 47; and Jürgen Golte, *Repartos y rebeliones: Túpac Amarú y la contradicciones del sistema colonial* (Lima: Instituto de Estudios Andinos, 1980), 47.

Table 4. Originario and Forastero Populations, by Bishopric, 1754

| Bishopric | Number of: | | Total | Percentage of Forasteros |
	Originarios	Forasteros		
Chuquisaca	11,589	15,359	26,948	57
Mizque	3,182	506	3,688	14
La Paz	10,550	13,644	24,194	56
Cuzco	20,711	12,053	32,764	37
Arequipa	3,083	667	3,750	18
Huamanga	8,587	1,933	10,520	18
Lima	17,720	5,371	23,091	23
Trujillo	12,788	5,387	18,175	30
Total	88,210	54,920	143,130	38

Source: Sánchez-Albornoz, *Indios y tributos*, 52.

uneven (see figure 5). On the puna, forasteros were clustered in the mining towns, particularly Potosí and Oruro. Even after a prolonged period of economic decline, these towns were still attracting migrants, vagabonds, seasonal workers (who often stayed on), and itinerant traders. Beyond them lay bleak lands where few forasteros settled. The villages scattered across the high steppes of Porco counted as migrants a little more than one-third of their Andean population; Chayanta's forasteros composed only 29 percent of the Indian population; and in Carangas, they constituted only 15 percent.[22] Highland forasteros were predominantly urban dwellers.

In the eastern kichwa tiers, rural forasteros were found in large numbers in Indian villages and on Spanish agricultural estates. They composed more than half the tributary population in the well-populated valleys and slopes along the eastern frontier, from the province of Larecaja in the north to Tarija and Chichas in the south. Some of these provinces were originally outside the boundaries of the provincias obligadas; from Toledan times, they had attracted economic refugees from the highlands. Other valleys, such as those in Chulumani and Cochabamba, drew migrants to commercial agrarian enterprises which offered shelter from tax burdens, at least until Viceroy Palata and his successors instituted "reforms." Migrants also gravi-

22 Golte, *Repartos y rebeliones*, 55. For a discussion of the regional distribution of forasteros throughout Peru, see ibid., 58 and 60. For an analysis of the relationship between the spatial distribution of forasteros and the patterns of social protest in 1780-1781, see Oscar Cornblit, "Society and Mass Rebellion in Eighteenth-Century Peru and Bolivia," in R. Carr, ed., *St. Antony's Papers*, no. 22 (Oxford: Oxford University Press, 1970), 9-44.

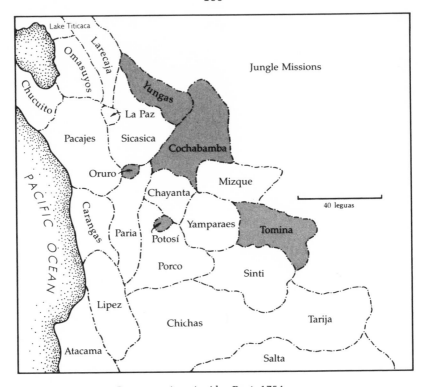

Figure 5   Forastero Concentrations in Alto Perú, 1754
Source: Adapted from Golte, *Repartos y rebeliones*, map 5.
Note: Shaded provinces are those in which 80 percent or more of the tributary
population was classified as forastero.

tated toward the villages that suffered sharp demographic declines.
The intensive maize agriculture in such valley communities as Sipesipe and Tiquipaya required (and could support) substantial numbers of settlers to replace their originarios who had fled and, even
more so, the victims of the epidemics in the second and third decades of the eighteenth century.

Of all the eastern provinces of Alto Perú, Cochabamba developed
the most extreme imbalance between native and forastero populations. Even by 1683, more than nine out of ten married male Indians
were listed as forasteros (table 5). The competition for Indian labor
between the Indian villages and the haciendas in the Toledan era had
been resolved in favor of the latter: more than two-thirds of the province's tributaries were living in Spanish towns or haciendas. Furthermore, within the Indian villages, forasteros outnumbered native in-

Table 5. Residence and Classification of Tributary Population of
Cochabamba, 1683 and 1786

Residence and Classification	1683		1786	
	Number	*Percentage*	*Number*	*Percentage*
Total tributary population	6,735	100	10,698	100
Spanish towns and haciendas	4,556	68	7,828	73
Pueblos reales	2,179	32	2,870	27
Originarios	411	6	433	4
Forasteros	1,768	26	2,437	23
All forasteros[a]	6,324	94	10,265	96

Sources: AGN, Sala 13, Padrones, 18.1.1, Leg. 41; 18.1.3, Leg. 43; 18.2.1, Leg. 46; 18.2.2, Leg. 47; and 18.2.3, Leg. 48.

[a] Forasteros in pueblos reales + all tributaries in towns and haciendas.

habitants by approximately four to one. One hundred years late, another census found still greater demographic imbalances in the region. Nearly three-quarters of the tributary population of the region resided in the Spanish towns and haciendas; and in the Indian villages, originarios were outnumbered by forasteros by almost six to one, and they constituted a mere 4 percent of the total tributary population.

These statistics demonstrate that, as colonial authorities had suspected, Cochabamba had become the preeminent province of forasteraje. Its Indian demographic profile was the result of the breakdown of the Toledan model of indirect rule. To a greater extent than in other provinces, rural migrants had been removed from the orbit of their communities. The pattern of ethnic identification in the region was decaying. Some valley Indians still maintained symbolic and material links to their original highland ayllus, but to an increasing degree they were differentiated according to their economic and social position in the local native hierarchy and by their fiscal status, rather than by their ancestral ethnic roots. Outside the peasant villages, sociocultural boundaries were even more blurred. As the forasteros assimilated themselves into the lower ranks of Spanish society, the sociocultural distance between "indio forastero" and "mestizo" (or "cholo") was diminished, and as reforms in the tribute and mita systems advanced, those boundaries were increasingly crossed. In the southern Andean world, then, Cochabamba was the most troublesome province for colonial authorities who were trying to resurrect the extractive institutions that had crumbled under the impact of Andean flight and resistance.

What Was To Be Done?

Almost from the outset, colonial authorities had tried to chart the crosscurrents of Andean migration. Particularly after the Toledan reforms impelled more of the native peoples to abandon their ayllus and communities, the motivations, destinations, and routes of Andean migrants occupied the thoughts and reports of Spanish officials. Viceroy Montesclaros, who in 1615 was the first to assess the magnitude of mita commutation and absenteeism, speculated about the movements of the cimarrones. He feared that many Indians vanished into the uncharted lands stretching into the jungle, where they were swallowed up by nature. Other migrants, he believed, melted into Spanish towns and mining camps, seeking work that conferred exemption from tribute and mita service. But the viceroy doubted that most Andeans, even those laboring in the mines, assimilated themselves successfully into the urban sector. Sooner or later, the migrants sought protection in rural settings: on the "estancias [ranches] and haciendas of Spaniards and rich Indians of other districts . . . where they eventually [acquire] the status of yanacona and free themselves of the mita." He estimated that, already in his day, about 25,000 yanaconas inhabited rural properties throughout Alto Perú.[23]

Later in the century, the Duque de la Palata, as part of his effort to revitalize the mita, identified three main destinations of the migrating Indians: Spanish cities and towns, the northern "free provinces" and eastern fringe areas outside the orbit of the mita, and Spanish and creole haciendas. He did not think that many Indians headed for Andean villages, except perhaps in the free provinces. Instead, they seemed to move into Spanish colonial society or into distant lands that had traditionally beckoned southern Andeans struggling to escape mita service and pursuing caciques. Palata focused especially on the Spanish hacendados who offered shelter to Indians from tribute and the mita. The hacendados were not the only ones to blame for the exodus of highland Andeans; like his contemporaries, Palata believed that the root of the forastero problem grew deep in the subsoil of village life, where Indians were abused by caciques, corregidores, and priests alike. But the problem of population dispersion, in the viceroy's view, was compounded by the greediness of hacendados who used property ownership to entice Indians into submission.

---

23 Zavala, *Servicio personal*, 2: 52, summarizing "Relación que el Marqués de Montesclaros, virrey del Perú, deja a su sucesor . . ."

Sometimes through false promises and coercive means, the hacendados captured a docile labor force and protected it behind barriers that even royal authority could not easily penetrate.[24]

Throughout the seventeenth century, the apologists for and beneficiaries of compulsory Andean labor at Potosí were haunted by the specter of powerful landlords draining highland Indian communities of potential mitayos. Times had changed since the halcyon days of Potosí's second silver boom, when the chacareros of Cochabamba had forged commercial alliances with merchants and mineowners at Potosí and all groups had capitalized on the export boom. As Andean migration and population decline grew worse over the course of the seventeenth century, particularly in its later decades, the azogueros of Potosí and the landlords of the eastern valleys increasingly looked upon each other as competitors for Indian labor. Their opposition intensified in the 1680s, as Palata moved to impose tribute on the forasteros. Hacendados throughout Alto Perú gave voice to their protests and discontent about the viceroy's reforms.[25]

A century had passed since Toledo had launched his agrarian policy in an effort to mediate the rivalry between Potosí's mineowners and the landlords of the eastern kichwa zone. But neither Toledo nor the Council of the Indies (with its ordinances of 1609) could prevent the redistribution of Indians between Indian communities and private agrarian estates. Nor were they able to establish parameters within which private enterprise might stabilize and thereby maintain the equilibrium achieved by the Toledan state between private and extractive modes of exploitation (see chapter 2). Nor was state power of any use in coping with high mortality rates among the subject population. The only viable political strategy, then, was to censure the perpetrators of abuse within the Indian community and to

24 Fuentes, *Memorias de los virreyes*, 2: 244ff.; Sánchez-Albornoz, *Indios y tributos*, 88-89; and Zavala, *Servicio personal*, 2: 186-187. Cf. the similar observations by a Lima oidor in 1644: "Some Indians . . . have fled to provinces so distant that they are never heard from again. They . . . are hidden and detained on the chácaras, ranches, [and] obrajes [textile workshops] . . . of owners, who are so powerful that neither corregidores nor mita captains can wrench [them] free" (quoted in Sánchez-Albornoz, *Indios y tributos*, 112, n. 37; my translation). On Andean migration to Spanish haciendas in the Cuzco region, see Magnus Mörner, *Perfil de la sociedad rural del Cuzco a fines de la colonia* (Lina: Universidad del Pacífico, 1978), 46-55. For a fascinating comparison with migration patterns and consequences among the Mayans, see Nancy Farriss, *Mayan Society under Colonial Rule* (Princeton: Princeton University Press, 1984), chap. 7.

25 Cole, "Viceregal Persistence," 48.

somehow contain the power of the labor-hungry hacendados. But how?

The most urgent issue in the seventeenth century was the deterioration of the mita. Long before Palata mounted his ambitious projects, Potosí's mining elite, audiencia magistrates, authorities in Spain and Peru, and clerics engaged in countless debates over how to ensure an abundant, cheap labor force for Potosí's silver mines. Various schemes were contrived to enhance the power of the state to recruit mitayos or to supplant the mita with the colonization of Potosí's hinterlands by Indians who would work "voluntarily" in the silver mines.[26] The most militant mineowners demanded no less than a second reducción, on the scale of the first (Toledan) reducción. They urged Viceroy Montesclaros to forcefully repopulate the official Indian villages with yanaconas and forasteros. Once the reservoir of compulsory laborers was restocked and mita obligations distributed more evenly, they argued, Indians would not have to be recruited so often nor driven so hard.[27]

However concerned Montesclaros was about the mita's decline, he was unwilling to mandate the resettlement of all forasteros inhabiting hacienda lands without taking into consideration the labor requirements of those agrarian enterprises. He intended to relocate only Indians on Spanish properties who were not performing "vital tasks" for the benefit of the kingdom. Like his predecessors, Montesclaros wanted to repopulate the Indian communities, but he refused to expel all recent migrants to the valleys. Instead, he proposed that barriers be erected to stop the flow of migrants between prov-

26 In 1610, the company of Jesuits at Potosí proposed a plan for colonizing the city's hinterlands with 25,000 Indians. They would be settled in the abandoned towns of Puna, Chaqui, and Yura, where they would engage in agriculture and also work for wages in the mines. The clerics believed that many Indians longed to escape the abuses they suffered in their own villages, and this scheme would both free them from the tyranny of their caciques and enable them to work in the mines without having to endure the hardships of the mita journey and the long absence from their villages, while at the same time providing a stable Indian labor force for the mines. Such a project would of course have required coordination and enforcement by the colonial state. It was never carried out. See Zavala, *Servicio personal*, 2: 45ff. The debates and regulations concerning mine labor run through all three volumes of that work. See also Arzáns y Orsúa y Vela, *Historia de la villa imperial*, and Cole, *Potosí Mita*.

27 "Parecer en materia de si conviene que los indios de la mita . . . asistan en ella y su comarca, o vengan de sus tierras como se ha fecho [sic] hasta aquí" (Apr. 1, 1610), report of a special commission of oidores of La Plata, cited and summarized in Zavala, *Servicio personal*, 2: 48-50.

inces. The obligated provinces would become quasi principalities, cordoned off from one another by border guards, sentinels, and toll gates. Corregidores would monitor the movement of Indians and expel vagabonds and migrants caught inside their territorial jurisdiction.[28]

This policy had a European derivation in medieval statutes banning overland travel and enforcing compulsory residence. Indeed, a few decades earlier, the English parliament under the Tudors had issued a series of ordinances forbidding vagrancy and vagabondage, a problem that had mushroomed out of control under the impact of the enclosure movement. But however difficult it may have been to enforce in the gently rolling English countryside, a statute limiting geographic mobility in the mountainous interior of Peru was pure folly. Even had the state equipped itself with militia, guards, and spiked gates at every crossroad, Andeans had countless ways of eluding the authorities in the rugged landscape that they knew so well.

As the quality of ore continued to deteriorate in the 1620s and 1630s, Potosí's mineowners demanded more action from the colonial state. Once again, they called for a second reducción. In 1634, the outspoken *procurador* (attorney) of Potosí, Sebastián de Sandoval y Guzmán, urged the crown to sacrifice the interests of the landowners for the benefit of silver mining and the entire kingdom. His tactical approach to the agrarian question was rather unique. He acknowledged the risks in and obstacles to a second reducción, and he admitted that it would provoke the wrath of chacareros and ranchers who saw their workers rounded up by colonial authorities and driven off to their original communities. Spaniards might even refuse to obey the royal orders. Some opponents of the plan had argued, too, that such a drastic measure might impoverish the Andean kingdom in the long run, leaving fertile lands lying fallow and herds untended. But the procurador proceeded to refute the objections to his proposal. In particular, he dismissed the warning that a second reducción would doom commercial agriculture. Hacendados, he suggested, could purchase African slaves to replace the Indians they lost. If there was still a shortage of labor, village Indians might then be or-

---

28 For further discussion of Montesclaros's schemes and policies with respect to the mita, see Zavala, *Servicio personal*, 2: 51-53. A contemporary of Montesclaros proposed that the state go one step further and issue internal passports to itinerant Indians—anticipating a device of social control that was to become common in Africa under European rule in the late nineteenth century.

dered to serve periodically in an agricultural mita (reminiscent perhaps of the Incaic mit'a of Cochabamba).[29]

Sandoval y Guzmán went so far as to challenge the very legitimacy of land ownership by Spaniards. He questioned the rights of landowners to acquire, by the payment of fees (*composiciones*), titles to parcels of vacant land that had belonged to Indian communities at the time of the Toledan reducción. He was especially outraged by an ordinance issued in 1631 that had permitted a new wave of land acquisitions. Thus, ironically, his interest in rejuvenating the mita by recolonizing highland Indian villages led him to a defense of communal Indian landholding interests. He questioned the definition of "vacant land" and the propriety of a royal order alienating parcels of community land simply because they lay fallow. He urged the crown to annul the sale of all village land to Spanish hacendados, even if it meant paying them indemnity from the royal treasury or treasuries of the communities whose land had been taken. In short, the salvation of the mita and hence of the silver industry of Potosí required, in his view, a two-pronged attack on the private agrarian sector: the expulsion of recent Andean immigrants from the haciendas and the return of community lands acquired by composiciones. Such a proposal posed a formidable threat to the hacendados.

But while imperial interests obviously had a stake in silver mining, the colonial authorities were not mere creatures of the mining elite. Even Toledo, who used state power to force Andean communities to subsidize Potosí's industry, ultimately tried to arbitrate between the private agrarian sector and the institutions that served the interests of the miners (see chapter 2). Nor was the audiencia of La Plata entirely in favor of mining interests when they conflicted with those of valley landlords. In 1611, the audiencia issued a defense of chacareros, arguing that Indians fled to the eastern valleys to escape the unbearable conditions in the mines.[30] Furthermore, viceroys and jurists knew full well that the azogueros themselves often collected cash payments in lieu of mitayos and pocketed the income rather than earmarking it for the wages of mingas. Such arrangements contributed to the decline in mining production and therefore in royal

29 Sebastián de Sandoval y Guzmán, "Pretenciones de la villa imperial de Potosí," cited in Cole, "Viceregal Persistence," 51, and Zavala, *Servicio personal*, 2: 98-103.

30 Saignes, "Polítícas étnicas," 11. The following year, the audiencia warned that to eject migrants in a second reducción "would destroy the chácaras and evaporate food supplies." Ibid.

revenue.[31] Calls for a second reducción, then, were met with skepticism and reluctance on the part of the viceregal authorities. Even in the 1650s, when the Council of the Indies did order a new repartimiento, its ambivalence toward the mining elite was reflected in its rejection of requests to reduce the price of mercury and the royal share of silver.[32]

The larger problem, however, was structural: even if the colonial state had thrown its full support behind the mining sector, its capacity to rebuild the earlier model of exploitation had been greatly reduced. Historians have written extensively about the colonial bureaucracy that had grown increasingly slack, ineffectual, and distant from imperial and even viceregal centers of power.[33] Steps by the Hapsburg rulers after 1678 to commercialize key colonial offices, such as systematically auctioning the post of corregidor, further removed power from viceregal authority. The post of corregidor was the highest provincial office in the viceroyalty, but it was subordinate to the viceregal and audiencia authority. However, the commodification of the post gave rise to a group of provincial bureaucrats whose authority and conduct were virtually unchecked. The diffusion of power among provincial authorities undercut the ability of the viceroy to intervene in local affairs or to mediate between conflicting interest groups. In comparison to Toledan times, the higher echelons of authority in Peru in the late seventeenth century seemed to be going into political retreat. The problem of the Hapsburgs' political lethargy was compounded, in the Andean area, by the geopolitical remoteness of Alto Perú.

The azogueros of Potosí could no longer count on an interventionist state to shore up the Toledan system. In 1670, Viceroy Conde de Lemos proposed that the mita be abolished. The proposal aroused

31 "Varios apuntes sobre asignación de indios . . . ," ANB, Minas, no. 1898 (Manuscritos Rück 575, Tomo 14), f. 67; Cole, "Abolitionism," 332.

32 Cole, "Abolitionism," 313-315.

33 See, for example, John Lynch, *Spain under the Hapsburgs: Spain and America, 1598-1700*, 2 vols. (New York: Oxford University Press, 1969), vol. 2; John Parry, *The Sale of Public Office in the Spanish Indies under the Hapsburgs* (Berkeley and Los Angeles: University of California Press, 1953); John L. Phelan, "Authority and Flexibility in the Spanish Imperial Bureaucracy," *Administrative Science Quarterly* 5 (1960): 47-65; John TePaske, "La crisis del siglo XVIII en el virreinato del Perú," in B. García Martínez, ed., *Historia y sociedad en el mundo de habla española* (Mexico City: Colegio de México, 1970), 263-280; and Guillermo Lohmann Villena, *El corregidor de Indios en el Perú bajo los Austrias* (Madrid: Ediciones Cultural Hispánica, 1957).

the azogueros' bitter opposition, and it was never put into effect.[34] Although Palata finally succeeded in matriculating forasteros, his plans to tax them and impose mita obligations came to naught. His successor, Viceroy Conde de la Monclova, rolled back the mita and tribute reforms, freeing the forasteros from tributary exactions for the time being. A more pointed example of the inconsistency of vice-regal policy could hardly be found. Where Palata was determined to take almost any step to introduce the mita into the northern and eastern fringe provinces, Monclova had little sympathy for the miners' dependence upon the state to force Andeans to work. Monclova never quite embraced abolitionism, but he managed to undo the work of his predecessor and to crush the hopes of Potosí's mineowners.[35]

Little wonder, then, that an azoguero living at the beginning of the eighteenth century might feel removed from and even disdainful of viceregal authority. Despite all the debate that had raged over the agrarian question, and despite all their demands for a new reducción, the mineowners never managed to wrest Andean migrants from the grip of the hacendados.

Toward the Subjection of the Forasteros

Between the decades of the 1680s and the 1730s, Potosí's mining industry experienced a deep recession, owing partly to the deteriorating quality of the ore and partly to the declining silver prices on the world market. Mineowners complained about the metals being extracted from the Cerro Rico: "Where before a load of metal weighing 50 quintales [hundredweights] yielded between 200 and 400 pesos corrientes, today [in 1734] it earns only 100 or 150 pesos, and it costs 100 pesos to extract, grind, refine, and cast that load of metal."[36] Moreover, the ore had to be mined from greater depths, with all the attendant problems of flooding, labor exhaustion, and cave-ins, and, to make matters worse, mercury shipments from Huancavelica were erratic. For a while, the crown diverted the flow of Spanish mercury from New Spain to Potosí. But as Potosí's industry deteriorated further, the crown cut off the supply of mercury from Spain, leaving Potosí's mills dependent upon Huancavelica's quicksilver.

34 See the detailed account in Cole, "Abolitionism."

35 Sánchez-Albornoz, *Indios y tributos*, chap. 3, and Cole, "Viceregal Persistence," 48-50.

36 Quoted in Zavala, *Servicio personal*, 3: 34.

Potosí's troubles translated directly into dwindling royal income. From a peak of 27,184,785 pesos during the first decade of the seventeenth century, net income from Potosí declined steadily and reached a low of 10,543,949 pesos in the last decade.[37] Taxes collected at Potosí were sent to Lima, where a portion was set aside to cover colonial government costs; the rest was sent on to Spain. Between 1651 and 1700, Potosí transferred 170,000,000 pesos to Lima. But the magnitude of the transfer was declining, gradually at first and then sharply. By 1770, the flow of surplus revenue had dried up altogether.[38] And as Lima's income dropped, so too did Spain's. During the second half of the seventeenth century, Peru sent 16,000,000 pesos to Seville, less than one-quarter of what it had remitted to Spain in the preceding half-century. That decline did not reflect simply the collapse at Potosí. A larger share of revenue was being kept in the colony to cover the growing cost of the bureaucracy and, especially, of military defense.[39] In addition, the *peruleros* (contraband traders from São Paulo) and other contrabandists siphoned off silver through illegal channels of trade.

The fiscal and mining problems of the Andean kingdom occurred at a time when England's agriculture and industries (textiles, shipping, and coal), as well as its domestic market, were expanding rapidly. England had also emerged the stronger military and diplomatic power following the War of the Spanish Succession (1700-1713). British contraband in the Western Hemisphere was getting out of control just when the Bourbon dynasty ascended to the Spanish throne. The Bourbons eventually were to introduce various schemes, based upon mercantilist thinking, to close the gap between the thriving economies of northern Europe and those of Spain's more backward regions (see chapter 8). But in the early eighteenth century, they still pinned their hopes on mineral exports and the flow of bullion from the New World. Furthermore, tribute revenues and income from the sale of offices were also deemed crucial. The crown's wish was to continue selling corregimientos, while still entrusting the corregidores with the task of raising more tribute monies for the royal treasury. How-

37 TePaske, "Fiscal Structure," 86, and Bakewell, "Registered Silver Production."

38 TePaske, "Fiscal Structure," esp. 77.

39 Lynch, *Spain under the Hapsburgs*, 2: 219-224; Herbert Klein and John J. TePaske, "The Seventeenth-Century Crisis in the Spanish Empire: Myth or Reality?" *Past and Present*, no. 90 (1981): 116-135; Javier Tord Nicolini, "Sociedad colonial y fiscalidad," *Apuntes* 4 (1977): 3-28.

ever preposterous that proposition might have seemed, it meant that officials in the Peruvian viceroyalty had to grapple once more with the vexing problem of the forasteros and, ultimately, with the agrarian question.

Viceroys and other royal authorities trying to generate more tribute income in Peru at that time faced formidable odds. Since Palata's day, the rural Andean world had undergone wrenching change. In the midst of the mining depression, epidemics of bubonic plague, influenza, and measles ravaged the land in 1719 and 1720, and again in the early 1730s. The indigenous population, which had been slowly declining during the seventeenth century, dropped precipitously in the early decades of the eighteenth, reducing Peru's Andean population to a quarter of its size at the time of the European intrusion.[40] The demographic curve turned gently upward in about 1740, but during the preceding decades, the human landscape was marred by epidemic, economic paralysis, and peasant penury.[41]

It was precisely the conjuncture of demographic disaster and mining recession that prompted Viceroy Marqués de Castelfuerte, who ruled from 1724 until 1736, to organize a new census count and an inspection of all the provinces. The rationale for the census count was to readjust tribute quotas in the wake of the epidemics, which would presumably be to the advantage of the tributaries. But Castelfuerte had another, more ominous motive. He believed many villages were "taking advantage" of the recent calamities to reduce their tax payments. His inspectors were therefore ordered to determine the true magnitude of population decline. Furthermore, they were to expose any corregidores, curates, and caciques who were pocketing tribute monies. Although Castelfuerte believed tribute embezzlement to be widespread, he wanted particularly to inspect those provinces where population decline seemed most dramatic and where he believed political malfeasance to be most blatant.

By these criteria, the province of Cochabamba provoked the viceroy's interest. Castelfuerte suspected foul play among the provincial authorities. He stated flatly that "the cause of the unfortunate decline [of tribute revenues] is embezzlement. Local authorities use the pretext of epidemic to hide Indians and exploit them in their own

40 Sánchez-Albornoz, *Indios y tributos,* 34; Noble David Cook, "La población indígena en el Perú colonial," *Anuario de Instituto de Investigaciones Históricas,* no. 8 (1965): 73-105.

41 A vivid description of social conditions in those years is found in a 1724 report by P. Manuel de Toledo y Leiva, rector of Jesuits in Huancavelica, in Vargas Ugarte, ed., *Pareceres jurídicos,* 168-183.

obrajes [textile workshops] and on their ranches and haciendas."[42] Behind the accusation lay a deep-seated distrust of private agrarian interests (which were beginning to emerge even within the matrix of village society). Once more, Cochabamba appeared as a region of recalcitrant landowners conniving to defraud the state of its tribute. Castelfuerte believed not only that tributaries were undercounted, but also that many Indians in the province were "passing" as mestizos—i.e., as people with one European parent, who were officially exempted from paying tribute. In his view, most people of mixed ancestry should be paying tribute, and he referred to them generically as *cholos*, who, as people with one European grandparent, were *not* exempted from paying tribute. Indeed, he protested that if cholos were exempt, Cochabamba "would be without tributaries."[43]

The viceroy's observations about the cholos reveal the ambiguity of sociocultural statuses in the eastern valleys and the extent to which the caste system had eroded. It suited the viceroy's purposes, of course, to attribute the apparent rapid growth of Cochabamba's mestizo population to the efforts of Andean peoples to evade royal tribute collectors. Castelfuerte believed that the "alleged mestizos" of Cochabamba were simply Indians and cholos who had exchanged their indigenous cultural garb for western clothing and identity. To his mind, the most permeable fiscal and racial boundary was that which separated cholos from mestizos. How could passage across this boundary be prevented in a region where ethnic and racial differentiation had long been blurred?

The extent to which *mestizaje* in Cochabamba was a phenomenon of transcultural movement is still a matter of conjecture. Future work with local parish records may reveal, for example, the magnitude of ethnic intermarriage in the region in the early eighteenth century. Meanwhile, there is only impressionistic evidence. We know that formal and informal unions had been taking place between Europeans and Andeans since early colonial times, and this has sometimes been given as the explanation for the size of the mestizo populations.[44] However, it is surely no accident that the region's

42 "Castelfuerte sobre la revisita a Cochabamba" (1731), AGI, Charcas, Leg. 343. On similar accusations levied against other corregidores in Alto Perú, see Arzáns de Orsúa y Vela, *Historia de la villa imperial*, 3: 192, 227-228, 260-261, and 271-272.

43 Castelfuerte to the crown, Apr. 29, 1731, AGI, Charcas, Leg. 343.

44 See, e.g., Humberto Guzmán Arze, *La realidad social de Cochabamba* (Cochabamba: Amigos del Libro, 1972), 36-37, and Guzmán, *Cochabamba*.

mestizo population seemed to increase most at those times when the colonial authorities were making renewed efforts to collect tribute from forasteros.[45] Beginning with Palata's regime and periodically thereafter, the status of forastero would lose its favorable position, and the only way its occupants could avoid tribute obligations was to slip into the category of mestizo.

The relative ease of passing as mestizo cautions against employing this term to define a social group, whether in terms of a common racial identity or a shared function, role, or position in the class structure. Like "forastero" and (to a certain degree) "originario," "mestizo" was fundamentally a fiscal category: one that defined an interstitial group that was different from "Indian" (the latter including "cholo") and that was therefore exempted from the rights and obligations assigned to Indians by the colonial state. The ambiguous and arbitrary status of mestizo in Cochabamba was reflected in later documents in which colonial authorities tried to describe or define exactly who was a mestizo. In the first regional census (1788) in which mestizos were separately counted, they were found to be 31 percent of Cochabamba's population (see table 13). The intendant Francisco de Viedma, under whose administration the census was conducted, listed the typical occupations of Cochabamba's mestizos: artisans, weavers of *tocuyos* (rough, unbleached cotton cloth), petty traders, and poor laborers in the central valleys. Other contemporary observers said that mestizos were also peasants who "leased land from the propertied and offered their labor in return."[46] Trial records from the same period show mestizos who were tenants (*arrenderos*) joining with Indian tenants, their neighbors, to denounce the abuses of a tyrannical landlord.[47] Tribute collectors even had difficulty separating mestizos from forastero tributaries. As one mestizo peasant so poignantly put it, "We [arrenderos] all live under the same wretched conditions."[48]

Whatever the problems of determining status, Castelfuerte was determined to systematize the collection of tribute. Specifically, he wanted to finally carry out Palata's plan to subject the forasteros

45 Sánchez-Albornoz, *Indios y tributos*, 169.

46 "Don Francisco de Hervoso y Figueroa, Obispo de Santa Cruz, sobre piezas sueltas de Santa Cruz" (1790), AGI, Charcas, Leg. 410, f. 8v.

47 "Exp. del yndígena Esteban Pablo contra su patrón Manuel Almarás en la hacienda Caporaya" (1795), AHMC, Leg. 1273.

48 "Real provisión sobre no ser yanaconas los indios de hacienda de Carasa" (1747), ANB, EC no. 6396.

to the payment of tribute. He also added a provision for the redistribution of some communal land to forasteros, creating thereby the new fiscal category of *forastero con tierra* (forastero with land), which carried with it an obligation to serve in the mita, as well as to pay tribute. According to Sánchez-Albornoz, this step was effective in bringing most forasteros into the tribute system.[49] Thus, the decade of the 1730s marked the end of the tax-exempt category of landless Indians. The new tax structure officially closed the agrarian loophole through which so many Andean migrants had sought relief from the pressures of village life. However, Castelfuerte's reforms were not enforced for another half-century, until after the Indian rebellions of 1781 and the reorganization of the colonial bureaucracy (see chapter 8).

Castelfuerte's reforms still required resolution of the question of the definition of the tribute-exempt category of mestizo. Again, the ambiguity rested with the cholos—those who could claim only one-quarter European ancestry. Castelfuerte's agents and inspectors were ordered not to give people of mixed ancestries the benefit of any doubt: if mestizo status could not be positively proven by parish records or by other means, the individual in question was to be assigned the status of forastero. In his single-minded pursuit of increased revenues, the viceroy was determined to unmask the "alleged mestizos" of Cochabamba and make that province an example of the new, stringent state policy toward tribute evaders.

To execute his reforms, Castelfuerte commissioned a royal inspection of the Cochabamba province. The visitador, Manuel Venero de Vera, arrived in Challacollo, on the western highland boundary of the province, in November 1730. His mandate was to expose tax frauds, particularly the underregistration of tributaries and the embezzlement of tribute monies. Many peasants feared that the inspector would register and assess them as forasteros unless they produced clear proof of mixed ancestry. Almost as soon as Venero de Vera registered new tributaries in the pueblos of Challacolla and Sicaya, rumors raced through the region to the effect that the inspector had "reduced" many mestizos to forasteros. Downriver from the towns under inspection, an angry crowd gathered in the central plaza of Capinota, one of the region's pueblos reales. Many of the protesters were mestizos, but they were joined by Andeans and by a few

49 Sánchez-Albornoz, *Indios y tributos*, 166, and Sánchez-Albornoz, *Population of Latin America*, 93.

Spanish patrons. The crowd soon turned into a violent mob that rampaged through the village and surrounding areas.[50]

Perhaps the crowd might have been contained had the royal inspector restricted himself to identifying the embezzlers of tribute funds and bringing order to the process of collection, and had he acted more prudently in the registration of forasteros. But Venero went in aggressive pursuit of people on the margins of the quasiracial categories. The situation was exacerbated by rumors that the corregidor was bribing Venero's aides and assistants so that they would overlook irregularities in the tribute registries. Thus, the tributaries would have to pay their dues, while the corrupt officials would go unpunished. Nor did the inspector improve his standing with the local population when he ordered the militia to crush the rebellion at Capinota. Venero's intransigence and blunders turned a local crowd action into a regional tax rebellion.

As the month of November drew to a close in 1730, crowds of peasants, artisans, and laborers collected in the towns of Quillacollo and Cochabamba. The few sympathetic creoles who had stood with the protesters earlier that month now withheld their support because of their fear of what might happen. The picture sketched in official reports of what did happen is indeed an ugly one of mob action, in which two hundred insurgents killed the alcalde (mayor) of Cochabamba and fifteen vecinos and then pillaged the towns, stealing and committing "unspeakable atrocities." Although the viceroy and the king admitted that the inept inspector had made mistakes, they characterized the uprisings as race wars between the cholos and mestizos and the white vecinos, who had always lived in fear of mestizo violence and hatred.[51] The mestizo rebel leader, Alejo Calatayud, had tried to legitimate his actions by claiming loyalty to the king and calling for "death to bad government" (a slogan that would echo throughout the southern Andes almost fifty years later). He and his comrades paid with their lives: they were strangled in the central

50 Most of the official documents pertaining to the 1730 tax rebellion in Cochabamba are in the AGI, Charcas, Leg. 343 and 344. For a detailed study of the rebellion, based primarily upon this documentation, see Patricia C. Hutchins, "Rebellion and the Census of Cochabamba, 1730-1732" (Ph.D. diss., Ohio State University, 1974).

51 "Real cédula a la audiencia de La Plata sobre la sublevación de mestizos de Cochabamba con motivo del empadronamiento de los indios," (1732), RAH, ML 9/1758, tomo 103. See also Scarlett O'Phelan Godoy, *Rebellion and Revolts in Eighteenth-Century Peru and Upper Peru* (Cologne: Bohlau, 1985), 74-80.

plaza and their dismembered bodies were strewn along the road as a gruesome warning to the restless plebe.

Yet the colonial authorities did not really believe that this barbaric punishment would serve to "discipline the masses." The viceroy recalled Venero and suspended the census count. He sent another inspector to the province a year later, but the registration of "alleged mestizos" as forasteros was ended. Instead, the tribute dues of forasteros were fixed at six pesos two reales—one of the highest forastero tribute rates in Alto Perú.[52] But from 1731 on, the authorities regarded the "mestizo province" of Cochabamba as a land of restless, refractory people who might turn seditious at any moment. Even the hacendados who had once willingly sheltered Andean migrants from tribute obligations and helped them pass into the ranks of cholos and mestizos, now watched warily over this "dangerous class." Cochabamba's peasantry and artisans had vividly demonstrated the limits of state power.

New Conditions and New Conflicts

In about 1740, a confluence of economic and demographic trends pushed the viceroyalty out of recession, and over the next sixty years, the Andean colonial economy experienced an uneven recovery. The Andean population also began to grow. Kubler's study of tribute records had indicated a vigorous rate of growth, but more recent studies have cast doubt on the reliability of his sources, and the weight of the evidence now is that there was a modest expansion of the Andean population during the second half of the eighteenth century, with considerable regional variation. As we shall see later, Potosí's population did not share in this growth.[53]

52 The total amounts of tribute owed by a community were adjusted from time to time in accordance with changes in the number of adult males. One such change took place in 1738, under Viceroy Villa García: AGN, Sala 13, 18.2.1 (1785).

53 George Kubler, *The Indian Caste of Peru, 1795-1940: A Population Study Based upon Tax Records and Census Reports* (Washington, D.C.: Smithsonian Institution, 1952); Sánchez-Albornoz, *Population of Latin America*, 110-111, and Sánchez-Albornoz, *Indios y tributos*, 34; Herbert Klein, "Peasant Response to the Market and the Land Question in the 18th and 19th Centuries," *Nova Americana*, no. 5 (1982): 103-134; Mörner, *Perfil de la sociedad rural*, chap. 1. For Cochabamba, see tables A-2 and A-3. On Potosí, see María del Pilar Chao, "La población de Potosí en 1779," *Anuario del Instituto de Investigaciones Históricas*, no. 8 (1965): 171-180.

This period was also marked by a gradual increase in agricultural production, particularly in subsistence crops. The analysis by Tandeter and Wachtel of tithes levied on grain grown on private lands (indigenous grains grown on communal lands were not subject to the tithe) in the archbishopric of Charcas shows that, after a sharp cyclical drop in the 1720s, there was a clear increase, beginning in the late 1730s and lasting until the early years of the nineteenth century, although it was not until after 1760 that agricultural production and tithe revenue reached the levels of the late seventeenth century (figure 6).[54] By the same token, however, the prices of agricultural products fell.[55] If Potosí's commodity market mirrored price trends in the

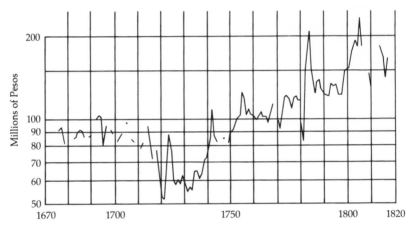

Figure 6   Value of Tithes in the Archbishopric of Charcas (La Plata), 1670-1820
Source: Enrique Tandeter and Nathan Wachtel, *Precios y producción agraria: Potosí y Charcas en el siglo XVIII* (Buenos Aires: Estudios CEDES, 1984), 72. Reproduced by permission.

54 This study—Enrique Tandeter and Nathan Wachtel, *Precios y producción agraria: Potosí y Charcas en el siglo XVIII* (Buenos Aires: Estudios CEDES, 1984)—is the first to chart prices for all of Alto Perú over the course of a century. However, several earlier studies examined agricultural production and price trends in different areas; see esp. Ruggiero Romano, "Movimiento de los precios y desarrollo económico: El caso de Sudamérica en el siglo XVIII," *Desarrollo económico* 1-2 (1963): 31-43; and Marcello Carmagnani, "La producción agropecuaria chilena: Aspectos cuantitativos (1680-1830)," *Cahiers des Amériques latines* no. 3 (1969): 3-21.

55 Romano, "Movimiento de los precios." Because of this price drop, which Tandeter and Wachtel confirmed in their work, tithes and agricultural output were inversely correlated. Thus, in order to infer the trend of agricultural production from tithe revenues, Tandeter and Wachtel charted the secular movement of tithes (*diezmos*) deflated by the annual index of agricultural prices as

rest of Alto Perú, then the general recovery and growth in agrarian production had a deflationary effect on prices, in contrast to the inflationary effect of Potosí's boom in early colonial days. This situation had great significance for the internal evolution of Cochabamba's agrarian class structure in the latter half of the eighteenth century (see chapter 5 and 6).

Beyond the fertile lands of Alto Perú, recovery was also manifest in the silver mines, both new and old. The expanding economies of Europe required increasing supplies of monetary metals to lubricate the trade with Asia, Africa, and the Americas. Repercussions were felt throughout Latin America, as prospectors staked out gold fields in Minas Gerais, struck rich silver deposits in Guanajuato, and revamped the interior works of older mines. As part of this change, the output of Potosí's mines, after many decades of decline, began to rise.[56] The growth in silver output was sustained, with some pauses and hesitations, until the Independence Wars broke out.

But the magnitude of the upturn in Potosí's production must have disappointed contemporaries who hoped for a bonanza on the scale and intensity of the second silver cycle of Toledo's day. The pace of expansion was much slower than it had been in the late sixteenth century (figure 7). Silver production doubled between 1740 and 1780, whereas during the peak decades of 1580 and 1590, it had more than trebled. In absolute terms as well, Potosí's recovery was only partial. Silver output rose only to the level achieved in the middle of the seventeenth century. During the decade of the 1790s, when the average annual output was higher than at any other time in the eighteenth century, the mint stamped three and one-half million pesos, far less than the seven million pesos minted by Potosí in a decade two hundred years earlier.[57] Thus, neither in scale of production of its mines nor in the size of its population did Potosí recover its former importance. Under the new stimulus of the world market,

---

well as by the index of moving averages of those prices, as registered in contemporary account books at Potosí. (However, the values shown in figure 6 are the actual, not the adjusted, values.) For a discussion of tithes as an indirect indicator of agricultural production in Cochabamba, see Brooke Larson, "Rural Rhythms of Class Conflict in Eighteenth-Century Cochabamba," *Hispanic American Historical Review* 60 (1980): 407-430.

56 Brading and Cross, "Colonial Silver Mining," 569; Enrique Tandeter, "La rente comme rapport de production et comme rapport de distribution: Le cas de l'industrie minière de Potosí, 1750-1826" (3rd Cycle Doctorate, Ecole des Hautes Etudes en Sciences Sociales, Paris, 1980), chap. 2.

57 Brading and Cross, "Colonial Silver Mining," 573 and 578.

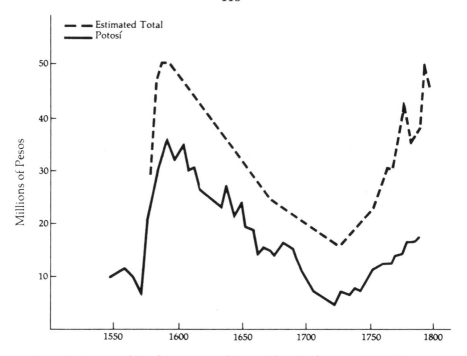

Figure 7   Estimated Total Peruvian and Potosí Silver Production, 1560-1800
Source: David Brading and Harry Cross, "Colonial Silver Mining: Mexico and
Peru," *Hispanic American Historical Review* 52(1972): 569; Reproduced by
permission.

mines were being opened everywhere. Where once the Cerro Rico
and surrounding mines of Porco (the province in which Potosí was
located) produced 70 percent of all Peruvian silver, in 1774 they
yielded only about 40 percent.[58] Furthermore, the crown seemed
rather indifferent to the fate of the Potosí mines. While it still
granted privileges to the azogueros and to the exploiters of the Potosí
mines in general, it increasingly pinned its hopes on the silver mines
of Mexico, which were proving to be far more competitive on the
world market.[59]

58 Major rivals were the new mines of Cerro de Pasco in Peru's central sierras.
See John Fisher, *Minas y mineros en el Peru, 1776-1824* (Lima: Instituto de Estudios Peruanos, 1977), 34ff.

59 Enrique Tandeter, "Forced and Free Labor in Late Colonial Potosí," *Past and
Present*, no. 93 (1981): 99-100; Arzáns de Orsúa y Vela, *Historia de la villa impe-
rial*, 3: 10ff. On Mexican silver mining in the eighteenth century, see David
Brading, *Miners and Merchants in Bourbon Mexico, 1763-1810* (Cambridge:
Cambridge University Press, 1971), 152.

In contrast to the Toledan era, no centralizing colonial state engineered Peru's economic growth in the mid-eighteenth century. Indeed, the resources and patrimony of the colonial state had diminished, as had its corresponding power to control a civil and religious clientele. Of course, the Bourbons continued to discuss plans to revamp the tribute system and enforce the institution of mita. But after the blunders of Castelfuerte, most viceroys gave up their grand designs for tribute reform and instituted, instead, piecemeal changes on the local level. Until the 1780s, the overall orientation of the state was a rentier one: it was content to sell offices to corregidores and allow power and perquisites to these provincial authorities in return for a steady, secure income. The crown's revenue from the sale of five-year terms of office increased, as corregidores themselves were able to realize a higher return on their investment in office. In the early 1750s, the crown further enhanced the value of corregimientos, and its own income, by granting corregidores the right to distribute a fixed volume of commodities to the Indians under their jurisdiction. This measure allowed the state to tax the value of the legal *repartimiento de mercancías*, giving the state yet another benefit from the system. But even before the crown institutionalized the repartimiento de mercancías, it had been inclined to tolerate the widespread practice among corregidores, for this nefarious activity provided the economic underpinnings of the commodification of the highest provincial post. There would be little incentive for a creole or peninsular to invest funds in the office if such lucrative activity were not available. Thus, the crown was inclined to turn its back on the shady dealings of the provincial officeholders, until measures of control became absolutely necessary.

The combination of decentralized rule and growing opportunity for mercantile gain created more room for extralegal enterprise as well. On paper, Spanish law continued to be, as Coatsworth has described it in Mexico, "full of restrictions, prohibitions and regulatory provisions governing labor relations, property rights, water allocation, permissible crops, minimum wages, tax obligations, and religious duties."[60] Nevertheless, in practice, the upper echelons of government in the Andes were remote and ineffectual. The locus of power was local or regional, and no "visible hand" of imperial power controlled the scope or direction of economic change. Private agrarian enterprises revived and flourished in the fertile valleys of coastal

60 John Coatsworth, "The Limits of State Absolutism: The State in Eighteenth-Century Mexico," in Spalding, ed., *Essays*, 35.

Peru, in the tropical eastern yungas, and in pockets along the southeastern frontier of Chuquisaca and Santa Cruz.[61] Obrajes, *chorrillos* (small, primitive textile workshops), and later tocuyo looms began to hum with activity, in spite of royal prohibitions and increased competition from European contrabandists. But more than the growth of small, productive enterprises across the Andes, this period of royal remoteness gave free rein to commercial ventures. Increasingly over the course of the eighteenth century, until the outbreak of rebellion in 1781, corregidores forged economic alliances with Lima's merchant elite and harnessed merchant capital to political power.

The interlocking interests of coastal merchants and corregidores were recognized by some contemporaries. In 1749, Jorge Juan and Antonio de Ulloa exposed the inner workings of the compulsory market, driven by the capital of merchants and the coercive tactics of corregidores.[62] Corregidores counted on Limeño merchants to contribute to the cost of office and to supply commodities. In return, the merchant-sponsor received a share of the profits.[63] This union of merchant capitalism and political force, which the crown legitimized in 1754, produced a vast compulsory market in commodities sold at artificially high prices to Andean peasants. Regional authori-

---

61 Historians are still charting the contours of commercial agriculture in eighteenth-century Peru and Alto Perú. Early studies tended to emphasize the stagnation of agriculture and trade; see, for example, Guillermo Céspedes del Castillo, "Lima y Buenos Aires: Repercusiones económicas y políticas de la creación del virreinato de La Plata," *Anuario de estudios americanos* 3 (1946): 667-874; and Oscar Febres Villarroel, "La crisis agrícola en el Perú en el último tercio del siglo XVIII," *Revista histórica* 27 (1964): 102-199. More recently, several historians have studied dynamic regional economies, where haciendas specialized in marketable crops for export to Potosí and other distant cities; see, for example, Nicolas Cushner, *Lords of the Land: Sugar, Wine, and Jesuit Estates of Coastal Peru (1600-1767)* (Albany: State University of New York Press, 1980). On the growth and labor needs of coca plantations in the yungas east of La Paz, see Herbert Klein, "Hacienda and Free Community in Eighteenth-Century Alto Perú," *Journal of Latin American Studies* 7 (1975): 193-220.

62 Jorge Juan y Santacilia and Antonio de Ulloa, *Noticias secretas de América* (Buenos Aires: Mar Océano, 1953). An English-language edition is available: *Discourse and Political Reflections on the Kingdoms of Peru*, ed. and trans. John J. TePaske and Besse A. Clement (Norman: University of Oklahoma Press, 1978).

63 Ibid. See also A. Moreno Cebrián, *El corregidor de indios y la economía peruana en el siglo XVIII* (Madrid: Instituto Gonzalo Fernández de Oviedo, 1977); Javier Tord Nicolini, "El corregidor de indios del Perú: Comercio y tributos," *Historia y cultura* (Lima), no. 8 (1974): 173-214.

ties and their agents forced Andean villagers to "accept" mules imported from the ranches of Tucumán, bales of cloth imported from Quito, baskets of yungas coca, brandy processed in coastal vineyards, and European textiles and trinkets. The pressure to pay off debts and to capitalize on political officeholding within a five-year period impelled the corregidores to use political means for mercantile ends. Their entrepreneurial behavior led to a diffusion of the marketplace from its loci in cities, towns, ports, mining camps, and transit crossroads to peasant villages in remote areas. The marketplace came, unbidden, to the Andean community. In the process, the merchant houses of Lima discovered an inland market so vast and lucrative as to help compensate for the end of their monopoly over transatlantic trade.[64]

Potosí's recovery in the middle decades of the eighteenth century mirrored the spontaneous development of informal enterprises that undermined the monopolistic control of azogueros. In production and commerce, small-scale, informal enterprises mushroomed in the mining towns, as mineworkers, too, took advantage of the rising demand for silver. Unlike the highly capitalized mercantile enterprises of the corregidores and their merchant collaborators, the mineworkers' production of silver was atomized among many small, illicit operations. In the eyes of Potosí's mining elite, the economic recovery was a mixed blessing, because it stimulated "internal competition" from an aggressive group of free mineworkers (mingas) who scavenged discarded ore from the slag heaps and, as before, stole chunks of ore from the interior veins.[65] The threat lay not only in their numbers, but in the degree to which they were able to exert control over both mineral extraction and refining.

The *kajchas* or "silver thieves" of Potosí organized themselves into work gangs led by skilled pickmen.[66] During the thirty-six hours

64 Spalding, *Huarochirí*, 202-203.

65 Enrique Tandeter, "La producción como actividad popular: 'Ladrones de minas' en Potosí," *Nova Americana* no. 4 (1981): 43-65; Tandeter, "Rente comme rapport de production," chap. 3, esp. 188-212. (All citations to chap. 3 of this work refer to a Spanish version, entitled "Mita, minga, y kajcha," kindly provided by the author.)

66 On the basis of contemporary estimates, Tandeter ("Mita, minga, y kajcha," 134) suggests that the number of kajchas fluctuated between about 2,000 and 4,000 between 1759 and 1782, the number being higher at the beginning of that period than at the end. On the problem of their control of the industry, see "Relación que hace don Manuel Amat . . .," cited and summarized in Zavala, *Servicio personal*, 3: 64; and Tandeter, "Producción como actividad popular."

or so on Saturday and Sunday when mining operations were required to cease, the kajchas entered the mines to recover chunks of ore they had concealed during the preceding week of legal labor or to cut and smuggle out fresh ore. The ore was brought to small-scale refiners, *trapicheros*, who processed it in mule-driven mills, more primitive affairs than the great water-powered mills of the azogueros. The refined silver was sold to the Banco de Rescates, following its establishment in 1752. Thus, even though *kajcheo* was illegal, the royal bank received the stolen ore, which in the late 1750s probably represented about 30 percent of all silver traded at Potosí.[67] Indeed, despite warnings from Potosí's corregidor, who saw a danger in allowing gangs of mineworkers to flout the law, higher royal authorities implicitly tolerated the practice, presumably because of the additional silver that it brought into commerce.[68]

In spite of the increase in world silver prices, therefore, the mining elite of Potosí feared a deterioration in its economic position. The state was unable or unwilling to put an end to the kajchas' activities, nor would it put in place the machinery to draft more mitayos, in order to raise their number above the 2,919 who worked at Potosí in 1754.[69] The mining elite dealt with this situation in one of two ways: by leasing their operations to others, or by squeezing more surplus value out of the mitayos under their control.[70] The latter was accomplished by shifting from wage work to piecework and then increasing the piecework requirement. A mitayo in the 1750s was required to haul five "sets" (*pallas*), each set equivalent to fifteen loads, during a period of five days or nights of work. Ten years later, each set was made the equivalent of thirty loads.[71] The only way a mitayo could cope with this increased demand was to mobilize auxiliary workers, among his kin or as temporary wage laborers, to carry some of the load. In other words, the mineowners shifted a portion of labor costs to the mitayo himself. Further, mitayos gave up their authorized rest weeks to work almost continually through their year at Potosí. Finally, as their sixteenth-century forebears had done, the

67 Tandeter, "Mita, minga, y kajcha," 136, and Tandeter, "Producción como actividad popular," 51-52.

68 Tandeter, "Mita, minga, y kajcha," 137-139, and "Producción como actividad popular," 56-57.

69 Tandeter, "Forced and Free Labor," 103.

70 Tandeter, "Producción como actividad popular," 45.

71 Tandeter, "Mita, minga, y kajcha," 84, and Tandeter, "Forced and Free Labor," 107.

mitayos depended upon assistance from members of their own families and their native communities. The harsher work regime mandated some kind of collective strategy at Potosí, both in the fulfillment of work quotas and in the daily struggle for subsistence.

From the mineowners' point of view, the forced speed-up of silver production made the difference between the success or failure of their enterprises. In 1790, the mitayos' average weekly wage was two reales less than that of the mingas, yet they had to deliver one-third more ore than the free laborers.[72] With a static labor supply at Potosí and an old technology, there was no way to increase silver output except by altering relations of production and bearing down harder on some workers. Tandeter contends that it was "the manipulation of [the work] quota which enabled the mines of Potosí to double their production between the 1740s and the 1790s."[73] When the mita was abolished after independence, the increased labor costs involved in shifting entirely to free wageworkers swallowed up the margin of profit and rendered the mines noncompetitive. Thus, the mita made possible the survival of the industry, but for those who were caught in its claws, it was a brutal existence.

During these decades of "slow, painful growth" at Potosí,[74] the political economy of colonialism developed its own momentum and moved in directions that did not always serve royal interests. After the long period of royal retreat, the colonial state in the Andes no longer possessed the internal cohesion, political program, or bureaucratic apparatus to contain or channel the currents of socioeconomic change. In theory, the state was still a direct, autonomous claimant on the resources of Andean communities, but in reality, the corregidores manipulated tribute collection for their own private gain. Tribute embezzlement reached scandalous proportions in the 1750s.[75] In theory, again, the state continued to protect the corporate

72 Tandeter, "Forced and Free Labor," 134; Francisco de Paula Sanz to Antonio Valdés, June 30, 1790, cited and summarized in Zavala, *Servicio personal,* 3: 75-76. For a description (and denunciation) of the quota system by Cochabamba's intendant, see Viedma, *Descripción geográfica,* 179.

73 Tandeter, "Producción como actividad popular," 107.

74 Enrique Tandeter, "Rent As a Relation of Production and As a Relation of Distribution in Late Colonial Potosí" (paper presented at the Eighth National Meeting of the Latin American Studies Association, Pittsburgh, April 5-7, 1979), 10.

75 In one case in the mid-1750s, corregidores and caciques in the Cuzco area siphoned off more than 50 percent of tribute dues: Tord Nicolini, "Corregidor de indios del Perú," 199. For more general discussions of corregidores and corrup-

integrity of Indian villages, but in fact, the corregidores engaged with impunity in all kinds of extortionist practices. On paper, the state was also still committed to coordinating the flow of forced migrants to Potosí, yet the mita continued to wither, particularly as work conditions worsened at Potosí and as more and more corregidores impeded the movement of mitayos. In short, the political apparatus of Peru in the mid-eighteenth century was in shambles: it neither ensured the functioning of the extractive institutions (tribute and mita) nor did it protect the subsistence economies that underpinned those institutions. And finally, the state did not have the leverage or authority to arbitrate effectively among conflicting colonial interest groups.

In the southern Andes, the crisis of political authority was manifest in the open antagonism between Potosí's mining elite and the corregidores, who had come to wield considerable power over the Indians under their jurisdiction. Although the mining elite itself stood on shaky moral ground, its members protested against the abuses perpetrated by the corregidores on the Andean peasants. The corregidores, however, were emboldened by royal tolerance and, after 1754, by the crown's sanction of their coercive mercantile activities. Increasingly, the corregidores crossed the threshold of "tolerable" or "acceptable" levels of extortion and began to threaten the interests of the mineowners themselves. They underregistered or hid tributaries, thus removing them from the mita labor pool.[76] They converted village Indians to permanent laborers on their haciendas and in their textile workshops.[77] The behavior of the corregidores provoked new

tion in an earlier period, see Lohmann Villena, *Corregidor de indios,* and Sánchez-Albornoz, *Indios y tributos,* chap. 3, esp. 95-99 and app. 2.

76 In the 1740s, for example, the corregidor of Cochabamba was accused of hiding many Indians from the royal tax collectors and defrauding the crown: AGI, Charcas, Leg. 367 (1746). The royal authorities in Huancavelica heard complaints about corregidores whose commercial activities were interfering with the mita; see the 1748 report of the governor, cited and summarized in Zavala, *Servicio personal,* 3: 39. On the case of a corrupt corregidor of Porco who was impeding the flow of tribute and mitayos, see Arzáns de Orsúa y Vela, *Historia de la villa imperial,* 3: 192, 227-228, 260-261, 271-272. The most important chronicle of the tactics of the corregidores is still Juan y Santacilia and Ulloa, *Noticias secretas.* Clerics were not immune from similar accusations; the azogueros declared that they were exploiting Indians and obstructing the flow of mitayos: "Exp. relativo a la averiguación de las entradas y gastos q. tienen los curatos de la provincia de Cochabamba" (1760-1761), ANB, Mano de obra, no. 788.

77 See, for example, the report of Castelfuerte in AGI, Charcas, Leg. 343, April 21, 1731.

waves of Andean migration.[78] In the 1770s, Viceroy Manuel Amat warned that corregidores were overburdening Indians with unwanted merchandise and driving them to desert their villages (see below).

The crown's attitude toward this set of issues was ambivalent. On the one hand, the crown recognized that the actions of the corregidores were adverse to its fiscal interests. On the other hand, it needed the considerable revenue from the *alcabala*, the "sales tax" on the value of a legalized repartimiento de mercancías.[79] Furthermore, the crown was unwilling to abandon the internal colonial market to the free play of market forces. Contemporary observers, even ones as astute as Juan and Ulloa, believed that Indians were by nature indolent and that they needed "pressuring" if they were to purchase the kinds and amounts of goods that the corregidores distributed. The alternative would be economic atrophy and decline. Wrapped in this philosophical cloak, the crown stood behind the corregidores and in 1754, as already noted, granted them the right to distribute a stipulated volume of goods at fixed prices to the people of their district.[80] Thus, the ambivalence of the crown was resolved in favor of a mercantile-political alliance, at least for the time being.

78 The corregidor of Cochabamba was also accused of driving Indians out of their villages and causing an increase in the number of ausentes: AGI, Charcas, Leg. 367, 1746. In 1753, of the 130 mitayos that Cochabamba's villages were supposed to dispatch, only 59 actually set off for Potosí: ANB, Manuscritos Rück, no. 131, ff. 107-110. Migration and absenteeism were not the results only of the commercial practices of the corregidores or their oppression of local populations; the periodic epidemics were also a factor. So also was the old problem of the *indios rescatados*, who purchased exemption from the mita by paying fees of 80 or 100 pesos to their caciques. The caciques would then hire forasteros or their own servants to serve on the mita for a fraction of the exemption fee. However, the hired forasteros often fled, thus aggravating the problem of drafting mitayos: "Avios sobre . . . el mejor régimen, establecimiento, y gobierno de la real mita . . ." (1762), ANB, Minas, no. 789.

79 Even Viceroy Amat, who perceived the danger of unregulated corregidor activities, noted that the taxes on the repartimiento de mercancías benefited the crown, but he was under no illusion that the taxes set limits on the volume or value of forcibly distributed merchandise: Manuel de Amat y Juniente, *Memoria de gobierno*, ed. Vicente Rodríguez Casado and Florentino Pérez Embid (Seville: Escuela de Estudios Hispanoamericanos, 1947), 189. The magnitude of this source of royal revenue is worth noting. In 1751, when the tax rate was 4 percent, the total value of alcabalas on the repartimientos in the viceroyalty was 217,160 pesos: John Fisher, *Government and Society in Colonial Peru: The Intendant System, 1784-1814* (London: Athlone, 1970), 14-15.

80 On the legalization of the repartimiento de mercancías, see Golte, *Repartos y*

To the mining elite, the corregidor, always a political rival, now appeared as an economic rival as well, in the competition for scarce Indian labor. The problem was an old one: since the early seventeenth century, the mita had not functioned at full capacity (see chapter 2). Potosí's mineowners historically had issued reclamations, registered protests, and demanded action to shore up the Toledan system. But conditions had now changed, and new protagonists had emerged in the struggle over Andean peasant labor. The mineowners' traditional enemies, the hacendados of the eastern valleys, had faded from the arena. As the private agrarian sector became entrenched and the state showed itself incapable of constraining Andean migration toward the eastern valleys and towns, or unwilling to do so, the scope and terms of the conflict began to shift as well. By the mid-eighteenth century, the debate was not fundamentally over the proper balance between two modes of exploitation (private and extractive) and the distribution of Indian laborers between them, and few azogueros demanded a "second reducción" or the massive expulsion of Indians from valley haciendas to highland villages, where they could be tapped for tribute and mita. At issue, rather, was the conduct of the colonial authorities who were responsible for collecting tribute and dispatching mitayos. After years of royal neglect and the accumulation of power in the hands of provincial and local bureaucrats, the corregidores and their collaboratos menaced mining interests. The eighteenth-century variant of the agrarian question, then, was the issue of the power of the local authorities who reached inside the Andean communities, exploited peasants for personal gain, and blocked the outflow of draft labor to the mines. When the invigorated Bourbon state finally took tribute and mining interests to heart again, in the 1780s and 1790s, it shifted attention to the alarming state of affairs within the Andean community. By then, the crown had abolished the post of corregidor, but, as we shall see in chapter 8, the social legacies of mercantile exploitation survived rebellion and the dismantling of the corregimientos.

Political Unrest in the Valleys

The crisis of colonial rule that gripped the viceroyalty in the mid-eighteenth century was played out, on a small scale, in the Cochabamba region. Tensions mounted in the region, as the burden of the

rebeliones, 84-85. The royal tariff of 1754 is published in ibid., 87 and 98-100, and in Moreno Cebrián, *Corregidor de indios*.

repartimiento de mercancías grew heavier. Peasants who inhabited communal lands were increasingly vulnerable to the corregidor's economic power. A group of Indians from the community of Tapacarí confronted the corregidor of Cochabamba in court. The suit unfolded in the late 1740s and early 1750s, the beginning of a thirty-year period during which Indians throughout Alto Perú waged judicial struggles against the authority of corregidores and their mercantile practices. The litigation initiated by the Tapacarí Indians illuminated the larger struggle over Andean peasant labor that fractured and weakened the colonial bureaucracy in this period.

Under the terms of the royal decree of 1754, the repartimiento de mercancías in Cochabamba amounted to 186,675 pesos in a five-year period during the 1770s—2,000 mules (25 pesos each), 4,000 *varas* of cloth from Quito (some at 7 pesos, some at 7 pesos 4 reales), 20,000 varas of rustic clothing (1 peso), 30 quintales of iron for plows (100 pesos), 10 *pearas* of coca (9 pesos per basket), and imported clothing of various sorts (total of 50,000 pesos).[81] In absolute terms, this was a larger value of commodities than was absorbed by any other province,[82] but since Cochabamba's population was also relatively large—about 26,500 Andeans lived in the province in 1754—the per capita value, about 7 pesos, was comparable to that in other provinces.[83] Of course, these figures do not include the value of goods forcibly distributed outside the legal limits.

The data indicate how involved the corregidor was in long-distance trade in colonial commodities. About 73 percent of the repartos were products from Andean workshops, estancias, plantations, and mines. The mules were probably supplied by the ranches of Salta and Tucumán in the south, while the *bayetas* (coarse woolen cloth) came from obrajes in the province of La Paz and the highlands to the north, closer to Cuzco.[84] The corregidor procured the finer "quiteño"

81 AGN, Sala 13, 18.1.5, Leg. 45. A *vara* was a measure of length approximately equal to thirty-three inches; a *peara* was a measure regarded as what could be carried by ten mules.

82 Spalding, *Huarochirí*, 202-205.

83 Golte, *Repartos y rebeliones*, 104-105. The value of the legal allotment of repartos in Cochabamba province represented about 3 percent of the total value of legal merchandise distributed by all the corregidores of Alto Perú.

84 In a discussion of the origin of the repartos in Peru, Golte (*Repartos y rebeliones*, chap. 3) argues that the forced participation of Andean peasants in trade stimulated an increase in the production of articles of consumption throughout the viceroyalty. The origin of repartos distributed in Cochabamba can be sur-

cottons from Lima merchants. The connection to coastal merchants was also important, since the corregidor had license to distribute 50,000 pesos worth of imported textiles. In allotting repartos for forced distribution, the corregidor didn't necessarily discriminate between subsistence products and luxury goods; Andean victims of the repartimiento often found themselves indebted to the corregidor for snuff boxes, combs, or buckles, along with the mules and baskets of coca they were compelled to "purchase."

Before the repartimientos were legalized, the corregidores had sought their "clients" in the pueblos reales, which were directly subordinate to the provincial colonial hierarchy. Deprived of even the tenuous protection of a landlord, whose self-interest lay in shielding his tenant-laborers from outside claimants, the village Indians were exposed to the corrupt, coercive practices of local authorities. Furthermore, the corregidor, by co-optation, pressure, or imposition of an outsider, used members of the native hierarchy as intermediaries in the distribution of commodities among peasant households. Finally, the repartimiento de mercancías required, for their effective functioning, that the corregidores intervene in the political affairs of the Andean villages, and that they establish a network of collaborators to facilitate the flow of commodities and enforce the debt obligations of Indian consumers.

The logic of compulsory exchange and the dependence of the corregidores upon Indian collaborators produced contradictory effects in the Andean villages. On the one hand, the behavior of the corregidores threatened the political autonomy of village life and infringed upon local traditions, and so provoked moral indignation among the Indians. Yet on the other hand, the villagers could not present a united front against the corregidores, for their moral outrage had to be directed not only toward them but also toward the native collaborators. Caciques were turned against each other, and the internal divisions in the Andean communities were sharpened. Sometimes, the expressions of moral indignation precipitated upheaval within a community, destroying any semblance of solidarity (see chapter 4).

For the present, it is sufficient to note the growing political unrest in the valleys during the time when the repartimiento de mercancías flourished. Long before the outbreak of the rebellions of 1781, the Indians of Tapacarí sought retribution from the audiencia for their

---

mised from the alcabala records that were systematically kept in the last two decades of the eighteenth century; for a detailed discussion, see Brooke Larson, "Economic Decline and Social Change in an Agrarian Hinterland: Cochabamba in the Late Colonial Period" (Ph.D. diss., Columbia University, 1978), 232–240.

suffering under the rule of Cochabamba's corregidor, Bartolomé Fiorilo Pérez. Some time during the 1740s, about 75 Tapacareños journeyed to La Plata, where they testified against the abuses perpetrated by the corregidor and his collaborators, both creole and native.[85] Although witnesses accused different individuals, their basic objection was to the use of force that penetrated to the heart of the community and reduced them to debtors. The mercantile-political alliance in the village exposed them to economic shocks from which they could not shield themselves. A seventy-year-old man accused Gerónimo de los Ríos, the corregidor's lieutenant, of distributing "with all the rigor and force of authority" brandy, iron, mules, rustic cloth, maize, sheep, and baskets of coca.[86] A bilingual though illiterate mestizo spoke out against the same lieutenant and against the cacique Pedro Condori, who had sold him grains and a mule for sixteen pesos on a six-month credit term; when he defaulted on his debt, the man was thrown into prison.[87] Another witness confessed to serving as an agent of the corregidor, out of fear of imprisonment. A group of forasteros testified that the corregidor had forced them to accept 100 varas of bayeta, at one peso each.[88]

The forced purchases were not all that the Tapacarí Indians were suffering from. They protested an "artisans' tax" that was levied on weavers even when they had no wool to spin or weave. They complained about the alcabalas imposed on the Indians of the ayllu Guaico, turning a sales tax into a head tax of four pesos. In effect, they were paying double tribute—to the king and to the local authorities.[89] The repartimiento de mercancías, then, was only the most prominent mechanism of extraction employed by the corregidores.

To the Indians of Tapacarí, the audiencia of La Plata seemed to offer the only means of protecting themselves against the corregidor's excesses. The viceregal authorities had lost their power to

---

85 "Juicio en grado de apelación sobre los capítulos que se lee a don Juan Guillermo Liro de Córdova, por el indio Blas Condori, sobre las tierras en el pueblo de Tapacarí," ANB, EC no. 46 (1753), f. 136 (hereafter cited as "Juicio de Liro de Córdova contra Condori"). Some of the litigation is also in "Exp. sobre los capítulos puestos a d. Bartolomé de Fiorilo," AGI, Charcas, Leg. 367 (1752-1756) (hereafter cited as "Exp. sobre . . . Fiorilo").

86 "Exp. sobre . . . Fiorilo," ff. 199-200.

87 Ibid. f. 205.

88 Ibid. f. 210.

89 Ibid. ff. 209-210.

shield, and so the Indians appealed to the judicial authorities as a last resort, invoking the norms guaranteeing communal autonomy and subsistence security in return for complying with state exactions. But once the repartimientos were legalized, the struggle could no longer be waged on moral grounds. The issue of an unjust use of force then became irrelevant. Instead, the Andeans began to base their pleas on the difficulty of meeting their obligations to outside authorities under such harsh conditions. Increasingly, it was coming down to a choice between redeeming debts to the corregidor, on the one hand, and paying tribute and serving the mita, on the other. The magistrates heard Indians threaten to join the thousands of others who had, over the years, cast loose from their villages and thrown off their yoke to the colonial state.[90] More than ever, the corregidor loomed as a menace to the social order of Alto Perú.

In the 1740s, when the Tapacarí Indians testified before the audiencia of La Plata, the magistrates were already antagonistic toward the rapacious corregidores of Alto Perú. Corregidor Fiorilo fit the stereotype well, and he soon found himself on the defensive against charges of fraud and corruption. Specifically, he was accused of charging excessive prices for repartos and of embezzling tribute payments. He requested that the audiencia order a royal inspection of the province. This was done, and, as he hoped, the royal inspector absolved the corregidor of malfeasance. But the Tapacarí Indians rejected the inspector's report. They complained that the vecino who was in charge of investigating whether the corregidor had underregistered tributaries had not conducted his own census count but had simply solicited lists of resident Indians from local hacendados. A lawyer pointed out on behalf of the Tapacareños that landlords chronically underregistered their forastero tenants. The oidores eventually indicted Fiorilo on two counts: hiding tributaries and overcharging Indians for repartos.[91]

This action provoked opposition far from the scene of the crime and the court. In Lima, the case against Fiorilo seemed to represent the mountain court's offensive against corregidores and their mercantile pursuits, in which Lima's merchant aristocracy was heavily involved. The merchants believed that the audiencia of La Plata, in-

---

90 "Exp. que tiene recurso de los indios de pueblos de Tapacarí, Mojosa, Yaco, y Cavari en Cochabamba y La Paz sobre derechos parroquiales . . .," ANB, EC no. 31. (1761). See also Golte, *Repartos y rebeliones*, 128-139, and Zavala, *Servicio personal*, 3: 51-65.

91 "Exp. sobre . . . Fiorilo," Cuadernos 3 and 7.

clined to favor the mining interests in the area, was turning into a forum in which Indians and other aggrieved people could make their protests, and they demanded that the Lima court, which had superior judicial authority, stem the tide that threatened the alliance of mercantile and political interests embodied in the figure of the corregidor.

Fiorilo himself appealed his case to the Lima court. The oidores of La Plata were slow in responding, and the viceroy accused them of deliberately stalling the judicial review process by failing to remit the proper papers to Lima. But in the end, Fiorilo was exonerated. In 1753, the Council of the Indies endorsed the decision to acquit the corregidor. However, although the council seemed to stand squarely behind the coastal mercantile and political elites of the viceroyalty, that is not all there was to its deliberations. One member of the council praised Fiorilo for his stern rule of the Cochabamba province. The corregidor, he said, may have indulged in corrupt activities at the expense of the royal exchequer, but he imposed ten years of "peace and order" on that volatile land.[92] Only about twenty years had passed, after all, since the bloody rebellion of Calatayud and the mestizos of Cochabamba, and the members of the council presumably had that in mind.

Nevertheless, the council failed to realize how dangerous the state of Andean affairs was becoming. The audiencia of La Plata was almost powerless, and the legitimacy of relations between the colonial state and the village peasants had been destroyed. In Cochabamba, where most Indians lived outside the village structure, the inflated power and the commercial activities of the corregidor were affecting peasants and the urban poor everywhere, not merely in the pueblos reales. In the 1760s and 1770s, voices of discontent were heard in new corners of the province, outside the Andean communities. In 1773, for example, Andean peasants who lived on haciendas in the parish of Yani, in the *partido* (district) of Ayopaya, brought a protest before the oidores of La Plata. They were supported by the testimony of a creole mayor who had served as an intermediary in the repartimiento and found himself a victim of debt because, even with threats and force, he was unable to distribute all the merchandise consigned to his district.[93] Five years later, the city council of Cochabamba rose up against its corregidor and denounced the practice of

---

92 Ibid., Cuaderno 3.

93 "Testimonio del expediente de teniente de Ayopaya contra el corregidor de Cochabamba," ANB, EC no. 139 (1773).

forcefully distributing goods in the province. The repartimiento must be abolished, the council members argued, because of "all the misery it causes all classes of people . . . threatening them with violence to accept an excessive quantity of goods they do not need; demanding payment before their credit term is over; and obligating others to serve against their own will as debt collectors for the corregidor."[94]

Toward the end of his administration (1761-1776), Viceroy Manuel Amat y Juniente issued a sober warning: "If the present situation continues, the kingdom will fall into ruin, the Indians will vanish . . ., lands will lie fallow, . . . and the mines . . . will be deserted. . . . no peace will reign if [corregidores] continue to persecute Indians."[95] And indeed, violent insurrection did break out throughout the southern Andes in 1780 and 1781, jolting the imperial bureaucracy out of its lethargy. It was only then that the Peruvian viceroy suppressed the repartimiento de mercancías, on the grounds of "the injuries and wrongs which they cause the Indians, whose complaints have flooded the tribunals."[96]

But the measure came too late to prevent a wave of violence from engulfing the land. From Cuzco to Jujuy, peoples of Andean and mixed ancestries joined the rebel guerrillas of Túpac Amarú, in the north, and Túpac Catari, in the south. Almost everywhere, the principal target of attack was the corregidor, the most despised symbol of corruption and exploitation. The uprisings destroyed the bureaucratic apparatus that had permitted the crown to retreat behind the unbridled greed of the corregidores and forsake its obligations to Andean communities.

Against this backdrop of political unrest and ultimately open rebellion, Andean peasants saw their communities threatened. In some villages, they managed to confront the forces of change with a measure of unity and solidarity. But in others, two centuries of colonialism had created disparate and irreconcilably hostile groups. The political tensions of the age magnified the internal class and ethnic divisions. In the Cochabamba valleys, at least, the conjuncture of political and economic forces in the middle and later decades of the eighteenth century could not but disrupt the web of village life.

94 AGN, Sala 9, Interior, 30.1.6, Leg. 4, Exp. 13 (1778).

95 "Relación que hace don Manuel Amat," quoted in Zavala, *Servicio personal,* 3: 61.

96 The quotation is from a proclamation by Viceroy Jauregui in December 1780, as quoted in J. Fisher, *Government and Society in Colonial Peru,* 21.

Andean
Village Society

Through the lenses of sixteenth-century documents, the historian can view an uneven, contradictory process of change in the southern Andes—a process in which Andean peoples accommodated and adjusted to some European elements and melded others with Andean traditions to ensure the social reproduction of their culture and communities. The insightful observations of Polo de Ondegardo and Hernando de Santillán, not to mention the native chroniclers, were richly textured with ethnographic detail that revealed keen sensitivity to the norms and customs of the autochthonous groups.[1] They interpreted the values and traditions of Andean societies to the European world and, in the process, documented the resilience and resourcefulness of those societies in the face of the powerful, destructive forces unleased by the arrival of the Europeans. The dialectic of native resistance through adaptation and change is also revealed in early colonial litigation and sometimes even in notarial records chronicling the prosaic or heroic activities of Andean peoples coping with the burdens imposed by the new colonial order. As we saw in chapter 1, such records may show the ways Indians imposed the logic of their own society on the Europeans by manipulating colonial law and concepts of justice to preserve or regain mitmaq colonies in

1 Polo de Ondegardo, "Relación de los fundamentos" and "Informe . . . al Lic. Briviesca de Muñatones"; Hernando de Santillán, "Relación del origen, descendencia, política, y gobierno de los Incas . . ." (1563-1564), in *Collección de libros y documentos referentes a la historia del Perú*, Vol. 9, ser. 2 (Lima: San Martí, 1927), 536a. The most important published indigenous source for seventeenth-century Peru is Poma de Ayala, *Primer nueva corónica*. On the conquest period, see Diego de Castro Titu Cusi Yupanqui, *Relación de la conquista del Perú* (Lima: Biblioteca Universitaria, 1570; 1975), and Frank Salomon, "Chronicles of the Impossible: Notes on Three Peruvian Indigenous Historians," in Rolena Adorno, ed., *From Oral to Written Expression: Native Andean Chronicles of the Early Colonial Period* (Syracuse: Syracuse University Press, 1982), 9–39.

distant maize or coca valleys, for example, or by accumulating capital to purchase land titles as another means of retaining their access to multiple ecological zones. Contemporary narrative reports and the recorded transactions and petitions of Indians in the sixteenth century paint a vivid picture of two societies in collision and demonstrate that Andean peoples were not immediately or absolutely crushed by the weight of colonial rule. Rather, they adapted, often in subtle ways, to the new circumstances in order to preserve small spaces for their traditional practices and beliefs.[2]

The ethnographic detail of sixteenth-century documents is often absent in those of the eighteenth century. In the earlier period, for example, different ethnic strands in the Andean social fabric would be identified, but eighteenth-century bureaucrats rarely bothered to differentiate the Carangas from the Caracaras or the Charcas. Cultural differences among the Andean peoples faded into the background as colonial authorities homogenized Andean peoples into a single category of "Indian," or else differentiated among them according to the territorial-administrative grid that their predecessors had established. The consolidation of a colonial regime, with ideological roots deeply embedded in an ethos of cultural and racial superiority, relegated indigenous cultural distinctions and rivalries to the margins of consciousness and life in this exploitative and conflictual social order. After the frontiers had closed and the intruders had effectively subordinated the indigenous peoples, the Spanish agents of empire no longer felt it necessary to deal with them as near equals or to exploit traditional native enmities. And with the imposition of Spanish hegemony, the opportunities for the Andean peoples to collaborate with the intruders or to manipulate colonial practices to advance their own tribal or ethnic interests against rival Andean groups gradually disappeared.

Thus, the relative absence of European references to indigenous ethnic diversity in the eighteenth century bespeaks the lack of importance that colonial authorities attached to cultural differences among Indians, rather than any process of fusion of various ethnic elements into one mass of "Indians." Indeed, some Andean groups retained their cultural integrity and identity into the late twentieth century.[3] Moreover, colonial civil authorities could afford to ignore

2 See the discussion of the dialectics of tradition and acculturation, resistance and accommodation, in Wachtel, *Vision of the Vanquished*, 140-168, 188-200.

3 See the rich ethnographic literature on contemporary Andean societies in the southern Andes, particularly O. Harris, "Kinship and the Vertical Economy" and

the meaning of culture for Andean peoples only as long as they did not threaten the social order. In periods of unrest, native rebels jolted colonial rulers out of their indifference and ignorance into sharp awareness of native consciousness and respect for the power of cultural identity. At such times, the rulers found that native Andean leaders could effectively manipulate cultural symbols and identities to inspire solidarity or to provide ideological justifications for insurgency. If Spanish authorities were to prevent the frequent Indian revolts from spreading, they had to anticipate the cohesive or divisive cultural forces at work in the heart of Andean rural society. However, in normal times, when natives passively expressed their resistance to colonial rule in daily actions or rituals that are largely hidden from historians, most high-level administrators were only dimly aware of the complexities of ethnic cultures or the beliefs and rituals that infused meaning into agricultural work and other ordinary actitivies.

In the same way, eighteenth-century European observers failed to appreciate the significance of hierarchy in Indian societies, perceiving it primarily in terms of European standards of status, function, or wealth. The dominant image was that of villages inhabited by homogeneous groups of barefoot peasants living perilously close to the margin of subsistence and ruled or governed by a privileged group of caciques. To European eyes, Andean societies were internally stratified either according to a native's relationship to the state or outside administrator (e.g. as tributary, mitayo, or cultural broker) or according to his access to local resources. The sensitive Spanish observers of the sixteenth century, who recognized the ideology and practice of reciprocity and redistribution that both governed and mitigated the relations of hierarchy and subordination among members of the same ethnic group had few counterparts in the eighteenth century. Moreover, the eighteenth-century records of the censuses (*padrones*) carried out by the colonial authorities concentrate their attention on the village unit, neglecting Andean self-definitions of kinship and community at either the subvillage or the transvillage level. Ayllus, mitmaq strands, and other native forms of affiliation do not readily appear in these census reports. After two centuries of colonial rule, ethnic and kinship affiliations were certainly harder to trace, but colonial authorities were not assiduously looking for them, either. As the Bourbons tightened and centralized state authority over In-

"Labor and Produce," and Platt, "Espejos y maiz" and "Role of the Andean Ayllu."

dian communities in the aftermath of the 1781 rebellions and tried to reverse the trend toward population dispersion and migration among the Indians, they were intent upon resurrecting the old Toledan model of the village. The search for more tributaries prompted royal authorities to redivide Andean settlements into discrete clusters of households. As Toledo had done two hundred years before (see chapter 2), Bourbon administrators in the late eighteenth century transmuted Andean concepts of space and association into Spanish territorial and administrative units although they continued to recognize native moieties, because these were useful subvillage units of governance and tribute collection. In many census records, villages were further divided into spatial and administrative subcategories, which sometimes overlapped with indigenous definitions of communal groups. In the cabecera village of Tapacarí, for example, census records grouped people into *anexos* (which vaguely corresponded to ayllus) and *estancias* (spatial clusters of peasant households).

The padrones, then, provide a kind of three-dimensional view of village society: a hierarchy of territorial and administrative units; clusters of originarios and forasteros; and a society atomized into individuals and households, whose fiscal status was determined by sex, age, and ascriptive status in the community of residence. Obviously, they are rich sources for the historian, but their administrative purpose of pinning down tributaries and holding in check the number of tax evaders and ausentes skewed the vision of most colonial observers in the late eighteenth century. Few among them caught sight of vestigial forms of vertical archipelagos or understood the contradictory forces that governed social relations among peasant households, extended kin groups, or moieties. For deeper comprehension of the texture of village society and the content of social relations, the historian must rely on judicial records that give voice to Andeans' expressions of protest, denunciation, or denial and that reveal, in moments of crisis, the moral sinews that held their societies together.

Even phrased in European or administrative terms, however, the Andean village remains a useful analytic construct through which to study the intersection of colonial forces of change and the actions and consciousness of Andean peoples responding to broader historical patterns. A principal unit of social control under colonial rule, the village was always a sensitive pressure point of the often contradictory forces of political economy to which Andean peasants responded, by acquiescence, transformation, or resistance. The village is also a point of departure for studying the ways in which Andean peoples initiated change and altered colonial society, sometimes imposing their own dictates or limits on the power of the colonial state or market when it threatened to violate their own material and cultural integrity.

And yet, while they might draw upon their cultural heritage, ethnic identity, and communal tradition to mitigate or defy the pressures of alien institutions, village Indians were more exposed to imperial policies and naked force than were those Indians who inhabited hacienda lands and whose relation to the outside world was mediated by a landlord. Village Indians had greater scope and authority in structuring the social and technical arrangements within their society to ensure subsistence to its members and to meet their obligations to the state, but they also carried many more burdens of obligations to claimants both outside and inside their community than did most peasants living on estates. Theoretically, village Indians who collectively shared the rights and responsibilities bestowed by community membership drew upon a wellspring of tradition and ideology that placed a premium on self-sufficiency and subsistence, reciprocity and community. These ideals set parameters of economic and social justice, which the Toledan state originally preserved in modified form. In the late colonial era, Andean peoples still invoked the traditional normative order to censure deviant behavior within their own societies and to challenge the legitimacy of authorities both inside and outside their communities. The extent to which those norms actually governed social relations among factions and individuals within village society, however, is only beginning to be explored in the historical literature.[4]

The Pueblos Reales in Flux

Probably more than most other Andean communities in the eighteenth century, Cochabamba's pueblos reales were marginalized, weak, and "contaminated" by outside economic and ideological in-

4 On social relations in village society during the latter half of the colonial period, see Spalding, *Huarochirí* and her earlier work, *De indio a campesino: Cambios en la estructura del Perú colonial* (Lima: Instituto de Estudios Peruanos, 1974); Stern, "Struggle for Solidarity" and "The Age of Andean Insurrection, 1742-1782: A Reappraisal" (paper presented at the Social Science Research Council/University of Wisconsin Conference on Resistance and Rebellion in the Andean World, 18th-20th centuries, Madison, Wis., Apr. 26-28, 1984); Sánchez-Albornoz, *Indios y Tributos*; Brooke Larson, "Caciques, Class Structure, and the Colonial State," *Nova Americana*, no. 2 (1978): 197-235; Rasnake, "Kurahkunah," chap. 3; and Daniel Santamaría, "La propiedad de la tierra y la condición social del indio en el Alto Perú, 1780-1810," *Desarrollo económico*, no. 66 (1977): 253-271.

fluences. The five villages (Tapacarí, Capinota, Sipesipe, El Paso, and Tiquipaya) were not equally decayed or factionalized, but in comparison to communities elsewhere in Alto Perú, which had preserved their ethnic identity, collective strength, and group self-sufficiency, they were in a sorry state. The historical roots of their malaise went back to the time of the conquest and the Toledan reforms, when royal villages were created, almost arbitrarily, out of an amalgam of ethnic splinter groups, both autochthonous and mitmaq (see chapters 1 and 2). In many cases, chieftains were named for their association with the Incas, not because they were the "natural" leaders of a particular ethnic polity. Such community cohesion and solidarity as existed were forged by the imperatives of the colonial situation. Leadership in the valleys was imposed from above and was dependent upon the support of encomenderos and, later, the colonial state. But even the sanction of community status by the Toledan state was not sufficient to protect the five pueblos from the advance of private landowning and the seepage of tributaries to the chácaras. Already internally fragmented in the late sixteenth century, the villages were increasingly confronted by European colonists who extended their control over the fertile lands, competed for access to water, and pressed against the frail boundaries of the Indian communities. By the early seventeenth century, private estates had gained the edge over the Indian communities in the competition for land and labor. By the end of the first decade of the nineteenth century, the five villages contained less than 25 percent of the "Indians" recorded in the tribute census (table 6). To be "Indian" in this region was, for the most part, to live under the domination of a landlord, side by side with peasants, traders, and artisans of mixed ancestry and ambiguous cultural origins.

The villages of Cochabamba were subject to another outside force

Table 6. Tributary Population of Cochabamba, 1683-1808

	1683	*1737*	*1786*	*1793*	*1808*
Total Tributary population	6,735	5,484[a]	10,773	8,854	11,718
Tributary population of the pueblos reales	2,179	1,918	2,864	2,935	2,859
Percentage of total in pueblos reales	32	35	27	33	24

Sources: See table A-1.
[a] Does not include tributary population of the district of Ayopaya.

during the colonial period: the influx of forasteros. As pointed out in chapter 3, the pueblos assimilated a large proportion of forasteros. Even by the time of Palata's census, the forastero population constituted about 80 percent of their inhabitants. Conversely, in four of the five censuses taken between 1683 and 1808, originarios and their families composed less than one-quarter of the villages' population (table 7). The social consequences of Andean immigration for the patterns of landholding and social relationships in those villages cannot be determined from the padrones alone, but it is likely that forasteros remained in their host villages for longer than a generation, at least during the second half of the colonial period. Most forasteros (or their forebears) originated in a distant, "foreign" village. While there may have been some "crossovers" between the categories of forastero and orginario, as Platt found for the villages of Chayanta, the preponderance of forasteros in the Cochabamba pueblos has to be explained primarily by in-migration and settlement.[5] In a material way, then, the forastero influx peopled the valley pueblos in the face of sharp population decline. But in so doing, they further fragmented the ethnic makeup of village society. While the villages may have assimilated forasteros through religious sodalities (cofradías) religious rituals, communal obligations, and intermarriage in the early period,[6] by the eighteenth century they were so "bottom heavy" with forasteros that there was but a small core group to perform that function. We may speculate then, that forasteros increasingly were "outsiders" in their host villages. The padrones of the eighteenth century assumed that forasteros had no landholding rights, or the attendant communal responsibilities, in their villages. They did have access to community resources through such economic relationships as paying rent or dues in return for usufruct rights or perhaps through the patronage of a cacique. But in neither case did they enjoy communal membership or share in the community's obligations to the state. Even after forasteros were converted to tributaries, they still found insulation from certain onerous burdens. But as a group of outsiders, they were subordinate to and dependent on the

5 Platt, *Estado boliviano y ayllu andino*, chap. 2. A major difference between Chayanta and Cochabamba, however, was the relatively small proportion of forasteros in the former. In 1754, the percentages of forasteros in Cochabamba and Chayanta were 83 percent and 29 percent, respectively: Golte, *Repartos y rebeliones*, 55.

6 Saignes, "Políticas étnicas," p. 13.

Table 7. Originario Population of the Villages of Cochabamba, 1683-1808

	1683		1737		1786		1793		1808	
Village	Number	Percentage of Total Population	Number	Percentage of Total Population	Number	Percentage of Total Population	Number	Percentage of Total Population	Number	Percentage of Total Population
Tapacarí	75	12.8	165	28.0	150	10.2	200	13.6	202	12.9
Sipesipe	65	16.8	68	25.0	68	17.0	156	37.1	133	36.1
El Paso	113	26.4	56	26.3	38	22.3	108	45.8	99	49.0
Tiquipaya	77	22.4	161	70.0	90	23.5	143	33.0	143	34.4
Capinota	81	19.3	187	30.4	87	19.2	83[a]	—	79	26.0
Total	411	18.9	637	33.2	433	15.1	690	23.7	656	23.0

Sources: AGN, Sala 13, Padrones, 18.1.1, Leg. 41; 18.1.5, Leg. 45; 18.2.2, Leg. 47; 18.2.5, Leg. 50; and 3.4.4, Leg. 54.
[a] Census report not available; this figure is the average of the figures for 1786 and 1808.

native authorities in their host villages. Forasteros, for the most part, inhabited the poorer and less secure niches of village society.

Another index of the villages' weak defense against outside forces was the impoverishment of their communal property. None of the Indian villages possessed a capital stock—valued in money—sufficient to guarantee a minimum income to community members in times of crop failure or to underwrite their tribute dues. It is true that the peasants of Capinota and Tapacarí retained access to high-altitude pastures and arable fields, as well as to warm, moist acreage suitable for maize cultivation, which afforded the kind of social insurance against drought, flood, frost, and blight upon which Andean peoples traditionally had depended. But colonial authorities measured the economic stability of villages in terms of the monetary value of their communal holdings and, particularly, the liquid capital in their treasuries. Periodically, colonial officials expressed concern about the decapitalized condition of the Indian communities and devised schemes to restock the villages' larders. They blamed the pauperization of village Indians not on the colonial system itself, but on corrupt corregidores, caciques, or landowners who drained the villages of their cash reserves.

In the 1770s, when colonial authorities were attempting to increase tribute-producing revenues, they spoke out once more against the burden on village treasuries. They admonished landowning families who still owed money to village Indians and ordered them to pay their debts. Many creole landowners in Peru had inherited mortgages that originally drew upon the treasuries of Andean villages and were subsequently swollen by unpaid interest at the rate of 5 percent per year. A royal inventory in 1776 showed a total of 120,000 pesos of such debts still outstanding; a single hacienda, one of several named Queroquero, owed 5,430 pesos to the village of Sipesipe—most of it interest that had not been paid for 181 years (see table A-4). Twenty years later, Francisco de Viedma was still complaining about these debts. He calculated that Indians had claims against hacendados for 202,365 pesos in principal and 579,044 pesos in interest. In his own intendancy, the five pueblos had liquid assets amounting to only 2,142 pesos; yet the village of Tapacarí alone was owed interest in the amount of 150,000 pesos.[7]

At the same time, the Indian villages of Cochabamba supported a

7 "Correspondencia con los gobernadores e intendentes de Cochabamba y La Paz" (July 24, 1797) AGI, Charcas (Ramo Secular), Leg. 436; and Viedma, *Descripción geográfica*, 183-187.

heavier tax burden than many other communities of the altiplano. The reason was that royal tax collectors in the late eighteenth century set the tribute rates of originarios according to the assessed market value and productivity of village lands. In Cochabamba's maize valleys, as well as in other eastern lowland regions, the originario landholders paid high tribute dues for usufruct rights to superior acreage.[8] The originarios of Capinota, who occupied what was considered to be some of the richest territory in the region, were assessed at 10 pesos 1.5 reales, and the rates for the originarios of the other villages were not much lower (see table 8). The originarios in the region had the option of delivering a portion of their dues in maize, but they probably did not exercise it very often, since the value of the crop was arbitrarily fixed at 12.5 reales per fanega—a value that was probably always lower than its market price. Whether they paid entirely in cash or partially in kind, the village Indians of the maize valleys paid about twice the annual tax that highland village Indians were assessed. The originarios of Pacajes, for example, paid only 5 pesos each in tribute, and the Indians of Chayanta, 4 pesos 7 reales. Even the landless forasteros of Cochabamba's maize valleys paid a higher rate (6 pesos 2 reales) than the landholding inhabitants of highland villages.[9]

The Indian villages of Cochabamba were not all equally impoverished or vulnerable to outside commercial forces. Sipesipe, El Paso, and Tiquipaya appeared to be in the worst state of decay (see table 9). El Paso, once the rich and prized encomienda of Polo de Onde-gardo, was almost extinct by the late eighteenth century. A mere 38 originarios inhabited the village in 1786, compared to the 684 tributaries registered by Toledo in 1573, although this population loss had been partly mitigated by the entry of forasteros, who numbered 192 by then. But mestizos and creoles outnumbered Indians of both categories in the village. During his inspection of El Paso in the 1780s, Francisco de Viedma described the village as a ghost town, abandoned by Indians who feared the mita or who never returned from the mines.[10] Viedma commissioned a royal inventory of village lands that were not being cultivated by village peasants and ordered them to be leased on five-year terms. The rent proceeds were to go to the

8 "Informe de la contaduría de retasa sobre la revisita del partido de Santa Cruz" (Feb. 25, 1793), RAH, ML, 9/1733, Tomo 78.

9 AGN, Sala 9, Justicia, 31.3.4, Leg. 7, Exp. 91 (1778), and AGN, Sala 13, Padrones, 17.6.1, 17.10.2, and 18.2.1, Leg. 46 (1786-1787).

10 Viedma, *Descripción geográfica*, 67-68 and 180.

Table 8. Annual Tribute Dues in Pueblos Reales, Census of 1785-1787

Pueblo Real	Originarios			Forasteros			Total for Pueblo Real[a]
	Monetary Tribute per Originario	Total Monetary Tribute	Maize (fanegas)	Monetary Tribute per Forastero	Total Monetary Tribute	Total Monetary Tribute	
Tapacarí	9/2	1,400	76	6/2		10,137	11,628
Sipesipe	9/7.5	617	50	6/2		2,081	2,757
El Paso	9/7.5	351	22	6/2		1,200	1,578
Tiquipaya	9/5	794	62	6/2		950	2,817
Capinota	10/1.5	—	—	6/2		—	3,167

Sources: AGN, Sala 13, Padrones, 18.2.1, Leg. 46; 18.2.2, Leg. 47; 18.2.3, Leg. 48.

Note: Monetary tribute per originario or forastero is given in pesos corrientes and reales; amount of total tribute is given in pesos corrientes.

[a] Including value of maize at officially fixed price of 12.5 reales per fanega. Total tribute payments given in primary source differ from calculated sums of tribute dues (including maize) for each pueblo.

Chapter 4

144

Table 9. Tributary Population of the Five Pueblos Reales of Cochabamba, 1573 and 1786

Pueblo Real	1573 Total	1786 Total	Originarios	Forasteros
Tapacarí	1,173	1,465	150	1,315
Sipesipe	819	401	68	333
El Paso	684	230	38	192
Tiquipaya	504	402	90	312
Capinota	419	366	87	279

Sources: "Tasa de la visita general de Francisco de Toledo," AGI, Contaduría, Leg. 1786; AGN, Sala 13, Padrones, 18.2.1, Leg. 46; 18.2.2, Leg. 47; 18.2.3, Leg. 48.

royal treasury. El Paso, along with its neighboring villages, Sipesipe and Tiquipaya, apparently had large tracts of such "excess lands" (*sobrantes de comunidad*).[11] Neither land shortage nor population density seemed to be an important factor in the exodus of originarios from El Paso.

El Paso was flanked on the southwest by Sipesipe, the ancient royal pastures and maize fields of the Incas and the fertile headlands of the valley, and by Tiquipaya on the east. As in El Paso, clusters of peasants cultivated irrigated lands in both those villages. The population was racially mixed, with natives composing 56 percent of the inhabitants of Sipesipe and 40 percent of Tiquipaya's population in the 1780s.[12] Among the native population, forasteros greatly outnumbered originarios in all three of these villages (table 9). Their influx into Tiquipaya brought the tributary population in 1786 to about 80 percent of the size of the tributary labor force in 1573. Sipesipe's tributary population, on the other hand, was still only half what it had been two centuries earlier.

The three villages had enjoyed little political or cultural insularity during the colonial period. Occupying some of the richest irrigated land in the entire region, they were a choice target of non-Andeans. Before the end of the seventeenth century, they had lost portions of their territory to colonial encroachers, who leased or squatted on parcels of land. Sipesipe had lost 27 percent of its tributary population to private landholders. Some of those peasants may have lived outside the boundaries of the pueblo, on estate land, while they continued to pay tribute dues to their community, but many others

11 "Informe del Augustín Antesana sobre las tierras de Sacpaya (pueblo de Capinota)" (Dec. 24, 1821), AHMC, Leg. 1068.

12 Viedma, *Descripción geográfica* 66–68.

probably were absorbed by Spanish landholders who leased or expropriated village lands along with their peasant inhabitants (mostly forasteros). Tiquipaya, too, had lost some of its maize lands and almost 20 percent of its resident Indian population to Spanish landholders.[13] The villages also were invaded by creole and mestizo traders, landholders, pack drivers, and artisans. In 1788, Tiquipaya was inhabited by more non-Andeans than by natives, and almost half of the total populations of Sipesipe and El Paso consisted of outsiders.[14] The incursion of outsiders probably intensified even further toward the end of the colonial era. In the Quillacollo parish, contiguous to the valley pueblos, the number of private landholding units increased from the sixteen listed in the 1786 census to thirty-three in the 1804 census.[15] By land reclamation and the advance of arable land, and by the internal division of Spanish-held property units, pressure on the pueblos became ever greater. Trial records from this period are replete with challenges and counterchallenges over land and, particularly, water rights. Typical was the struggle of Tiquipaya to prevent the wealthy and powerful hacendado and merchant family, Boado y Quiroga, from siphoning off precious water flowing down from the mountains. Boado y Quiroga controlled fields situated upland from the village and was able to divert the stream to his own lands. The Indians claimed they had rights to the *mita de agua* for ten days and nights each month during the growing season, rights which they contended had been ratified by the colonial court in 1647.[16] But even under the invigorated Bourbon state, following the 1781 rebellions, the villages could not count on the state's protection against the forces of attrition (see chapter 8). Situated in the heartland of the maize valleys, densely populated with peasants, smallholders, and hacendados, the three pueblos reales could do little to shield themselves.

West and southwest of the Valle Bajo, where the valleys narrowed and followed the flow of the rivers cutting their way through the mountains, lay Capinota and Tapacarí (see figure 1). Less is known about Capinota than about any of the other pueblos of Cochabamba.

13 AGN, Sala 13, Padrones, 18.1.1, Leg. 41, and 18.1.3, Leg. 43.

14 Viedma, *Descripción geográfica*, 66-68.

15 Sánchez-Albornoz, *Indios y tributos*, 178.

16 Land transactions, stock holdings, and other fragments of information about the Boada y Quiroga family's wealth are found in local notarial books of the second half of the eighteenth century. See also, "Los caciques de Tiquipaya sobre la mita de agua . . ." ANB, EC no. 46 (1793).

Geographically separated from the central valleys by a small mountain range, the village was somewhat protected from the advance of Spanish landholding that was occurring there. Yet it was not an isolated village. Its fertile lands flanked the Arque River, which carved a trade corridor through the mountains. The village served as a way station for travelers and traders en route to Chuquisaca and Potosí, and it was the point of departure for the caravan of pack animals and mitayo families that left the province each year for the mines. Sheltered by the mountains, watered by the river, the valley of Capinota was one of the most fertile corners of the region. Its peasants cultivated high-quality grain and alfalfa in the alluvial soil and tended fruit orchards. The rivers powered local mills, owned by creoles, where Indians ground their corn. In years of abundant harvest, Capinota peasants probably marketed a portion of their crop in the market town of Arque, the next town up the river toward the western puna. Capinota's excellent agricultural conditions and the town's location attracted many settlers. More than one thousand people, variously labeled as Spaniards, cholos, and mulattoes, lived among the village's 2,400 Indians in 1788.[17] Some of those people were transient pack drivers, who stationed themselves in the town of Capinota while they waited for business. Others owned mills in the area or leased parcels of village land. Two large Spanish haciendas occupied land inside the village territory and supported 220 forasteros (table 10). Consequently, the peasants of Capinota sometimes were forced to fight to protect their rights to the mita de agua and their herds and pastures. In 1788, Juan José Paniagua, one of the wealthier landowners in the province, claimed title to certain Indian lands on the

Table 10. Indian Population of the Village of Capinota, 1787

	Moiety of Anansaya	Moiety of Urinsaya	Total
Originarios	156	218	374
Forasteros with land	45	16	61
Total landed tributaries	201	234	435
Forasteros without land			1,446
On estancias (n = 28)			1,044[a]
On haciendas (n = 2)			220
In villages (n = 2)			182

Source: AGN, Sala 13, Padrones, 18.2.3, Leg. 48, ff. 606-607.
[a] Including 112 forasteros at the ranch and mill of Sicaya.

17 Viedma, *Descripción geográfica*, 67-68.

ground that they had not previously been cultivated—a tactic frequently employed by local hacendados and one that was similar to the justification being used in North America around the same time.[18] Paniagua had cleared a hillside field for the planting of maize and had built a reservoir and canals to irrigate the field. The Indians accused him of seizing their animals that were grazing in the vicinity.[19]

While hacendados were testing the borders of village autonomy and territory, highland caciques challenged the authority of the caciques of Capinota in a land dispute that had its origins in early colonial times. The subparish of Arque, San Cristóbal de Sicaya, was inhabited by a small group of Carangas mitimaes who were associated through kin ties to their nuclear village of Toledo, located in the highland province of Paria. This was probably the strongest surviving ethnic network in the Cochabamba province that still bound lowlanders to their highland kin groups, administrative boundaries notwithstanding. These mitimaes, numbering only 112 persons in 1787, still possessed rich lands, herds, and grain mills in the "hacienda Sicaya," as it was listed in the padron.[20] The caciques of Capinota apparently accepted their presence as forasteros in the subparish, but in the 1780s the highland caciques claimed jurisdiction over them and argued that they should have originario status, since the mitimaes' land rights had originally been granted by the highland caciques. If this claim were upheld, the highland caciques would then be entitled to the revenue from the mitimaes. On the other hand, it was in the interest of the caciques of Capinota to apply European standards of village membership: they considered the mitimaes to be immigrants—forasteros who had settled on village land that rightfully belonged to their own people of Capinota and who therefore owed taxes as forasteros to the village of Capinota. Classification of the mitimaes of Sicaya as forasteros of Capinota meant a heavier tribute burden on them, for although forasteros usually paid tribute at a lower rate, in this case the forasteros of Cochabamba were considered to have access (through the payment of rent) to such high-quality acreage that they were assessed at a higher rate than

18 On land claims in North America based on a European interpretation of "vacant" lands, see Robert F. Berkhofer, *The White Man's Indian* (New York: Knopf, 1978), 119ff.

19 "Exp. por el indio pral. José Tastara contra Juan José Paniagua por daños . . . que le hace en sus sementeras, con sus ganados," AHMC, Leg. 999 (1788).

20 AGN, Sala 13, Padrones, 18.2.2, Leg. 47 (1787).

most originarios in Alto Perú. As mitimaes of the highland village of Toledo, the Sicaya Indians would owe the crown five pesos annually, but as forasteros in the fertile river valley, they paid the standard forastero rate of six pesos two reales. It is hardly surprising, therefore, that a royal inspector resolved the dispute in favor of Capinota's caciques.[21] In doing so, he obliterated one of the region's last vestiges of vertical landholding articulated through kinship ties.

Capinota was divided into moieties (parcialidades): an upper division, Anansaya, and a lower division, Urinsaya. These groups were administered separately by their own caciques, who were responsible for delivering tribute and dispatching mitayos. Urinsaya was the larger of the two, but the originario population of both these parcialidades did not amount to more than 20 percent of Capinota's Indian households (see table 10). The originarios has access to lands on various tiers of the vertical landscape within the village territory, though their holdings were concentrated on the alluvial plain that fanned out from the river banks. Forasteros, on the other hand, were dispersed among the hillsides, where they cultivated maize, wheat, and potatoes in drier soil and tended their herds. They lived and worked in the units listed in the padrón as estancias, which did not seem to be subordinated to caciques of either moiety.

The pattern of settlement was quite different in the village of Tapacarí.[22] The town of that name was located at the confluence of two rivers, which irrigated nearby lands, nibbled away at the hillsides, carved passageways through the cordillera, and flooded their banks for three months each year during the rainy season, isolating the town from the central valleys. The territory of Tapacarí was vast, stretching across some 4,733 *fanegadas* of mostly unirrigated land at altitudes ranging from 8,200 to 14,800 feet. (A fanegada was the area of land that could be sown with a fanega of seed.) Few non-Indians inhabited the village, but forasteros outnumbered originarios even more than in the other pueblos reales of the province (see table 9). The parcialidad of Anansaya was larger than that of Urinsaya. Outside the immediate environs of the pueblo of San Augustín de Tapacarí, members of Anansaya were distributed among forty estancias, those of Urinsaya among only twenty estancias (see table 11). According to Sánchez-Albornoz, on only three of these estancias did members of the two parcialidades mingle with each other. By and

21 "Exp. sobre que se cobre el tributo de indios forasteros en Arque (pueblo de Capinota)," AHMC, Leg. 1256 (1786).

22 Sánchez-Albornoz, *Indios y tributos*, 173-176.

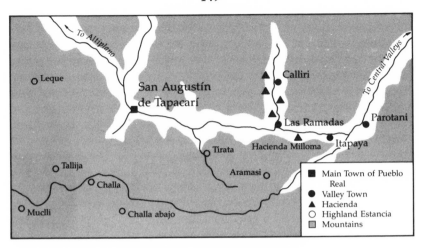

Figure 8   The Pueblo Real of Tapacarí

large, the members of Anansaya lived in Tapacarí proper and in the anexos and estancias of its hinterlands (Tallija, Guaico, Chicmuri, and Tirata). The originarios and forasteros of Urinsaya also cultivated lands near the town of Tapacarí, but many forasteros of Urinsaya inhabited remote estancias of Muclli or occupied land on haciendas in the Spanish parishes of Calliri and Ramada, two islands of white settlement to the east of the community. The dispersion of forasteros among the numerous estancias shows how far settlement conditions had deviated from the original Toledan model of the nucleated village.

Still more striking is the degree of integration of originario and forastero families. Forasteros lived in all the estancias, outnumbering originarios there by nearly nine to one, but there was at least one originario family in almost every estancia as well. A detailed census of the anexo of Tallija illustrates the pattern (see table 12). In each of the seven estancias there were between one and three originario households, along with an average of thirty forastero families.

This pattern of distribution of forasteros and originarios among Tapacarí's estancias and anexos raises important questions about the relations of production and exchange in the village. Sánchez-Albornoz speculates about a hierarchical relationship between originarios (who perhaps served as overseers) and forasteros.[23] If that was the case, how deep was the social divide between these groups? Were

23 Ibid., 175.

Table 11. Places of Settlement of the Tributaries of Village of Tapacarí, 1786

Parish	Parcialidad of Anansaya				Parcialidad of Urinsaya			
	Settled Places	All Tributaries	Originarios	Forasteros	Settled Places	All Tributaries	Originarios	Forasteros
Tapacarí								
San Augustín	1	9	0	9	1	8	2	6
Estancias	40	411	53	358	20	137	29	108
Tallija								
Anexo	1	54	3	51	—	—	—	—
Estancias	7	119	7	112	—	—	—	—
Guaico								
Anexo	1	14	1	13	1	39	6	33
Estancias	16	233	18	215	—	—	—	—
Chicmuri								
Anexo	1	25	1	24	1	18	0	18
Estancias	3	44	2	42	4	25	3	22
Tirata								
Anexo	1	30	5	25	—	—	—	—
Estancias	6	83	5	78	—	—	—	—
Itapaya								
Anexo	1	48	9	39	1	37	5	32
Estancias	3	9	0	9	2	21	0	21
Muclli								
Anexo	—	—	—	—	1	19	0	19
Estancias	—	—	—	—	4	61	0	61
Ramada								
Haciendas	—	—	—	—	5	21	1	20
Calliri								
Haciendas	—	—	—	—	16	307	0	307
Number of tributaries in anexos[a]	—	180	19	161		121	13	108
Number of tributaries in estancias	—	899	85	814		244	32	212
Number of tributaries in haciendas	—	0	0	0		328	1	327
Total number of tributaries		1,079	104	975		693	46	647

Source: Adapted from Sánchez-Albornoz, *Indios y tributos*, 174. (Differences between the figures in this table and those in other tables on related subjects are due to differences in the primary sources used.)

a Including the town of San Augustín.

Table 12. Distribution of the Population of Anexo of Tallija, 1798

Location	Adult Males			Adult Females			Minors	
	Tributaries	Reservados[a]	Ausentes	Married	Unmarried	Widowed	Adolescent Boys	Others
Village								
Originarios	3	0	0	2	1	0	1	4
Forasteros	69	13	2	69	27	29	15	140
Estancias								
Yarbicoya								
Originarios	3	0	0	3	3	0	0	3
Forasteros	13	3	1	11	5	3	0	31
Antagacua								
Originarios	3	0	0	3	0	0	0	6
Forasteros	34	6	4	31	7	8	8	58
Challoma								
Originarios	2	0	0	3	0	0	0	1
Forasteros	12	3	0	12	3	1	3	17
Casilliri y Caramarca								
Originarios	1	1	0	2	1	0	0	3
Forasteros	11	1	0	11	3	1	4	17
Guaylla								
Originarios	1	0	0	1	1	0	0	3
Forasteros	3	0	0	3	0	1	1	8
Challa Abajo								
Originarios	3	0	0	3	0	0	0	8
Forasteros	34	9	3	32	2	3	8	51
Challe del Medio								
Originarios	3	0	0	3	0	0	2	5
Forasteros	36	7	3	33	7	7	8	68
Total	231	43	13	222	60	53	50	423
Originarios	19	1	0	20	6	0	3	33
Forasteros	212	42	13	202	54	53	47	390

Source: AGN, Sala 13, Padrones, 18.3.2, Leg. 52 (1798).
[a] Elderly or disabled (exempt from tribute).

forasteros an underclass of landless and dependent peasants? Or did tributary status have little bearing on the social relations of production and the conditions of life in the village? Did class relations and social differentiation perhaps cut through the village social hierarchy in different ways?

Obviously, the static picture of village society provided by the padrones reveals very little about these relations or about the normative order that legitimated them. But judicial records containing the testimony of Andean peasants and village authorities open perspectives on the internal tensions, alignments, and conditions of life and work in the villages. As we saw in chapter 3, Tapacarí around midcentury was caught in the throes of a bitter struggle between two cacique families. That feud began to intensify under the rule of the corregidor Fiorilo Pérez, who threw his support behind one of the rival caciques and meddled in internal village affairs. Moreover, Fiorilo and his collaborators imposed repartos on Tapacarí peasant households and aroused the resentment of Tapacareños by intensifying the economic pressures on them. On the surface, the judicial records chronicle the peasants' protest against their common enemy, the corregidor, but they also reveal the deeper crosscurrents and conflicts in Tapacarí society, where caciques fought each other to preserve their authority and legitimacy and where peasants resisted the burdens they bore at the expense of their own well-being.

A Cacique Rivalry

Beginning in the 1740s and lasting for twenty years or more, a bitter rivalry raged between two cacique families in the village of Tapacarí. The protagonists were on the one hand, Pedro Condori, a cacique of Urinsaya, and his son Blas; and, on the other, Juan Guillermo Liro de Córdova, son and heir of a former cacique of Anansaya who had been stripped of his authority by the corregidor Fiorilo.[24] The central issue in the dispute was the control of village lands. Pedro Condori and Liro de Córdova accused each other of expropriating communal lands, whose fruits were supposed to meet the subsistence needs of village peasants in times of need or tribute deficits and to supply mitayo caravans. The privatization of these lands was a violation of

---

24 "Juicio de Liro de Córdova contra Condori." Other sources pertaining to this feud are in AGI, Charcas, Legs. 367 and 525. Information about the Liro de Córdova family and its holdings and political status in Tapacarí is found in wills and property transactions in local notarial records, cited in note 65. See also AGN, Sala 9, Tribunales, 37.3.6, Leg. 9, Exp. 164.

Andean principles (sanctioned by the colonial state) governing their management, use, and redistribution, and it was held to be corroding the moral economy of Tapacarí. Perhaps more important, a cacique trying to win the sympathy and support of the magistrates in the court of La Plata knew the land issue mattered to the colonial authorities. As pointed out in chapter 3, there was at this time growing concern that caciques and corregidores were carving haciendas out of community land and tying Indians down, hiding them from tax collectors and obstructing the flow of mitayos to Potosí. The feuding caciques were aware of this issue.

In one of the court cases that marked the dispute, Pedro Condori described the rich pastures and bountiful crops of Tapacarí. He listed thirty-three wheat fields, seven patches of white and dark maize scattered across the *quebradas* (ravines) and hinterlands and in the puna, eight parcels of quinoa land, fourteen fields of potatoes, and two "chacras" of ocas. He estimated that the community harvested more than 1,400 fanegas of wheat in an average year and 2,000 fanegas in a good season. So endowed, the peasants of Tapacarí should have been able to meet their tribute obligations without strain. And yet, Condori said, Tapacarí tributaries were always in arrears.[25]

The problem, he argued, lay in the way the community's productive resources were distributed. He charged that the Liro de Córdova family had cornered most of the reserve land, and to prove his accusation, he presented an inventory of the "excessive amount" of land in Liro de Córdova's possession: the hacienda Aparumiri, comprising irrigated and dry lands on the outskirts of Tapacarí; the hacienda and chacra of Amaru; the chacra of Tirata, located in the highlands of Tapacarí (listed in a later padron as an anexo); the estancia Escalera, with fields of barley, quinoa, and ocas; and the estancia Quenuasunturu.[26] Condori accused Liro de Córdova of "ruining their generation" of Indians and threatening the community's economic integrity by parceling out its lands to his followers and minions—all of them outsiders, whom Condori described as follows:

> They are only newly arrived forasteros, but because they are his partisans and part of his faction, they enjoy and possess many parcels of land and privileges which they readily abuse, so that

25 "Juicio de Liro de Córdova contra Condori," ff. 6 and 19.

26 Ibid., ff. 19-20; AGN, Sala 13, Padrones, 18.2.2, Leg. 47 (1787). The estancia Escalera is listed in the 1787 census under the anexo of Guiaco; the estancia Quenuasunturu is not listed in that census at all.

you could almost call them hacendados, for they sow 30 to 40 fanegas of wheat seed and they leave other lands fallow, and these people have many other Indian tenants who work for them in exchange for land rights.[27]

In later testimony, Blas Condori admitted that the Condori family also possessed "a parcel of irrigated and dry land and a second plot of potato land in the [Tapacarí] estancia of Guari." He justified these holdings on two grounds: that he had made capital investments in them (presumably to improve them and enhance their value), and that they were payments for his service in the mita twice during his life, once as a mitayo and once as a captain.[28] Thus, we have a curiously twisted argument from this cacique: while he defended the community's right to preserve its communal resources and denounced Liro de Córdova for privatizing "reserve lands," Condori himself considered land to be a commodity whose value could be increased through capital investment. And he claimed his ownership rights on contradictory grounds: his individual entrepreneurial activities and his "service to the collectivity."

Liro de Córdova responded both by defending himself and by making countercharges against Pedro Condori. Some parcels of land ("one in the river valley and pasture land in the puna") he declared he had purchased with cash. He admitted that some of his properties were located within the boundaries of the pueblo real, but said that they were "modest holdings" whose yields benefited the entire community. On the other hand, he spoke of Condori's "great number of chacras" (he listed six estancias) and said they were illegally held because "he neither pays tax nor covers the expenses of the community." What more could the magistrates expect, Liro de Córdova asked, from an Indian who possessed the title of cacique not through inheritance but through appointment by a corrupt corregidor?[29]

Thus, Liro de Córdova did not deny that both he and Condori held community lands in their personal domain, but he insisted that he had rightfully inherited those lands, that he was the poorer of the

---

27 "Y siendo yndios foranos adbenedizos solo por ser parciales y de facción suya gosando y poseen cantidad de tierras y unos provilegios que se abusan de manera que se pueden llamar hazendados pues siembran 30 y 40 fanegas de trigo y para otras tantas dejan para hacer barbechos y estos tienen muchos yndios arrimados a quienes les dan tierras por su trabajo" "Juicio de Liro de Córdova contra Condori," f.4.

28 Ibid., ff. 4-5.

29 Ibid., f. 35.

two rivals, and that his succession to the cacicazgo had not bestowed a patrimony in crops or other forms of community wealth. On the contrary, he had managed the cultivation of his lands using his own seeds and remunerating the labor of Indians.

> When I entered the government they gave me none of the crops that amounted to more than 900 fanegas of wheat, besides potatoes and oca, which are planted in abundance; all those products were collected by Blas Condori . . . , and I did not receive even a grain of seed. I sowed fields with my own seeds, paying for the communal labor of the Indians, as is customary, at one real per day's work.[30]

Liro de Córdova also assured the court that the fruits of his lands were used to satisfy community obligations: to cover tribute debts caused by death, absenteeism, and deprivation. They fed the village during the festivities (*hospicios*) when the corregidor visited Tapacarí, and they were stored for consumption by the mitayos who gathered for six or eight days in the town of San Augustín before setting off for Capinota and Potosí.[31]

In explaining why Tapacarí showed tribute deficits almost every year, Liro de Córdova stressed the sharp fluctuations in the wheat crop from year to year. "There is no doubt . . . that this year I planted 79 or 80 fanegas of wheat, but its yields vary . . . Even if it is a bumper crop and each fanega of seed bears 10 fanegas of fruit, we will only harvest 700 or 800 fanegas of wheat. We take out a fifth of this grain to dry in the granaries for next year's seed."[32] The village's tribute debts therefore could not be reliably paid with surplus crops. It was not a question of land expropriation, according to Liro de Córdova, but simply the fickle hand of Nature that determined how well Tapacarí could meet its obligations to the state.

Putting aside the verbal warfare between the caciques, there was a genuine issue of land concentration among the native elite in the village of Tapacarí. Condori made reference to wealthy Indians—he

---

30 "Quando yo entré al gobierno no se me dió parte en los frutos que esttaban existenttes que pasaron de nobicientos fanegas de trigo fuera de papas y ocas que son los efecttos que se siembran en mas abundancia y que toda dha porcion de efecttos se la cogió y recogió Blas Condori con su madrastra . . . de forma dhas. siembras las mandé hazer con mi propia semilla pagando a los indios su trabajo en lo que es costumbre a real por día." Ibid., f. 32.

31 Ibid., ff. 4-5.

32 Ibid.

called them "proto-hacendados"—who planted thirty or forty fanegas of wheat seed on lands they individually controlled.[33] Perhaps his
self-interest warped his view of land-tenure patterns, but the unequal access to seeds and arable lands was confirmed many years later
by an outsider. The intendant Francisco de Viedma, following a visit
to the village in the mid-1780s, made the observation that "the lands
that the originarios hold are unjustly and unreasonably distributed;
some [originarios] do not hold the two *topos* of land stipulated by the
royal statutes, while the caciques and principales have 50, 60, or
more fanegadas of land"[34]

Viedma was referring to a native landed oligarchy which by virtue
of its status and power, had access to abundant resources. Condori,
and later Liro de Córdova, exposed illegitimate landowners other
than native members of the political hierarchy. The caciques alluded
to the mechanisms of land distribution whereby some forasteros
were granted land in the village in return for favors or loyalty to their
patron. As was mentioned earlier, forasteros theoretically had an im-
personal, contractual relationship with other inhabitants of the village. They perhaps cultivated the same potato and wheat fields, but
as rent-paying tenants, their relationship to nature was mediated
through the market. In some cases, which are occasionally documented in notarized wills and court records, forasteros gained landholding privileges in their host villages through marriage to an endowed widow or to a young female member of a local ayllu or
village.[35] But such prospects were unlikely under conditions where
forasteros vastly outnumbered originarios. Marriage to originario
women in Tapacarí (or in the other pueblos) probably did not propel
many landless forasteros into positions of economic security or village membership in this period. Astute alliances with one or another
cacique probably afforded a more open avenue for receiving land assignments (*asignaciones*) in the village, particularly at times of intense rivalry and factionalism.

Behind the land question and the allusions to corrupt patronage
lurked the issue of economic tyranny. Tapacarí's political fissure in
the 1740s and 1750s revealed the accumulated grievances of its local
people, and the accusing caciques were among the best chroniclers
of the outrages inflicted (by their rival) on village peasants. Blas Con-

33 Ibid., f. 4.

34 Viedma, *Descripción geográfica*, 64.

35 See, for example, "Autos sobre el dro. a las tierras de Pultintiri (Tiquipaya)"
AHMC, Leg. 1140 (1752).

dori charged that each person on the potato estancias of Lower Challa, Upper Challa, Antagua, Tallija, Apo, Muclli, and Guaylla was "obligated to cultivate 25 or 30 cargas of potatoes, which were later dried on the highest hillside and turned into chuño."[36] The pastoralists of the puna also paid rent (yerbaje) on the lands grazed by their llama herds. Those who owned mares, he claimed, had to pay ten or twelve reales a year, and all the peasants of the puna were required to purchase wheat harvested from Liro de Córdova's estates at fixed prices and on short-term credit. Condori said a group of hilacatas executed Liro de Córdova's orders and collected rent on his behalf.[37] The hilacatas to whom Condori referred may have been originario adult males assigned to live among the clusters of forasteros and to serve as sentinels and as nodes of social control in a network that bound the town of San Augustín de Tapacarí (center of the native hierarchy) to the remote estancias of the puna.

Yet even if this were so, it would hardly constitute the entire picture of Tapacarí's social hierarchy. The categories of originario and forastero were, of course, Spanish colonial constructs designed for fiscal and administrative purposes. However, as we have seen, some forasteros apparently managed to acquire land rights and employ tenants and sharecroppers, while Viedma observed many originario households living on the margin of subsistence. Thus, the status of originario alone did not determine a family's rights to seeds, lands, water, or herds or define its relations to the native hierarchy or to the resident forasteros. Many, perhaps most, members of the originario minority seemed to be impoverished, subordinated, and vulnerable to claimants both inside and outside the village.[38]

The rival caciques were uncharacteristically subdued on this point, but many originario witnesses decried their own inferior status and miserable living conditions. Widows claiming an authorized exemption from tribute and mita were particularly courageous in their denunciations of the caciques. One such widow, María Santuza, complained in 1758 that

> at present I am paying tribute because I refuse to leave my house to fulfill mita duties. I must give domestic service to that governor [Liro de Córdova] and other nobles of the pueblo. If I re-

36 "Exp. sobre . . . Fiorilo," f. 210.

37 "Juicio de Liro de Córdova contra Condori," ff. 34-35.

38 The intendant Viedma (*Descripción geográfica*, 173-174) later confirmed this impression, although he stressed the injustices that originarios suffered at the hand of religious authorities in the village.

fused to pay tribute they would seize my lands. To cultivate the reserve land of the community, I am obliged to lend six yoke of oxen, a plowshare, and laborers [*gañanes*] to plow, thresh, and gather the harvest. I never owed these obligations in the past, but now many widows and tributaries must pay them out of fear of the governors.[39]

She alluded to obligatory and coerced "rent" (in labor and kind) extracted from menfolk as well. Another widow told the magistrates that her husband had faithfully paid his tribute dues but still found himself obligated to render personal services to the cacique's lieutenant for one year. The woman claimed that her husband had helped to dig the irrigation ditches and construct the roof, walls, and patio of the lieutenant's hacienda in Tapacarí. After it was built, he spent the rest of the year as a domestic servant in the new estate. The widow said he had received no pay except for a daily ration of food.[40] Her words were echoed in the testimony by other originarios—men and women, cultivators and artisans, members of Anansaya and Urinsaya.

This record reveals a village torn apart by protracted factional disputes and sharply divided between an Indian minority wielding considerable economic power and a mass of peasants struggling for their livelihood. At first glance, it seems to contradict the impression left by the padrones that Tapacarí had withstood outside pressures more successfully than the smaller pueblos reales of the Valle Bajo. It is certainly true that the people of Tapacarí had managed to preserve their territory and shield themselves from an influx of non-Indians. Judged by this criterion, the village of Tapacarí had been able to reproduce its social system over two centuries of colonial rule. But the community had experienced profound internal transformations that had weakened its defenses against private accumulation and incipient class divisions in the interior of village society. Furthermore, the feud between cacique families had created a rift in Tapacarí that exacerbated social tensions and revealed the resentment that many peasants felt for members of both the native and the Spanish hierarchies. The peasants' testimony against the caciques and their clientele exposed a web of relations that bound them to their "overlords" through rent, obligatory loans of draft animals, domestic servitude,

39 "Juicio de Liro de Córdova contra Condori," ff. 22-23.
40 "Exp. sobre . . . Fiorilo," ff. 217v.-219.

and rotative field work on cacique-controlled lands.[41] Perhaps agrarian labor relations in the village still assumed reciprocal forms, but the social content had changed. Customary labor prestations had become *servicio personal* in the eyes of many peasants, and work on so-called community lands no longer guaranteed subsistence rights. When the cacique feud broke out, many peasants in Tapacarí took advantage of it to seek retribution in the colonial courts.

Class Relations and Colonial Legitimacies

The weak communal tradition and crisis of authority in Tapacarí left the village vulnerable to the divisive forces of class. Yet the advent of class differences and property ownership in Tapacarí did not entirely transform Andean social relations, based as they were on principles of kinship and reciprocity. The peasants managed to preserve some room for the reciprocal relations and collective work activities that knitted individuals and households into the traditional social fabric. Indians of the estancias probably maintained access to resources at different ecological tiers through reciprocal trading or labor arrangements with other estancias or with kinsmen. Work parties continued to be the norm on certain lands and at certain times in the agricultural cycle. The imperatives of subsistence agriculture and the need to pool risks and provide for insurance against crop failure ensured the survival of reciprocal labor relations, quite apart

41 There was, besides the caciques, another hierarchy, closely interwoven with the native one, that was an important source of tension in Tapacarí in the eighteenth century: the secular and regular clergy. San Augustín was the seat of an Augustinian monastery, and originario households were drafted, on a rotational basis, for a year of labor on the monastery's lands. Peasant families also subsidized the secular clergy. In an extensive list of grievances submitted to the court in 1796, Tapacarí Indians complained of the excessive labor services demanded by their parish priests whom they served as pack drivers, escorts, cooks, handymen, and field laborers. In addition, the petitioners challenged the custom of sponsoring religious festivities on the terms mandated by the priests. According to Indian testimony, the clerics appointed originario families each year to serve as patrons (*alfereces*) of one of the ten saints of the village. The annual cost per family of this patronage ranged between forty-seven pesos (in the subparish of Itapaya) and eighty-five pesos (in the village of San Augustín). Tapacareños complained that these parish dues "ruined even the more prosperous families." "Representación de los indios principales de Tapacarí . . . " (Sept. 26, 1796), RAH, ML 9/1675, tomo 20, f. 277. See also "Exp. que contiene recurso de los indios de Tapacarí sobre los derechos parroquiales . . . ," ANB, EC no. 31 (1761), and "Exp. sobre los abusos de los indios de Tapacarí . . . ," AGI, Charcas, Leg. 525 (1779).

from their ideological and ceremonial meanings. Modes of peasant livelihood called for some degree of collective decision-making about seed varieties, crop rotation, irrigation, and land and labor usage.[42] But these relationships are often not visible to historians; only in moments of stress or conflict do they sometimes come to light.

One such moment in the life of an Andean peasant household was the departure of a family for the mines of Potosí. When enrolled in the mita, a peasant family had to extricate itself from the multiple reciprocal relations that bound it to other households and had to entrust its meager resources to kinsmen who could be called upon in times of need. Such an arrangement might be phrased in Andean or commercial terms, but it rested on the principle of mutual aid. One example of such a caretaking arrangement comes from the village of Capinota in 1742. Called up for the mita, Ysidro Condo asked his son-in-law to safeguard his cattle, in return for which Condo would bring him maize, salt, and ají. This particular arrangement, tidy and even mercantile in form, eventually led to a lawsuit wherein Condo accused his relative of selling the cattle.[43] But what of the myriad other arrangements peasants made with their kinsmen, neighboring households, or ayllus, if they were to entrust their herds, lands, hut, and perhaps even children to others before they set off for the mines?

It is also conceivable that while the burdens of tribute and repartos turned peasants against members of the ethnic elite, they sometimes reinforced "horizontal" reciprocal or collective relationships. During the dispute between the two Tapacarí caciques which was discussed above, Pedro Condori accused Liro de Córdova of charging excessive ground rent to the potato cultivators of a highland estancia.[44] But that rent was paid by the entire estancia, not by individual peasant households. Among the rural forasteros of Tapacarí, such Andean forms of collectivity and reciprocity took root outside of traditional kinship and cultural contexts; there was no common ancestor-god, cultural heritage, or ethnic identity on which they could be grounded. They were born of a material and moral necessity to widen the range of subsistence options available.

But mutuality and reciprocity among peasants in the rural hinterlands of Tapacarí had little effect upon cacique rivalries or class

42 Halperin and Dow, *Peasant Livelihood*, esp. chaps. 2, 3, and 12.

43 "Testimonio del yndígena Ysidro Condo" (1742), AHMC, Leg. 1062.

44 "Juicio de Liro de Córdova contra Condori," ff. 4-5.

cleavages in the village. As we saw earlier, there was a privileged clique of natives who had accumulated wealth and entrenched themselves in the community as patrons of loyal factions, upon whose members they bestowed gifts of land and other resources. An incipient Indian landholding elite, certainly identifiable by Viedma's day, had distorted the traditional distribution of resources and violated the traditional normative order. Class tensions were already evident during the course of the feud between the caciques, who probably used the resources at their disposal to reinforce alliances with their clienteles. But by thus obtaining short-term economic and political gains, the caciques undermined their social standing in their own moieties. They could hardly pretend to serve as stewards of the community's norms and resources, mediators of disputes and conflicts, and overseers of the equitable distribution of lands and water, when they were clearly serving their own material and political interests. Their interstitial position in colonial society had always been a source of tension and contradiction. But once those contradictions were turned inward toward the collective well-being and undermined the self-sufficiency and subsistence autonomy of the peasants, reducing them to servicio personal or to supplicants of their own caciques, the village authorities had forsaken their moral stature. At a time when external pressures were growing and the corregidor was intervening more directly in village life, it was no longer possible for the caciques to balance colonial extraction against Andean legitimacy. In buttressing their own power and economic security through accumulation within the matrix of the community, they had sacrificed their integrity and authority. Once the feud was channeled through the courts and Tapacareños began to testify about conditions of life and work in the village, the caciques found themselves in the peculiar position of defending themselves to the magistrates of the audiencia. More than ever before, the caciques needed the support of the colonial rulers, when the greatest challenge to their position emanated from below—from the discontented, refractory peasantry.

But what was the criterion of a cacique's right to govern in the middle of the eighteenth century, in the opinion of the audiencia of La Plata? In conflicts between hereditary chiefs and those appointed by corregidores, who were seen as too ready to intervene in village life, the oidores were inclined to be on the side of tradition and noble lineage. Liro de Córdova did indeed attack Condori as an impostor, foisted on the community by Fiorilo. But the issue involved more than the question of inheritance versus appointment, for in villages throughout Alto Perú Indians were often appointed to serve as temporary chiefs (*caciques interinos* or *caciques gobernadores*) by colonial authorities, who took into consideration the quality of leadership and the comportment and usefulness of the appointees. Caciques had to carry out their duties within their villages, as well as meet their obligations to the state; they had to command their own people's respect and obedience, but they also had to ensure the delivery of tribute dues and mitayos. Furthermore, they were under increasing pressure to show that they would be able to make up any tribute deficits with their own personal wealth. Thus, Condori and Liro de Córdova had to both demonstrate their wealth to the magistrates and deny its origins in exploitative enterprises which violated the very Andean norms they were expected to respect and preserve.

Liro de Córdova, the deposed hereditary cacique, contended that he possessed the "finances necessary to guarantee the village's tribute."[45] The list of assets he presented was impressive: the hacienda Yllataco in Quillacollo and several houses nearby and in Tapacarí, and in the estancia Amaru; a quantity of silver plate; 50 oxen, 60 cows, 1,200 sheep, 70 horses, a mule train consisting of 10 animals, 8 mules equipped to transport wine, 15 burros, 8 riding mules, and 3 riding horses; and 360 fanegas of wheat and 40 fanegas of maize.[46] In addition, he named a half-dozen Indians who he said were willing to help him post bond for the tribute dues with the value of their own property or cash. Some of these bondsmen were principales of Tapacarí, but at least one, Bernardo Mamani, was an outsider, the brother of Sipesipe's cacique.[47] For his part, Condori warned the oidores about the insolvency of his rival's bondsmen and the sad little farm of 20 fanegadas of rocky, dry soil that Liro de Córdova called a hacienda. Condori declared that he would be able to cover tribute deficits through his own enterprise and his long-distance commercial ventures.[48]

The caciques' claims of prosperity and business acumen differed sharply from their uneasy, inconsistent testimony about their landholdings in the village. Neither one admitted that he controlled parcels of land in the village and charged rent in labor services. As we have seen, Condori said that estancia Indians paid Liro de Córdova

45 "Exp. sobre . . . Fiorilo."

46 Ibid., f. 55.

47 Ibid.

48 Ibid., ff. 66v.-73.

excessive rents, but Liro de Córdova said he enjoyed a benevolent relationship with the peasants who tilled his "reserve lands." How, he asked the magistrates, could he make Indians pay rent and forsake their right to pasture their herds and gather firewood on these lands? "The Indians may be poor, but they are aware of their legal obligations and would defy such [unjust] orders."[49] Nor did he force them to purchase wheat, he insisted, although he sold them wheat they needed to stock up for long journeys (presumably to Potosí). Liro de Córdova dismissed these charges with an economy of words. His use of the labor of Indians and their animals he explained in these words:

> In many other villages it is customary to oblige Indians to ride their mares to the wheat field and lend them for threshing the grain; the Indians must also help plant the seed and gather the ripened crop . . . ; but I never use my authority as governor to force people to work even when the crops are cultivated on community lands. My actions are infused with the spirit of Christianity . . . ; I solicit horses from village members and ask to borrow them. I also pay the Indian horse owners and give gifts . . . like jugs of aguardiente. And during the festivities on the day we thresh I give them abundant amounts of food and chicha.[50]

It is reasonable to assume that both Liro de Córdova and his traditional rival appreciated the symbolic importance of reciprocal gestures and generosity in their dealings with native laborers. Even when labor relations were essentially coerced and conflictual, the caciques probably supplied the food and drink to their workers that most hacendados customarily provided to their own peons at harvest time. But on an ideological level, Liro de Córdova tried to legitimate his authority in the eyes of the colonial magistrates by invoking Christian ideals as well as Andean norms of social behavior. His testimony projected the self-image of a native lord whose generosity took the specifically Andean form of gift-giving, supposedly part of an ongoing reciprocal relation with the village Indians, who then willingly contributed their horses and labor for the collective good. In presenting his case, Liro de Córdova obviously sought to narrow the social distance between himself and the peasants of Tapacarí and to camouflage the coercive nature of the labor that many Tapacareños testified to.

Throughout the trial, Condori and Liro de Córdova disputed each

49 "Juicio de Liro de Córdova contra Condori," ff. 4-5.

50 Ibid., f. 28v.

other's opinion about the capacity of Tapacarí's agricultural yields to cover tribute deficits. Condori claimed sufficient reserves existed; his rival denied it. Yet, as we have seen, both caciques declared themselves wealthy enough to personally make up any deficits. However, testimony by the caciques themselves and by originarios provide a very different picture of who bore the chronic burden of the village's tribute debts. Liro de Córdova stated that the caciques normally appointed thirteen originarios each year to collect tribute from each anexo in the parcialidades. These people, not the cacique, were responsible for covering the uncollected balance of the tribute quota. Liro de Córdova admitted that each of these "halacatas," as he called them, had accumulated debts for outstanding tribute dues, ranging from one hundred to three hundred pesos.[51] At other points in the trial, Pedro Condori similarly stated that the Indians whom he had appointed as tax collectors during the previous four years collectively owed him more than four thousand pesos.[52] Apparently, the practice of shifting the debt burden to these appointed collectors (*cobradores*) was common throughout the eighteenth century.[53] But the caciques, eager to prove to the magistrates their magnanimity, befitting Andean lords, assured them that they had seen to the prompt delivery of tribute dues, without imposing undue hardship on the debtors or the community. Condori told the judges that he raised tribute money by selling his own wheat in Arequipa and in the yungas of La Paz. He described his actions as personal sacrifices made to avoid selling community stocks or "confiscating the goods [of the cobradores] as I should have done" to meet the tribute payments.[54]

It is not known how often the caciques actually did cover tribute deficits out of their own assets. Condori's statement suggests that cobradores at least were at risk of losing their goods when there were deficits. The widow María Santuza told the oidores of her fear that her lands would be seized if tribute payments were not met (see

51 "Exp. sobre . . . Fiorilo," f. 64.

52 Ibid., passim, esp. ff. 64, 64v., and 66v.

53 Following the 1781 rebellions, provincial authorities often appointed caciques interinos to oversee tribute collection; their ability to cover tribute deficits was a necessary qualification for such an appointment. "Exp. sobre las elecciones de caciques interinos de Capinota," ANB, EC no. 72 (1796). On the economic hardships facing the cobradores, see AGN, Sala 9, Interior, 30.4.6, Leg. 30, Exp. 39 (1791), ff. 39-39v.

54 "Exp. sobre . . . Fiorilo," ff. 64v.-66v.

above). Other witnesses at the trial acknowledged personal debts to one of the caciques, and the means of their redemption can only be surmised. But caciques probably manipulated the terms of credit and debt among village Indians to their advantage. In their own testimony, however, they concealed their power over debtors by casting the relationship in an Andean mold: Through their alleged generosity, they were "saving" the Indians who failed to deliver the amount of tribute assigned them. The quest for colonial legitimacy forced them to try to reconcile the contradictions and conflicts between their economic power and patronage in the community, on the one hand, and their professed conformity to Andean norms of governance and authority (as sanctioned by the colonial state), on the other.

The audiencia of La Plata, and eventually the Council of the Indies, held for Liro de Córdova and reinstated his right of succession to the cacicazgo in the late 1750s.[55] Little is known of the family's activities for a couple of decades afterward, but by the 1780s, it had achieved control over both moieties. Sebastián Francisco, Juan Guillermo's son by his first wife, administered Anansaya, and Sebastián Francisco's son-in-law, Matías Quispe, was cacique of Urinsaya (see figure 9). The family had extended its holdings inside and outside the village of Tapacarí. According to private family records (which were unaffected by the need to present a favorable picture to the court), their properties included the haciendas Milloma and Casavinto in

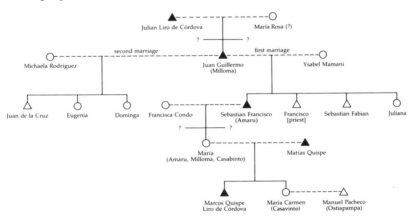

Figure 9   Genealogy of the Liro de Córdova Family of Tapacarí
Note: Shaded figures represent individuals who held the office of cacique. Names of haciendas owned by individuals are shown in parentheses.

55 Ibid., Cuaderno 1.

the parish of Las Ramadas, downriver from Tapacarí. The Casavinto estate included wheat lands and six grain mills; its assessed market value of 26,563 pesos made it one of the larger haciendas in the region. The purchase price of Milloma had been 24,000 pesos; Juan de la Cruz Liro de Córdova, son of Juan Guillermo by his second marriage, had paid it with the help of a loan of 12,000 pesos from a Carmelite convent.[56] A 1782 account book listed five other holdings: three haciendas of Sebastian Francisco Liro de Córdova and two chacras of Quispe and his wife.[57] Their total yield amounted to 541 fanegas of wheat and 47 cargas of potatoes—a poor harvest that must have suffered from the aftermath of the 1781 rebellion. Nonetheless, the estimated market value of the crop represented about three-quarters of the value of tribute owed by the originario population.[58] In addition, Juan de la Cruz Liro de Córdova owned 1,500 head of cattle that grazed on pasturelands in the estancia Aparumiri (the same estancia that Blas Condori had accused Juan Guillermo Liro de Córdova of possessing in 1758).[59] In the estancia of Amaru, María, daughter of Sebastian Francisco, owned grain mills and lands.[60] But the family's most extensive tract of land in Tapacarí was Añaguaiani. In 1782, the overseer reported that its wheat crop amounted to 253 fanegas. As was customary, he stored the grain, urging the caciques to sell it quickly because "the rebels continue to invade Tapacarí."[61]

The caciques ran their agrarian enterprises much like any other large landlord did. They entrusted management to a creole overseer, Fontanilla, who kept records of their holdings, harvests, and returns. During the harvest period, he hired between fourteen and forty-seven jornaleros for fourteen successive days to cut and gather the wheat

---

56 "División de la hacienda y molinas de Milloma . . .," AHMC, Leg. 1062 (1791); "Testamento de doña María Liro de Córdova," AHMC, Leg. 1090 (1792) (hereafter cited as "Testamento de doña María Liro de Córdova"); "Exp. de Juan de la Cruz Liro de Córdova . . . sobre la nulidad de la venta de tierras 'Casavinto,' " AHMC, Leg. 1256 (1782) (hereafter cited as "Exp. de Juan de la Cruz").

57 "Cuaderno de cuentas dadas . . . de las cosechas de las sementeras de los caciques de Tapacarí," ANB, EC no. 84 (1782) (hereafter cited as "Cuaderno de cuentas").

58 "Cuaderno de cuentas."

59 "Exp. de Juan de la Cruz."

60 "Testamento de doña Maria Liro de Córdova." The mills, alone carried an assessed market value of 18,000 pesos.

61 "Cuaderno de cuentas."

and between twenty-seven and thirty men for three days to load the grain on pack animals and carry it to the storage huts. To thresh and winnow the wheat on days when the wind was favorable for carrying away the chaff, Fontanilla called upon "all the people of [the estancias] Yrpuma, Guanuara, and Escalera."[62] In private, the caciques and their creole administrator viewed their properties as commercial ventures. Away from the scrutiny of rivals and oidores, there was no allusion to reciprocity between caciques and the peasants who worked on their lands.

Despite ritual gestures to nativism, this native elite was very Hispanic in its way of life. Not only did a creole look after its properties and a convent lend it money. At least two children of Juan Guillermo were educated in creole schools.[63] Several kin married mestizos or creoles, and others intermarried with cacique families of Capinota and other pueblos reales. At least one member of the family, María, had a mulatto slave as her personal servant. María's wealth also included lands, mills, herds, and all manner of textiles, including rich velvets from the capitals of Europe and *polleras* (layers of full skirts) made of fine bayeta—a luxurious amalgamation of two cultures.[64]

This, then, is the unequivocal evidence of an extraordinarily wealthy cacique family that had amassed property and power in Tapacarí between the 1740s and the outbreak of the Andean rebellion of 1781. The Liro de Córdovas had emerged from the trials with the support of the highest colonial authorities. Over the next couple of decades, the family took advantage of this legitimation to advance its economic interests. Precisely during the peak period of repartimientos de mercancías, the Liro de Córdovas extended their hold over community resources. It is not unreasonable to assume, therefore, that the processes of privatization and internal differentiation in Tapacarí accelerated in the decades prior to the 1781 uprisings.

But in the context of village society, even one like Tapacarí, which was historically weakened by ethnic fragmentation and factionalism, indigenous authority that rested on class domination and colonial legitimation was always subject to the threat of social alienation and rejection. As Hispanicized native landholders, the caciques were hardly distinguishable from other members of the colonial hier-

62 Ibid.

63 "Exp. de Juan de la Cruz."

64 "Testamento de doña María Liro de Córdova."

archy. Moreover, they were regarded as people who had rejected or forsaken their Andean heritage to serve their own class interests and those of the state. Their lip service to Andean ways notwithstanding, the Liro de Córdovas represented the colonizers, and thus they occupied a vulnerable position in their own society. The events of 1781 fully exposed the caciques to the scorn and hatred of their people. When rebellion finally erupted in Tapacarí early in 1781, the caciques became despised outcasts.

In the last days of February, a group of Andeans gathered together near the village of Challa, near the mountain pass where the road crossed the provincial border. One Sunday morning, as mass was being held, they swept down from the mountains and invaded San Augustín de Tapacarí, the seat of the pueblo real. The rebels killed the parish priest and several hundred other people, although Sebastian Liro de Córdova and Matías Quispe had been warned and had fled at dawn. Following the attack, the rebels retreated to the mountains, regrouped, and then attacked the Liro de Córdovas' hacienda Milloma, turning it into their fortress. The hacienda was located in the river valley, and, by controlling it, the rebels were able to cut off Tapacarí proper from the lower river basin and the central valleys of Cochabamba. Communication was also impeded by nature for it was the rainy season, and the swollen river made it difficult for troops to come to the aid of the besieged pueblo. The month of March was punctuated by bloody battles between the Andean rebels and the royalist troops. In their first foray from the provincial capital of Cochabamba, creole militiamen drove the insurgents out of Milloma and back into the mountains. In the meantime, however, other rebel bands closed in upon the village of Tapacarí and repelled the Spanish attacks. The corregidor then dispatched a second major expedition, which managed to recapture Tapacarí after a fierce and costly battle.[65]

Not a great deal is known about the alliances, tactics, or leadership of the rebels who seized San Augustín. But there is no mistaking the enmity between the rebels and the ethnic elite of Tapacarí. The caciques entrusted their valuables and 2,000 pesos in cash to a wealthy

65 "Sublevación de los indios de Tapacarí," AHMC, Leg. 1275 (1781), "Ynformación sumaria producida sobre las alteraciones de la provincia de Cochabamba en 1781," Archivo de la Biblioteca de la Universidad Mayor de San Andrés (La Paz), no. 97, f. 6; AGN, Sala 9, Intendencia, 5.8.2, Leg. 1 (July 3, 1782); Lillian Estelle Fisher, *The Last Inca Revolt, 1780–1783* (Norman: University of Oklahoma Press, 1966), 160-162, 166-167. Besides the rebellion focused on Tapacarí, there were local uprisings that same year in Arque, Colcha, Cliza, and other places.

vecino outside the village in order "to protect their property from the pillage of the Indian rebels."[66] When the rebellion had been crushed and royal inquiries began, a young mestizo woman testified boldly about the hostility that Tapacareños felt toward the cacique clan.

> Indian rebels came from Challapata and Ayopaya killing Spaniards and all white people. . . . Their first enemies were the caciques . . . who hid their possessions before they fled . . . The caciques, Don Sebastian Córdova and Don Matías Quispe, are very rich men and in all parts of this land the Indian insurgents hunt the rich to rob them and take their lives. I have heard many Indians say that the main objective of the rebels was to kill these caciques, especially Córdova, for being the compadre of the priest and for concealing the tariff [of the repartimiento de mercancías] in order to rob the Indians. It is rumored that the caciques stole from originario principales, too. They have controlled power for many generations.[67]

These observations, impressions, and rumors indicate only the shadowy outlines of this rebellion, one that articulated with the earlier and concurrent struggles that unfolded in the highlands under the legendary leadership of Túpac Catari and Túpac Amarú.[68] But they also reveal the gulf that separated the masses from the ethnic elite in Tapacarí, an elite so entrenched and so distant, with its Christian-Hispanic ways, that it could not fend off the rebels with

66 "Exp. . . . sobre la restitución de pesos pertenecientes a los caciques . . . ," ANB, EC no. 78 (1781).

67 "Sublevación de los indios de Tapacarí," AHMC, Leg. 1275 (1781), ff. 6-9v.

68 The literature on the Túpac Catari and Túpac Amarú rebellions and associated local uprisings is growing rapidly. See Leon Campbell, "Recent Research on Andean Peasant Revolts, 1750-1820," *Latin American Research Review* 14 (1979): 3-49; Alberto Flores Galindo, ed., *Túpac Amarú II: 1780* (Lima: Retablo de papel, 1976); Scarlett O'Phelan Godoy, "La rebelión de Túpac Amarú: Organización interna, dirigencia y alianzas," *Histórica* 3 (1979): 89-121; Scarlett O'Phelan Godoy, "Tierras comunales y revuelta social: Perú y Bolivia en el siglo XVIII," *Allpanchis*, año 13, vol. 19 (1983): 75-91; and O'Phelan Godoy, *Rebellions and Revolts*. Recent studies of the ideological aspects of the Túpac Amarú and Túpac Catari rebellions include Jorge Hidalgo Lehuedé, "Amarus y cataris: Aspectos mesiánicos de la rebelión indígena de 1781 en Cusco, Chayanta, La Paz, y Arica," *Revista Chungará*, no. 10 (1983): 117-138; Stern, "Age of Andean Insurrection," and Alberto Flores Galindo, "Buscando un Inca" (paper presented at the Social Science Research Council/University of Wisconsin Conference on Resistance and Rebellion in the Andean World, 18th-20th centuries, Madison, Wis., Apr. 26-28, 1984).

its own partisan defenders. Instead, the caciques moved out of the orbit of the pueblo real into Spanish territory—the only safe haven under the circumstances. The caciques became exiles, dependent on the colonial militia and state for their protection.

Thus, the earlier judicial victory of the Liro de Córdovas was a Pyrrhic one. Colonial legitimation ultimately proved their undoing in the uprisings of 1781. While it gave them a new lease on life, allowing them to accumulate great personal wealth in the village, it further eroded the traditional relationships between the ethnic elite and ordinary Tapacareños. The caciques' power and material security no longer depended upon their social prestige in the village or on their ability to command the labor and loyalty of peasants through a process of reciprocal (though asymmetrical) exchanges. Kinship and community, as defined in Andean terms, had lost their meaning in Tapacarí, and Tapacareños, both originario and forastero, saw the native elite violating traditional norms. As the pressures of repartimiento bore down harder on peasant households and stretched subsistence patterns to the breaking point, and as the Liro de Córdovas acquired title to some of the best lands and herds in Tapacarí, there seemed little the village Indians could do to block the ascent of an Indian landed oligarchy. But when Andean rebels mobilized throughout the southern Andes early in 1781, the moment of peasant reprisal in Tapacarí had arrived. The local insurgents exposed the fragility of ethnic power and authority that had come to be based primarily on class relations and colonial legitimation.

Haciendas
and the Rival
Peasant Economy

Despite the ambivalence of the early colonial state toward private landownership in the maize valleys, Spanish colonists extended their control over Cochabamba's valleys and highlands until they occupied most of the fertile areas, encircling the five pueblos reales. By the 18th century, rural life in most parts of the region revolved around the hacienda, where a dispossessed and dependent peasantry worked for the landlords in return for access to the means of subsistence. Whether they worked the lands of a great estate or turned in a share of the crops they grew on a small plot, the peasants of the haciendas were bound to their landlords in a web of mutual obligations (and antagonisms) that was relatively impervious to the colonial state. Indeed, this was the source of the ambivalence of Toledo and his successors, who feared a permanent "loss" of village peasants to the private domain.

The state's perspective—that the haciendas secluded peasants from the extractive institutions of colonial society—led to an image of mute, docile, dependent people eking out a precarious livelihood under the control of an omnipotent landlord. Much of the early literature on seigneurial relations, particularly on Mexican haciendas, reinforced this view.[1] In the Andean context, the peasants appeared

1 This was particularly the case in the classic study by François Chevalier, *La formation des grands domaines au Mexique: Terre et société aux XVIe-XVIIe siècles* (Paris: Institut d'Ethnologie, 1952). More recent literature has challenged this interpretation. Three surveys of that literature and discussions of the research and debates surrounding the Mexican, and more generally the Spanish American, hacienda are Magnus Mörner, "The Spanish American Hacienda: A Survey of Recent Research and Debate," *Hispanic American Historical Review* 53 (1973): 183-216; Eric Van Young, "Mexican Rural History since Chevalier: The Historiography of the Colonial Hacienda," *Latin American Research Review* 18 (1983), 5-61; and Enrique Florescano, "The Formation and Economic Structure of the Hacienda in New Spain," in Leslie Bethell, ed., *The Cambridge*

to be Indians who had forsaken their rights and obligations to their own communities and the right to act or speak as members of their ethnic family. In theory, they were atomized and directly subordinated, through property and patron-client relations, to a master. They had no claim on either Andean or colonial legitimacy, such as their counterparts in Tapacarí did. There was apparently little recourse but to submit or accommodate.

Yet colonial authorities themselves contradicted their own stereotypes of the hacienda peasants when they reflected on the Cochabamba tax rebellion of the early 1730s (see chapter 3). The exploitative relations that emerged on the haciendas did not escape resistance and challenge, even when the peasants had "voluntarily" agreed to the rent or labor arrangements. Like the village peasants, tenants on haciendas sought to protect their subsistence security, but their struggle was focused on the terms of land tenure and rent. Occasionally, the conflicts were channeled through the courts, affording glimpses of the peasants' perceptions of their rights and obligations.

But it was the proliferation of a commercially oriented peasantry in the central valleys rather than direct political confrontations, that constituted the greatest threat to the landowning class. Rural smallholders who leased patches of hacienda land engaged in petty trade and crafts in addition to their agricultural activities. Periodically, they entered the market as sellers of small food surpluses or specialized commodities. The resulting myriad of economic enterprises, small in scale and precapitalist in nature, changed the contours of the regional economy. For some peasants, this diversification substantially lessened their dependence on the landlords and mitigated the effects of harvest failure. But for the landowning class, the advent of a commercially active peasantry, which increasingly controlled cereal production on the estates, undermined its economic power and challenged its monopoly of grain surpluses.

As class relations became more intricate in the eighteenth century, the social geography acquired texture and variation. Increasingly, the region seemed to be composed of two subregions: on the one hand, the central valleys, and on the other, the western highlands and river valleys that reached upland toward the altiplano. The western highlands and river valleys served as trade corridors between the altiplano and the central valleys, but they were not caught up in

History of Latin America (Cambridge: Cambridge University Press, 1984), 2: 153-188.

the economic trends that swept across the central valleys. In fact, some western areas, such as Ayopaya, seemed more disconnected from the central valleys than ever before. In contrast, the three central valleys (Valle Bajo, Sacaba, and Cliza) were the site of numerous haciendas and smallholdings, Spanish towns and pueblos, and primitive manufactories and workshops. The region's economic pulse beat there, where a growing peasant population produced, distributed, and consumed staple goods that flowed through a network of commercial arteries. Contemporary census reports reveal the subregional patterns of agriculture, industry, and trade in eighteenth-century Cochabamba.

Charting the Social Geography

The European sojourners and administrators, weary after weeks of travel by mule or horseback across the altiplano, must have been relieved and delighted upon arriving in Cochabamba valley, to find a temperate climate and a fertile land inhabited by many Spaniards and creoles. Like Vázquez de Espinosa more than a century earlier, Cosme Bueno wrote in the 1740s that Cochabamba had every right "to call itself the granary of Peru, because it produces in abundance all kinds of seeds in a benign and healthy climate. . . . Streams of good water irrigate the fields and fertilize the valleys where there are more than 300 haciendas."[2] Some forty years later, Francisco de Paula Sanz, then administrator of the royal tobacco monopoly, inspected the province and described it as "one of the most beautiful places I have seen in all the viceroyalty. [The capital city] is surrounded by country houses [*quintas*] whose lands are cultivated, ringed by fruit orchards, and bathed by the waters of two rivers, the Tamborada and the Rocha."[3] Though Paula Sanz submitted the report in 1783, he had toured the parishes of Cochabamba shortly before the western districts were convulsed by the rebellions of 1781. His report reflected an unwarranted optimism about the region's vitality and social order. Indeed, Paula Sanz discussed the state of agriculture and industry without mentioning the quality of life or hu-

2 Cosme Bueno, "Descripción de las provincias pertenecientes al arzobispado de La Plata" [1740s], in Manuel de Odriozola, ed., *Colección de documentos literarios del Perú* (Lima: A. Alfaro, 1872), 3: 123-124.

3 "Copia de la descripción de la provincia de Cochabamba que hizo el . . . d. Francisco de Paula Sanz," RAH, ML, 9/1725, tomo 70 (Sept. 21, 1783). (Cited hereafter as "Descripción de Cochabamba").

man conditions in the valleys. He was content to catalogue the economic activities of the "one hundred thousand souls" who inhabited the province.

Less than ten years later, Francisco de Viedma, the first head of the intendancy of Santa Cruz de la Sierra (which had absorbed the province of Cochabamba), wrote his well-known description of the region, a description marked by great concern for detail. Viedma spent several years traveling through the parishes and collecting data before producing his account in 1788.[4] Unlike Paula Sanz, he was deeply disturbed by the poverty and human need he had seen all around him. In the wake of the rebellions, the scandalous behavior of the corregidores, and the drought of 1784, Viedma refused to ignore the penury of peasant life, the deep class divisions, and the precarious balance of class forces in local society.

Viedma deplored the conditions he found, all the more because the region's special ecological niche in the Andean landscape seemed to have offered a happy alternative, in European eyes, to the harsh climate and austere life of puna Indians. "Upon hearing a geographic description of the entire province, who would not consider it to offer the greatest possibilities for human happiness on earth? And upon hearing of the region's abundant resources and population, who would not wonder why [the region] has suffered such calamities?"[5] It was a question that Viedma tried to answer now and again in his long report. This report was essentially a compilation of statistics and observations which, when added to Paula Sanz's report, yields a picture of zonal variations in the three central valleys of Cochabamba and the outlying western districts.

Viedma's report provided the first complete census and socioracial profile of the province. It showed that 125,245 people inhabited the five partidos of the province—about 7 percent of the total population of the viceroyalty (table 13).[6] It confirmed earlier impressions of the

4 Viedma, *Descripción geográfica*. There is some confusion about the year that this report was written. Although it is dated 1793, Nicolás Sánchez-Albornoz discovered correspondence from Viedma indicating that it was actually completed in 1788 (personal communication and *Indios y tributos*, 167). The intendancy of Santa Cruz de la Sierra stretched across the vast, relatively unexplored jungle lowlands east of the Andean escarpment and beyond the lowland town of Santa Cruz. However, its heartland continued to be the densely populated "high valleys" of Cochabamba and the western river valleys and highlands of Arque, Tapacarí, and Ayopaya that bordered the altiplano to the west.

5 Viedma, *Descripción geográfica*, 159.

6 Golte (*Repartos y rebeliones*, 42) has estimated that the population of Alto and Bajo Perú at the time was about 1,800,000.

Table 13. Socioracial Distribution of the Population of Cochabamba Province, by Partido, 1788

	Total		Socioracial Category					
Partido	*Number*	*Percent*	*Spanish*	*Mestizo*	*Cholo*[a]	*Indian*	*Mulatto*	*Black*
Cochabamba (Cercado)[b]	22,305	17.8	6,368	12,980	0	1,182	1,600	175
Sacaba	7,614	6.1	1,249	2,290	0	3,805	269	1
Tapacarí	26,937	21.5	3,277	6,280	1,597	14,770	996	17
Cliza	37,615	30.0	6,682	12,192	0	16,355	2,366	20
Arque	22,137	17.7	1,238	3,936	1,286	15,158	496	23
Ayopaya	8,637	6.9	1,275	1,493	0	5,620	247	2
Total								
Number	125,245		20,089	39,171	2,883	56,890	5,974	238
Percentage								
of total		100.0	16.0	31.3	2.3	45.4	4.8	0.2

Source: Viedma, "Descripción geográfica," AGN, Sala 9, Intendencia, 5.8.5, Aug. 10, 1793. This is the original manu-script on which the subsequent Bolivian publication was based. As Sánchez-Albornoz has pointed out (personal com-munication and *Indios y tributos*, 167), several of the population figures given in the manuscript were printed incor-rectly in the published Bolivian version.

[a] Officially defined as persons of one-quarter "white ancestry."

[b] The Cercado was the district of the provincial capital—i.e., the city of Cochabamba and its environs.

acculturative pressures in this region. Cochabamba had a larger pro-portion of real or alleged mestizos—nearly one-third of the popula-tion—than most other provinces of Peru. Less than half of the prov-ince's inhabitants were classified as Indians, even by Viedma, who, as intendant was intent upon increasing tribute revenue. By way of comparison, about 21 percent of the population of the entire viceroy-alty was mestizo and about 60 percent, Indian.[7] Acculturative influ-ences were most marked in the Cercado district of Cochabamba proper, where mestizos outnumbered Indians by more than ten to one, and in the valley of Cliza, where there were about three-quar-ters as many mestizos as there were Indians. Some 25,000 mestizos (nearly two-thirds of all the mestizos in the province) lived in these two partidos, and so did about two-thirds of the province's 20,000 Spaniards. Large numbers of Indians, on the other hand, were found in the western river valley of Arque and the partido of Tapacarí. Of those Indians who lived on Spanish rural properties or in towns out-side the jurisdiction of the five pueblo reales, about 60 percent lived in the Spanish parishes of the three central valleys.

The Cercado

The town of Cochabamba, with its surroundings, was still the province's center of power and commerce in the late eighteenth cen-

7 Ibid.

tury, even though it was not the largest district in population. It was the provincial capital, nesting in the rich alluvial plain that received the waters from the two higher valleys of Sacaba and Cliza and from the northern and western quebradas of the Valle Bajo. Situated at an altitude of 8,200 feet, the city of Cochabamba and its hinterlands were surrounded in the west and north by the Cordillera Oriental and the towering peaks of Tunari, whose snows fed the volcanic lakes and streams that irrigated the bottomlands and cooled them during the summer months of November through January. To the east of the city rose the small mountain chain of San Pedro, separating the Valle Bajo from the valley of Sacaba. Low-lying hills to the south also cut Cochabamba off from the higher valley of Cliza. The city was strategically situated at the axis of the three central valleys connected by two narrow corridors—one leading to Sacaba and the frontiers beyond, the other leading to the vast, open valley of Cliza and points southeast.

The climate and the drainage by mountain streams helped make the Valle Bajo one of the richest arable areas in Alto Perú. Sandy, rocky soil, poor in organic materials, was found in higher parts of the valley, especially at the base of the northern cordillera, but in the central parts of the valley, alluvial deposits and ravines left by torrents and flooding after the rainy season were high in organic nutrients. The alluvial soil, with low levels of salinity, gave the highest crop yields in the valley. Agrarian studies of the Valle Bajo in the twentieth century show that in this valley, 70 percent of flat cultivable land were irrigated (though only 20 percent of all valley land had an abundant supply of water).[8] The evidence of agricultural conditions in the eighteenth century is, of course, less clear-cut. Both Paula Sanz and Viedma alluded to the lands of the Cercado as the richest in the province. "Extensive irrigation allows [cultivators] to plant vegetables, strawberries and fruit trees, and fodder in great abundance," Viedma observed in 1788.[9] Maize and wheat were also cultivated on irrigated land in the district, though many farmers allocated drier, less fertile lands to their wheat and potato crops. Yet despite relatively high yields, agrarian enterprises in the Cercado district provided a small portion of the region's grain production. The Cercado had 18 percent of the province's total population and yet

8 Carlos Camacho Saa, *Minifundia, Productivity, and Land Reform* (Madison, Wis.: Land Tenure Center, 1966), 16.

9 Viedma, *Descripción geográfica*, 46.

produced only about 8 percent of all its tithed grain.[10] Perhaps many cultivators devoted themselves to horticultural and other crops that were not tithed, or perhaps the Cercado's urban concentration left relatively little room for agrarian activities.

Viedma reported that the Cercado boasted fourteen large haciendas, "which resemble small villages inhabited by Indians and mestizos who till the soil of their rancherías as tenants of the landowners who possess them."[11] He was probably referring to the largest haciendas in the city's immediate environs—haciendas such as Calacala, with 34 adult Indian males; Queruqueru, with 34; Sivingani, with 21; Caracoto, with 39 tributary families; and the enormous Santa Vela Cruz y Tamborada estate, with 112 tributaries in 1786. These were surrounded by smaller holdings, listed as *pertenencias*, which supported only two or three Indian families and perhaps a few other peasants who were not registered in the tribute system.[12]

Not all the Indians resided on haciendas, however. According to the 1802 padrón, about a thousand of them lived in poor urban barrios, such as Colpapampa, Caracota, and the hillside of San Sebastián, or outside of town, on the Pampa de las Carreras, for example.[13] Many Indians leased plots of land from the monasteries in order to grow their own food. Others worked as domestic servants, craftsmen, or traders. Many Indian and mestizo men and women were self-employed or did piecework, spinning and weaving rustic cotton textiles. Viedma wrote that "in the city [of Cochabamba] and many towns throughout the province, [people] manufacture the ordinary cotton cloth that they call *tocuyos* for local consumption and for

10 Average tithes collected during the five-year period from 1806 to 1810 provide a rough guidepost to the relative magnitudes of grain production among the different partidos (excluding the pueblos reales, which did not pay full tithes). In the Spanish valley zone, for example, there was a considerable difference between the amounts of cereal produced in the Cercado district and the Cliza valley. While Cliza was drier in parts than the eastern end of the Valle Bajo, the district produced significantly more grain than did the smaller, more densely populated Cercado area.

11 Viedma, *Descripción geográfica*, 45.

12 AGN, Sala 13, Padrones, 18.2.1, Leg. 46 (1786-1787), ff. 104v.-106v., and 18.3.3, Leg. 53 (1802). Whereas Viedma focused his attention on the more opulent estates, tribute collectors inventoried large and small properties alike, in search of tributaries. The 1802 padrón, for example, listed thirty-one rural properties in the Cercado where tributaries lived and worked.

13 AGN, Sala 13, Padrones, 18.3.3, Leg. 53 (1802), f. 212.

export to the highlands, Tucumán, and even Buenos Aires.[14] The 1801 census listed one cloth factory in Cochabamba where twenty-four adult men and thirty-five adult married women operated the treadle looms and spinning wheels.[15]

Though these Indians were assimilated into urban life, engaging in all kinds of commercial pursuits and sometimes seeking opportunities to shed their ethnic identity and free themselves of tribute dues, many members of the urban plebe never learned to speak Spanish. Viedma observed that the urban poor of Cochabamba spoke no other language than Quechua, and he expressed concern that Quechua was seeping into the speech of "respectable women."[16] This was to be expected, since these women dealt directly with servants and with the market women every day of their lives. The large influx of urban or semiurban Indians and mestizos would inevitably affect European culture, to the consternation of this erudite and proud Spaniard. Yet the poor urban dwellers of Cochabamba did not constitute a homogeneous acculturated group that had adopted and diluted the norms and customs of the dominant class. Many natives clung to fragments of their own culture in the midst of urban life. In the very heart of the Cercado district, for example, parcels of land called *yncacollos* still belonged to the "comunidad de yndios de Tapacarí y Capinota," according to the 1802 census.[17]

The concentration of town dwellers in the Cercado made it the largest commercial center in the region. According to Paula Sanz, "there are many prosperous vecinos, food is abundant, and all kinds of cloth are traded here."[18] Viedma concurred in his report: "You can find all the necessities of life in the plaza every day of the week; food is very moderately priced, including meat and bread and all kinds of vegetables, fruits, and fowl. . . . From distant provinces, they bring in salt, dried fish, wines, aguardientes, and sugar."[19] But the intendant pointed out that the merchants imported very little wine (in contrast, it might be added, to Potosí's enormous import trade in spirits) because of the peculiar passion for the chicha which local women distilled from maize. Viedma seemed scandalized by the volume of

14 Viedma, *Descripción geográfica*, 47.

15 AGN, Sala 13, Padrones, 18.3.3, Leg. 53 (1802), f. 212.

16 Viedma, *Descripción geográfica*, 46.

17 AGN, Sala Padrones, 18.3.3, Leg. 53 (1802), f. 212.

18 "Descripción de Cochabamba," f. 2.

19 Viedma, *Descripción geográfica*, 46.

consumption of this alcoholic drink. He estimated that, each year, 200,000 fanegas of maize were turned into chicha and drunk by the "vulgar" and even by the "decent" people in the region.[20]

The Partido of Tapacarí

Not far west of the city of Cochabamba lay the much smaller Spanish parish of Quillacollo. It was bordered on the north by the pueblos reales of El Paso and Sipesipe and on the south by serranía. The parish of Quillacollo was in the partido of Tapacarí; it occupied most of the Valle Bajo, except for the Cercado and the western ravine and highlands of the pueblo real of Tapacarí. It was the main parish of haciendas and the westernmost extension of legal Spanish land occupation. As such, it may be contrasted with the town of San Augustín de Tapacarí, where few Spaniards lived. In his study of the partido of Tapacarí, Sánchez-Albornoz describes San Augustín and Quillacollo as two poles, one Indian and the other Spanish, competing for land and labor.[21] In geographic and commercial terms, however, Quillacollo was more oriented to the eastern end of the valley than to the western. It lay along the royal highway that connected the river valleys of Arque and the altiplano to the capital city and points east. Although Quillacollo had its own market on Sundays, the parish sent some of its grain surpluses to Cochabamba, Arque, and Oruro.[22] Textiles and agriculture occupied most of its laborers. Viedma mentioned that "no other town [in the province] dedicated itself as much to cloth weaving." He estimated that five hundred cholos and mestizos were engaged in this craft as artisans or wage workers in the factory owned by Pedro del Cerro, which made bayeta and ordinary cloth.[23]

20 Ibid., 47. The consumption of chicha gave much of the stimulus to the cultivation of maize. Viedma may have exaggerated the volume of chicha consumption, but his emphasis on its importance to maize production was well founded. The most highly valued irrigated lands in the central valleys were usually earmarked for maize, and the best fields yielded two harvests in good years. By contrast, wheat was usually grown on tracts of unirrigated land in the cooler highlands. The first known figures on maize and wheat production in the region were published in the Dalence census of 1846, which showed that the department of Cochabamba produced 189,136 fanegas of wheat and 476,794 fanegas of maize in a "normal" year. See José María Dalence, *Bosquejo estadístico de Bolivia* (La Paz: Editorial Universidad Mayor de San Andrés, 1975), 238.

21 Sánchez-Albornoz, *Indios y tributos*, 172-173.

22 "Descripción de Cochabamba," f. 3.

23 Viedma, *Descripción geográfica*, 67.

Sacaba

While the parish of Quillacollo was noted for its textile work-shops, the valley of Sacaba—which lay on the other side of San Sebastian hill from Cochabamba—was famous for its wheat crop, an "abundant and superior wheat crop" said Paula Sanz, "that feeds the capital city."[24] In parts of the Sacaba valley, settlers had introduced a system of mixed farming, whereby animal husbandry and pastoralism in the highlands and cereal cultivation in the valleys were mutually dependent, striking a delicate ecological balance similar to that in many grain regions of preindustrial Europe.[25] Landlords carved out large tracts of land in the valley for the cultivation of wheat, maize, and fodder crops. Since the Sacaba River was dry most of the year, the vecinos had their workers construct reservoirs in the northern highlands above the Sacaba valley, which caught rainwater during the summer. Canals and ravines channeled water from these reservoirs and from small streams to the valley estates during the dry season. As in many regions in the Andes, creole landlords adopted the native custom of distributing scarce water in turns according to a strict time schedule. The elaborate irrigation system in Sacaba mitigated the otherwise wide variation in crop yields, "so that in general, the harvests are good."[26] Viedma reported that rural Indian, mestizo, and mulatto tenants cultivated superior qualities of wheat, maize, and alfalfa on Sacaba's largest haciendas. These peasants often had access to their landlords' pastures at higher elevations: "in the cordillera, the tenants keep their sheep and cattle in estancias."[27] Each year, the shepherds drove their animals down to the valley, where the animals would graze on and fertilize the recently harvested fields. Some landlords took advantage of the annual journey by requiring the pastoralists to work in the fields, cutting the last of the ripened wheat. For example, the herders of Ucuchi, an estancia tucked away in the remote cordillera to the north of Sacaba, were expected to work for a month on the valley lands of their lord to fulfill a labor obligation demanded of them as part of their rent. In

24 "Descripción de Cochabamba," f. 2.

25 B. H. Slicher Van Bath, *The Agrarian History of Western Europe, 800-1850* (London: Edward Arnold, 1963); Joan Thirsk, ed., *The Agrarian History of England and Wales (1500-1640)* (Cambridge: Cambridge University Press, 1967), vol. 4, chaps. 2 and 3.

26 Viedma, *Descripción geográfica*, 53.

27 Ibid.

addition, they paid rent in kind and money to their landlord each year.[28]

Cliza

A small mountain chain separated the Sacaba valley from the Cliza, the largest of the three central valleys. Stretching some thirty miles long and an average of seven miles wide, the Valle Alto of Cliza lay at an altitude of 8,700 feet. Because of its altitude, Cliza suffered from a chronic shortage of water. Its shallow rivers virtually disappeared during the dry season, though they frequently flooded during the rainy season. (It is telling that even after the agrarian reform of the 1952 revolution, many peasants of Cliza were unable to reorient the traditional maize and potato cultivation to intensive horticulture because of a lack of irrigation.)[29] The deficiency of water, together with a scarcity of alluvial deposits, meant consistently lower yields than in the Sacaba and Cerado parishes, greater fluctuations in yields from one year to the next, and diminishing returns from the soil after fewer years of cultivation. In the early nineteenth century, the market value of unirrigated maize and wheat land was only between 10 and 20 percent of the market value of the permanently irrigated soil in the most desirable valley zones. An inventory of the hacienda Chullpas in the Cliza valley, made shortly after independence, showed that its most valuable land was assessed at a rate nine times higher than its least valuable cultivated land (table 14).

Several factors may have compensated for the limited supply of water in the Valle Alto. First, its sheer territorial size, a total 150,000 acres, allowed landlords and peasants to increase production expanding the area of arable land. The narrow belt of land skirting the mountains was traditionally planted with wheat, while maize and potatoes were usually cultivated in the more fertile, partially irrigated central and eastern valley zones. Second, the proximity of higher elevations allowed peasants to cultivate tuber crops; oca, for example, should be planted in small patches of dry land and in soil

28 "Arriendos y tasaciones (con sus obligaciones, tareas, yuntas, urcas y leña) de los arrenderos de la estancia Ucuchi," AHMC, Leg. 1096 (1801-1808).

29 Camacho Saa, *Minifundia*; Leonard E. Olen, *Cantón Chullpas: A Socio-Economic Study of the Cochabamba Valley of Bolivia* (Washington, D.C.: Foreign Agricultural Reports, 1948); Richard W. Patch, "Social Implications of the Bolivian Agrarian Reform" (Ph.D. diss., University of Michigan, 1956).

Table 14. Assessed Value of the Hacienda Chullpas, in Cliza, 1828

Type of Property	Number of Fanegas	Price per Fanega (pesos)	Value
Permanently irrigated maize land	26	450	11,700
Partially irrigated maize land	30	250	7,500
Cultivable land outside hacienda	12	240	2,880
Unirrigated maize land	84	100	8,400
Unirrigated wheat land	154	50	7,700
Uncultivated rocky soil	30	30	900
Saltpeter	41	20	820
All land			39,900
Buildings, tools, and house			3,200
Total			43,100

Source: "La venta y remate pública de la hacienda Chullpas," AHMC, Leg. 1083 (1827).

with a high salt content.[30] Potatoes were also cultivated; they required less acreage than maize and far less than wheat (though labor requirements were heavy), and their growing cycle was somewhat different from that of maize and wheat. Potatoes could be planted starting in late September and harvested in late March or April, whereas maize and wheat were usually sowed and harvested a little later in the valleys (see figure 10). Even the limited cultivation in the serranía surrounding the Cliza valley afforded some insurance against the caprices of nature and the fluctuations of the yields of unirrigated valley acreage.[31] Finally, Cliza had rich grazing lands, especially in the central zone, which supported abundant herds of cattle and oxen, sheep, mules, and horses.[32] Livestock provided manure and draft power for plowing the extensive grain fields and for hauling freight. The supply of meat, wool, and tallow was secondary to those functions.

In the late eighteenth century, the Cliza valley was the most populous and productive zone in the province. Some 37,600 people, 30 percent of the province's inhabitants, lived in the valley's parishes of Tarata, Punata, Paredón, and Arani (see table 13). In 1786, the partido of Cliza had the largest concentration of Indians in the province, having experienced probably the greatest increase in that segment of

30 Guillermo Urquidi, Monografía del departamento de Cochabamba (Cochabamba: Tunari, 1954).

31 Olen, Cantón Chullpas, 35-36.

32 Viedma, Descripción geográfica, 76.

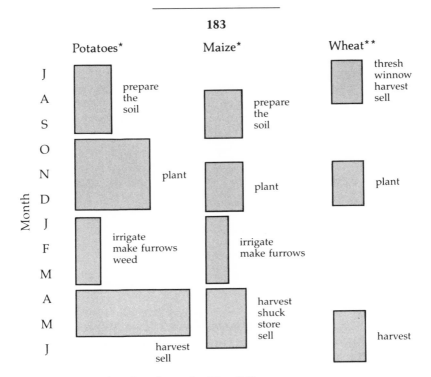

Figure 10   Agricultural Cycles in the Cliza Valley
Source: Bryan Anderson, unpublished. (I am grateful to the late Bryan Anderson
for making this chart available.)
Note: Width of bar indicates relative intensity of labor input.

the population among all of Cochabamba's partidos during the preceding century (table 15). The size of its population and territory
made Cliza the largest agricultural producer, to judge by the average
tithe revenues: In the first decade of the nineteenth century, the partido of Cliza (which was under the ecclesiastical jurisdiction of the
bishopric of Santa Cruz) generated 39 percent of the tithe income
from the five partidos of Cochabamba province.[33] Viedma reported
that most of the 17,000 Indians (as well as a substantial number of
mestizos) lived on "an infinite number of haciendas, which appear
to be small hamlets."[34] Although Viedma had despaired of enumer-
ating all these rural properties, royal tax collectors in 1802-1808
listed 153 haciendas and 24 estancias and small holdings (*sitios*)
throughout the Cliza valley. Some were indeed hamlets, like the ha-

33 Derived from data in ANB, MI, tomo 2, 6-VI (1825).

34 Viedma, *Descripción geográfica*, 77.

Table 15. Change in Indian Population of Partidos of Cochabamba between 1683 and 1786

Partido	Number of Indians		Percentage Change
	1683	*1786*	
Cercado	1,170	4,182	+ 257
Sacaba	866	3,805	+ 339
Tapacarí	5,693	14,766	+ 159
Cliza	3,581	16,227	+ 353
Arque	2,922[a]	14,906	+ 410[b]
Ayopaya	9,759	5,420	− 44
Total	23,991	58,122	+ 142

Sources: AGN, Sala 13, Padrones, 18.1.1, Leg. 41 (1683); 18.1.3, Leg. 43 (1683); 18.2.1, Leg. 46 (1786); 18.2.2, Leg. 47 (1786); 18.2.3, Leg. 48 (1786).

[a] No data for Caraza.

[b] This increase is inflated because of the absence of the Indian population of Caraza in the data for 1683.

ciendas Cliza and Chullpas, where 954 and 200 Indians, respectively, lived alongside a comparable number of nontributary peasants.[35] Others were merely clusters of pastoralists in the higher altitudes.

Although visitors to the Valle Alto were impressed by its opulence, all but the most perfunctory or optimistic of them expressed concern about population growth, poverty, and unemployment. Viedma observed that because of overpopulation, there was not enough industry "to occupy so many idle hands."[36] Colonial authorities during this period were acutely aware of the growing pressure on valley resources, and they proposed various schemes to alleviate it (see chapter 7).

But if Cliza was a zone of a proliferating peasantry of Indians and mestizos, and of extremes of wealth and poverty, it was also an area of intense commercial and artisan activity. As we shall see, in years of abundant harvest, many peasants who leased or sharecropped parcels of land sold their own small surpluses in local ferias in the valley. The Cliza feria, in particular, became a bustling livestock and grain market every Sunday morning. Cliza was also noted for its domestic chicha industry. Other industries flourished in the valley, including glass blowing and the manufacture of soap, gunpowder, and textiles.[37]

35 AGN, Sala 13, Padrones, 18.3.4, Leg. 54 (1802-1808).

36 Viedma, *Descripción geográfica*, 77.

37 Ibid., and "Descripción de Cochabamba," f. 2.

Arque

In the western reaches of the province, the land gathered into folds that formed rugged, arid mountains in western Tapacarí, Arque, and Ayopaya. This jumble of mountains cut off the region's broad, fertile valleys and principal towns from the altiplano and the main arteries of trade along that high plateau. The bulk of Cochabamba's population was isolated by the eastern sierras that formed the most rugged and inaccessible extension of the cordillera. Traversing the province from west to east, travelers would begin their journey on the high plateau surrounding the city of Oruro and gradually work their way down precipitous switchback trails until they eventually encountered shallow streams that joined at lower elevations to form the Tapacarí and Arque rivers, which cut and twisted their way through the mountains and eventually flowed into the Río Grande. There were two main passageways through the cordillera to the central valleys: one went through the pueblo real of Tapacarí; the other and more traveled one went through the valleys of Capinota and Arque.

The western partido of Arque was a district of sharp ecological contrasts wrought by the numerous tributaries and rivers that had gorged out moist, fertile, warm valleys. Peasants planted some of the province's best maize and fruit crops in the valleys of Caraza, Capinota, and Arque. But the partido also had the highest number of estancias. Thousands of Indians inhabited the hills and remote high valleys of Arque, where their sheep and cattle could graze and they could plant traditional highland crops undisturbed by the river-valley traffic or the competition for access to superior quality soil.[38] In the fertile quebradas, at elevations ranging between 7,900 and 9,200 feet, some fifty-odd hacendados took advantage of their favorable location and the abundant river water to cultivate grains for export to Oruro and other provinces. Hacendados who owned lands near the banks of the Arque and Colcha rivers built canals and dams to chan-

---

38 The partido of Arque apparently had the greatest number of property units inhabited by tribute-paying Indians of any of Cochabamba's districts. Consequently, although the growth of its Indian population between 1683 and 1786 probably paralleled that of the Cliza valley, Arque's Indian population was distributed more widely: an average of only nine tributary families inhabited each rural property. On the other hand, Arque's mixed-race population was relatively small compared to the number of mestizos in Cliza and the Cercado. Thus, the overall demographic profile of Arque was one of a predominantly Indian population, distributed between a few large grain estates and milling operations located in the river valley, on the one hand, and a multitude of smaller properties, including many estancias, scattered across the mountainous interior of the partido, on the other. (For a discussion of Arque's only pueblo real, Capinota, see chap. 4.)

nel the water to irrigate their fields and to harness the power of the rivers, which ran swiftly after the rainy season, to drive their grain mills. Almost one-third of the grain mills in the province of Cochabamba were located along the banks of Arque's waterways. In the parish of Arque proper, thirteen hacendados were registered in a 1799 survey as owners of sixty-two mills, each of which represented considerable capital investment. In the poorer parish of Colcha, upriver from Arque, nine hacendados operated thirty-one mills.[39] The lands and mills of Arque, located along the trade corridor connecting the central valleys to the altiplano and blessed with water power, gave some landowners of the parish a critical advantage in the marketing and processing of maize and wheat destined for the colder lands of the altiplano provinces (see chapter 6). Furthermore, landowners in the parishes of Arque and Colcha exercised control over most of the water power and the arable and pasture land in those parishes, even if they didn't monopolize grain marketing or pack driving. Curiously, though, Viedma reported in 1788 the existence of mitmaq lands still controlled by the Indians of Challacollo, whose principal ayllus were located in the province of Paria.[40] Most of the Indian land in the Arque parish was high pasture, but Viedma also mentioned the existence of twelve *fanegadas* of irrigated maize lands, which yielded a rich and abundant crop after a good growing season.[41] But even though vestiges of precolonial land patterns remained, Arque nevertheless had become an important Spanish trade route that connected grain haciendas, mills, and highland markets.

Ayopaya

In the northeast corner of the province of Cochabamba lay Ayopaya, the most isolated and varied of the partidos. The western part of the district was bordered by the cordillera, and most lands in Ayopaya were situated well above 10,500 feet. Ayopaya's landscape of snow-covered peaks, cold, wind-swept puna, and pastureland resembled that of Sicasica and other highland provinces to the west. But in deep crevices and in the northern escarpment, where steep moun-

39 "Real visita a las molinas de grano," AHMC, Leg. 1213 (1799).

40 Viedma, *Descripción geográfica*, 70.

41 Ibid. Viedma added that the land was "administered by the cacique of that pueblo [Challacollo], whose products . . . must be worth more than 1,000 pesos . . . [as much] as if he owned [the land] through rights of primogeniture." In later years, the Indians leased some of their lands and mills to a creole: "Exp. seguido a nuevo remate . . . de la hacienda y molinos de Arque," ANB, EC no. 7 (1816).

tains sloped down to the tropical yungas, the land was extremely fertile. Some of Ayopaya's eighty-six haciendas were located in these pockets, and they produced cash crops such as sugar cane, cotton, ají, maize, peanuts, and tropical fruit. In the dry land at high elevations, most hacendados raised stock and cultivated wheat and potatoes. Life seemed bleak on these estates, even to the seasoned traveler of the Andes. After touring the district, Viedma observed that "the human condition is even worse in Ayopaya than in the other districts. The Indians shoulder the burden of agricultural work and are at the mercy of tyrants whose only title of authority is that of 'employer.' "[42] And if living conditions were not sufficiently depressed, the recent Indian rebellions had left visible scars all over the countryside; Viedma saw the charred ruins of many haciendas and chapels.

Against this grim contemporary description, the partido's Indian population loss is thrown into bold relief. In 1683, Ayopaya's native population of 9,759 was the largest in the province. However, over the next century, the number of Indians declined by 44 percent, to 5,420 in 1786 (see table 15). Much of this loss was probably due to emigration, especially adult Indian men.[43] The reasons for Ayopaya's loss of native population are not hard to discover. Viedma's description of the exceptionally harsh conditions of life on Ayopaya's highland estates would support the proposition that most emigrants in the late eighteenth century were refugees from poverty and landlessness. An alcalde of Yani in 1773, decried the intolerable burdens that a rapacious corregidor had placed upon the local population and also alluded to deepening impoverishment in the backlands of Ayopaya.[44] Indirect evidence suggests that many peasants of Ayopaya sought better lives on the thriving coca plantations (*cocales*) of Chulumani, northeast of the city of La Paz. Thus far, there is no demographic study of Ayopaya's population movement that can be compared to Klein's monograph on seasonal labor migration between the alti-

42 Viedma, *Descripción geográfica*, 57-58.

43 In comparison to the Indian population in other partidos (outside the pueblos reales), Ayopaya's native population had the most imbalanced sex ratio (66.6 adult and adolescent males per 100 adult females), the highest proportion of widows (24 percent), and a relatively high proportion of absent tributaries (13 percent). AGN, Sala 13, Padrones, 18.2.1, Leg. 46 (1786); 18.2.2, Leg. 47 (1786); 18.2.3, Leg. 48 (1786).

44 "Testimonio del expediente de teniente de Ayopaya contra el corregidor de Cochabamba," ANB, EC no. 139 (1773).

plano province of Pacajes and the yungas, but that study does not show the powerful attraction the cocales exerted on the highland Indians and the intensive labor requirements of those enterprises.[45] There is reason to believe that the yungas also drained the native population from the highland estates of Ayopaya in the second half of the eighteenth century. The two principal European informants, Viedma and Paula Sanz, commented on the strong trade currents between Ayopaya's highland haciendas and the flourishing coca enterprises in the tropical lowlands. In 1781, Paula Sanz mentioned that the maize and wheat farms of Ayopaya's four parishes fed "the pueblos of the yungas and the city of La Paz"; and later Viedma reported that llamas, alpacas, goats, sheep, horses, and cattle grazed on "excellent pastures in the estancias of Ayopaya, and the export of cattle to the yungas is very profitable," and he described the mestizo mule drivers (*arrieros*) who brought grains, flour, and dried meat from Ayopaya to La Paz.[46] It is not unreasonable to conjecture that, while "sheep ate men" on the bleak steppes of Ayopaya over the course of the eighteenth century, those native peasants who sought relief from the grinding poverty of the partido followed the new trade route and cattle trail to the tropical lowlands, where they settled and worked for a spell on the coca plantations before moving on—or dying.

Peasant Smallholding

The complexity and variety of tenure arrangements on eighteenth-century estates in Cochabamba defy any attempt to construct a typology of agrarian enterprises along classic European lines. Some historians have identified Latin American analogues of feudalism: e.g., the wheat and cattle estates that Chevalier described for a region of seventeenth-century Mexico.[47] Some haciendas undoubtedly resembled the *Gutsherrschaft* type of manorial organization that devel-

45 Klein, "Hacienda and Free Community."

46 "Descripción de Cochabamba," f. 3, and Viedma, *Descripción geográfica*, 57-58.

47 Although Chevalier was not the first historian to conceptualize the Mexican hacienda in terms of the European manorial economy, it was he who, as Van Young has pointed out, "brought the great estate down from the level of abstraction to that of historical reality," and in the process described seigneurial relations that bound peasants to their lord and cloistered them on autarchic estates: Van Young, "Mexican Rural History," 9ff. For a more theoretical treatment of feudal enterprises in Poland, see Witold Kula, *An Economic Theory of the Feudal System* (London: New Left Books, 1976).

oped in certain regions east of the Elbe River in the seventeenth century, under the stimulus of the cereal export trade. In this model, landlords cultivated large territorial units by drawing on the labor of a servile peasantry.[48] One hacienda in the Cochabamba province that fit this model was that of El Convento, in the Caraza valley. It was owned by Augustinian monks, and its labor force consisted of seventy-eight yanacona families, whose status was permanent and inherited, along with a number of tenants, who at least theoretically had more leeway to negotiate tenure arrangements.[49] However, El

[48] There is some disagreement about the nature of land tenure in an enterprise of the *Gutsherrschaft* type, but most historians agree that it was organized around the direct cultivation of the demesne by service tenants, who engaged in corvée labor and also had tiny cottage holdings. The estate was a micropolitical unit: power was held primarily by the landlord, and tenants were subject only indirectly to a territorial prince. Perhaps the first systematic attempt to make explicit comparisons between this form and Latin American haciendas was Cristobal Kay, "Comparative Development of the European Manorial System and the Latin American Hacienda System: An Approach to a Theory of Agrarian Change for Chile" (D. Phil. diss., University of Sussex, 1971); see also Cristobal Kay, "Comparative Development of the European Manorial System and the Latin American Hacienda System," *Journal of Peasant Studies* 2 (1974): 69-98. Other discussions of the *Gutsherrschaft* enterprise are Slicher van Bath, *Agrarian History of Western Europe*, 156-157 and passim; and Perry Anderson, *Passages from Antiquity to Feudalism* (London: New Left Books, 1974), part 2, esp. 246-265. The comparison between certain "hacienda regions" in Latin America during periods of expanding agricultural export trade and the seigneurial system on eastern European estates during the wheat export boom has been a theme of interest to several other historians as well; see, for example, Mario Góngora, *Encomenderos y estancieros: Estudios acerca de la constitución social aristocrática de Chile después de la Conquista, 1580-1660* (Santiago: Editorial Universitaria, 1970), 121-122; and Mörner, "Spanish American Hacienda," 211-212.

Just as Europeanists have interpreted the "second serfdom" as a response to the stimulus of the export market in grains, Latin Americanists have seen the intensification of coerced labor on rural estates in the context of market stimuli and the inadequate or insecure supply of cheap labor. See, for example, Macera, "Feudalismo colonial americano"; Eric Hobsbawm, "A Case of Neo-Feudalism: La Convención, Peru," *Journal of Latin American Studies* 1 (1969): 31-50; Carmagnani, "Producción agropecuaria chilena"; and Mario Góngora, *Origen de los inquilinos de Chile central* (Santiago: Editorial Universitaria, 1960). However, there is no consensus about the extent to which landlords restricted the mobility of their rural laborers through debt or other mechanisms. On this subject, see Gibson, *Aztecs*, 252-255, and Arnold J. Bauer, "Chilean Rural Labor in the Nineteenth Century," *American Historical Review* 76 (1971): 1059-1082, and "Rural Workers in Spanish America: Problems of Peonage and Oppression," *Hispanic American Historical Review* (1979): 34-63.

[49] "Real provisión sobre no ser yanaconas los indios de la hacienda de Carasa,"

Convento's relatively heavy reliance on yanacona labor distinguished it from most other haciendas of the time.

On most haciendas where the owner continued to administer the demesne, seigneurial relations covered a broad spectrum of tenure arrangements. Labor prestations were important components of rent, and tenants usually also paid cash and delivered shares of their harvests, however meager. Extra services, such as domestic labor, might also be woven into this web of obligations. But the amount and mechanics of labor rent varied significantly. One hacienda might require the seasonal migration of highland herders and cultivators down to the hacienda's valley lands, where they would work for a month in the maize or wheat fields.[50] On another, a dozen Indian households had fixed labor obligations, and the mayordomo hired seasonal wageworkers during harvest time to help cut and gather the wheat and cart it to the mill and then to the city of Cochabamba.[51] On still others, each tenant household was responsible for recruiting extra workers during the planting and harvest seasons if the household was unable to meet its obligations unaided.[52] In many cases, this responsibility forced tenants to sublet parcels of their leaseholds

---

ANB, EC no. 6396 (1747). On the hacienda of La Leguna, in Punata, a landlord tried to rent out his tenants to his landowning neighbors. In 1772, the tenants filed suit against him, charging that he was trying to force them into "yanaconazgo." The tenants complained that the landlord even bestowed new surnames on them, so that their very identity would be lost. "Bernardo y Pablo Sola, indios de Cochabamba, sobre pretender sujetarlos de servidumbre de yanaconazgo . . .," ANB, EC no. 216 (1772).

50 "Arriendos y tasaciones . . . de los arrenderos de la estancia Ucuchi," AHMC, Leg. 1096 (1801-1808).

51 "Exp. por doña Francisca de Valencia y Cabrera contra Ygnacio Beltrán sobre la administración de la hacienda Parotani," AHMC, Leg. 1090 (1807).

52 "Exp. por el indígena Estaban Pablo contra su patrón Manuel Almarás en la hacienda Caporaya," AHMC, Leg. 1273 (1795). This strategy of shifting the burden of mobilizing and paying labor to tenant households was a common practice in other parts of Latin America as well; see, for example, the discussion of rent obligations on estates in the León region of the Bajío in David Brading "Estructura de la producción agrícola en el Bajío, 1700 a 1850," in E. Florescano, ed., *Haciendas, Latifundios, y plantaciones en América latina* (Mexico City: Siglo XXI, 1975), 128, and David Brading, *Haciendas and Ranchos in the Mexican Bajío: León, 1700-1860* (Cambridge: Cambridge University Press, 1978), 113-114. For a more general discussion of the variety and combinations of forms of rent payment, see Magnus Mörner, "A Comparative Study of Tenant Labor in Parts of Europe, Africa, and Latin America, 1700-1900," *Latin American Research Review* 5 (1970): 3-15.

to members of a marginal labor force (*arrimantes*) who would reciprocate by working for them during the busy seasons. In that way, a
tenant family might break the limits imposed by the household size
(and number of productive laborers) to carry a heavier burden of rent
labor. From the landlord's viewpoint, this method shifted the burden
of labor recruitment from the manager and owner to the peasant
household. Thus, even on estates where labor obligations bore down
hard on peasant households, there was usually an intricate network
of obligations binding peasants to the landlord, as well as to other
peasant families with differential rights and access to hacienda resources.

In contrast to the *Gutsherrschaft* form of organization was the
Grundherrschaft form, in which the landlord leased his entire estate
to a large number of small-scale cultivators, who paid him rent in
cash or shares of the crop. This, too, had its parallels in the Cochabamba valley. In part because of the custom of dividing inheritance,
property units rarely survived intact during their transmission across
generations; rather, the drift was toward fragmentation of ownership. Under such circumstances, labor services were less useful than
cash tenancies and sharecropping. However, this diffusion of production among peasant households was still a long way from peasant
proprietorship and from the creation of a kulak class.

Most haciendas were probably operated with some combination of
demesne agriculture on a limited scale and peasant smallholding on
the bulk of their land. Landlords often reserved parcels of the most
fertile wheat and maize lands, whose harvest went directly into the
hacienda storehouses for future consumption, tithes, or sale. The
rest of the land would be distributed among the resident tenants,
thus using hacienda resources as payments to a permanent labor
force.[53] A detailed inventory of Aramasi, a middle-sized hacienda lo-

53 A previous study has emphasized "hacienda resource payment" as a strategy
of landlords to avoid having to make cash payments to permanent or seasonal
laborers. Landlords allowed peasants to graze their animals on the estate's pastures, cultivate parcels of arable land, collect firewood or ichu grasses, etc. Over
the long term, this strategy may have increased the relative power of tenants,
who had "cheap access to hacienda resources and at the same time could not be
prevented from leaving the estate." Juan Martínez Alier, "Relations of production on Andean haciendas," in Kenneth Duncan and Ian Rutledge, eds., *Land
and Labor in Latin America: Essays on the Development of Agrarian Capitalism in the Nineteenth and Twentieth Centuries* (Cambridge: Cambridge University Press, 1977), 146. A pioneering work on the internal relations between
rival peasant and landlord economies within a rural property unit is Rafael Ba-
raona, "Una tipología de haciendas en la sierra ecuatoriana," in O. Delgado, ed.,

cated in the Spanish parish of Calliri, provides an anatomy of that estate's internal land divisions.[54] In 1784, its assessed market value was 9,653 pesos. Like most haciendas, it had a large expanse of pasture and scattered pieces of arable land at varying altitudes across the highlands. It also included moist valley land, where maize was cultivated, though it had much less of such land than many other haciendas situated in the central valleys. Aramasi combined the raising of livestock with cereal and potato cultivation. The landlords owned no grain mills, but they had considerable assets in draft animals (40 plow oxen) and freight animals (12 burros), as well as 100 sheep. Aramasi's wheat yield in 1784 amounted to 268 fanegas—a poor return, no doubt, in that year of severe drought. Among the tenant population were about eighty or ninety Indians,[55] together with an unknown number of mestizo tenants. Together, the tenants occupied, or had access to, more than half of the hacienda's arable land, in addition to the open pasture in the highlands (see table 16). The largest single category of land was the area leased to arrenderos, which constituted 45 percent of the hacienda's territory. The "owner's land" represented only 7 percent of the estate's area, although almost 30

Table 16.   Land Use on the Hacienda Aramasi in Calliri, 1784

	Area	
Land Use	*Fanegadas*	*Percentage*
Total hacienda	409[a]	100.0
Demesne land	150	36.7
Owner's land	30	7.3
Hacienda land	120	29.3
Under lease	212	51.8
Indian administrator's land	12	2.9
Indian maize land	15	3.7
Land cultivated by arrenderos	185	45.2
Unclaimed or waste land	47	11.5

Source: "Hacienda Aramasi," AHMC, Leg. 1066 (1784).
[a] Excluding open range land.

Reformas agrarias en América latina (México City: Fondo de Cultura Económica, 1965), 688-694.

54 "Tasación de la hacienda Aramasi, en el valle de Calliri," AHMC, Leg. 1066 (1784). The estate, owned by Mónica Berbete Corilla y Paniagua, was located in the lower reaches of the Tapacarí River valley. Its lands bordered the hacienda Milloma, owned by Tapacarí's cacique family, the Liro de Córdovas (see chap. 4).

55 AGN, Sala 13, Padrones, 18.3.4, Leg. 54 (1808), f. 181.

percent was categorized as "hacienda land," whose yields probably were used to cover operating costs (including liens and debts). Thus, it is clear that most of the hacienda's resources were under peasant control. On paper, the hacienda appeared to be a cohesive property unit under central administration, but the fragmentation of land tenure meant, in effect, decentralized agricultural production.

The details of Aramasi's tenure pattern suggest a high degree of internal differentiation among the rural tenants (see table 17). The individual leaseholds ranged in area from five fanegadas to seventy, and in total assessed value from 36 pesos to 525. Moreover, some lands were cultivated collectively by the arrenderos; these were most likely irrigated maize fields, whose yields were the source of chicha for ceremonial festivities. Finally, some lands were leased to the two Indian authorities, alcalde and the hilacata, who performed such functions as mediating rent relations and coordinating cultivation of the collective maize lands, as well as carrying out certain religious duties. This political/religious hierarchy probably overlapped with the hierarchy based on differential access to land. The hacienda peasants thus managed to combine household production with communal production along traditional lines.

Table 17. Area and Value of Leased Lands on the Hacienda Aramasi, 1784

Arriendo	Area (fanegadas)	Assessed Value (pesos)	
		Per Fanegada	Total Value
Calanchulpa	35	15	525
Ocororuni	10	10	100
Luiuluiuni	6	6	36
Guañagagua	20	8	160
Tacocolpa	15	10	150
Torrini	20	10	200
Taconi	15	10	150
Ychocollo	20	8	160
Ajuri	15	15	225
Tacocuchi	8	12	96
Copafina	10	15	150
Vilca	6	12	72
Santa Rojas	5	10	50
Chapiloma	25	8	200
Quesera	70	8	560
Lands of the hilacata	8	10	80
Lands of the alcalde	4	10	40
Communal maize land	15	24	360

Source: "Hacienda Aramasi," AHMC, Leg. 1066 (1784).

Chapter 5

194

It would be overly simplistic, therefore, to see land tenure and labor arrangements on the haciendas exclusively in the European mold of *Gutsherrschaft* or *Grundherrschaft*. Hacienda organization in eighteenth-century Cochabamba was variegated and fluid, and different patterns could be found simultaneously on a given estate. Tenants usually paid rent in some combination of cash, kind, and labor prestations. In return, they often received payment in hacienda resources, "gifts" of food and drink, and sometimes cash wages. If there was any single most common pattern, it was sharecropping. On both large and small haciendas, tenants often worked certain lands "in company" with the landowner. In many cases, the sharecropped lands were subsidiary parcels, apart from the main *arriendo* for which the tenant paid rent. The landowner usually furnished seeds, draft animals, and tools in exchange for half or more of the harvest, though there were also many other arrangements.[56] Sharecropping thrust agricultural production almost entirely into the hands of peasant cultivators, marginalizing the economic role of the property owner. At the same time, it provided a measure of subsistence security to the smallholder, by sharing the risk of crop failure between the cultivator and the landlord. This was particularly important on temporal lands, where yields fluctuated widely. Thus,

56 Sharecropping arrangements were generally made in verbal contracts, but court suits, wills, and estate inventories give us some information about their terms. Some of the arrangements were fairly formal and relatively equitable. For example, a widow who inherited part of the hacienda Mamanaca, in the parish of Tarata, entered into a *sociedad* (association) with her sharecropping "partner." She agreed to supply the land, seeds, oxen, and plow; her partner provided his "work, industry, and assistance," paid half of the fixed costs of production, and was liable for part of the estate's debts. The harvests were to be divided evenly, but a part of the tenant's share went to cover his half of the fixed costs. "Doña Juana de Dios Urquidi en sociedad con d. Manuel Balencia," AHMC, Leg. 1423 (1790).

On the hacienda Liquina, in the Cliza valley, the owner—also a widow—supplied only the land, while her tenant partner had to provide the seeds, tools, and animals. This widow complained that, despite her impoverishment and lack of liquid capital, she was unable to sell her "mulattoes," since her tenants were "really more cholos than mulattoes" and were therefore considered free men and women. "Exp. por doña Juana Ysabel Garrido Morales contra doña Marañón," AHMC, Leg. 1175 (1761).

On still another hacienda, Chacarilla, sharecroppers worked with day laborers. The tenants sharecropped some of the estate's lands, providing seeds as well as their labor. But during the harvest, the landlord also brought in five day laborers (*peones jornaleros*), who provided only their labor in return for a small fraction of the crop. "Tasación de la hacienda Chacarilla," AHMC, Leg. 1144 (1803).

tenants who owed fixed rents, which could easily take two-thirds of their harvest in a bad season, could look to their sharecropped lands for some relief. The landlord, on the other hand, had to reduce the amount of product he could claim in a year of calamity. In many cases, though, even sharecropped lands provided slim protection against a subsistence crisis when weather conditions were especially bad.

The multiplicity of sharecropping arrangements on the Cochabamba haciendas brings to mind the process of increasingly intricate tenure patterns that Geertz has described for parts of Indonesia during its colonial period.[57] Borrowing the concept "involution" from its original aesthetic context, Geertz used it to characterize tenure systems that grew more encrusted and complicated, like a spider web that neither grows nor shrinks, but becomes ever more intricate in detail. There was an internal dynamic to land-tenure arrangements, although the changes did not fundamentally alter agrarian class relations, either in the Indonesian context that Geertz studied or in eighteenth-century Cochabamba. Instead, the arrangements developed, as Geertz put it, "through technical hairsplitting and unending virtuosity," giving them a kind of gothic texture.[58] From within the formal agrarian structures of property ownership in Cochabamba was emerging an active peasantry seeking subsistence niches and negotiating for as much economic autonomy and security as it could wrench from the landowners. The elaboration of tenure patterns reflected the increasing presence of small-scale cultivators in the province and the diffusion of agricultural resources among them.

One force behind the dispersion of production units was the fragmentation of property ownership. Evidence of this phenomenon, one that plagued hacienda agriculture in many parts of Spanish America, is found in wills, notarized records of land transactions, padrones listing property units and their owners that can be traced through several decades, and estate inventories.[59] Records of *hijuelación*, the

---

57 Clifford Geertz, *Agricultural Involution: The Processes of Ecological Change in Indonesia* (Berkeley and Los Angeles: University of California Press, 1963).

58 Ibid., 81-82.

59 Although uncatalogued and unorganized, the notarial books and the records of judicial proceedings housed in Cochabamba's municipal archive provide rich documentation of land-tenure arrangements, land transactions, inheritance patterns, and encumbrances on landed property. The documents are full of examples of people buying, selling, bequeathing, inheriting, and encumbering small,

bequest and subdivision of property, in the late eighteenth century offer examples of the dismemberment of rural properties as they were willed to a widow, several offspring, and members of the regular and secular clergy who were expected, in return, to remember their benefactor in their prayers. Real-estate transactions also show the movement of land titles, not only and not primarily to whole estates, but to bits and pieces of them.[60] A survey of property boundaries and deeds made in 1748 revealed that fragmentation of ownership had proceeded quite far even by then. Landowners frequently claimed several scattered plots of land, while lands registered as a single property unit often listed multiple owners. The hacienda Mamata in the Cliza valley, for example, was owned by five individuals, each of whom paid the tax on a part of the estate. A neighboring hacienda, Liquina, also had several owners.[61] Records of formal ownership often provide only ambiguous evidence of real economic power and landlord-tenant relations, but this diffusion of property suggests that the landowning class was losing its grip on the institutional foundations of its power. Increasingly, it was engaged in internal competition for control over property units that were crumbling under the weight of the Spanish partible-inheritance laws, accumulated indebtedness, and uncertain returns on agricultural investment.

Yet, in eighteenth-century Cochabamba as in colonial Indonesia, the trend toward small-scale agricultural production had less to do with land-ownership patterns than with the way land was worked. Geertz's emphasis on the elaboration of labor relations on estates

---

scattered pieces of property. The notarial books, in particular, contain numerous accounts of land transactions involving fragments of haciendas.

60 The records of rural real-estate transactions in Cochabamba in 1781 show that only three out of eighteen transfers involved the sale of an entire hacienda; the other fifteen sales involved small plots of ground. In 1785, the real-estate market was brisker, but of the thirty-eight recorded land sales, only ten were whole haciendas. AGN, Sala 13, Contaduría, 27.1.1 (1781) and 27.1.5 (1785).

61 The survey listed 121 hacendados, who paid a total of 5,486 pesos in taxes and fees, ranging from 10 pesos, for several fanegadas of poor land, to 400 pesos, for several haciendas in Cliza that belonged to one individual. But almost three-quarters of the property owners paid less than 50 pesos in settlement fees for various small, dispersed properties. "Composiciones y amparos de haciendas, tierras, y estancias de Cochabamba por D. José Antonio de Zabala," ANB, EC no. 100 (1748). Tribute collectors also sometimes noted the internal fragmentation of ownership. In the 1803 padron of Punata, for instance, the hacienda-estancia complex known as Tambillo y Chirusicollo was listed as being owned by several families. AGN, Sala 13, Padrones, 8.3.3, Leg. 53 (1803), f. 56.

applies equally well to the maize valleys of Cochabamba. It was economic involution "from below": the gradual dispersion of hacienda resources among a dense peasant population that engaged in intensive cultivation of maize on parcels of land that often yielded two harvests a year. These small-scale cultivators rarely appear in contemporary sources, but their proliferation signaled a divisibility of agricultural inputs and outputs that continued to characterize agrarian patterns in Cochabamba into the twentieth century.[62]

Peasants Confront a Landlord

Yanaconaje was the bedrock of the rural labor force on Cochabamba's early haciendas. Reluctantly recognizing the need of hacendados to have an assured supply of labor, the Toledan state institutionalized subservient labor relations on the grain haciendas in the eastern valleys of Alto Perú. Although nominally free, the yanaconas were reduced to the status of dependent, immobile workers whose inferior position was passed down through the generations, sentencing their progeny to similar lives of hardship and stigmatization. But Andean migrants from the highlands moved into the Cochabamba valleys over the course of the seventeenth and eighteenth centuries, and as their numbers grew, yanaconaje receded into the background. By the end of the colonial era, yanaconas constituted only about 3 percent of the Indians in the region, and nearly all of them lived on large haciendas in the Cliza valley. Of the 1,393 yanaconas counted in 1805, the Augustinian hacienda of Achamoco alone was home to 78.[63] A few equally formidable enterprises, most of them also under control of a monastic order, had managed to preserve their property

62 Studies of land tenure in the Cliza valley on the eve of the 1952 revolution have shown the region polarized between large neofeudal estates, such as the monastic hacienda Cliza, and estates in an advanced degree of fragmentation, such as the neighboring hacienda Chullpas. Although the hacienda Cliza is better known, it was probably more the anomaly. See Patch, "Social Implications," and Olen, Cantón Chullpas. A major research project on the peasant economy and regional differentiation in the valleys and highlands of Cochabamba has recently been undertaken by a group of sociologists and anthropologists under the direction of Jorge Dandler. A description of the research design and a discussion of preliminary findings can be found in Centro de Estudios de la Realidad Económica y Social, Programa de investigación sobre la economía y desarrollo regional de Cochabamba (La Paz: CERES, 1981, mimeograph).

63 AGN, Sala 13, Padrones, 18.3.3, Leg. 53 (1802-1808); and 18.3.4, Leg. 54 (1802-1808), f. 64; AGN, Sala 9, Intendencia, 5.8.7, Leg. 6 (1805).

and to shield the vestiges of their servile labor force from the disintegrating forces of change.

Meanwhile, on the 680 or so rural properties scattered across the province's five partidos, most of the workers were arrenderos—tenants, as distinguished from the bonded yanaconas. Their relationship to the owner was, at least theoretically, mediated through the market. They were supposed to be free to negotiate the terms of rent in accord with certain regulations, and their rent was supposed to bear some relationship to their access to hacienda resources and land-use rights, although in the late eighteenth century the colonial state tried to standardize rents by pegging them to the size and assessed value of leaseholds.[64] But in fact, neither the market nor the state determined the relations between landlords and tenants. It was, rather, the force of custom which determined peasant expectations of landlord behavior and the (unequal) exchanges between them.[65] Although norms varied from hacienda to hacienda, and over time, it was widely expected that landlords would afford tenants some access to hacienda resources in addition to their individual arriendos: perhaps the right to collect firewood, to graze sheep on the estancia, or to call upon the landowner for cash advances or credit. Assistance in the event of famine or personal misfortune, and gestures of generosity and of ritual kinship at particular moments in the life course of a faithful tenant, were unwritten forms of patronage and protection that peasants had come to expect of their landowners. Although acutely aware of class cleavages, rural tenant laborers counted on their lords to provide a small cushion against subsistence crisis, a symbolic measure of security that legitimated the tradition and terms of tenancy. When the terms of exchange shifted sharply

---

64 In Mexico at about the same time, the standard ground rent was ten pesos per fanega of cultivated land: Brading, *Haciendas and Ranchos*, 75 and 198.

65 Scott, *Moral Economy of the Peasant*, 179ff. In the last years of the eighteenth century, tenants sometimes resorted to judicial tactics in an effort to bring about a degree of landlord compliance with royal regulations, when they believed that custom no longer served their interests. Yanaconas, however, were considered to be subordinated and bound to the person of the landowner and to the property. Custom forbade them to negotiate over the terms of their status; even their subsistence came directly from their overlords, in the form of stipulated rations of food and clothing. RAH, ML, 9/1962, tomo 37 (Nov. 19, 1794), f. 289v. On the maintenance and breakdown of patron-client relations on some haciendas around the turn of the twentieth century, see Erick Langer, "Labor Strikes and Reciprocity on Chuquisaca Haciendas," *Hispanic American Historical Review* 65 (1985): 255-278.

against them and a landlord abused his power, it was not uncommon for peasants to resist, through flight or direct political confrontation.

One of the more visible conflicts in the region erupted in 1795 on the grain hacienda of Caporaya, located in the valley of Caraza. Judging by the padron of 1786, Caporaya was a middle-sized estate, inhabited by some two dozen Indian families and probably a considerable number of nontributary tenant households. By custom, the smallholding tenants of Caporaya had provided various labor services to the landlord, and they also worked some parcels of land "in company." In 1781, the property had been sold, and the new owner, Manuel Almarás, had tried to impose harsher terms. In the eyes of the tenants, he thus violated the norms that had governed rent relations on the hacienda up until then. Speaking in Quechua, one Ygnacio Condori (who bore no relation to the cacique of Tapacarí) described the labor prestations demanded of him and other arrenderos. A translator dictated his testimony to the court notary, who recorded it in the third person.

> This year they [the arrenderos] planted [on the demesne] some 40 fanegas of wheat, two fanegas of maize, and twelve of barley. This work is a heavy burden to bear, but they must also weed, harvest, thresh, winnow, shuck the corn and move the grain to the storage huts. For his labor, he [Condori] is paid one-half a *real* [per day], along with usufruct rights to three *viches* of maize land and three fanegadas of wheat land.[66]

These terms were much worse than the previous ones. Another tenant added:

> Under the old labor arrangement, each Indian contributed only two yoke of oxen, along with the plowmen [*gañanes*], and he who had no yoke to lend could satisfy his obligation with his own labor in the wheat, maize, and quinoa fields. But in the last four or five years that Almarás has owned this property . . . each Indian must contribute eight yoke of oxen and the plowmen, even if he has none.[67]

Another arrendero also complained of the demand for "eight yoke of oxen accompanied by peones," in addition to the extra eight days

---

66 "Exp. por el yndígena Esteban Pablo contra su patrón Manual Almarás en la hacienda Caporaya," AHMC, Leg. 1273 (1795), f. 7v. A *viche* was an area of land equivalent, in the Cochabamba region, to about one-sixth of a fanegada.

67 Ibid., ff. 9v.-10.

of field work they did "without wage or any compensation." Furthermore, Almarás required each tenant to gather firewood for the hacienda and for the townhouse in Cochabamba.[68]

These heavier labor obligations placed additional burdens on other members of the household as well, since they had to make up for the labor thus lost on their subsistence plots. Yet at the same time, Almarás also forced arrendero women and children to work for less than the customary compensation for their labor. Women were put to work "spinning and weaving and fermenting maize flour, for making chicha."[69] They also performed various subsidiary tasks on the estate, such as preparing for the customary festivities at threshing time (*la trilla*). Unlike the seasonal field work of men, women's rent labor was continuous. And, according to the aggrieved tenants, the women were subject to harsh discipline by the hacendado's wife, who managed the obraje and, they said,

> keeps Condori's wife almost a perpetual slave, spinning cotton and wool. She hardly finishes spinning one bag of wool, when she is handed another. She receives only one real, instead of the customary day's pay of two reales . . . The wife of Almarás forces all the women on the hacienda to weave . . . but they get no payment except a little salt or wheat.[70]

The children's task was to tend the landlord's livestock. The tenant households had to take turns in supplying a child to serve as shepherd for a month in the distant estancia lands. One tenant complained that the children had to sleep for a month outdoors on the cold puna, keeping vigil over the master's flocks. If a tenant had no child to spare, he had to hire a neighbor's son to serve. Although this type of labor obligation was not uncommon, it was usually paid for at the rate of one peso a month, but Almarás paid only four reales.[71]

Behind the expressions of moral indignation, the broad outlines of the labor regime of this hacienda, can be discerned. Peasant testimony about work obligations before the new regime suggests how heavily the entire tenant household was burdened. Aside from the obligations accruing to arrendero households that corresponded loosely to the size and quality of their leaseholds, there was an im-

68 Ibid., f. 1v.

69 Ibid., f. 1.

70 Ibid., ff. 7v and 10.

71 Ibid., f. 10.

plicit division of labor by age and sex. The witnesses made frequent references to the "old ways," before Almarás purchased the property, when the men tilled hacienda land while their women spun and worked the treadle looms in the hacienda's workshop. There seemed to be a consensus that this arrangement was not unjust, nor was it regarded as objectionable that the arrenderos lent yoked oxen and plowmen on certain days of the year.

But Almarás failed to honor an implicit code of reciprocity. He demanded more labor and gave less in return than had been the case in the past, and in the process he jeopardized his own legitimacy and status. In effect, he violated the tenants' rights by demanding servicio personal and thereby reducing the status of free arrenderos to one of intolerable servitude. Until the moment these tenants challenged the authority of the landowner, peasant defiance was met with lashings and other physical abuse. In protest, Condori, at one point in the testimony, proudly declared himself to be a free person, not a "miserable yanacona."

The confrontation that broke out on this hacienda was provoked by the transfer of ownership. A new master, driven by greed or perhaps simply unschooled in the nuances of patron-client relations, aroused the moral outrage of his tenants and unwittingly sabotaged his own enterprise. But tenant agitation was not unusual in Cochabamba in the late colonial period. Growing population pressure on irrigated valley lands, heavier alcabalas and tribute, meager and fluctuating harvests, and growing landlord reliance on income from their tenantry combined to sharpen tensions between peasants and landlords. The form and content of such conflicts probably varied considerably from one hacienda to the next, and most of them never reached the colonial courts. But the strong presence of the state, following the great Indian rebellions, and its renewed effort to intervene in the private domain, probably encouraged some peasants to engage in "judicial politics" against their immediate overlords, even at great risk to their own future. Just as Andean peoples once protested the excesses of corregidores who violated the royal regulations on repartos, so rural tenants pressed their cases against extortionary landlords by measuring their obligations against royal regulations. The arancel introduced in the court proceedings against Almarás specified that a tenant was required to pay ten pesos and to work for two days for the landlord for each fanegada of irrigated maize land that he cultivated; a fanegada of wheat land was worth two pesos and two-fifths of a day's work; a fanegada of barley land, one peso and one-fifth of a day's work; and the site of the tenant's hut, one day of work.[72] Thus, a standard was provided by which peasants could protest the claims of a landlord or bargain for more favorable rent terms.

Furthermore, it was in the interest of the Bourbon state to pay attention to peasant grievances in order to prevent them from taking flight. Intent upon taxing forasteros residing on haciendas in the region, the Bourbons wanted to curtail the movement of Indian peasants in the valleys. The tenants knew how to exploit that fear. The peasants of Caporaya warned colonial authorities that their tyrannical lord "was driving all the miserable Indians to distant places in Vallegrande and the yungas, which is hurting the royal treasury."[73] Another witness threatened to flee the hacienda and follow the tracks of other refugees to unknown places in Ayopaya.[74] They realized that the colonial state had a stake in stabilizing agrarian class relations, even in the confines of the hacienda, and their bargaining position in the late eighteenth century was thereby improved (see chapter 8).

Peasants As Traders and Artisans

In contrast to the stark antagonisms of peasant-landlord relations that were exposed in the courtroom, class tensions in the marketplace seem diffuse and opaque. Yet it was probably in the realm of distribution, and specifically in the growing participation of rural smallholders in the product market, that peasants (in the aggregate) most affected the balance of class forces in the region. In the ordinary pursuit of a livelihood, peasants of the central valleys came out from under the weight of their rent obligations to participate in local markets. At weekly ferias, they congregated before dawn and haggled until well past midday over prices of wheat and maize, potatoes, coca, tocuyo and bayeta cloth, raw cotton and wool, salt, tallow, ají, fruits, sugar, cows, sheep, goats, mules, and oxen. Some of these transactions took the form of barter.

The central marketplace in the region was found on the outskirts of Cochabamba on Saturday mornings. Satellite markets flourished on Sundays in the towns of Quillacollo and Cliza; Tarata's feria took place on Tuesdays. Contemporary Europeans commented on the abundance of staples in the marketplace of Cochabamba: "Every day

72 AHMC, Leg. 1273 (1795), f. 23. Sharecropping Indians were exempt from these obligations.

73 Ibid., f. 1.

74 Ibid., f. 7v.

you can find . . . foodstuffs in the plaza selling at very moderate prices; the bread is as cheap as the meat, and there is every kind of vegetable, fruit, and fowl."[75] Indian traders (*manazos*) provisioned the towns with meat, after slaughtering the cattle they had driven from pastures in Mizque and Vallegrande. Most of the traders were women: *bayeteras* and *algodoneras*, who sold cloth, yarn, and cotton, and *capacheras*, who peddled vegetables, fruits, breads, and other items from their baskets and mantas.[76]

The rhythm and volume of commerce in staples were subject to the vagaries of agricultural conditions, of course. It was therefore still a shallow and periodic product market in which the smallholders participated, and a bad season could virtually eliminate them from the scene. In fact, as we shall see, the landowning class counted heavily on occasional harvest failures to make their much larger profits. But the advent of regular peasant markets in the central valleys signaled the emergence of a channel outside the channels controlled by landlords and large merchants, through which peasants could trade among themselves on their own terms and in accord with their own marketplace etiquette.[77] Peasant smallholders also diffused the

---

75 Viedma, *Descripción geográfica*, 46.

76 "Encabecimiento de mercaderes y comerciantes," AGN, Sala 9, Intendencia, 27.3.4 (1793-1794).

77 The development, internal dynamics, and social significance of retail or subsistence marketplaces in regional economies in Spanish America is a topic that has not yet attracted the attention of many historians. Assadourian's structural analysis of the internal market that revolved around the export economy of Potosí points to the importance of such studies, but analyses of regional marketing networks are still the domain of anthropologists. However, the historical and ethnographic work of Sidney Mintz has opened new perspectives on the topic; see, for example, his "Caribbean Marketplaces and Caribbean History," *Radical History Review*, no. 27 (1983): 110-120. This study, concerning the development of an internal market system in Jamaica during the eighteenth and nineteenth centuries, complements Mintz's earlier, conceptual work on "horizontal" class linkages that are reinforced by exchange relations in periodic peasant markets: "Internal Market Systems As Mechanisms of Social Articulation," in V. F. Ray, ed., *Proceedings of the 1959 Annual Spring Meeting of the American Ethnological Society* (Madison: University of Wisconsin Press, 1959), 20-30. On the notion of commodity exchanges governed by an egalitarian market etiquette, see Karl Polanyi, *The Great Transformation: The Political and Economic Origins of Our Time* (Boston: Beacon, 1944), 46-47. For contemporary analyses of peasant markets in the Cuzco region and the role of monetary transactions and reciprocal exchange, see Antoinette Fiorvanti-Molinié, "Multi-Levelled Andean Society and Market Exchange: The Case of Yucay (Peru)," in Lehmann, ed., *Ecology and Exchange*, 211-230. On ferias in contemporary Cochabamba, see Wolfgang Schoop, "Los ciclos rotatorios de los comerciantes ambulantes en las ferias se-

sources of supply for local towns in the region. The multiplicity of smallholders and the economic involution of tenure relations also fragmented into many small pieces the units of agricultural distribution, rendering small traders more vulnerable to harvest fluctuations. The imagery of an antlike economy, so often used to describe the regional economy of Cochabamba today, captures part of the picture of the petty commodity production and trade that was beginning to flourish at the time. Periodic market participation reinforced the economic viability of the peasant family economy by diversifying its subsistence activities. Yet from the perspective of agrarian class relations—the insertion of peasants as traders and artisans into the regional economy cut deeply into the economic power of landlords. Not only were landowners losing their grip on the distribution of hacienda resources inside their estates, but they were also witnessing a multitude of small-scale producers entering the commercial circuits and eroding their commercial monopoly.

This competition from peasant producers stimulated considerable commentary and complaint by landowners and municipal authorities. They grumbled about the overabundance of food crops, the depressed cereal prices, and the sluggish grain market (see chapter 6). The unregulated bread market was the greatest source of dissatisfaction. "There is no control over price, weight, or quality in the sale of meat and bread; people sell wherever they like in this city, and however they can," wrote Viedma in 1788. [78] Thirty years later, cabildo members were still complaining about the "anarchic" bread market.[79] They worried about all the bread sellers who did not belong to the bakers' guild. After harvesting their wheat and maize and turning it into flour, many peasants then procured the necessary firewood and aniseed, baked the dough in their own earthen ovens, and sold the bread from baskets on the streets of Cochabamba and other towns. According to council members, Cochabamba and other valley towns were ringed with earthen ovens. In 1824, Intendant Martín Ruíz de Somocurcio lamented the situation:

> Nowhere else in the world are the essentials of life sold without being properly weighed. Only in Cochabamba are the people disposed to accept whatever an old, usurious haggler is willing to

manales de los valles de Cochabamba," *Arbeitspapiere* (Universität Bielefeld), no. 13 (1978).

78 Viedma, *Descripción geográfica*, 46.

79 "Informe . . . sobre la contribución de harinas . . .," Dec. 1, 1817, in *Digesto de ordenanzas, reglamentos, acuerdos, decretos, de la municipalidad de Cochabamba* (Cochabamba: Heraldo, 1900), 3:242-247.

give them for their money. The infinite expansion of the guild [of breadmakers] and the fact that most are mestizos and of the most miserable station in life are insuperable obstacles to regulating the sale of this vital necessity.[80]

The intendant probably expressed the feeling of many government officials, after some forty years of attempts to establish an effective municipal grain market. At least since the arrival of Viedma in 1784, intendants had tried to assert government control over retail grain sales and to levy a tax on the flour purchased by members of the bakers' guild. "From the beginning of my term," Viedma wrote in exasperation, "I wanted to regulate [the meat and bread] trade . . . but I failed in spite of all my efforts."[81] In 1817, the cabildo compiled a list of 450 bakers, who annually purchased 20,000 fanegas of corn flour and between 40,000 and 50,000 fanegas of wheat flour. By issuing licenses to the bakers, the municipal government once more tried to restrict the number of people selling bread and to regulate the prices and quality of flour and bread.[82] In 1824, during the last years of colonial rule, Intendant Ruíz de Somocurcio proposed yet another scheme to control the sale of grain, a plan that was clearly in the interests of Cochabamba's largest landowners, some of whom served on the town council.

Ruíz de Somocurcio called for the formation of a joint stock company, the Sociedad de la Panadería Pública, (Public Bakery Association), which would exercise a monopoly over the sale of bread in the city. The intendant argued that this course of action would allow the state to raise needed revenue through levies on the wholesale purchase of flour, while granting a monopoly on the retailing sale of bread to a few of the city's wealthiest vecinos—those who purchased company shares at five hundred pesos each.[83] Although the plan was never implemented, the proposal itself is interesting. The intendant, seeking to raise 50,000 pesos annually from the local population to supply funds for the royal army, realized that one of the greatest favors he could do for the wealthier hacendados of Cochabamba was to give them a monopoly over the local grain trade, wiping out the competition they faced from the petty merchants and producers by

80 "Don Martín Ruíz de Somocurcio al cabildo," Mar. 8, 1824, in *Digesto de ordenanzas*, 3:272.

81 Viedma, *Descripción geográfica*, 46.

82 "Informe . . . sobre la contribución de harinas . . . ," 3:242-247.

83 "Don Martín Ruíz de Somocurcio al cabildo," 3:272-280.

dismantling the numerous ovens that ringed the city.[84] The small-scale producers who sold bread directly to the consumer would be forced out of the market. The municipal procurator, who represented the community before the cabildo, criticized the intendant's proposal, arguing that it would hurt the region's poor farmers, who were already destitute from more than a decade of intermittent warfare. The procurator advocated "absolute, free trade" in the region.[85] The minutes of the last council meetings of the colonial era show that the procurator had some sympathizers among the more antiroyalist members of the cabildo, though others perceived the existing grain market as almost barbaric, serving no one's interest—no one's, that is, except that of the "poor farmer."

Open-air markets at dawn, swarming with haggling peasants; caravans of llamas and traders trekking down from the western highlands during harvest season to barter in the valley ferias; mule trains loaded with sacks of flour en route to Oruro after a good harvest; the fluid movement of perishable commodities across the open valleys: these were the signs of a regional marketing system that local authorities failed to harness or stamp out. For some peasant producers, participation in the rural marketplace made possible individual accumulation, and the very existence of the markets must have created opportunities for some to manipulate the terms of exchange to their own advantage. Thus, while the emergence of peasant markets eroded the economic power of the landholding class, it advanced the process of social differentiation within the peasantry. A thin layer of petty commodity producers and traders in the valleys probably prospered and accumulated small patrimonies, which they bequeathed to their children. Their legacies are rarely documented, but the occasional will that surfaced during a legal dispute among the heirs or that found its way into a notarial book does reveal something about the sources and limits of peasant prosperity in Cochabamba of the late eighteenth century.

The most detailed testament of a peasant located among the trial records in the municipal archive of Cochabamba was written by a mestizo arrendero, Ramusa Almendras, who lived on the hacienda Chimboata in the Cliza valley.[86] Her daughter identified her as an

84 Ibid., 272.

85 "Sr. gobernador intendente al rey," May 7, 1824, in *Digesto de ordenanzas* 3: 282-284.

86 "Testamento de Ramusa Almendras de la hacienda Chimboata," AHMC, Leg. 1055 (1810).

elderly tenant of the estate, who, with the help of her children, had tended sheep and cattle and "worked hard to increase her possessions." After her husband abandoned the family, fleeing as a "fugitive from the law," Ramusa hired her son-in-law and others to help in the field work on her rented lands. Though there is no mention of commercial activities, the peasant woman must have engaged in them to some degree, for she had managed to accumulate a modest amount of wealth. Her net worth was estimated at 260 pesos at the time of her death, and her small legacy consisted of stored wheat, maize, potatoes, and quinoa and sheep, goats, oxen, mules, and horses. She had done well, by contemporary standards, but she had never acquired title to even a small piece of arable land in her own name.

The few wills, hacienda inventories, and notarial records available indicate that some peasants did acquire, through purchase or inheritance, a "small area" of maize land or a parcel of temporal land in the highlands. It was not unknown for a landlord to bequeath small plots of land and a few animals to his faithful yanaconas.[87] But even among the more prosperous peasants, land acquisition was no easy proposition, if only because land was so expensive. One fanegada of partially irrigated maize land, for example, was assessed at 250 pesos in the late eighteenth century—the approximate monetary worth of all of Ramusa Almendras's worldly possessions. Land purchase thus required either substantial amounts of cash or access to credit, and these were largely restricted to the local landholding elite (see chapter 6).[88]

[87] For example, Don Vicente Caero of the hacienda Muela bequeathed "good land, not stony waste land" and some animals to his two yanaconas and their children: "Testamento de don Vicente Caero," AHMC, Leg. 1213 (1756).

[88] Colonial sources rarely give the occupation of parties engaged in land transactions. The main clue as to whether title to property was being acquired by a peasant is a reference (or lack of reference) to the sociracial status of the purchaser. Usually, records of property transfers mentioned the "race" of the buyer if he was mestizo, ladino, cholo, or Indian. In the late colonial era, few titles passed into the hands of Indians or mestizos, according to the notarial records. In contrast, notarial records of the 1830s and 1840s routinely registered the occupation of both the buyer and the seller of land, and it was not unusual for peasants, laborers, and artisans to acquire or rent small properties in those years. A typical case was the purchase in 1840 of five and a half viches of land in the hacienda Oronata, with rights to the mita de agua for two hours every fifteen days, by a weaver and his wife, a seamstress: "Venta de tierras de sra. Bartolina Nava," AHMC, Leg. 1410 (1840). In 1833, a peasant (*labrador*) and his wife, a spinner (*hilandera*), signed a five-year lease for two estancias in the mountains

Perhaps the most important obstacle to peasant accumulation was simply the fact that most peasants lived at the mercy of seasonal and cyclical fluctuations of crop yields. Subsistence insecurity, the universal bane of peasant existence, made the equilibrium of the peasant family economy persistently precarious. Growing population pressure on the unirrigated lands, which suffered first and most severly from a shortage of rainfall, exacerbated the situation. Viedma's concern about "idle hands" and the "growing mixed-blood population" in the late eighteenth century reflected these problems. For many peasant households, even "normal" harvest fluctuations could bring hardship. During the fifteen years between 1786 and 1800, a period of relatively moderate fluctuations, the price of a fanega of maize went up as high as twenty-eight reales and down as low as sixteen reales per fanega (see figure 11 below). Even for those smallholders who endured (or capitalized on) chronic economic insecurity, a severe drought or other calamity could spell ruin. In the late eighteenth and early nineteenth centuries, the region experienced three subsistence crises: one associated with the 1781 rebellions; a second during the drought of 1784; and a third which was the result of a prolonged drought around 1804. These disasters transformed many peasants into beggars and paupers and destroyed the wealth of even those peasants who had had the makings of petty rural proprietors.[89]

The insecurity attendant upon small-scale agriculture, together with the growing opportunities for petty commerce in the towns and

bordering the pueblo real of El Paso: "Contrato de arrendamiento de tierras," AHMC, Leg. 1376 (1833), f. 223. Future research may find that peasant proprietorship was more common after independence. It may also be true, however, that the acquisition of land titles by peasants and artisans was more frequent in the late colonial period than the notarial records indicate. It seems likely that the intensified tax pressures on peasant households, together with the economic disruptions caused by war and agricultural crises, impeded the process of land acquisition by smallholders in the last decade of colonial rule.

89 A more detailed discussion of agricultural fluctuations and of their differential impact on the peasant and landowning classes is found in chap. 6. See also Larson, "Rural Rhythms of Class Conflict." On agricultural cycles and the secular stagnation and decline of staple prices in eighteenth-century Alto Perú, see Tandeter and Wachtel, *Precios y producción agraria.* The most systematic, long-term analysis of agricultural price and production trends pertains to eighteenth century Mexico; see the pioneering work of Enrique Florescano, *Precios del maíz y crisis agrícola en México, 1708-1810* (Mexico City: Colegio de México, 1969); Brading, *Haciendas and Ranchos,* chap. 8; and Richard L. Gardner, "Price Trends in Eighteenth-Century Mexico," *Hispanic American Historical Review* 65 (1985): 279-326.

ferias of the central valleys, motivated many peasants to diversify their economic activities. Though short of capital and land, and lacking the economic autonomy that land ownership might have bestowed, many rural people applied their "idle hands" to primitive manufacturing. When peasants could no longer assemble a variety of lands in different ecological niches or call upon their community for aid in times of stress, they found new forms of social insurance: selective engagement with commodity production and exchange, and a combination of agriculture, pastoralism, trade, and manufacturing. Thus, in the Cliza valley and on the outskirts of Cochabamba, a family of maize cultivators might also manufacture chicha and sell it to other peasants at the ferias. Wheat growers in the Sacaba valley crafted rustic furniture for sale in the nearby towns. Rural laborers in the Quillacollo parish made tocuyo (see chapter 7).

When, in 1774 and again in 1780, colonial authorities sought to increase alcabalas and regulate overland trade in the viceroyalties of La Plata and Peru, they encountered strong opposition from the popular classes of Cochabamba. It was the cholo peasant-artisans of the central valleys, particularly of Cliza, who launched the most visible protest. The "guilds of tocuyo weavers, tailors and shoemakers, ironmongers, and soapmakers" were part of the "popular commotion," and local officials worried about their power to "disturb the peace." Indeed, the procurador advised against the tax increases, because of the "poverty, indigence, and scarcity in which most inhabitants of this province find themselves living."[90] Like their forebears who revolted against the threat of tribute levies in the 1730s, the smallholder-artisans in the 1770s and 1780s constituted a powerful political force against tax reforms.

As petty commodity producers, the valley peasants were remolding the contours of the regional economy, diversifying production and evolving a network of peasant markets. They were giving shape to an emerging peasant economy, one that was outside the domain of the traditional Andean community and that has made a deep imprint on the region down to the present day. Most important, they were forging a rival economy that increasingly encroached on the economic power of the landowning class.

90 "Exp. seguido con motivo del amago de revolución en Cochabamba, con datos de los impuestos que de cobran de los frutos de la tierra," ANB, EC no. 57 (1781); and "Informe del corregidor sobre los pasquines y la comoción popular en Cochabamba," AGI, Charcas, Leg. 505 (1774).

The Landowning Class: Hard Times and Windfall Profits

In the early colonial period, grain haciendas sprang up like mush-rooms around the cities and towns and some mining camps—wher-ever town dwellers concentrated in large numbers and preexisting Andean settlements posed little obstacle to the overseas colonizers. Two hundred years later, in the late eighteenth century, most hacen-dados were still supplying food to nearby urban areas. Given the growing population, some landowners could count on rising property values to secure more loans or to press for more rent.

But in general, times were hard for the owners of the grain and livestock estates of Andean America, or so at least they complained. The secular stagnation and decline of agricultural prices in Alto Perú during the second half of the eighteenth century narrowed the mar-gin of return on grain sales. Many hacendados, including those in Cochabamba, found themselves confronting competition from a class of smallholders (mostly tenants and sharecroppers) who period-ically brought small quantities of staples to the market, depressing the prices of those crops. The centrifugal effect of Spanish partible-inheritance laws compounded the problem. By the late eighteenth century, the transmission of land ownership through inheritance had fragmented many property units into parcels and pieces and had re-duced haciendas to mere paper units of reckoning. But the effects of these internal corrosive forces on the landlord class depended ulti-mately upon the profitability of agriculture and upon the strength of regional and extraregional markets.

Grain Haciendas in Decay

Almost everywhere in eighteenth-century Spanish America, land-lords complained of low returns on capital investment in grain agri-culture. In his survey of agrarian studies, Mörner found that the average return on capital invested in agriculture (including specialized crops) did not exceed 6 percent at that time.[1] Most agricultural enterprises, particularly grain haciendas, were burdened with multiple liens—mortgages and various "annuities" (annual payments on charitable bequests and other "pious works")—that siphoned off large portions of income. Haciendas in the Mexican province of Oaxaca, for example, carried accumulated debts that absorbed as much as two-thirds of the capital value of those estates.[2] Brading postulated that "the [Mexican] fortunes created in mining and commerce were invested in land, there to be slowly dissipated or to be gradually transferred into the coffers of the Church."[3] Of course, the fact that most landlords were deep in debt to the church cannot be ascribed simply to competition from small-scale cultivators, mismanagement of the enterprise, or conspicuous consumption by a "prestige-oriented" class. Many landowners complained that the high costs of production absorbed most of the returns they got from the sale of their staple crops. One Martín de Garmendía, a hacendado of Cuzco province, said that "for every peso paid for a unit of grain, five percent is paid for annuities and rent, ten percent covers tithes, 20 percent pays salaries and wages, and 40 or 50 percent covers transport costs."[4] Although his cost accounting is perhaps incomplete, unrepresentative, and even inaccurate, Garmendía's estimate of freight costs is striking. It emphasizes the formidable logistical obstacles faced by the owners of grain estates who tried to reach beyond the markets in their immediate vicinity. Similarly, Florescano found that most grain enterprises in central Mexico during the eighteenth century were handicapped by poor roads, high transport costs, and extremely narrow markets.[5] The hacendados of the Bajío who built irrigation works and turned maize patches into wheat fields were among the fortunate few who could take advantage of the expanding

1 Mörner, "Spanish American Hacienda," 204; see also Magnus Mörner, "Economic Factors and Social Stratification in Colonial Spanish America, with Special Regard to Elites," *Hispanic American Historical Review* 63 (1983): 335-370.

2 William Taylor, *Landlord and Peasant in Colonial Oaxaca* (Stanford, Calif.: Stanford University Press, 1972), 140-142; see also Arnold J. Bauer, "The Church and Spanish American Agrarian Structure, 1765-1865," *Americas* 28 (1971): 78-98.

3 Brading, *Miners and Merchants*, 219.

4 Quoted in Magnus Mörner, "En torno a las haciendas de la región del Cuzco desde el siglo XVIII," in Enrique Florescano, ed., *Haciendas, latifundios, y plantaciones* (Mexico City: Siglo XXI, 1975), 363.

5 Florescano, *Precios del maíz*, 88ff.

market in staple crops. Like the early chacareros of Cochabamba who supplied cereal to Potosí during the sixteenth-century silver boom, the landlords of the Bajío set out to conquer the staple markets of Guanajuato, America's eighteenth-century silver capital in Mexico. The thriving grain estates in the province of León in the Bajío apparently were among the exceptions that proved the rule.[6]

If most hacendados found their agrarian operations limited by geographical barriers and capital scarcity, landlords throughout the Andes saw their situation deteriorate sharply after 1780. The crown's decision to create the viceroyalty of La Plata in 1776 and then to open Buenos Aires to direct trade with all Spanish ports in 1778 increased foreign competition manyfold and diverted the flow of silver toward Buenos Aires. Merchants in southern Atlantic ports channeled European goods to Alto Perú and beyond to Cuzco, Arequipa, and even Lima. Although Cuzco and the coastal sugar and cotton plantations and vineyards continued to send products to Alto Perú after 1780, those commodities were often traded for European textiles rather than for unminted or coined silver, as had been customary in earlier times.[7] To make matters worse, the flood of European textiles undermined the interregional trade in rustic cloth that was produced in Andean obrajes and workshops. The Cuzco region, among others, suffered a sharp decline in the export of textiles.[8]

Meanwhile, as the traffic across the pampas grew heavier, the merchants of Buenos Aires competed with hacendados throughout the Andes for cargo animals, especially mules. During the six years between 1776 and 1781, the estancias of Salta and Córdoba exported 70,000 mules (at eight to nine pesos per animal) to Peru, and between 1790 and 1800, another 30,000 (at thirteen to sixteen pesos per mule).[9] Mules became scarce and expensive in many parts of Peru,

6 Brading, *Haciendas and Ranchos.*

7 J. Fisher, *Government and Society in Colonial Peru,* 133; Céspedes del Castillo, "Lima y Buenos Aires"; and Febres Villarroel, "Crisis agrícola en el Perú."

8 Mörner, "En torno a las haciendas," 357; and Mörner, *Perfil de la sociedad rural.* For a comprehensive and fascinating study of rural society in the Cuzco area, see Luís Miguel Glave and María Isabel Remy, *Estructura agraria y vida rural en una región andina: Ollantaytambo entre los siglos XVI y XIX* (Cuzco: Centro de Estudios Rurales Andinos "Bartolomé de la Casas," 1983).

9 John Lynch, *Spanish Colonial Administration, 1782-1810: The Intendant System in the Viceroyalty of the Río de la Plata* (London: Athlone, 1958); Nicolás Sánchez-Albornoz, "La saca de mulas de Salta al Perú, 1778-1808," *Anuario del Instituto de Investigaciones Históricas,* no. 8 (1965): 261-312.

and freight costs rose accordingly. Moreover, the crown's determination to raise state revenue in the colonies prompted it to increase the sales (alcabala) and transit taxes on most colonial items of trade, and muleteers had a difficult time evading these taxes after the state built customs houses at strategic points along the most heavily traveled routes.

Agrarian interests in the southern Andes were also dealt serious blows by native insurgents in 1780 and 1781. In Cochabamba and other regions, rebels destroyed haciendas and mills, burned crops, and slaughtered landlords' herds. The royal armies sometimes struck back by burning the crops and stealing the livestock of Indians.[10] Rebellions also often broke out along main commercial arteries; the insurgents blocked trade routes between the central valleys of Cochabamba and the altiplano, for example, and cut off food supplies to Oruro and other highland markets.[11] Viedma reported that, several years later, many landowners of Cochabamba had still not recovered from the losses they suffered during the rebellion.[12]

Imbued with the doctrines of the physiocrats and vested with enhanced authority by the crown, Viedma and other intendants who arrived in the Andes in 1784 turned their attention to the ailing regional economies of their districts. As instructed in the Ordinance of Intendants (1782), they set about the tasks of inspecting their intendancies and gathering information on population, roads, commerce, industry, and Indian villages. In their reports, they described sluggish markets, underproductive estates, and depressed agricultural prices in a rich land of abundant and varied vegetation.[13] Some authorities traced the root cause of Peru's agricultural decline to the disposition of labor. Macera has argued that the frequent complaints of labor scarcity in eighteenth-century Peru were not related to the Indian population curve, which after all was on the upswing again.[14]

10 Campbell, "Recent Research on Andean Peasant Revolts," 27.

11 Ibid., 28; and Mörner, *Perfil de la sociedad rural*, 119ff.

12 He mentioned, for example, that in 1787, newborn calves had still not replenished the herds of cattle lost during the Indian uprisings. AGN, Sala 9, Intendencia, 5.8.4, Leg. 3, May 1, 1787.

13 Viedma's report is analyzed in chap. 5. A brief summary of it may also be found in Tibor Wittman, "Sociedad y economía de Cochabamba: La 'Valencia del Perú' en 1793," *Revista de Indias*, no. 31 (1971): 367-376. On the intendancies in Lower Peru, see J. Fisher, *Government and Society in Colonial Peru*; for Alto Perú, see Lynch, *Spanish Colonial Administration*.

14 Macera, "Feudalismo colonial americano," 168ff.

Contemporary observers said that the problem lay in the work habits of native peoples. In 1751, the crown echoed this opinion: "The indolence, sloth, and laziness of those natives towards all kinds of work is notorious."[15] Along with the colonial authorities, the crown feared that, with the abolition of the repartimiento de mercancías, the Indians would slip back into their idle ways. The intendant of Arequipa, in his report, confirmed that Indians had become more inactive since 1781, and he declared that the crown must prod them to work if Peru's economy was to flourish again.[16]

Viedma was one of the intendants who expressed alarm about the decay of Alto Perú's economy and specifically of its granary, Cochabamba. He made many comments about the contrast between nature's bounty and the human misery he saw around him. His reports were filled with descriptions of vagrants, abandoned highland towns, decaying haciendas, and an impoverished population that consumed chicha in excess. But unlike many of his colleagues, Viedma ascribed the decline to narrow markets and a "crisis of overproduction." In his view, peasant laziness was not necessarily congenital, but was rather a social malaise that crept over the land as monetary incentives weakened and markets became glutted. In his 1788 report, Viedma wrote:

> Agriculture is one of the most important sectors of the economy; but it is necessary to search for outlets so the cultivator's labor will always be justly remunerated. There is little use in cultivating more wheat and maize [in Cochabamba] when experience has shown us that the lack of demand in the outlying provinces has depreciated the price of these products, such that the price of a fanega of wheat or maize does not reach even one peso. . . . We must be aware of this overabundance [of grain] in order to be able to find a solution to the problem; for this is the fundamental cause of people's sloth and laziness. As people attain the means of subsistence so as not to be forced to gaze at the ancient face of hunger, they are content with [the traditional crops like] maize, potatoes, and ají . . . as they pass through a

15 Edict of June 15, 1751, quoted in Golte, *Repartos y rebeliones*, 84.

16 Victor M. Barriga, *Memorias para la historia de Arequipa*, 4 vols., (1786-1791) (Arequipa: La Colmena, 1941-1952), 1: 107-108; also cited and summarized in Zavala, *Servicio personal*, 3: 91-92. On similar views, recast in liberal ideological terms, among nineteenth-century Chilean landowners, see Arnold J. Bauer, *Chilean Rural Society from the Spanish Conquest to 1930* (Cambridge: Cambridge University Press, 1975), 148.

languid and licentious life. It would not be so were these fruits scarce.[17]

Viedma was here expressing his view of the causes of economic backwardness, revealing how influenced he was by neomercantilist currents of thought. Yet he himself had observed at first hand that peasants in the crowded valley of Cliza had turned to handicrafts to supplement their meager income from farming; and the "hamlets of arrenderos" who lived in the Cercado district were among the legions of petty traders who converged upon the ferias of Cochabamba, Quillacollo, and other towns. Thus, Viedma's empirical observations of economic activity in the central valleys (see chapter 5) did not seem to support his precepts about peasant lassitude and depressed grain prices. Certainly the landless laborer who received the statutory daily wage of two reales hardly considered food prices to be "deflated"; nor from a regional perspective could grain prices in Cochabamba be considered exceptionally low.[18] When Viedma addressed the problem of idle and redundant laborers, he was articulating the viewpoint of his class—one that interpreted economic decline in terms of overproduction and lack of market demand and price incentive. Yet even while they tried to plumb the causes of "peasant lethargy," Viedma and his fellow landowners paradoxically found themselves challenged by increasing competition from a profusion of small-scale cultivators.

Perhaps it is not surprising, then, that the intendant rarely reported to the Consulado, the royal trade guild in Buenos Aires, the problems of scarcity or high food prices in the region. In 1784 and 1804, when all of Alto Perú was beset by severe, prolonged drought and by famine and bands of wandering beggars, Viedma did write of human misery and hardship. In a series of reports about agricultural conditions between 1785 and 1800, however, he stressed the region's abundant grain supplies and reserves and the moderate prices of food. In September 1796, for example, he reported that the harvest of that year, together with grain stored from the previous year, had inundated the local market. Peasants in the neighboring highland provinces also enjoyed favorable planting conditions in those years, and the intendant noted that Cochabamba's farmers therefore shipped

17 Viedma, *Descripción geográfica*, 159-160.

18 The average price of grain in Cochabamba was about eighteen reales in an ordinary year, while in the Bajío it hovered around fourteen reales. Brading, *Haciendas and Ranchos*, 184.

little grain to the highlands. He reported that "even Cochabamba's inflated and numerous population would be incapable of consuming all local [food crops] over the next two years."[19] Even when the weather was bad, as in the early months of 1787, the intendant predicted no serious food shortage in the region, for he declared that sufficient grain had been stored from previous harvests to feed the local population adequately. He continued to remain confident during the poor harvest of 1787. On September 1, he reported that much of the crop had died for lack of rainfall, but he considered current grain prices (twenty-two reales per fanega of maize) to be relatively low nevertheless, again because of the existence of grain reserves that people could draw on.[20] (For additional details, see table A-5.)

This pattern of one or two successive years of ordinary to abundant harvests followed by a year of poor harvest, due to extensive flooding, as in 1788 and 1797, or to drought, as in 1792 and 1807, recurred with almost uncanny consistency between 1785 and 1800. Yet despite this variation, Viedma never reported serious shortages of wheat or maize. When frost and drought ruined the crops (especially in the highlands) in 1792, Viedma assured the Consulado that maize was still readily available, at the price of twenty-four reales a fanega. So it was also in 1797, 1799, and 1800. Yet prices in those years were fluctuating widely (see figure 11). Perhaps Viedma was assessing the significance of the fluctuations not from the peasant's and wage laborer's point of view but from the perspective of landlords finally able to dispose of some of their surpluses.

One of the best informants about the profitability of haciendas in Cochabamba was Juan Felipe Negrón, who had come into possession of the hacienda Chullpas in the Cliza valley, an estate that Viedma had purchased earlier (in 1805) in the hope of founding an orphanage on the grounds. After Viedma's death in 1809, his widow sold most of the property. Following the Wars of Independence, the estate was assessed at 50,084 pesos, most of it in the form of some four hundred fanegadas of land, especially its irrigated maize fields (see table 15 above). Chullpas was unquestionably one of the wealthiest and largest estates in the region, yet when it was auctioned off in 1828 (bringing 55,125 pesos), it seemed to be in a sorry state. Its buildings and mills were crumbling, and the property carried various ecclesiastical benefices and liens amounting to 30,000 pesos—more than half of its assessed value. Furthermore, the estate had not weathered

19 AGN, Sala 9, Intendencia, 5.8.3, Leg. 2, Sept. 6, 1786.

20 Ibid., 5.8.4, Leg. 3, Sept. 1, 1787, and Dec. 31, 1787.

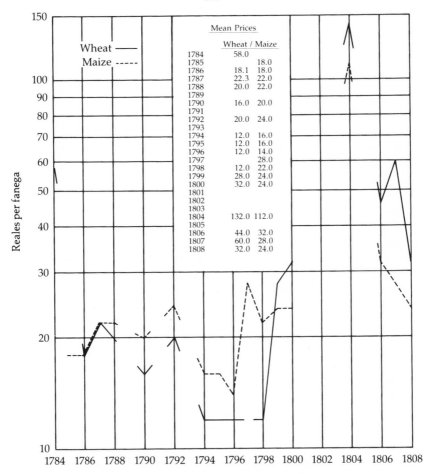

Figure 11   Wheat and Maize Prices in Cochabamba, 1784-1808
Sources: AGN, Sala 9, Intendencia, 5.8.3, Leg. 2; 5.8.4, Leg. 3; 5.8.5, Leg. 4;
5.8.6, Leg. 5; 5.8.7, Leg. 6; 5.9.1, Leg. 7; and 5.9.2, Leg. 8.

the transition to republican rule very well. Between the last colonial
census in 1804 and the time Negrón registered a complaint about
property taxes in 1828, the resident Indian population had declined
from 207 to 70.[21]

Negrón spoke of a serious problem that faced many landowners in

21 AGN, Sala 13, Padrones, 18.3.3, Leg. 53 (1804); "Don Juan Felipe Negrón, vz.
de Potosí, se remató . . . la hacienda Chullpas (cantón de Toco)," AHMC, Leg.
1360 (1828); "Venta y remate público de la hacienda Chullpas," AHMC, Leg.
1083 (1827).

the late colonial period. Access to water made the difference for him between the possibility of prospering or the near-certain prospect of falling deeper into debt. Negrón captured what water he could from the Toco and Quaiculi rivers to irrigate his maize fields, but neither he nor his predecessors had invested in the construction of irrigation ditches, reservoirs, or sluices to ensure a more reliable supply of water. He complained that the system of rotational irrigation (the mita de agua) did not provide sufficient water to allow him to harvest two crops a year. Thus, unlike some of his more fortunate neighbors, Negrón had to cope with the uncertainties of rainfall. According to his own accounts, a spectacular harvest of 3,000 or 4,000 fanegas of wheat and maize might be followed the next year by a "normal" yield of 2,000 fanegas, with prices in a good year at about ten to twelve reales per fanega and in the normal years at sixteen to eighteen reales. Gross income in a good year would therefore be between 4,000 and 5,000 pesos; in the normal years, between 4,000 and 4,500 pesos. Negrón estimated that his production costs in a good year would be 3,000 pesos, but only 1,500 pesos in an ordinary year. Consequently, net income in a good year represented between 2 and 4 percent of the value of the land, while in an ordinary year it represented from 5 to 6 percent—although all those figures are somewhat higher than was actually the case, since Negrón failed to include in his production costs the amounts required for annuities, interest on his debts, and seed for the following year.[22] However crude Negrón's accounts may have been, they revealed the inner logic of demesne agriculture: landlords reaped their highest returns when the weather was unfavorable and prices were thereby higher.

Deprived of distant markets and of any incentive to increase agricultural production, the landlords of Cochabamba turned inward and developed a system of storage and distribution that was adapted to the conditions of harvest fluctuations. When drought, frost, or flood reduced competition from the smallholding cultivators, the large landowners (individual and corporate) who had stored grain from previous years had a chance to profit considerably. From this perspective, it is understandable why Viedma reported that, even after moderately poor harvests, there was no serious shortage of food in the region. The large landowners were able to turn the vicissitudes of nature to their own advantage.[23] It was commonplace, in times of

22 AHMC, Legs. 1083 and 1360, f. 231.

23 Florescano, *Precios del maíz*, has shown how landlords in central Mexico were able not merely to take advantage of high prices but even to create them.

food shortage, for them to release their stores of grain onto the market in small quantities, or else to increase their exports to the western highland markets, in order to keep the price up. That is what the cabildo of Cochabamba, for example, discovered during an inspection of the granaries of haciendas in the Cliza and Cochabamba valleys that had been prompted by the drought of 1784.[24]

The landowners who benefited most from crop failures were those who controlled extensive irrigation works that continued to water their maize fields even after several weeks of little rainfall or who at least had the political leverage and authority to command access to periodic distribution of scarce water. As Negrón acknowledged, "It doesn't matter whether maize sells for five or six pesos if it withers on the stalk for lack of irrigation; in that case, an hacendado is apt to lose everything."[25]

During an inspection of flour mills in several parishes in 1799, royal authorities had occasion to interview many hacendados who operated water-driven mills on their estates. The owners expressed their dissatisfaction with the prospect of paying a tax of one real per fanega on the grain they milled. The owners were also worried about their access to water. Especially for those who had invested substantial amounts of capital in their milling enterprises—a typical mill was assessed at between 3,000 and 4,000 pesos in the late eighteenth century—the supply of water was critical. How landowners fared in the struggle over water depended partly on the location of their mill in relation to the quebrada, where streams had carved out mountain ravines and spilled down into the valley bottomlands. One miller, José de Severicha y Foronda, complained that the landowners who had higher land frequently siphoned off the river water upon which he depended to power his grain mills. Consequently, he was able to operate the enterprise only five months out of the year for lack of water, and under these conditions, he told the inspector, he rarely made a profit. In fact, Severicha presented detailed accounts to prove that only the earnings from properties he owned in the Cliza valley made it possible for him to operate his mills in Quillacollo. If he were not so fortunate as to own haciendas in Cliza, he said, he could never pay his debts or prevent the foreclosure of his property. "For the truth is that the earnings of a poor asendado [sic] are hardly sufficient to cover costs and to allow him to retain the title of 'asen-

24 "El procurador general al cabildo," Feb. 10, 1784, in Digesto de ordenanzas, 3: 128.

25 "Venta y remate público de la hacienda Chullpas," AHMC, Leg. 1083 (1827).

dado' when asendados spend more than they earn.'[26] It is very likely
that Severicha exaggerated his case and professed poverty in order to
dissuade the inspector from levying the tax. Yet the inspector who
toured the mills compiled a catalogue of complaints concerning the
risks and costs of the milling enterprises. Even under optimal conditions of abundant harvests and plentiful water supplies, mills operated only three to six months a year. Returns fluctuated sharply
from one year to the next, and millowners feared floods even more
than drought. In the words of one millowner in the river valley of
Tapacarí, "Milling depends upon rainfall, and drought can silence all
the wheat mills in the region; but when torrential rains swell the
rivers and spill over the banks, all traffic and trade with highland
Indians ceases and many mills are destroyed."[27]

These millowners and hacendados were expressing the discontent
that landowners felt in most regions of narrow, circumscribed markets. Like peasants whose very subsistence and petty mercantile accumulation were jeopardized by the fluctuation of harvest yields,
landlords themselves could not break loose from the cycle: their profits from agriculture were derived from scarcity, high prices, and the
subsistence needs of the peasant class. If hacendados diversified their
operations and invested in several mills, they might partially make
up for the low returns on the sale of maize and wheat after plentiful
harvests by the fees they charged for turning peasants' grain into
flour. But returns on their capital investment were always vulnerable to the weather.

In addition to their concerns about water, weather, and competition from small-scale cultivators, many landowners also perceived a
deeper threat from the commercial opening of Buenos Aires in 1776
and especially from its opening to direct trade with Spanish ports
after 1778. Of course, the hacendados had little fear of direct competition from Spanish agrarian enterprises. The problem, rather, was
that the traffic in silver and in European goods in the port of Buenos
Aires drew heavily upon the freight animals, particularly the mules
and horses raised on the grasslands of Salta and Córdoba. Muleteers
drove fewer pack animals northward into the Andes to sell to hacendados and local merchants. Wholesale merchants of the southern
port city began to assume control of the means of overland transport
in the viceroyalty, leaving many regions with acute shortages of
mules and horses.

26 "Real visita a las molinas de grano," AHMC, Leg. 1213 (1799).

27 Ibid. (interview with Mariano Vergara).

In Cochabamba, landowners had not been able to replenish all the horses and mules lost during the Indian uprisings, when the city had dispatched a large band of militia to La Paz to break the rebels' stranglehold on that city. In the 1780s and 1790s, hacendados saw the price of mules rise from between fifteen and twenty-five pesos to more than thirty-five pesos. The shortage of freight animals alarmed Viedma and other provincial authorities, and they protested the situation in reports and letters to the consulado in 1800 and 1801.[28] Only the wealthiest landowners owned enough pack animals to transport their own harvest to distant markets. Most property owners and small-scale producers were unable to transport their grain, even when periodic shortages forced up staple prices considerably, except by the use of professional pack drivers or other intermediaries who owned mule trains. This scarcity of pack animals conferred an additional advantage on the region's large landowners and merchants.

In Viedma's view, the new trans-Atlantic trade arrangements posed another, perhaps more serious, threat to the local landowners. In 1788, he wrote: "Spanish goods are regularly imported to this city [Cochabamba]. Luxury is fashionable now, and many consume [Spanish] articles of trade, occasioning the flight of money, which the province can ill afford."[29] In the same report, he estimated that the local population spent 200,000 pesos on European merchandise, about 35 percent of the total value of all (colonial and European) imports in 1788.[30] When checked against yearly alcabalas on imports, Viedma's estimate appears to be much too high.[31] Furthermore, the amount of European goods that traders brought into the province varied considerably from year to year. But Viedma's criticism of hacendados who lived beyond their means, frittering away their income on such items as Spanish silks, was not surprising under the circumstances.

Indeed, insolvency of landowners was a matter of some concern in the 1780s. In 1783, the cabildo of Cochabamba took note of the encumbrances and debts that burdened most estates in the region and expressed alarm that, two years after the Indian uprisings, many ha-

28 AGN, Sala 9, Consulado, 4.6.4, tomo 14 (1800 and 1801), especially ff. 56-56v.

29 Viedma, *Descripción geográfica*, 47.

30 Ibid., 144.

31 For details, see Larson, "Economic Decline and Social Change," 230-240.

cendados had still not resumed payment of their obligations to creditors.[32] Some forty years later, at the time of independence, an angry landowner who decried government plans to tax property owners remarked that "Those who call themselves landowners in this province actually own a ridiculously small part of their property; in most cases, landlords whose estates are worth ten, fifteen, or twenty thousand pesos own less than a third of the property."[33]

Wills and inventories (*tasaciones*) of family properties in the late eighteenth and early nineteenth centuries show that, in most cases, between one-third and one-half of the total assessment was encumbered by loans and various forms of obligations to the church (*obras pías* and *capellanías*). As historians have shown for other regions, encumbrances on rural properties tended to accelerate the turnover of property, for by assuming the payment of obligations, purchasers could buy the real estate for a smaller cash outlay.[34] In transfers of property ownership in Cochabamba in the 1780s, the average purchaser paid cash for only about 50 percent of the assessed value of the property.[35] Property sales usually included the transfer of all or most debt obligations to the new proprietor. Sometimes loan contracts forbade the subdivision of property, but most of them stipulated only that the hacienda be kept up and the assessed property value maintained. When several heirs inherited an encumbered hacienda, they frequently assumed a portion of the debt obligations, in accordance with the value of their share of the inheritance.[36]

The largest moneylenders in Cochabamba province were its seven monasteries. At the time of independence in 1825, the sum of their outstanding loans was more than 600,000 pesos (table 18). Church liens on property that year were worth a little more than the estimated value of the province's exports in 1788.[37] The monasteries extended credit (*censos*), with the property as collateral, at a fixed interest rate of 5 percent annually. Sometimes credit was extended in perpetuity (*censos en compra*) in exchange for an annual fee paid to

32 AGN, Sala 9, Intendencia, 5.8.2, Leg. 1 (1783).

33 ANB, Ministerio del Interior, Prefectura de Cochabamba, vol. 2 (1825).

34 Mörner, "Spanish American Hacienda," 198.

35 AGN, Sala 13, Contaduría, 21.1.1 (1781) and 27.1.5 (1785).

36 See, for example, the division of the hacienda Muela among several heirs, in "Hijuelación de la hacienda Muela, en Arani," AHMC, Leg. 1067 (1817-1833).

37 The total value of the province's exports in 1788 was estimated to be 620,906 pesos. Viedma, *Descripción geográfica*, 156.

Table 18. Principal and Interest of Loans
Held by Cochabamba's Monasteries, 1825

Monastery	Principal		Annual Interest	
	Amount (pesos)	Percentage of Total	Amount (pesos)	Percentage of Principal
Santa Clara	222,480	34.9	7,662	3.4
San Augustín	117,919	18.5	4,066	3.4
Santa Theresa	114,625	18.0	3,779	3.3
Santo Domingo	79,912	12.5	3,296	4.1
San Francisco	54,199	8.5	1,672	3.1
La Merced	38,653	6.1	1,223	3.2
La Recolección	9,720	1.5	406	4.2
Total	637,508	100.0	22,104	

Source: ANB, Ministerio del Interior, tomo 2, no. 236 (1825).

the monastery; in other cases, the loans were made for a seven-year term.

The richest ecclesiastical institution in Cochabamba, and the largest lender, was the Franciscan convent of Santa Clara, located in the city of Cochabamba. In 1825, it held 222,480 pesos in mortgage loans, more than one-third of the value of all ecclesiastical loans in the province that year. Santa Clara was a large nunnery, with a resident population of sixty-three nuns and their personal servants.[38] The "sisters of the black veil" who graced the courtyards of Santa Clara were mostly the daughters of wealthy hacendados, who paid the convent a "dowry" (in effect, an entrance fee) of between 1,000 and 3,000 pesos and sometimes in addition pledged an "endowment" of annual payments. Such, for example, was the arrangement under which Tomasa Liro de Córdova, daughter of the cacique of Tapacarí, Guillermo Liro de Córdova, entered the convent on the eve of the Túpac Amarú uprisings.[39]

Santa Clara built its financial empire, however, not so much on the proceeds from its dowries or benefices as on the reinvested profits of its agrarian enterprises. The convent was probably the largest landowner in the Cochabamba province during the eighteenth century. In 1648, Francisco de Varga bequeathed to it twenty fanegadas of rich, irrigated maize land in the Cliza valley. The assessed value

38 Viedma, Descripción geográfica, 38; Gabriel René Moreno, Ultimos días coloniales en el Perú (La Paz: Juventud, 1970), 172.

39 AHMC, Leg. 1444 (1780), f. 718.

of the hacienda Cliza in that year was 40,000 pesos.[40] Over the next century, the convent's financial managers invested in neighboring land and properties. By the early nineteenth century, the nunnery's hacienda Cliza extended across 860 fanegadas of bottomland. In 1825, the minister of the interior in the newly established republic registered 565,400 pesos as the total assessed property value of Santa Clara. The estate's wheat and maize fields alone were estimated to be worth more than 300,000 pesos, and sale of the harvested crop brought in 17,000 pesos in that year alone.[41] Nothing was said at that time about the size of its labor force, but in the last colonial tribute census in 1803, the resident Indian population numbered almost one thousand.[42] In terms of its wealth, size, and income, this latifundium dwarfed other estates in the region.

There was no central registry of ecclesiastical real estate, but occasional references make it clear that other orders had substantial investments in land as well, if to a lesser degree than the Franciscans. The Augustinians held lands in the village of Tapacarí, and they owned the wealthy hacienda El Convento in the valley of Caraza, where sixty-three yanaconas served the mendicants in 1747,[43] and the hacienda Achamoco in the parish of Tarata in the Cliza valley, where seventy-eight yanaconas lived and worked in the early nineteenth century.[44] The Dominicans owned lands and mills on the large hacienda Vinto on the outskirts of Quillacollo.[45] A Carmelite convent owned high-altitude pasture and crop lands and tropical lowlands in the parish of Yani (partido of Ayopaya), and in the early nineteenth century it leased out the hacienda Yani to someone who planted potatoes in its puna land, maize in warm, sheltered niches, and sugar cane in the tropical, low-altitude acreage.[46] The Jesuits,

40 Damian Rejas, *Tercer centenario de la fundación del Monasterio de Santa Clara (1648-1948)* (Cochabamba: Universal, 1948), 5-6.

41 ANB, Ministerio del Interior, tomo 2, no. 236 (1825).

42 AGN, Sala 13, Padrones, 18.3.4, Leg. 54 (1803).

43 "Real provisión sobre no ser yanaconas los indios de la hacienda de Carasa," ANB, EC no. 6396 (1749).

44 "Exp. por el Convento de San Augustín . . . sobre la devolución de las haciendas de Hachamoco en arrendamiento," AHMC, Leg. 1175 (1806).

45 AHMC, Leg. 1457 (1765), f. 510.

46 "Exp. por Ciprián Cartagena contra la administración del Monasterio del Carmen sobre . . . la hacienda de Yani," AHMC, Leg. 1062 (1782); AGI, Charcas, Leg. 236, Nov. 8, 1724 (on the foundation of the Santa Teresa convent and the

too, had made inroads into the Cochabamba valleys before 1767.[47] In some parishes, like Caraza and Cliza, monasteries owned some of the best lands and probably ran the most efficient and profitable agrarian enterprises. The Augustinian friars, for example, rarely parceled out their land to arrenderos, but instead maintained tight control over a servile yanacona population.

Notwithstanding these investments in land and the shrewd management of estates, however, it is probable that most ecclesiastical capital, including the assets of Santa Clara, was in the form of loans. At least from the perspective of the cash-hungry individual landowner, at once heir to a splintered estate and beset by rising freight costs and fierce competition over irrigation water, it would seem that the friars and the women of the black veil collectively monopolized the supply of loan capital and rural credit in the late eighteenth century. No wonder, then, that at the time of independence, many landowners expressed hostility toward their pious creditors and often renounced their obligation to redeem their debts to them.[48]

Pressed from below by peasant producers during years of good harvests and from above by the claims of ecclesiastical creditors, many landowners gave up management of their agrarian enterprises and lived off the rent from their tenants. When Viedma and cabildo members bemoaned the decay of agriculture, they spoke for landowners who were witnessing the erosion of their economic position in local society. Some hacendados did improve their estates by building irrigation ditches and small reservoirs to increase productivity and enhance their ability to profit during seasons of scanty rainfall.[49] Others, like Almarás of the hacienda Caporaya, tried to extend the area of arable land and to press their tenants for more labor time to sow the new acreage (see chapter 5). But many other landowners, perhaps the majority, considered only two options to be economi-

hacienda Yani; Adolfo de Morales kindly allowed me to consult his notes on the contents of this document).

47 Several large estates that had been owned by the Jesuits, such as the haciendas Calliri, Paucarpata, Marquina, and Quirquiavi, were later mortgaged or leased as *obras pías* by the *Junta de Temporalidades*, and the income from the properties was used to support orphanages and other charities. AGN, Intendencia, 5.8.2 (1802).

48 ANB, Ministerio del Interior, Prefectura de Cochabamba, vol. 2 (1825).

49 For example, in the 1770s and 1780s, the owners of the hacienda Muela, in the Cliza valley, invested in irrigation works for "many fanegadas of land": "Exp. por don Juan de Díos Mariscal contra Pedro Pablo Lara," AHMC, Leg. 1099 (1772-1787).

cally viable. As a wealthy cleric said in his will, his heirs could either parcel out his land (*usufructar*) among small-scale tenants, who would work the land as sharecroppers or pay rent in labor or cash, or else lease the entire estate (*arrendar*) to another landowner, a prosperous peasant, or the former overseer.[50] For a landowner burdened with debt and with little access to cash or further credit, the latter was often the more attractive alternative.

In some cases, a landowner had to lease his estate to avoid foreclosure. In a contract drawn up in 1780, the owners of the hacienda Ayguaico in Cliza explained that they were forced to lease "the hacienda, its houses and gardens, and all its lands," including "13 fanegadas of fertile maize land cultivated by Indian sharecroppers," in order to pay debts amounting to more than 4,000 pesos to the convent of Santa Clara. The owners, three brothers, were to supply the first year's seeds, and the leaseholder (*arrendatario*) would make an immediate payment of 250 pesos "in order to free the hacienda from seizure by creditors [*censualistas*]" and would also pay an annual rent of 400 pesos, as well as covering the costs of maintaining and improving the hacienda.[51]

Where a landowner was unable to raise funds for investment, a short-term lease might serve as an alternative way to make improvements on his land. The owner of the large hacienda La Banda in the Arque, for example, stipulated in a lease contract that the arrendatario was to "improve the hacienda, mills, and garden" of the estate; if that requirement were not met, the rent would be raised by fifty pesos (to two hundred pesos) at the end of the two-year lease.[52]

The other means by which a landowner could generate income from land was through a *censo enfiteútico* (or *venta enfiteútica*). Like

50 "Testamento de Blas Mendez de Rueda," AHMC, Leg. 1450 (1781).

51 "Contrata de arrendamiento de la hacienda Ayguaico," AHMC, Leg. 1444 (1780). In contemporary parlance, *arrendamiento* referred to a formal lease arrangement, whereby a written contract stipulated the terms of exchange. Most such contracts ran for two to nine years, although the arrendatario usually had the right to terminate the contract at midpoint. Leaseholders usually had to post bond for the rent, which generally ranged between 5 and 8 percent of the property's assessed value. In addition, they also assumed the burden of the property's fixed costs. Thus, an arrendatario was usually a person of some economic means and social standing. In contrast, a tenant or renter (arrendero) was a peasant who merely paid a customary rent in labor, cash, and/or kind for the right to use one or several parcels of arable land and pasture for one year.

52 "Contrata de arrendamiento de la hacienda La Banda," AHMC, Leg. 1450 (1793).

the arrendamiento, the censo enfiteútico gave the buyer access to land and its product in return for an annual cash payment, but in this case the arrangement was to endure for the lifetime of the buyer (and sometimes would be continued by his heirs as well).[53] Such contracts were most frequent in the last years of the colonial period, when the increasing difficulty in securing loans and the indebtedness of many of Cochabamba's landowners probably made the prospect of a steady income over a long period of time seem quite attractive.

Tithes As a Mode of Accumulation

Despite the pressures on landowners in the late eighteenth century, a few individual hacendados still managed to accumulate wealth. Negrón, the Cliza hacendado who has been mentioned before, alluded to the existence of an elite that controlled large tracts of rich, permanently irrigated lands and that prospered while other landowners and peasants saw their crops wither if the rains were late or light. Many of these propertied men also exploited the opportunities afforded by tithe collection. A shrewd "tithe farmer" would gather together grain reserves from many peasants and hacendados in a particular parish and then dispose of them at times when prices were highest, especially in the arid highlands, where drought often etched deep scars in the landscape.

Every year, about twenty tithe farmers (*diezmeros*) bid for the right to collect roughly one-tenth of a parish's grain harvest (except in the parishes of the Indian communities, where they collected somewhat less than a tenth). The amount of tithe revenue which the church received depended on the final auction price of the tithe. The revenue from Cochabamba's parishes that were in the archbishopric of Charcas ranged between 25,000 and 40,000 pesos during the last decades of the eighteenth century and the first decade of the nineteenth; the parishes in the Cliza valley, which were part of the bishopric of Santa Cruz, usually produced between 10,000 and 25,000 pesos more.[54] The amount a prospective tithe farmer was willing to bid depended on his expectations of financial gain, and those expectations were influenced to some degree by the outlook for the coming

53 "Censo enfiteútico de la hacienda Coñacoña," AHMC, Leg. 1270 (1774); "Censo enfiteútico de la hacienda Marcavi," AHMC, Leg. 1360 (1840), f. 162v.

54 Larson, *Explotación agraria*, 132-137.

harvest. A comparison between tithe revenues and Viedma's reports on planting conditions will show the relationship.

In 1785-1786, Viedma said planting conditions were favorable (table A-5); as may be seen in figure 12, tithe revenue for 1786 amounted to about 23,000 pesos—a relatively low sum, with the parishes in the Cliza valley especially contributing little. In 1786-1787, planting was late because of drought, and Viedma predicted a poor harvest in two trimester reports in late 1786 and early 1787; tithes rose to 42,000 pesos. The next year, 1787-1788, cultivators enjoyed good rainfall, and an abundant harvest was expected. In 1788, tithe income dipped slightly. Thus, there seemed to be an inverse correlation between the anticipated volume of grain production and the amount of tithe revenue. Between 1774 and 1809, tithe revenue peaked sharply twice: in 1783-1784 and in 1803-1804. Tithe farmers paid the church 114,000 pesos in 1784 and 122,735 pesos in 1804, which were both years of extreme food scarcity. At the end of 1804, Viedma wrote that thousands of peasants had been forced off their lands in search of food to eat. The other side of the picture was that considerable profits accrued to a few speculators, who were able to sell the maize they had stored or collected in tithes for as much as 112 reales per fanega that year. Florescano's conclusion that, in Mexico, landlords gained at the expense of peasants during times of crop failure is applicable to Cochabamba as well.[55]

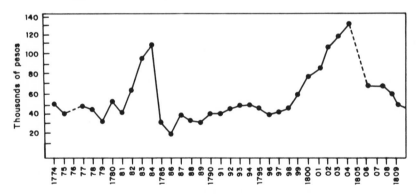

Figure 12   Tithe Revenue from Cochabamba's Parishes, 1774-1810
Source: Derived from data in Larson, "Economic Decline," 437-440.
(Parishes in the districts of the Cercado of Cochabamba, and in Sacaba, Tapacarí, Arque, Ayopaya, and Cliza only.)

55 The auction price of tithes reflected anticipations of the market value of grain, not its actual volume or value after harvest, and it is therefore but a crude

It is difficult to realize that, even in the midst of famine, tithe farmers still managed to expropriate one-tenth of the harvest of peasant households. Some peasants must have found ways to resist the tithe collector's demands. Many of the beggars who flocked to the soup kitchens opened by Cochabamba's two nunneries in 1804 were undoubtedly peasants who had abandoned their fields to avoid tithe, rent, and tribute exactions, as well as to feed themselves. One may imagine that tithe collectors were not a little nervous about their own safety as they made their rounds, forcing peasants to open their near-empty storage huts and surrender part of the crop, sometimes including even the seeds saved for next year's planting. But the evidence is that tithe collectors suffered no financial loss during famine periods. They were known to seize anything of value, preferring livestock if they could not find sufficient grain.

There is not yet sufficient information with which to calculate precisely the rate of return that tithe farmers received, but there is one important clue. In 1774, a royal treasury official argued that many tithe farmers managed to avoid paying the alcabala of 4 percent (later raised to 6 percent) on the value of the tithe. Furthermore, this official proposed that tithe farmers be taxed on the value of the grain sold, rather than on the auction price. In the course of his argument, he pointed out the considerable difference between the two amounts:

> If the tax were levied on the sale of tithed grain, royal revenue would increase; for the tithe farmer who bids 10,000 pesos for the right to collect the tithe in a parish will often sell the grain he collects for 15,000 or 16,000 pesos.[56]

This suggests a 50 or 60 percent rate of return. The significance of that rate is the more striking in view of the facts that the rate of return on most loans was fixed at 5 percent and that the rate of return on the capital value of agricultural enterprises in Cochabamba was rarely more than 4 or 5 percent. In fact, the profit on tithe farming was more than an investor could reasonably hope to realize in any other activity in the region. Under these circumstances, tithe

and indirect indicator of the relationship between grain production and prices. For other studies of tithe revenue and agricultural price fluctuations, see Carmagnani, "Producción agropecuaria chilena"; Bauer, "Church and Spanish American Agrarian Structure"; Brading, *Haciendas and Ranchos*; and Tandeter and Wachtel, *Precios y producción agraria*.

56 "Autos . . . contra el alferéz real . . . sobre los diezmos," AHMC, Leg. 1213 (1774).

speculation was the most "rational" form of economic behavior on the part of the landed elite.

The mechanics of tithe farming also stimulated realignments within the landowning class. Members of the propertied class who wanted to participate in the tithe venture had to close ranks. Each year they bid, the tithe farmers were required to post a bond. Since a considerable portion of their own property was often already burdened by encumbrances, prospective speculators usually turned to other landowners for help in posting this bond, and usually this meant those among their kinfolk, fictive (or ritual) kin, and in-laws who possessed unencumbered land. A study of the surnames and kin ties of frequent tithe speculators in the late eighteenth and early nineteenth centuries strongly suggests that members of the wealthiest landed families tended to trade places from year to year as speculators and bondsmen. In 1790, for example, everyone who successfully bid to collect tithes named at least one bondsman, and at least one-third of these bondsmen were a spouse, an in-law, a sibling, a cousin, or a parent.[57]

The forty or so individuals who were involved in tithe farming each year belonged to a fairly exclusive club. The entry requirements were the usual ones: property assets and good connections. Thus, the effect of this enterprise on the social hierarchy was to sharpen the differences within the landowning class between the small, interlocking elite of tithe speculators and the larger number of insolvent landowners who lived primarily off the proceeds of rents from their tenantry. Tithe farming also gave the upper tier of the landholding class economic leverage over peasant smallholders, since it allowed speculators to manipulate the terms of exchange to their own advantage when scarcity gave them a monopoly over the grain market. For tithe farmers, the cycles of natural calamity compensated, in some measure, for the secular stagnation of agricultural prices and the competition of smallholders in "normal" years.

For speculators and landowners, then, "rentier strategies" of accumulation tended to alter the significance of private property in perhaps subtle but important ways. Where once the valley chacareros and hacendados had been on the moral and political defensive against a colonial state that sought to subordinate private agrarian

---

57 Kinship links were reconstructed by matching the surnames on tithe records against those in the records of notarized economic transactions of other kinds. Many of these surnames appeared as diezmeros and bondsmen on tithe lists in the postindependence period as well.

enterprise to an extractive model of exploitation, the landowners of the late eighteenth century no longer needed to buttress their case with titles, fees, and court cases legitimating land ownership and occupation. Where the structure of land ownership had once led to large-scale grain production destined for export to Potosí, hacienda ownership in the eighteenth century did not necessarily imply demesne agriculture or guarantee profits on grain exports. As we saw in chapter 5, the structure of land ownership was only an imprecise guide to the pattern of agrarian production and class relations. The accumulative strategies of landowner-speculators suggest that landed property was valued not as a factor of production but as an indirect means of securing cash and credit. Above all, unencumbered land was valued as collateral: the qualification for entry into tithe farming and other forms of investment requiring insurance. Within the small circle of landowners able to take heavy risks on speculative ventures, the "circulation of collateral" allowed a degree of flexibility. Landowners who could not post bond on a risky investment at one moment might call upon kinsmen to put up collateral for them, and the favor would be reciprocated at some later date. Under these circumstances, of tight credit and cash and an ever-shrinking pool of unencumbered land to serve as collateral, kinship and reciprocal relations within the landowning elite served as important instruments of economic defense, which could be brought into play to serve the interests of landowners who had abandoned large-scale grain production as the principal source of accumulation.

Elusive Markets of the Altiplano

Francisco de Viedma may have been aware of the competition between small-scale farmers and large landowners in the Cochabamba valley, but the intendant was more concerned about the declining demand for the valley's produce in the "outlying provinces." Yet his own evidence seems to contradict his conclusion that Cochabamba had no market outlet for its staples. In the same report of 1788 in which he lamented the withering of demand in the outside provinces, he estimated that the region had "exported" in that year 200,000 fanegas of wheat and maize, worth some 450,000 pesos (at the relatively high unit price of two pesos two reales). This represented 75 percent of all commodities shipped out of the province along the western trade routes to the altiplano. In addition, pack drivers carried an estimated 160,000 fanegas of flour, worth 40,000 pesos, from the mills of Arque and Tapacarí to the western districts and points beyond. On the other hand, according to Viedma's figures, the region's wide variety of handicrafts accounted for less than 20 percent of the total value of commodities going to extraregional markets; the value of tocuyo exports, for example, was 75,000 pesos, or 12 percent of the region's out-going trade. Despite its economic diversification in the eighteenth century, Cochabamba still provided inhabitants of the altiplano and the highland towns primarily with maize and wheat.[58]

The overproduction that disturbed Viedma thus had not meant a return to a "natural economy" or to subsistence production. Viedma's views simply reflected the landlords' feelings about their weakening mercantile position as provisioners of the mining town. Viedma expressed the frustration of many large landowners, who felt that, in most years, the mining markets were beyond their commercial reach. Entrusted with the task of stimulating agriculture in their intendancies, Viedma, Paula Sanz, and other Bourbon administrators acted on the premise that success in this task depended upon the export of crops and handicrafts to the mining towns. Paula Sanz, in his report of 1794 on the importance of mining and the mita at Potosí, declared that hacendados in the most fertile regions of the viceroyalty had fallen on hard times. Wheat grew abundantly in the provinces of Cochabamba and Chayanta, he said, and yet landlords did not prosper, because of the declining price of wheat at Potosí. He complained that the price did not go above thirty-two reales per fanega and sometimes went as low as twenty reales.[59]

Although Viedma opposed Paula Sanz's proposal to extend the mita, he shared his colleague's belief that without the stimulus of cash derived from trade with the mining towns, the colony would inevitably decline. Viedma's hope for his region's economic recovery

58 Viedma, *Descripción geográfica*, 137. It may be that the prominence of cloth in Cochabamba's export trade was even greater than Viedma's figures indicate. Only a few years later (1794), Paula Sanz estimated the value of Cochabamba tocuyos shipped to Potosí at 40,000 pesos (see table 19), and since Potosí was probably the major market for Cochabamba textiles, it is unlikely that the region exported almost the same value of cloth to other extraregional markets.

59 Paula Sanz, "Contestación al discurso [sobre la mita]," cited and discussed in Zavala, *Servicio personal*, 3: 104. On the secular stagnation and decline of prices in Alto Perú during the second half of the eighteenth century, see Tandeter and Wachtel, *Precios y producción agraria*, and chap. 3 above. On trade and commerce at Potosí, based on the Paula Sanz census, see Marie Helmer, "Commerce et industrie au Pérou à la fin du XVIIIe siècle," *Revista de Indias*, no. 10 (1950): 519-526.

was shaped by his perception of Cochabamba's earlier prosperity. "There is no doubt," he wrote in 1788, that "no other province is so rich in fruits" as Cochabamba.

> The region is a natural provider for the puna provinces, where nature has been so miserly with her blessings on the infertile and arid earth. Yet it is a land of bald hills and cold winds which hides glittering riches in its veins. If those riches could but be discovered and pulled from the depths of that deep earth, we would see the renaissance of an era of prosperity. Cochabamba would need no branch of industry other than the cultivation and export of wheat and maize.[60]

However, legend as much as entrepreneurial spirit shaped contemporary consciousness about the possibilities of the mining economy. The tales of Potosí's wealth during the second silver boom two centuries earlier led the Bourbon reformers to picture an age of unlimited opportunity that blessed the most fortunate adventurers and the shrewdest entrepreneurs. Yet, even as German technical advisors converged on the mineral-rich mountain in the 1780s to introduce the latest technology, the mountain itself stood as testimony to decadence. Much production had been abandoned to gangs of weekend scavengers, and whole sections of the city, which once teemed with 150,000 people, were now pockmarked with deserted huts. Despite the fact that Potosí still imported large quantities of goods from other parts of the viceroyalty, the town had not recovered its earlier commercial power. In comparison to the volume, intensity, and profitability of trade in the late sixteenth century, Potosí's market in staple goods had withered considerably. Paula Sanz estimated that the city had imported, from both elsewhere in the colony and Europe, less than four million pesos worth of goods in 1794—less than two-thirds the value of imports in 1603.[61]

---

60 Viedma, *Descripción geográfica*, 164-165.

61 "Descripción de la villa," 380; AGI, Charcas 697, Socasa, Nov. 19, 1794. (A printed copy of the census of trade of 1794 made by Paula Sanz may also be found in AGN, Biblioteca, *Telégrafo mercantil* 1 [1801].) Paula Sanz noted that his estimate excluded one million pesos worth of chicha and between 100,000 and 200,000 pesos worth of livestock; elsewhere in the report, however, he said that the value of chicha sold in the city amounted to only 203,515 pesos. See also Zavala, *Servicio personal*, 3:106, and Helmer, "Commerce et industrie au Pérou." In a recent study by Tandeter and his colleagues, comparing the figures of the 1794 census of trade to alcabala records on goods imported to Potosí in 1793, it was found that the census greatly overestimated the value of wines and

As intendant of Potosí, Paula Sanz was convinced not only that recovery was possible for the mining town but also that it would lead to economic renewal for all of Alto Peru.[62] Even in 1794, Potosí still attracted 2,806,700 pesos worth of goods. Most of these commodities (80 percent) were produced within the colony, even though in smaller proportion than had been the case in 1603 (90 percent). The largest suppliers of goods to Potosí were the vineyards of Moquegua (see table 19). Muleteers and merchants, probably conducting most

Table 19. Origin and Value of Imports to Potosí, 1794

	Value	
Place of Origin	*Pesos*	*Percentage*
Moquegua	1,111,000	39.6
Europe	600,000	21.4
Environs of Potosí	405,000	14.4
Cuzco	280,900	10.0
La Paz	103,000	3.7
Atacama, Lipez	59,000	2.1
Cochabamba[a]	54,000	1.9
Chuquisaca[b]	31,000	1.1
Chichas	30,000	1.1
Lima	27,800	1.0
Paraguay	25,000	0.9
Oruro	17,000	0.6
Other areas	63,000	2.2
Total	2,806,700	100.0

Source: AGI, Charcas 697, Socasa, Nov. 19, 1794.
[a] Goods imported from Cochabamba consisted of tocuyo cloth (40,000 pesos), coca (10,000), wooden furniture (2,000), hides (1,000), and soap (1,000).
[b] Most of the goods imported from Chuquisaca consisted of semitropical commodities that had actually been produced in the missions of Mojos and Chiquitos and then shipped to Chuquisaca, taxed there, and reexported to Potosí.

aguardiente and underestimated the value of coca, thus inflating the importance of large-scale imports of high-priced commodities and deflating the importance of the fragmented trade in coca, which was partially controlled by Indians and mestizos. (Enrique Tandeter et al., "El mercado de Potosí a fines del siglo XVIII," in Harris, Larson, and Tandeter, *Participación indígena*, 379-424.) Nevertheless, this study confirms the decline of Potosí's mercantile power between the late sixteenth and the late eighteenth centuries. Moreover, the recovery of the mining industry in Potosí did not bring about a corresponding increase in trade. As Tandeter's earlier research had shown, the increase in the output of silver was accomplished by "squeezing" the mitayos, whose wages were insufficient to support any large volume of trade (see chap. 3).

62 Paula Sanz, "Contestación al discurso," in Zavala, *Servicio personal*, 3: 104-107.

of their business from Arequipa, moved aguardiente and wine across the cordillera to the mining town. The "environs of Potosí" provided the town with low-priced commodities like salt, quinoa, resin and pitch, wood, and explosive powder. Most long-distance trade involved either specialized cash crops (coca, sugar, and cacao) or textiles (bayetas de obraje and tocuyo).

In Cochabamba, it was the artisans, not the cultivators or landowners, who capitalized most on Potosí's market. Weavers sent 40,000 pesos worth of cloth, and carpenters and soap-makers also sold their products there. Except for a small supply of inferior quality coca, no crops were recorded as being sent from Cochabamba to the mines. However, that may only be because the crown levied no alcabala on the sale of wheat and maize and thus no tax record was kept on their movement. It seems likely that there was a considerable, though "invisible," trade in grain, as Viedma's 1788 report suggested.

Patterns of interregional trade in cereal became vividly clear during periods of food shortage. In 1781, for example, colonial authorities declared an emergency in Potosí and requisitioned food crops from surrounding provinces. Supplies of flour began to dwindle dangerously in August of that year. By late September, wheat reserves in the city's storehouses had diminished to one thousand fanegas, enough to supply the city for only eight days. Indian rebels had managed to close down the royal highway across the altiplano, cutting off all traffic and trade to Oruro and Potosí. Peasant armies were swarming over the countryside, stealing grain from hacienda granaries to provision themselves and their comrades. In Potosí, it was reported that eight hundred Indians had converged on the town of Chunguri (located in the temperate lowlands near Ayquile, in Mizque) to seize grain. "They proceeded to provision themselves without paying for it, [which is not surprising,] considering that these people are known for their lawlessness and sedition; perhaps they seized the grain to aid their other Indian comrades, who want to throw off the yoke and end the subjugation of which they have been victims."[63] Other insurgents stole or seized food and animals in Pitantora and other valleys in the province of Chayanta.

Members of the municipal government invoked a 1582 ordinance that required cultivators and landowners within a twelve-league radius of Potosí to transport and sell their harvest to the municipal

63 Exp. 550, AGN, Sala 9, Hacienda, 33.2.2, Leg. 23 (1781), f. 13v.

council in years of severe food shortages.[64] (The ordinance had been enacted to undermine the monopoly that wholesale merchants had tried to establish over the grain trade.) The council also mandated that all landowners in the four provinces of Porco, Chayanta, Tomina, and Yamparaes transport and sell one-half of their harvest to Potosí.[65] These measures failed to overcome the food shortage, and the audiencia of La Plata in 1782 extended them to the provinces of Cochabamba, Tarija, and Chichas.[66]

The harvests of Porco, Chayanta, Tomina, and Yamparaes were the hope of Potosí authorities not only in times of scarcity, but also, apparently, in normal years. The landlords of Cochabamba found plenty of competition during most years from wheat cultivators in the provinces of Chayanta and Pitantora. A contemporary wrote that "the best wheat is cultivated in Pitantora, and the grain trade is the most opulent branch of commerce. . . . Pitantora regularly provisions Potosí with flour, though many neighbors from Carangas, Paria, and Porco travel to Chayanta to negotiate big grain deals during the harvest season."[67] This report probably underestimated the importance of the Chayanta ayllus as suppliers of grain to the market of Potosí. These ayllus marketed large quantities of wheat at the mines well into the nineteenth century, before the advent of free-trade policy and of Chilean wheat imports weakened their competitive position. Platt's study of Chayanta has underscored the crucial role that the ayllus played as suppliers of wheat and other food crops.[68] Part of their success derived from the fact that they still had access to lands in multiple ecological tiers: lands in the puna and valleys, often separated by several days' walk. During the entire colonial period, they preserved a high degree of collective self-sufficiency.

The ayllus historically had been closely integrated into the mining town's economy through multiple mercantile links, but they had retained control over the distribution of the communal resources, risks, and surpluses related to their commercial activities. In fact,

64 BNB, AP, tomo 5 (1585-1590), f. 309v.

65 Exp. 550, AGN, Sala 9, Hacienda, 33.2.2, Leg. 23 (1781), f. 17.

66 "Sobre la escasez de granos en Potosí," ANB, Sublevación de indios, vol. 5 (1782).

67 Pedro Vicente Cañete y Domínguez, *Guía histórica, geográfica . . . del gobierno e intendencia de la provincia de Potosí* (1789) (Potosí: Colección de la Cultura Boliviana, 1952), 246.

68 Platt, *Estado boliviano y ayllu andino*, chaps. 1 and 2.

the kurakas commercialized wheat production on communal lands in order to pay tribute to the colonial (and later, the early republican) state. Thus, mercantile activities were traditionally subordinated to collective needs and responsibilities. They did not intensify the processes of internal differentiation within ayllu society. The "kuraka model of mercantilism" that Platt describes had a logic quite distinct from the processes of mercantilization that were at work within Tapacarí society (see chapter 4).

From the perspective of Cochabamba's hacendados, already pressed by the smallholders and petty traders in the valleys, the commercial activities of the Chayanta ayllus were yet another source of commercial competition in a time of shrinking and unstable market demand. In addition, the haciendas of Pitantora and of other valleys in Chuquisaca, Tomina, and Yamparaes enjoyed closer proximity to Potosí's market. Increasingly, the profits from trade in Cochabamba grains were contingent upon the conditions of supply, and particularly on the fluctuation of harvest yields.[69] Crop failure in the highlands and valleys favored Cochabamba's landowners in two ways. First, it reduced or eliminated the competition from the small-scale producers and traders who normally participated in local retail markets. Second, it forced more highland Indians to trade directly with the landowners and tithe speculators who, for the time being, monopolized the supply of grain.

Intendant Viedma was quite aware of the oscillation of market demand in the "outside provinces." In the late months of 1786, as officials began to forecast a poor growing season, the optimistic Viedma commented that profit would compensate for the hardship wrought by prolonged drought in the highlands.[70] A while later, he wrote that "the scarcity of water usually drives many people down from the nearby provinces and impels them to purchase the provisions necessary for their own subsistence."[71] In 1792, he again reported drought, and he noted that it always took its toll first in the altiplano. In the valleys and quebradas, landowners could draw water from reservoirs and mountain streams during the early phase of a

69 For a discussion of the significance of harvest fluctuations and the dynamics of internal markets in precapitalist societies, see Pierre Vilar, "Réflexions sur la 'crise de l'ancien type': 'Inegalité des recoltes' et 'sous-développement'," in *Conjoncture économique, structures sociales: Hommage à Ernest Labrousse* (Paris: Mouton, 1974), 37-58.

70 AGN, Sala 9, Intendencia, 5.8.3, Leg. 2, Jan. 3, 1787.

71 Ibid.

drought. Thus, landlords whose crops survived the dry spell and who stored their reserves could expect Indians to come down from the parched cold lands of Paria and Sicasica in search of food.[72]

We still know little about the nature or magnitude of commercial transactions during the food crises that struck every few years in the late eighteenth century. Viedma's observations suggest that the puna Indians were forced into the market to obtain small quantities of grain that their own cracked soils could not yield. However, it is probable that many highland Indians trekked down into the valleys of Cochabamba to obtain food even in bountiful years. One glimpse of this trade is given by a creole miller who lived in the town of San Augustín de Tapacarí. In 1799, he told the royal mill inspector about his enterprise.

> The Indians who wander through this quebrada come from the intendancies of La Paz and Puno. They purchase grain and grind it into flour during the three months of harvest [June, July, and August]. Most do not return for at least another year . . . and in the month of September and thereafter, few Indians bring their grain to be milled. This is the usual rhythm of the mill industry in the parishes of Tapacarí and Paria. The mills depend upon rainfall, and drought halts most wheat mills. On other occasions, it rains so heavily that the river floods, and the puna Indians cannot travel down through the ravines and gorges to purchase grain and grind it in our mills.[73]

If the highland Indians regularly came down into the valleys to obtain maize, wheat, ají, or other crops, why did Cochabamba's landlords and tithe speculators depend so heavily upon shortages to reap large returns? It is probably because in years of normal or abundant harvest, the highland Indians had the option of bypassing the large grain dealers and dealing directly with small-scale peasant producers and traders in the ferias. By doing so, highland Indians retained some control over the terms of exchange. It is quite likely, for example, that many highland Indians bartered salt, quinoa, and potato seeds with the small-scale maize cultivators of the central valleys. But even when they were closed out of this trade, enterprising landlords,

72 AGN, Sala 9, Intendencia, 5.8.5, Leg. 4, Apr. 30, 1792.

73 "Real visita a las molinas de grano," AHMC, Leg. 1213 (1799).

speculators, and merchants were able to resort to other advantages they had—for example, the proximity of grain mills, or their freedom from municipal price regulations.[74]

The towns of Arque and Tapacarí offered several such advantages, which turned them into marketplaces dominated by wholesale grain dealers. First, the towns were located to the west of the central valleys—out of the commercial orbit of most small-scale grain cultivators, who could not afford to pay the costs (four or five reales per fanega) of shipping maize there from the Cliza valley.[75] Second, municipal authorities gave up trying to regulate prices in those towns. Viedma complained in 1787 that it was "impossible to regulate prices in Arque, as it is a port town to the western provinces, where prices fluctuate according to the volume of export."[76] Third, the towns were situated along river gorges and surrounded by grain mills. Seed and flour could be purchased in one marketplace, often from one grain merchant, without the need of traveling another two or three days eastward into the central valleys of Cochabamba. Not surprisingly, grain traders could fetch considerably more for their product in Arque and Tapacarí than in Cochabamba.[77]

In the eighteenth century, then, the so-called export trade in Cochabamba grains had its terminal point in the "port towns" of Arque and Tapacarí. Except perhaps when grain prices were unusually high, merchants and speculators were rarely willing to pay the cost of freight to market their grain in the cities of the altiplano. Instead, they sent some grain to the western river valleys, stored the rest in granaries on the outskirts of town, and then waited for chang-

---

74 It was not uncommon for hacendados and millowners in the valley of Arque to try to "capture" trade and commerce with the transient Indians en route through the valley. In 1715, the corregidor of Cochabamba accused the creole hacendado Luís Paniagua and other landowners and millers of forcing highland Indians to purchase maize from them. Ironically, the official also accused the Indians of Sicaya, who owned a hacienda and mills in the pueblo real of Capinota, of forcing other Indians to grind their wheat and maize in their mills. "Exp. de la audiencia de Charcas sobre los perjuicios que los hacendados infieren a los indios forzándoles a moler sus granos . . . ," ANB, Minas, tomo 147 (1715).

75 "Apelación interpuesta por López Roque, indio tributario de Arque," ANB, EC no. 24 (1759).

76 AGN, Sala 9, Intendencia, 5.8.4. Leg. 3, Sept. 1, 1787, f. 4.

77 For example, in 1792 a fanega of wheat cost twenty reales in the city of Cochabamba and twenty-four reales in Arque. AGN, Sala 9, Intendencia, 5.8.5, Leg. 4, Apr. 30, 1792, f. 3.

ing conditions to improve their market position. During the months after harvest, especially in years of drought, the large landlords of Cliza and other parts of the central valleys stationed their Indian and mestizo agents, porters, and watchmen in Arque and Tapacarí to oversee the storage and marketing of their crops.[78] In those years when the highland Indians were forced to deal with the large grain merchants, the market towns of Tapacarí and, particularly, Arque flourished with activity. They became the nexus between the worlds of the highland Aymara Indian and the valley creole landlord-speculator.

The Cochabamba landowners in the late colonial period faced the same logistical barriers that existed for grain hacendados in other parts of the Andes. In spite of the economic recovery of Potosí and Oruro, those markets did not generate the demand that had once stimulated large-scale grain production and exports from the Cochabamba valleys. Conditions had changed since Vázquez de Espinosa's time, when Cochabamba was said to have sent a million pesos worth of grain to Potosí each year. The age of long llama caravans and mule trains carrying food crops up the Arque River gorge through alpine passes to Potosí was no more.

Although he may not have realized it, Viedma's diagnosis of Cochabamba's "crisis of overproduction" reflected the long-term structural transformation of the regional economy and of its position in the internal market of the southern Andes. On the one hand, the diffusion of supply among a growing population of small-scale producers eroded the position of landowners and merchants, creating an alternative basis of commercial exchange among valley peasants as well as between them and the Indians migrating from distant highland villages. On the other hand, the large grain farmers and merchants were more and more moved to the margin of the long-distance grain trade with Potosí. The nature of Potosí's economic recovery, based primarily upon more intensive exploitation of the mine laborers, and the rise of Chayanta ayllus and grain estates in the southern valleys of Chuquisaca and Porco as provisioners of the mining market undercut the position of Cochabamba's grain export-

---

78 A description of marketing arrangements comes from a priest who accused his Indian agent in 1758 of stealing grain (the defendant stated that the loss was due to rodents in the granaries). In the course of the trial, both the priest and the agent referred to the existence of Indian middlemen in Arque who served as agents for hacendados of the Cliza valley. "Apelación interpuesta por López Roque, indio tributario de Arque," ANB, EC no. 24 (1759).

ers, particularly in the last years of the eighteenth century, when pack animals were becoming scarce in the region.[79]

Thrown on the defensive, landlords and merchants resorted to commercial and speculative strategies designed to exploit the precariousness of peasant agriculture, especially among highland Indians. Valley landowners who owned permanently irrigated maize fields were in a particularly advantageous position for capitalizing on the trade with Arque and Tapacarí. A poor harvest would not only drive more Indians down from the highlands; it would also wipe out the small surplus that otherwise allowed many valley arrenderos to participate in the ferias as petty traders. The profits of the wealthy landowners and tithe speculators therefore rode on the periodic subsistence crises of the peasantry.

But while landowners never gazed at the ancient face of hunger, the uncertainties of and dependence upon periodic agrarian crises irritated them. Some of them proposed reformist schemes; the influence of the Bourbons and the growing interest in rejuvenating the regional economy stirred hopes and sparked new initiatives. For a while, there seemed to be pragmatic remedies for the region's economic malaise.

79 It may well be that the city of Oruro was a more important market for Cochabamba's grain in the late eighteenth century than was Potosí, but so far there has been little research into this trade. There was almost no reference to the Oruro market in the documents consulted for this study.

The Spirit
and Limits
of Enterprise

When Don José Gómez Merino made his rounds as administrator of the royal tobacco monopoly in the 1790s, he would gaze out of the carriage window at the seasonal forests of cornstalks that were neatly framed by narrow ribbons of sunlit water. He must have felt some frustration as he pondered the potential of cultivating specialized crops that would burst the rigid constraints on the local market. Instead of maize sucking the rich nutrients from the soil simply to nourish the local plebe, Cochabamba's fertile lands could turn the province into a local Andalucía, with a thriving viticulture or orchards of olive trees yielding crops for export to lucrative distant markets. Such marketable commodities as wine, olive oil, hemp, or flax would break the region's economic stalemate and integrate it into a dynamic colonial market economy, to the benefit of the region's innovative landowners and merchants.[1]

Gómez Merino's ideas were skeptically received, but they were part of a new spirit of enterprise that emerged among a small circle of colonial administrators and landowners late in the eighteenth century. After the creation of the intendancy in 1784, and before the onset of the famine crisis of 1804, visions of economic reform and growth beguiled a few would-be entrepreneurs and administrators,

---

1 Gómez Merino did draw up detailed proposals for regional economic reform, calling for state promotion of viticulture, olive-tree cultivation, and the production of hemp and flax. See "Plan de administración de la provincia de Cochabamba presentado por D. José Gómez Merino al Virrey D. Pedro Melo de Portugal, en el que trata del comercio, industria, y agricultura de la provincia," RAH, ML 9/1667, tomo 12 (n.d., early 1790s), ff. 81-89; and "Plan de desarrollo agrícola, industrial, y comercial para la provincia de Cochabamba presentado por D. José Gómez Merino," RAH, ML, 9/1667, tomo 12, July 17, 1794, ff. 223-226. Viedma vigorously objected to these proposals: see "Sobre el plan de desarrollo presentado por Gómez Merino," AGN, Sala 9, Intendencia, 5.8.5 (1796).

who thought they saw a way out of the region's economic stagnation, endemic poverty, and involuted land-tenure pattern. It seemed to point eastward, toward the largely unsettled, uncharted tropical lowlands that had been conjoined with the corregimiento of Cochabamba to form the intendancy of Santa Cruz de la Sierra. The heartland of Cochabamba was now enveloped by an administrative territory that not only embraced the tropical lowlands around Santa Cruz but also extended northward into the Amazonic basin lands of the Mojos Indians. The perceived potential of lowland agriculture drew the attention of reformers away from the tiresome problems of grain agriculture and peasant "idleness" in the central valleys. There would be no need to rationalize agricultural production on valley haciendas (with the inevitable resistance that it would provoke), when a verdant frontier beckoned. If tapped, tropical resources might offer a mercantile solution to the decline of the landowning class.

But the promise of prosperity did not only lie beyond the remote eastern precipice that dropped off into the jungle. For a few years, a small number of merchants realized high returns on an unlikely commodity produced in the very interior of the peasant economy. Fortuitous circumstances in the late 1790s suddenly turned the rustic cotton textile called tocuyo into a commodity that was in demand all over the viceroyalty of La Plata. This "poor man's cloth," woven on the looms of Cochabamba, had a commercial appeal that was the envy of all wholesale dealers. Even beyond the immediate material returns, the commercialization of tocuyos sparked the imagination of reformers who saw in textile manufacturing the potential for sustained regional economic growth—it was no further away than the weaver's workshop on the edge of town. The problems and possibilities of economic reform in Cochabamba were determined as much by the region's natural and human resources and its agrarian class structure as by imperial political and economic forces.

All across the Andes in the late 1780s, a new breed of professional bureaucrat communicated a spirit of reform and interpreted the royal will to improve social conditions in the colonies and weave them more tightly into the web of Bourbon absolutism. Some royal officials emphasized political integration and royal control, with little regard for economic reform. Others sought to rationalize and centralize administration in their districts only within a context of economic change and regional growth. Inevitably, these latter administrators confronted the contradictions of economic and political reforms that were influenced by Spanish mercantilism and dictated by the imperatives of an imperial state. But the arrival of practical reformers, ostensibly to rejuvenate regional economies, was bound to inspire dreams and kindle hopes. Cochabamba's intendant, Francisco de Viedma, was such an individual. His humanism, ambitions, and energy inspired the imagination of what might be—if only his economic plans were implemented. His dreams of economic recovery, and his attempt to reconcile regional interests with those of the Bourbon state, would eventually dissolve in disillusionment. But for a while, Viedma carried the ideals of the Spanish Enlightenment and mercantilism to the backwaters of the empire, where they caught the fancy of a small regional elite.[2]

Viedma was very much a man of his times, influenced by the European doctrines of mature mercantilism, with its stress on production and trade.[3] Like the well-known reformist ministers of Philip V and Charles III, Viedma appreciated the fact that Spain's economic and political strength depended upon the injection of specie into manufacturing and agriculture. Yet he was fully aware that a nation's wealth could no longer be measured simply in terms of the quantity of specie, as the sixteenth-century bullionists had contended. Contemporary economic thinking prescribed a large dose of state intervention to stimulate agricultural production, manufacturing, and commerce. Mercantilists were in agreement that the state had to promote production in order to establish a favorable balance of trade, while also maintaining terms of trade that were advantageous to producers in the mother country. In Viedma's homeland, a campaign was underway to promote wool and cotton manufacturing and to tear down the internal and overseas barriers that stifled commerce. The opening of Buenos Aires to direct trade with Spain and the creation of the viceroyalty of La Plata were but two reforms that marked Spain's new determination to knit the colonies more closely into the fabric of Spanish metropolitan economy—theoretically, for the benefit of both parties.[4]

2 There is not yet a biography of this exemplary administrator, but see the prologue written by Hector Cossío Salinas to Viedma, *Descripción geográfica*, 11-26. On intendants and the reform era, see J. Fisher, *Government and Society in Colonial Peru*, and Lynch, *Spanish Colonial Administration*. On reforms affecting the audiencia, see Mark A. Burkholder, "From Creole to *Peninsular*: The Transformation of the Audiencia of Lima", *Hispanic American Historical Review* 52 (1972): 395-415.

3 The keystone study of mercantilism is Eli Heckscher, *Mercantilism*, 2 vols. (New York: Macmillan, 1955). An important historiographical critique of the concept is D. C. Coleman, ed., *Revisions in Mercantilism* (London: Methuen, 1969).

4 For economic policies in Spain, see Earl J. Hamilton, *War and Prices in Spain, 1651-1800* (Cambridge: Harvard University Press, 1947). On economic and intel-

Far from the salons and academies of Spain, Viedma hoped to apply his wisdom and his knowledge of political economy to the rejuvenation of the fields and workshops of Cochabamba, a region he was convinced offered as much potential for development as any region of Spain. As we saw in the last chapter, he attributed many of Cochabamba's economic problems to the withering of the mining-town markets for its maize and wheat. He hoped, almost wistfully, for a silver boom that would transform the internal commodity market of Alto Perú. But Viedma was a pragmatist as well as a dreamer, and he developed an integrated plan to diversify Cochabamba's economy. He wanted to steer the regional economy away from its dependence on grain farming by developing a local mining industry, expanding the textile industry, and introducing specialized crops that could overcome the logistical obstacles to long-distance, overland trade. If mineral operations were successful, he believed, Cochabamba would be free of its dependence on distant markets for cash accumulation. But even if they failed, the intendant was convinced that the production or procurement of tropical agricultural products (cacao, coca, sugar) would revive the region's export capacity and channel specie into the pockets of local entrepreneurs. The challenges were to persuade members of the local elite to put up the necessary risk capital and to replace the old sources of cash.[5]

Tropical Horizons

Viedma looked beyond the eastern frontier of European settlement to the tropical and subtropical lowlands for solutions to the economic malaise that afflicted the hacendados of the central valleys. If

---

lectual trends in eighteenth-century Spain and America, see Robert J. Shafer, *The Economic Societies in the Spanish World, 1763-1821* (Syracuse: Syracuse University Press, 1958); Richard Herr, *The Eighteenth-Century Revolution in Spain* (Princeton: Princeton University Press, 1958); J. Muñoz Pérez, "Los proyectos sobre España e Indias en el siglo XVIII: El proyectismo como género," *Revista de estudios políticos*, no. 81 (1955): 169-185; Stanley Stein, "Reality in Microcosm: The Debate over Trade in America, 1785-1789," *Historia ibérica*, no. 1 (1976): 111-119; David Brading, "El mercantilismo ibérico y el crecimiento económico en la América latina del siglo XVIII," in Florescano, ed., *Ensayos sobre el desarrollo económico*, 293-314; J. Muñoz Pérez, "La publicación del reglamento de comercio libre de Indias de 1778," *Anuario de estudios americanos* 4 (1947): 615-664; and Henry Kamen, "El establecimiento de los intendentes en la administración española," *Hispania* 24 (1964): 368-395.

5 For a critical assessment of Viedma's report on the regional economy, see chap. 5. Among other such reports, those of Gómez Merino (see n. 1) and Tadeo Haenke stand out. The latter's proposals for the promotion of textile manufacturing are discussed below.

landowners were to diversify agriculture and invest in specialized crops, they would inevitably have to colonize those lands, on the far side of the treacherous divide, to the east and north of their safe, familiar valleys. This was not an empty terra incognita; rather, the lowlands were sparsely populated by numerous tribes of hunters, gatherers, and fishermen, many of whom had been "reduced" (see chapter 2) and grouped into "nations," as the Spaniards called them. Four of these nations—the Mojos, Chiquitos, Chiriguanos, and Yuracarees—lived in nucleated settlements in several different ecological zones of the lowlands.[6]

Viedma had a two-pronged plan for bringing commerce and civilization to the tropical frontier. First, colonial authorities would have to incorporate the lowland tribes into the mercantile economy. Second, the tropical regions would be colonized by agrarian entrepreneurs and by Indians and mestizos relocated from the densely populated valley of Cliza and the Valle Bajo to the new lowland plantations.

Viedma's tracts on the history and potential prosperity of the lowlands demonstrate the scope of his vision and ambitions.[7] Although he did not know the jungle missionary settlements at first hand, he carefully studied the reports, censuses, and maps that charted the location and size of the lowland communities and the exportable resources (see figure 13). There were the Mojos villages, strung like beads along the remote northern rivers and tributaries that drained into the Amazon basin. A map drawn in 1769 showed seventeen reducciones of Mojos;[8] however, in a report made in 1788 by Lázaro de Ribera,

6 There is a substantial literature on the lowland tribes in the eighteenth century, particularly the Mojos and Chiquitos peoples. See, for example, Josep Barnadas, "Las reducciones jesuitas de Mojos," *Historia boliviana* 4 (1984): 135-166; David Block, "Links to the Frontier: Jesuit Supply of Its Moxos Missions, 1683-1767," *Americas* 37 (1980): 161-178; Georges Desdevises du Dezert, "Les missions des Mojos et des Chiquitos de 1767 à 1808," *Revue hispanique* 43 (1918): 365-430; and Gabriel René Moreno, *Catálogo del archivo de Mojos y Chiquitos* (1888) (La Paz: Instituto Boliviano de Cultura, 1976).

7 Although his report on Cochabamba is far better known, Viedma devoted at least as much effort to writing about the pueblos and reducciones of the tropical frontier. Many of his reports and letters on the Indians and the Spanish colonizers of the lowlands are included in the Bolivian edition of his *Descripción geográfica*. However, the confusing organization of the book makes it difficult to distinguish one document from another and to identify their archival origins. Where a cited document does not appear to be part of *Descripción geográfica*, its title or subtitle will be given.

8 "Mapa que comprende las misiones de Moxos y Chiquitos," AGI, sección 5,

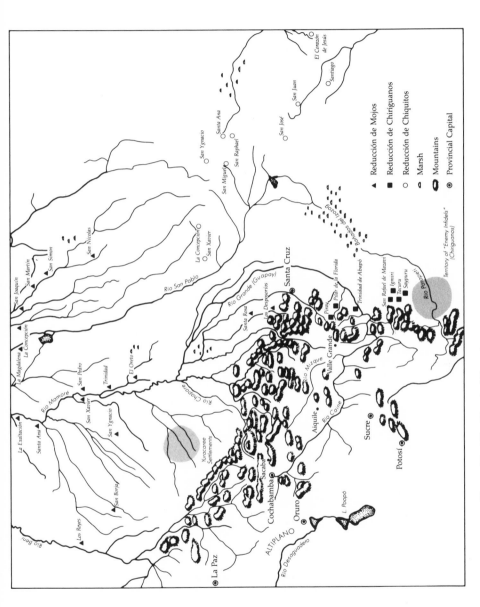

Figure 13   The Tropical Frontier
Source: Adapted from the map in "Mapa que comprende las misiones de Moxos
y Chiquitos," AGI, Sección 5, Charcas 502, no. 78 (1769).

governor of the Mojos province, only eleven such villages were re-corded.[9] Not more than 22,000 people lived in these settlements.[10] Located deep in the tropical forest, they were believed by Viedma to be potentially the most prosperous villages. The rich soil and humid climate would be favorable for crops of sugar, maize, rice, yucca, and fruits, which could be transported by river raft during certain seasons of the year.[11]

To the southeast of the tropical forest lay scattered settlements of Chiquitos, who were maize cultivators and herders inhabiting hot savannahs that extended as far north as the eighteenth parallel, where grasslands gradually gave way to dense, tropical undergrowth. The Chiquitos' villages were reached only by long overland treks nearly to the outer edge of Spanish territory. The 18,840 people who inhabited ten Chiquitos pueblos in 1788 attracted the attention of colonial authorities more for their strategic proximity to the Portuguese settlements of Mato Grosso than for the resources they controlled. As long as the Chiquitos were properly administered and remained loyal vassals, they served as a first defense against Portuguese encroachments.[12]

The Yuracarees inhabited the tropical lowlands of the present-day province of Chaparé, to the northeast of Cochabamba. Two priests from the Cliza valley managed to "reduce" and convert many Yura-carees in the 1760s and 1770s, but neither Viedma nor Ribera offered any estimate of their numbers. Viedma foresaw lucrative plantations and trade in the territory of the Yuracarees, so close to the central valleys of Cochabamba, if new trails were blazed and their villages opened up to trade with the higher, temperate maize valleys.[13]

Charcas 503, no. 78 (1769). The locations of mission settlements on this map are shown in figure 13.

9 On the report and administration of Lázaro de Ribera, see Alcides Parejas, "Don Lázaro de Ribera, gobernador de la provincia de Moxos (1784-1792)," *Anuario de estudios americanos* 33 (1976): 949-962.

10 Viedma, "Ventajas que resultan a los mismos indios . . . dándoles en libertad como los demás del Perú . . .," in his *Descripción geográfica*, 209 (cited hereafter as Viedma, "Ventajas").

11 Ibid., 211.

12 Viedma, "Males que padecen estos indios, privándoles de la libertad y perjuicios que se infieren a los vecinos de Santa Cruz," in his *Descripción geográfica*, 200 (cited hereafter as Viedma, "Males"), and Viedma, "Ventajas," 209.

13 Viedma, "Nueva reducción de San Carlos, de indios de la nación de Yuracarees," in his *Descripción geográfica*, 127.

The most famous inhabitants of the tropical slopes of the cordillera were the Chiriguanos. In the sixteenth century, even in the zeal to extend commercial coca cultivation deeper into the tropics, there was anxiety about provoking the wrath of the fierce Chiriguano warriors. Indeed, the Incas themselves had fortified the eastern borders of their empire specifically to guard against the Chiriguanos.[14] Over three centuries, Spanish missionaries had managed to pacify many Chiriguano tribes, and the founding and survival of the city of Santa Cruz was testimony to their partial success at "domesticating" the Chiriguanos. Yet even in the 1780s and 1790s, the Spaniards feared for their lives in the territory around the Parapetí River. Tacuarembo, Sauce, Piriti, Ubau, Iquacti, Timboy, and Parapetí were indicated as lands of "enemy infidels," where neither Christianity nor civilization had penetrated. Repelled yet fascinated, Viedma described these fearsome heathens, with their painted bodies, leather skins, and bows and arrows, in vivid detail. He was most disdainful of their idleness, "their habits of consuming chicha and lying about in hammocks,"[15] and he was determined to advance the cutting edge of Christendom into this bastion of barbarism.

Yet, even if the persistence of heathenism among the Chiriquanos irked this moralistic Christian, he took comfort in the success of several missionary settlements situated to the south of Santa Cruz. The town of Trinidad de Abapó, in particular, was a model missionary community of industry and self-sufficiency, and Viedma made it a showcase for his proposed reforms of the other lowland villages. The people of Abapó tended livestock and cultivated small amounts of cotton to supply their own textile workshops. Priests had established "spinning schools," where spinsters and young girls kept themselves occupied in "useful tasks." Young boys attended a separate school, where they studied the Scriptures and learned to read and write or were trained as weavers or carpenters. The town had a healthy economy, in Viedma's view, because it exported some of its goods to Santa Cruz and Chuquisaca. But more than its economic success, Viedma praised Abapó for the moral foundations upon which it rested—for its "spiritual, temporal, and economic govern-

14 "Visita a Pocona," and *Repartimiento de tierras*, 14 and passim. On the Chiriguano frontier in the sixteenth century, see Thierry Saignes, "Une frontière fossile: La cordillère chiriguano au XVIe siècle," 2 vols. (3rd cycle doctorate, University of Paris, 1974).

15 Viedma, "Descripción y estado de las reducciones de los indios chiriguanos," in his *Descripción geográfica*, 239.

ment." He saw the mission town as a beacon of light in a sea of darkness where moral turpitude, sloth, and sensuality seemed to flourish as luxuriantly as the tropic vegetation.[16]

For Viedma, the question of frontier development had a historical dimension which made it all the more urgent. Industry and the social fabric of life in the mission communities had deteriorated sharply since the expulsion of the Jesuits from Spanish America in 1767. Viedma had only praise for the Christian education, government, and economic enterprise that the Jesuits had given to their Indian wards. In the villages of the Mojos and Chiquitos, the order had patiently chaperoned their trustees along the path from barbarism to civilization and, in the process, raised their material standard of living. With the loss of these dedicated missionaries, the villages had been deprived of their moorings and had cast about on the seas of corruption and indolence. The secular priests assigned to administer the villages after 1767 were responsible for the "desolation, inactivity, vice, and perversity" that reigned thereafter.[17] When civil administrators finally took note of the situation in the early 1780s, a "new plan of government" for the mission Indians was formulated by Ribera. But while Intendant Viedma lauded the aim of this plan—to turn over the administration of the villages to civil authorities—he nevertheless opposed it, on the ground that merely to "transfer the economic government from ecclesiastical to secular hands" left untouched the main problem, which was the colonial authorities' control over the distribution of crops and goods produced by the Indians.

> They deposit all their precious manufactures in the hands of their administrators, who keep the closest accounting to prevent the Indians from hiding their wares; in return, the Indians receive most wretched clothing of skins and food to eat; for while the Indians are permitted to keep maize, bananas, yuccas, and fruits, they must surrender their other crops, such as cacao, coffee, sugar, and . . . beeswax.[18]

Furthermore, the civil administrators required the Mojos people to carry their tribute in canoes, paddling many days against the current,

16 Viedma, "Gobierno espiritual, temporal, y económico de las antiguas reducciones,"in his *Descripción geográfica*, 242-244.

17 Viedma, "Males," 194.

18 Ibid., 202, 203. On Ribera's plan, see also Parejas, "Don Lázaro de Ribera," and Barnadas, "Reducciones jesuitas," 160-162.

to Port Jones or Port Paila and from there to trek overland to the royal receiver in Santa Cruz.[19]

Against popular opinion on the matter, Viedma proposed that the lowland Indians be granted a degree of economic autonomy. The issue at hand was the Indians' capability for self-government and communal self-regulation. Where there was no cultural tradition of community; where warrior tribes had managed to fend off the Incas, restricting the eastern edge of Tawantinsuyu to the high valleys of Cochabamba, Pocona, and Tarija; and where the jungle and the arid plains made sedentary agriculture a futile endeavor, there was ample room for skepticism. Indeed, Viedma himself did not challenge the judgment of the early ecclesiastics who, in the sixteenth century, had said that the lowland Indians were "incapable of governing themselves, unlike the rest of the Indians in the kingdom of Peru."[20] It was for that reason that the Jesuits had been given the task of domesticating them. But times had changed, and Viedma argued against the perpetuation of their wardship under civil administrators. To support his case, he invoked philosophical and juridical arguments, from the preachings of Bartolomé de las Casas to the legal code of Juan de Solórzano, which sanctioned the freedom of America's native sons and daughters.[21] With painstaking detail, he described the legal status of tributaries and yanaconas, to demonstrate that, unlike them, the lowland Indians continued to live in a state of unfreedom that was unjust and without cause.[22]

However, even if they had a moral claim to freedom, it might still be questioned whether, "after so much time in the reducciones, . . . they were civilized and capable of trading their own fruits and goods and of paying tribute."[23] Lacking first-hand evidence with which to make his case, Viedma drew on the empirical observations of Ribera concerning the moral character of the Mojos and Chiquitos. For Ribera himself had praised the Mojos as "the most able, industrious, and loyal vassals that the king had in all his kingdoms."[24] But whereas Ribera concluded that the Indians deserved protection from

19 Viedma, "Males" 203.

20 Ibid., 195.

21 See Juan de Solórzano Pereira, *Política indiana*, 5 vols. 1647 (Madrid: Iberoamericana, 1930).

22 Viedma, "Males," 191-203.

23 Ibid., 195.

24 Ibid., 201.

unscrupulous traders and the corrupt influences of commerce, Viedma argued that the Mojos were skilled artisans and traders who were capable of defending their own interests. Indeed, Viedma projected a utilitarian and acquisitive image of *homo economicus* onto the lowland native. Despite centuries of subservience, the lowland Indians were capable of "rational action." All that was necessary, in the intendant's view, was to tear down the barriers of protection, unlock the missions' resources, and release the Indians from wardship. The returns from trade would encourage the lowland natives to work harder in agriculture and industry. Eventually, their economy would flourish and the lowland villages would become models of economic progress.

To Viedma, then, the mission towns of the jungle offered an opportunity for the development of industrious villages, from which tropical commodities and the products of native handicrafts could be produced for export to urban centers throughout the viceroyalty. The crops to be grown might replace imports from distant lands. The Indians in these villages were "disposed" toward commerce and industry, and they were uncontaminated by the sloth and corruption of Cochabamba's mestizos and cholos, "who are not motivated by noble causes, the glory of a prize, the fear of punishment, or even the hardships of neediness."[25] Whatever the mixture of Rousseauian innocence and yeoman industriousness with which Viedma characterized the lowland native, his proposal was rather unorthodox. At a time when the crown was designing ways to shield highland villages from extortionist traders, in the aftermath of the 1781 rebellions and the abolition of the repartimiento de mercancías, Viedma was pressing for "free trade" with the mission Indians. While the intendants were expected to resurrect some features of the Toledan model of village society throughout Alto Perú, Viedma went further and advocated assimilationist policies that would integrate the jungle Indians into the market economy.

Perhaps it was a radical plan.[26] But in Viedma's mind, it held much hope for the stimulation of the sluggish economies along the eastern frontier. Once the lowlands entered the "modern age" of trade, industry, and cash-crop agriculture, the merchants and entrepreneurs

---

25 Viedma, "En que se hacen demostrables las muchas proporciones que presenta la naturaleza a la mayor prosperidad de la provincia," in his *Descripción geográfica*, 168.

26 However, Viedma's opposition to Ribera's plans was supported by the Council of the Indies in 1805. Barnadas, "Reducciones jesuitas," 160.

of Cochabamba and other nearby areas would take advantage of the new situation. Their geographical proximity to the tropical frontier would allow them to serve as middlemen in the traffic between jungle and highland. Eventually, new trade routes would penetrate the unexplored riverways and cross the eastern savannahs that bordered Portuguese territory. Viedma even envisaged a major lowland highway stretching from the Parapetí River (after the last barbarous Chiriguanos had been conquered) to the town of Jujuy. This new road would throw open a hitherto inhospitable land to progress, prosperity, and Christianity.

But trade was not enough to propel Cochabamba out of its economic lethargy. Viedma wanted the lowland regions to be colonized by rich landowners willing to risk investment in plantation agriculture. He thought the possibilities for commercial agriculture were endless: cacao plantations would displace imports from Caracas and Guayaquil; coca fields would rival the established cocales of the yungas east of La Paz; rice paddies, cotton fields, and sugar plantations would substitute jungle crops for coastal imports. Alto Perú's tropical frontier would be turned into the central source for all the specialized agricultural commodities traditionally imported from distant lands. It was an ambitious plan, but Viedma was convinced that the penetration of tropical lands would allow a few enterprising planters to reap high returns on their investment and would provide a way for the upper tier of Cochabamba's landowning elite to leave grain cultivation to their peasant tenants and initiate new agricultural enterprises where they would presumably have more control over the terms of exchange.[27]

Viedma focused his plan of jungle colonization on two areas: the hinterlands of the city of Santa Cruz and the newly opened territory of the Yuracarees. In the region around Santa Cruz, colonization had already taken root. Many of the huge ranches in the vicinity of the

27 Viedma, "Gobierno espiritual, temporal, y económico de las antiguas reducciones," in his *Descripción geográfica*, 262, and "Ventajas," 219. Viedma also proposed the administrative breakup of the intendancy into two parts, one centered around the old corregimiento of Cochabamba and the other around the city and frontier hinterlands of Santa Cruz. (p. 213.) Much documentation on the lowland tribes in the late Bourbon period is lodged in the Real Academia de Historia, in Madrid. See, for example, "Documentos referentes al gobierno de las misiones de Mojos y Chiquitos después de la expulsión de los jesuitas," RAH, ML, 9/1733, tomo 76 (1777-1780), ff. 37-48, "Informe del obispo de Tucumán . . . sobre las reducciones de los Yuracarees, cerca de Mojos y Cochabamba," June 10, 1804, RAH, ML, 9/1731, tomo 76, ff. 27-36.

town had cane fields, and the region exported small quantities of a sugar of inferior quality sugar to the western highlands. Viedma had learned of a recent discovery that sugar flourished in the rich top soils of the tropical forest. Thirteen years after deforestation and the beginning of cultivation, the cane still thrived there. (On the drier plains, in contrast, the soil was exhausted after only three or four harvests of sugar cane.)[28] However, the sugar mills in the region were among the most primitive in America. These mills (*trapiches*), driven by mules, lost a large part of the cane juice. The problem of technological backwardness was compounded by land-tenure customs that, Viedma believed, discouraged sugar planters from investing capital in more modern machinery. No landholder in Santa Cruz had a title of ownership, since the lands had never been divided and distributed among the earliest settlers. Instead, the landholders were in the position of "homesteading" [*dominio precario*], and this lasted only "as long as they have livestock and cultivate their lands [*chacos*]."[29] The absence of private property and the inability to transmit property rights by inheritance were the principal factors responsible for the region's economic stagnation, in the intendant's view. Viedma believed that with a new set of property laws, the landholders would be more inclined to improve their mills and cut back the forests to extend their cane fields.

But Viedma harbored even greater hope in a plan to develop the Yuracaree territory near the Chaparé River. Located to the north and northeast of Cochabamba, the Yuracaree lands already had attracted the interest of many hacendados of Cliza. The two priests from Cliza who had reduced and converted the Yuracarees had also cleared patches of forest to plant coca. By Viedma's time, fifty-two cocales had been established in one area of the Chaparé River basin. Most coca enterprises failed after several years, however; the intendant explained these failures in terms of poor cultivation and storage methods.[30] In his opinion, progress and development mainly depended upon the education of the farmers, the diffusion of technical skills, and the acquisition of modern equipment.

Curiously, the labor question did not figure prominently in Viedma's grand scheme. Yet intensive labor, both permanent and seasonal, would be needed to clear the land, plant the cane and coca,

28 Viedma, *Descripción geográfica*, 112.

29 Ibid., 113 and 163-164; AGN, Sala 9, Intendencia, 5.8.6, Leg. 5, Oct. 12, 1798.

30 Viedma, *Descripción geográfica*, 135-136 and 162.

and harvest the crop. Given the past difficulties in exploiting the Indians, Viedma can hardly have assumed that these labor needs would be satisfied by the Indians. (In fact, his only apparent concern in this regard was to end the bondage of captured Chiriguano Indians, who were bought and sold publicly in an unregulated slave trade that still thrived in Santa Cruz.)[31] His proposed solution to the labor problem was the massive migration and resettlement of peasants from the crowded central valleys of Cochabamba. Viedma saw this as an opportunity for them, too:

> For the Indians who till the soil on the pitiful parcels of land the owner gives them, there will be an alternative to the misery that burdens people in their lowly station in life; the mixed bloods who compose the majority of Cochabamba's population will be employed as laborers, and they will be forced to forget their idle ways.[32]

Thus, the colonization of the lowlands would alleviate the social and demographic pressures in the heartland of Cochabamba. With remarkable foresight, Viedma's scheme anticipated, by almost two centuries, the opening of the Chaparé jungle to small-scale colonizers who cultivated coca and other crops for the markets of Cochabamba. Like Viedma's plan, state-directed colonization in the middle of the twentieth century was designed to shift peasant population from Cliza and the Valle Bajo to the sparsely populated tropics. The intendant had the imagination to realize that colonization was not only a commercial opportunity but also a safety valve for restless peasants beset by the uncertainties of subsistence agriculture. Harnessing the jungle to commercial enterprise was a solution to widespread poverty, vagrancy, and threats to the public order.

If Viedma's plan seemed extravagant, he nevertheless recognized that practical measures had to be taken before people would risk their capital in it. The most serious and immediate need was for transportation. The direct route to the Yuracarees was hazardous, exposing travelers to the perils of cold and treacherous mountain passes. "The trail is one of the most torturous ones in the kingdom

---

31 "Auto del gobernador intendente de Cochabamba . . . prohibiendo el servicio personal de indios llamados 'piezas sueltas' de Santa Cruz," Aug. 17, 1787, RAH, ML, 9/1733, tomo 78, ff. 95-98; and "Informe del yntendente de Cochabamba [sobre] encomiendas de Santa Cruz, sus yndios, y su tributo," RAH, ML, 9/1733, tomo 78, May 13, 1792, ff. 139-153.

32 Viedma, *Descripción geográfica*, 162.

of Peru," Viedma admitted. The icy winds and avalanches endangered "particularly those poor people who migrate down to the jungle to work on the coca haciendas"; the mountainous route offered no pasture for pack animals, and water was extremely scarce.[33] The alternative route—across the high valleys of Cliza and Mizque, descending into Santa Cruz, and then downstream by river raft—could take as long as four or five months to traverse. Ever since the 1760s, local officials had been petitioning the audiencia of La Plata for permission to build a road from the city of Cochabamba to the region of the Chaparé and the Yuracarees, and Viedma added his weight to this plea. He argued that direct access to the Yuracaree missions would vitalize trade between the high maize valleys and the new coca plantations and would bring traders into contact with the Yuracaree and Mojos communities. Merchants would exchange maize for coca and other tropical commodities, which Cochabamba middlemen would then ship to the mining towns and cities.[34] The royal treasury, the traders, and the packdrivers of Cochabamba would all reap profits from this trade. Furthermore, Cochabamba "would avoid the annual loss of 98,000 pesos exchanged for some 14,000 baskets of coca imported from La Paz." Viedma realized that the coca dealers of La Paz, by the same token, would seek to prevent the construction of a road to the Yuracarée forests and the development of a major coca-producing region there. But he tried to convince the crown that such competition would be healthy for the economy of Alto Perú: first, because it would lower the price of coca and therefore the cost of sustaining mineworkers at Potosí; and second, because the population of La Paz would then not depend so heavily upon the proceeds from coca and would turn to other economic pursuits, such as mining.[35]

The political and merchant elites of Chuquisaca objected even more strongly than those of La Paz to Viedma's proposal to build a road down into the jungle. As long as Santa Cruz was the only point of passage to the northern jungle missions, Chuquisaca—the seat of the audiencia of La Plata—benefited the most from the jungle traffic. Chuquisaca was also a central transit point between Santa Cruz and Potosí, and the flow of tropical commodities from the lowlands to Potosí generated a considerable amount of tax revenue for the local

33 Ibid., 134-135.

34 Ibid., 160-165, and Viedma, "Ventajas," 210-211 and passim.

35 Viedma, *Descripción geográfica*, 162.

treasury. The new road would divert much of this traffic away from Chuquisaca and to Cochabamba. The elites of Chuquisaca had no wish to cede the city's privileged position to a rival.[36] Monopoly and privilege were considered the principles of economic advantage, no matter how many proposals set forth the ideals of unregulated trade and technological innovation. The precepts of mercantilist thought posited a static economy, in which one port's gain was another's loss. The hot, wet forests of the Chaparé River basin may have adjoined Cochabamba, but Chuquisaca's trade monopoly over the Santa Cruz route to the lowlands blocked any direct linkage between the two regions. This conflict illustrates how, even apart from imperial policy, the politics of regionalism could stifle the economic initiative of reformists. Viedma encountered an intransigent group in Chuquisaca that thwarted his efforts to advance the frontier of colonial settlement into the untapped forests.

Another impediment was that investors would be reluctant to sink scarce capital into enterprises that offered no guarantee of success. Viedma's plans met with considerable skepticism among the local creole elite, accustomed to speculative ventures in tithes, usurious investments, and rent income.[37] While they may not have analyzed their notions of economic life, most merchants and landowners probably held fast to the mercantilist preconceptions of a "prevailingly inelastic demand ... changeable not so much by economic forces as by the dictates of authority."[38]

In a world where most people still lived at the margins of subsistence, where roads were few and treacherous, and where even Potosí's apparent recovery was attenuated by a sustained population decline that weakened market demand in that town, most people perceived the feebleness of market demand even for exotic tropical commodities. The entry of commercial capital into the eastern frontier, either through trade with mission Indians or through plantation agriculture, would not take place without state intervention on behalf of such enterprise. Even embedded in Viedma's plans, stressing individual initiative as they did, was the implicit assumption of state support. Obviously, if exchange relations between the mission Indians

---

36 "Yncidente importante sobre la apertura de un camino desde Cochabamba a los yndios Yuracarees, y comunicación con las misiones de Moxos," RAH, ML, 9/1723, Tomo 68 (1807), ff. 91-94.

37 See chap. 6, and Lynch, *Spanish Colonial Administration*, 79.

38 D. C. Coleman, "Eli Heckscher and the Idea of Mercantilism," *Scandinavian Economic History Review* 5 (1957): 19.

and itinerant traders, were to be established on the basis of free trade, the state would have to dismantle the protective barriers that stood in its way. If plantations were to sprout in the jungle, the state would have to sanction private property, open up access to the lowlands, and help provide cheap labor.

The problem of labor supply was also serious. Colonization and the cultivation of sugar, cotton, and coca, were all labor-intensive activities, requiring large amounts of cheap labor long before they realized a return. Viedma offered no plan for labor recruitment, but he expected the plantations to draw their workers from the under-employed laboring poor of the central valleys. Implicit in his scheme is the principle of extra-economic coercion. How else but through corvée labor would the "redundant" mestizo and cholo population "be forced to forget their idle ways" through hard work on the plan-tations? Would it require a new rotative system of forced labor, an imposed relocation of people to the lowlands, or perhaps merely the enactment of vagrancy laws that would legitimate the removal of "idle" Indians and mestizos to the plantations? Viedma never cared to follow his proposals through to their logical conclusions. But he anticipated the structural limits on new enterprise in the jungle, and he implicitly accepted the need for state action to provide cheap la-bor to the fledgling plantations. Political force, more than market incentive, would determine the feasibility of his plans.

Thus, when Viedma found that the state was fundamentally indif-ferent to his proposals, he was unable to attract creole interest in them. The crown's inertia only deepened the skepticism of his own constituency. The landowning elite, even those who enjoyed some degree of liquidity, were content to invest in a variety of local enter-prises and leave the commercial conquest of the tropics to the fertile imaginations of "progressive" reformers. It would take another two hundred years for Viedma's plan to be realized. In the meantime, however, events far from the valleys created overnight a bonanza for the local textile industry. In 1796, entrepreneurial attention was sud-denly drawn to the tocuyos.

War and the Textile Boom

During his tour of the province in the 1780s, Viedma noticed with keen interest the considerable number of workshops where spinning wheels and looms hummed with activity. Cochabamba had a prim-itive industry that supplied rustic cotton cloth to local consumers. That this regional industry had eluded most European observers in the past is not surprising: it was primarily a cottage industry, dispersed among the huts and workshops of peasant families. Like so many other primitive textile industries in early modern Europe, the manufacture of tocuyos in Cochabamba got its start in the effort of peasants to diversify the basis of their livelihood. Sometimes textile production was carried out as part of the rent that tenants owed to a hacendado, but probably in most cases, peasant families independently engaged in making tocuyos for their own use and for exchange in the ferias and towns in the central valleys. Bayetas were also sold in the ferias, but most of them were imported from the provinces near La Paz, Chucuito, and Cuzco.[39] In contrast, tocuyos were a local product that clothed and bandaged the laboring poor.[40] Their manufacture was a by-product, during the late colonial era, of the subsistence pressures on smallholding peasants, on the one hand, and the growing opportunity for retail commerce in the markets of the central valleys, on the other. In pursuit of subsistence security, peasants had turned to part-time trade and artisanry.[41]

Contemporary sources give no precise estimates of the number of people engaged in cloth production and marketing in Cochabamba.

39 A sample of entries in the royal alcabala records of Cochabamba showed a wide variety of goods being imported into the region. (The sample consisted of every fifth entry during seven two-year spans—1777-1778, 1782-1783, 1787-1788, 1792-1793, 1797-1798, 1802-1803, and 1807-1808—for a total of 1,313 entries.) However, such common items of consumption as bayetas, rough clothing, and coca predominated. Bayetas alone constituted about 30 percent of the value of all imported taxed goods. Their main origins were the regions of La Paz, Oruro, and Cuzco. Highland textiles might have been one major item of trade between highland and valley peasants (who exchanged it for maize and other valley products). For a more detailed discussion of the alcabala sample and the import trade into the region, see Larson, "Economic Decline and Social Change," 234-240. There were, of course, obrajes on many haciendas (see chap. 5), but the commercial production of woolen textiles on rural estates seems to have been relatively minor in scale. It is notable that Viedma's only mention of such an enterprise concerned the decline and abandonment of the region's most famous obraje, Hulincate, in the Sacaba valley (*Descripción geográfica*, 53).

40 "Memoria de don Juan Carrillo de Albornoz," Apr. 15, 1804, AGN, Sala 9, Intendencia, 30.7.5, Leg. 56, Exp. 6 (hereafter cited as "Memoria de d. Juan Carrillo de Albornoz"); and Barriga, *Memorias para la historia de Arequipa*, 1: 53. Barriga's report is summarized in Zavala, *Servicio personal*, 3: 86-89.

41 For a brief discussion of peasant economic diversification into craft production in Europe, in response to the forces of population pressure and capital shortage, on the one hand, and the growth of retail marketing networks, on the other, see Slicher van Bath, *Agrarian History of Western Europe*, 217ff.

In 1788, Viedma mentioned that five hundred cholos and mestizos occupied themselves in cloth manufacturing in the parish of Quillacollo.[42] Tocuyo weavers were also found in the partidos of the Cercado and Tarata, in the Cliza valley. In 1804, two years after the end of the textile boom, Juan Carrillo de Albornoz mentioned the figure of three thousand weavers.[43] However, the British envoy, John Barclay Pentland, stated in 1827 that some twenty thousand people were involved in textile production at its height (presumably in the late 1790s).[44] That may well be a gross overestimate, or perhaps Pentland was including spinners as well as weavers.

In any event, it appears that the scale of tocuyo production in Cochabamba was greater than that of any other region in the Andean world in the last years of the eighteenth century. Arequipa was the nearest rival, but in the late 1780s, for example, Arequipa's intendant reported that its weavers generally produced about 124,000 varas of cloth each year, while Viedma estimated Cochabamba's cloth exports at the time to be 300,000 varas annually—and that presumably does not include the cloth sold or bartered in local marketplaces.[45] The observations of Tadeo Haenke, a German naturalist who resided in Cochabamba for many years, confirms the impression of the strength of the textile industry in Cochabamba: "The province . . . consumes [as much cotton] in its looms as all the other [provinces] combined."[46]

Despite the importance of the industry, curiously little information has been left to us about the forces and relations of production in it. Most contemporary observers focused attention on the primi-

42 Viedma, *Descripción geográfica*, 67.

43 "Memoria de d. Juan Carrillo de Albornoz."

44 United Kingdom, Foreign Office, 61/12, General Consulate, John B. Pentland, *Report on the Bolivian Republic 1827*, f. 176 (hereafter cited as Pentland, *Report on the Bolivian Republic*).

45 Barriga, *Memorias para la historia de Arequipa*, 1:53; Viedma, *Descripción geográfica*, 137, 139-141.

46 Tadeo Haenke, "Memoria sobre el cultivo de algodón . . .," in *Telégrafo mercantil*, AGN, tomo 2, no. 36 (1801), f. 291. Haenke estimated the annual importation of cotton into Cochabamba at between 30,000 and 40,000 *arrobas* in about 1799. In 1788, Viedma had put the figure at 11,000 arrobas (*Descripción geográfica*, p. 145). However, in 1798, at the height of the boom, Viedma also estimated that some 30,000 arrobas of raw cotton were entering the province each year (AGI, Charcas, Leg. 436, Apr. 3, 1798). An arroba was equivalent to about twenty-five pounds.

tive conditions under which people worked. In Haenke's words, equipment was "poorly constructed," and the laborers lacked "the use of those [English] machines that facilitate and abbreviate different tasks."[47] The machinery that was turning the cities of Manchester and Belfast into the textile workshops of the world and launching England's industrial revolution was not to be found in the Cochabamba valleys.

As is typical in a cottage industry, different members of the family participated in distinct phases of production. Women and children worked in the preparatory phase: cleaning, plying, and spinning the cotton into yarn.[48] A peasant woman would purchase or otherwise obtain raw cotton from a cotton merchant (*algodonero*) and fashion it into yarn in the spare moments of her agricultural work day. The central task of weaving was man's work, and it required some skill, investment in a treadle loom, and considerable blocks of time. Women and children then completed the job, stretching and sometimes dying the finished cloth. Unless production was on consignment, women also took on the responsibility of marketing the cloth. Symbolically, perhaps, weaving enjoyed primacy in the hierarchy of tasks. But the auxiliary tasks—preparing, spinning, and stretching the cotton—required more labor time. As a result, female spinners generally outnumbered male weavers by more than three to one. Together, they constituted an army of invisible textile laborers who blended silently into the rural landscape.

Cochabamba's tocuyos readily competed in the urban markets of Alto Perú against the cotton cloth from Arequipa and the dyed cottons of Quito, but most trade remained local and in the hands of small-scale peddlers. Merchant capital did not capture a significant portion of the tocuyo trade until the last decade of the eighteenth century. Several factors inhibited the development of the large-scale production and distribution of tocuyos before that. The administrative and commercial reorientation of Alto Perú, away from Lima and the Pacific coast and toward Buenos Aires and the Atlantic coast, increased the flow of Spanish goods to the new viceroyalty of La Plata. Following the division of the Peruvian viceroyalty and the abolition of the repartimiento de mercancías, the docks of Buenos Aires were increasingly laden with bolts of Catalan cloth destined for markets in the interior. The Bourbon "free-trade" reforms of 1778, along with generous state subsidies, led to a rapid growth of

47 Haenke, "Memoria sobre el cultivo de algodón," f. 293.

48 Ibid., f. 293; Pentland, *Report on the Bolivian Republic*, f. 176.

the textile industry in Spain; in only a decade, between 1775 and 1784, the production of cotton textiles increased threefold.[49] Moreover, the cotton cloth that came off the looms of Barcelona were superior in quality to the rough homespuns of Cochabamba and Arequipa. Finally, English merchants were selling cotton cloth and the rustic calicoes of India throughout the viceroyalty. These contraband textiles leaked through southern Atlantic ports and were smuggled across the Brazilian frontier. They were ubiquitous and invariably undersold domestic cotton textiles. No wonder, then, that Francisco de Viedma complained in 1788 that the importation of European cloth was "draining the province of scarce money."[50] The result was that the price of tocuyos in Alto Perú began a drop in about 1771 that continued for the next two decades.[51] Local merchants saw no promise of return in trying to sell tocuyos in distant markets. Its production was left in the hands of petty producers and traders who were trying to eke out a livelihood.

But every so often during the eighteenth century, imperial rivalries and trade wars caused a sudden turn of fate. In 1796, Great Britain declared war on Spain and sent its navy into the mouth of the La Plata River, sealing off the port of Buenos Aires. This economic isolation, in the midst of Spain's imperial crisis, created a market for tocuyos that had never existed before. Across the pampas, in Chile, and in Alto Perú, urban consumers were forced to seek local supplies of cotton, woolen, and linen textiles.[52] Tocuyos broke through the previous constraints, supplying markets as distant as Buenos Aires.

49 James C. La Force, Jr., *The Development of the Spanish Textile Industry, 1750-1800* (Berkeley and Los Angeles: University of California Press, 1965), 15.

50 Viedma, *Descripción geográfica*, 47.

51 Tandeter and Wachtel, *Precios y producción agraria*, 27 and 29-30.

52 See Pedro Santos Martínez, *Las industrias durante el virreinato, 1776-1810* (Buenos Aires: Editorial Universitaria de Buenos Aires, 1969), esp. chap. 2; and Jose María Mariluz Urquijo, "Noticias sobre las industrias del virreinato del Río de la Plata en la época del Marquéz de Aviles (1799-1810)," *Revista de historia americana y argentina* 1 (1956-1957): 85-118; Ricardo Caillet-Bois, "Un ejemplo de la industria textil colonial," *Boletín del Instituto de Investigaciones Históricas* 14:20, nos. 67-68 (1936): 19-24; and Assadourian, *Sistema de la economía colonial*, 191-208. For comparisons with the impact of the trade wars on colonial textile production, particularly cotton cloth, in Mexico, see Brading, "Mercantilismo ibérico," 312, and esp. G. P. C. Thomson, "The Cotton Textile Industry in Puebla during the 18th and 19th centuries," in Nils Jacobsen and Hans-Jürgen Puhle, eds., *The Economies of Mexico and Peru during the Late Colonial Period, 1760-1810* (Berlin: Colloquium, 1986), 169-202.

Even the upper classes now had to be content with the itchy tocuyo cloth for their undergarments.[53]

Under this stimulus, the volume of production of tocuyos began to climb. In 1788, Viedma had estimated that cloth worth 60,000 pesos left Cochabamba for "outside provinces" (excluding Mizque). In 1798, Pedro Canals, the provincial treasurer, stated that registered tocuyo exports in the previous year were valued at 88,085 pesos (at the unit price of two reales per vara, the unit price Viedma reported in 1788).[54] This represented a 47 percent increase in less than ten years. The treasurer further estimated that in the first three months of 1798, tocuyo exports amounted to 46,156 pesos—more than three times the value of tocuyos exported in the same three-month period in 1788. Although both Viedma and Canals reported the unit price of tocuyos to be two reales per vara, the price rose during the war years to two and a half reales and more.[55]

But while demand was great, the factor market was still a bottleneck for Cochabamba textile producers and merchants. Raw cotton came from the Peruvian coast, around Moquegua and Arequipa. Supply was erratic, and during the war, the price climbed steeply. An arroba of cotton that cost about two pesos four reales in 1788 cost as much as six pesos ten years later.[56] Cotton imports caused a heavy cash outflow, estimated to amount to 180,000 pesos in 1798.[57] It was the cotton planters and algodoneros who were capitalizing most on the tocuyo bonanza.

The reformers, who had always had their sights set on the tropical frontier, saw a solution to the problem: cultivate cotton in the low-

---

53 Haenke, "Memoria sobre el cultivo de algodón," f. 293, and AGN, Alcaldía, 1799 (according to a personal communication from Susan Socolow).

54 Viedma, *Descripción geográfica*, 137; "Correspondencia con los gobernadores e intendentes de Cochabamba y La Paz," Apr. 16, 1793, AGI, Charcas, Leg. 436.

55 In the 1780s, a vara of tocuyo rarely sold for more than one and one-half reales; by 1799, it normally fetched two and one-half reales. In Buenos Aires, the price stabilized at around three and one-half reales during the shortage. Tandeter and Wachtel point out, however (*Precios y producción agraria*, 30) that this price increase was a modest one in historical terms. It merely returned the price to the levels before 1770, when European competition began to depress them.

56 Viedma, *Descripción geográfica*, 145; "Correspondencia con los gobernadores e intendentes de Cochabamba y La Paz," Apr. 3, 1798, AGI, Charcas, Leg. 436.

57 Viedma, *Descripción geográfica*, 145. In 1827, Pentland (*Report on the Bolivian Republic*, f. 180v.) noted that most raw cotton imported from the Peruvian coast for Cochabamba's looms was sold in the marketplaces of Paria and Tapacarí.

lands of Santa Cruz and vertically integrate the tocuyo industry. This would not only make textile manufacturing more profitable but would also promote the colonization of the jungle. The backward linkages of the cloth industry would at last open up the frontier to commercial agriculture. Viedma was enthusiastic about this idea, and he petitioned the viceroy and the king for permission to cultivate cotton in the region of Santa Cruz. But it was Tadeo Haenke who most ardently championed the cause of cotton cultivation in the region. In 1799, he wrote an essay (published in the *Telégrafo mercantil* of Buenos Aires in 1801) presenting the case to the royal authorities. He deplored the region's dependence on coastal cotton imports and reminded the crown of the importance of the tocuyo industry for the entire colony during the blockade.

> During the present war, tocuyos have been the only resource of these interior provinces. With the end of communication with Europe . . . many people would have gone about naked had it not been for Cochabamba's tocuyos. In consideration of all the circumstances . . . it is necessary to stimulate the cultivation of cotton in every way possible and to develop the textile industry that is now in its infancy.[58]

But how could Haenke expect the crown to sanction the expansion of manufacturing in Cochabamba when it favored Spanish textiles and promoted their export to the colonies? Haenke confronted this issue head on, arguing that the tocuyos posed no competition to Spanish cloth. Spanish and colonial textiles appealed to two different markets: the imports to the creole elites who could afford their higher cost, and the tocuyos to the poor. Thus, metropolitan and colonial textile industries were complementary, not competitive. If any imperial power competed with local textile manufactures, it was England, which was beginning to distribute India's crude cottons. But in any event, Haenke argued that the demand for all kinds of textiles in the viceroyalty was beginning to outpace the supply, even under normal trade conditions.[59]

If Haenke thought there was little reason to prohibit local cotton cultivation and manufacture, he saw one compelling reason why the industry had to survive and grow. Like Viedma, Haenke was concerned about poverty and social unrest in the central valleys. In the burgeoning textile industry, the growing mass of marginal small-

58 Haenke, "Memoria sobre el cultivo de algodón," f. 293.

59 Ibid., ff. 291-292.

holders and landless laborers could find subsistence security. In 1799, textiles constituted the one sector of the local economy that could absorb greater numbers of impoverished peasants seeking subsidiary work outside of agriculture.[60] If the industry survived the end of the European blockade, it might offer a solution to the region's anemic economy.

The day of reckoning came only a year after Haenke's report was published. With the signing of the Peace of Amiens in 1802, the British lifted their blockade. The sharp increase in alcabala revenues from imports in 1804 and 1805 signaled the renewed influx of European cloth, as well as other goods, into Cochabamba.[61] In 1806, the British invaded La Plata and reopened the continent to contraband trade. In the meantime, all of Alto Perú had suffered acutely from harvest failures and famine. As early as 1804, the optimistic and ambitious proposals of Haenke were already unrealistic. The authorities in Cochabamba tried to adjust their thinking to cope with the unfolding crisis.[62]

An 1804 report on the state of the tocuyo industry, and its prospects, reflected the newly conservative thinking on regional economic reform. Written by Juan Carrillo de Albornoz, a wealthy creole merchant and member of the cabildo of Cochabamba, the report stated almost matter-of-factly that many of the region's 3,000 looms had fallen silent and the industry was virtually dormant.[63] At issue, therefore, was not cotton cultivation or the vertical integration of the industry, but simply its survival under the impact of European

60 Ibid., ff. 293-294.

61 Revenue from alcabalas on Spanish goods rose from 2,852 pesos in 1802 to 8,887 pesos in 1805. However, it dropped off sharply in 1806, to 2,443 pesos, presumably because of the British invasion of Buenos Aires and the collapse of overseas Spanish trade. AGN, Sala 13, Cajas Reales, Leg. 23 to 34 (1801-1806). (For complete figures on alcabala revenues on imported and colonial goods carried into Cochabamba, see Larson, "Economic Decline and Social Change," 447.) The problem of European competition with colonial textile producers was compounded by increased Catalan demand for Peruvian cotton. It became more difficult and more costly to procure the raw materials needed to produce tocuyos in the region. Thus, Cochabamba faced "double competition" from the privileged and stronger metropolitan cotton industry of Barcelona after the Peace of Amiens.

62 On the condition of the tocuyo industry, see AGN, Sala 9, Consulado, 4.6.4, tomo 14, Apr. 15, 1804, ff. 80-80v. For a discussion of regional economic decline during the first decade of the nineteenth century, see chap. 8.

63 "Memoria de d. Juan Carrillo de Albornoz."

competition. Carrillo de Albornoz proposed tighter regulations on tocuyo weavers to improve and standardize the quality of the cloth. He wanted to restrict manufacture to guild members who operated looms that had a stipulated number and size of combs. Given sufficient quality control, the tocuyos might appeal to the upper classes and break through the class barrier that had limited their market. Reminiscent of the English Statute of Artificers of 1563, which tightened guild regulations over the woolen-cloth industry in reaction to the collapse of the export boom,[64] this proposal was a medieval remedy. It did not threaten metropolitan interests or challenge royal policy; it simply tried to restrict cloth production to "professional" weavers so that tocuyos might compete against the finer cottons of Europe. The class bias implicit in the proposal is obvious: the industry would neither employ nor clothe the laboring poor, but rather would serve the interests of the wholesale merchants and a small guild of *tocuyeros* who complied with municipal regulations. Control over production would pass entirely into the hands of the mercantile elite and municipal authorities.[65]

To a certain degree, that had begun to happen spontaneously under the impact of the textile boom. During the war years, merchants discovered that tocuyos were yielding high returns, and they injected capital into the marketing of both raw cotton and finished cloth. In Buenos Aires, tocuyos fetched prices high enough to more than offset the costs of the overland transport that was necessary during the blockade.[66] Those who stood to profit most were the merchants who monopolized the carriage trade. The shortage of pack animals in the region, which had existed ever since the 1780s, threw much of the long-distance trade in tocuyos into the hands of a privileged few.[67] In fact, the situation was serious enough to have led local authorities to register complaints with the consulado of Buenos Aires in 1801.

64 See F. J. Fisher, "Commercial Trends and Policy in Sixteenth-Century England," *Economic History Review*, 1st ser., 10 (1940): p. 113.

65 Carrillo's proposal was supported by Viedma and, in 1806, it won the endorsement of the consulado. "Memoria de d. Juan Carrillo de Albornoz," and Santos Martínez, *Industrias durante el virreinato*, 43.

66 That had been one of Carrillo de Albornoz's arguments: "Memoria de d. Juan Carrillo de Albornoz," f.86.

67 Tandeter and his collaborators estimate that approximately 50 percent of the trade in tocuyos to Potosí in the year 1793 was conducted by a few large merchants. Enrique Tandeter et al., "El mercado de Potosí a fines del siglo XVIII," in Harris, Larson, and Tandeter, *Participación indígena*, 409.

They declared that, even when the merchants agreed to carry cargo for other traders and artisans, they charged fees far in excess of the stipulated rates, and they demanded cash advances.[68] Such practices excluded many small-scale producers or traders from the long-distance tocuyo trade.

If large-scale merchants monopolized the channels of supply to distant markets, they probably also had some impact on relations of production during the textile boom. Rather than rely on the fluctuating supply and uneven quality of cloth that came off the looms of the many rural artisans, some merchants distributed raw cotton to selected artisans and then marketed their finished cloth. For the best of these artisan-clients, the merchants probably even provided financing. An occasional legal dispute brings such credit and debt relations to light. One of the most acrimonious disputes involved Carrillo de Albornoz himself, who sought to collect 295 pesos of a loan of 1,200 pesos he had made to a tocuyo *maestro*.[69] One can only speculate about the extent to which artisans lost their economic autonomy to merchant creditors or gradually abandoned agriculture to make their living (and meet their debt obligations) through more or less full-time craft production. Haenke alluded to the growth of an urban artisanate in a passing observation that "inferior classes of people are able to earn the better part of their subsistence from [the textile] industry."[70] Thus, the injection of merchant capital into the tocuyo trade probably accelerated social differentiation among the craft producers, widening the gulf between the rural cottage weavers and an urban group of artisans.

But the emergence of an urban artisanate was doubled edged. For while the urban, professional weavers, who constituted an informal guild, benefited more from the textile boom than their rural counterparts, they were probably also increasingly subordinated to merchant capital. There is little evidence that the profits in the industry "trickled down" to the producers. Indeed, more than ever, urban artisans were now vulnerable to the shifting winds of the colonial market.

68 Pedro Ariscain to consulado, Dec. 10, 1800, AGN, Sala 9, Consulado, 4.6.4, tomo 14; Ariscain to consulado, Feb. 15, 1801, ibid.; and Juan Carrillo de Albornoz to consulado, Apr. 15, 1804, ibid.

69 "Autos por el regidor de . . . D. Juan Carrillo de Albornoz contra María Vargas (madre del maestro de tocuyo) en cuanto a un préstamo de 295 pesos," AHMC, Leg. 1213 (1804).

70 Haenke, "Memoria sobre el cultivo del algodón," f. 291.

Merchant involvement in the manufacture and distribution of tocuyos during the war years suggests that a rudimentary "putting
out" system was beginning to develop, in response to increased market demand. However, while some merchants may have created a
clientele of producers, merchant capital did not alter production in
any significant way. Merchants did not concentrate production in
factories, hire wage workers, or acquire machinery with which to
rationalize the productive process. In other words, the shift toward
urban-based artisan production in the late 1790s did not contain the
germ of capitalist relations. The accumulative strategy of the merchants was to monopolize the supply of pack animals rather than to
invest in production. Furthermore, the merchants diversified their
investments and holdings, always hedging their bets against sudden
misfortune or a downturn in the market. Notarial records show that
wealthy wholesale merchants like Juan José Eras y Gandarillas, Francisco García Claros, Francisco Ventura Valiente, and Juan Carrillo de
Albornoz owned large parcels of land, speculated in tithes and
bonded one another, and engaged in moneylending. They also held
prestigious political posts or occupied high ranks in the local militia.
Despite their financial capacity and the climate of reform, merchants remained locked in their old ways, unwilling to plow their
wealth into manufacturing.

Beneficiaries of the de facto barriers of protection, the merchants
knew that their profit on tocuyo exports was at the mercy of international events, which could once again flood the viceroyalty's marketplaces with European cloth. An additional deterrent to investment was the firm royal resistance to proposals to grow cotton in
Santa Cruz and Mizque. Clearly, then, there was little alternative
but to confine investment in tocuyos to the distributive realm, so
that capital could be quickly withdrawn or diverted when the collapse came and Spanish America's market was delivered, once more,
to the European cloth manufacturers. That way, when peace was followed by the flood of Spanish textiles, Cochabamba's merchants
could shift from exporting tocuyos to importing Catalan's fine linens
and cottons.[71] The local merchants could make such adjustments;
the artisans would be left to fend for themselves.

71 Thomson's research on the cotton textile industry of Puebla provides an illu-
minating comparison with Cochabamba's crafts. Although significantly more
developed, the Mexican cotton industry suffered similar political and market
constraints in the eighteenth century. Even when the cotton textile industry
thrived in Mexico, also during the imperial trade wars that cut off European imports, the local merchant class assiduously avoided capital investment in pro-

During the 1780s and 1790s, economic reformers and pragmatic entrepreneurs discovered the limits of enterprise in the colonial context. As they sought ways to alter agrarian class relations and break the "class stalemate" between peasants and hacendados in the central valleys, they came up against economic, political, and ideological obstacles to regional economic growth. Those obstacles were not peculiar to Cochabamba, but they stood out starkly to contemporary observers because the potential for economic growth in the region seemed so great. The proximity of tropical resources and the textile boom inspired proposals for economic reforms and briefly raised hope. The economic thinking of the time, combined with events on the world scene, suggested that sustained growth was possible even within the constraints of imperial rule and a shallow, unstable colonial market. But nowhere in the Andes was there greater disparity between economic plans and action, between ambitions and reality. What was to be a colonial showcase of industry and agriculture had collapsed, by 1804, into a morass of drought, famine, and misery.

So far as Alto Perú was concerned, the Bourbon decades were a period of frustrated economic reform. Behind the promise of reform there lurked a stronger colonial state bent upon extracting more surplus in the form of higher tribute and taxes on economic activity. While innovative individuals may have looked to new enterprises to stimulate the regional economy, the Bourbon state sought ways to harness the Indian communities, once more, to the mining industry of Potosí. More than ever, Spain needed fresh revenue with which to finance the empire and beat back the British.

duction. Like the Cochabamba workshops, the industry of Puebla did not undergo internal reorganization or modernization during the brief boom periods before independence. It, too, was dealt a serious setback by the Peace of Amiens and the re-emergence of Barcelona as the major European supplier of cotton cloth. However, Thomson also shows how Puebla's textile manufacturing did grow and begin to transform its internal productive organization in the middle of the nineteenth century, thus taking a divergent path from Cochabamba's craft industry. See Thomson, "Cotton Textile Industry in Puebla," and his "Puebla between Mine and Metropolis: Three Cycles of Growth and Decline, 1532-1850" (paper presented at the Seminar on Economic Imperialism and Latin America, University of London, Nov. 5, 1979).

The Ebb Tide
of Colonial Rule

The shift in the global balance of imperial forces in favor of British hegemony posed a grave threat to Spain's overseas territories and lent a sense of urgency to the Bourbons' reformist ideals. In the third quarter of the eighteenth century, the Bourbons hastened to export those reforms to Spanish America, where an "enlightened Spanish absolutism" might fortify the colonies against British encroachment. The introduction of reforms signaled the end of a long period of neglect and the reconstitution of a centralized, interventionist colonial state that primarily served the interests of the empire and the metropolitan elites. But the reforms also touched the everyday lives of most people in the colonies. The face of empire showed itself in myriad ways: in newly formed militias, in toll houses and an army of tax collectors, in ubiquitous tribute officials, and in a growing number of officious *peninsulares* who occupied many of the highest posts.

Principal among the latter were the intendants appointed to replace the corregidores and to administer the new, enlarged administrative units. The intendants were the linchpin of imperial reform, as they were vested with broad responsibilities in matters of justice, finance, war, and general administration. Where the viceroy once enjoyed supreme power over fiscal affairs, the intendant now assumed responsibility for the management of royal tax collection in his own territory. Where once the audiencia tended to all important judicial matters, the intendant might adjudicate disputes or dispense justice in certain situations. The concentration of power in the hands of (for the most part) Spanish intendants was one mechanism of tightened royal control over the colonial hinterlands.[1]

1 J. Fisher, *Government and Society in Colonial Peru*; Lynch, *Spanish Colonial Administration*; Burkholder, "From Creole to *Peninsular*"; Leon G. Campbell,

The obverse of these changes was, of course, a reduction in the power and jurisdiction of other colonial authorities. Viceroys lost some jurisdiction over fiscal matters, and colonial magistrates found their juridical authority impinged upon by vigorous intendants who did not hesitate to mix their executive and judicial functions. Within the colonial political elite, the reforms provoked or exacerbated conflicts on all levels: individual, institutional, cultural, and ideological. For most creole authorities, therefore, the reforms were a mixed political blessing: they threatened to undermine traditional authority and prestige, even though they also promised to strengthen the bureaucracy as a whole and grant it broader powers. A strong colonial state was going to be resurrected on a weak foundation of elite factionalism, jurisdictional disputes, and petty rivalries.[2]

All of this was manifested in Alto Perú. Four intendancies were carved out of the western altiplano provinces and the eastern grain valleys and tropical lowlands, and the new intendants undercut the authority of the viceroy—whose power had in any case never effectively penetrated the interior mountain provinces—and undermined the semiautonomy of the audiencia of La Plata as well. Not only did the four intendants serve as a countervailing force to the magistrates, since they were directly subordinate to the superintendant of Buenos Aires; they also took over some of the judicial functions of the oidores. Furthermore, the new audiencia of Buenos Aires absorbed some of the powers of the older, inland court.

In this new situation, the factionalism and tensions endemic to late colonial rule in Alto Perú turned some of the proposed economic reforms into highly charged political and moral issues. When the Bourbons forced colonial authorities to come to grips once again with the labor problem at Potosí, for example, they were plunged into a bitter debate over the attributes of a functioning mita. At base, it was a political struggle, cloaked in ideological garb, but it recalled the ideals of Toledo's era some two centuries earlier, and it diverted the attention of authorities from the brutal social effects of increased

The Military and Society in Colonial Peru, 1750-1810 (Philadelphia: American Philosophical Society, 1978).

2 Góngora, *Studies in the Colonial History of Spanish America*, chap. 5, esp. 174-175. For a prime example of the endemic jurisdictional disputes among colonial authorities in the Bourbon years—the rivalry between Victorián de Villava, president of the audiencia of La Plata, and Intendant Francisco de Viedma over the power of the latter—see Lynch, *Spanish Colonial Administration*, 253.

colonial taxation until, by the end of the first decade of the nine-teenth century, it was too late.

The Poverty of Reform

Compared with the spectacular growth of Mexico's silver mines in the late eighteenth century, Potosí's slow recovery was unimpressive to the Bourbons, all the more so as world silver prices were pegged to production costs in the most productive mines of Mexico. Silver mining at Potosí was not particularly profitable in the late eighteenth century, and it no longer attracted entrepreneurs in possession of capital or courage. Some administrators pinned their hopes for increased production on the technical assistance offered by the German Nordenflicht expedition (1788-1789) to Potosí.[3] For others, labor was the critical factor.

As discussed in chapter 3, the proliferation of small-scale, independent miners had weakened the bargaining position of the azogueros, who had reluctantly come to accept kajcheo as a necessary evil if the free mingas were to work at all. Increasingly, mine owners and renters fell back on the piecework system (see chapter 3) to squeeze more labor time out of the dwindling number of mitayos at Potosí. But the intensification of exploitation in the mines had intrinsic limits, if the labor force was to reconstitute itself from day to day and week to week. Azogueros complained that the heaps of discarded ore and earth bore no more nuggets of silver that could be plucked from the rubble. If production was to increase, ore had to be cut from deeper lodes in the mountain. Mineowners needed more ore pickers and carriers if production was to be sustained, and the arrendatarios who leased mines were desperate for more workers.[4] Thus, if the Bourbons were serious about stimulating mineral production and royal revenues, they would, according to many reformers in Alto Perú, have to increase the number of mitayos who could be subjected to the regimen of piecework. Once again, the mines needed forced subsidization by Andean peasant economies.

The intendant of Potosí, Juan del Pino Manrique, was one who

3 Rose Marie Buechler, "Technical Aid to Upper Peru: The Nordenflicht Expedition," *Journal of Latin American Studies* 5 (1973): 37-77; Marie Helmer, "Mineurs allemands à Potosí: L'expédition Nordenflycht (1788-1789)," *La minería hispana e iberoamericana* 1 (1978): 513-528.

4 Cañete y Domínguez, *Guía histórica*; Tandeter, "Rente comme rapport de production," chapts. 3 and 4.

argued for an amplified mita. Pino Manrique opposed royal instructions to model Potosí's renovation after the successful Mexican mines that functioned without forced labor. He believed that, given Potosí's inferior quality of ore and its uncompetitive position, its survival demanded a revitalized mita. He rejected the alternative of abandoning the Cerro Rico to the kajchas, who already infested the mines and chipped away at their interior works. Mining would succumb to an underground world of anarchy if some measure of power were not restored to the mining elite. Control over a compulsory labor force, subject to tareas, would widen the margin of gain and dislodge the mingas from their semiautonomous place in the industry.[5]

The argument, of course, was not new. But times had changed since the debate over the logistics and morality of the mita in the early seventeenth century. Perhaps out of fear of provoking Indian unrest only fifteen years after the great rebellion, or perhaps inspired by the fashionable ideals of the Enlightenment, some colonial authorities expressed reservations about the proposals of Pino Manrique. After all, Mexico's success had proven that colonial mining could prosper without a system of forced labor. There might be a less onerous way of inducing peasants to take their turn in the silver mines. A climate of ambivalence clouded the issues, and political resentments and rivalries that had not existed during the earlier debate added fuel to the fire.

The main protagonists in the renewed debate, which took place between 1793 and 1797, were Francisco de Paula Sanz, successor to Pino Manrique as intendant of Potosí, and Victorián de Villava, president of the audiencia of La Plata. Presiding over a weakened court, Villava turned against the azogueros and, in his "Discourse on the Mita of Potosí," challenged Potosí's intendant to justify the mita in terms of the common good of the colony.[6] Following the precepts of mercantilism, Villava asserted that agriculture and industry were the foundation of the economy. He contended that a monoculture, revolving around the production of the "universal commodity,

5 "Representaciones del gobernador de Potosí, Pino Manrique, sobre la ordenanza de minería," June 16, 1786, cited and summarized in Zavala, *Servicio personal*, 3: pp. 71-74; Tandeter, "Rente comme rapport de production," 279-304.

6 Victorián de Villava, "Discurso sobre la mita de Potosía" (1793) in Ricardo Levene, *Vida y escritos de Victorián de Villava* (Buenos Aires: Peuser, 1946), xxx-xxxiv.

money," was unhealthy when agriculture and industry stagnated. And why should the mining elite receive a special subsidy while industrious subjects engaged in agriculture and industry were left to their own devices? Other mines survived without benefit of a mita; so should Potosí.

Villava's assumption that Andean mining enterprises could thrive without mitayos challenged conventional thinking about the nature of the Indian. It was because of this basic issue of the "moral character" of the native, as Zavala has remarked, that Villava introduced Enlightenment ideals into his discourse:

> Look with shame upon those historians who, lacking philosophy and politics, have been so weak as to doubt the rationality of those miserable people [the Indians]. To this day, most look upon Indians as children or machines. Yet education makes of a man the person he wishes to be. An Indian transplanted to London could become a loyal and eloquent member of the opposition party, or [in Rome], a wise counselor to the pope.[7]

Villava's compassion and idealism set him apart from his peers and made him the leading spokesman against such institutions as the mita. He denied the prevailing belief that "racial inferiority" explained why Andeans shunned mine work or appeared passive and sullen before their colonial masters. In his view, the greed and despotism of the colonizers had forced the Indians to acquire "unattractive" character traits.

Villava's views were rather unorthodox even compared to the thinking of open-minded men like Viedma. The two men shared similar outlooks on many subjects, including an admiration for the Jesuit management of mission Indians in times past. Curiously, however, Viedma hedged on the issue of the mita. "I leave this sensitive issue to a pen other than mine," he wrote in 1788.[8] Although he apparently had no intention of advocating abolition, he did raise his voice against certain "excesses" related to the institution. Viedma was troubled, for example, by the plight of mitayos who re-

---

7 This paraphrase of Villava's argument is found in Zavala, *Servicio personal,* 3: 101. The content of the entire debate is discussed in great detail in ibid., 3: 100-128.

8 Viedma, *Descripción geográfica,* 178. See Viedma's descriptions of the tarea system and other hardships faced by mitayos in ibid., 178-180. See also ANB, Minas, tomo 129, no. 1177, Dec. 12, 1794, and "Exp. de los mitayos de Capinota sobre los tributos," ANB, Minas, tomo 129, no. 1170 (1792).

turned to an uncertain fate in their village, and he protested the suffering of valley Indians who had to live and work in the harsh climate of the puna. But Viedma's comments were pragmatic in tone; they lacked the philosophical depth or moral conviction of Villava's writings. Moreover, Viedma and Villava were political rivals, even more than they were intellectual companions.[9]

In the 1790s, however, Villava confronted the entrenched interests of Potosí's economic and political elites. Among their leaders was the intendant, Paula Sanz, surely a worthy opponent. Paula Sanz had traveled extensively throughout Alto Perú and had compiled statistics and notes on many aspects of the area.[10] He knew how to capitalize on his worldliness. He cast himself as a pragmatist, cut from a different cloth than the armchair philosopher Villava, who rarely left the stuffy chambers of the Chuquisaca court.

His proposed strategy was to expand the mita (or the "new mita," as it was called) and to impose tighter regulation on compulsory labor. Together with Pedro Vicente Cañete y Domínguez, Paula Sanz issued the so-called Caroline Code, based upon Toledan ordinances and other legislation and intended to correct the worst abuses suffered by the mitayos. The mita would be "cleaned up" and expanded to incorporate more Indians. Furthermore, the tarea system would not be left to the dictates of individual greed and violence; it would be regulated and rationalized. Much as the crown had tried to do in the 1750s with the repartimiento de mercancías, the intendant now proposed to regulate the tarea regime while granting it legal sanction.[11]

In 1794, Paula Sanz, invoking his authority as intendant, ordered the dispatch of 184 Indians from the pueblos of Pocoata and Aymaya, in the province of Chayanta, to serve as mitayos to two miners, Luís de Orueta and Juan Jaúregui, who had invested in new mining equip-

9 See Zavala, *Servicio personal*, 3: 155.

10 Ibid., 3: 102-103. One of Paula Sanz's reports is discussed in chap. 5. His chief ally, Cañete y Domínguez, wrote the definitive report on Potosí, *Guía histórica*. See also René Arce, "Un documento inédito de Pedro Vicente Cañete en torno a la controversia de la nueva mita de Potosí," in Martha Urioste de Aguirre, ed., *Estudios bolivianos en homenaje a Gunnar Mendoza* (La Paz, 1978, mimeograph), 119-124.

11 Rose Marie Buechler, "Mining Society of Potosí, 1776-1810" (Ph.D. diss., University of London, 1974), chap. 3; Tandeter, "Rente comme rapport de production," chap. 5; Zavala, *Servicio personal*, 3: 102-107; Buechler, "El intendente Sanz y la 'mita nueva' de Potosí," *Historia y cultura* (La Paz), no. 3 (1977): 59-95.

ment under the guidance of a member of the Nordenflicht expedition. At the same time, he assailed the secular priests of the Indian communities of Alto Perú for their "hypocrisy" in opposing the mita, and obstructing the recruitment of mitayos. Paula Sanz scorned the prelates, who, he said, preached against the injustices of the mita while subjecting their native parishioners to tyrannical rule, compulsory labor, and extortion.[12] It was an assault that recalled the earlier attacks against the corregidores during the heyday of the repartimiento de mercancías (see chapter 3). But the corregidors had long since been banished, and it was now the local religious authorities who were responsible for the mita's decline, even while the Indian population was growing. Not surprisingly, Paula Sanz pushed the clerics squarely into the political camp of Victorián de Villava. What had begun as a polemic and a rivalry between Villava and Paula Sanz became a political and ideological battle that implicated the church.[13]

The intendant's order to dispatch new mita companies aroused the priests and missionaries in Chayanta. The irate prelates hastened to La Plata, where they found the sympathetic ear of Villava. The court suspended the intendant's order in March 1795, and this decision was affirmed by the viceroy a month later. In addition, several rebellious caciques in Chayanta who had been deposed during the struggle over the mita were ordered reinstated. Subsequent orders from Madrid and Buenos Aires sought to restrain the power of Paula Sanz to expand the mita in his intendancy.[14] These actions were probably motivated, in part, by fear of worsening the situation in an already volatile province. There was little moral impulse behind them; the crown was basically indifferent to the Caroline Code and did not seriously entertain abolitionist options. It simply wanted to navigate a less treacherous course in the economic revitalization of Potosí.

Instead of applying naked coercion to increase the flow of migrant peasants to Potosí, the intendants of Alto Perú were to pursue basic agrarian reforms aimed at reconstituting the Indian villages around Toledan principles. In the aftermath of the 1781 rebellion and the dismantling of the corregimientos, the time was ripe for community reform and renovation. Village society had degenerated to its nadir

12 Buechler, 'Intendente Sanz," 61 and 63; Zavala, *Servicio personal*, 3: 11 and 116.

13 Buechler, "Mining Society of Potosí," chap. 4.

14 Zavala, *Servicio personal*, 3: 100 and 126; Lynch, *Spanish Colonial Administration*, 182-183.

during the last years of the repartimiento and the Indian wars. Now that the corregidores had been banished and the native rebels exterminated, the Bourbons believed that social reform was possible. The intendants were charged with adjudicating disputes and keeping peace in the villages, and, more fundamentally, with managing community resources.[15] The distribution of community lands and funds was made the explicit prerogative of the intendants. The Bourbons were not willing to leave these vital matters in the hands of native authorities (or of local prelates, for that matter). The crown sought to enhance the political leverage of the intendants so that they could shield Andean villages from outside threats and facilitate the extraction of surpluses from them. The royal mandate was to distribute community lands more equitably, but behind it was the threat of heavier taxation and mita recruitment. Compared to the crude tactics of Paula Sanz, the reformist strategy of extraction probably seemed more prudent and effective.

Francisco de Viedma was one of the few intendants who took up the challenge to implement land reform in the Indian communities. From the beginning of his term, he expressed concern about the extreme imbalances in community land distribution and tribute categories. As noted in chapter 3, the first Indian population census taken after the Indian uprisings revealed that landholding originarios made up only about 15 percent of the village population. The overwhelming majority of Indians were dependent leaseholders, or at least so they claimed to the tribute collectors. Viedma's tour of the villages alarmed him further, for he suspected that caciques like the Liro de Córdovas of Tapacarí were controlling the distribution of community lands in their own interests.[16] The decay of communal landholding was even more advanced in the valley pueblos of Sipesipe, El Paso, and Tiquipaya, where Indians hardly outnumbered mestizos and creoles any longer. Thus, the intendant advocated the restoration of the corporate village much along the lines of Toledo's blueprint. He hoped to distribute lands more democratically among village Indians, with little regard for their cultural or social links to their communities. The result would be the passage of landless forasteros into the status of landholding originarios. Viedma justified his plan on fiscal and moral grounds: by generating "more tribute monies . . . the land reform would allow the Indians to break their

15 J. Fisher, *Government and Society in Colonial Peru*, chap. 4; Lynch, *Spanish Colonial Administration*, chap. 8.

16 Viedma, *Descripción geográfica*, 182; see also chap. 4.

bonds of slavery and escape the misery they suffer as dependents of the few originarios who have land."[17] State intervention would reverse the process of class differentiation in the villages and guarantee the means of subsistence to a servile Indian peasantry. Viedma glossed over the fact that the reform would subjugate originario peasants more directly to state obligations.

As is so often the case with such efforts, the intendant's land reform fell far short of its goals. The 1793 padron revealed that the number of originarios in Cochabamba increased by 79 percent since 1786, from 339 to 607 (see table 20). Yet forasteros still outnumbered originarios by more than three to one. Moreover, the impact of the land reform was uneven. Land was widely redistributed in Sipesipe, El Paso, and Tiquipaya, but in the cabecera pueblo of Tapacarí, where land was most concentrated among the originario population, the reform was less effective.[18] Perhaps Viedma was unwilling to challenge the power and authority of the Liro de Córdova clique that still ruled Tapacarí. After all, that village had erupted in 1781, and its rebels had divided the province into two parts for several months. Viedma may have felt that he could not afford to dislodge the caciques and

Table 20. Composition of Tributaries in Pueblos Reales of Cochabamba, 1786 and 1793

Pueblo Real	Total Number of Tributaries	Forasteros	Originarios Number	Originarios Percentage
		1786		
Tapacarí	1,465	1,296	169	11.5
Sipesipe	381	316	65	17.1
El Paso	219	190	29	13.2
Tiquipaya	424	348	76	17.9
Total	2,489	2,150	339	13.6
		1793		
Tapacarí	1,468	1,268	200	13.6
Sipesipe	420	264	156	37.1
El Paso	236	128	108	45.8
Tiquipaya	433	290	143	33.0
Total	2,557	1,950	607	23.7

Sources: AGN, Sala 13, Padrones, 18.2.1, Leg. 46; 18.2.2, Leg. 47; and 18.2.5, Leg. 150.

17 Viedma, *Descripción geográfica*, 64.

18 See chap. 4, and Sánchez-Albornoz, *Indios y tributos*, 180-185.

risk losing their loyalty and collaboration at a moment when heavier taxation required strong rule and the financial bonding of tribute dues. In any event, it is ironic that the Liro de Córdovas emerged from the reform with more material wealth rather than with less. Records show that they were granted royal licenses to build and operate grain mills in the Tapacarí River valley in the late 1790s.[19] Evidently, the land reform was adjusted to local circumstances. Egalitarian distribution may have been the ideal, but it was applied only where royal interests so dictated.

Land redistribution was not the only mechanism by which Viedma tried to alter the social hierarchy of the Indian villages. He wanted to reverse the centuries of pauperization of the villages by building up their capital stock and then purposefully managing the dispensation of the funds. His main project was Tapacarí. Community funds would be obtained from two sources: interest on outstanding mortgage loans, which had accumulated over many years of delinquent payment; and the sale of wheat cultivated on communal lands.[20] Viedma was not specific about which lands would be earmarked for communal production or about the role that the caciques would play in the communal efforts to rebuild the municipal treasury. On the contrary, what is striking about his proposal is the implicit separation of the village elite from the proposed reforms. Viedma apparently wanted to intervene directly in the village economy to ensure that surplus harvests were marketed for the benefit of the community as a whole.

Viedma therefore, proposed the establishment of a "neutral" administrative body (composed of himself, two treasurers, a member of the cabildo, and the royal protector of Indians) to oversee the use of the communal funds. In his view, the funds were to serve three purposes. First, they would underwrite tribute deficits. The state would no longer be so dependent upon the personal assets of the caciques to post bond for the value of tribute, nor would cobradores find themselves in debt following their rounds of tribute collection. Second, the community would spend a portion of its monies for the pur-

19 In 1798, for example, Matías Quispe won a royal license to build two grain mills on the outskirts of the pueblo real, in recognition of his "punctual and efficient" handling of tribute collection. AGN, Sala 9, Tribunales, 37.3.2, Leg. 124, Exps. 18 and 27 (1798).

20 AGI, Charcas, Leg. 436, "Instrucción que forma . . . Francisco de Viedma para el gobierno de los monte-píos," July 20, 1798, AGI, Charcas, Leg. 436. (See also table A-4).

chase of basic goods (mules, iron, tools, and cloth) at wholesale prices for resale to peasant households, eliminating the fees of middlemen.[21]

Finally, the funds would be used to restore a measure of community welfare to Tapacarí. They could be allocated to purchase supplies for departing mitayos or to make loans to peasant families in stress. Although he never conceptualized his plan in such terms, Viedma was proposing to take over the traditional responsibility of the ethnic elite to tend to the well-being of all community members. The traditional basis of cacique legitimacy had long disintegrated in Tapacarí, as hierarchical relations were no longer governed by Andean ideals of reciprocity and redistribution (see chapter 4). Viedma felt it was incumbent upon the state to shield village peasants from their own native overlords as well as from outsiders. Tapacarí's new *monte-pío* (pious works) would serve as a halfway house of charity and insurance, providing the needy with emergency resources and underwriting the value of communal tribute. The Bourbon state would undertake to restore the traditional rights of community members to a minimum of subsistence security as long as their caciques met their obligations to the state.

The issue of legitimate Andean rule in the villages, which had been raised in the middle of the eighteenth century by the eruption of feuds and the pressures of the repartimiento (see chapter 4), continued to vex Viedma and other intendants. In Tapacarí, as seen earlier, there was a prolonged political struggle between the Condoris and the Liro de Córdovas over the right to moiety rule. The intendants were unwilling to leave the question of cacique legitimacy to the ad hoc decision making of the audiencia. Furthermore, barely a decade had passed since the rebellions, and the state needed to monitor closely the succession to power in the villages. The Ordinance of Intendants, enacted in 1782, restored many of the Toledan regulations governing the accession to and transmission of ethnic authority. For example, members of the village hierarchy (alcaldes, cobradores, etc.) were to be elected by natives in the community, and the position of cacique was to go only to members of a noble line-

21 The Ordinance of Intendants (1782) outlawed the repartimiento de mercancías, and at the same time authorized the establishment of government-run shops in which Indians could purchase goods at regulated prices and on credit. The law was opposed by most intendants; only Viedma and the intendant of Paraguay took concrete measures to implement it. See Lynch, *Spanish Colonial Administration*, 196-199.

age.[22] But whereas in Toledo's day noble lineages produced numerous heirs, in the 1790s many villages could not come up with direct descendants of noble ancestors. Viedma complained that "the decadence of the Indians and the lack of legitimate succession is the cause of confusion and chaos [in selecting caciques]."[23] Without caciques of noble lineage to inherit the staff of office, it was left to the subdelegado to select candidates for the cacicazgo. Sometimes, the local authority appointed a native; on other occasions, subdelegadoes nominated two or three "appropriate candidates" from among whom the village could elect one. According to Viedma, local Spanish authorities employed various means of maneuvering certain individuals into positions of power in the village hierarchy, although the crown tried to limit this by stipulating that colonial authorities could appoint caciques interinos or "governors" only if no legitimate heir could be identified.[24]

Royal authorities were also granted the power to intervene in villages where the cacicazgo was in dispute among blood relatives of a former cacique. The members of a parcialidad may have had the right to choose a cacique from among several claimants, but the intendant or the subdelegado had the right to pass judgment on the "eligibility" of the candidates, thus preserving a mechanism by which colonial authorities could manipulate the ethnic hierarchy of villages. An heir to the cacicazgo was also supposed to prove himself fluent in Spanish and skilled in agriculture and crafts.[25] In practice, however, very little had changed since the middle of the eighteenth century. Local royal authorities sought candidates who were close kin to the former cacique and who were wealthy enough to underwrite their moiety's tribute dues. In an age of heavier taxation, this latter qualification was especially important, lest the subdelegado find himself in arrears to the royal exchequer. In the 1790s, the subdelegado of Arque explained to the judges of the audiencia that

22 These matters were dealt with in arts. 10 and 11 of the ordinance. See also "Exp. sobre los indios que deben elegir sus alcaldes," ANB, EC no. 245 (1796), and "Exp. sobre los indios alcaldes en Carangas," ANB, EC no. 247 (1796).

23 "Exp. de elecciones de caciques interinos de Capinota," ANB, EC no. 72 (1796).

24 "Exp. por Clemente Choque sobre el dueño del cacicazgo," ANB, EC no. 48 (1796), f. 15.

25 "Exp. con la nomina de las elecciones de alcaldes indios," ANB, EC no. 136 (1794); "Confirmación de indios de la elección de alcaldes de Oruro, año de 1795," ANB, EC no. 24 (1795), f. 6.

he appointed caciques only if they could guarantee the entire tribute quota;[26] and in court battle in Santiago de Berenguela, a creole litigant admitted that an Indian had been named sole candidate for the cacicazgo because "he is the legitimate grandson of Don Diego Condorena and because he could underwrite the royal tribute debt for the value of 12,000 pesos."[27] In spite of the royal proclamations to the contrary, material assets still outweighed kinship and service to the community in the selection of native candidates for the village hierarchy.

Another important attribute for a cacique was proven loyalty to the crown. The litmus test was the Indian's behavior during the 1781 rebellions. Rebel leaders had been executed, but in the lingering climate of fear and suspicion, the slightest indication that a prospective cacique had sympathized with the insurgents could be disabling. Subdelegados could rule out a candidate because of a report of suspicious behavior a decade earlier. Intravillage disputes over the cacicazgo sometimes led to accusations of sedition during the general uprisings. One such case occurred in Capinota during the mid-1790s, when Ygnacio Condo challenged the subdelegado's choice of a distant cousin, Guillermo Condo, as cacique.[28] Ygnacio claimed to be the legitimate heir upon his father's death in 1782. However, because he was too young at the time, the cacicazgo passed to his uncle, Tomás Condo. In the meantime, Ygnacio served as a mitayo and then as a principal. When his uncle died, the cacicazgo was passed to his cousin, the cacique of Anansaya and an enemy of his family. Ygnacio declared that Guillermo, his father, and a brother had been traitorous in 1780 and 1781, having traveled through villages inciting Indians to rebel, in alliance with the Chayanta rebel leader, Tomás Catari. Ygnacio's own father, a cacique at the time, had remained loyal and fled to the city of Cochabamba to hide from the rebels. Ygnacio's story was disputed by his cousin, and the subdelegado ruled in Guillermo's favor. The trial reveals how the legacy of rebellion and war could feed into ethnic rivalries and power struggles at a time when the state was trying to control the village hierarchy.

The basic purpose of the reforms of the late eighteenth century

26 "Exp. sobre que don Augustín Jascata hace renuncia del cargo de cacique . . . de Capinota," ANB, EC no. 158 (1808).

27 "Exp. por Nicholás Condorena sobre el derecho al cacicazgo de . . . Santiago de Berenguela," ANB, EC no. 158 (1799).

28 "Exp. sobre que don Augustín Jascata hace renuncia del cargo de cacique . . . de Capinota," ANB, EC no. 158 (1808).

was to resurrect, in modified form, the extractive model of exploitation that Toledo had introduced into the Andes some two centuries earlier. The Bourbons sought to rebuild the twin pillars of that model, the institutions of tribute and the mita, and to initiate a new cycle of taxation. But there was much to be done at the village level before the apparatus of extraction could function. If the state was once again to enforce the extraction of tribute and the flow of migrants to the silver mines of Potosí, it would have to protect the subsistence base of Andean communities much more diligently than it had in the recent past. The abolition of the repartimiento de mercancías and the displacement of the corregidores were important first steps. Further, as in Toledo's day, the intendants were ordered to intervene in the internal affairs of the villages and to mediate the relations between caciques and peasants. The state was to penetrate to the very heart of the community to alleviate the social ills that had resulted from almost two centuries of neglect and abuse.

But if the Bourbons' reforms looked very much like Toledo's ordinances, the social landscape of the Indian villages was not at all the same. The villages were sharply differentiated in their degree of self-sufficiency, cultural cohesiveness, and adherence to traditional norms governing relations of production. Many villages in Alto Perú had proved relatively resilient in maintaining their unity and cultural integrity against the forces of attrition and fragmentation.[29] But colonialism had sapped the internal resources and broken down the moral fiber of many other villages. In Cochabamba, the decay of communal traditions in the pueblos reales put to test the effectiveness of the Bourbons' social reforms.

For all his ambition and innovation, Viedma's administration had little impact on village society. His land reform did no more than paper over class divisions and increase the tribute rates of many former forasteros. It did not release peasants from subservience to prosperous, powerful, landholding Indians. Furthermore, Viedma's call for the payment of outstanding interest on the mortgage loans that had been issued by the villages could not be enforced. Heavily indebted landowners objected to making interest payments on loans contracted by their grandfathers or great-grandfathers. The regulations on cacique succession were manipulated by subdelegados,

---

29 Indeed, many communities had not only maintained their self-sufficiency but had even flourished by marketing wheat at Potosí and by preserving the tradition of dual residence in puna and valley zones. See Platt, *Estado boliviano y ayllu andino*, chap. 1.

much as corregidores had done earlier (see chapters 3 and 4). Even the intendant's efforts to shield the villages from coercive mercantile practices proved ineffective.[30]

In short, Viedma's reforms failed. Yet the tragedy of the Bourbon decades lay not so much in the failure of the state to redistribute community resources more equitably or to protect the villages from exploitation, but rather in its spectacular success in draining revenue from the native subjects. Where the social reforms failed, the fiscal reforms launched a new cycle of extraction that left the villages more impoverished than ever.

The Bankruptcy of Reform

Beginning in the 1770s, the Bourbons took systematic measures to generate more tax revenue in the Andes. The creation of the viceroyalty of La Plata was but one administrative change that decade designed to curtail contraband and siphon off more revenue from the colony. Tribute and taxes on mining were still the major sources of royal income in the southern Andes, but the state was turning increasingly to other sources. By the first decade of the nineteenth century, the financial burden of empire was beginning to weigh heavily on the merchant, mining, and landholding elites.

From the imperial point of view, the need to increase revenue from the colonies arose out of the desire to strengthen royal authority over them and to deter mercantile and military encroachment by England and her ally, Portugal. To increase revenue required in turn that the colonial economy be stimulated in ways that were not detrimental to the economic interests of the metropolitan elite. An overhaul of the fiscal system was also in order. It was in this last area of reform that the Bourbons achieved their greatest success in the viceroyalties of Peru and La Plata.[31]

---

30 These problems were not peculiar to Cochabamba, of course. Elsewhere in Peru, as Fisher has pointed out, "many subdelegates, especially in the sierra, continued the repartimientos and other abuses, and the intendants, as a result of indifference or impotence, or both, failed to check their activities." J. Fisher, *Government and Society in Colonial Peru*, 91. The problem of corruption was widely discussed in the 1780s by several intendants. They pointed to the lack of suitable candidates for the low-prestige post of subdelegado. In 1784, the bishop of Santa Cruz deplored the unsuitable character of most subdelegados in the Cochabamba region. Rather than "professionalize" this level of the bureaucracy, the crown granted the post to local landlords and petty officials with appropriate connections. Lynch, *Spanish Colonial Administration*, 76-77.

31 Fisher notes that "the general condition of the [Peruvian] viceregal exchequer

The need for increased revenue became particularly acute with the creation of the viceroyalty of La Plata in 1776. The sparse settlement of the pampas and the lack of economic activity except for cattle ranching and the export of hides made the extensive zone south of Tucumán a relatively unprofitable region. Without tax revenues from the northern provinces of Alto Perú, the new viceroyalty would have been economically unviable. Indian tribute and taxes on trade and silver mining were the main sources of the cash needed to pay the high cost of maintaining a bureaucracy and of protecting the Atlantic coastline from Portuguese and British interlopers.[32]

Even in times of peace, Buenos Aires drained funds from the interior provinces. In 1790, for example, Potosí transferred 818,768 pesos to the viceregal treasury at Buenos Aires.[33] Part of that money originated in Potosí itself—from mining taxes, tribute, and customs duties. Another part probably derived from revenue raised in the subordinate territories of La Paz, Cochabamba, and La Plata, which the Potosí authorities collected and transmitted to Buenos Aires.[34] Cochabamba was not the highest revenue producer in the viceroyalty. Potosí, with its mining taxes; La Paz, with its high tribute revenues (more than twice those of Cochabamba in 1790, and 80 percent of La Paz's total tax revenues in that year); and Buenos Aires, with its rich returns from customs duties, all generated more income for the state. But together, the four intendancies of Alto Perú supported the import-export trade of the port of Buenos Aires and helped to offset the annual deficits in the Buenos Aires treasury. In 1790, this deficit amounted to 123 percent of income that year; the revenue received from the interior provinces reduced it to 108 percent of income.[35]

---

improved considerably between 1782 and 1787.": J. Fisher, *Government and Society in Colonial Peru*, 118. Lynch argues that, while the overhaul of the fiscal machinery was only partly successful in the viceroyalty of La Plata, "it gave a unified and vigorous stimulus to honesty and efficiency": *Spanish Colonial Administration*, 131.

32 In 1790, mineral taxes generated 1,102,642 pesos (32 percent of the total revenues 3.4 million pesos that year); commercial imposts, 749,617 pesos (22 percent); and tribute, 562,528 pesos (16 percent). Herbert Klein, "Structure and Profitability of Royal Finance in the Viceroyalty of the Río de la Plata in 1790," *Hispanic American Historical Review* 53 (1973): 444. Klein estimates that at least two-fifths of royal expenditures went to maintain the viceroyalty's bureaucracy. Ibid., 455.

33 Ibid., 451.

34 Ibid., 463.

35 Ibid., 453.

Yet even with that help, the viceregal treasury was in a chronic state of indebtedness. In 1790, almost 40 percent of all viceregal expenditures went to maintain the bureaucracy. In fact, the viceroyalty was barely able to pay for its own maintenance and military security. Although it was the second largest taxation zone in the entire empire after New Spain, the viceroyalty of La Plata nevertheless remitted little income to Madrid. Although the royal revenues generated in the viceroyalty of La Plata were more than 20 percent of the revenues raised in New Spain, the southern viceroyalty sent to the mother country tax monies that amounted to only about 6 percent of Mexico's remittances. The tax revenue from the interior provinces of Alto Perú was therefore crucial for the maintenance of this Spanish colony.[36]

Why, then, were the Bourbons so determined to increase royal income in the southern zone if so little revenue actually reached the metropolis? Part of the reason lies in Spain's need to defend the Atlantic coast, as part of the struggle against England in the New World, and to close the river basin area to British and Portuguese contraband trade. This was particularly important because La Plata was a potential market for Catalan textiles and other metropolitan goods. In other words, to the people of Alto Peru, higher taxes would mean increased commercial competition from Spanish manufacturers.

The advent of new taxes and fiscal policies had far-reaching effects on the economy and society of Cochabamba. Shortly before the creation of the intendancy, royal administrators had begun to reorganize the provincial treasuries of Alto Perú. Previously, the Potosí treasury had served as the central treasury for all of the provinces of Alto Perúa. Royal income from Cochabamba flowed into that *caja principal*, which then remitted a portion of the revenue to the viceregal treasury in Lima. In 1773, the crown established two other treasuries in Charcas: one in La Plata and the other in Cochabamba. Three years later, with the creation of the viceroyalty of La Plata, the treasury at Buenos Aires became the *tribunal mayor de cuentas*, or principal accounts office, although Potosí's treasury continued to be the central accounting office for Alto Perú. There was also a network of subsidiary treasuries (*cajas surbordinadas*) throughout the Viceroyalty, each of which sent its accounts and part of its income to either Potosí or Buenos Aires. Cochabamba was one such caja subordinada, sending its excess revenue to Potosí.[37]

36 Ibid., 456.

37 On the fiscal reforms under the Bourbons, see Klein, "Structure and Profita-

Extant records of these treasuries show that gross royal income in Cochabamba increased five and a half times between 1757 and 1809 (see figure 14). Part of that increase reflected the fact that after the establishment of Cochabamba's treasury in 1773, the province of Mizque remitted its revenue there. But Mizque's economy was in decay and its tributary population was small, so the province could not have been an important revenue producer. The increase in Cochabamba's revenue derived mainly from improved methods of collection, additional taxes that weighed more heavily upon the elite, and the increase of tributary population in the central valleys. After 1780, royal authorities levied a 6 percent ad valorem tax (alcabala) on the sale of goods, local tribute collection was systematized, and the state imposed a host of new taxes on commercial activities. Despite poor harvest conditions in the early 1780s, the state extracted an increasingly large surplus from the province.

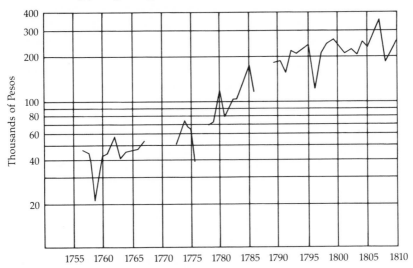

Figure 14 Gross Royal Income from Cochabamba, 1757-1809
Sources: See table A-6, and AHMC, Leg. 1175 (1757-1767).
Note: Gross royal income includes uncollected taxes and residual income from previous years.

bility,"441-443; Lynch, *Spanish Colonial Administration*, chap. 6; Guillermo Céspedes de Castillo, "Reorganización de la hacienda virreinal peruana en el siglo XVIII," *Anuario de historia del derecho español* 23 (1953): 329-369; and Pedro Santos Martínez, *Historia económica de Mendoza durante el virreinato, 1776-1810* (Madrid: Universidad Nacional de Cuyo, 1961), chap. 6. For the instructions on account keeping published by the crown in 1784, see "Nuevo método de cuenta y razón para la real hacienda en las Indias," reprinted in *Revista de la Biblioteca Nacional* (Buenos Aires) 4 (1940): 267-318.

The effect of the fiscal reforms on tribute was particularly dramatic. Tribute revenue rose from an annual average of less than 50,000 pesos between 1780 and 1784 to an annual average of almost 100,000 pesos in the quinquennium 1800-1804, though it subsequently declined as a result of the famine of 1804 (see table A-6). From the imperial perspective, this increase was the most notable achievement of Viedma's administration. Ever since the 1730s, royal agents had tried to increase tribute revenue in the Cochabamba valleys. Forasteros were made liable for tribute in that decade, but authorities were notably unsuccessful in collecting the tax (see chapter 3). Viedma's feat in managing to wring substantially more tribute money out of the Cochabamba peasantry was not a minor one, since tribute made up more than 40 percent of the total income of the provincial treasury (see table A-6).

The effect of the tax reforms on the peasantry was quite different. Only a few years after the abolition of the repartimiento de mercancías, tribute obligations began to depress the economic conditions of forastero households. The more rigorous procedures of tax collection left fewer places to hide. Between 1786 and 1808, royal agents fanned out over the territory on four separate occasions to hunt for tributaries and prospective tributaries. In Cochabamba, tax collectors were aided by Viedma, who toured the countryside and conducted his own census (see chapter 5). The fiscal reforms also widened the gap between the tax burdens of the valley peasants and those of the highland natives in the rest of Alto Perú. Since the Indians of the maize valleys were considered to have access to acreage of higher quality than that available to their highland counterparts, they paid premium rates. Landless forasteros of Cochabamba were expected to pay six pesos two reales a year—more than most landholding originarios of the puna paid.[38] This was the reason why the Carangas Indians of Sicaya, near the valleys of Capinota, fought to retain their vertical ties to their highland community of Toledo; although the quality of the land there was poorer than that in most valley areas of Cochabamba, their status as originarios would have meant lower tax rates (see chapter 4).

Alcabalas, the taxes on trade and commerce, constituted about 15

---

38 A visitador who made an inspection of Cochabamba in 1793 noted that forasteros were not supposed to pay more than seven pesos in tribute each year and that in most provinces of Alto Perú they paid only five pesos, except in Potosí, where they often paid seven. "Informe de la contaduría de retasas sobre la revisita del partido de Santa Cruz," Feb. 25, 1793, RAH, ML, 9/1733, tomo 78, ff. 170-172.

percent of royal income from the province. The "royal ninth" (*real noveno*), a tax of 11 percent levied on tithes, was an important source of revenue (see table A-6), but it was the alcabalas that were the heaviest burden on producers and traders. As part of the Bourbon reforms, tax farming was replaced with methods of direct collection, toll houses were established along the river trade routes of Arque and Tapacarí, and in 1780 the rate of alcabalas was raised to 6 percent from its previous level of 4 percent. Alcabala revenues increased sharply in the 1770s and again in the late 1780s, after the region had recovered from the rebellions. This was a period of relatively sluggish trade and generally stagnant prices, so the increased revenue from alcabalas simply reflected the higher rate and the stricter enforcement. In 1774 and again in 1780, wealthy merchants and rural craftsmen briefly united in opposition to the reforms, and there were some incidents of mob action (see chapter 5).[39]

By 1800, the region's population had endured twenty-five years of tax reforms. The overhaul of the fiscal machinery and the establishment of a provincial treasury in Cochabamba had produced spectacular results. But it also imposed relentless pressure on most people and drained the region of scarce capital at a time when Viedma was trying to rejuvenate its economy. Above all, increased tribute income—the main source of royal revenue in Cochabamba—cut into the subsistence production of peasants, even as the regional economy began to deteriorate after the turn of the nineteenth century. In good times and bad, the peasant family had to meet its obligations to the state. Spanish absolutism made no concessions to human misfortune, even when drought struck and famine stalked the arid land.

Early in 1805, Viedma wrote despairingly to the consulado of Buenos Aires:

> We have had a serious shortage of water during the last five years, especially in the past year. There are not voices to express the calamity and hunger that the miserable Indians and mestizos suffer, such that they must beg to live. Agriculture, the only livelihood of these people, has not yet yielded its fruits. The tocuyo trade has decayed, and public works have ceased due to a

---

39 "Testio. del procurador gral . . . ," AGI, Charcas, Leg. 505 (1794). See above, chap. 5, no. 90. There was much contemporary debate over the exemption of Indian traders from alcabala levies; see "Exp. del recurso hecho por Don Manuel Maruri c/ el gob. de Potosí sobre que no le embarase el cobro de dhas alcabalas de los indios . . . ," ANB, Minas, tomo 149, no. 81; "Documento sobre la exención de la alcabala que debe gozar los indios," ANB, EC no. 141 (1779).

shortage of capital. Everything is lamentable. People wander in masses, begging in the towns and countryside. They eat roots of withered grass in order to survive. . . . [They] are wandering corpses, and many collapse, dead from starvation.[40]

Viedma's description could have applied to any region of Alto Perú. Authorities reported that the highland peasants suffered even more acutely, particularly near the salt pans of Lake Poopó, where even in good years the arid altiplano yielded only quinoa and bitter potatoes. They reported an increase in mortality rates, the extermination of livestock, and the total loss of the harvest, including next year's seeds. Everywhere, people had turned to begging and scavenging, eating wild roots and wood in their quiet desperation.[41]

This crisis pierced the veil of Bourbon "enlightenment" and revealed the imperatives of imperial rule. In 1805, in the midst of human misery, an executive order to all intendants, caciques, and alcaldes demanded that they account for the decline of tribute revenues and the delay in the remittances. Local authorities were reminded that tributes were due promptly on January 25 (the Christmas installment) and June 25 (following collection on San Juan's Day). No excuse was acceptable, neither natural calamity nor human deprivation.[42]

The subsistence crisis of the first decade of the nineteenth century broke the peasant family economy, fragmented Andean communities, and destroyed regional economies. Revenue from tribute and economic activity plummeted as a result. In Cochabamba, royal income from tribute, alcabalas, and novenos reales declined after 1804 and did not recover for the rest of the decade. Tribute dropped sharply, from 465,368 pesos in the 1800-1804 period to 277,560 pesos in the 1805-1809 period. Where tribute had represented almost half of all royal income in Cochabamba during the earlier period, it represented only 36 percent in the later one (see table A-6). As tax revenue from economic activity and tribute dried up, the provincial treasury, in a search for other sources of income, even taxed the upper classes (see below). Nevertheless, the treasury's net income

40 AGN, Sala 13, Cajas Reales, 5.8.7, Jan. 13, 1805.

41 "Exp. de yndios de Carasa solicitando el convento de San Augustín les rebajen el arriendo por la calamidad del año, AHMC, Leg. 1099 (1804); AGN, Sala 9, Intendencia, 5.8.7, Feb. 15, 1804, and Feb.-Mar., 1805. See also chap. 6.

42 "Exp. sobre que los caciques cobradores pasen a pagar sus cobranzas a la tesorería," ANB, EC no. 198 (1805).

dropped sharply after 1802, and between 1804 and 1808, royal expenditures outstripped royal income. Moreover, the treasury was sending a larger and larger proportion of its revenue out of the region, to the superordinate treasures of Buenos Aires and Potosí and, after 1803, to the newly established treasury of Santa Cruz. What was more ominous, tax collections were lagging. Uncollected tax liabilities nearly doubled between 1795-1799 and 1800-1804 and increased by another 50 percent in the next five-year period. The amount of uncollected taxes averaged 32,494 pesos a year between 1805 and 1809.[43] Just when Buenos Aires was draining off more royal income from Cochabamba, more and more people were simply evading the tax collectors.

The growing burden of imperial finance reflected the militarization of colonial society during the first decade of the nineteenth century. The royal revenue itemized as *otras tesorerías* (other treasuries), in the debit column of the ledger, was earmarked for expenses outside the province. The precise destination of these funds cannot be traced, but most of them probably went to defray military costs in the River Plate region. It is surely no accident, for instance, that a huge increase in otras tesorerías, from approximately 92,800 pesos in 1806 to 141,900 pesos in 1807, followed immediately upon the British invasion of Buenos Aires.[44] Intensified efforts to militarize the intendancies of Alto Perú also absorbed more royal revenue in this decade. Royal expenditures on military salaries, for example, rarely surpassed 4,000 pesos annually before 1800, but in 1807 and again in 1809, they were about 79,000 pesos.[45]

In 1807, the provisional junta of the royal treasury in Cochabamba met to organize the "war effort." The junta planned to stockpile supplies of wood, iron, gunpowder, and other materials needed for the local production of weaponry.[46] Although the intendancy of Santa Cruz de la Sierra was buried in the interior of the colony, hundreds of miles from Buenos Aires, its uncharted eastern frontier bordered Portuguese territory and thus was a point of penetration for both the

43 AGN, Sala 13, Cajas reales 27.4.4, Leg.236 (1795); 5.5.3, Leg. 18 (1796); 27.5.2, Leg. 240 (1797); 27.5.4, Leg. 241 (1798); 27.6.1, Leg. 243 (1799); 5.6.1, Leg. 22 (1800); 5.6.2, Leg. 23 (1801); 5.6.3, Leg. 24 (1802); 5.6.4, Leg. 25 (1803); 5.7.1, Leg. 28 (1804); 5.7.3, Leg. 30 (1805); 5.8.1, Leg. 34 (1806); 5.8.4, Leg. 37 (1807); 5.9.1, Leg. 40 (1808); 5.9.5, Leg. 44 (1809).

44 AGN, Sala 13, Cajas reales, 5.8.1, Leg. 34 (1806), and 5.8.4, Leg. 37 (1807).

45 AGN, Sala 13, Cajas reales, 5.8.4, Leg. 37 (1807), and 5.9.5, Leg. 44 (1809).

46 AGN, Sala 9, Intendencia, 5.9.1, Sept. 4, 1807.

Portuguese and their British allies. Emergency measures were called for if the intendancy was to be protected from the "heathen enemy."

That meant, essentially, that more royal revenue had to be squeezed out of the local population. For the first time, religious institutions, wealthy merchants, and landowners in the central valleys of Cochabamba were taxed. The region's monasteries, convents, and cofradías were required to pay 15 percent on the value of interest on loans and on the sale of their properties.[47] In 1808, as Napoleon's armies swarmed over the Iberian peninsula, the treasury forced the region's monasteries to "lend" it cash, in the amount of 19,462 pesos.[48] Persons inheriting property worth more than 2,000 pesos had to pay either 2 or 4 percent of the value of their inheritance, depending on their relationship to their benefactor.[49] Other vecinos found themselves cajoled or coerced into lending money to the government.[50] As it turned out, these fiscal pressures came at the beginning of a long period of insurgency that would plunder and exhaust the regional economy until the last vestiges of Spanish imperial rule were finally destroyed in 1824 and 1825.

The crisis years between 1804 and 1808 closed the chapter of Bourbon reforms in Alto Perú and initiated the long period of insurgency that culminated in Independence. In the Cochabamba region, the social impact of two decades of reform was contradictory. On the one hand, class antagonisms were intensified. Agrarian class relations deteriorated sharply, as large numbers of rural people were struck by famine and destitution. Class polarizations were never so nakedly exposed as in 1804, when tithe dealers paid record prices to capitalize on the scarcity and soaring prices of maize and wheat. Peasants saw tithe speculators and large landowners feeding on their misfortune. Crop failures eliminated the smallholders as sellers in the

---

47 AGN, Sala 13, Cajas reales, 5.7.3, Leg. 30 (1805), and 5.8.4, Leg. 37 (1807). This measure was applied to the entire colony. See Brian Hamnett, "The Appropriation of Mexican Church Wealth by the Spanish Bourbon Government: The 'Consolidation of Vales Reales,' 1805-1809," *Journal of Latin American Studies*, 1 (1969): 86-91.

48 AGN, Sala 13, Cajas reales, 5.9.1, Leg. 40 (1808).

49 Ibid.

50 In early 1807, Cochabamba's largest merchant, Francisco Ventura Valiente, donated five hundred pesos for "extraordinary expenses in the defense of the capital" against the British invaders. He also supplied one thousand varas of tocuyos for bandages. AGN, Sala 9, Intendencia, 5.9.1 (1807).

marketplace and brought a temporary restoration of agrarian mono-
ply to landowners, merchants, and diezmeros. Social tensions in the
region were compounded by the collapse of the tocuyo trade after
1802, for not only did the collapse hurt the artisans and merchants
involved in the textile industry, but the bonanza that preceded it had
concentrated wealth in the hands of a few merchants able to capitalize on the long-distance overland trade. Artisans were marginalized
from the wholesale trade, and many fell into debt and dependence
upon merchant-creditors (see chapter 7). During the years ushering
in the nineteenth century, the terms of exchange shifted against the
plebe and peasantry.

On the other hand, the great disparity between the ideals of reform
and the harsh reality of reform left a bitter legacy that turned most
people in the region against the Bourbon state. The disillusionment
with imperial rule gave the region's wealthy and poor something in
common that was potentially explosive. The Andean inhabitants of
the pueblos reales saw that the reforms had failed to restore the economic autonomy of their villages or correct the extreme imbalances
in the internal distribution of communal resources. Instead, they
faced a more coercive, extractive state apparatus, and one without
the power or willingness to provide the patronage that the Toledan
state had offered in return for tribute and mitayos. Worse still from
their point of view was the moral ignominy of a colonial state that
demanded more tribute during the worst famine in memory. Meanwhile, class privilege offered less and less immunity from royal taxation. The wealthy were being ferreted out as sources of income with
which to meet military needs. But even before the Napoleonic invasion of Spain, the regional elite had begun to see false promises in
the economic reforms proposed by their innovative intendant. Promises of frontier colonization and industrial growth disintegrated before royal opposition and regional rivalry. By 1804, the horizons of
potential entrepreneurs had narrowed and disillusionment had set
in. There seemed to be no road out of the region's economic quagmire, after all.

Thus, while the conjuncture of economic crisis and growing disillusionment did not forge a popular movement or unite landowners
and peasants, it may have created a common ground. But then, for a
short period between 1810 and 1812, extraordinary circumstances
would unite the rich and the poor in an insurgency movement
against royal troops. Creole landowners struck out from Cochabamba to defeat the royalists in the town of Aroma, on the altiplano,
while in the heartlands of the region, Andean and cholo peasants

brandished primitive arms and tools against the invading Spanish cavalry. Fragile bonds of solidarity momentarily turned the region of Cochabamba into a symbol of anticolonialism and the center of Alto Perú's struggle for independence.[51]

To end the story of agrarian conflict and change in colonial Cochabamba on this note would, perhaps, create false expectations. Class tensions and contradictions were not subsumed for long in the decolonization movement. Populist myths concerning participation in the independence struggles in Cochabamba tend to obscure the class conflicts that surfaced again after fifteen years of intermittent fighting had finally brought victory. The war brought many changes, particularly in the composition of the landowning elite and the ownership of valley lands. But it did not shatter the agrarian class structure or release the peasantry from the burdens of heavy taxation. On the contrary, the new state was built on the fiscal foundations of the old, and a new cycle of tributary extractions was set in motion.

But if the creole state resurrected, in an altered form, a political economy of colonialism, it also inherited a refractory peasantry in the maize valleys, who historically had demonstrated the limits of state power. That had happened, dramatically, in the tribute rebellion of 1730. But more often, peasants had shaped the contours of class society in the region, and confronted the injustices of colonialism, in their everyday activities, prosaically rather than heroically. The local tradition of resistance was not one of visible, collective action guided by native or class ideology. Rather, peasant defiance was expressed in minor acts of resistance, such as slipping through the interstices of the tribute system. Over time, these silent strategies of "passive resistance" had challenged the model of colonial exploitation based on caste and turned the Cochabamba region into a symbol of its erosion. When the creole state tried in the 1830s to impose that model once again, it encountered the limits of its capacity to discipline the valley peasants. The legacy of peasant resistance threatened the continuity of the neocolonial order.

51 Guzman, *Cochabamba*, pp. 126-129; Charles Arnade, *The Emergence of the Republic of Bolivia* (Gainesville: University of Florida Press, 1957), 32-37; and René Arce, *Participación popular en la independencia de Bolivia* (La Paz: Colegio Don Bosco, 1979).

Colonial Legacies
and Class Formation

Like so many social historians, I often searched, while in Bolivia, for visible links to the colonial past in contemporary rural society. I was eager to find material artifacts that would make rural colonial society seem less abstract and textureless. Such vestiges of the past were not hard to find. During a hike early one Sunday morning into the quebradas of Sacaba, I came upon an ancient grain mill, owned and worked by a local peasant and his young son. A walk on the outskirts of the city of Cochabamba led to a half-eroded hacienda, now inhabited by poor migrant families; it was an estate registered in the eighteenth-century notarial books I had been working with. An eight-hour truck ride up the Tapacarí riverbed deposited me in San Augustín de Tapacarí, a village of thatched-roof huts, perched precariously on a hillside at the confluence of rivers, that once claimed to be the province's most important pueblo real and a major trade route to the western altiplano.

But I found more vital and vivid legacies of the past in the small peasant enterprises and weekly ferias that still thrive in the central valleys. The presence of the colonial past is to be found, for example, in Cliza's marketplace on Sunday, where thousands of peasants congregate from dawn until midday, haggling in Quechua over the prices of sheep, potato seed, and coca. It is also to be found in the peasant families of Punata, who are cultivators, peddlers, and chicha-makers; and in peasant households such as the one I visited in Sacaba, where the household head weaves bayeta, and his wife markets it, when agricultural work does not occupy them. Contemporary scenes of a robust peasant economy, based on *producción parcelaria* (small-scale agriculture) and a strong commercial orientation, are not byproducts of the 1953 agrarian reform. They harken back to colonial times. As we saw, a distinct peasant economy began to assume form and force in the later part of the eighteenth-century,

295

emerging from, and accelerating, the fragmentation of rural property units and the erosion of the economic power of landowners.

But there is a darker scene, far from the valleys, that also stands as mute testimony to the historical evolution of agrarian class relations in eighteenth and nineteenth-century Cochabamba. Today, in the mine shafts of San José, on the outskirts of Oruro, and in the tin mines of Siglo XX-Uncía, a large number (perhaps a majority) of the workers are the sons or grandsons of Cochabamba peasants. In the early twentieth century, these migrant peasants from the valleys composed the body of an incipient industrial proletariat that extracted crude ore from the new or "modernized" mines that fed the industrialized nations with the tin, tungsten, lead, and copper that they craved.

These are contrasting images: an enterprising peasant family that combines agriculture, craft production, commerce, and occasional day labor, and a mine worker whose father severed his roots in the land and cast his fate with the demons of the industrial underworld. The contrast would seem a contradiction in historical terms, one that feeds into the on-going debate over the impact of capitalism on Latin American peasantries.[1] On the one hand, the region may be seen as a symbol of the resilience and resourcefulness of a peasantry that is famous for its diversified economy. Even today, there is little agrarian capitalist enterprise in Cochabamba; small-scale peasant and artisan production still reigns supreme. It is the petty commod-

---

1 The basic issue in the debate is whether the peasant economy has the capacity to survive and reproduce itself under dependent capitalism, or will gradually disappear as capitalist relations penetrate the countryside. The two principal schools of thought revolve around the early debates over the transition to capitalism in the Russian countryside. Latin American exponents of "peasantization" are influenced by the principal work of A. V. Chayanov, *The Theory of the Peasant Family Economy*, ed. and trans. D. Thorner, B. Verblay, and R.E.F. Smith (Homewood, Ill.: Irwin, 1966); those who argue that peasants tend to become proletarians usually take, as their conceptual point of departure, V. I. Lenin, *The Rise of Capitalism in Russia* (Moscow: Progress, 1974). Much of this controversy is cast in terms of "articulating modes of production" and the relative importance, functional symbiosis, and inherent historical tendencies of interpenetrating modes of production. See Foster-Carter, "Modes of Production Controversy." For summaries of the issues and debate as they relate to Latin America, see Alain de Janvry, *The Agrarian Question and Reformism in Latin America* (Baltimore: The Johns Hopkins University Press, 1981), esp. chap. 3; Alain de Janvry and L. A. Couch, "El debate sobre el campesinado: Teoría y significación política," *Estudios rurales latinoamericanos* 2 (1979): 282-295; and Richard L. Harris, "Marxism and the Agrarian Question in Latin America," *Latin American Perspectives* 5 (1978): 2-26.

ity producer who supplies the towns and cities across the region.[2] From a short-term regional perspective, the historical resilience of the peasant class looms large. Yet, on the other hand, the region expelled peasants into the capitalist export sector; they became the main source of a dispossessed labor force in mining around the beginning of the twentieth century. The decomposition of the peasantry spawned a nascent industrial proletariat.

From a long-term historical perspective, these apparently contradictory tendencies—the social reproduction of the peasantry and its simultaneous erosion—are simply two aspects of the process of advancing social differentiation within the peasant class. As throughout the colonial past, so also in the postindependence period, peasants were both protagonists in their struggle for a livelihood and for just terms of exchange and also the objects, often the victims, of historical forces and ecological pressures that threatened their precarious existence and often forced them to surrender to the harsh terms of the labor market. In some cases, migration to wagework in the mines brought supplementary income that strengthened the viability of the peasant family economy. But in countless other cases, valley peasants and rural laborers succumbed to the emerging industrial regime out of desperation. For many rural cultivators, the erosion of sources of subsistence during the nineteenth-century was the most important legacy of colonialism. It was this legacy that created, out of those at the bottom of the rural social heap, an industrial proletariat.

In the following pages, by way of conclusion, I will gather together the various strands of the preceding analysis of class formation under colonial rule in the Cochabamba region. I will then turn to explore the contradictory processes of social differentiation within the Cochabamba peasantry, as it confronted a neocolonial order and then the penetration of foreign capital in the late nineteenth century.[3]

2 Jorge Dandler Hanhart, "Diversificación, procesos de trabajo, y movilidad espacial en los valles y serranías de Cochabamba," in Harris, Larson, and Tandeter, *Participación indígena*, 639-682. Dandler's research on the peasant family economy in different zones of the region of Cochabamba is part of a team project under the auspices of the Centro para el Estudio de la Realidad Económica y Social (CERES).

3 The aim of this chapter is heuristic: to broadly interpret regional agrarian change in the nineteenth and twentieth centuries and to suggest future directions of research for testing these interpretations. For many of the ideas explored in this chapter, I am indebted to Tristan Platt and Ramiro Molina Barrios, for

Historical Roots of Agrarian Classes

As this study has shown, the origins of agrarian class formation date to the early colonial period. During the later part of the sixteenth century, a class structure based upon the private control of land and the expropriation of surplus from economically dependent peasants took root in the valleys. The development of this precapitalist agrarian order, however, was neither an inevitable nor an irrevocable response to the European invasion and the incursion of market forces. The early European colonizers were extraordinarily successful in their efforts to impose control over Indian land and labor in the valleys, but in many surrounding regions, particularly in the highlands and across the altiplano, the advance of private landownership and class relationships did not occur until the later part of the nineteenth-century. Andean ethnic groups continued to have collective access to land in exchange for some degree of compliance to the tributary demands of the colonial state.

In the Cochabamba region, a peculiar configuration of conditions made it possible for Europeans to overcome Andean resistance and establish a firm foothold in the valleys by the 1570s and 1580s. The precolonial heritage of Inca rule and mitmaq settlement in the region impeded the ability of Andean peoples to forge ethnic alliances and block European encroachment following the Spanish Conquest. On the one hand, the Cochabamba valleys afforded fertile niches for ethnically diverse mitmaq colonies scattered throughout the region. Cochabamba was an ethnic frontier area, where pockets of Aymara peoples extended the vertical archipelagos of their powerful altiplano kingdom into the eastern reaches of the maize valleys and beyond into the tropical lowlands. It sheltered a mélange of ethnic settlements, both mitmaq and autochthonous, that coexisted uneasily with each other until the arrival of the Europeans. On the other hand, the Valle Bajo was annexed directly by the Incas and turned into a principal granary of Tawantinsuyu. Under a highly centralized, elaborate organization of labor prestation, both permanent and transient ethnic groups cultivated maize for the Incas.

This combination of centralized Incaic rule and atomized ethnic settlement in the valleys created a precarious situation, which the Europeans began to exploit in the 1540s and 1550s. The military phase of the conquest seemed to shatter the Incaic agrarian regime,

---

allowing me to read parts of their study (in manuscript form), *Qollaruna: El origen social del proletariado del estaño* (forthcoming).

as the transient laborers fled upland, leaving a few Incaic lords beholden to encomenderos for their status as Indian intermediaries and their continued authority to rule (at a local level). Among the mitmaq colonies, there could be no unified ethnic resistance to Spanish penetration. The conquest had upset the delicate balance of power that had obtained among the diverse Aymara and Quechua-speaking ethnic groups in the region. In the transition to colonial rule, highland-based Aymara polities struggled to recover traditional rights to valley lands. Many of those Indians who remained in the Valle Bajo after the collapse of the Inca state were thrown on the defensive against the aggressive pursuits of highland Indians. To defend their hold over valley resources and their authority over Indians, local caciques (as the Europeans now called them) sought legitimacy and protection from their new European overlords. In the absence of political and moral consensus and ethnic solidarity, valley Indians became extremely vulnerable to Spanish exploits. This became increasingly clear in the 1570s, 1580s, and 1590s, when they realized that Spanish chacareros, not Aymara lords, posed the gravest threat to their existence. But by then, the balance of forces had tipped in favor of a growing number of aggressive landowners.

The emergence of class relationships in the region, however, cannot be understood simply in terms of Andean and European alliances and conflicts at the regional level. The consolidation of the colonial system of exploitation, based primarily upon modes of indirect rule, set in motion deeper currents of socioeconomic change in the region. As it centralized power in the 1570s and 1580s, the colonial state became the principal claimant of the labor of its Andean subjects. On an ideological level, the colonial state tried to establish its authority among Andean lords by granting them certain privileges and legitimating certain "customary rights and obligations" of all Andean peoples who lived in state-sanctioned villages. Most important, the state validated their collective right to a minimum degree of subsistence security, at the same time that it rationalized Indian settlement and land tenure in ways that would facilitate tribute collection. This was part of the Toledan system of indirect rule in the southern Andes that was designed to subsidize both the colonial bureaucracy and the mining industry at Potosí. In the short term, the power of the colonial order seemed impressive. Between 1570 and 1620, the southern Andes became the premier source of the commodity money for an expanding world market economy, and Potosí became a commercial magnet and a source of circulating medium that stirred up the regional economies of the Andes. Both indigenous and Spanish areas of settlement were drawn into the expanding orbit of Potosí's market.

Mercantile forces therefore played a fundamental role in the transformation of social relations and the development of agrarian classes in Cochabamba. Spanish chacareros, driven by the commercial opportunities emanating from Potosí, organized agricultural production for export to the mines. They attracted Indians from nearby pueblos reales and employed them as jornaleros, sharecroppers, and tenants. As time went on, many landowners reinforced their hold over a servile labor force of yanaconas. The creation of a dependent rural labor force thus accompanied the growth of livestock ranches, the spread of wheat fields, and the intensive production of maize on irrigated lands (with techniques inherited from the Incas). These developments signaled the formation of a regional economy responsive to the inflationary market in food crops created by the silver bonanza. But, it is worth underscoring, the penetration of the market in this part of the Andes was not the causal determinant of Cochabamba's early agrarian transformation. The advent of commercial capitalism in the southern Andes was neither inexorable nor sufficiently powerful to destroy traditional forms of Andean social organization in all areas. Nor was the power of the colonial state a determining force capable of transforming Andean lifeways. Theoretically, it established some mechanisms to preserve the economic autonomy of ethnic groups at the level of ayllu or village. That the Cochabamba region departed so radically from its precolonial social patterns during Potosí's second cycle of silver production in the late sixteenth century was in part the consequence of Andean ethnic fragmentation (intrinsic to mitmaq settlement patterns) and of the political vacuum left by the collapse of Inca control over valley lands. In contrast, throughout nearby highland regions, most Indians retained some degree of collective economic control over land and labor prestations.

On the other hand, Cochabamba was certainly not unique. In other areas along the eastern valleys and slopes of the cordillera, similar circumstances eroded the power of Andean groups before the advance of Spanish landowners. Europeans took advantage of splintered and weak ethnic settlements in the valleys of Larecaja, Chuquisaca, Tomina, and other kichwa areas to expropriate choice lands in temperate climes. Even farther afield, in the regions of Huamanga and Arequipa, for example, strong parallels may be drawn. But in each area, the precolonial heritage was different; the particular configuration of ethnic settlements was specific to the region;

and the social dynamics and consequences of struggle between Andeans and Europeans varied. Cochabamba was perhaps an extreme case of weak Andean resistance to European settlement; the strong Inca presence there had created a brittle, hierarchical social order that could not survive the initial military defeat. The origins, if not the evolution, of early agrarian class formation in Cochabamba therefore were rooted as much in the precolonial past as in the expansion of an internal market that incorporated the southern Andes into the world economy.

Over the course of the seventeenth and eighteenth centuries, the evolution of agrarian classes in the region took on a dynamic of its own. Potosí's mercantile power faded with time, and, over the long term, Cochabamba was increasingly subject to pressures that reflected the failure of the Toledan model of colonial rule in Alto Perú. The region's large forastero and mestizo population was only the most visible sign of the erosion of the state-organized extractive system. It was this group of forastero and mestizo peasants that eventually had the greatest impact upon the agrarian class structure in the valleys. Through their prosaic pursuits of a livelihood, peasant families created the elements of a viable, alternative economy within the institutional confines of the hacienda system of landholding and labor control. In so doing, they slowly and almost silently began to alter the contours of the regional economy and society during the late colonial and postcolonial periods.

The analysis of the emerging peasant economy in eighteenth-century Cochabamba situated the dynamics of regional class relations in the broader context of economic stagnation and decline and fragmented political rule. Although Potosí's output began to recover modestly in the second half of the century, following a secular slide, its power as a market for the wheat and maize products of the valleys remained weak and erratic. Furthermore, most staple prices declined or stagnated during this period, and Cochabamba's landlords confronted aggressive commercial competition from the ayllus of Chayanta, which virtually captured the wheat trade to Potosí in the late part of the century. The diminished scope, stability, and intensity of interregional trade in grains had come to transform the economic logic of commercial agriculture in eighteenth-century Cochabamba. Increasingly, demesne agriculture depended upon cyclical harvest failures and shortages to force up prices. Landlords with large grain reserves, tithe speculators, and cultivators who controlled permanently irrigated bottomlands all found themselves in position to capitalize on drought. Mercantile accumulation pivoted on scarcity, which both created need and eliminated small-scale producers from the marketplace.

But those moments of calamity and profit were infrequent. In the intervals, landlords sought short-term solutions to the cumulative pressures of market contraction, capital shortage, debt, and property fragmentation. One apparent solution was found in a rentier strategy. Increasingly, landlords parceled out hacienda resources to their tenants in a multiplicity of forms. Tenants were enmeshed in a web of obligations, in return for which they might cultivate leaseholds, share common pasture, collect firewood, or sharecrop potato or maize fields. As a result, property rights often corresponded only loosely to the mosaic of de facto landholding rights and the way the land was worked. Haciendas came to be internally colonized by a growing population of arrenderos. Over the longer term, landlord adjustments to secular decline created an opportunity for peasants to reconstitute a subsistence economy within the confines of the estate. Sooner or later, as custom became entrenched, the expansion of peasant smallholding on estate lands encroached on the power of landlords to determine the disposition or use of their resources and sometimes even the terms of exchange with their tenants.

In the shifting balance of class forces, peasant smallholders devised creative solutions to the problems of subsistence insecurity, involving a shrewd manipulation of available resources, human reciprocities, and market initiatives.[4] Andean forms of labor-sharing, barter, and insurance all served to support traditional social relations of production. But so, too, did commercial enterprise. The particular weight or balance of market and nonmarket strategies at any given time depended on a peasant family's particular equilibrium of resources and needs. In the drier highlands, peasants living on haciendas usually tried to assemble parcels of land in different ecological zones. Crop diversification, to spread risk and extend the family's

---

4 Dandler Hanhart, "Diversificación," and the presentations at the weeklong CERES seminar, "Valles y serranías de la región de Cochabamba," (Cochabamba, July 29-August 2, 1981). See also similar analyses of the "open" family economy in the Montaro and Yanamarca valleys of central Peru, in Norman Long and Bryan R. Roberts, eds., *Peasant Cooperation and Capitalist Expansion in Central Peru* (Austin: University of Texas Press, 1978); Norman Long and Bryan R. Roberts, *Miners, Peasants, and Entrepreneurs: Regional Development in the Central Highlands of Peru* (Cambridge: Cambridge University Press, 1984); and Florencia Mallon, *The Defense of Community in Peru's Central Highlands: Peasant Struggle and Capitalist Transition, 1860-1940* (Princeton: Princeton University Press, 1983), 209 ff.

reach across complementary agricultural zones, cast their subsist-ence strategies in traditional Andean terms. In the valleys, the re-creation of "micro-verticality" to diversify crops and diminish risk was less viable. In fact, in the Valle Bajo, where permanent irrigation often yielded two maize harvests a year, peasants concentrated on one crop and hired extrafamilial hands to harvest it. In the drier val-ley of Cliza, peasants diversified from maize into livestock and po-tatoes. But in both valleys, small-scale, intensive agriculture was usually insufficient to support a household, so peasants engaged in a host of nonagricultural activities. They sold crops both locally and in distant marketplaces, and, more important, they created a net-work of retail markets where staple commodities were traded in kind or for cash. The ferias were arenas of "horizontal exchange" among members of the same class, rather than urban colonial mar-ketplaces where the logic of commercial capitalism governed ex-change.

In terms of both production and exchange, therefore, we see the dim outlines of a peasant economy in formation during the late colo-nial period. It was composed of dependent smallholders, most of whom still had no title to land but were gradually wresting control over productive resources and nibbling away at the edges of demesne agriculture. Peasants were turning into artisans, traders, and some-times petty usurers. On a regional scale, they were creating an incip-ient rival economy that narrowed the commercial opportunities and conditioned the mercantile tactics of Cochabamba's landed elite. Al-ready by the late eighteenth-century, the valley peasantry was a force to be reckoned with.

Yet the very historical processes that gave substance and form to this distinctive peasant class, that deepened the interpenetration of subsistence and commercial activities, also placed intrinsic limits on its economic autonomy. However shrewd and flexible peasant families might be in their livelihood strategies, and however much they tried to balance their subsistence requirements against recipro-cal obligations to kinsmen or neighbors, they lived and worked out-side the cultural and material context of Andean village society. They may have practiced reciprocities, but those practices were embedded in a class context. In their daily pursuit of a livelihood or their struggle against the enduring injustices and humiliations of being Indian in colonial society, or living in the shadow of a patrón, most valley peasants faced the world alone. They did not have re-course to the material and ideological traditions of Andean commu-nities to defend themselves against the incursion of outside claimants, the arbitrary demands of a landlord, or the ravages of natural disaster. There was no communal tradition of group self-sufficiency, reciprocity, and distribution to buffer the peasant household against subsistence threats or to contain class forces. Valley peasants had no means of calling upon the moral economy of their ancestral kin and ethnic groups to collectively confront the outside world whenever it turned hostile. In short, the absence of a strong ethnic heritage in the valleys left most peasants without economic autonomy or symbolic integrity.[5]

The relative weakness and vulnerability of valley peasants eking out a subsistence outside the ayllu context is especially evident when judged against Andean ideals of self-sufficiency, reciprocity, and collectivity. As was discussed in chapters 3 and 4, those ideals had ceased to govern or mediate social relations in many Andean villages by the early seventeenth-century. Indeed, Andean migration into the Cochabamba valleys during the seventeenth century was one important consequence of the strains and distortions of village life under the impact of colonial rule. In the Cochabamba region, village society organized around the reducciones had decayed considerably by the eighteenth century.

Yet, at base, this judgment of the vulnerability of valley peasants to the corrosive forces of class, state incursion, and subsistence threat is not made against some utopian ideal. It is set in the specific conditions of life and work in the ayllus of the neighboring province of Chayanta at the end of the colonial period. Among the six ayllus of Chayanta—once the locus of powerful ethnic groups who served as the Inca's privileged warriors—the communal tradition and segmentary organization continued to thrive. Platt's study of these ayllus during the nineteenth century reveals the extent to which they had preserved their unity, group self-sufficiency, and traditional moral economy.[6] The material foundations of their communal tradition rested on their dual-residency patterns. The ayllus controlled lands in the puna and in the valley, extending their reach across several ecological tiers of the vertical landscape. Through kinship and reciprocity, the communities enjoyed almost the full gamut of Andean agriculture: they had access to both the tuber staples of the highlands and the maize agriculture of the valleys. The vertical dis-

5 For similar discussions in different contexts, see Scott, *Moral Economy of the Peasant*, 40-43; and Mallon, *Defense of Community*, 330 and 342.

6 Platt, *Estado boliviano y ayllu andino*, chap. 1 and 2 and "Role of the Andean Ayllu." See also O. Harris, "Labor and produce."

position of family labor between puna and valley, the patterns of transhumance, and the intricate networks of reciprocity were all co-ordinated by village norms, customs, and ceremonial/agricultural calendars.[7] To be sure, the ayllus did not exist in an egalitarian paradise. Conflicts, rivalries, and processes of social differentiation marred village life and had to be channeled in nondestructive ways. But the ayllus did manage to harness commercial forces without allowing them to destroy the internal social fabric of communal life. They ensured a subsistence niche to all their members, and they protected their collective interests against outside threats. In short, they faced the world, for the most part, as ethnic collectivities.

Beyond Colonialism

The dissolution of the colonial state and the transition to republican rule in Bolivia posed a major threat to the peasants of Chayanta and other highland regions where the ayllu had adapted and reproduced itself under colonial rule. In the aftermath of war, as President Andrés Santa Cruz tried to shape the new government in the late 1820s, there were plans to abolish tribute and, in effect, end the ideological basis for ayllu landholding. Eventually, the mining recession and the fiscal crisis of the fledgling national government forced the state to fall back on the institution of tribute as its main source of revenue. Reestablished in 1831 (and abolished only much later, in 1882), tribute levied upon Indians made up about 60 percent of government revenues by the middle of the nineteenth century.[8] In real and symbolic terms, state-sponsored extraction served as the mainstay of the new republic until the mining industry once more began to grow. There were monetarist devices for providing governmental revenues during this period as well. In 1830, the state issued a debased silver currency (*moneda feble*) as a temporary solution to its chronic financial deficit. This political economy, however shaky and unstable in the 1830s and 1840s, had many affinities with the former colonial state. It was grounded in mercantilist ideology, tempered by

7 See the sources cited in n. 6. On the role of "ethnic time," tribute, and market participation among the ayllus of Lipez, see Tristan Platt, "Calendarios tributarios e intervención mercantil: La articulación estacional de los ayllus de Lipez con el mercado minero potosino (siglo XIX)," in Harris, Larson, and Tandeter, *Participación indígena*, 471-558.

8 Sánchez-Albornoz, *Indios y tributos*, 217, and Herbert S. Klein, *Bolivia: The Evolution of a Multi-Ethnic Society* (Oxford: Oxford University Press, 1982), 105.

its neocolonial dependence upon tribute. In its policies of official and de facto protectionism, it also shielded Bolivia's internal economy from foreign commercial penetration.[9]

The strong continuities of the republican state with colonial policies toward tribute and corporate landholding preserved the ideological underpinnings of traditional state-peasant relations. All across highland Bolivia, wherever the ayllu thrived, Andean peoples viewed the restoration of tribute as legal confirmation of their collective right to hold land. It served as symbolic endorsement by the state that their way of life might still be preserved, even as other things changed.[10] Indeed, the people of Chayanta sought to maintain their tribute obligations to the state, for tribute simply represented one side of the traditional, asymmetrical "pact of reciprocity" that had always governed relations between the ayllus and the state. In return for tribute, the Chayanta peoples received state sanction that legitimated and preserved their economic autonomy and cultural heritage. Furthermore, their collective control over village resources and their traditional role in the wheat market gave those ayllus considerable leeway in coping with tribute burdens. Ethnic leaders spread the burden, made internal adjustments in tribute categories, and marketed communal harvests to mitigate the pressures of tribute and rationalize the allocation of community resources to meet their tribute obligations.[11] These ayllus had advantages in their ecological endowments and cultural cohesion, but recent research documents the survival of ayllus across much of highland Bolivia at least until the advent of free-market policies in the late nineteenth century.[12] Not only did Andean communities persist well into the century; they even experienced population growth (although tributary popu-

---

9 Platt (*Estado boliviano y ayllu andino,* chap. 1) argues that traditional patterns of interregional wheat trade survived the transition to republican rule largely because of the protectionist effects of currency devaluation and the high costs of overland transport from the coast. It also appears that, after the first rush of English traders onto the scene in the late 1820s, foreign competition in textiles somewhat receded. In any event, the artisanal production of cotton cloth in Cochabamba was not eliminated. See Brooke Larson, *Explotación agraria,* chap. 5.

10 Sánchez-Albornoz, *Indios y tributos,* p. 204.

11 Platt, *Estado boliviano y ayllu andino,* chap. 2.

12 Erwin P. Grieshaber, "Survival of Indian Communities in Nineteenth-Century Bolivia" (Ph.D. diss., University of North Carolina, 1977), and "Survival of Indian Communities in Nineteenth-Century Bolivia: A Regional Comparison," *Journal of Latin American Studies* 12 (1980): 223-269.

lation rose in most highland provinces of Bolivia between the census years of 1838 and 1877).[13]

In the Cochabamba region, where the communal tradition was historically weak and private modes of surplus extraction had predominated since early colonial times, the patrimony of a colonial or neocolonial state had little meaning. The state had no moral power to grant land to its forastero tributaries inhabiting hacienda lands. At most, judicial institutions might serve a mediating function in peasant-landlord conflicts over rent. But in general, tribute represented naked extraction to the valley smallholder. Historically, the incursion of the state had long since upset the social equilibrium in the valleys; caste had decayed and forasteros were hardly distinguishable from cholo or mestizo peasants.

When the republican government of Bolivia resurrected the tribute institution in 1831, only a century had passed since the tax rebellion in Cochabamba. That uprising of valley mestizos against tribute levies had precluded, for almost fifty years, the systematic collection of head taxes in the province. The Bourbons had finally generated more tribute during the two decades (1786-1808) of fiscal reorganization. But tribute was still not an accepted institution. In fact, heavier taxation had coincided with a period of regional economic decline and ultimately a famine. The intrusive Bourbon state had produced penury and painful memories among the valley peasants.

Much had changed since then. Peasants of the central valleys had experienced fifteen years of warfare, during which they had tasted the fruits of victory for a while. Their protonational sentiment and participation in the independence movement had raised expectations about a new social order that would finally shatter the institutions of mita and tribute. They suspected, moreover, that a republican state would be unable to single out the forasteros from the mixed-blood population in a countryside where almost everyone spoke Quechua. The legend and memory of Calatayud warned against state infringement on the perceived rights of cholos and mestizos in Cochabamba.

A phenomenological analysis of peasant perceptions of the creole state and the injustice of the new tribute system awaits the inquiries of another historian. But the forms and effects of peasant resistence to republican tribute can perhaps be seen in the census records. Un-

---

13 Grieshaber, "Survival of Indian Communities" (1977) and "Survival of Indian Communities" (1980); Platt, *Estado boliviano y ayllu andino*, 62-70; Klein, "Peasant Response to the Market."

like the case in the highlands, the tributary population of Cocha-bamba was vanishing during the middle decades of the nineteenth-century. The number of tributaries declined by 38 percent between 1838 and 1877, from 11,067 to 6,828.[14] Some of that decline was pro-duced by excess deaths caused by an epidemic around 1856, but some of it was due to peasant flight and "passing" into the ranks of cholos and mestizos. In areas like the Cercado and the Cliza valley, where racial and cultural amalgamation was most extensive, the de-cline of tributary population was sharpest[15]; and the drop in tributar-ies living outside the five pueblos reales was steeper than the decline within the villages.[16]

It is not clear either how Indians evaded the new tribute regime or the extent to which the creole state disrupted the equilibrium of peasant households in the valleys in the nineteenth century. In the 1830s and 1840s, peasant defiance in the valleys did not take the form of collective action. Resistance was expressed individually and silently, in the clandestine actions of peasants who somehow shed their ascriptive ethnic status. The forasteros slowly vanished, as mestizaje spread.[17] But the sharp divergence between the success of

14 Grieshaber, "Survival of Indian Communities" (1977), 138, 140, and 142; "Survival of Indian Communities" (1980), 236 and 244. Grieshaber's work was based upon the following Indian census records of Cochabamba, housed in the ANB: Arque, no. 5 (1850); Ayopaya, no. 13 (1844); Cercado, no. 21 (1850); Cliza, no. 23 (1831), nos. 24 and 25 (1846), and no. 26 (1850); Punata, no. 30 (1867); Tapacarí no. 31 (1828), nos. 32 and 33 (1844), no. 34 (1851), and nos. 35 and 36 (1867); Tarata, no. 37 (1872); and Cochabamba, no. 40 (1834) and no. 41 (1844).

15 Tributary population declined by 78 percent in Cliza and 75 percent in the Cercado, compared to the overall decline of 38 percent. For sources, see n. 14.

16 Hacienda tributaries declined from 4,284 in 1838 to 1,843 in 1877 (a 57 per-cent decrease). Pueblo real tributaries dropped from 6,783 in 1838 to 4,985 in 1877 (a 19 percent decrease). These estimates are Grieshaber's (see n. 14). It is difficult to assess overall Indian population trends, however, since census-takers often failed to register women and children after about midcentury: Klein, "Peasant Response to the Market," 116.

17 It is suggestive that the two complete censuses of the region (Viedma's, in 1788, and the Bolivian state's, in 1900) show that in roughly the area occupied by the colonial province of Cochabamba, total population increased from about 125,000 to 248,000, while the proportion of "whites" increased slightly (from 16 to 18 percent), and that of "Indians" decreased from 45 to 23, whereas "mestizos and cholos" increased from 33 to 51 percent. (The residual category of "others" increased from 5 to 7 percent.) Contemporaries talked about the gradual "whitening" of the rural population, as Indians declined and the "whiter" mixed blood population expanded. See chap. 5, esp. Table 13, and, for 1900, Federico

the tributary regime in the highlands and its failure in the valleys points to different peasant perceptions of the moral authority of the republican state. Compliance in the highlands and resistance in the valleys can be understood only in the light of the different social legacies of colonial rule. For many highland ayllus, tribute symbolized state protection of communal lands even after the independence wars were won. But in the Cochabamba valleys, the primacy of agrarian class relationships had marginalized the patron-state and undermined its ability to extract tribute. It had nothing to offer the peasant family that was eking out a precarious existence outside the village context.

In the 1870s and 1880s, the neocolonial, mercantilist regime gave way to a new political economy of the free market. As Mitre has shown, those decades were a historical watershed that reintegrated Bolivia into the world market economy as both a mineral producer and a market for imported food crops.[18] Silver mining entered a phase of rapid growth between 1873 and 1895, which paralleled in volume of output the second silver cycle of Toledo's times.[19] New mines in Huanchaca and Colquechaca disgorged silver, and they called for a more highly skilled, stable labor force, anchored to the site of production, to work its machines and meet the regimented work schedules. Other, smaller, preindustrial mines required only seasonal or unskilled workers who worked on a contract basis. The labor requirements of the new mines continued to grow after the turn of the century, as tin replaced silver and industrial metals became profitable to export.

The modernized silver industry depended on railroads to carry crude ore to the Pacific coast and overseas, and at the same time the rails opened the interior of Bolivia to Chilean wheat imports and other foreign staples. Rails linked the port of Antofagasta to Pulacayo and Uyuni in 1889 and advanced across the altiplano to Oruro in 1892. By the turn of the century, railroads had created an alternative circuit of trade revolving around the exportation of crude ore and the importation of wheat.[20] In 1890, the consumers of La Paz

---

Blanco, *Diccionario geográfico de la República de Bolivia*, 4 vols. (La Paz: Oficina Nacional de Inmigración, 1901), vol. 2.

18 Antonio Mitre, *Los patriarcas de la plata: Estructura socioeconómica de la minería boliviana en el siglo XIX* (Lima: Instituto de Estudios Peruanos, 1981).

19 See Klein, *Bolivia*, 298-299 (table 2).

20 J. Valerie Fifer, *Bolivia: Land, Location, and Politics since 1825* (Cambridge: Cambridge University Press, 1972), 66-70.

could purchase Chilean wheat for less than they paid for wheat hauled over the mountains by mule from Cochabamba.[21] Contemporary observers worried about the impact of the new imports on Bolivia's small-scale, primitive industries. In the marketplace that sprang up near railroad junctions, foreign imports displaced tocuyos and flour from Cochabamba, the bayetas from Oruro, and sugar from Santa Cruz.[22] Small-scale traditional trade networks survived where foreign imports did not reach or where popular patterns of consumption (of maize, for example) still depended on internal sources of supply. But the advent of rail transportation reoriented the western altiplano to the world market, away from the eastern valleys and serranías that had traditionally provisioned them.[23]

The final element in the historical watershed was the state's "project of national integration." As the silver oligarchy consolidated its control over the national government, the ideology of capitalism provided new guideposts for state policy.[24] To unfetter the economy, shift the tax base to productive enterprise, and unlock the nation's human and natural resources, the state reversed its policy toward communal landholding and tribute and began to enforce the commodification of ayllu lands. Between 1874 and 1882, communal property and tribute were legislated out of existence. At the same time, a tax was levied on the assessed value of land to replace the tithes and *primicias* (taxes on Indian crops and livestock). Thus, there was no relief from taxation for native landholders. But more than ever before, the ayllus were vulnerable to market forces. Communal landholding was forsaken by the liberal state for the ideals of a free market economy. In many areas near La Paz, the enforcement of the 1874 Law of Expropriation unleashed commercial forces and accelerated the advance of latifundios across the altiplano.[25]

21 Mitre, *Patriarcas*, 176; Grieshaber, "Survival of Indian Communities" (1977), 228.

22 Platt and Molina Barrios, *Qollaruna*, 5.

23 Ibid., 8; Platt, *Estado boliviano y ayllu andino*, 68-70.

24 Platt, *Estado boliviano y ayllu andino*, chap. 3; Herbert S. Klein, *Politics and Political Change in Bolivia* (Cambridge: Cambridge University Press, 1969), chaps. 1 and 2; and Marie-Danièle Demelas, "Darwinismo a lo criollo: El darwinismo en Bolivia, 1880-1910," *Historia boliviana* 1 (1981): 55-82.

25 Silvia Rivera, "La expansión del latifundio en el altiplano boliviano," *Avances*, no. 2 (1978): 95-118. For a critical assessment of Rivera's argument, see Gustavo Rodríguez Ostría, "¿Expansión del latifundio o supervivencia de las comunidades indígenas? Cambios en la estructura agraria boliviana del siglo

But the tradition of communal solidarity in some areas of Bolivia, such as Chayanta, proved stronger than the land reform. The state threatened in Chayanta what Platt described as "an entire social and cultural order in which the Andean ecology, production and marketing calendars, residence patterns, and tributation to the state all meshed into a rhythm of social activity,"[26] and the ayllus responded violently. What began as an attack on a local tax collector, a regional representative of the state, eventually escalated into a series of uprisings that culminated in the so-called "Caste War" of 1899. This was followed by the elaboration of a program of "cultural liberation and ethnic revindication" that recalled the rebellions of 1781.[27] For the moment, state efforts to fragment the ayllus were thwarted in this corner of the Andes.

The policies of the state had entirely different social consequences for rural society in the Cochabamba valleys. There, the threat did not lie in the state's *ex-vinculación* laws forbidding communal landholding, and it did not provoke ethnic resistance to the commodification of village lands. On the contrary, the valley pueblos reales (Sipesipe, El Paso, and Tiquipaya) were broken up into parcels of land that were put on the market as early as 1878.[28] Neighboring hacendados purchased some of these parcels, but more often they were sold to peasants and artisans who purchased, on average, less than a hectar each. Between 1886 and 1894, about 60 percent of village land passed into the hands of small-scale cultivators. The easy transition to legalized private landholding and the dissolution of those pueblos reales after four centuries are evidence of the long process of internal decay of community life and norms in the villages. Long before republican laws sanctioned the privatization of village land, the pueblos reales had fragmented into de facto smallholdings, cultivated by a growing number of mestizos.

In contrast to the quiescence of the valley peasantry, the landowning elite reacted strongly against the policies of taxation and free trade. They felt themselves the victims of the new property taxes (*catastros*) that shifted more of the tax burden to the creoles. The new taxes cut into their returns on commercial agriculture and dis-

---

XIX," *Serie: Historia*, Working Paper no. 1, Instituto de Estudios Sociales y Económicos (IESE), Universidad Mayor de San Simon (Cochabamba, 1983).

26 Tristan Platt, "Liberalism and Ethnocide in the Southern Andes," *History Workshop*, no. 17 (1984): 12.

27 Ibid., 15. See also Platt, *Estado boliviano y ayllu andino*, chap. 4.

28 Rodríguez Ostría, "Expansión del latifundio," 11.

couraged land concentration and improvement. Moreover, in the 1920s, levies on the production of chicha depressed local demand. People turned to contraband liquors, and maize, the staple and symbol of valley agriculture since time immemorial, thus lost a large part of its market. To the landowners, however, the weight of taxes was minor compared to the impediments to interregional trade. The free-trade policies of the state represented "a protectionist policy in favor of other countries, and against Bolivia, for imported foodstuffs like wheat flour."[29] Not only did the importers pay but a modicum of tax; they also enjoyed relatively low freight costs. It was a common joke that Buenos Aires was closer to Europe than Cochabamba was to Santa Cruz. The valley landowners felt a growing economic isolation from the rest of Bolivia, especially the markets of the altiplano. The region was situated in the geographic center of the populated backbone of the nation, and yet it was cut off from the markets of La Paz, Oruro, and the mines. Who could afford freight costs to haul wheat, when imported grains were both superior in quality and cheaper? The landlords also were shut out of the subsistence marketplaces and traditional circuits of trade among valley cultivators and highland traders. The surviving large estates demanded a large volume of monetarized transactions, if such deals depended on periodic crop failures and high grain prices. However, the traditional cyclical rhythm of mercantile accumulation by large valley landlords was broken by the advent of foreign competition and cumbersome taxes.[30]

29 Octavio Salamanca, *La crisis en el departamento de Cochabamba* (Cochabamba: Ilustración, 1927), 36.

30 In 1901, Blanco noted that the interregional trade of Arque, where once "the Indians of . . . La Paz and . . . Puno came to buy large quantities of wheat and maize.," had "lost all its importance since the introduction . . . of flour from Chile which, in spite of its inferior quality, is preferred for its low price." Blanco, *Diccionario geográfico*, 2: 10. Many of Cochabamba's large landlords responded to the foreign competition by shifting from wheat to maize production. Until 1917, most maize was produced for the manufacture of chicha, but then, with the arrival of the railroad, hacendados discovered new commercial opportunities in the production of maize alcohol. During the 1920s, the region's maize production continued to increase as more of the crop was turned into alcohol. By 1927, however, the supply of grain alcohol outstripped the demand. Furthermore, government toleration of contraband trade in imported alcohol, stiffer taxes on maize and chicha, and increasing freight costs combined to drastically reduce the margin of returns on large-scale agriculture. For more detailed discussion, see Ricardo Azogue Crespo, Gustavo Rodríguez, and Humberto Bolares,

The landlord view was perhaps best expressed by the hacendado and essayist Octavio Salamanca. In 1927, Salamanca published an essay criticizing the national government for its destructive and unjust policies toward agriculturalists in the valley. Though he claimed to speak for all cultivators, both large and small, his assessment of the agrarian problem reflected his class biases. It was his opinion that the 50 percent increase in taxes during the previous five years was devastating to large landowners. Over the same period, maize consumption had fallen sharply, depressing prices. The "scissors" effect of higher fixed costs and declining prices was destroying the valley hacienda. The shortage of credit and capital in the region exacerbated the problem, since it meant that landowners could not obtain the loans they needed to cover short-term deficits and tide them over until times improved. Just as peasants in the valleys once dreaded the arrival of the tribute census taker, now landlords feared the property-tax assessor. Indeed, the property tax affected the rich more than the poor, for large landowners could not elude it as easily as smallholders could. That, at least, is what Salamanca seemed to suggest when he said that "practically all taxes are paid by the whites."[13] Thus, the state's assault on "white landowners" threatened to undermine the very foundations of class society in the valleys and to doom the hacienda to extinction.

There was another dimension, however, to the agrarian problems in Cochabamba during the early twentieth century, having to do less with the state or the market than with the internal dynamics of class. More than ever before, landlords were being squeezed from below by peasant smallholders. Across the central valleys, peasants were purchasing parcels of land. Estates were in an advanced state of fragmentation. In a pamphlet published in 1931, Salamanca estimated that, out of the province's total population of some 400,000 people, about 120,000 owned urban and/or rural property. Salamanca believed that one half of them "are those whom we call Indians, because they cultivate the land, . . . but who are really mestizos and cholos."[32] The advance of peasant proprietorship was so rapid that Salamanca believed that the old hacendado families were being "dispossessed" of their estates. In the cantón of Colcapirgua, for exam-

---

"Cochabamba: El proceso histórico de su constitución como región, 1900-1930," part 3 *Los Tiempos*, Jan. 23, 1986, pp. 2-3.

31 Salamanca, *Crisis en el departamento de Cochabamba*, 38.

32 Octavio Salamanca, *El socialismo en Bolivia* (Cochabamba: Bolívar, 1931), 185-186.

ple, there were 2,000 small properties. Only sixteen haciendas had survived, and the largest counted only seventeen tenants. In the Cliza valley, the so-called piqueros (owners of small amounts of property) were proliferating, as more and more peasants invested their meager savings in land titles.[33] Here, then, was another aspect of the state of affairs in agriculture: the consolidation and legitimation of peasant smallholdings at a time of depressed agricultural profits. The incursion of the peasants into the legal structure of property holding threatened to destroy the material and ideological basis of agrarian exploitation that had governed class relations in the valleys for four centuries.

But how, in a period of depressed markets and heavy taxes, did peasants manage to acquire land? Salamanca showed the methods that were used. While he idealized the "harmonious" relations between landlords and tenants in the valleys, he also believed that landlords bargained over the terms of rent from a weak position. Tenants, he argued, were in a favorable position to acquit themselves of their labor obligations and to concentrate on the cultivation of potato or maize lands. They also sharecropped large tracts of hacienda land and surrendered only half of the crop to their landlords. Thus, in Salamanca's view, even colonos were able to accumulate money to purchase small plots of land. It was common for tenants to continue leasing hacienda land while they acquired parcels of their own until they had finally established economic independence.[34] Salamanca's analysis reveals more about the class outlook of beleaguered landlords than it does about the conditions of tenancy, for it shows how weak some hacendados seemed to consider themselves to be before the advance of their own tenantry.

Salamanca particularly admired the ability of peasant families to blend subsistence and commercial activities. Against the somber picture of hacendados abandoning their enterprises, his description of a buoyant peasant economy stands out in bold relief. He had obviously observed the myriad facets of the economy in the valleys:

> Recall that at least half the landowners are mestizos. . . . They do not abandon their properties . . . but as land alone does not yield enough to satisfy their basic needs, they engage in com-

33 Ibid. Evidence of widespread *piquería* in parts of the Cliza valley is found in Olen, *Cantón Chullpas*, and in oral testimony of peasants in Tiraque and Chillichi (personal communication by anthropologists María Lagos and Bryan Anderson, respectively).

34 Salamanca, *Socialismo en Bolivia*, 187-188.

merce. While the men work in the fields or work for wages in a nearby city, the women shepherd the flocks, spin, weave, make *huiñapo* and chicha, sell fruits, and trade their products in the mines and cities of the altiplano.[35]

These activities generated small amounts of capital, which the women carefully hoarded, away from their men who might squander it in the chicherías. Here, then, in the delicate equilibrium of the peasant household as a unit of production and consumption lay the source of petty capital accumulation, "in these savings lies the explanation for the enormous territorial subdivision of the valleys," concluded Salamanca.[36]

Salamanca was acutely aware of the threat that a robust peasant economy presented to the local property structure. He focused on the ability of peasant households to gain freedom from rent as they acquired properties. But historically, processes of social differentiation are never one-sided or unilinear. Peasant prosperity could easily be reversed by a natural or personal calamity. Even "independent" smallholders rarely lived much above the threshold of subsistence insecurity. Ominously, there was, during the late nineteenth and early twentieth centuries, growing population pressure on productive resources in the central valleys. The subdivision of valley lands reflected not only enhanced peasant purchasing capacity, but also the growing hunger for forest, water, and fertile land. Between the Viedma census of 1788 and the first complete regional census in 1900, the population had almost doubled.[37] Salamanca commented on the shrinking supply of good valley land, the problem of erosion,

35 Ibid., 188. (*Huiñapo* referred to the balls of fermented dough used to make chicha.) More than twenty years earlier, in 1907, the *Círculo comercial cocha-bambino* had made note of the preponderance of small-scale traders in the export of maize, chicha, flour, potatoes, vegetables, and other products to the altiplano towns. It estimated that 75 percent of this commerce was controlled by "people of the village and the countryside." Most of them came from the area around Punata, Cliza, and Tarata in the Cliza valley. (Cited in Azogue Crespo Rodríguez, and Bolares, "Cochabamba," 2.) For a study of the contemporary peasant family enterprise in one subregion, see Francis R. Cajka, "Peasant Commerce in the Serranías of Cochabamba, Bolivia" (Ph.D. diss., University of Michigan, 1979).

36 Salamanca, *Socialismo en Bolivia*, 189. For a brief discussion of the internal decomposition of haciendas in the Cliza valley prior to the 1953 agrarian reform, see Jorge Dandler Hanhart, "El desarrollo de la agricultura, políticas estatales, y el proceso de acumulación en Bolivia" (typescript, 1981), 45-56.

37 See n. 17 above.

and the increasing density of population.[38] In particular, the problem of deforestation had worsened since the turn of the century, when the increase in chicha production began to require greater quantities of charcoal. Thus, the spread of peasant proprietorship was also accompanied by signs of ecological deterioration, fractionalization of output, and pauperization of many smallholders. Bits and pieces of land were bought and sold, but this did not lead to an even distribution of resources. Smallholders often bequeathed their parcels of land to their children, dispersing them among many heirs. While some families accumulated a few worldly possessions, some pack animals, a patch of potato land here and of maize land there—perhaps as they continued to work on the landlord's demesne—others slipped into the ranks of landless laborers, squatters, or subtenants. Among the peasantry, land tenure relations became increasingly stratified.[39]

As the process of social differentiation advanced, it created more precarious conditions for peasants who could neither purchase land nor secure the customary patronage of their landlords who were now increasingly looking to "sell out." A group of "redundant" laborers was beginning to emerge that found no secure subsistence niche in the region. Across the valleys around the turn of the century, therefore, labor arrangements became more intricate and elaborate. In much the same way that Geertz describes for Indonesia,[40] the laboring poor in Cochabamba entered into a great variety of labor agreements—leasing, subcontracting, pawning, jobbing, and wage work. More and more, they turned to the tertiary sector.[41] Where that failed to provide a livelihood, they set off to find work in the mines and salt fields beyond the western cordillera. Over the course of a century, the cumulative effects of the region's economic involution had created conditions favorable to the expulsion of poor peasants and day laborers into the expanding export sector, once wage work was available.[42]

38 Salamanca, *Socialismo en Bolivia*, 187.

39 Two earlier studies of Cliza describe cross-sections of rural society and show the various strata of tenants, squatters, and piqueros in the 1930s and 1940s: Olen, *Cantón Chullpas*, and Patch, "Social Implications," 22-29.

40 Geertz, *Agricultural Involution*, 99.

41 A report issued in 1907 estimated that 50 percent of the labor force in Punata, Cliza, and Tarata were arrieros. That may be an exaggeration, but the observation underscores the prevalence of nonagricultural activities among the "part-time" peasants in the Cliza valley. See Azogue Crespo, Rodríguez, and Bolares, "Cochabamba," 2, and Dandler Hanhart, "Diversificación," 20-21.

42 Platt and Molina, Barrios (*Qollaruna*, 28-30) speculate that peasant migration

The outlines of patterns of migration out of the valleys around the turn of the century have only recently come to light, especially in the research of Platt and Molina Barrios.[43] Their analysis of mining-company records on the work force of the largest tin mine in Bolivia, Llallagua-Uncía, reveals a preponderance of mine workers from the Cochabamba valleys. This confirms Harris and Albó's briefer study of industrial mine workers, in which they noted the large-scale migration of Cochabamba peasants and former peasants to mines in Norte Potosí (as Chayanta was now called).[44] The influx of valley peoples into the mining camps created "islands" of Quechua-speaking cholos and mestizos in the heart of Chayanta. Where the peasants of Chayanta resisted proletarianization and continued to this day to work in the mines only temporarily and under limited conditions,[45] Cochabamba migrants often cast their fate with the mines and forged the new industrial proletariat of tin mining.

The predominance of Cochabamba miners in Llallagua-Uncía was already evident in the 1920s, the decade of Cochabamba's so-called "agrarian crisis." But the exodus had actually began much earlier, probably sometime in the 1880s and 1890s, well before the development of the tin mines. To date, there has been little research on the westward migratory movement from the valleys, but several contemporary observations and the study of Platt and Molina Barrios provide important clues to the early wave.[46]

During the thirty-year boom (1880-1910) in nitrate production in Bolivia's "lost lands" of the Atacama desert, poor peasants left the

---

from Cochabamba followed upon a period of subsistence crisis in the peasant economy. They suggest that part of the deterioration in the standard of living was due to the contraction in demand for the foodstuffs that valley peasants had traditionally traded to highland peoples. Yet Salamanca (*Socialismo en Bolivia,* 187-188) mentions peasant commerce in the mines as one important source of petty accumulation, and Platt and Molina Barrios (*Qollaruna,* 20) themselves show that Cochabamba products continued to be sold in the marketplace of Uncía. The evidence is clearly still too preliminary and fragmented to permit more than speculation about the intensity or causes of the crisis in the peasant economy.

43 Platt and Molina Barrios, *Qollaruna,* esp. chap. 2.

44 Olivia Harris and Xavier Albó *Monteras y guardatojos. Campesinos y mineros en el norte de Potosí* (La Paz: Centro de Investigación y Promoción del Campesinado, 1975), 22, 26-27.

45 Ricardo Godoy, "From Indian to Miner and Back Again: Small-scale Mining in the Jukumani Ayllu, Northern Potosí, Bolivia," (Ph.D. diss., Columbia University, 1983); Harris and Albó, *Monteras,* 84; Platt and Molina Barrios, *Qollaruna,* 30-31; and Harris, "Labor and produce," 91-93.

46 Platt and Molina Barrios, *Qollaruna,* 25-26.

valleys for the mines. On the barren coast of Chile, they extracted nitrate for export to Europe and North America, where it was used for explosives and fertilizer.[47] In 1907, a report on the agriculture in Cochabamba expressed alarm at the growing number of impoverished peasants who had been forced to abandon their parcels of land and move to the Chilean coast: "So numerous are those who emigrate from Cochabamba that, within a few years, they will represent the industrial progress of a fatherland that is not theirs."[48] Two years later, a local newspaper, *El heraldo*, again reported widespread movement out of the region. The editor considered the cause to be the depressed level of agricultural prices and the glutted grain market, and he estimated that several thousand people had left the valleys since the beginning of the decade.[49]

When job opportunities on the coast dried up shortly before the First World War, and even more so afterward, Cochabamba's laborers began to return to Bolivia. In 1911 and 1914, local newspapers in Uncía and Oruro noted, with some anxiety, the flood of Cochabambinos and other Bolivians returning from the nitrate fields.[50] Some may have hoped to purchase land in the valleys, but many others now felt themselves to be permanent wageworkers and sought work in the new tin industry. From white saltpeters to black mines: they moved from an extractive industry on the wane to one just beginning to expand. It did expand over the next decade, but it did not do so enough to absorb these additions to the labor force. The swelling supply of valley migrants seeking wage work on the altiplano was beginning to outpace demand during the second and third decades of the twentieth-century.[51]

47 Fifer, *Bolivia*, 73-74. The "lost lands" were the coastal territories ceded to Chile after Bolivia's defeat in the War of the Pacific (1879-1883).

48 José Aranibar, "Proprietarios, conductores, y clase menesterosa al frente de los años agrícolas," *Boletín agrícola del Ministerio de Colonización y Agricultura*, no. 18 (1907), 101. (I am grateful to Gustavo Rodríguez for bringing this article to my attention.)

49 Cited in Azogue Crespo, Rodríguez, and Bolares, "Cochabamba," 2.

50 See Platt and Molina Barrios, *Qollaruna*, 24-25.

51 Platt and Molina emphasize this oversupply of labor, which was a circumstance favorable to the early phase of mining industrialization in Bolivia. In sharp contrast, the Cerro de Pasco mining company of the central sierra of Peru suffered from a chronically inadequate and unstable labor force (because of the low wages). In Bolivia, there was less of a need to "break" the peasant subsistence sector, wage caste war against the ayllus of Chayanta, or deploy coercive

Peasants into miners: however dramatic the transformation seemed to be in this particular region in the early twentieth-century, peasant ties were never completely cut. Furthermore, repercussions of these waves of migration were felt everywhere in the valleys. Directly or indirectly, through kin, neighbors, or landlords, peasants were drawn into the industrial orbit of the mines even if they never set eyes on the bleak encampments of Llallagua-Uncía or San José. Stories and rumors about the conditions of life and work in the mines began to filter back to the valley. Peasants had cousins and friends who, after only seven or eight years in the shafts, began to vomit up pieces of their blackened lungs in a slow agony of death. They heard gruesome reports of a massacre of mineworkers in Uncía in 1923. But they also heard about bold protests of miners during the 1920s. A sense of militancy, forged around an emerging class identity and solidarity, was in the air. While many peasants in Cochabamba may not have quite understood the circumstances of the brutal struggle in the distant mines, a growing number of smallholders in Cliza and the Valle Bajo began to appreciate the force and meaning of class conflict.[52] The mines were beginning to cast a new, more ominous shadow across the valleys. Cochabamba peasants themselves would soon begin to mobilize for social justice, preparing the ground for revolution and reform just a few years hence.

On the temporal horizons that stretch into the past, opening generous expanses of historical time, historians can always find the social continuities or discontinuities they seek. The *longue durée* per-

mechanisms of labor recruitment such as *enganche* (though it did function in Bolivia). For comparison with Peru, see especially Mallon, *Defense of Community*, chaps. 5 and 6; Adrian DeWind, *Peasants Become Miners: The Evolution of Industrial Mining Systems in Peru* (New York: Garland, 1987); and Long and Roberts, *Miners*.

52 On the development of class ideologies and the political mobilization of miners, see especially June Nash, *We Eat the Mines and the Mines Eat Us: Dependency and Exploitation in Bolivian Tin Mines* (New York: Columbia University Press, 1979). On the influence of mining politics on valley peasants, see Harris and Albó, *Monteras*, 26-27 and 37ff.; Jorge Dandler Hanhart, *El sindicalismo campesino en Bolivia: Los cambios estructurales en Ucureña* (México City: Instituto Indigenista Interamericano, 1969); and Jorge Dandler Hanhart, "Politics of Leadership, Brokerage, and Patronage in the Campesino Movement of Cochabamba, Bolivia" (Ph.D. diss., University of Wisconsin, 1971). See also James Kohl, "The Cliza and Ucureña War: Syndical Violence and National Revolution in Bolivia," *Hispanic American Historical Review* 62 (1982): 607-628, and Andrew Pearse, "Peasants and Revolution: The Case of Bolivia," *Economy and Society* 1 (1972): 255-279, 399-424.

spective of social reality in preindustrial Europe over three or four centuries leaves the strong impression that the structure of social relationships in the countryside was resistant to crises, shocks, and internal contradictions. From this perspective, the historian may invoke the power of geography, culture and civilization, economy and state, class or colonial relationships, or attitudes (*mentalités*) as structural constraints that slowed the tempo of historical change over the long term. Cast in this Braudelian framework, human societies seem to be endowed with a permanence and coherence that are almost impervious to human action. "Some structures . . . become stable," writes Braudel, "[and] get in the way of history, hinder its flow, and in hindering it shape it."[53]

Yet that same contemplation of a vast sweep of time can bring into focus a different historical landscape, one marked by discontinuities and change. From far above the surface of political events and short-term economic fluctuations, a long-term vision of history brings to light the sharp outlines of economic and social trends that move together or at odds with each other, shaping time in the image of cycles and intercycles and occasionally punctuating it by the force of a structural crisis. Such a vision, following the movement of several simultaneous tendencies imbues history with motion, ebb and flow, contradiction and change. It locates within social structures the elements of their own disequilibrum and the potential for their transformation; it reveals the fragility of the basis of economic life; and it grants the power of human agency to people trapped inside enduring social relationships that seem eternal. The trans-conjunctural perspective may be primarily economic, which traces cyclical time and charts the shifting direction or tempo of secular trends that produced significant social consequences. Or it may focus on human relationships that both condition and were conditioned by the larger political and economic environment. Through this conceptual lens, long-term history makes visible the power of people to alter social structures and shape their own world, even if they did so unconsciously and "not always as they wanted." Social history that widens the scope of historical time into several centuries can still chart the currents and eddies of structural change, insurrectional threats to the social order, and shock waves that reverberate through seemingly static or brittle social and mental structures. In so doing, it brings to light precisely the impermanence, sometimes the evanescence, of

53 Fernand Braudel, *On History* (Chicago: University of Chicago Press, 1980), 130.

social structures and relationships that otherwise seem carved in stone.

This long-term perspective on agrarian conflict and change in the Cochabamba region has found deep currents of socioeconomic change amidst striking continuities. In spite of the strong presence of Europe in the region since the sixteenth-century, the enduring influence of mining on the regional economy, and Cochabamba's continued importance as a food producer for western highland Alto Perú, the social organization and texture of rural life and the region's functional role in the economic totality were full of historical motion and subject to conjunctural pressures. The presence of historical change in continuity is best illustrated by Bolivia's two major mining cycles. In the first, in the late sixteenth-century, the valleys were closely integrated into the silver export industry and were indirectly subjected to the imperatives of the world market and the logic of mercantile capitalism. Cochabamba's nexus to the mines was maize and wheat, and its emergent role as the region's granary conditioned, in some measure, the mercantilization of productive relations, based on servile labor. In the silver cycle of the late nineteenth-century, the regional economy once more became closely tied to the mining sector, but its role as food producer during the era of mercantile capitalism had diminished. Cochabamba had become primarily an exporter of people, who no longer could cling to the husk of a penurious peasant existence.

Where the origins of Cochabamba's agrarian class society in the sixteenth century lay in the peculiar legacies of Incaic rule and the imperatives and contradictions of mercantile colonialism, the subsequent evolution of agrarian class relations within the region created the social conditions for the emergence of an incipient proletariat for the nitrate fields and tin mines outside it around the turn of the twentieth century. Cochabamba, once the region of refuge for Andean migrants seeking respite from the pressures of colonialism, became a region of flight, where the pressures and tensions of class forced peasants to submit to the degradation and dangers of mining. Out of the ebb and flow of class conflict and the historical processes of social differentiation, the region had turned from an exporter of grains in the late sixteenth-century to an exporter of people in the late nineteenth-century.

Cochabamba: (Re)constructing a History

Rereading and Remembrance

From the distance of a decade or more, I can see the unfolding of my own intellectual journey, and perhaps that of my generation of Andean social historians, in the shifting designs and layering of this study of Cochabamba. Like many other regional/social histories written in the 1970s and 1980s, this book took its initial conceptual shape as part of an ongoing dialogue with Marxian paradigms. Committed to political economy perspectives yet wary of reductive models, this study set out in search of Andean peasant agency and the local dynamics of landlord and colonial power. It did so through history, not theory, however, and I chose to banish most theoretical questions to the footnotes or bury them in the book's overarching narrative structure. My first aim was to write a long-term regional history of Cochabamba—uncluttered by theoretical propositions—where none had existed before. But at each stage of research, writing, and revision, I inevitably used this regional case study to mediate political economy perspectives and social history, as well as to engage comparative Andean themes. Reading *Cochabamba* retrospectively is to remap part of the Andean historiographical landscape of some fifteen or twenty years ago, which gave the book meaning and shape at the time of its production.

The original dissertation proposal, written in the early 1970s, set out to examine the historical impact of mining cycles on an "agrarian hinterland" of the Andes. The case that caught my attention was Potosí—the starkest example of an export economy fueling the expansion of mercantile capitalism in Europe during the sixteenth and seventeenth centuries—and one of its primary grain suppliers, the region of Cochabamba. The importance of the Potosí-Cochabamba commercial nexus became apparent to me in my previous archi-val research project (for the M.A. thesis) on sixteenth-century trade and commerce at the mining town. But the full conceptual signifi-cance of Potosí's influence on "the formation of an interior colonial market economy" became clear during the mid-1970s, in a series of articles published by Carlos Sempat Assadourian.[1] Building on his research (and influenced strongly by the prominent historiographic debates over Indian demography, overseas trade, mining cycles, and hacienda formation in colonial Mexico), I floated a hypothesis that this early colonial commercial nexus served as a powerful incen-tive to Spanish colonizers, who gradually turned Cochabamba into an enclave of seigneurial landlordism and commercial grain agricul-ture. The main research project was to trace over time the unfolding relationship between the Cochabamba region and the mining econ-omy, and specifically to explore the socioeconomic effects of Potosí's decline on this outlying agricultural region. I set out to examine whether the down-cycle of mining relaxed its hold on the region and what this "agrarian decompression" might have meant for class re-lations in Cochabamba. Eighteenth-century Cochabamba would pro-vide a regional laboratory within which to examine the endogamous processes of class formation and class struggle, the institutions and practices of the regional hacienda elite, the making of a distinctive mercantile regional economy, and the cumulative historical impact of peasant strategies of livelihood and resistance. And, indeed, much of this book remains faithful to the original aims of the study (see especially chapters 5 and 6).

Yet in the course of research, the limits of "dependency" and "capi-

1 My first fortuitous contact with Carlos Sempat Assadourian's work came in 1972, when Herb Klein handed me a mimeographed article entitled, "Potosí y el crecimiento de Córdoba en los siglos XVI y XVII." (Typescript. Published in *Cuadernos de historia social y económica* 8 (1971): 1-19.) Still relatively un-known among North American historians, he burst on the scene as an economic historian and theorist of colonial Latin America with his contribution to the famous volume, *Modos de producción*, published in Buenos Aires in 1973, the same year I arrived there to begin my research. See the notes of chapter 2 for a broader range of his publications and their influence on my own analysis. For recent historiographic discussions of Sempat Assadourian's influence on the field of Andean history, see Steve Stern, "New Directions in Andean Economic History: A Critical Dialogue with Carlos Sempat Assadourian," *Latin American Perspectives* 12 (1985): 133-148; and Brooke Larson, "Andean Communities, Politi-cal Cultures, and Markets: The Changing Contours of a Field," in Brooke Larson, Olivia Harris, and Enrique Tandeter, eds., *Ethnicity, Markets, and Migration in the Andes: At the Crossroads of History and Anthropology* (Durham: Duke University Press, 1995), 5-54, esp. 14-18.

talist world system" paradigms became increasingly clear to me. Global and regional interactions were crucial, but they had to be inserted into the preexisting world of the southern Andes if their historical significances for Andean peoples were to be understood. Colonialism had to be studied not as a teleological force but as a fundamentally contested historical process—stubbornly acted upon by both factious colonial elites and Andean peasants and lords. Class categories had to be complicated by ethnic and cultural questions. And everyday forms of peasant subsistence and resistance had to be linked to indigenous cultural practices and meanings. In a word, class analysis had to be inserted into dynamic transregional Andean-colonial contexts and "an ethnic dimension built into the oppressions, patterns of adaptation and resistance, collective grievances and aspirations . . ." that shaped Andean peasant history.[2] Of course, these ethnohistorical revelations were not bolts from the blue, however much I might have wished them to be. As with all conceptual doubts and shifts, they came slowly and painfully out of the scholarly conversations, collaborations, and debates that were beginning to forge a small interdisciplinary community of scholars and activists in the Andes just about the time I packed up my research proposal and took off for the archives.[3]

2 The quote comes from Steve Stern's important methodological essay, in which he exhorts historians of peasant politics to integrate ethnicity into their class-driven analyses; see "New Approaches to the Study of Peasant Rebellion and Consciousness: Implications of the Andean Experience," in Stern, ed., *Resistance, Rebellion, and Consciousness in the Andean Peasant World, 18th to 20th Centuries* (Madison: University of Wisconsin Press, 1987), 3-25, quoted from 16.

3 Already by the early 1970s Andean studies was becoming the locus of interdisciplinary dialogues among archaeologists, anthropologists, and historians, and much of this new research activity converged on questions of native Andean responses to early colonial rule. Four landmark studies stand out for their conceptual recasting of early colonial Andean history around that time: James Lockhart's innovative prosopographical use of notarial records to depict distinctive social groups of "early Spanish Peru" (*Spanish Peru, 1532-1560: A Colonial Society* [Madison: University of Wisconsin Press, 1968]); Nathan Wachtel's Anna-lesque study of indigenous (mostly Andean) structures and responses to Spanish conquest and colonialism, first published in French in 1971 (*La vision des vaincus: Les Indiens du Pérou devant la conquête espagnol, 1530-1570* [Paris: Editions Gallimard, 1971]); John Murra's ethnographic reading of two early Spanish *visita* records for insights into Andean inter-ecological and cultural practices, specifically their "vertical archipelago" patterns of ethnic organization (published in several articles, including his extended essay entitled "El 'control vertical' de un máximo de pisos ecológicos en las economías de las sociedades andinas," in Iñigo Ortíz de Zúñiga, ed., *Visita a la provincia de León de Huánuco en 1562*

The book's conceptual recasting was also an intrinsic part of the process and outcome of archival research. As many a novice historian discovers, initial research designs (those pretty schemes that sometimes get us modest funding) have a funny way of disassembling on the way through the archive! But perhaps my generation of *marxisant* social historians who trundled off to provincial and local archives carrying paradigms in our knapsacks had an especially difficult transition to make, as we tried to negotiate two sorts of epistemological exercises—one deductive, the other inductive. On the one hand, we had come of intellectual age in the post-Vietnam era of politically engaged research, and many of our historical projects implicated burning ideological issues of the day. In my own case, I wanted to use colonial agrarian history to challenge some of the tenets of dependency and world-systems theory within a Marxian framework of social history and class struggle. On the other hand,

---

[Huánuco: Hermilio Valdizán, 1972], 2:429-476; reprinted in John Murra, *Formaciones económicas y políticas del mundo andino* [Lima: Instituto de Estudios Peruanos, 1975]: 59-116); and Karen Spalding's pioneering ethnohistorical work on the internal transformations of rural indigenous society under colonial rule (see especially, "Social Climbers: Changing Patterns of Mobility among the Indians of Colonial Peru," *Hispanic American Historical Review* 50 [1970]: 645-664; and "Kurakas and Commerce: A Chapter in the Evolution of Andean Society," *ibid.*, 53 [1973]: 581-599). Taken together, these studies began to bring history and anthropology, structuralism and culturalism, into conceptual proximity.

This field development did not come all at once, however. For much of the early 1970s, in fact, Andean ethnology remained insulated by its single-minded pursuit of singular Andean ecological and cultural properties, often analyzed in isolation from larger historical processes. Marxian social scientists working on the Andes, on the other hand, rarely bothered to engage cultural or ethnic issues in their ongoing debates over the role of the peasantry in transitions to dependent capitalism and/or revolutionary mobilizations. This breach was demonstrated dramatically at two international scholarly conversations in 1973 and 1974. While Andean anthropologists converged on Toronto in 1973 to puzzle out Andean kinship practices and the very conceptual parameters of the *ayllu*, Latin American Marxists gathered the next year in what became a historic panel debate on *modos de producción* and the place of the peasantry in the transition to capitalism. As I have discussed at length in a recent essay, this bipolar, Janus-like view of the colonial and postcolonial Andean world challenged a new generation of Andean scholars in the late 1970s and early 1980s to work within and across this epistemological divide in creative and interesting ways (Larson, "Andean Communities, Political Cultures, and Markets: The Changing Contours of a Field," in Larson, Harris, and Tandeter, eds., *Ethnicity, Markets, and Migration in the Andes*, 5-54). For a synoptic state-of-the-field essay on field developments in Andean ethnology during the 1970s, see Frank Salomon, "Andean Ethnology in the 1970s: A Retrospective," *Latin American Research Review* 17 (1982): 75-128.

like most historians, I had an aversion to determinisms of all kinds. I was attracted to the emerging genre of regional/social history because it directed historians' attention inward and downward toward the local, the specific, and the processual. In our efforts to bridge that gap between grand theory and human agency, between timeless truths and thick descriptions, social historians strove to put flesh on bloodless abstractions, content into categories, and names on numbers. Or, as William Roseberry put it, to situate our work at the intersection of history, political economy, and culture.[4]

Once ensconced in the archive, far from the theory-ladened study groups and graduate seminars that had once crowded my graduate student days in New York City, my own project gradually shed its grand design in search of a deeper understanding of the driving forces of colonial economic life. I was chastened by the enormous variety, complexity, and unevenness of colonial source material, with which I hoped to test models of grave polemical importance. Equally daunting was the prospect of inferring patterns and trends from disparate bodies and broken series of quantitative data (tithe revenues, alcabala tax series, Indian population registries and tribute revenue, royal treasury income, notarized land and debt transactions, etc.). What could such dry statistics possibly reveal about social agency, local power relations, or regional ethnic and class structures? Official records, problematic colonial texts in their own right, were distressingly silent when read in isolation from the regional and historical context which I was only beginning to construct. As with most of the new regional histories of the late 1970s and 1980s, there was no historiographical foundation upon which to build a study of eighteenth-century Cochabamba or, for that matter, even a history of eighteenth-century Bolivia! It soon became apparent that if I were going to be able to glean social-historical insights from quantitative sources, catch glimpses of peasant agency, or evaluate the significance of colonial census records (by reading *between* and *behind* the numbers as well as by charting demographic trends), then these quantitative sources had to be read critically against a tapestry of qualitative sources gathered from every niche of the documentary record (from the high imperial reports and letters of Bourbon royal administrators to the tedious transactions of notaries recording the stuff of everyday economic life).

Like many other colonial historians, I made the pilgrimage to the

4 William Roseberry, *Anthropologies and Histories: Essays in Culture, History, and Political Economy* (New Brunswick: Rutgers University Press, 1989), 26-27.

Archivo General de Indias in Seville in search of imperial directives and judicial court cases from the Audiencia of Charcas that eventually found their way to the Council of the Indies. I also had the opportunity to work in Argentina's (then, still well-serviced) Archivo General de la Nación in Buenos Aires, a crucial repository of late colonial documentation for the Viceroyalty of La Plata (including Alto Perú after 1776). But the heart of the research project focused on local and regional-level agrarian life and required my gaining access to local and municipal archives. There awaited me, I sincerely hoped, the mother lode of documentary riches. After eight months of research in Argentina and Spain in 1973 and early 1974, I set off by train across the pampas for the Andes. Cochabamba's archives, I had heard, were still closed to the public, so I arrived there determined to wage a campaign to open them. Little did I imagine that it would take me to high government ministries in La Paz in search of letters and directives, and back again to the antechamber of the mayoral palace in Cochabamba, where I waited along with a dozen local peasant petitioners, day after day, for an audience with the appropriate municipal authorities; or that it would require a mastery of the labyrinthian partisan politics of Cochabamba in order to identify political officials (and their party affiliations) who might have the leverage and sympathy to take up my cause. Eventually my appeal reached the desk of the mayor, who ordered the archive opened to me on a limited basis. (I was soon joined in the archive by a local genealogist eager to trace his family's white aristocratic roots back to the sixteenth-century Spanish city of Toledo.)

The municipal archive of Cochabamba proved to be worth the long wait. Its uncatalogued *legajos* yielded bits of social and economic data which afforded, every once in a while, a glimpse into the political and moral quandaries of the age and the kinds of conflicts that seemed to cleave local society.[5] As always, there were some disappointments. I was forbidden to read early colonial documents in the municipal archive because of an ongoing dispute among local politicians over the official year of the city's founding—that is, whether the Villa Real de Oropesa, as Cochabamba was originally named, was founded in 1571 or 1574. (The stakes apparently were high, as two successive mayors quarreled over the appropriate year to celebrate its

5 The municipal archive has since been staffed, reorganized, and catalogued by professional historians (and occasionally an archivist). For a published catalogue of part of its collection, see Raimundo Schramm, "Archivo Histórico de Cochabamba: Índice de documentos sobre indios y tierras (siglos XVI, XVII y XVIII)," *Revista Andina* (1990).

400th anniversary, and which of them would have the honor of presiding over it!) And months later, the prioress of Cochabamba's most famous nunnery, Santa Clara, informed me that their archive had gone up in smoke one year during the fiery festivities of San Juan. (True or not, I was stopped in my tracks.) Still, there was enough archival material about the minutiae of agrarian life to counterbalance the remoteness of statistical and imperial documentation gathered from the archives of Seville, Lima, and Buenos Aires.

As I think back to those days, I am struck by the optimism and perseverance that most Latin American social historians brought to their endeavors. In dogged pursuit of untapped archival riches, we sought access to local, provincial, parish, cacique, and private family archives, whose worm-eaten documents had never before seen the light of day. Like panning for tiny nuggets of gold, the work often required random sifting through uncatalogued documents to gather bits of information on everyday transactions, which might or might not add up to discernible social or economic patterns, illuminate the historical memories of indigenous litigants, or lead down the elusive trail of a local hacienda family (whose lineage quite often disappeared suddenly into the lost folios of an itinerant scribe). Although postmodernist anxieties about subjectivity and (inter)textuality were not part of the conceptual baggage of most historians in the 1970s and early 1980s, there were profound lessons to be drawn from the very experience of doing archival work under such conditions. The randomness of research in unorganized archives; the intrinsic difficulties of reading colonial litigation that often went on for decades, involved indigenous plaintiffs and witnesses whose testimonies were muffled and mediated by Spanish-speaking authorities, and had no clear resolution (at least as recorded in the document); emerging clues in colonial judicial records suggesting the widespread practice of dissimulation among Andean Indians, who learned quickly how to make colonial statistics lie in order to lighten the burdens of Indian tribute and mita; and, above all, the vast documentary silences about marginalized subjects of colonial history and whole aspects of economic and political life that lay hidden beneath long periods of social quiescence—all these accumulated insights and experiences which came out of the very process of archival work sharpened our critical interpretive approaches to colonial documents. Not only did the new social history integrate agency into structural analyses of colonial and class exploitation, but it also produced anxieties about the possibility of recovering and rendering histories of indigenous, slave, and laboring peoples who left few, untainted documentary traces. This emerging methodological self-consciousness anticipated later post-modernist and subalternist concerns about subject positionality, the instability of meaning, and the power of language in constructing colonial hegemony (and occasionally empowering dissident popular cultures).[6] But it did not paralyze Latin American social historians of the late 1970s and 1980s from harvesting a rich crop of peasant and labor studies. Over that decade historians acknowledged the profound impact of imperialism and capitalism on economic life in the so-called periphery, but they also began to liberate informal small-holding and laboring peoples from the shadows of the dominant labor institutions and to constitute them as historical agents. The new literature gave us a kaleidoscopic view of the protean and contentious smallholding economies springing up in the crevices and contradictions of colonial labor institutions—ranging from the autonomous marketing sphere of "proto-peasantries" living on slave plantations in eighteenth-century Jamaica and Haiti; and the refractory silver "thieves" who literally carved out their own small fortunes and economic claims from the faltering mining monopolies of eighteenth-century Potosí; and the proliferating *rancheros* across the central valleys of late colonial Mexico; to the "proto-smallholders" inhabiting Cochabamba's villages and haciendas in the late eighteenth and nineteenth centuries. While most analyses focused attention on subaltern economic strategies and coercive labor processes, they began to broach issues of peasant politics, culture and power, in effect anticipating the linguistic turn of the 1990s.[7]

6 For an insightful essay on historicizing trends and challenges in Latin American and African studies during the 1980s, see Steve Stern, "Africa, Latin America, and the Splintering of Historical Knowledge: From Fragmentation to Reverberation," in Frederick Cooper et al., eds., *Confronting Historical Paradigms: Peasants, Labor, and the Capitalist World System in Africa and Latin America* (Madison: University of Wisconsin Press, 1993), 3-20. For a clear and critical introduction to postmodernist theories and aesthetics, see David Harvey, *The Condition of Postmodernity: An Enquiry into the Origins of Cultural Change* (Oxford: Basil Blackwell, 1989). The recent influences of the Indian Subaltern Studies Group on history is discussed in the "AHR Forum on Subaltern Studies" in the December 1994 issue of the *American Historical Review*, and for Latin American history, in particular, in Florencia Mallon's piece, "The Promise and Dilemma of Subaltern Studies: Perspectives from Latin America," 1491-1515.

7 The examples cited come from the following studies: Sidney Mintz, "Slavery and the Rise of Peasantries," *Historical Reflections* 6 (1979): 213-242; Sidney Mintz, *Caribbean Transformations* (Chicago: Aldine, 1974); Sidney Mintz, "The Rural Proletariat and the Problem of Rural Proletarian Consciousness," *Journal of Peasant Studies* 1 (1974): 290-325; Enrique Tandeter, *Coercion and Market: Silver Mining in Colonial Potosí, 1692-1826* (Albuquerque: University of New

Nowhere were the historiographical challenges and opportunities greater than in the reinvigorating field of Andean studies during the late 1970s and early 1980s. Once the insular domain of ethnologists and archaeologists, the field was infiltrated by a new generation of historians and anthropologists working at the edges of their disciplines. A critical strain of Andean anthropology began to historicize Andean cultural forms as social constructions rooted in specific material and symbolic struggles and adaptations under colonial and republican rule. Increasingly, anthropologists turned from grand homologies to regional, local, or community-based studies to trace intra-Andean processes of cultural conflict and change and to understand their dynamic insertion into broader imperial (or national) structures.[8] Andean historians were moving in similar directions, as they turned their analytical focus inward toward the rural peasant world and the myriad challenges it posed to regional and imperial elites in specific historical moments.[9] This cross-disciplinary effort

---

Mexico Press, 1993), esp. chap. 3; Frans J. Schryer, *The Rancheros of Plisaflores: The History of a Peasant Bourgeoisie in Mexico* (Toronto: University of Toronto Press, 1980); and this work on Cochabamba. For reflective appreciations of Latin American social history of the 1980s and its challenges to Wallerstein's world-system theory, see Steve Stern, "Feudalism, Capitalism, and the World-System in the Perspective of Latin America and the Caribbean," in Frederick Cooper et al., eds., *Confronting Historical Paradigms: Peasants, Labor, and the Capitalist World System in Africa and Latin America,* 23-83; and William Roseberry, "Beyond the Agrarian Question in Latin America," in Cooper et al., 318-370.

8 The "new" ethnohistory of the Andes made its debut in a 1978 special edition of Annales, devoted to innovative interdisciplinary studies of Andean society, both past and present. An English-language version was subsequently published in John V. Murra, Nathan Wachtel, and Jacques Revel, eds., *Anthropological History of Andean Polities* (Cambridge: Cambridge University Press, 1986). The new ethnographic and historical work on Norte Potosí being done by British anthropologists Olivia Harris and Tristan Platt opened new perspectives on the historical resilience and adaptations of ayllu-based Andean communities and cultural values in that region of Bolivia. See especially, Olivia Harris, "Labour and Produce in an Ethnic Economy: Northern Potosí, Bolivia," in David Lehmann, ed., *Ecology and Exchange in the Andes* (Cambridge: Cambridge University Press, 1982), 70-96; and Tristan Platt, "The Role of the Andean *ayllu* in the Reproduction of the Petty Commodity Regime in Northern Potosí (Bolivia)," ibid., 27-69. Platt's 1982 ethnohistorical study of nineteenth-century Chayanta had an enormous impact in constituting indigenous peoples as historical subjects in the political life of the Bolivian republic during the liberal era. See Platt, *Estado boliviano y ayllu andino: Tierra y tributo en el Norte de Potosí* (Lima: Instituto de Estudios Peruanos, 1982).

9 Andean social-regional history, a field that barely existed in 1970, acquired an extraordinary richness and density over the 1980s and early 1990s. In the

provided a critical forum in Andean studies for my generation of scholars, because it began to engage the variant determinisms inherent in both structuralist approaches to Andean culture and ethnicity (sometimes reified as *lo andino*) and in Marxian theories of penetrant capitalism in the Andean periphery.[10]

The redefinition of Andean research priorities was also rooted in the explosive political situations in Peru and Bolivia, which provoked new interest in agrarian and indigenous themes and broke down the false dichotomies separating academics and politics. Even historians working on the "remote colonial past" often found themselves drawn into larger political debates about the implications of their studies for understanding contemporary forms of colonial oppression, agrarian transformation, peasant politics, and rural social move-

---

making of this book, I engaged in critical dialogues with the ongoing research of historians working in two areas of Andean social and/or ethnohistory: the formation of the early colonial state and society (esp. Karen Spalding's *Huarochirí: An Andean Society under Inca and Spanish Rule* [Stanford: Stanford University Press, 1984]; Steve J. Stern, *Peru's Indian Peoples and the Challenge of the Spanish Conquest: Huamanga to 1640* [Madison: University of Wisconsin Press, 1982]; Thierry Saignes, *Los Andes orientales; Historia de un olvido* [Cochabamba: CERES, 1985]; and Nicolás Sánchez Albornoz, *Indios y tributos en el Alto Perú* [Lima: Instituto de Estudios Peruanos, 1978]); and the regional or local history of mining and hacienda economies, peasant and wage labor relations, agrarian cycles, and everyday forms of peasant livelihood and social reproduction under late colonial rule or republican rule (e.g., Florencia Mallon, *The Defense of Community in Peru's Central Highlands: Peasant Struggle and Capitalist Transition, 1860-1940* [Princeton: Princeton University Press, 1983]; Enrique Tandeter, "La rente comme rapport de production et comme rapport de distribution: Le cas de l'industrie minière de Potosí, 1750-1826," 3rd cycle doctorate, Ecole des Hautes Etudes en Sciences Sociales, Paris, 1980 [recently revised and published in English as *Coercion and Market: Silver Mining in Colonial Potosí, 1692-1826* [Albuquerque: University of New Mexico, 1993]]; and Juan Martínez Alier, "Relations of Production on Andean Haciendas," in Kenneth Duncan and Ian Rutledge, eds., *Land and Labor in Latin America: Essays on the Development of Agrarian Capitalism* [Cambridge: Cambridge University Press, 1977], 141-164). I also drew methodological and comparative inspiration from the Annales school's *longue duree* approach to agrarian harvest cycles and rural patterns of social unrest, especially as it was applied by Enrique Florescano to Mexican regions during the eighteenth century. See Florescano, *Precios de maíz y crisis agrícola en México, 1708-1810* (Mexico City: Colegio de México, 1969).

10 For an insightful assessment of the new Andean social history produced during the 1980s and its challenges to "traditional" Andean ethnology, see Deborah Poole, "Antropología y historia andina en los EE.UU.: Buscando un reencuentro," *Revista Andina* 10 (1992): 209-245. See also Charles Walker, "La historiografía en inglés sobre los Andes: Balance de la década del 80," *Revista Andina* 9 (1991): 513-528.

ments. In Peru the military-populist regime of Velasco (1968–1975), followed by a decade of escalating military and political violence in the 1980s, shaped a whole generation of historically minded "peasant-ologists" critical of authoritarian policies of rural modernization and land reform, the persistence of peasant poverty, and the aims of the Peruvian national project to marginalize Indians through violent suppression of their ethnic difference. But it was Bolivia's wrenching changes and struggles, and the political schisms and debates they generated, that influenced the course of my own evolving research on colonial Cochabamba. The crucible of military dictatorships under Banzer (1971–1978) and later García Meza (1980–1982), followed by the restoration of a weak neoliberal regime determined to dismantle the remnants of the authoritarian-populist project left over from the Revolution of 1952, catalyzed political debates and grassroots social movements among peasants, laborers, and intellectuals throughout the country. Even the archive did not provide sanctuary from the everyday manifestations of political repression and unrest in those times: peasant roadblocks and marches, activist Bolivian colleagues suddenly disappearing into exile or worse (and then sometimes re-surfacing briefly in sunglasses and wigs), candlelit conferences held clandestinely during military curfews and blackouts, and the ubiquitous machine-gun-toting military man in downtown Cochabamba were commonplace. But it was the cultural politics and discourses emanating from *katarismo*, a new social movement based in La Paz, that was to have the most critical and enduring impact on the political and intellectual life of Bolivia during the early to mid-1980s. Specifically, katarismo's agenda of ethnic (i.e., Aymara and Quechua) revindication called for a critical historiography that would place indigenous peoples (and ethnic issues) at the very center of Bolivia's modern political history. The decolonization of historical knowledge also called for the collectivization of research methods and dissemination across ethnic and linguistic boundaries. Following precedents established by progressive Jesuits in La Paz, katarista-inspired scholars began to create alternative idioms and venues (Aymara-language radio soap operas devoted to historical dramas about Tupac Katari, for example; roving guerrilla theaters; history comic strips; bilingual historical studies; an Aymara oral history archive) to disseminate their work. As a political-cultural movement, katarismo has undergone enormous flux and change over the past fifteen years, but its contribution to the field of Andean studies has been enormous.[11]

11 Most notably, the Taller de Historia Oral Andina (THOA) has produced a series of studies and built an impressive oral history archive of Aymara and Quechua

In retrospect, I can better appreciate the powerful revisionist historiography that Aymara intellectuals were forging in La Paz at about the same time I was busily studying a region of Bolivia that might have been across the sea from the highland territory of katarismo. Indeed, the early 1980s now appear to have been a crucial moment in the articulation of an alternative, ethnically plural nationalism that ripped into post-revolutionary statist experiments of land reform, modernization, and nationhood.[12] The bitter legacy of violence and repression under Banzer and García Meza during the 1970s and early 1980s intensified the need for critical introspection about the recent revolutionary past and its disintegration into successive

testimonies gathered by the collective. See, for example, the following THOA studies: *El indio Santos Marka T'ula* (La Paz: Ediciones del THOA, 1984); *Mujer y lucha comunaria: historia y memoria* (La Paz: HISBOL, 1986); *Los constructores de la ciudad* (La Paz: Ediciones del THOA, 1986); and "Santos Marka T'ula," Aymara-language radio-novel in 90 episodes, broadcast by Radio San Gabriel (La Paz), 1987. An important precedent was set by the Jesuit institution, El Centro para la Investigación y Promoción del Campesinado (CIPCA), which broadcast a historical novel entitled "Tupak Katari" in the 1970s. CIPCA continues to publish and disseminate all sorts of scholarly works on Bolivian indigenous peasants and workers.

Among the important new historical studies, see Roberto Choque, *La sublevación de Jesús de Machaqa* (La Paz: Chitakolla, 1986); Choque et al., *Educación indígena: ciudadanía o colonización?* (La Paz: Aruwiyiri, 1992); Carlos B. Mamani, *Taraqu 1866-1935: Massacre, Guerra y Renovación en la biografía de Eduardo Nina Qhispi* (La Paz: Aruwiyiri, 1991); and Victor Hugo Cárdenas, "La Lucha de un pueblo," in Xavier Albó, ed., *Raíces de América: El mundo Aymara* (Madrid: Alianza Editorial, 1988), 495-534. Taken together, these studies recuperated the highland heritage of neocolonial violence and indigenous resistance that intensified between 1880 and 1930—a chapter in the turbulent history of Bolivian liberalism and nationalism that had remained buried until very recently. On the reconstruction of Bolivian history through an "autonomous vision of the indigenous past," see Silvia Rivera C., "Sendas y senderos de la ciencia social andina," *Autodeterminación: Análisis histórico-político y teoría social* 10 (1992): 83-108. Her own work, *"Oppressed but Not Defeated": Peasant Struggles among the Aymara and Qhechwa in Bolivia, 1900-1980* (Geneva: UNRISD, 1987), remains one of the first and most fundamental studies in this new ethno-historiography.

12 At base, Andean ethnic-cultural critiques of oligarchic, populist, and neo-forms of liberalism denounce its violent deployment of anti-Indian policies, aimed at destroying indigenous territories, autonomies, and identities while perpetuating (and concealing) ethnic and class forms of oppression in the name of modernity and modernization. In particular, indigenous movements protest the imposition of a "national culture" of mestizaje, through which a small creole elite has tried to claim hegemony by defining indigenous cultures within the nation-state as obstacles to national development and integration. See Wankar (Ramiro Reinaga), *Tawantinsuyu: 5 siglos de guerra ghewaaymara contra Espana* (La Paz: MINKHA, 1978); and Rivera, *"Oppressed but Not Defeated."*

dictatorships. To most Bolivians, the 1952 "nationalist revolution" still represented Bolivia's most important experiment in modern nation-building, thanks to its historic multiethnic, multiclass alliance of militant mineworkers and Cochabamba peasants, under the leadership of progressive middle-class political leaders. More than any other region, Cochabamba symbolized both the hearth and the grave of this nationalist political project. For beginning in the 1930s its peasants had led the struggle against the landed oligarchy: they organized agrarianist unions, invaded local haciendas, and eventually pressured populist-nationalist regimes to implement extensive agrarian reform (which, when put into effect starting in 1953, carved smallholding and communal properties out of ex-hacienda land). Yet less than a decade later, in 1964, Cochabamba was also the site of the infamous "military-campesino pact" that buttressed the military regime of General René Barrientos and paved the way for a wave of repressive dictatorships thereafter. The long-term legacies of these state-driven populist pacts seemed bitter, indeed, even for Cochabamba peasants.[13] The resurgent ethnic movements of the late 1970s and 1980s excoriated Bolivia's revolutionary-nationalist project for imposing a "hegemonic mestizo model" (and its liberal economic precepts) on this pluriethnic society, whose indigenous peoples still nurtured communal ideals and memories in many parts of the altiplano.

This insurgent Aymara critique had acute political relevance in the early 1980s. For just as Bolivia was restoring a fragile democracy after a decade of dictatorship, it confronted the harsh onset of "neoliberalism," that widely touted, U.S.-promoted, free-trade solution to Latin America's earlier state-led era of nationalism and developmentalism imported into Bolivia and other parts of Latin America during the 1980s and 1990s. Untempered by populist policies and rhetoric, this latter-day version of free-trade liberalism represented a complete capitulation to postindustrial global capitalism. Deregulation, deindustrialization, and cooperative drug-control policies were bitter medicines Bolivian government officials had to swallow if they

13 In January of 1974, three months before I arrived to begin my fieldwork, Cochabamba peasants were brutally massacred by the military for setting up roadblocks and cutting off the city's food supplies in protest of tax hikes and price policies. For an overview of Bolivian history, particularly the revolutionary-nationalist era, see Silvia Rivera, *"Oppressed but Not Defeated."* For standard histories of the Bolivian revolutionary era, see Herbert S. Klein, *Bolivia: The Evolution of a Multi-Ethnic Society* (New York: Oxford University Press, 1982); and James Malloy, *Bolivia: The Uncompleted Revolution* (Pittsburgh: University of Pittsburgh Press, 1970).

were to succeed in obtaining foreign loan and investment capital. To Bolivia's new ethnic militants, however, it was bitter irony that the same MNR political leaders (no less than Victor Paz Estenssoro), who had presided over the earlier populist/developmentalist phase of national integration, were now managing a Reagan-style revolution of economic deregulation, which basically denationalized and dismantled the same tin mines and disemployed the same mineworkers (or their sons) that had once represented the triumph of Bolivian nationalism over imperial capitalism in the early 1950s. In this politically charged climate, Aymara-based neo-indigenismo became a force in national politics, filling the vacuum left by the crisis of Marxism, populism, and nationalism.[14]

The rise of militant ethnic movements in Bolivia also gathered strength from positive international developments. Disparate indigenous rights movements had cropped up across the Americas during the 1970s. Some flourished and eventually consolidated themselves into high profile pan-Indian movements during the late 1980s and early 1990s, thanks in part to converging international interests in biodiversity and rain forest conservation, cultural survival, and human rights issues. Suddenly even Latin America's "non-Indian nations" had strong indigenous rights' advocates forging international alliances with nongovernmental organizations. In Bolivia, the convergence of ecological and ethnic movements in 1990 abruptly shifted the locus of struggle away from the traditional combat zone of the altiplano to the peripheral tropical lowlands during the his-

---

14 Xavier Albó, "Making the Leap from Local Mobilization to National Politics," *Report on the Americas* 29 (1996): 16. Scholarly critiques of "creole" liberalism and neoliberalism, past and present, came from a variety of sources, including the traditional Left. For a sample of recent political dialogues about the nationalist revolution of 1952, ideological and historical reverberations between liberalism and neoliberalism, and the role of the unions and leftist political organizations in Bolivia, see the special issue of *Autodeterminación* on the history of the Bolivian Left (6-7 [1988]), and the issue on Liberalism/Neoliberalism (9 [1991]).

To many critics on the Left, the greatest challenge confronting Bolivia's neo-indigenismo (reflected in the factional and ideological battles fought within katarismo and more generally, in its broad-based union, the CSUTCB) was to conjoin ethnic-culturalist and class-union strategies and goals in the search for solidarity against the new economic austerity measures of free-trade liberalism. The strong heritage of class/syndicalist politics among different sectors of indigenous and non-indigenous laborers (particularly the militant industrial tin miners of Siglo XX, Catavi, Oruro and other cities, as well as the incidents of peasant strikes, roadblocks, the terrible massacre of Cochabamba peasants in 1974) seemed to call for broad political agendas inclusive of both cultural and economistic demands.

toric "march for territory and dignity," in which 700 men and women from lowland tribal groups walked 400 miles from the Amazon rain forest through the snow-capped Andes on route to La Paz. The bitter symbolism of 1492/1992 provoked another powerful ritual protest in the indigenous counter-quincentenaries that multiplied in the cities and towns across Bolivia on 12 October 1992. But these dramatic political theaters tend to obscure the grassroots ethnic mobilizations that gathered momentum across the altiplano over the late 1970s and early 1980s.

Here, then, in the intellectual projects of katarismo was the chance to recover a powerful counterhegemonic tradition to liberal ("ethnocidal") nation-building projects that had dominated Bolivian history and historiography until then. Aymara intellectuals reconstructed Bolivia's tumultuous political past, not in terms of the usual clichés chronicling Bolivia's succession of caudillos, nor even as an epic of heroic mining/peasant struggles against Bolivia's oligarchic ruling class, but rather as a series of violent political and cultural struggles spearheaded by militant caciques beginning in the 1780s, intensifying again after 1880, and continuing into the 1980s. The principal protagonists at war were Bolivia's liberal oligarchy and its indigenous communities. And the stakes continued to be enormous: was the Bolivian nation to be modeled after western-liberal ideals of cultural homogenization and citizenship (vis-à-vis the peculiarly Latin American national-cultural project of reified mestizaje) or reordered around the principles of ethnic pluralism, cultural self-determination, and "ayllu democracy"?[15] The clash between katarismo and neoliberalism in the mid-1980s was turning out to be the most recent manifestation of that historic struggle.

Hindsight often brings clarity to the ambiguities and arbitrariness surrounding life's everyday experiences, choices, and positions. Although there were moments when I came face to face with the

15 On the suppression of indigenous history and memory by the official populist historiography and ideology, see Luís Antezana H., "Sistemas y procesos ideológicos en Bolivia," in René Zavaleta M., ed., *Bolivia Hoy* (Mexico: Siglo XXI, 1983), xxx; on the polarity between "liberal democracy" and "ayllu democracy," see Silvia Rivera, "Democracia liberal y democracia de ayllu: El caso de Norte Potosí, Bolivia," in Carlos Toranzo Roca, ed., *El difícil camino hacia la democracia* (La Paz: Instituto Latinoamericano de Investigaciones Sociales, 1990), 9-52. For an acute historical comparison of Mexico, Bolivia, and Peru's divergent national struggles to build hegemonic populist regimes, based on official mestizo projects, see Florencia Mallon, "Indian Communities, Political Cultures, and the State in Latin America, 1780-1990," *Journal of Latin American Studies* 24 (1992): 35-53.

growing intellectual and ideological breach that separated traditional Andeanists and Aymara ethnic nationalists from Marxist peasant-ologists (most of whom seemed to be working in the valleys of Cochabamba), I must confess that the routines of archival research followed by the solitary work of writing, succeeded then by the en-cumbrances of untenured university life and a growing family in the United States, shielded me from most of the heat and fallout from these ongoing political and ideological struggles in Bolivia at the time. Yet even while I lived and worked in Cochabamba, strong ideo-logical and regional traditions continued to polarize anthropological-historical discourses among Bolivianists.

My immediate contact with these poles of Andean politics and scholarship came in the form of my collaborative work with Cocha-bamba-based anthropologists and sociologists in the summer of 1981. It was a partisan introduction to the "peasantology" side of the deep divide I was beginning to perceive. In that year, I returned to Cochabamba to collaborate with a team of anthropologists led by Jorge Dandler and Jorge Balán, in their study of the contempo-rary patterns of peasant livelihood and social reproduction. Inhabit-ing another conceptual universe from that of the contentious ethnic politics of La Paz, these fieldworkers were interested in contempo-rary class-driven processes of peasantization—namely, the economic adaptability and viability of Cochabamba's peasant families and their continuing ability to provision the towns and cities of Cochabamba amid the ecological, demographic, and economic pressures of rural smallholding.[16] On a theoretical level, this project engaged ongoing agrarianist debates in Latin America over peasantization versus pro-letarianization. Leaning toward the peasantization side of the Marx-ist equation, it argued that Cochabamba's peasant economies were living proof of Latin America's vital small-scale cultivators, artisans, and laborers who constantly adapted to regional and distant mar-kets in order to avoid abject surrender to the forces of proletarian-ization. The project produced a series of important monographs on the changing internal composition of peasant household economies, the growing informal sector of the regional economy, shifting gender relations, participation of peasants in coca production in the tropi-

16 See Jorge Dandler, "Diversificación, procesos de trabajo, y movilidad espa-cial en los valles y serranías de Cochabamba," in Harris, Larson, and Tandeter, eds., *La participación indígena en los mercados surandinos: Reproducción y transformación en los siglos XVI-XX* (La Paz: CERES 1987), 639-682. The project was cosponsored by the Centro para el Estudio de la Realidad Económica y Social (CERES).

cal region of Chapare, and the new migratory networks connecting Cliza and other towns and villages across Cochabamba's Valle Alto to distant wage jobs (now, no longer in the mining camps of high-land Bolivia or the Chilean coast, but in the mushrooming construction industry in and around the city of Buenos Aires). These anthropological studies found that Cochabamba's peasant-laborer diaspora now encompassed the Argentine capital almost a thousand miles to the south.

That summer field experience changed the way I thought about colonial Cochabamba. Coaxed out of the shadows of the past into the sunshine of contemporary peasant life, I began to perceive the vague outlines of certain long-term historical patterns and continuities that had nearly eluded me in the archives. For the first time I began to reassemble fragmented evidence of agrarian patterns in the late colonial past through an interdisciplinary dialogue with anthropologists working on contemporary peasant economy and society. What my sources seemed to be suggesting about the submerged, barely discernible smallholding economy of the late colonial period, for example, was thrown into bold relief by my colleagues' fieldwork on peasant economics in contemporary Cochabamba. And they learned, too, that contemporary peasants were the heirs of economic and political traditions that may have stretched back into the colonial past. On the other hand, I was becoming increasingly aware of the epistemological and political chasm separating the valley peasant-ologists of Cochabamba from the highland nativists of La Paz and Norte Potosí. Often, political and scholarly differences were couched in regional terms. But behind those regional contrasts lay conceptual and ideological differences over the importance to be attached to "class" or "ethnicity" as the axis of analysis—and political action. At times this chasm reflected the insularity of regional approaches and the lack of sustained intellectual dialogue, rather than the heat and noise of sustained polemic.[17] It is telling, for example, that in our collaborative study of Cochabamba peasant economies in 1981, we

17 Gustavo Rodríguez's research on nineteenth-century liberalism and land-holding in Cochabamba was perhaps the first attempt to critically engage the question of regional difference among Bolivian oligarchies and peasant struggles. See his "Expansión del latifundio o supervivencia de las comunidades indígenas? Cambios en la estructura agraria boliviana del siglo XIX," *Série: Historia*, Instituto de Estudios Sociales y Económicos (IESE), Working Paper no. 1 (Cochabamba: Universidad de San Simón, 1983). He directly addressed the 'altiplano model' developed in Silvia Rivera, "La expansión del latifundio en el altiplano boliviano," *Avances* 2 (1978): 95-118.

sought comparative perspectives, not in the ethnic economies and politics of Bolivia's altiplano regions but in the mestizo/mercantile peasant-miner traditions of the distant Mantaro valley of central Peru (being intensively studied by anthropologists Norman Long and Bryan Roberts).[18]

It was impossible and undesirable, in any event, to work in Bolivia without wrestling with the deeper implications of these variant regional histories and discourses. In the case of this unfolding study, Paceño-based ethnic politics and historiography helped me to recast my regional history by locating it in the dynamic, complex world of the southern Andes—at the analytical intersection of mercantile forces, Spanish imperialism, and preexisting Andean political cultures in transition. I no longer approached the study of haciendas, markets, and peasants in early colonial Cochabamba as "logical outcomes" of European commercial penetration, colonization, and assimilation, but as historical products involving a long and complicated European and indigenous scramble for fertile kichwa lands (as well as power, privilege, and authority) in the chaotic aftermath of the Spanish conquest. If the Cochabamba valleys were perhaps more predisposed to European colonization than other regions, then the reasons (I conjectured) had as much to do with Incaic legacies, ethnic politics and imperial conflicts, and with peasant migratory and subsistence strategies, as they did with the advance of European mercantile colonialism or with the region's natural endowments (see chapters 1 and 2).[19] In making the pre-Conquest Andean world the

18 Norman Long and Bryan R. Roberts's research on the Montaro region of Peru did much to advance the argument about peasant strategies of communal reproduction and articulation with dependent capitalist sectors, in contradistinction to Leninist teleologies about proletarianizing tendencies. See their edited volume, *Peasant Cooperation and Capitalist Expansion in Central Peru* (Austin: University of Texas, 1978). Norman Long served as a consultant to the Cochabamba project in the early 1980s.

19 Although we still lack an in-depth study of Cochabamba's late-Incaic/early colonial transition, José Gordillo and Mercedes del Río have published and analyzed a hitherto unknown Toledan inspection and census, dating from 1573. This *visita* of Tiquipaya sheds fascinating light on post-Conquest Indian demographics, household composition, and ayllu settlement patterns; the first encomiendas and *tierras de repartimiento* of Tiquipaya (later, one of the region's five pueblos reales); and the regional peculiarities of Inca power and society in this valley before the Conquest. The document confirms much of what Nathan Wachtel discovered about itinerant labor flows into the region, Inca control over royal grain production, and post-Conquest disruptions. But for the first time, researchers have been able to do extensive demographic analysis of an early colonial

Chapter 10

conceptual point of departure, I was also inspired by the pathbreaking research of Karen Spalding on Huarochirí, Steve Stern on Huamanga, and Thierry Saignes on Larecaja. In these regional colonial studies, Andean ethnic groups—in all their variety and diversity— were becoming proactive historical subjects and the Conquest itself was no longer construed as an event but as a protracted process of struggle and transformation, in which the actions of Andean peoples conditioned the evolution of colonial structures. The motor forces of change in my own regional study became the deep, historical contradictions intrinsic to the social strategies and struggles among regional elites, Andean peasants, and the imperial State. Some battles were played out on imperial fields of power; others were thrashed out at the regional level; and still other conflicts simmered beneath the surface of everyday ethnic and class relations. Over time, they seemed to have undermined the institutional pillars of colonialism: caste and the landed estate. Thus, whereas my initial research project had set out to study the destructive impact of external imperial forces on the region, the revised book version explored the dialectics of structure and agency in shaping the endogamous processes of colonial and class formation.[20]

---

indigenous settlement in this region, drawing important implications about the transition from Inca to Spanish rule. One of their more intriguing hypotheses points to the importance of a royal Inca nunnery (*acllahuasis*) in Tiquipaya, making it perhaps a crucial site of Inca political control through the appropriation and redistribution of virgin women among the southern Collasuyu. See Gordillo and del Río, *La visita de Tiquipaya (1573): Análisis Etno-Demográfico de un Padrón Toledano* (Cochabamba: UMSS, 1993). See also the important recent work of Mercedes del Río on sixteenth-century Tapacarí: "Simbolismo y poder en Tapacarí," *Revista Andina* 8 (1990): 77-106.

20 As mentioned earlier, this book is now part of a growing Andean "historiography of resistance," to borrow Poole's phrase. This literature has grown, deepened, and diversified over the 1990s, although Andean peasant histories on the nineteenth century are being produced in more abundance now than they were ten or fifteen years ago. An important synthesis of the early colonial historiography and its implications for broader issues concerning the Toledan state is Kenneth J. Andrien's "Spaniards, Andeans and the Early Colonial State in Peru," in K. Andrien and R. Adorno, eds., *Transatlantic Encounters: Europeans and Andeans in the Sixteenth Century* (Berkeley: University of California Press, 1991), 121-150. For a more encompassing, reflective assessment of the field of indigenous-centered colonial history, in the context of current indigenous social movements and debates, see Steve Stern, "Paradigms of Conquest: History, Historiography, and Politics," *Journal of Latin American Studies* 24 (1992): 1-34; reprinted in the second edition of Stern, *Peru's Indian Peoples and the Challenge of Spanish Conquest* (Madison: University of Wisconsin Press, 1993), xxi-liii.

But if this book (and the new Andean historiography of which it was a part) tried to mediate imperial/world market forces and Andean agency, political economy issues still served as its conceptual center. Although the book did not set out to challenge the tenets of cultural determinism, the implicit elements of critique cropped up throughout: for example, in the analysis of intra-Andean conflicts, cacique rivalries, and disputed claims of Indianness in eighteenth-century Tapacarí, which belied the idealism of a seamless "moral economy" governing Indian communal relations (chapter 4); in my discussion of the extractive policies of the Bourbon state, particularly during the devastating drought of the early 1800s, which exploded the myth (deployed by defensive highland ayllus in the Liberal era) of a benevolent "tributary pact" legitimating Spanish rule[21] (chapter 8); and in my rendering of peasant practices of tribute evasion and mestizaje during the eighteenth and nineteenth centuries, which suggested a de-Indianizing political and cultural logic at work among the valley's smallholding peasantry, quite at odds with the defensive ethnocommunal strategies of the ayllus of Chayanta and other highland peoples (chapter 9). On this last point, the book made an implicit argument about divergent colonial legacies, enduring regionalisms, and plurality of Andean peasant politics in Bolivia. As I began to realize, Cochabamba posed a strong regional counterpoint to the ayllu-centric politics and histories of highland peoples. I saw in this case the potential for understanding alternative forms of peasant labor, subsistence strategies, and struggle that had developed *outside* a colonial-Indianist tradition. And yet my emphasis on regional economic and political issues limited the parameters of my research into peasant politics and political consciousness in late colonial Cochabamba; they were largely intuited from the regional-

21 Aside from ongoing negotiations and conflicts over royal tribute policies in the late colonial era, the tithe (broadly defined) proved to be another crucial political and discursive domain of struggle. Rather than analyze tithes as an economic index of agricultural production (see my discussion of Tandeter and Wachtel's study in chapter 3) or as a speculative venture that complements other economic activities of a regional elite (see chapter 6), social historians are beginning to look at the contentious politics of tithing as a window onto deeper conflicts over colonial jurisdictions, legitimacies, and identities in Alto Perú. The protagonists in this drama included not only disparate secular and ecclesiastical authorities as well as imperial and local elites, but also highly differentiated peasant groups—in particular, communal landholders and a variety of tenant cultivators (*arrenderos*). See Rossana Barragán and Sinclair Thomson, "Los lobos hambrientos y el tributo a Díos: Conflictos sociales en torno a los diezmos en Charcas colonial," *Revista Andina* 11 (1993): 305-345.

historical context. Furthermore, I posed the comparison between Cochabamba's aggressively mercantile, de-Indianizing peasants and Chayanta's ayllu-Indianist politics in the nineteenth century mainly as a heuristic device in order to underscore the diverse forms of peasant labor and struggle in the Bolivian Andes. For while the book tried to liberate Andean peasant agency from the stranglehold of structuralism, and while it hinted at the kinds of political concerns and values that animated local conflicts over land, labor, and taxes, it did not grant analytical priority to the ways in which peasants and other laboring people in the valleys forged political traditions, social networks, and identities out of local experiences and struggles. As I discuss below, it is precisely these kinds of issues that now need to be integrated into the framework of this regional history.

But this is to leap ahead of the story. For amid the ideological firestorms in Bolivia in the early 1980s, Andean histories like this one would be read and critiqued by politically engaged scholars for their utility in understanding and judging contemporary peasant movements in Bolivia.[22] Among Bolivian social scientists and activists seeking a usable past, the prevailing regional dichotomy (particularly in its more generic forms of valley/highland or mestizo/Indian dualities) became symbolic—not necessarily of the complexity and plurality of Andean political culture but of the ideological poles in modern Bolivian politics. In its most reductive form, this binarism counterposed two mutually exclusive cultural heritages—and irreconcilable political imaginaries—that seemed to boil down to the acceptance or rejection of market capitalism, agrarian reform privileging peasant smallholding, and integrative nationalism. From the valley perspective, peasantologists perceived in Cochabamba's history the hopeful signs of a resilient adaptive peasantry which could, and would, resist the social forces of proletarianization (against the predictions of most orthodox Marxists), while they struggled for small measures of economic autonomy and justice. For militant ethnic nationalists, on the other hand, Cochabamba's regional history was emblematic of peasant quiescence, assimilation, and co-optation—the evils of colonialism and modernity which had thwarted highland ethno-communal ideals (communal land reclamations, cultural self-determination, and pluriethnic conceptions

22 Spanish translations of this study (in essay form) began circulating in Bolivia in 1978. Inexpensive, "pocket-copies" of my collected essays, entitled *Explotación agraria y resistencia campesina en Cochabamba* (Cochabamba: CERES, 1983; 1984) went through two editions of 1,000 copies each. The Spanish-language version of this book was published in Bolivia in 1992, by CERES.

of nationhood). Where many kataristas wrote off Quechua-mestizo peasantries as corrupt clients or penny capitalists, they heralded "the awakening of the giant," armed with a communal memory and destined to follow in the footsteps of the insurgent rebel leader, Tupac Katari. Two hundred years after the six-month siege of La Paz, latter-day Aymara nationalists would rise up to lead Bolivia out of the quagmire of failed nationalism, mestizo hegemony, and neoliberalism.[23]

23 In a subtle way, the polarity between highland/valley and ethnicity/class positions is revealed in the pair of articles on modern Bolivian peasant politics in Stern's 1987 edited volume, *Resistance, Rebellion, and Consciousness*. Xavier Albó's analysis of the origins, strength, and hope of the katarista movement highlights the deep historical roots and continuities of ethnic/communal ideology and practice among the *colla* peasants still living in traditional communities. He then draws the "historic contrast" to valley peasants, who inherited a very "weak communal tradition." By deploying this "historical-structural contrast" between the Cochabamba valleys and the La Paz altiplano, Albó deduced the essential cultural and ideological attributes of each kind of peasant society, which shaped their distinctive political traditions and contemporary political consciousness (the "open" *classista* politics of individualist, land-hungry peasants in the Quechua valleys as opposed to the communal anti-state *etnicismo* of the Aymara highlands). At base, he lays the tragedy of the 1952 revolution at the feet of corrupt creole reformers and their clientelistic (and vulnerable) peasant allies who tried to impose western forms of nationalism on this profoundly pluriethnic society. See Albó, "From MNRistas to Kataristas to Katari," in Stern, ed., *Resistance, Rebellion, and Consciousness*, 379-419.

In contrast, Jorge Dandler and Juan Torrico contribute a painstakingly researched ethnography of Ayopaya peasant politics in the late 1940s, in which they vindicate and explain why peons of one feudalistic hacienda in this highland area of Cochabamba tried to forge a paternal pact with the populist president, Villarroel, and lay claim to their rights as citizens. Theirs is a poignant case of hacienda-based peasants deploying both their indigenous identity to call for, and participate in, the first National Indigenous Congress, held in 1945, *and* their rights as citizens to build an agrarian movement to break the bonds of feudal servitude and forced labor. No less important, these anthropologists bring the historical memories and interpretations of Ayopaya leaders to bear on their analysis. See "From the National Indigenous Congress to the Ayopaya Rebellion: Bolivia, 1945-1947," in Stern, ed., *Resistance, Rebellion, and Consciousness*, 334-378.

It is precisely this kind of cultural and social history, grounded in the local experiences and memories of the peasant participants themselves, that is needed to break down prevailing political/regional binarisms (and deductive approaches) which still characterize much political and scholarly discourse. For a friendlier reading of the Albó article, as well as an eloquent call for future historical and anthropological research that moves beyond the nativist/nationalist schism, see Stern, "Introduction to Part IV," in *Resistance, Rebellion, and Consciousness*, 327-333.

A recent North American study that reproduces these familiar highland/valley, ethnic/class antinomies is by Dwight R. Hahn, *The Divided World of the*

The ethnic/class debate has continued to animate various democratic and emancipatory projects in Bolivia during the past decade. But changing historical conditions have compelled scholars and activists to reframe many of the issues surrounding peasant social movements and the Bolivian nation-state. Ironically, as neoliberalism has taken its toll among the rural and urban poor in Bolivia, state policies and discourses have become more accommodating to the ideals of ethnic pluralism and popular participation. At the same time, katarismo's influence has waned and ethnic politics have grown more pluralized, complicated, and (some would argue) compromised with certain sectors of the Bolivian state. Militant katarismo has had to temper and adapt its political strategies and discourses to fit the changing times. In the meantime, neoliberalism (and the withering of the international Left) has nearly defanged the militant mineworkers' unions, leaving few hopeful prospects for a resurgence of class-driven movements, at least for the present. As always in Bolivia, though, the most visible signs of change spring directly out of popular politics and discourses, and the 1990s has been a decade of diversifying and deepening popular mobilization. Since the early 1990s, indigenous groups from Bolivia's tropical lowlands have taken center stage in developing ecological and indigenous-rights movements, thus expanding the scope and content of ethno-communal politics. The 1990 march of lowland native groups for "territory and dignity" directed national attention to submerged and forgotten ethnic issues. Furthermore, the proliferation of subaltern populisms defies conventional race/class dichotomies. New strategies of "popular participation" in local electoral politics have spread among the sprawling Aymara communities of urban immigrants in El Alto and La Paz. For the first time in history, the voters of Bolivia elected a vice president who is an educator and activist of Aymara origin; and the Bolivian constitution now formally recognizes the principle of ethnic pluralism. Gender identities linked to class issues have galvanized women's advocacy groups, in poor urban neighborhoods, agricultural cooperatives, marketplaces, and industrial belts throughout Bolivian cities. And nontraditional political groups, such as the coca growers of Cochabamba's Chapare region, have seized the offensive against the state's neoliberal policies and, in particular, the U.S.-driven coca eradication campaign. This rapidly changing

---

Bolivian Andes: A Structural View of Domination and Resistance (New York: Crane Russak, 1992).

political scene has catalyzed a new cycle of political and scholarly rapprochement, rethinking, and revision in the past several years.[24]

Stepping back from the immediacy and urgency of Bolivian scholarly politics and polemics, I want to reengage these debates about the regional-historical formation and legacies of peasant politics and political consciousness in Bolivia from the standpoint of the historiographic present. Building on the foundations I laid in the original book, I want to harness some of the issues and approaches of the new cultural and political historiography of the 1990s to this specific regional case. This conceptual recasting therefore owes much to innovative scholarship in Latin American rural history, particularly to those searching historical analyses that explore subaltern politics and political culture over long periods of time.[25] But it does

[24] For example, Bolivian scholarship in the 1990s has increasingly historicized and engendered approaches to ethnic identity-making. See, for example, Rossana Barragán, *Espacio urbano y dinámica étnica: La Paz en el siglo XIX* (La Paz: HISBOL, 1990), and her article on "implicit" ethnic and gender identities under colonial or neocolonial state formation, entitled "Entre polleras, lliqllas, y ñañacas: Los mestizos y la emergencia de la *tercera república*," in S. Arze et al., eds., *Etnicidad, economía y simbolismo en los Andes* (La Paz: HISBOL, 1992), 85-128. See also Thérèse Bouysse-Cassagne and Thierry Saignes, "El cholo: actor olvidado de la historia," in S. Arze et al., eds., *Etnicidad*, 129-144. It is significant that on the quincentennial (October 1992), the new Bolivian journal, *Autodeterminación*, dedicated an entire issue (vol. 10) to the theme of "Lo mestizo, lo nacional." This journal issue provoked intense debate in Bolivia over this long-disparaged, if not long-forgotten, theme. New historical research in La Paz also engages issues of ethnicity, nationalism, and citizenship. See, for example, the collective volume: Roberto Choque et al., *Educación indígena: ciudadanía o colonización?* and Silvia Rivera's important essay on liberalism and internal colonialism, "La raíz: Colonizadores y colonizados," in Xavier Albó and Raúl Barrios, eds., *Violencias encubiertas en Bolivia* (La Paz: Aruwiyiri, 1993), 1: 27-142.

[25] See, for example, the pathbreaking studies of Flores Galindo, *Buscando un Inca: Identidad y Utopia en los Andes* (Lima: Editorial Horizonte, 1988); Silvia Rivera, *Oprimidos pero no Vencidos;* various contributions in Stern, ed., *Resistance, Rebellion, and Consciousness in the Andean Peasant World;* Erick Langer, *Economic Change and Rural Resistance in Southern Bolivia, 1880-1930* (Stanford: Stanford University Press, 1989); Joanne Rappaport, *The Politics of Memory: Native Historical Interpretation in the Colombian Andes* (Cambridge: Cambridge University Press, 1990); Gavin A. Smith, *Livelihood and Resistance: Peasants and the Politics of Land in Peru* (Berkeley: University of California Press, 1989); and Roger Neil Rasnake, *Domination and Cultural Resistance: Authority and Power among an Andean People* (Durham: Duke University Press, 1988). Important recent studies include Florencia E. Mallon, *Peasant and Nation: The Making of Postcolonial Mexico and Peru* (Berkeley: University of California Press, 1995);

not invalidate political economy approaches. In my view, we still need their macro-explanatory perspectives and tools to analyze the structures and ruptures of empire and postcolonial nation-making. Obviously, the study of imperial and world-market forces is key to understanding the intrinsic tensions of colonial life, which in turn shaped regional dynamics of power, agency, and struggle.[26] But the recent turn to linguistic and cultural analysis has proved to be an important supplementary tool, and it is beginning to endow Andean studies in particular with a new conceptual landscape that is richer, more diverse, and more interactive than the older bipolarized world of valleys and highlands, colonizers and colonized, landed elites and peasants, haciendas and ayllus, mestizos and Indians, Quechuas and Aymaras. New historical subjects are springing up in different social networks and niches of the rural and urban Andes. Gendered and occupational groups, ethnically hybrid peoples, ritual specialists and peasant intellectuals, urban ayllus, and itinerant and transient subcultures now populate the pages of historical studies. These emerging historical subjects and subjectivities confront prevailing wisdoms in a variety of ways (often reverberating with the earlier cycle of debate in the late 1970s and 1980s). For example: rural Andean communities, once pristine and autonomous, are now examined for their complicated internal hierarchies and conflicts over the meanings of their own communal heritage, authority, justice, and belonging. Andean ecological practices of "verticality" are now integrated into broader material and symbolic approaches to Indian participation in colonial and regional market systems. And Andean "cultures of opposition" now appear to have inserted themselves into broader political movements or ideologies (insurgent, hegemonic, or otherwise).[27] Inher-

---

Mark Thurner, *From Two Republics to One Divided: Contradictions of Postcolonial Nationmaking in Andean Peru* (Durham: Duke University Press, 1997); Sinclair Thomson, "Colonial Crisis, Community, and Andean Self-Rule: Aymara Politics in the Age of Insurgency" (Ph.D. diss., University of Wisconsin, 1996); and Cecilia Mendez, "Rebellion without Resistance: Huanta's Monarchist Peasants in the Making of the Peruvian State: Ayacucho, 1825-1850" (Ph.D. diss., State University of New York at Stony Brook, 1996).

26 The challenge to integrate "searching analyses of peasant economic strategies and labor processes within much more dynamic, flexible and open-ended visions of peasant politics, social networks, and culture" is insightfully discussed in Stern's introductory essay, "Africa, Latin America, and the Splintering of Historical Knowledge: From Fragmentation to Reverberation," in Frederick Cooper et al., *Confronting Historical Paradigms*, 3-20; quoted from 14.

27 See Poole, "Antropología y historia en los EE.UU."; Brooke Larson, "Andean

ently political and cultural, and yet still grounded in the specifics of regional political economy, this new research agenda raises fascinating questions about the historical significance of peasant and popular political cultures in polarized colonial and class contexts like Cochabamba. Methodologically, it brings the focus of inquiry back to that dynamic point of intersection where history, political economy, and culture converge at the regional level. And in the case of this specific regional history, it provides me with an opportunity to map the rough contours of peasant and popular political culture onto the original template of Cochabamba's long-term colonial and agrarian history. This is the task I have set for myself in the remainder of this chapter.

Cochabamba Revisited

Let me begin the task by confronting a crucial question that lies dormant in this study: how, under the constraints of colonialism and class, did Cochabamba peasantries construct social identities and alterities through their manifold cultural, political, and economic practices in the context of regional agrarian change? I do not pretend to answer this question below. But drawing on the research advances of other scholars and my own critical reflections, I attempt to outline the cultural and political possibilities presented to Cochabamba peasants and laborers in their unfolding social history, with an eye on the eventual emergence of militant peasant agrarianism in the early twentieth century. Exploring the constitutive elements of peasant political consciousness in the context of long-term regional history invites multiple research topics and approaches. But I want to focus my attention on three specific analytical domains of history, politics, and culture: (1) the rise of informal sites of peasant popular culture and collectivities located in the economic and discursive interstices of colonial/class power relations during the eighteenth and nineteenth centuries; (2) the dialectics of dominant and popular culture and power on the spacial and ethnic borderlands of mestizaje in the same period; and (3) the transformation of everyday forms of power struggles and popular culture into a radicalizing peasant movement in the early part of the present century.

By interweaving these strands of analysis, I want to argue that the

Communities, Political Cultures, and Markets: The Changing Contours of a Field," in Larson, Harris, and Tandeter, eds., *Ethnicity, Markets, and Migration in the Andes*, 5-53; and John Gledhill, *Power and Its Disguises: Anthropological Perspectives on Politics* (London: Pluto Press, 1994), esp. chaps. 5-7.

contradictory historical dynamics of polarizing class relations and eroding colonial-caste power in eighteenth- and nineteenth-century Cochabamba helped make flourish an expansive interstitial cultural and economic domain. The scope and significance of "Qochala popular culture" were shaped by long-term historical-regional processes, and by the moving poles of power and meaning as they evolved over time in the Cochabamba region. But rather than focus attention on the specifics of colonial or class forms of domination (as the original study does), I want to focus here on the elusive sinews and sites of local power and contestation that seemed to flourish at the margins. In substance, I argue that this dynamic open-ended subculture incubated everyday forms of peasant-plebeian politics and discourses, which exploded occasionally during the eighteenth and nineteenth centuries—often in the form of gendered, municipal conflicts over immediate economic and civic issues. The region's emerging political traditions of "cultural mestizaje," forged by a sprawling, heterogeneous valley population of itinerant peasants, artisans, marketing women, and laborers, laid the basis for potentially subversive, deeply anti-colonial discourses that were to become the staple of everyday politics and struggle long before peasant migration to the mines, rural syndicalism, and class consciousness took root and spread across the valleys in the 1930s and 1940s. If future research confirms the outlines of this hypothetical argument, then it will have to critically reengage broader historical questions concerning the origins and significance of contemporary peasant movements in Cochabamba and their relationship to the revolutionary-nationalist project of Bolivian state-making in the mid-twentieth century. But for the moment, let me try to unpack the constitutive elements of Cochabamba's peculiar phenomenon of "cultural mestizaje" in the late colonial and later liberalizing eras.

Sites and Sinews of Qochala Culture

From the outset, this research agenda calls into question my earlier premise about peasant politics and consciousness in the region. Placing the Cochabamba peasantry in broad temporal and spacial context, I argued in chapter 9 that most of the region's rural laborers, including village peasants, lived outside the institutional and cultural bounds of communal society and therefore had little recourse to the moral and legal collectivism of ayllu life. Historically stripped of their ancestral territorial rights, hereditary lords, sacred lineages and ancestors; deprived of colonial corporate privileges under the república de indios; subject to the daily oppressions and contradictions of class and colonialism; and not yet endowed with militant class consciousness, Cochabamba's peasants "faced the world alone" in the late eighteenth and nineteenth centuries—at least in a metaphorical sense. Were I writing this book today, I probably would advance the following thesis: that while Cochabamba's peasantry did not inherit primordial ethnic identities or invoke colonial corporate privileges as strategies of defense, they actively adapted and reconstructed communal and political relations through their quotidian practices of adaptation, survival, and struggle. My premise: that popular culture and politics (and more generically, "cultural mestizaje") must be seen as intrinsic to the wider material and social processes of imperial rule, class formation, and local conflicts over water, land, and peasant labor. This book implies as much at various points in the narrative, but a long-term history of subaltern mestizo political culture in Cochabamba, and its significance for understanding contemporary peasant movements in the region and the nation, has still to be written.

An initial research task, then, invites us to explore the patterns and processes through which peasants, plebeians, and laborers broke down their isolation and came together in multiple, overlapping sites of work, ceremony, and struggle. Prevailing notions that Indian migration and uprootedness, their absorption into insular haciendas, or their cultural contamination by mercantile practices, placed intrinsic limits on peasant political action and consciousness have to be put to rest. For such assumptions deny the collective agency and the identities of generations of rural folk apparently clever enough to devise livelihood strategies (bundled together in an incipient "rival peasant economy"), but incapable of creating alternative social spaces and identities. Rather than viewing eighteenth- and nineteenth-century Cochabamba primarily in terms of everyday forms of peasant livelihood and hacienda land-labor relations, I want to rethink the region as a vivid laboratory for inquiring into peasant and plebeian efforts to craft communities, collectivities, and identities amid the polarizing agrarian pressures and colonial crisis in the southern Andes. We need not reduce this task to one of simply uncovering an alternative "moral economy" governing horizontal relations among hacienda and smallholding peasantries. But we do need to locate the multiple, embedded sites of popular culture, power, community, and identity formation in the specific context of regional history and political economy in order to understand how culture, power, and economics continually interacted with and transformed each other over time.

The broad regional picture that emerges is one of cultural contradiction, diversity, and ambiguity in the late colonial era. On the one hand, the province encompassed starkly different microeconomies and cultures—from the insular haciendas and enforced servitude of highland Ayopaya to the crowded central valleys where haciendas coexisted and competed with an emerging, heterogenous sector of smallscale agriculturalists, artisans, traders, and laborers (see chapter 5). On the other hand, while this was an era of intensified pressures on valley land and water, tithe speculation and tax squeezes, cyclical harvest crises, and Bourbon repression and reform, it did not imply the absolute immobilization of servile laborers, their retreat into subsistent poverty, or the absence of middle peasants, smallscale merchants, muleteers, or artisans successfully competing in local retail markets.[28] Indeed, there are subtle indications throughout

28 For a contrary view, see Robert H. Jackson, *Regional Markets and Agrarian Transformation in Bolivia: Cochabamba, 1539-1960* (Albuquerque: University of New Mexico Press, 1994). Putting a different spin on the original title of my own book, Jackson locates Cochabamba's fundamental "agrarian transformation" in the 1890s, and explains it in terms of the adverse effects of Bolivia's new open-trade policies, railroad links to the coast, and anti-Indian agrarian reform laws. All these forces conspired to "radically [transform] the structure of land tenure," such that "by the 1920s the hacienda was no longer the dominant form of land tenure as in other parts of Bolivia" (p. 86). In spite of Jackson's contentious stance, my own conclusions (chapter 9) also point to the late nineteenth century as a critical moment of accelerated agrarian change.

Where we differ is in our interpretive views of late colonial Cochabamba. In part, it is simply an artifact of our research designs and strategies: whereas I focused my analysis of class formation and agrarian change on the late colonial period, Jackson targets the late nineteenth century, arguing that Cochabamba's genuine agrarian transformation came in "his era," not "mine." The problem with his effort to colonize one historical conjuncture is twofold: first, he finds himself compelled to argue for agrarian stasis and continuity throughout the mid to late colonial period (". . . changes in land tenure and rural labor relations only occurred in the middle and late nineteenth century, and not the late colonial period, and they were related to the decline of Bolivia's mining economy and the Cochabamba grain trade in the decades following Bolivian independence" [p. 195]). While he correctly points to the lack of serial data documenting Cochabamba's export trade to Potosí and other highland cities in my own study, he extrapolates from some of the very same published data I use (e.g., the famous Viedma 1788 census, which according to Nicolás Sánchez-Albornoz, is incorrectly dated 1793) to bolster his counterargument that Cochabamba's extra-regional wheat trade continued to flourish during the late eighteenth century. Second, Jackson adduces economic and political factors as the short-term precipitants of regional decline and land tenure changes, but leaves little analytic space for peasant agency in this regional history—except perhaps during the dramatic dissolution of the hacienda regime and the profusion of smallholders and syndicalists in the early twentieth century.

this study that as Cochabamba's peasant, artisan, and plebeian populations were becoming more differentiated and culturally mixed, they were also inventing traditions, spinning social networks, contesting colonial coercions, and remaking their own ethnic identities in ways that expanded the scope of their humdrum lives well beyond the backside of their draft oxen. There was a flexibility and dynamism to many peasant households which allowed them to gain ground (metaphorically, if not literally) through their diversifying productive, commercial, and wage-labor strategies. Much of this buoyancy came from intensive local demand (and wavering extraregional markets) for valley maize, chicha, and textiles. Without denying the atomizing forces of poverty, power, and repression, then, we need to follow peasants into their everyday social experiences of work, ceremony, and struggle, and seek out the ways they interacted with political and cultural communities beyond the village or hacienda gate.

On a more methodological note, this dynamic and diverse regional context cautions against static or homologous conceptions of "peasant culture." I prefer to use the more open-ended, ambiguous term, "popular culture," both because it widens the analytic compass to include a whole variety of gendered, ethnic, and occupational groups, whose lifeways, allegiances, and identities tended to undermine preconceived dichotomies (rural/urban, peasant/laborer, Indian/mestizo) in this regional context, and because the term implicitly references itself to dominant (and contested) forms of power and meaning. As Gil Joseph and Daniel Nugent argue, [popular culture] cannot be conceptualized in terms of its intrinsic qualities, but rather [it] must be seen "in relation to the political forces and culture(s) that engage it."[29] Concretely, our challenge is to understand how diversifying, heterogenous clusters of rural and urban laborers continuously engaged in the production and contestation of meaningful practices in the context of wider social, political, and ideological struggles.[30]

29 Gil Joseph and Daniel Nugent, "Popular Culture and State Formation in Revolutionary Mexico," in Joseph and Nugent, eds., *Everyday Forms of State Formation: Revolution and the Negotiation of Rule in Modern Mexico* (Durham: Duke University Press, 1994), 3-23, quoted from 15.

30 I use this regional case to suggest ways to search out the elusive, hidden, and dispersed sites of microcollectivities and informal communities that seemed to be embedded in the myriad routines and realms of everyday life—particularly in the fluid, interethnic spaces of this regional society. These were material and discursive arenas where subordinated groups of peasants and laborers engaged in the production and contestation of cultural practices, meanings, and identities. Hardly seamless, consensual, or even oppositional, popular culture (as I

In practical terms, then, this agenda calls for shifting the analytical locus to the potential sites and forms of popular culture, community, and identity-making on the outer edges of colonial and hacienda economic power. Two overlapping material and discursive domains of subaltern community-building seem particularly salient for eighteenth- and nineteenth-century Cochabamba: (1) the development of ritual-political institutions, practices, and networks that

---

am conceptualizing it here) was both a historical product of long, complicated histories of struggle, survival, and creative adaptation under colonial rule, as well as an ever unfolding process of internal adaptations and conflicts among subaltern actors themselves, over the boundaries and content of communal belonging, intracommunal inequalities, and cultural alterities. As I suggest later in the essay, this notion carries with it an implicit methodological agenda. As many historians have long argued, the study of subaltern cultures cannot be wrenched from the complicated contexts of power and domination that encased them. But nor can colonial or class power relations be understood in isolation from the political and cultural challenges, improvisations, and accommodations emanating from below. As Marxist cultural historians have reminded us from time to time, hegemony is (was) not a static mind-numbing system of dominance (based on the coercion and consent of the masses), but an active process which, in the familiar phrase of Raymond Williams, ". . . has continually to be renewed, re-created, defended, and modified . . . [because] it is also resisted, limited, altered, and challenged by pressures not at all its own" (Williams, *Marxism and Literature* [Oxford: Oxford University Press, 1977], 112). Historicizing Gramsci's notion of hegemony as a set of politically charged linkages and tensions between popular cultures and power-building, a younger generation of Latin American anthropologists and historians have turned their attention to the "dialectics of cultural struggle" (or, multiple sites, agents, and mediums of cultural conflict and production) as a conceptual pathway into *both* the historical formation (and transformation) of local political cultures and the struggle to maintain, reproduce, or reconstruct elite dominance. This political-cultural agenda has converted "marginal," "parochial," "prepolitical," "inchoate," and "inarticulate" groups of preindustrial laborers and peasants—all but invisible to the historian's eye until quite recently—into crucial political (and politically conscious) subjects, who continuously engaged and construed their wider political world in manifold and significant ways (to paraphrase Steve Stern's widely quoted axiom, in his "New Approaches to the Study of Rebellion and Consciousness," 9). Understanding the dynamics of popular culture and peasant political agency also sharpens our view of the vexed and violent histories of nation-building in the Andes and elsewhere. For as peasants and laborers engaged in their quotidian practices of survival, struggle, and community-building, as they grappled with the meanings and moralities of imperial (later, national) rule, they inevitably exposed the tensions and vulnerabilities of power. Among those Latin Americanists who have theorized "hegemony," peasant politics, popular culture, and state formation in the context of their own deeply researched historical case studies, see especially Florencia Mallon, *Peasant and Nation: The Making of Postcolonial Mexico and Peru*, chaps. 1 and 10.

drew dispersed rural peasants into the orbit of mestizifying/Indian-izing urban parishes, towns, and cities across the central valleys; and (2) the articulation of peasant networks and exchanges through emerging "popular markets" which circulated people, commodities, ideas, and loyalties. Neither provincial "mestizo" towns nor peasant markets were unique to the region, of course. But Cochabamba's historical geography, migratory streams, and diversifying economy (concretely, the region's concentration of provincial cities, towns, and villages in the valley basins; its itinerant traditions of petty marketing, muleteering, and laboring; the everyday interconnections among rural textile weavers, traders, and independent artisan groups; the thick layering of peasant leaseholders living on local haciendas; and the uneven expansion semi-independent rural smallholders—particularly toward the end of the nineteenth century) incubated new economic and cultural strategies and identities among rural immigrants, thriving urban artisan and plebeian groups, and emerging ritual and political elites at the lower ranks of culturally defined hierarchies. This social ecology must have created all sorts of interdependencies and mutualities, tying rural people together and giving rise to new forms of cooperation and exchange, which may have mediated and bridged ethnic and economic differences among heterogeneous "popular groups" and bound them tentatively together amid polarizing class and colonial pressures. It also created niches for urbanizing indigenous cultures to flourish. However, I would argue that we view these quotidian domains of popular political culture and community formation as neither "alternative" nor "autonomous"—that is, as lying outside of, or in opposition to, the institutional and discursive parameters of dominant creole culture. Even in its original emphasis on hacienda formation, mestizaje, and peasant economic strategies, this regional history makes a strong case against such a proposition. But nor should we consider the region's emerging Quechua-mestizo communities and identities to have been either fully assimilative or totally subordinant to creole power and practices. Rather, it makes more sense to approach the study of pueblerino barter-markets and ritual-religious politics (and the emerging forms of power and identity they engendered) as material and discursive spaces of fluid—one might even say, strategic—in-betweenness and ambiguity, where power, meaning, and identity were rendered more indeterminant, relational, and contestable.

Consider, for example, the trade fairs, festivals, and local political rituals that probably accompanied the spread of towns and settlements across the crowded valley basins during the late eighteenth century. The hearth and hub of this culturally hybrid, pueblerino world, these towns and small cities (Quillacollo, Tarata, Sacaba, the provincial capital of Cochabamba, etc.) hosted peasant ferias, artisan communities, and merchants, as well as a steady stream of deracinated peddlers, casual laborers, *arrieros*, and pilgrims passing through. Valley towns and cities also were nodes of connection and confluence: regional trade circuits, labor migration patterns, and religious festivals all converged on the valley towns. Popular religious ceremonies, for example, attracted market hawkers, political notables, and celebrants into the same frenetic sphere of ritual activity, political negotiation, and cultural exchanges. Somewhat removed from the crucible of colonial or hacienda power, these "offstage" settings were sites of cultural crossover, impromptu actions, and social bonding that gradually gave rise to new political, religious, and institutional arrangements improvised from both Andean and European cultural values and symbols. One footpath toward this "interior hybrid world" leads into local cultural practices and meanings embedded in colonial institutions like *cofradías, cabildos,* and *compadrazgos* (or, confraternities, local town councils, and extended kin networks, respectively).[31] How did these institutions transmute through culture, space, and time? Or to pose the question in context: how did urbanizing, "mestizifying" Indians (or Indianized mestizos)

---

31 Thierry Saignes, "Indian Migration and Social Change in Seventeenth Century Charcas," in Larson, Harris, and Tandeter, eds., *Ethnicity, Markets, and Migration in the Andes,* 187. I am indebted to Thierry Saignes's hypothesis that "it seems very likely that it was particularly the system of festive duties (*cargos*) organized in the ayllus according to the Catholic ritual that made possible the rapid integration of all its members, both native and migrant, with their mixed origins and categories" (187). I am applying his hypothesis to Cochabamba, of course, which shared some characteristics with the valleys of Larecaja, Saignes's region of study.

For a wide-ranging set of historical cases and interpretive approaches to civil-religious institutions, see Albert Mayers and Diane Hopkins, eds., *Manipulating the Saints: Religious Brotherhoods and Social Integration in Post-Conquest Latin America* (Hamburg: Wayasbah, 1988); William Taylor, "Cofradías y cargos: An Historical Perspective on the Mesoamerican Civil-Religious Hierarchy," *American Ethnologist* 12 (1985): 1-26; and Rafael Varón, "Cofradías de indios y poder local en el Perú colonial: Huaráz, siglo XVII," *Allpanchis* 20 (1982): 127-166. The ethnographic literature on contemporary cargo systems is vast, but see the early classic by Frank Cancian, *Economics and Prestige in a Maya Community: The Religious Cargo System in Zinacantán* (Berkeley: University of California Press, 1965); and for a succinct discussion of the Andean cargo system, see Catherine J. Allen, *The Hold Life Has: Coca and Cultural Identity in an Andean Community* (Washington, D.C.: Smithsonian Institution Press, 1988), 115-119.

transform the social functions and meanings of those institutions and incorporate them into their own changing cultural frameworks of understanding and practice? To what extent did they serve as emerging axes of local networks and identities, articulating town and country, plebeian and artisan, into small ritual-political "cells"? Did local fiesta-*cargo* systems (rotative civil-religious officeholding by means of sponsoring Christian festivals) provide the social basis upon which mixed groups of indigenous and non-indigenous peoples redefined communal boundaries, hierarchies, and identities? And did these emergent forms of popular religiosity and prestige hasten "the demise of [ethnic] kingdoms and hereditary lords," as Thomas Abercrombie suggests they did for the highlands of Oruro?[32]

As Abercrombie's formulation indicates, historians have already begun to broach these questions within the broader context of Andean demographic flux, transculturation, and the erosion of hereditary ethnic lineages. Yet we still lack an understanding of these intersecting long-term forces: the restructuring of ritual-political hierarchies and identities around local cargo systems and the crisis of traditional cacicazgos in the Andes. Crosscutting regional patterns complicate the picture. In the northern Andes, hacienda and obraje labor needs, massive migratory movements, and the looming crisis of hereditary cacicazgo spurred the fragmentation, reorganization, and dislocation of indigenous politics and religion by the mid-seventeenth century.[33] In Lower Peru, elaborate, independent cofradías apparently became the basis of communal politics and rituals much earlier than in the highland provinces of Alto Perú, where (in La Paz at least) they remained "flexible, locally varied, and probably only partially integrated."[34] This broken historical terrain obscures our vision of the long-term transformation of Andean political culture and the shift from hereditarian forms of authority to local, rotative civil-religious hierarchies. Did the shift become apparent in the draconian reforms of the early Toledan era, amid the massive Indian migration and *forasterismo* of the seventeenth century, in the era of economic compression and political intrusion around the mid-

32 Abercrombie, "To Be Indian, To Be Bolivian: 'Ethnic' and 'National' Discourses of Identity," in Greg Urban and Joel Sherzer, eds., *Nation-States and Indians in Latin America* (Austin: University of Texas, 1991), 95-130, quoted from 105.

33 Karen Vieira Powers, *Andean Journeys: Migration, Ethnogenesis, and the State in Colonial Quito* (Albuquerque: University of New Mexico, 1995).

34 Thomson, "Colonial Crisis, Community, and Andean Self-Rule," 79.

eighteenth century, as a result of Bourbon repression and reform immediately following the Túpac Amarú rebellions, or in the age of high Liberalism under a centralizing nation-state? Andeanists have rooted Andean political transformation in these various historical moments, but only recently have historians like Karen Powers and Sinclair Thomson begun to trace, and explain, the long-term process of cacicazgo decline and the gradual reconstitution of communal civil-ecclesiastical hierarchies in the northern and southern Andes, respectively.[35]

35 Karen Powers, *Andean Journeys*, chaps. 4 and 5; and Sinclair S. Thomson, "Colonial Crisis, Community, and Andean Self-Rule," esp. 85-93.
On seventeenth-century indigenous migration and labor patterns, the high-land-valley connections, the resettlement and reintegration of forasteros in host communities, and cultural transformations of indigenous communities, see the body of work by the late Thierry Saignes, cited in chapters 1, 2, and 3, and his more recently published essay, "Indian Migration and Social Change in Seventeenth Century Charcas," in Larson, Harris, and Tandeter, eds., *Ethnicity, Markets, and Migration in the Andes*, 167-195. See also Luís Miguel Glave, *Tra-jinantes: Caminos indígenas en la sociedad colonial, siglos XVI/XVII* (Lima: Instituto de Apoyo Agrario, 1989); and Ann Zulawski's important new work on indigenous labor and migration in seventeenth-century Oruro and outlying rural areas, *They Eat from Their Labor: Work and Social Change in Colonial Bolivia* (Pittsburgh: University of Pittsburgh, 1995). On the reintegration of forasteros in rural and urban communities of seventeenth-century Cuzco, see Ann M. Wightman, *Indigenous Migration and Social Change: The Forasteros of Cuzco, 1520-1720* (Durham: Duke University Press, 1990). These studies provide rich regional and local contexts for analyzing the reconfiguration of indigenous and Hispanic ritual-political meanings and practices in the midst of vast demographic shifts.
For a sample of the explanatory and temporal frameworks that Andean historians have deployed in their studies of the crisis and decline of Andean colonial cacicazgos, see Sánchez-Albornoz, Powers, Saignes, Glave, and Wachtel (*Le retour des ancetres: Les Indiens Urus de Bolivie XXe-XVIe siecle: Essai d'histoire regresive* [Paris: Gallimard, 1990]), on the seventeenth-century demographic, economic, and political dynamics of the legitimacy crisis. Historians who root the general crisis of colonial cacicazgos in the mid-eighteenth-century crunch of corregidor/reparto politics and extractions include Golte (*Repartos y Rebeliones: Túpac Amarú y las contradicciones del sistema colonial* [Lima: Instituto de Estudios Peruanos, 1980]), Spalding (*Huarochirí*), Larson (chapters 3 and 4 of this book), Stern ("The Age of Andean Insurrection, 1742-1782: A Reappraisal," in his *Resistance, Rebellion, and Consciousness*, 29-33, esp. 73-76), and more recently, Thomson, "Colonial Crisis, Community, and Andean Self-Rule." Still others point to the brutal shock waves of the 1781 rebellions and post-rebellion Bourbon reforms and repression, which legally abolished hereditary lordships and provoked all sorts of local reprisals against caciques in the era spanning the post-rebellion repression and the Independence era. See especially the work of David Cahill, "Caciques y tributos en la sierra del sur del Perú después de la rebelión de

Not surprisingly, Andean ethnohistorians appraise this Andean political transformation from sharply different vantage points. Some Andeanists argue that the decline (and later abolition) of hereditary Andean lordships dealt a lethal blow to long-standing ethnic lineages and politics, while others view it in terms of internal cultural readjustments and the reinvigoration of Andean political culture as the locus of power gradually shifted from the apex to the base of ethnic-colonial hierarchies.[36] From the vantage point of Bolivia's eastern belt of valleys, where ethnically fragmented indigenous communities often pursued aggressively integrative strategies, the profusion of local civil-religious hierarchies would seem to represent the reintegration of local political culture and power around a more "contractual type of sociability [and authority]."[37] Significantly, Thierry Saignes found that seventeenth-century Cochabamba—Alto Perú's main region of refuge—had already come to the attention of religious authorities for its "innumerable religious fraternities of Indians and Spaniards in their separate towns."[38] We still know little about their internal workings or long-term effects on the economic and ritual life of villages, towns, and haciendas in colonial Cochabamba. And in any event, those "separate towns" mentioned in the inspector's 1632 report had disappeared for all practical purposes by the late eighteenth century. But we need to reconceptualize the cofradías, cabildos, and compadrazgos—Saignes's "three significant Cs of social change"—as something more than just colonial institutions corrupting and supplanting Andean lineages, lordships, and communal lifeways. Resituated in ethnically fragmented and economically polarized regions like Cochabamba, they may have served as venues through which forasteros, mestizos, and other "outsiders" reintegrated themselves

---

los Túpac Amarú," *Actas del XVII Simposio de Historia Económica* (Lima, 1986); and Rasnake, *Domination and Cultural Resistance.* On the nineteenth century, see Andrés Guerrero, "Curagas y tenientes políticos: lay ley de la costumbre y la ley del estado (Otavalo, 1830-1875)," *Revista Andina* 7, no. 2 (1989): 321-365; and Tristan Platt, "The Andean Experience of Bolivian Liberalism, 1825-1900." For a synthetic interpretation that glosses over temporal processes, see Abercrombie, "To Be Indian, To Be Bolivian."

36 For the latter position, see especially Sinclair Thomson, "Colonial Crisis, Community, and Andean Self-Rule," and Roger Rasnake, *Domination and Cultural Resistance.*

37 Saignes, "Indian Migration and Social Change in Seventeenth Century Charcas," 189.

38 Cited and quoted in Saignes, *ibid.,* 187. The quotation is drawn from a report entitled *Memorial y relación de las cosas tocantes al reina del Perú* (Cochabamba, 1632) issued by the Franciscan inspector, B. de Cárdenas.

into the economic, political, and ritual rhythms of their "host communities," wove complex inter-town and inter-regional rotative systems, and gradually came to authorize new social forms of power, belonging, and identity.

Specific questions spring to mind: did the advent of trade fairs, fiestas, and pilgrimages in the valleys' towns and cities create an ethos of egalitarianism, ethnic fusion and vertical alliances, and perhaps even an inclusive language of community in this highly differentiated, mobile society? To what extent did popular religion and commerce momentarily collapse class and racial boundaries and meld social groups into something approximating a coherent whole? Such occasions were, to be sure, "no more than a rough and ready egalitarianism, a social fiction that was evanescent yet necessary in a [colonial] polity characterized by a horribly skewed distribution of wealth."[39] David Cahill's description of Corpus Christi celebrations in late eighteenth-century Cuzco also pertains to popular religiosity in Cochabamba. But however evanescent, these institutional and informal expressions of popular religion map another methodological route into the internal cultural workings of power, community, and identity formation.

Take, for example, the case of Cochabamba's most famous pilgrimage site, the shrine of the Virgin of Urkupiña. Local legend tells us that beginning in the seventeenth century, Quechua Indians trekked from distant highland estancias to worship the mestizo "Virgin of Urkupiña" (the name of this now-famous cult is taken from the Quechua phrase, *orqopiña,* meaning "she is already on the hill"). According to local stories, a mestiza Virgin and her child appeared sometime in the seventeenth century near the sacred Qota spring on a hillside on the outskirts of the city of Quillacollo. Although they were never sighted by anyone but a young shepherd girl, their images were "imprinted" on sacred stones, which the pilgrims hauled down the hillside to the altar of the Church of San Ildefonso. They also built their own hidden shrine among the hill's outcroppings, near the sacred spring. Overlooking the town of Quillacollo, yet located slightly beyond the strictures of Catholic ritual, this sanctuary became a spatial and ritual borderland where pilgrims made their offerings to the Virgin and the *huacas* (the sacred stones and spring) of the hillside. The pilgrims paid homage to both Christian and indigenous

39 Cahill, "Popular Religion and Appropriation: The Example of Corpus Christi in Eighteenth Century Cuzco," *Latin American Research Review* 31 (1996): 67-110, quoted from 80.

deities, by offering sacred stones—symbols of the ancestors, life, and fertility—to the Madonna and her child. And their ritual journey bridged two symbolic spaces, the hillside shrine and the parish chapel. But what, we may ask, was the Virgin's significance to variegated social groups at the intersection of urban and rural society? Did the festival of Urkupiña prefigure, and eventually confirm, the mercantile practices of artisans and peasants in the eighteenth and nineteenth centuries, long before the postrevolutionary Bolivian state appropriated and transformed Urkupiña into a symbol of commodity fetishism and national folklore?[40] Did Quillacollo's trade and artisan guilds officially sponsor the Virgin's festival, recasting her as the patron saint of the pious urban plebe? Or, did Urkupiña remain an ambiguously indigenous symbol until well into the twentieth century? Clearly we need to probe her changing and contested significations, for I suspect that this unique icon encouraged the integration and identification of peasantries with a larger imagined community that lay beyond the narrow confines of their everyday work life. Urkupiña was perhaps one of the more inclusive religious icons that indigenous, mixed-race, Hispanic, and other groups fashioned out of an amalgam of liturgical teachings and Andean beliefs. In providing a sacred space for disparate rural and urban groups to celebrate and worship, the Virgin necessarily became a hybrid, eclectic, syncretic symbol. Neither strictly subversive nor hegemonic, Urkupiña's sacred powers and ethnic identity were variously (and vicariously) interpreted and claimed by competing social groups in this institutional, spatial, and ethnic frontier.

Cochabamba's rotative, retail marketplace was another interstitial, interethnic site of cultural innovation and social networking. Located at the intersection of overlapping circuitries, urban-based ferias constituted, in the words of Linda Seligmann, "the border marking the separation between the urban and rural spheres and the

40 Now one of Bolivia's most famous national-religious celebrations (rivaled only by Oruro's Carnival and La Paz's Fiesta del Gran Poder), Quillacollo's cult of the Virgin of Urkupiña has not yet been the subject of a long-term cultural history. But see María L. Lagos's splendid ethnohistorical study of the cult as "contested cultural terrain" over the past thirty years, during which time it has been transformed into the premier national symbol of petty commodity capitalism and upward mobility: "'We Have to Learn to Ask': Hegemony, Diverse Experiences, and Antagonistic Meanings in Bolivia," *American Ethnologist* 20 (1993): 52-71. My brief discussion draws from her article, esp. pp. 55-57. See also Gustavo Rodríguez O., "Fiestas, poder, y espacio urban en Cochabamba, 1825-1917," *Siglo XIX, Revista de Historia* 13 (1993): 95-118.

nexus in which they intersect[ed]."[41] Furthermore, in the Andes as in Mesoamerica, small-scale, rotative marketing often worked in tandem with festive cycles, since the ritual calendar created sieve-like demand for chicha, choclo, potatoes, and other foodstuffs, and local festivals in turn drew thousands of pilgrims, peddlers, and consumers into their orbit. As David Cahill notes for eighteenth century Cuzco, "trade circuits and migratory labor patterns were to a large extent coterminous with the spatial distribution of pilgrimage venues . . . [such that] the 'sacred topography' was simultaneously a commercial network."[42] We might reasonably expect therefore that Cochabamba's exploding sector of itinerant middlemen (from the trade guilds, middling merchants, and *comerciantes ambulantes* to itinerant pack drivers) deployed colonial cargos, pilgrimages, and ritual kinship to weave extensive, if tenuous, webs of alliance and exchange among far-flung peasant villages (including dependent smallholders inhabiting hacienda lands). Cochabamba's ferias also existed apart from those carnivalesque moments of festivity and consumption, and their cycles, rhythms, and intensities responded to the dictates of the agricultural cycle, in turn complicated by municipal and mercantile intrusions. Indeed, the ferias served as nodes in the informal circuitry of goods and people throughout the valleys as early as the late eighteenth century.

This, at least, is my premise in chapter 5. But whereas this book approaches the topic of peasant marketing primarily in terms of peasant subsistence strategies and agrarian class relations, my concern here is to explore the potential cultural implications of small-scale mercantile strategies for the rise of new social groups, networks, and subjectivities, as well as for the broader historical formation of a distinctive regional political culture. My premise of course is that the participation of peasants in retail markets did not signify their surrender to the dictates of rational choice theory. Andean historians have established that, in spite of sharp temporal, regional, and ethnic differences, Andean repertoires of "resistant adaptation" and survival included the selective participation in a wide variety of trading and market activities from early colonial times.[43] And in any event,

---

41 Linda J. Seligmann, "To Be In Between: The Cholas as Market Women," *Comparative Studies in Society and History* 31 (1989): 694-721, quoted from 698 and 703.

42 Cahill, "Popular Religion and Appropriation," 78-79.

43 This is one of the central premises of our coedited volume, *Ethnicity, Markets and Migration in the Andes.* See especially Steve Stern's conceptual contribu-

Cochabamba's eighteenth-century grain markets were hardly spheres of competitive "free" trade, subject as they were to hacienda monopolies, transport problems, coerced trade, tithe speculation, price-fixing, and municipal regulations (chapter 6). Peasant participation was irregular at best, and brokerage played a vital role in articulating rural and urban commerce.

But my point is more methodological in nature: that we need ethnohistorical perspectives on peasant-based ferias as hard-won historical and cultural achievements; that we should approach them not as a structural outcropping of regional economic history but as ongoing social, conflictual processes in which transient, heterogeneous groups of village and hacienda peasants, laborers, peddlers, artisans, muleteers, porters, and a plethora of other cultural/economic brokers managed to carve out subaltern, interstitial spaces in order to exercise a little leverage over the scope, terms, and ongoing relations of exchange among themselves. We can borrow some elements from Mikhail Bakhtin's idea of marketplace subculture as a semi-autonomous domain encouraging gestures that were "frank and free, permitting no distance between those who came in contact with each other, and liberating from the norms of etiquette and decency imposed at other times."[44] Indeed, peasant fairs were both temporary refuges from hegemonic codes as well as sites of periodic conflict and confrontation between marketplace "transgressors" and dominant elites. But as many anthropologists have demonstrated, peasant fairs are/were also highly ritualized and moralized microfields of force, wherein small-scale, ambulatory market vendors and their

---

tion to the idea of an ambiguous, contradictory "colonial-Andean logic," through which ethnic groups selectively incorporated and reworked European-colonial mercantile practices, while trying to redeploy their own ayllu resources in order to take advantage of emerging colonial product markets and hedge their bets against the uncertainties and pressures of colonial rule ("The Variety and Ambiguity of Native Andean Intervention in European Colonial Markets," *ibid.*, 73-100). The term "resistant adaptation" is Stern's, although it derives from his discussion of Andean peasant politics in his article, "New Approaches to the Study of Rebellion and Consciousness." For a fascinating applied case of ethnic management and mediation of indigenous market participation, see Tristan Platt, "Ethnic Calendars and Market Interventions among the Ayllus of Lipes during the Nineteenth Century," in Larson, Harris, and Tandeter, eds., *Ethnicity, Markets, and Migration in the Andes*, 259-296.

44 See his *Rabelais and His World* (Bloomington: University of Illinois Press, 1984), 10. Quoted in Marisol de la Cadena, "Race, Ethnicity, and the Struggle for Self-Representation: Deindianization in Cuzco, Peru (1919-1992)," (Ph.D. Diss., University of Wisconsin, 1996), chap. 4, p. 2.

peasant clients distanced themselves from dominant practices and ideologies of coerced transactions (tribute, rent, mita, repartos, etc.) and reconstructed their own moral codes of equivalency and community.[45] If we are to understand the historical and cultural processes by which popular markets became constitutive spaces of subaltern culture, community, and identity-making within the dominant regional economy, we need to turn our primary attention to the social formation of specialized intermediaries—market vendors, peddlers, itinerant traders, etc.—whose unique social position, economic activities, and cultural practices elaborated extensive kinship and commercial networks, perpetuated an egalitarian market ethos (wherein unequal exchange was negotiated within the discursive [if fictive] framework of reciprocity), and eventually came to define themselves as a gendered, re-ethnicized community of mestizas (or, sometimes, cholitas).

A rich body of ethnographic literature illuminates the vital role that market women perform in rotative, retail peasant marketing systems throughout the Andean highlands today.[46] With the explosion of the informal sector in Bolivia and Peru, women peddlers, hawkers, vendors, shopkeepers, and beggars have also become a prominent part of the urban economic landscape. Many have learned to manipulate government bureaucracies, laws, and language to facilitate transactions or assert their collective rights. For the novice traders seeking to establish themselves, however, their advantages derived mainly from their cultural affinities with, and ties to, their rural communities of origin. For, as Seligmann argues, "the unique

45 See Sidney Mintz, "Men, Women, and Trade," *Comparative Studies in Society and History* 13 (1971): 247-269; Judith-Maria Buechler, "The Dynamics of the Market in La Paz, Bolivia," *Urban Anthropology* 7 (1978): 343-359; Linda J. Seligmann, "To Be In Between: The Cholas as Market Women," 706-709; Brooke Larson and Rosario León, "Markets, Power, and the Politics of Exchange in Tapacarí, c. 1780 and 1980," in Larson, Harris, and Tandeter, eds., *Ethnicity, Markets and Migration in the Andes*, 224-256, esp. 246-248; Marisol de la Cadena, "Race, Ethnicity, and the Struggle for Self-Representation," chap. 4; Florence Babb, *Between Field and Cooking Pot: The Political Economy of Marketwomen in Peru* (Austin: University of Texas, 1989); and Hans Buechler and Judith-Maria Buechler, *The World of Sofiá Veláquez: The Autobiography of a Bolivian Market Woman* (New York: Columbia University Press, 1996).

46 Aside from the sources listed above, see also Susan Bourque and Kay Warren, *Women of the Andes: Patriarchy and Social Change in Two Peruvian Towns* (Ann Arbor: University of Michigan Press, 1981); June Nash, *"We Eat the Mines, and the Mines Eat Us": Dependency and Exploitation in Bolivian Tin Mines*, 2nd ed. (New York: Columbia University Press, 1993); and Billie Jean Isbell, *To Defend Ourselves: Ecology and Ritual in an Andean Village* (Austin: University of Texas Press, 1978).

social position of *cholas* and their remarkable capacity to travel cultural and trade routes between rural and urban centers provide us
with an opportunity to examine why, rather than becoming fully acculturated or assimilated in national society, they have formed ties
of solidarity among themselves and with rural communities of indigenous peasants."[47] Even the most casual traveler to Bolivia today
cannot help but notice the distinctive dress of urban market women
(often mislabeled by tourists as "Indians"). They stand out amid
the mass of haggling humanity, thanks to their elaborate (regionally
varied) clothing code: white top hats (until recently, worn in most
ferias of the Valle Alto and Bajo), *polleras* (layered cotton or velvet
skirts), aprons, striped *aguayos*, earrings, and money purses dangling
from their layered petticoats. Clothing (and other implicit ethnic
markers) serve a crucial function in assigning legitimate membership in marketplace culture and in the collective self-representation
of cholitas (not all of whom are market vendors). But whereas ethnog-
raphers have mapped the social topography of contemporary peasant marketplaces, and their ubiquitous mestiza intermediaries, we
still lack historical understandings of how many market women expanded the meanings and boundaries of mestizaje and empowered
themselves as a gendered community of comerciantes of various
sorts.[48]

---

47 Seligmann, "To Be In Between: The Cholas as Market Women," 695. Drawing on a whole body of ethnographic research, as well as her own fieldwork,
Seligmann shows "the socially calculated efforts of different sectors of the indigenous population to create the conditions for both reciprocal and unequal
exchange [relations] simultaneously," and the position and ability of market
women to "manipulate reciprocity to obtain commodities for market exchange"
(708). In a recent study, Marisol de la Cadena argues against the idea of mestiza market women as cultural straddlers; instead, she analyzes how Cuzqueña
market women redefined indigenous practices and self-identities as dignified
"urban indigenous mestizas" who, although they enjoyed better social conditions
and wielded power over rural ("Indian") peasants, never renounced or ruptured
indigenous forms of self-representation ("Race, Ethnicity, and the Struggle for
Self-Representation," esp. chap. 4).

48 But very suggestive studies include Rossana Barragán, "Entre polleras, lliqllas,
y ñañacas: Los mestizos y la emergencia de la tercera república"; Olivia Harris, "Ethnic Identity and Market Relations: Indians and Mestizos in the Andes,"
in Larson, Harris, and Tandeter, eds., *Ethnicity, Markets, and Migration in the
Andes*, 351-390; Silvia Rivera, "Los desafíos para una democracia étnica y genérica en los albores del tercer milenio," in Silvia Rivera, ed., *Ser mujer indígena,
chola o birlocha en la Bolivia postcolonial de los años 90* (La Paz: Ministerio de
Desarrollo Humano, 1996), 17-84; and Elizabeth Peredo Beltrán, *Recoveras de los
Andes: La identidad de la chola del mercado* (La Paz: ILDIS, 1992).

New research on Cochabamba takes up this task, to a certain degree. An important study by Gustavo Rodríguez and Humberto Solares argues that a distinctive Qochala "culture of chicha" began to lodge itself in the bosom of Cochabamba's landlord society in the late nineteenth century.[49] They root their argument in the region's economic reorientation toward the retail trade in maize and chicha, which created enormous demand for peasant women in the fermentation process of chicha production. (Peasant women gathered together in what we might call "chewing bees" to masticate balls of corn flour.) Depending upon their precarious position as tenants, landholders, and/or laborers in the local economy, most peasants had little room to maneuver in order to take advantage of local market demand for chicha. But some small-scale landowners, market women, and other intermediaries apparently did manage to seize the opportunity and establish *chicherías* along the carriage roads and on the edges of towns and cities. In broad terms, Rodríguez and Solares's argument is consistent with the political-economic findings of Robert Jackson, whose recent book chronicles the advancing fragmentation of land tenure, the collapse of Cochabamba's long-distant grain markets, the decline of the old hacienda regime, and the reorientation of Cochabamba's grain production around segmented local and regional markets after the 1880s.[50] As local demand for maize and chicha expanded, haciendas competed against small-scale farmers and brewers for a share of the local market, and landlords tried to compensate for the collapse of extraregional markets in wheat by reorienting production toward local and regional markets. But they never managed to take control of popular economic supply lines or the expanding urban chicha economy in the late nineteenth century.

Here, then, was an expanding economic sphere in which some mestiza entrepreneurs reinforced their ties to outlying peasant suppliers and consumers, who themselves frequented urban ferias and festivals. Many mestizas probably wielded considerable amounts of cash and credit to secure their webs of kinship and clientelism, and their economic activities both articulated and symbolized (in both popular and elite representations) the growing cultural proximity and

---

49 Gustavo Rodríguez Ostría and Humberto Solares Serrano, *Sociedad Oligárquica, Chicha, and Cultural Popular* (Cochabamba: Editorial Serrano, 1990). See also the detailed regional study by Humberto Solares Serrano, *Historia, espacio y sociedad, Cochabamba, 1550-1950: Formación, crisis, y desarrollo de su proceso urbano* (Cochabamba: CIDRE, 1990), tomo 1.

50 Jackson, *Regional Markets and Agrarian Transformation in Bolivia.* See also chapter 9, this book.

tensions between country and city, peasant and plebe, Indian and cholo, as the region's grain market turned inward in the late nineteenth century. Along with the prodigious variety of women traders, the "mestiza" brewers mediated and shaped the rise of a working class/plebeian subculture that increasingly transgressed the sociospatial boundaries of "white society." Increasingly, urban working-class barrios and the open-air marketplace (the famed *la cancha* in the city of Cochabamba) became sites of confrontation between market vendors, chicherías, and municipal authorities. For the chicheras not only imported the Indianized maize economy into the core of urban life, but they elaborated new customs, rituals, and conventions—and probably created no small amount of disorderliness—associated with the chicha brewery/pub. These pubs were mainly for itinerant peasants, packdrivers, tradesmen, and urban laborers to drink and socialize.[51] But, as Rodríguez and Solares argue, they were also exotic havens for patriarchs seeking respite from the stifling conventions of elite society. Presided over by their mestiza proprietors, the urban chichería was an intimate, yet power-laden space of ritualized consumption and conviviality, where peasants, plebeians, and patricians momentarily came together to drink chicha from earthen bowls, eat *lengua picante*, dance with local mestiza women, gamble, and generally make merry. Perhaps a bit like public festivals, the valley chicherías were unique social microcosms of interclass, interethnic mingling, wherein the rituals and symbolisms associated with the chichería created a fictive ethos of democracy (and a dynamic site of multiethnic contact) that was perhaps unthinkable for the more rigidly racist society of La Paz in the same period. But if the urban chichería (much like the brothel) was a place where white male oligarchs sometimes chose to mix and cavort with the mestizo and Indian plebe, such class and racial boundary crossings were very much in keeping with patriarchal privileges and prerogatives. And if the pubs were "symbolic oases" of multiethnic contact and fusion, they may have served more to mask social differences than to subvert them.

In the larger context of city life, therefore, the chichería occupied

51 Scholars are beginning to study mestiza brewers and market vendors as political subjects asserting their rights to autonomy and respect in the intensifying municipal urban struggles over creole projects of modernity and state formation. See Marisol de la Cadena, "Race, Ethnicity, and the Struggle for Self-Representation," and Gena Hames, "Negotiating Honor: Sexual Slander among Chicheras, Its Market Manifestations, and the Role of the State in Early Twentieth Century Bolivia," (paper presented at the American Historical Association, New York City, January 2-5, 1997).

an extremely ambiguous position in regional society, as judged by Cochabamba's elites in the late nineteenth century. On the one hand, the chichería was a fixture of the social landscape—a watering hole for the masses and (male) elite, alike. More important, the proliferating pubs were symptomatic of the expanding local market for maize and chicha, offering some economic relief to landlords who had seen their own profits decline from the collapse of extraregional grain markets after 1880. The pubs were also proving to be an intermittent source of municipal revenue.[52] On the other hand, the invasion of urban chicherías, street vending, and itinerant marketing practices symbolized social danger, degeneracy, and decay in an increasingly ethnicized, plebeianized urban landscape at a time when modernity gripped the political imaginary of would-be modernizing elites.[53] In short, the chichería seems to hold a multifaceted and highly charged significance in the remaking of Cochabamba's political economy and culture in the late nineteenth century. And poised at the very center of this emerging political culture stood the figure of the white-top–hatted, streetwise mestiza entrepreneur. Indeed, as I will argue shortly, the mestiza of Cochabamba became a multivalent symbol of the intense struggle over regional (and later, national) authenticity and representation in the late nineteenth and early twentieth centuries.

Before we proceed, however, allow me a caveat. As should be clear from my discussion so far, the historically constructed social networks and communities (the nodes of popular culture and connectedness) I have mapped were not enclaves of ethnic fusion or egalitarianism existing on the margins of dominant society. They, too, were rent by fissions, conflicts, and strife that vexed and factionalized all rural Andean communities in transformation (see chapter 4). Furthermore, rural and urban poor constructed their own cultural codes and taxonomies (often borrowing and reworking elite images and idioms of race) to differentiate themselves from elites, from each other, and from other subordinate "others." As Florencia Mallon reminds us through her theorizing and by way of her own case studies of regional political cultures in mid-nineteenth-century Mexico: "[r]ural communities were never undifferentiated wholes but historically dy-

52 On the Bolivian alcohol industry, tax policies, and their impact on Cochabamba corn production more generally, see Jackson, *Regional Markets and Agrarian Transformation in Bolivia*, 108-123.

53 Rodríguez and Solares, *Sociedad Oligárquica, Chicha, y Cultural Popular*, 70-81.

namic entities whose identities and lines of unity or division were constantly being negotiated."[54] Ethnic primordialisms and communal utopianism have no analytical place here. Instead, the challenge is to probe the internal political-cultural dynamics of subaltern groups seeking to define and defend the boundaries and meanings of community, hierarchy, and alterity, and to situate the dynamics of interstitialized political culture in the regional-historical context of polarizing class relations.

In late eighteenth-century Cochabamba, the emerging Quechua-mestizo ritual-political practices and associations, as well as the sinews and spaces of peasant/plebeian marketplace culture, were overlapping domains of everyday discursive production, wherein people created their own contingent moral understandings of belonging and exclusion. Rural and urban religious brotherhoods practiced ritual reciprocities and rotated the obligations of political-religious life among the male elders, for example, but the offices of *alferéz, alcalde, cobrador,* and *hilacata* generally excluded the formal participation of peasant women and youth. Urban craft guilds had their own pecking orders, fraternal codes, and closed-door policies, which were publicly acknowledged through their own sponsorship of fiesta-cargo rituals. On the other hand, the micropower and identity politics of Cochabamba's petty mercantile culture seemed to be more fluid, open-ended, and ambiguous—at least in terms of gender relations. Whole interior sections of the marketplace were feminized spaces, dominated as they were by mestiza market vendors (particularly the meat vendors), ambulatory peasant traders, food sellers, and chicheras. As mentioned earlier, the boom in small-scale maize and chicha production in the late nineteenth century catapulted many peddler women into positions of modest power and prosperity, and they wove extensive networks of commerce, kinship, and clientelism across the countryside.

But there were divisive social forces at work as well that kept women out of certain trade, transport, and artisan sectors. For example, mercantile middlemen often elaborated informal racial taxonomies to buttress their economic power over their rural *"indiocito"* dependents. In a recent essay, Olivia Harris argues that in the nineteenth-century Andes, mestizaje lost its formal colonial function and significance (as a legal and fiscal category) and came to be equated with urbanizing, mercantile middle sectors, whose commerce depended almost exclusively on their exploitative transactions

54 Florencia Mallon, *Peasant and Nation*, 11, esp. chap. 3.

with rural "Indian" agricultural producers. Many Andean middlemen and women invoked dominant notions of "mestizaje" and "whiteness" to distance themselves from their own impoverished "Indian" origins, to leverage their commercial (often extortionary) transactions among the rural poor, and to move up the employment ladder. Thus, Harris argues, late nineteenth-/early twentieth-century reformulations of mestizo identity (and self-identity) devalued the currency of Indianness (increasingly synomymous with subsistent poverty and degraded labor) and further polarized Indian/mestizo identities.[55] But here again, gender crosscut ethnic (self-)representations. As I argued earlier, where self-identified cholitas remained enmeshed in rural life, *cholaje* would continue to represent an ambivalent middle ground that strategically bridged rural and urban, Indian and mestizo categories. And, indeed, hegemonic racial codes usually reflected this same ambiguity—only cast in negative terms—by associating cholaje less with urban mestizaje (perhaps en route upwardly toward creole "whiteness" and/or *vecino* status) than with its original degradated condition of rural Indianness (and more generally with rural backwardness and barbarism).

Shifting strategies of racial-ethnic othering also penetrated the interior recesses of rural peasant life in certain times and places, although historians have only begun to study the intimate workings of gendered and ethnic inequalities at the level of peasant household.[56] Did peasant families racialize gender differences in response to the widening economic gap and cultural resources of their own kin? To take a hypothetical example from this regional case: did the rapid opening up of industrial labor migration from the Cochabamba valleys to distant Chilean nitrate fields and Bolivian mining camps in the late nineteenth and twentieth century deepen gender inequalities within economically diversifying rural households? If Marisol de la Cadena's suggestive study of provincial Cuzco holds true for Cochabamba (and other Andean regions), the migratory men from Cochabamba may have come to claim a "mestizo" identity associated with their newfound geographic, economic, and linguistic

55 Harris, "Ethnic Identity and Market Relations," esp. f. 364.

56 See an early ethnographic study of gendered "cholification" in June Nash's study, *We Eat the Mines, the Mines Eat Us*, 311-316; see also Steve Stern's pathbreaking study of gender relations, ethnocultural dynamics, and the formation of political culture in plebeian, Hispanicized, and rural indigenous regional contexts of eighteenth-century Mexico: *The Secret History of Gender: Women, Men, and Power in Late Colonial Mexico* (Chapel Hill: University of North Carolina Press, 1995), esp. chap. 6.

mobility, while in relational terms, they ascribed an essential (and inferior) Indianness to their Quechua-speaking womenfolk. Left behind in their rural villages to tend the family's fields, herds, and children, the peasant women of Chitapampa (and perhaps also Cochabamba?) became "more Indian" in local parlance.[57] On the other hand, the engendering of race (always perspectival, relational, and contingent) also went in multiple directions and served varied, contradictory purposes in different microcontexts. In this regard, we have to bear in mind regional idiosyncrasies. It is quite plausible to assume, for example, that Cochabamba's urbanizing market women manipulated racial concepts (mestizaje and cholaje, in particular) to legitimate their own ascendant economic status, relative to that of their menfolk, both within their own families and communities, and in the wider mercantile sphere. Indeed, contemporary popular wisdom holds that "when a woman is cultivating potatoes on her plot of land she is a peasant, but when she goes to Cochabamba to sell her potatoes she is a chola."[58] These musings about gendered constructions of ethnicity and class in the context of internal jockeying and divisiveness await new research, of course, but in my view these are the kinds of research strategies that promise to blast open rigid race/class binarisms left over from earlier debates.

Colonial Power and the Micropolitics of Mestizaje

In this section, I want to step back from the canvas and reinsert Qochala popular culture into the broader landscape of colonial power, politics, and political economy in eighteenth- and nineteenth-century Cochabamba. I am not interested here in construing popular culture simply in order to celebrate it (or, to upgrade my methodology). Rituals of resistance that go nowhere reveal very little about history, regardless of whether we are concerned with massive political ruptures or the intricate dynamics of local power and knowledges. But I am concerned with the *historical formation* of political culture— with the manifold ways that this region's highly variegated rural

57 Marisol de la Cadena, " 'Women Are More Indian': Ethnicity and Gender in a Community near Cuzco," in Larson, Harris, and Tandeter, eds., *Ethnicity, Markets, and Migration in the Andes*, 329-348.

58 Susan Paulson, "Familias que no 'conyugan' e identidades que no conjugan: La vida en Mizque desafía nuestras categorías," in Silvia Rivera, ed., *Ser mujer indígena, chola, o birlocha en la Bolivia postcolonial de los años 90*, 87-162, quoted from 87. I am grateful to Susan Paulson for sending me this book from Bolivia.

and urban populations struggled to make, and remake, their own informal cultural communities, social networks, and political-moral understandings as part of a problematic, contested political process of domination and struggle. This research priority calls for closer attention to peasant and popular political discourses which unsettled or negotiated the idioms, rules, and actions of their various overlords in specific fields of force. Here and there, in the pages of this book, we catch glimpses of the ethical premises and experiential knowledges upon which peasants pressed their local claims and grievances: in the 1740s and 1750s, Tapacarí peasants judged the transgressive behavior of their own caciques against local practices of communal responsibility (chapter 4); and the peasants of the hacienda Caporaya had a keen awareness of the difference between enserfment and freedom, and of customary "fair labor" practices governing landlord-peasant relations on that estate (chapter 5). These are but two instances of conflict in an agrarian society that never seemed to reach the boiling point in the late eighteenth century. We need much more research into the perennial conflicts over land, labor, water, herds, rent, and taxes—not only because they marked the pulse of rural life in this polarizing regional economy but also because they left a fragmented documentary record which contains the discursive elements of peasant political consciousness.[59] Notwithstanding postmodern

59 Confessing my own aversion to unmoored postmodern-speak, I have looked to historians and anthropologists (and others) who engage theory and methodology of peasant social action, politics, and political struggle in the context of their own ongoing empirical field/archival work. Over the years, I have drawn critical inspiration from the evolving work of James Scott, as he gradually shifted the loci of analysis in his successive studies from social action (both collective and quotidian) to the conflict-laden social constructions and contestations of power and meaning in everyday agrarian life. (See his trinity of peasant/popular culture political studies: *The Moral Economy of the Peasant: Rebellion and Subsistence in Southeast Asia* [New Haven: Yale University Press, 1976]; *Weapons of the Weak: Everyday Forms of Peasant Resistance* [New Haven: Yale University Press, 1985]; and *Domination and the Arts of Resistance: Hidden Transcripts* [New Haven: Yale University Press, 1990].) However, as historians know all too well, Scott's interpretive search for the "hidden transcripts" of peasant political consciousness in the second and third books still revolved around the primacy of agrarian class conflict, which mostly took the form of implicit, individualist, verbal, or symbolic attacks and counterattacks (Scott's "everyday forms of ideological warfare"). Moreover, his task of recovering peasant political consciousness was made considerably easier by the fact that his "historical subjects" (at least those whom he studied in the Indonesian region of Sedaca for his book, *Weapons of the Weak*) were/are located in the ethnographic present. As Eric Van Young has pointed out, cultural historians of peasants and other marginal groups

anxieties (and Subaltern School directives) about excavating peasant political discourses from official documents, Andean historians have begun to unearth subterranean peasant political understandings and idioms, which trafficked selectively and ambiguously in the legal, political, and symbolic language of colonial and republican elites.[60] Their search for the fragments of peasant political thinking in the Andes has not yielded a unifying, "authentic," or "alternative" political imaginary, nor even coherent discourses of discontent among humble peasant petitioners or litigants in one region or moment in time. But, in the words of Mallon, the new political historians of the Andes are revealing the extent to which Andean peoples "engaged in conflict over power and meaning . . . [and thus] helped define the contours of what was possible in the making of nation-states."[61] How local Andean peoples framed the issues, defined their rights, and contested authority are historical questions that must be grounded in the cumulative social experiences of struggle, adaptation, and community-making. This observation holds particularly for integrative ethnic borderlands, where peasants and rural laborers did not readily premise their political strategies on the ideals of ethnic-ancestral lineage or legal colonial-corporate privilege. Their traditions of peasant migration and itinerance, social differentiation, and transculturation imparted perhaps a more diffuse, informal, and impromptu tone to communal identities than in many parts of the monolingual, ayllu-dominated altiplano. But that fact did not consign Qochala peasants (or other valley peoples) to ethnic effacement, cultural isolation, or social anomie until the fictive moment of politi-

---

face the more daunting task of reading written texts (usually official records of some sort) as highly mediated fragments of subaltern social experience of removed dead people, who wrote no histories of their own, and of massaging these fragments into coherent political premises. See Van Young's essays on Mexican popular culture, peasant politics, and political projects during the Independence era, which speak to broader epistemological issues vexing social and cultural historians these days: "The Cuautla Lázarus: Double Subjectives in Reading Texts on Popular Collective Action," *Colonial Latin American Review* 2 (1993): 3-26; and "To See without Seeing: Historical Studies of Peasants and Politics in Mexico," *Mexican Studies/Estudios Mexicanos* 6 (1990): 133-159.

60 See the various contributions in Stern, ed., *Resistance, Rebellion, and Consciousness in the Andean Peasant World;* Florencia Mallon, *Peasant and Nation: The Making of Postcolonial Mexico and Peru;* and Mark Thurner, *From Two Republics to One Divided: Contradictions of Postcolonial Nationmaking in Andean Peru.*

61 Mallon, *Peasant and Nation,* 9.

cal awakening and awareness finally shattered their quietism one postcolonial day.[62] As I have tried to suggest, local peoples rearticulated ethnic, class, and gender identities to structure their own internally dynamic communities and networks in a variety of quotidian, power-laden contexts. Working from that premise, our task, then, is to piece together patchworks of political ideas, rhetorical strategies and tropes, and social memories and hopes (to map a "language of contention," to borrow William Roseberry's term)[63] in order to understand in a very approximate way how Cochabamba's rural and urban folk construed the wider colonial world and their rightful places in it.

There is another methodological implication in my discussion of popular culture and peasant politics, and that is to open the analytical angle wide enough to encompass both rural and urban political life in the region. My earlier discussion of popular culture mapped the possible points of convergence that drew Indians and mestizos, peasants and plebeians, countryside and town, into the same cultural and economic orbit from time to time. Political ideas, symbols, and allies also flowed through those transregional arteries and across geocultural borders, so that trouble in the city might soon lead to insurgent (or repressive) action in the countryside (and vice versa). In plotting the political activities and ideas that reverberated among the peasants and popular classes of central Cochabamba, we need to look beyond isolated, discrete forms of political struggle to the connective tissues of regional political life that occasionally brought peasants, laborers, and artisans into the same political and discursive arena, where they might forge common interests and themes to carry them into battle.

This item on the research agenda is important, if self-evident, because of the long-standing research priority granted the highland Indian rebellions of the early 1780s. Much historiographic effort has gone into mapping the social topography of Indian rebellion in the 1780s and then pinning explanatory models onto the spatial patterns of rebellion and nonrebellion throughout the southern Andes. More recently, Steve Stern and others have shaken up these reductive paradigms by advancing explanatory analyses of the absence of indigenous rebellion in much of the Andes during the insurgent years

---

62 For just such an interpretive scheme, see Xavier Albó, "From MNRistas to Kataristas to Katari," esp. 380-381.

63 William Roseberry, "Hegemony and the Language of Contention," in Joseph and Nugent, eds., *Everyday Forms of State Formation*, 355-366.

of 1781–1782.[64] But for the southern Andes, where the fault line of rebellion/nonrebellion seemed to follow the geocultural divide between highland and valleys, the remains of cultural determinism still tends to counterpose Aymara communitarian rebels (armed with millenarian dreams) to the putatively peaceful valley peasants living within the safety of landlord paternalism. A new generation of ethnohistorians working on Aymara regions of Bolivia in the late colonial era are only now beginning to unseat that assumption.[65] And the case of Cochabamba should offer a healthy dose of skepticism as well. For if we survey the broad landscape of peasant and plebeian mobilizations across the eighteenth and early nineteenth centuries, we expose the fallacy of bifurcating the Andean peasant world into opposing telluric camps—the militant Indians of the "harsh highlands" and the passive peasants of the "gentle valleys." (We need to be cognizant of regional variations, of course, but we must also beware of the implicit politics of variant regional discourses in Bolivia.)

What comes into view instead is an equally restless province, but one whose locus, timing, and forms of popular politics and mobilization differed markedly from rural highland patterns. If Qochala peasants and plebeians did not rise up in massive rebellion in 1780–1781, "mestizos" and others did set cities and haciendas on fire in the tax revolt of 1730; other riots, road blocks, and tax protests provoked colonial reprisals again in the 1770s and early 1780s, under the intensifying pressure of new extortions and coercions; and, just as the liberalizing port cities of Spanish America were breaking free of Spanish imperial rule, these valleys exploded again in a popular uprising in May of 1812—this time, in sedition against the royalist army

64 Steve Stern, "The Age of Andean Insurrection, 1742-1782: A Reappraisal," in his volume, *Resistance, Rebellion, and Consciousness in the Andean Peasant World*, 34-93. See also his prescriptive methodological essay that accompanies this historiographic appraisal in the same volume. See also the work of Scarlett O'Phelan Godoy, *Rebellions and Revolts in Eighteenth Century Peru and Upper Peru* (Koln: Bohlau Verlag, 1985), and her *La gran rebelión en los Andes: De Túpac a Túpac Catari* (Cuzco: Centro Bartolomé de las Casas, 1995).

65 See Sergio Serulnikov, "Disputed Images of Colonialism: Spanish Rule and Indian Subversion in Northern Potosí, 1777-1780," *Hispanic American Historical Review* 76 (1996): 189-226, as well as his forthcoming Ph.D. dissertation on the same subject; and Sinclair Thomson, "Colonial Crisis, Community, and Andean Self-Rule." See also Oscar Cornblit, *Power and Violence in the Colonial City: Oruro from the Mining Renaissance to the Rebellion of Túpac Amaru (1740-1782)* (New York: Cambridge University Press, 1995).

of Goyeneche. Significantly, the locus of Cochabamba's late colonial mobilizations was the emerging pueblerino culture of valley towns, barrios, and marketplaces. And their leading protagonists were identified variably as mestizos, cholos, plebeians, artisans, and/or market women—all of whom cropped up in colonial records as the unruly mestizo plebe, or "alleged mestizos." We don't yet know how these outbreaks of violence articulated indigenous and mestizo peasantries, nor the ways in which local political leaders linked their own interests and grievances to broader political themes, nor even the protagonistic role of artisan or plebeian intellectuals during the protests. But there are enough clues to suggest that Bourbon taxation and regulation were at the very heart of these "mestizo mutinies." It is uncertain how deeply these escalating tax rebellions ran in the late colonial era: did they simply turn the impending imperial crisis to their own immediate ends, or did they begin to appropriate and interpret Enlightenment discourses of liberalism, republicanism, and citizenship, thereby planting the seeds of popular (anticolonial, antioligarchic) projects of nation-building which would surface in the later decades of the nineteenth and early twentieth century? My intuition is that many peasants, artisans, and laborers did begin to fashion the elements of anticolonial practices over the course of the eighteenth century, which began at least as early as the 1730 tax rebellion and culminated in the mobilization of mestiza women (and a few of their menfolk) in opposition to Spanish rule in 1812, at the end of a terrible decade of drought, hunger, and heavy taxation (see chapter 8).[66]

Turning from rural to urban sites of popular mobilization in eighteenth-century Cochabamba also lays bare the points of contestation at the most vulnerable edges of Spanish colonial power. As this book has argued, Cochabamba's swelling "mestizo" population was the Achilles' heel of the colonial state for much of the seventeenth and eighteenth centuries. Its "alleged mestizos" were construed by

66 Very little historical research focuses on the insertion of peasants and other popular groups in the independence movement, but see René Arze A., *Participación popular en la independencia de Bolivia* (La Paz: Colegio Don Bosco, 1979), and Charles Arnade, *The Emergence of the Republic of Bolivia* (Gainesville: University of Florida Press, 1957). More recently, Tristan Platt has published an essay on the indigenous political imaginary and iconography of the emerging republic: "Simón Bolívar, the Sun of Justice, and the Amerindian Virgin: Andean Conceptions of the Patria in Nineteenth Century Bolivia," *Journal of Latin American Studies* 25, part I (1993): 159-189.

colonial elites as thinly disguised Indian tax evaders, and the valleys always seemed to lie just beyond the reach of the tributary state. Shifting tides of Indian migration, rampant transience (later dubbed vagrancy), collapsing categories of caste, and massive tax evasion exacerbated the internal divisions within the colonial elite. Formal debates usually revolved around the "Indian problem," as the entire Toledan project rested on the extraction of indigenous labor and tribute in Alto Perú (see chapter 3). The last decade of the eighteenth century, in particular, hatched a series of intense policy and moral debates over the Indian question—understandably, the primary focus of elite anxiety only a decade or so after the indigenous insurrections of 1781. But the emerging mestizo problem also proved a source of tension. In regions where itinerant, unregulated practices began to encroach on the cultural boundaries of elite society, creole intellectuals felt compelled to reexamine the ontological place and destiny of mestizos. Again, this regional case proves exceptionally rich. We catch glimpses of competing imperial agendas to contain and channel mestizaje. On the one hand, the imperatives of imperial taxation in Alto Perú drove Bourbon administrators to pursue mestizos as potential re-Indianized, landholding tributaries. On the other, local visionary reformers like Viedma and Haenke dreamed of converting "mestizo" farmers and casual laborers into an industrial labor force on modern plantations and textile manufactories (chapter 7). Within the parameters of this debate, we can perhaps capture the particularism of the southern Andes in the late eighteenth century. For I sense that Andean colonial authorities and local elites were far more troubled and divided over the "mestizo problem" than were their counterparts in, say, central Mexico, where the labor force was composed predominantly of "*castas*" and other people of mixed ethnic origins by the eighteenth century and where large-scale coercive Indian labor schemes had long since disappeared.[67] Not so in Alto

---

67 This is not to argue that colonial authorities in New Spain were not concerned about problems of social discipline, deviance, and unruliness and the threat of riot, particularly in mining towns. Swelling working-class subcultures demanded new forms and strategies of state discipline: see Susan Deans-Smith, "The Working Poor and the Eighteenth Century Colonial State: Gender, Public Order, and Work Discipline," in Beezley et al., eds., *Rituals of Rule, Rituals of Resistance: Public Celebrations and Popular Culture in Mexico* (Wilmington, Del.: Scholarly Resources, 1994), 47-76, and a host of similar studies in that volume, as well as selected Foucauldian approaches to power in the Josephs and Nugent volume on *Everyday Forms of State Formation*. See also R. Douglas Cope, *The Limits of Racial Domination: Plebeian Society in Colonial Mexico City, 1660-*

Perú, where Bourbon reformism after 1782 boiled down to a proposed revamping of the Toledan mita/tributary regime, repressing Indian rebels, and reinforcing caste. As long as colonial caste (specifically, the Indian república) still served as a powerful tool of colonial power and extraction, mestizaje would symbolize its limits or decline, the site at which ethnic markers had to be buttressed and policed. And, indeed, this would continue to be the case in Bolivia during much of the nineteenth century.

We need to hone this analysis of colonial power even further, however. If mestizaje in the Andes magnified the tensions and vulnerabilities inherent in a colony built on racial oppositions, and if it increasingly encapsulated the uprootedness, hybridity, and plebeianization of the colonized cultural landscape, then it must have called forth elite discourses of moral reform, discipline, and civilization—harbingers of race science and other discourses of modernity that would crystallize in the late nineteenth century. Certainly, we know that Viedma and other authorities were alarmed by the moral and social decay of city life, the intrinsic depravity of mestizos, and the anarchy of the spreading informal market. Already by the late colonial period, elites and plebes were engaged in low-intensity warfare over the control of public space and the boundaries of respectability, and it would intensify in the late nineteenth century. We need more studies rooting the genealogy of race and class discourses, and the ways in which elite constructions of race/class categories intermingled and informed each other over time in specific Andean regions.[68] This regional case is no exception. For I suspect that as

---

1720 (Madison: University of Wisconsin Press, 1994), for discussion of the urban bread riots and disciplinary reprisals taken by seventeenth-century colonial authorities of Mexico City.

68 Along with many European travelers' reports, mid-nineteenth-century *costumbrista*-style paintings often rendered intricate ethnic hierarchies carefully encoded by means of physiognomy, costume, body language, and context. These paintings were perhaps still closer to the Enlightenment spirit of encyclopedic cataloging of ordered "racial types" characteristic of the late eighteenth century than they were to the reductive binary categories of race science that would follow in the late nineteenth century. In any event, the interpenetration of gendered, ethnic, and class categories was already evident in the masterful watercolors of Bolivia's premier costumbrista painter, Melchor María Mercado, in the middle decades of the nineteenth century. In one painting depicting the "transport of chicha," Mercado depicted a proud, well-appointed mestiza chichera leading her retinue of laborers and servants en route to the market or pub. Her social-ethnic inferiors included (in descending order): her dwarflike keeper of the keys, a ponchoed cholo ("mozo de la aldea") bent double from the weight of the chicha vat

much as anywhere else in Latin America, mestizaje was a vexed and multivalent metaphor upon which elites hung their hopes, hatreds, and fears about the future of the race and the nation. Most colonial powerholders probably represented the "mestizo" as a regressive influence, embodying racial contamination, moral degeneration, and low-classness. But perhaps some of the region's dissident intellectuals saw in mestizaje the potential for moral progress, racial improvement, and advancing civilization. In any event, these concerns were common to most modern statist/civilizing projects in Latin America: the need to turn unruly plebes and peasantry into disciplined workers, soldiers, and taxpayers; to impose municipal control over public space, informal economies, and disorderly ceremonies; to rid the cities of superstition, crime, and vice; and to extend control over the forms of family organization, sexual practices, and moral and hygienic instruction. By these means, elites would police the social boundaries of race and class, modernize social life, centralize state power, and thereby better secure their dominance amid social change and uncertainty. In such endeavors, gender proved crucial, of course, since sexual practices were the crux of "race mixing" and all its social by-products. Abiding by the norms of patriarchy (which exempted elite men from sexual responsibility), the new forces of modernity, discipline, and reform targeted the urban-dwelling "mestizas," who became the objects of modernity's experiments and opprobrium. In regions like Cochabamba, where small-scale women producers and traders were the visible vanguards of an intrusive popular economy and culture in urban "white territory," the mestiza became a highly charged symbol of ethnicized space, racial degeneracy, sexual license, and economic mobility. Poised at the intersection of gender, race, and class boundaries, she magnified elite anxieties and legitimated new, more intimate forms of power. The discursive and institutional violence inherent in colonial state (re)formation may have taken more subtle forms in Cochabamba and

---

he hauled on his back, followed by an erect, but barefoot Indian porter carrying a large chicha jug on his head, and finally trailed by a small barefoot, indigenous peasant woman engaged in spinning wool. See Melchor María Mercado, *Albúm de paisajes, tipos humanos y costumbres de Bolivia, 1841-1869* (Sucre: Banco Central de Bolivia, 1991); and Silvia Rivera, "Los desafíos para una democracia étnica y genérica en los albores del tercer milenio," 36-37. For comparative regional and temporal reference, see J. Jorge Klor de Alva's essay on *casta* painting in colonial Mexico: "Mestizaje from New Spain to Aztlán: On the Control and Classification of Collective Identities," in *New World Orders: Casta Painting and Colonial Latin America* (New York: Americas Society, 1996), 58-72.

other relatively quiescent regions in the late eighteenth century, but they previewed postcolonial civilizing state activities in classifying, condemning, and controlling the growing urban plebe and its "invasive" popular cultures.[69]

Collective Peasant Political Agency

Mapping political culture onto the template of long-term agrarian class formation advances the analysis well beyond the parameters of peasant *economic agency,* which lies at the core of this book. Whereas the book illuminates their "politically neutral" livelihood and migratory strategies, their local everyday struggles over land-labor-taxation issues, and their individualist (often, ethno-racial) strategies of tribute evasion, the political cultural perspectives I have sketched here seek to understand the historical constitution of peasants as politically alert subjects, as bearers of cultural values, and as builders of informal social networks and identities in the course of their quotidian

---

69 This discussion draws much inspiration from Philip Corrigan and Derek Sayer's discussion of Modern English state formation as a contested cultural project and process (see their book, *English State Formation as Cultural Revolution* [Oxford: Basil Blackwell, 1985]), and from Ann Laura Stoler's critical appreciation of Foucauldian approaches to power in the context of European constructions of race and gender in colonial settings, particularly where colonial anxieties concentrated on people of mixed origins or other "ambiguously positioned interstitial groups." See her *Race and the Education of Desire: Foucault's "History of Sexuality" and the Colonial Order of Things* (Durham: Duke University Press, 1995), esp. 105-107, 133ff.

On the struggle over urban space, social discipline, public hygiene, and sexuality in the context of nineteenth-century state formation and modernity projects, see Donna J. Guy's study of Argentina: *Sex and Danger in Buenos Aires: Prostitution, Family, and Nation in Argentina* (Lincoln: University of Nebraska Press, 1991).

On the Andes, especially in regards to plebeian mestiza women, see the sources cited in note 45. Specifically on Cochabamba, see Gustavo Rodríguez O. and Humberto Solares S., "Fronteras interiores y exteriores: Tradición y modernidad en Cochabamba, 1825-1917," in Henrique Urbano, ed., *Tradición y modernidad en los andes* (Cusco: Centro Bartolomé de las Casas, 1992), 75-93. Once again, however, most recent quasi-Foucauldian approaches to disciplinary and socializing forms of state power focus on the Mexican case. For samples, see R. Douglas Cope, *The Limits of Racial Domination: Plebeian Society in Colonial Mexico City, 1660-1720;* Joseph and Nugent, eds., *Everyday Forms of State Formation;* and Beezley et. al., eds., *Rituals of Rule, Rituals of Resistance.* An overarching research review and agenda is mapped by Jeffrey W. Rubin, "Decentering the Regime: Culture and Regional Politics in Mexico," *Latin American Research Review* 31 (1996): 85-126.

lives and struggles. For heuristic purposes, I have sought to insert the book's triangular axis of land-labor-tribute struggles (thrashed out between peasants, hacendados, and colonial elites) into a broader field of force, one in which heterogeneous rural, urban, and itinerant groups negotiated and struggled over power, identity, and meaning from a variety of subaltern positions in this regional society. Regional specificity continues to loom large in this interpretive scheme. I have suggested that it was perhaps the central valleys' brisk, multi-ethnic traffic in people, goods, and ideas during the late eighteenth and nineteenth centuries that tended to erode Indian peasant isolation, born of poverty and discrimination, and weave disparate rural and urban peoples into intricate circuitries and integrative popular cultures, which crystallized around the open-air Quechua market-place and pueblerino ritual-political activities.

This hypothesis carries methodological implications: first, it suggests that historians focus more attention on the urban roots and transregional routes of popular politics and discourses in the mid- to late eighteenth century. We need new studies on the variety and multiplicity of popular actions, intellectuals, ideas, and identities that sprang from the lower ranks in the crucible of late colonial rule. Second, we need to probe the interior recesses of Bourbon state power, as it became caught on the horns of recidivist Toledan schemes of tribute reactivation and progressive, protocivilizing reforms aimed at socializing (even assimilating) interstitial racial, laboring groups that fit into neither republic (of "Indians" or of "Spaniards"). Cochabamba's "alleged mestizo" subculture was a clear site of discursive and political confrontation; it is a crucial laboratory for examining popular and elite struggles over power and meaning under late colonial rule in the Andes. Third, Cochabamba's long-term history of peasant "resistant adaptation" without rebellion (particularly the fact that the region remained dormant during periods of highland insurgent Indian movements) challenges Andean historians to specify and explain those infrequent (and perhaps still unidentified) moments of political crisis and popular mobilization, when contentious popular cultures did cohere around political and moral themes and thus challenged the basis of landlord and/or colonial authority.

The methodological value of such moments is, of course, inestimable. For they usually provide historians with rare documentary glimpses into the political lives, actions, and thinking of popular insurgents (or bystanders) whose lives got caught up in the chaos of the time. Wars, military coups, indigenous rebellions, endemic banditry, and urban riots not only wrenched power away from elites and thrust rebels into positions of empowerment and authority for a treacherously short time, but they were often, as Florencia Mallon shows, intense moments of "discursive construction," in which subaltern, middling, and ruling groups negotiated all kinds of fragile vertical and horizontal alliances, pacts, and truces in order to pursue their own goals.[70] Even when the surface calm was never broken, the very threat of war, taxation, or rebellion sometimes catalyzed communal consensus out of conflictive and inchoate situations. And from above, besieged colonial authorities or dissident elites often felt compelled to appease local peasant/plebeian actions and projects through transitory populist pacts or strategic benign neglect.[71] Either way, these were singular historical moments of peasant political and discursive mobilization that beam light onto the otherwise shadowy landscapes of quotidian popular political cultures.

Glancing back across the centuries, it is possible to identify three such moments in Cochabamba's history: the 1730 peasant and plebeian tax rebellions associated with the artisan intellectual, Alejo Calatayud; the amorphous mestizo crowd actions mobilized against the invading royalist armies in early 1812; and the explosive agrarianist movement that surfaced in the central valleys during the 1930s, and later escalated into a series of road blockades, labor strikes, and land invasions during the late 1940s and early 1950s. More than a transitory political moment or event, however, this third rupture has to be contextualized in broader structural and narrative terms. In my view, it represents the historic transformation of local peasant and popular cultures into a sustained agrarian movement (whose locus of power and self-representation was the rural *sindicato*), which, in turn, transcended its own regional origins to forge alliances with militant mine unions and dissident populist groups. In so doing, it moved Cochabamba's history of local peasant politics and political culture onto a new plane of collectivized forms of populist and class struggle that placed it squarely within the national political arena. It is this slow uneven transformation of local, popular political culture

70 Mallon, *Peasant and Nation: The Making of Postcolonial Mexico and Peru.*

71 On populist pacts, political betrayal, counterhegemonic peasant politics, and the contested state-building as an ongoing political process of domination, negotiation, and resistance, see Florencia Mallon, *Peasant and Nation,* esp. chap. 8, "The Intricacies of Coercion: Popular Political Cultures, Repression, and the Failure of Hegemony," 247-275. On late Mexican colonial policies of strategic appeasement of rebellious villages in Oaxaca and elsewhere, see William Taylor, *Drinking, Homicide, and Rebellion in Colonial Mexican Villages* (Stanford: Stanford University Press, 1979).

into an insurgent social movement around the turn of the twentieth century that I want to briefly consider in the concluding pages of
this essay.

How and why did Qochala peasants' politics and political culture
congeal into a radical agrarianist movement, complicated by urban
overtones of redemptive mestizaje, and ultimately force its popular
agenda onto this politically fractured, ethnically plural nation in the
early to mid-twentieth century? How did they articulate centuries-
long traditions of land-labor struggles with broader ideologies of liberalism and populism, thereby nationalizing local agendas and identities, while simultaneously radicalizing elite nationalist projects in
the 1930s, 1940s, and early 1950s? This question demands research
on the deep political traditions, politics, and discourses of laboring
peoples in the valleys, not rehashed reductionism read backward
onto history from presentist concerns or ideological positions. For
if we now recognize that peasant ideologies and discourses were
not inherent in ethnic, class, or regional structures, nor simply re-
gurgitated ideologies fed to "awakening" peasants by savvy populist
politicians, we have still to study the history of Qochala peasants
as political subjects. That they managed to gather consensus among
themselves, fashion coherent languages of class or citizenship, and
give political meaning to their deep "underground traditions" of peasant smallholding, mestizaje, and diasporic networks were hard-won
historical achievements that helped break the back of the Bolivian
landed oligarchies, redefine the boundaries of national belonging,
and propel Bolivia onto a unique historical trajectory—one that di-
verged sharply from the enduring racist authoritarian projects of
other Andean nations in the mid-twentieth century.[72]

72 How Cochabamba peasants struggled to find their collective political voice
is a crucial question that demands fresh historical research. Interestingly, there
is a new generation of political historians pursuing diverse political cultural
approaches to subaltern revolutionary politics and discourses in the early and
mid-twentieth century. See the following forthcoming dissertations: Laura Gotkowitz, "Within the Boundaries of Equality: Race, Gender, and Citizenship in
Bolivia (Cochabamba, 1880-1953)" (Ph.D. diss., University of Chicago, 1997);
José M. Gordillo, "Ethnicity, Politics, and Power: Post-Revolutionary Peasant
Struggles in the Valley of Cochabamba, 1952-1964" (Ph.D. diss., State University
of New York at Stony Brook); and Roberto Fernández, "The Chaco War, Bolivian
Nationalist Discourses, and the Peasant" (Ph.D. diss., State University of New
York at Stony Brook).
    There is an ample scholarship on the revolution, produced by an earlier gen-
eration of anthropologists and sociologists who tackled the question from various

To broach this broad historical question, we need to bring the rural peasantries (in all their differentiated variety) and the motley crowds of urban artisans, plebes, and laboring poor of Cochabamba into one unified field of vision. The region's deeply rooted political culture and rural-urban circuitries would seem to require it. We also need to root the question, not in the shallow sands of political events (the catharsis of the Chaco war, etc.) but in the deeper currents of agrarian and political transformations which began to quicken in the late nineteenth and early twentieth centuries (see chapter 9).

Out of the rural sector—with its long, contentious history of land and labor conflicts and the slow, uneven advance of peasant smallholding (particularly after 1880)—probably came popular

---

vantage points. The interpretive syntheses of the late Bolivian revolutionary and philosopher, René Zavaleta Mercado, continue to define many of the issues and debates about revolutionary pacts and hegemonic projects in the first half of the twentieth century. See especially his *Lo nacional-popular en Bolivia* (Mexico City: Siglo XXI, 1986) and *Bolivia: El Desarrollo de la Conciencia Nacional* (Mexico City: n.p., 1967).

The pioneering regional study of peasant politics in Cochabamba is, of course, Jorge Dandler's early ethnographic work on campesino syndicalism and clientelism. He looked to the crisis of the Chaco War (1932-1935), and its galvanizing impact on peasant political consciousness, to explain the rise of postwar peasant syndicalism and vertical political alliances in the Cochabamba valleys. His oral informants narrated poignant stories about Cochabamba peasants who returned home from the tropical trenches, armed with new ideological weapons and a deep sense of patriotic entitlement, to lay claim to their rights to lands, schools, unions, and suffrage. Dandler was also concerned with showing how vertical relations of clientelism controlled and channeled peasant mobilizations, effectively neutralizing them.

In regard to Dandler's explanatory emphasis on the impact of the war on regional class and political dynamics, I am not disputing the obvious here: that the Chaco War catalyzed popular mobilizations across the country and set the stage for the rise of powerful "popular-national" alliances, which ultimately redefined Bolivia's political landscape in the 1940s and 1950s. But I am suggesting that if we are to understand how Cochabamba peasants (and other peasantries) construed their experiences as laborers, soldiers, and citizens, envisioned Bolivian nationhood, and hitched their own local struggles to emerging multiclass, multiethnic projects, we need to widen the time frame beyond this singular moment of crisis and rupture, plumb the depths of local political culture and economy in the postcolonial and prewar era, and attempt to recover the subterranean political traditions, voices, and visions of Qochala peasants in their pursuits of livelihood, community, and justice. See Dandler, *El sindicalismo campesino en Bolivia: Los cambios estructurales en Ucureña* (Mexico City: Instituto Indigenista Interamericano, 1969); and his *Local Group, Community, and Nation: A Study of Changing Structure in Ucureña, Bolivia, 1935-52* (Madison, Wis.: Land Tenure Center, 1967).

interpretations of yeoman liberalism, which began to link proliferating practices of smallholding and migrant labor to broader ideologies of proprietorship and free trade, class solidarities, and questions
of citizenship.[73] Other valley peasants probably deployed legal and

73 Robert Jackson's work suggests that the period between the devastating
drought of 1878-1879 and the eve of the Chaco War (1932-1935) saw the weight of
power shift dramatically against the landholding oligarchy, hastening the parti-
tion of hacienda lands and the rise of independent smallholders, and unmooring
more peasants from the crushing routines of hacienda life (Jackson, *Regional
Markets and Agrarian Transformation in Bolivia: Cochabamba, 1539-1960*, esp.
chap. 4). It was also an era of intensifying social differentiation, migration, and
dispersion among valley peoples (see this book, chap. 9), which reinforced diasporic linkages between the highlands and valleys, between mining camps and
maize fields. We should not underestimate the impact of these economic changes
on Qochala peasant discourses and practices, and their potential articulation to
broader political movements in the age of High Liberalism (c. 1880-1930). It will
take patient spade work, however, because the Cochabamba region remained
relatively quiescent during that era, overshadowed by the explosive violence
across the altiplano that raged between defensive ayllus, aggressive latifundias,
and a modernizing state determined to dismantle the remnants of corporate
indigenous territories.
   Yet there seemed to be a subterranean, but equally "subversive," struggle being
waged against the oligarchic basis of landlordism in the Cochabamba valleys in
the same period. Indeed, there may have been two cycles of land parcelization
and redistribution. The first, top-down "formal" agrarian reform institutionalized
de facto smallholding in Cochabamba's Indian communities, by effectively
throwing them onto the land market. Robert Jackson found, for example, that
". . . the number of smallholders in Cochabamba Department proliferated, especially in the former community territory. After 1874, thousands of small properties came into existence in the territory of the former communities, especially in
the Valle Bajo, and, to a lesser degree, in the haciendas created during the colonial period" (*Regional Markets and Agrarian Transformation in Bolivia*, 87). A
second, bottom-up "informal" agrarian reform was probably marked by the slow,
uneven incursion of peasant smallholders into the hacienda domain and their
pursuit of titles to usufruct plots of land. If this indeed was the case, then we
need to reconsider how peasants may have subverted the original purposes of
the 1874 land reform to pursue their own local interests and agendas—either by
challenging the basis of landlord power and/or by redefining and reconstituting
communal property-rights. In other words, to what extent did peasants begin
to fashion individualist strategies of land acquisition into a broader articulated
agenda of political and economic rights? And how did they construct political
discourses and alliances around their emerging expectations? These questions
still beg to be answered.
   For an extremely suggestive article on the regional particularism of liberal
reforms and their impact on land fragmentation and acquisition among the
Indian communities of the central valleys, see the first-rate piece by Gustavo
Rodríguez O., "Entre reformas y contra-reformas: Las comunidades indígenas en el Valle Bajo cochabambino (1825-1900)," in Heraclio Bonilla, ed., *Los*

discursive tactics to reconstitute communal property out of private and/or municipal holdings, perhaps even in subregions where no institutionalized "Indian community" had ever existed.[74] These local discourses surely must have opened the symbolic chasm separating the valley's *piqueros* (whose small parcels of land gave them a measure of freedom and dignity) from the remaining *colonos*, whose formal conditions of service tenancy tied them to a degraded colonial-Indian past. It is significant perhaps that the very words *colono* and *colonaje*[75] entered the vernacular only in the late republican era—when serfdom, colonialism, and Indianness became increas-

Andes en la encrucijada: Indios, comunidades, y estados en el siglo XIX (Quito: FLACSO, 1991), 277-335. For a later period, see the historical-ethnographic study of Tiraque, a peasant community on the eastern edges of the Valle Alto, by María L. Lagos, *Autonomy and Power: The Dynamics of Class and Culture in Rural Bolivia* (Philadelphia: University of Pennsylvania Press, 1994).

74 For example, Laura Gotkowitz has identified a communal land reclamation campaign among indigenous caciques in the Vacas community in the region of Arani during the early twentieth century. She traces their logic of using the 1874 anticommunal, agrarian reform law (a liberal instrument promoting individual property rights) to defend their absolute right to "communal" land against the municipality of Cochabamba, which owned and rented the Vacas lands to private investors. Significantly, these land claims were intimately tied to indigenous claims to citizenship, legal equality, and literacy in their campaign. (See Gotkowitz, "History, Property, and Race: The Cacique Movement in Cochabamba, Bolivia, 1914-1932" [paper presented at the American Historical Association, Atlanta, January 4-7, 1996].) In her dissertation, Gotkowitz links local indigenous struggles for land and citizenship in Vacas and Tapacarí to the broader, pan-Altiplano network of *"caciques apoderdos"* loosely united in their struggle for lands, fair labor practices, and education in the early decades of the twentieth century (personal communication).

75 The term appears earlier, but it did not come into widespread usage until the late nineteenth century. Service tenants carried other labels in colonial times, most notably *arrendero*. The formal conditions of colonaje were elaborately codified in the early twentieth century. In general, colonos held parcels of hacienda land in usufruct and grazing rights in exchange for labor services and payment in kind. Much *indigenista* literature documented unfree labor conditions on haciendas; see, for example, Rafael A. Reyeros, *El pongueaje: La servidumbre de los indios bolivianos* (La Paz: Universo, 1949). Alberto Rivera argues that servile labor relations prevailed on haciendas in the more remote highlands of the Cochabamba region, whereas hacendado control over land and labor in the crowded valleys had decayed considerably by the early twentieth century. Jackson's work corroborates this finding. See Rivera, *Los terratenientes de Cochabamba* (Cochabamba: CERES, 1992), 88; Jackson, "Decline of the Hacienda in Cochabamba: The Case of Sacaba Valley, 1870-1929," *Hispanic American Historical Review* 69 (1989): 259-281; and Jackson, "Evolución y persistencia del colonaje en las haciendas de Cochabamba," *Siglo XIX* 3 (1988): 145-162.

ingly associated in liberal and nationalist rhetoric with a regressive past and an impoverished rural present in the minds of dissident elites and social-climbing smallholders and merchants. Grounded in Cochabamba's fluid, mestizifying political culture, and caught up in the advancing frontier of peasant smallholding, popular political discourses often deployed Indianness as a gloss on rural poverty, immobility, and servitude, rather than as an empowering discourse of colonial-corporate privilege and communal identity.[76] Furthermore, the new migratory circuits that routed wayward peasants out of the crowded, fertilizer- and water-starved valleys to distant wage work—either up over the mountains to the Chilean nitrate mines or, later, to the booming tin mines of the western altiplano, or down into the newly opened eastern tropics of the Chapare—provided exit routes from rural servitude and Indianness, although not necessarily from poverty. Through all these experiences and struggles, Qochala peoples must have elaborated discursive frameworks which, in one way or another, challenged the basis of paternal absolutism and asserted their rights as free laborers to negotiated, contractual labor arrangements because, as the Caporaya peasants had asserted to the colonial courts more than a century earlier, ". . . we are not *yanaconas*" (chapter 5). Indeed, it seems that popular notions of social contract, property, and nationhood were beginning to frame a new grammar of politics which both reinforced rural Indian otherness and simultaneously created the basis for alternative popular constructions of class and citizen identities. The task of future historical research is to explore how peasants rearticulated customary smallholding practices into a formal political right—one that directly implicated (in their own local formulations) broader themes of freedom, modernity, and citizenship.

But if popular constructions of land, labor, and citizen rights emanated from rural traditions of struggle and adaptation, equally powerful and mutually interacting political forces bubbled up from the towns and cities. In the urban domain, questions of political autonomy, public space, and civil society were probably more germane. The towns and cities had always provided a partial shelter from the brutalities of rural labor and colonial extraction. They also exercised

76 María Lagos writes of the region of Tiraque that even after the 1952 revolution replaced "Indian" with the label "campesino" in official and public discourses, dominant and popular idioms continued to associate rural areas with "backwardness" and "Indianness." Indeed, colloquial truisms often referred to the "Indian" lurking within the campesino, and "Indian" and "cholo" were usually the insults of choice in heat of vernacular battles. Lagos, *Autonomy and Power*, 152-153.

centripetal force, pulling indigenous peasantries into their commercial and ceremonial orbits throughout the seasons and cycles of the year. As I have argued, rural/urban dichotomies tended to crumble amid the itinerant streams of people, goods, and communication that crisscrossed the valley basins. That also meant that the "racial geography" of these shared urban spaces was highly charged, ambiguous, and contested. Imperial and municipal authorities were vexed to find ways to freeze racial categories, not to mention tax, regulate, discipline, and reform the plebeianized peasants and laborers invading their urban spaces. Furthermore, the cities' municipal granaries served as symbols of oligarchic economic power and monopoly, especially when harvest failures and hunger drew peasants into the city demanding food.[77] But I would wager that it was the direct and arbitrary power that municipal elites exercised over the urban artisans, peasants, and plebes that had the greatest potential to openly *politicize* their preexisting informal networks and communities which had been built up through local customs and practices over many generations. Popular urban intellectuals were also well positioned to forge contingent coalitions and mediate across ethnic, linguistic, and class boundaries in strategic moments of crisis. Although the content of their political agendas may have been more diffuse and flexible than that of the emerging agrarian movements, it probably revolved around political issues of taxation, autonomy, and the right to coexist in the shared spaces of civil society. If so, then we need to trace the parallel route that these popular urban discourses paved to larger nationalist issues of citizenship, democracy, and national identity. For historically, their socially transgressive behavior and protean interstitial identities had undermined cultural geography of colonial (later, creole) "white" society.[78] In the early twentieth century, the question still held: would the plebe finally be allowed into, or be barred from, the city (and by extension, the emerging nation)? These discursive battles have important implications for rethinking the scope and content of prerevolutionary politics in this region and in Bolivia as a whole.

Perhaps it should not surprise us, then, that it was the Qochala mestizas, so often the target of Cochabamba's civilizing campaigns, who eventually emerged as crucial protagonists in this struggle. As

77 Jackson, *Regional Markets and Agrarian Transformation in Bolivia*, 19; Rodríguez and Solares, *Sociedad Oligárquica, Chicha, and Cultural Popular*, 135-137.

78 See Gustavo Rodríguez and Humberto Solares, "Fronteras interiores y exteriores."

I argued earlier, it was their aura of ethnic ambiguity, sexuality, and transgression that made them so vulnerable to civilizing missions, and at the same time so elusive. To most elites, lower-class mestizas represented the advancing edge of low-classness, vulgarity, promiscuity, and other evils associated with the plebe. But they also wielded considerable economic power over the horizontal flow of cash, goods, credit, and loyalties in the central valleys. Earlier generations of mestiza women had forged a political legacy of struggle and community that stretched back in time to the Independence wars. In the 1880s, the chicheras and market women confronted aggressive municipal "street-cleaning" campaigns; and other skirmishes over municipal power and autonomy must have unsettled urban life every so often in the early twentieth century, as modernity turned its moralistic guns on the socially proximate, urban plebe.

Indeed, in the early 1900s, hegemonic nationalist discourses once again engendered mestizaje as an ambivalent, antagonistic symbol. From conservative oligarchs to pro-Indian *indigenistas,* the plebeian mestiza embodied racial degeneracy, moral decay, and social danger, just as she had in late colonial times. Loaded with negativity, the vilified mestiza buttressed exclusionary oligarchic projects of all kinds in the 1910s, 1920s, and 1930s. Its opposite, the reified mestiza, served as the linchpin of populist variants of nationalism. She was proving to be a versatile metaphor of universal motherhood and homogenized nationhood (she was the mythical breeder, after all, of a racially improved "whitening" population). In this discursive battle over the dilemmas of race and national identity, Bolivian elites were deeply divided. As many historians have shown, the hegemonic mestizo model of nation-building that achieved apotheosis in postrevolutionary Mexico resonated throughout much of Latin America in the 1920s and 1930s. It served as the unifying mythology of national identity, which conflated race, class, and nation into one homogenized (and hegemonized) whole through the partial incorporation of popular cultures. (As a prop of national identity in postcolonial societies, the homogenizing mestizo model simultaneously scripted "Indians" and "Africans" out of the nation.)[79] But the official reifica-

79 See J. Jorge Klor de Alva, "The Postcolonization of the (Latin) American Experience: A Reconsideration of 'Colonialism,' 'Postcolonialism,' and 'Mestizaje'," in Gyan Prakash, ed., *After Colonialism: Imperial Histories and Postcolonial Displacements* (Princeton: Princeton University Press, 1995). For a tightly argued comparative study of failed and functional "hegemonic mestizo models" in Peru, Bolivia, and Mexico, see Florencia Mallon, "Indian Communities, Political Cultures, and the State in Latin America"; on Ecuador, see Ronald Stutzman, "El

tion of mestizaje did not serve as an effective instrument of nation-making in Bolivia—either before or after the early 1950s (as the rise of katarismo/neo-Indianismo so plainly and painfully demonstrated in the 1980s).[80] The Bolivian case cautions against taking a top-down in-strumentalist view of mestizaje as a "legitimating device" in the ser-vice of authoritarian-populist pacts. Even in Cochabamba (Bolivia's "mestizo" region par excellence), it remained a highly contested, an-tagonistic ethnic (self-)identity that was strongly rooted in the gen-dered urban subculture of the marketplace, pub, and street, as well as in the ongoing struggle between plebeian women and elite "white" society over the mestizas' claims to cultural and economic self-determination in the heart of urban society. The struggle of Qochala women to define and redeem their own ethnic identity implicated much more than just local issues of mestiza autonomy and respect-ability, however; for they seemed to be challenging the exclusionary premises of oligarchic nationalism in the early twentieth century. In this sense, historians need to reconsider the emancipatory potential of bottom-up efforts to "class-ify" and engender mestizaje as a col-lective self-identity in specific regional contexts of class struggle and community-building.[81]

In a recent study, Laura Gotkowitz charts the way. She exam-ines the efforts of urban market women in early twentieth-century Cochabamba to convert mestizaje from a stigma into a symbol of national honor and identity.[82] She traces the threads of competing historical and aesthetic interpretations of the legendary "heroinas" of Cochabamba, who were remembered for their courageous leader-ship in Cochabamba's 1812 uprising against the invading royalist

Mestizaje: An All-Inclusive Ideology of Exclusion," in Norman E. Whitten, Jr., ed., *Cultural Transformations and Ethnicity in Modern Ecuador* (Urbana: Uni-versity of Illinois Press, 1981), 45-94.

80 See Marta Irurozqui, *La armonía de las desigualdades: Elites y conflictos de poder en Bolivia, 1880-1920* (Cusco: Casa Bartolomé de las Casas, 1994).

81 These reflections draw much inspiration from the papers and conversations that took place among Marisol de la Cadena, Laura Gotkowitz, Kathryn Burns, and myself at the Latin American Studies Association panel on "Mestizas: Poli-tics and Gender in Peru and Bolivia" (Washington, D.C., September 27, 1995). I have also benefited enormously from reading Marisol de la Cadena's dissertation, "Race, Ethnicity, and the Struggle for Self-Representation: De-Indianization in Cuzco, Peru (1919-1992)," and from my ongoing dialogues with Laura Gotkowitz.

82 Laura Gotkowitz, "Mestiza Protagonists in Pre-revolutionary Cochabamba" (paper presented at the Latin American Studies Association, Washington, D.C., September 28-30, 1995).

army. As her analysis unfolds, we begin to perceive how lower-class women struggled in the 1920s and 1930s to take back ownership of this mythologized event and recast the nation's founding mothers in their own ethnic and class image. Elite representations of romanesque literary muses (fashionable among polite society in the 1920s) gave way in the 1930s and 1940s to scruffy plebeian-ized heroines *de pollera*. From an instrumentalist point of view, it might be argued of course that this transfiguration of the heroines represented the rise of an elite discourse romancing the mestiza; or perhaps it simply marked a political change at the top—the result of a symbolic concession of the Bolivian state in order to co-opt their loyalty. Certainly, the post-Chaco war period saw populist attempts at maneuvering and co-optation, and Gotkowitz shows us how the Villarroel regime of the 1940s officiated over the national consecration of Cochabamba's plebeianized mestiza heroines as the conflated symbol of nationhood and motherhood. But her analysis also reveals the extent of grassroots participation in these unfolding interpretive battles over Bolivia's national origin myth. By laying claim to a place of honor in the nation's pantheon of icons, Qochala market women were seeking the public respect and right of self-representation they had always been denied. More importantly, their struggle to reclaim their revolutionary-patriotic heritage extended the possibility of national identity and inclusion to other silent, subordinated women in Bolivia. Along with mobilizing peasant laborers on the crumbling haciendas of Cochabamba, these urban laborers were fighting to become the authors of an imagined political project—both past and present—that would embrace Bolivia's marginal groups as vital political and historical subjects. Their search for political inclusion in the Bolivian nation-state would eventually converge and compete with broader populist movements during the late 1940s and early 1950s.

The historical outcome of these struggles did not guarantee a place in the sun for Bolivia's newly enfranchised indigenous peasants and popular sectors. That the fragile revolutionary-populist project of 1952 foundered and disintegrated after 1964 is all too evident today. Yet the return to authoritarian political rule in the late 1960s and 1970s does not negate Cochabamba's deep political-cultural heritages of struggle, or the hard-won achievements of its peasants and plebeians who did construct popular political identities and discourses around notions of freedom, autonomy, mestizaje, and nationhood. Nor, however, does it deny the historic difficulties of negotiating an inclusive national project in a deeply divided neocolonial society like

Bolivia. The country's postcolonial legacies and its deep regionalized histories (and discourses) of peasant struggle have facilitated divide-and-rule policies to this day. But rethinking this regional history from the political/historiographical perspective of the mid-1990s renews my hope in the dignity, dynamism, diversity, and power of Bolivia's popular political cultures, in Cochabamba and elsewhere, to forge political traditions out of their everyday lifeways and to alter the course of their nation's political history.

Appendix

Table A-1. Annual Average of Tithes in the Archbishopric of Charcas (La Plata) from 1599 to 1607, by District

District	Pesos Corrientes	Percentage
Cochabamba	15,222	15.9
Yotala	11,007	11.5
Pitantora	9,756	10.2
Tomina	8,021	8.4
Matacas	7,442	7.8
Mizque	6,098	6.4
Paspaya, Pilaya	5,844	6.1
Oroncoto	5,784	6.0
Alcantari	5,183	5.4
Poopó	4,241	4.4
Guata	3,607	3.8
Potosí	3,152	3.3
Tarija	2,735	2.9
Moxtoro	1,923	2.0
Terrado	1,754	1.8
Soroche, Pocopoco, Luxe, Tarabuco, and Yocala	1,676	1.8
Potolo	236	0.2
Atacama, Chucuito	102	0.1
Chacras of Cochabamba, Paria, and Carangas	1,023	1.1
Chacras of La Plata province	855	0.9
Total	95,661	100.0

Source: "Diezmos del arzobispal de la Plata, 1599-1607," AGI, Charcas, Leg. 153.

Table A-2. Indian Population of Cochabamba Province, 1683-1850

Year	Total Indian Population	Tributary Population
1683	26,420[a]	6,735
1737	—	5,484[b]
1752	26,531	5,778
1786-1787	58,402	10,773
1792-1793	57,580	8,760
1804-1808	59,277	11,718
1850	46,587[c]	6,046[d]

Sources: For 1683, AGN, Sala 13, Padrones, 18.1.1, Leg. 41, and 18.1.3, Leg. 43. For 1737, AGN, Sala 13, Padrones, 18.1.5, Leg. 45. For 1752, José Antonio de Velasco, *Memorias de los virreyes que han gobernado el Perú*, vol. 4, appendix, pp. 9-11. For 1786-1787, AGN, Sala 13, Padrones, 18.2.1, Leg. 46; 18.2.2, Leg. 47; and 18.2.3, Leg. 48. For 1792-1793, AGN, Sala 13, Padrones, 18.2.3, Leg. 48; 18.2.4, Leg. 49; and 18.2.5, Leg. 50. For 1804-1808, AGN, Sala 13, Padrones, 18.3.3, Leg. 53, and 18.4.4, Leg. 54. For 1850, ANB, Padrones, Cochabamba.
[a] Does not include non-tribute-paying Indians in the parish of Caraza.
[b] Does not include tributary population of the district of Ayopaya, which probably numbered about 400.
[c] Does not include Indian population of Sacaba, and population of Ayopaya is based on the 1844 census.
[d] According to the *Tribunal General de Valores*, tributary population of Cochabamba in 1856 was 9,437 (personal communication from Nicolás Sánchez-Albornoz).

Appendix

Table A-3. Indian Population of Cochabamba Province, by Partido, Selected Years from 1683 to 1871

Year	Total Indian Population	Number of Tributaries	Number of Ausentes	Ausentes as a Percentage of Tributaries
		Partido of the Cercado		
1683	1,170	311	—	—
1737	1,516	254	—	—
1786	4,182	893	25	2.8
1792	4,421	866	75	8.7
1802	4,273	850	242	28.5
1850	3,224	507	329	64.9
		Partido of Sacaba		
1683	866	209	—	—
1737	—	211	—	—
1787	3,805	673	12	1.8
1791	3,397	592	59	10.0
1797	4,577	706	152	21.5
1804	3,194	533	102	19.1
		Partido of Tapacarí		
1683	5,693	2,161	—	—
1737	—	1,573	—	—
1786	14,766	3,089	113	3.7
1793	15,584	3,144	257	8.2
1798	16,806	3,315	480	14.5
1804	15,820	3,032	724	23.9
1844	18,240	3,477	762	21.9
1851	16,845	3,389	897	26.5
		Partido of Cliza		
1683	3,581	812	—	—
1737	7,478	1,382	—	—
1786	16,227	2,769	38	1.4
1792	16,355	2,769	38	1.4
1797	17,553	3,098	558	18.0
1803	17,345	3,519	368	10.5
1805	—	2,763	584	21.1
1831	—	1,566	—	—
1846	7,344	956	1,310	137.0
1850	4,487	718	1,567	218.2
		Partido of Arque		
1683	2,922[a]	1,079	—	—
1737	—	1,506	—	—
1787	14,906	2,488	—	—
1792	14,722	2,504	513	20.4
1798	15,088	2,932	322	11.0
1804	12,913	2,692	505	18.8
1850	13,861	2,783	1,989	71.5

Table A-3. Indian Population of Cochabamba Province, by Partido, Selected Years from 1683 to 1871 (*cont.*)

Year	Total Indian Population	Number of Tributaries	Number of Ausentes	Ausentes as a Percentage of Tributaries
		Partido of Ayopaya		
1683	9,759	2,163	—	—
1737	—	558	—	—
1787	5,420	845	111	13.1
1792	5,700	973	209	21.5
1807	6,214	1,172	259	22.1
1844	5,670	1,032	112	10.9
1871	—	513	—	—

Sources: See table A-2.

a Does not include non-tribute-paying Indians in the parish of Caraza.

Table A-4. Debts of Hacendados to Pueblos Reales of Cochabamba, 1776

Lending Community	Property Mortgaged	Original Owner	Present Owner	Date of Original Mortgage	Principal of Loan (pesos)	Total Outstanding Debt (pesos)
Pocona (Mizque)	Chuchupunata (Cliza)	Francisco de Medrano	?	1590	5,980	?
Sipesipe	Sununpaya (Cliza)	Juan Sánchez Macías	Francisco Saavedra	1586	1,200	1,001
Santiago de Cotagaita (?) (Mizque?)	mills of hacienda Pocoata (Cliza)	Fernando de Soria	?	1676	1,400	5,950
Sipesipe	Coñacoña, Guaicanaio	Pedro Maldonado	?	1549	300	772
Sipesipe	Calacala, Queroquero[a]	Francisco de Ynojosa; Juan Osorio	?	1576	198	300
Sipesipe	Queroquero[a]	Alonso de Escobar	?	1594	600	5,430
?	Queroquero[a]	Cristóbal de Arébalo y Diego Perea		1584	100	955
Sipesipe	Colcapirgua	Juan Sánchez Macías	?	1586	100	945
?	Samaca, Motefato	Andrés de Rivera	?	1579	180	?
Sipesipe	"unas haciendas"	Pedro de Baraona	?	?	426	?
Sipesipe	?	Francisco de Ynojosa; Juan de la Reinaga	Miguel de Rosales	1567	229	?

Source: "Testimonio de la nómina general de deudores de la Caxa Gral. de censos de comunidades de Indios . . . de la real audiencia de . . . Charcas, año de 1776," document no. C2518, BN.

[a] There were three different haciendas bearing the name of Queroquero.

Table A-5. Viedma's Reports on Grain Prices and Planting and Harvest Conditions in Cochabamba, 1784-1808

Year	Months	Price (reales per fanega)		Planting and Harvest Conditions
		Wheat	*Maize*	
1784	Sept.-Dec.	58	—	Poor harvest; flooding
1785	Jan.-Apr.	32	20	Abundant rain followed by dry planting
	May-Aug.	32	16-20	season; good yield foreseen
	Sept.-Dec.	25	16	
1786	Jan.-Apr.	14-17	16	At beginning of harvest, sufficient grain
	May-Aug.	19-20	16-20	to supply local population for two
	Sept.-Dec.	19-20	20	years; little grain exported; planting late, poor harvest foreseen
1787	Jan.-Apr.	16	20	Little rain, but previous year's harvest
	May-Aug.	25	22	kept most agricultural prices from ris-
	Sept.-Dec.	26	24	ing drastically; conditions favorable for planting; good harvest expected for next year
1788	Jan.-Apr.	20	22	Too much rain; much maize seed rotted in moist soil
1790	Jan.-Apr.	16	20	
1792	Jan.-Apr.	20	24	Little rain; good harvest expected only for irrigated crops; grain supply sufficient for local population due to abundant grain supplies from past years
1793	July-Dec.	—	—	Poor harvest; prices stable because of abundant grain stored from past harvests
1794	Jan.-Apr.	12	16	Heavy rains; good harvest
	June-Sept.	12	16	
1795	Jan.-Apr.	12	16	Abundant harvest
	June-Dec.	12	16	
1796	Jan.-June	12	14	Good harvest
1797	July-Dec.	—	28	Poor maize harvest, but scarcity avoided by grain stored in municipal granary
1798	Jan.-June	12	22	Abundant rainfall; heavy yields
1799	July-Dec.	28	24	Poor harvest, but little scarcity; prices slightly higher than usual
1800	July-Dec.	32	24	Serious shortage of water; drought destroyed much of wheat crop
1804	July-Dec.	132	112	Second successive year of drought, worst in history of Cochabamba; almost all crops lost; severe famine
1806	Jan.-June	40-48	32	Poor weather, but prices have declined;
	July-Dec.	40	32	good harvest foreseen
1807	July-Dec.	60	28	Little rainfall; planting delayed; poor harvest expected; prices slightly higher
1808	July-Dec.	32	24	Hot and dry weather; planting delayed; poor harvest foreseen

Sources: AGN, Sala 9, Intendencia, 5.8.3, Leg. 2; 5.8.4, Leg. 3; 5.8.5, Leg. 4; 5.8.6, Leg. 5; 5.8.7, Leg. 6; 5.9.1, Leg. 7; and 5.9.2, Leg. 8.

Table A-6. Sources and Amounts of Royal Income in Cochabamba, by Quinquennium, 1775-1809

	1775-1779[a]		1780-1784		1785-1789[b]	
	Amount (pesos)	Percentage	Amount (pesos)	Percentage	Amount (pesos)	Percentage
Indian tribute	122,578	49.3	241,809	44.7	202,899	44.0
Alcabalas	64,302	25.9	110,610	20.5	76,883	16.7
Reales novenos	11,999	4.8	29,359	5.4	20,551	4.5
Taxes on bureaucratic offices and salaries	40,152	16.2	109,863	20.3	90,331	19.6
Civil offices and salaries						
Sale of offices	4,493	1.8	5,025	0.9	6,133	1.3
Income tax	—	—	—	—	78	<0.1
Pension fund	—	—	273	<0.1	675	0.2
Military offices and salaries						
Fund for invalids	126	<0.1	572	0.1	260	<0.1
Pension fund	2,393	1.0	21,176	3.9	8,635	1.9
Ecclesiastical offices and salaries						
Inheritance tax	—	—	—	—	23,539	5.1
Tax on vacant higher-clergy posts	3,571	1.4	18,373	3.4	2,523	0.6
Tax on vacant lower-clergy posts	24,249	9.8	56,923	10.5	31,515	6.8
Income tax	1,496	0.6	2,802	0.5	12,948	2.8
One-month tax on clerical salaries	1,828	0.7	1,917	0.4	1,557	0.3
5-percent tax on clerical salaries	1,996	0.8	2,802	0.5	1,075	0.2
Surtax	—	—	—	—	1,393	0.3
State monopolies	3,792	1.5	13,960	2.6	7,742	1.7
Tobacco	—	—	—	—	—	—
Mercury	—	—	—	—	568	0.1
Playing cards	—	—	—	—	—	—
Stamped paper	3,792	1.5	13,960	2.6	7,174	1.6
Miscellaneous	5,651	2.3	34,895	6.5	62,511	13.6
Real hacienda en común	494	0.2	600	0.1	1,297	0.3
Otras tesorerías	455	0.2	—	—	—	—
Tax on possessions of deceased persons	—	—	—	—	301	<0.1
Tax on Jesuit property	—	—	23,276	4.3	53,630	11.6
Tax on sale of lands and titles	—	—	821	0.2	2,350	0.5
Fines	100	<0.1	150	<0.1	44	<0.1
Military defense tax	—	—	5,449	1.0	—	—
Alcances de cuenta	—	—	110	<0.1	171	<0.1
Diversos	4,602	1.9	4,489	0.8	4,718	1.0
Total	248,474	100.0	540,496	100.0	460,917	100.1

Sources: AGN, Sala 13, Cajas reales, 5.2.5, Leg. 1 (1775 and 1776); 5.2.6, Leg. 2 (1777 and 1778); 5.3.1, Leg. 3 (1779 and 1780); 5.3.2, Leg. 4 (1781 and 1782); 27.1.1, Leg. 218 (1783); 5.3.3, Leg. 5 (1784); 5.3.4, Leg. 6 (1785); 5.3.5, Leg. 7 (1786); 27.2.2, Leg. 224 (1787); 27.2.3, Leg. 225 (1788); 5.4.3, Leg. 11 (1789); 27.3.2, Leg. 229 (1790 and 1791); 5.4.6, Leg. 14 (1792); 27.3.3, Leg. 230 (1793); 27.4.3, Leg. 235 (1794); 27.4.4, Leg. 236 (1795); 5.5.3, Leg. 18 (1796); 27.5.2, Leg. 240 (1797); 27.5.4, Leg. 241 (1798); 27.6.1, Leg. 243 (1799); 5.6.1, Leg. 22 (1800); 5.6.2, Leg. 23 (1801); 5.6.3, Leg. 24 (1802); 5.6.4, Leg. 25 (1803); 5.7.1, Leg. 28 (1804); 5.7.3, Leg. 30 (1805); 5.8.1, Leg. 34 (1806); 5.8.4, Leg. 37 (1807); 5.9.1, Leg. 40 (1808); and 5.9.5, Leg. 44 (1809).

1790-1794		1795-1799		1800-1804		1805-1809	
Amount (pesos)	*Percent-age*	*Amount (pesos)*	*Percent-age*	*Amount (pesos)*	*Percent-age*	*Amount (pesos)*	*Percent-age*
437,495	52.8	460,314	48.5	465,368	49.4	277,560	29.8
141,533	17.1	136,242	14.3	126,835	13.5	93,299	10.0
43,451	5.2	27,749	2.9	43,713	4.6	26,049	2.8
93,181	11.2	145,836	15.4	129,161	13.7	92,783	10.0
4,570	0.6	983	0.1	3,183	0.3	2,426	0.3
2,902	0.3	1,886	0.2	2,037	0.2	2,183	0.2
4,687	0.6	9,594	1.0	8,966	1.0	2,636	0.3
4,744	0.6	3,940	0.4	3,510	0.4	5,981	0.6
6,636	0.8	26,179	2.8	2,966	0.3	1,779	0.2
—	—	—	—	3,925	0.4	9,596	1.0
7,857	0.9	46,131	4.9	9,832	1.0	43,204	4.6
23,490	2.8	33,722	3.5	81,356	8.6	16,784	1.8
19,324	2.3	1,616	0.2	—	—	428	<0.1
3,926	0.5	2,907	0.3	526	<0.1	2,582	0.3
6,033	0.7	4,582	0.5	6,374	0.7	3,855	0.4
9,012	1.1	14,296	1.5	6,486	0.7	1,329	0.1
38,690	4.7	32,781	3.5	58,824	6.2	22,388	2.4
—	—	20,000	2.1	36,800	3.9	6,000	0.6
27,571	3.3	818	<0.1	—	—	—	—
—	—	—	—	—	—	534	<0.1
11,119	1.3	11,963	1.3	22,024	2.3	15,854	1.7
75,001	9.0	147,128	15.5	117,791	12.5	419,059	45.0
20,984	2.5	78,188	8.2	74,542	7.9	239,089	25.7
602	<0.1	14,779	1.6	8,696	0.9	156,204	16.8
4,783	0.6	2,262	0.2	906	<0.1	—	—
—	—	—	—	—	—	—	—
5,944	0.7	1,797	0.2	220	<0.1	123	<0.1
261	<0.1	285	<0.1	117	<0.1	113	<0.1
20,544	2.5	27,607	2.9	13,064	1.4	509	<0.1
517	<0.1	4,978	0.5	1,771	0.2	1,324	0.1
21,366	2.6	17,232	1.8	18,475	2.0	21,697	2.3
829,351	100.0	950,050	100.1	941,692	99.9	931,138	100.0

Note: Discrepancies in totals of percentages due to rounding.

[a] Except 1777, data for which are missing.

[b] Except 1787 and 1788, data for which are missing.

Glossary

alcabala	ad valorem tax (6 percent after 1780) on the sale of slaves, real estate, tithes, and many commodities
alcalde	mayor; member of the *cabildo*; royal official who administered a rural district (*partido*), often after purchasing the office (replaced by *subdelegado* in 1784)
arancel	a royal proclamation regulating prices, rent, wages, etc.
arrendatario	person, usually a creole, who leased a hacienda, mill, or large tract of land, with its tenantry, for a stipulated rent over a period of several years
arrendero	a tenant, usually an Indian or mestizo, who cultivated land on a hacienda and paid rent in labor, kind, and/or money
arriero	muleteer
arroba	a measure of weight, equivalent to about twenty-five pounds
asignación	assignment of landholding rights to *originarios* in an Indian village
ausente	a missing or absent tributary
ayllu	formally, an endogamous lineage claiming descent from a common ancestor; in practice, the basic kin unit of Andean native society, which held title to land, organized cooperative labor teams, and performed other collective functions
azoguero	owner of a silver refinery (literally, "mercury man," so called because mercury was used in refining silver)
bayetas	rough unbleached woolen cloth
cabecera	the principal village of a *pueblo real*
cabecera del valle	the highest part of a valley, where lands were usually irrigated
cabildo	municipal council
cacicazgo	Indian chieftainship

caja de comunidad	treasury of an Indian pueblo, which was supposed to finance tribute deficits as well as supply mortgage capital to Spaniards acquiring land
caja real	royal treasury
cajón	a tank for refining silver by amalgamation, large enough to hold fifty *quintales* of milled ore
capellanía	an ecclesiastical benefice, which yielded 5 percent annually on the principal
carga	a measure of volume, equivalent to about six bushels
censo	a loan or credit guaranteed by collateral, usually land, bearing 5 percent interest
censo en compra	a mortgage loan negotiated at the time of purchase of land
censualista	a person or association providing a *censo*
chácara	a small estate or grain farm; also, in the eighteenth century, *chacra* (from the Quechua word *chajra*, farming, sowing, land)
chicha	Andean alcoholic beverage, usually made from maize
cholo	in the eighteenth century, a person formally defined as being "three-quarters Indian and one-quarter white"; later, a person of mixed Andean and European ancestry generally
chuño	"freeze-dried" potatoes, processed in high-altitude zones with extreme diurnal temperatures, making it possible to preserve them over a long period of time
cobrador	*originario* assigned by a cacique to collect tribute in an Indian village
composición de tierras	royal inspection and validation of land titles
corregidor	Spanish magistrate and administrator of a district (*corregimiento*); the post was abolished in the early 1780s
corregidor de indios	magistrate in charge of a rural Indian district
diezmo	one-tenth; tax levied on grain
efectos de Castilla	European (mainly Spanish) imported goods
efectos de la tierra	goods imported from other colonial provinces
encomendero	Spanish colonizer who was granted by the crown the right to collect tribute from one or more native communities and was expected, in return, to protect the welfare of the inhabitants

estancia	a highland property where grazing was usually combined with potato cultivation
fanega	a measure of volume that varied by region but was generally equivalent to about 1.6 bushels
fanegada	a measure of land area that varied by region and by soil fertility but generally referred to the amount of land needed to sow one fanega of seed
feria	open-air weekly retail marketplace
forasteros	Indians living in a community other than that of their original kin group and having no landholding rights in the host community (distinguished from *originarios*); in Cochabamba, they lived in Spanish towns and on Spanish haciendas as well as in *pueblos reales*
huaca	Andean deity believed to take the form of a mountain peak, rock, cave, water, or other natural object
kajcha	a silver thief, usually a *minga* who scavenged silver ore on weekends and sold it
kichwa	temperate valley zone where maize was the principal crop during Incan times
kuraka	Andean ethnic lord (the term was later replaced by the Spanish term "cacique")
legua	a measure of length, roughly the distance a horse could walk in an hour (approximately 2.5-3 miles)
maica	irrigated maize land
minga	wageworker in the mines
mit'a	literally, in Quechua, a turn at some task; more generally, the Andean system of rotating turns of service in the performance of community labor or the rendering of service to the Incan emperor
mita	colonial institution of rotation draft labor, particularly for work in the silver mines of Potosí (from the Quechua term *mit'a*)
mita de agua	an irrigation system that delivered water to designated properties, usually those of hacendados, for a specified number of hours a week or month
mitayo	an Indian laborer serving in the *mita*
mitimaes	Indian colonizers sent by their ethnic group to cultivate land in different ecological zones and at some distance from their homeland; also, Indians sent by the Incas to colonize recently conquered territories
mittayoc	seasonal migrant laborer who cultivated maize on Incan lands
obraje	primitive textile factory or workshop

obras pías	works of charity, usually sponsored by the Spanish crown
originarios	Indians still living with their original kin group and having the rights and responsibilities of *ayllu* membership (distinguished from *forasteros*)
parcialidad	moiety of an Indian village, usually composed of two sections, Anansaya (the upper half) and Urinsaya (the lower half)
partido	subdivision of a *corregimiento*; an administrative district composed of several parishes
peara (de mulas)	the load of goods carried by a "standard" mule train, usually consisting of ten mules
peso corriente	a silver coin weighing one ounce; the standard monetary unit for ordinary transactions, subdivided into eight reales
peso ensayado	the standard monetary unit of account in the early colonial era, subdivided into twelve reales
primicias	literally, "first fruits"; a tax levied on Indian crops and livestock
provincias obligadas	provinces from which *mitayos* were recruited
pueblo real	Spanish term for an Indian district, including a principal (*cabecera*) village and its surrounding rural settlements; there were five *pueblos reales* in eighteenth-century Cochabamba (Tapacarí, Sipesipe, El Paso, Tiquipaya, and Capinota)
puna	cold, dry lands at altitudes of 12,000 feet or more
quebrada	mountain gorge through which a stream flows down to the central valleys
quintal	a measure of weight, equal to four *arrobas*
quinto	the "royal fifth"; a tax levied on the silver extracted from the mines of Potosí
ramo	treasury account
real noveno	the "royal ninth"; a tax of 11 percent levied on tithes, which in turn were based on the estimated value of a region's agricultural production in a given year
reducción	forced resettlement program of Viceroy Toledo to bring dispersed Andean groups together into nucleated villages of Spanish design in order to facilitate state control and collection of tribute
repartimiento de mercancías	forced distribution of merchandise to Indians, usually on credit, by a *corregidor* or his agent
reservados	old and disabled men who were exempt from tribute and mita duty
residencia	judicial review of the conduct of a *corregidor* or other official at the end of his term in office

subdelegado	highest appointed official of a *partido*
temporal	dry land where wheat was usually cultivated
tocuyero	a weaver of *tocuyos*
tocuyos	rough unbleached cotton cloth
vara	a measure of length, approximately equivalent to thirty-three inches
veintena	one-twentieth; tax levied on wheat sown on Indian lands
viche	an area of land, equivalent in the Cochabamba region to about one-sixth of a *fanegada*
yanacona	a retainer who served the Incan emperor or an ethnic lord as a life-long servant
yanacona colonial	an Indian servant, miner, or agricultural laborer removed from his ayllu and bound to a Spanish overlord
yanaconaje	institution of personal servitude (see *yanacona* and *yanacona colonial*)
yungas	low-altitude tropical lands, generally on the eastern slopes of the Andes; specifically, in Alto Perú, the coca-producing region bordering the province of La Paz; also, the people inhabiting such regions

Archival Material

Manuscript Collections

BOLIVIA
Archivo Nacional de Bolivia, Sucre (ANB)

A superb repository of documents for the audiencia of Charcas and for Bolivia during the nineteenth century, this archive provides both fine-grained descriptive materials on the Cochabamba region and indispensable sources on mining, government, the Indian population, and the political culture of the dominant elites during the colonial period. Under the direction of Gunnar Mendoza, the archive's holdings have been meticulously catalogued and indexed. The major categories of documentary sources consulted for this study are listed below.

Sección de Tierras e Indios
Expedientes y correspondencia (EC) consist of royal edicts, civil and criminal court records, petitions, grievances, inspector's reports, and other documents. They are exceptionally rich sources for the study of Andean society, land transactions and disputes, and government policy. Included among the documents in this category are:
"Visita y composición de tierras y estancias en Cochabamba." 1748. EC no. 100.
"Juicio en grado de apelación sobre los capítulos que se lee a Don Juan Guillermo Liro de Córdova, por el indio Blas Condori, sobre tierras en el pueblo de Tapacarí." 1753. 136 ff. EC no. 46.
"Real provisión del cobrador de tributo de Sipesipe, con petición que el cacique exije el padrón . . ." 1754. EC no. 25.
"Informaciones hechas . . . sobre el número de indios mitayos . . . que se deben marchar a Potosí." 1755. EC no. 23.
"Quejas al rey de indios de Tapacarí, Mojosa, Yaco, y Cavaxi . . .

sobre los execivos [*sic*] derechos que se les cobra en sus entierros, matrimonios . . ." 1761. EC no. 31.

"Indios de Cochabamba sobre el pretender de sujetarlos a servidumbre de yanaconazgo en la hacienda de la Laguna." 1772. EC no. 216.

"Diligencias e averiguaciones de los bienes sustraidos a los caciques de Tapacarí." 1781. EC no. 36.

"Cuaderno de cuentas de las cosechas de las sementeras de caciques de Tapacarí." 1782. EC no. 84.

"Exp. sobre las elecciones de caciques interinos de Capinota." 1796. EC no. 72.

"Exp. sobre el remate de alcabalas de harinas de trigo y maíz." 1803. EC no. 3.

Sección de la audiencia de Charcas

Expedientes and correspondencia deal with such issues as taxes and treasury administration, corruption among colonial authorities, tithes and other ecclesiastical concerns, conditions of bridges and roads, disputes over land sales, commerce, and grain shortages. Similar to the expedientes concerned with Indian affairs, these records are full of rich detail about aspects of regional society. For a sample of the material on Cochabamba in the late colonial period, see EC no. 32, 37, 49, 72, and 79.

Mano de obra—Minería

This manuscript collection provides information on the export of labor and goods to Potosí from outlying rural districts and on all aspects of mining society.

Padrones de indios

This archive contains a series of Indian census records of Cochabamba for the following partidos and years: Argue, 1850; Ayopaya, 1844; El Cercado, 1850; Cliza, 1831, 1846, and 1850; Punata, 1867; Tapacarí, 1828, 1844, 1851, and 1867; Tarata, 1872; and Cochabamba, 1834 and 1844. These records, particularly several *catastros*, provide information about Indian landholding patterns in the region.

Administración de Mariscal Sucre

Catalogued under Sucre's Ministry of the Interior (MI) is rich information on monastic wealth in the region around the time of independence. See especially MI, vol. 1, no. 7, and vol. 2, no. 9.

Escrituras públicas (EP)

Of special interest are the books kept by three royal notaries—Juan Luís Soto, Gáspar de Rojas, and Lázaro de Aguila. They recorded transactions of all kinds, and their books reveal the intensity and variety of trade and commerce at Potosí during the early years after its founding in 1545.

Archivo Histórico Municipal de Cochabamba, Cochabamba (AHMC)

The municipal archive of Cochabamba was closed to the public at the time of my arrival in the city in 1974, because the documents were unorganized and uncatalogued. However, with the help of numerous people who appreciated the importance of archival research and who wrote letters, made phone calls, and campaigned on my behalf for the better part of two months, I was able to gain access to the archive, and shortly afterward I was joined by several local historians. Since then, the archive, which is housed in the Palacio de la Cultura in downtown Cochabamba, has been opened to the public.

The citations of material from this archive refer to the original number on the outside of the legajo (file) in which the document was found. The archive is currently being organized and many of the documents have been catalogued, so that citations in this text may not correspond to the new archival designations. However, I have identified most documents by a short, descriptive title and a date as well as by a legajo (Leg.) number.

The files include local trial records, complaints, wills, inventories, and petitions that provide microscopic views of rural life, commercial transactions, inheritance patterns, kinship ties, credit and debt relations, land tenure patterns, rent payments, tithe transactions, and myriad other facets of local society. Absent were the cabildo records. Apparently, manuscript copies of the libros de cabildo are not extant, although excerpts have been published in the *Digesto de ordenanzas*. Another disappointment was to discover that the records of the Monastery of Santa Clara apparently had been destroyed.

Archivo de la Biblioteca de la Universidad Mayor de San Andrés, La Paz

"Ynformación sumaria producida sobre las alteraciones de la provincia de Cochabamba en 1781." No. 97, 1781.

PERU

Biblioteca Nacional, Lima (BN)

"Testimonio de la nómina general de deudores de la Caxa Gral. de censos de comunidades de Indios . . . de la real audiencia de . . . Charcas, año de 1776." Document no. C2518.

ARGENTINA

Archivo General de la Nación, Buenos Aires (AGN)

As is well known, the AGN houses abundant documentary material on Alto Perú, particularly during the period of the viceroyalty of La Plata (1776-1810). The documents are catalogued by year, subject, and place.

Sala 13 (Cajas reales)

These treasury records include royal customs house records (*Guías y cuentas de alcabalas*) and Indian census records (*Padrones*); for Cochabamba, they span the years from 1773 to 1809, with only three annual records missing. The cajas reales consist of bound volumes, *Cuentas mayores de caja* and *Cuentas mensuales de caja*, which respectively include yearly and monthly entries of tax income and expenditures. In addition, unbound volumes, *Relaciones juradas*, available for only some of the years, give more detailed breakdowns of royal income and expenditures. The treasury records also include separate accounts of royal income from alcabalas—the tax on sales of most goods, real estate, and slaves, and the auction price of tithes. These records list the types, volume, and unit market value of goods imported into the province, and usually the merchants involved in the transactions and the origin of the merchandise (or sometimes a previous custom house where registered). They also record the value of tithes for each parish in the province each year and the 6 percent ad valorem tax that tithe collectors paid on their tithe investment. Treasury accounts consulted were 5.2.5, Leg. 1, through 5.9.7, Leg. 46. The unbound treasury and alcabala records for the region are found in Contaduría, Cuerpo 27, Legs. 218-250.

The padrones of Cochabamba are located in 18.1.1, Leg. 41 (1683), through 18.3.4, Leg. 54 (1804-1808). (See appendix tables A-1 and A-2.) The earliest Indian census found for Cochabamba in this archive dates from 1618-1619: 17.10.4, Leg. 40, books 1 and 2.

Sala 9 (Intendencia, Justicia, Criminales, Consulado, etc.)

There is abundant and varied material pertaining to the economy, society, and governance of the intendancy of Santa Cruz de la Sierra (which incorporated the old corregimiento of Cochabamba) in these sections of the AGN. An important series of reports are the trimester and semester records kept by the intendant, Francisco de Viedma, on harvest conditions, crop prices, and grain supplies for the years from 1784 to 1808 (see Intendencia, 5.8.2 through 5.9.2). Extensive records on the royal tobacco monopoly exist, as well as varied materials on such problems as Viedma's efforts at administrative and economic reform, expropriated properties of the Jesuits, the cost and recruitment of militiamen, royal taxes on grain mills and real-estate transfers, the difficulties of tribute and alcabala collection, contraband trade, tocuyo exports, shortages of pack animals, cabildo members, merchants and shopkeepers, and the appointment, responsibilities, and corrupt practices of subdelegados.

SPAIN
Archivo General de Indias, Seville (AGI)

Among the important documents on Alto Perú in this collection, particularly valuable are several early treasury records on tithes (see Charcas, Leg. 153, Diezmos del arzobispal de la Plata, 1599-1607) and on tribute on the yanacona population of Alto Perú (see Contaduría, Leg. 1818, Jan. 31, 1666). There is abundant correspondence concerning the bishopric of Santa Cruz (Charcas, Legs. 152, 153, 219, 375, 387, 388, 407, 408, 409, and 410). On the tax rebellion of 1730-1731 in Cochabamba, see Charcas, Legs. 343 and 344. On the conflicts in the pueblo real de Tapacarí and complaints about the corregidor, Bartolomé Fiorilo Pérez, in the middle years of the eighteenth century, see Charcas, Legs. 367 and 436. Numerous other documents on Cochabamba, which contain information on aspects of rural Indian society and protests carried up through the audiencia of La Plata to Madrid, are catalogued in the sections of Charcas and Justicia.

Real Academia de Historia, Madrid (RAH)

Colección Mata Linares (ML)

The most important sources for this study are the series of reports written by Francisco de Viedma, José Gómez Merino, Pedro Canals, Lázaro de Rivera, Tadeo Haenke, Francisco de Paula Sanz, and others on aspects of the region's economy and potential development. These reports, contained in this collection, were part of the Bourbon effort to promote commercial agriculture, improve road conditions, systematize tax collection, and so on (see chapter 7). There is also in this collection a wealth of documentary material on the Yuracaree, Moxo, and Chiquito settlements in the tropical lowlands and on the controversy over whether to transfer the seat of the bishopric of Santa Cruz to the city of Cochabamba.

ENGLAND

British Library, London

United Kingdom. Foreign Office 61/12. John B. Pentland, *Report on the Bolivian Republic. 1827. Microfilm.*

INDEX

Index

About the Author

Brooke Larson is Associate Professor of History at the State University of New York at Stony Brook and the past director of the Latin American and Caribbean Center. She has published several books in Bolivia and is coeditor of *Ethnicity, Markets, and Migration in the Andes: At the Crossroads of History and Anthropology* (Duke University Press, 1995).

Library of Congress Cataloging-in-Publication Data
Larson, Brooke.
Cochabamba, 1550–1900 : colonialism and agrarian transformation in Bolivia / Brooke Larson.
p. cm.
First ed. has title: Colonialism and agrarian transformation in Bolivia. Includes bibliographical references and index.
ISBN 0-8223-2061-4 (cloth : alk. paper).—ISBN 0-8223-2088-6 (pbk. : alk. paper)
1. Agriculture—Economic aspects—Bolivia—Cochabamba Region—History.
2. Peasantry—Bolivia—Cochabamba Region—History.   3. Mercantile system—Bolivia—Cochabamba Region—History.   4. Cochabamba Region (Bolivia)—Rural conditions.   5. Cochabamba Region (Bolivia)—Politics and government.
I. Larson, Brooke. Colonialism and agrarian transformation in Bolivia.   II. Title.
HD1870.c62L37   1998
305.5′633′098423—dc21   97-29926
                                                                                                        CIP